Comprehensive
LOTUS® 1-2-3®
Release 4 for Windows™

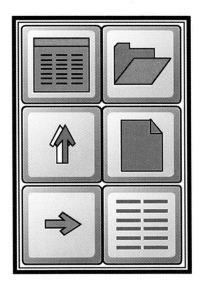

Comprehensive
LOTUS® 1-2-3®
Release 4 for Windows™

Roger Hayen
Central Michigan University

A
Susan
Solomon
Book

Course
TECHNOLOGY

Course Technology, Inc. *One Main Street, Cambridge, MA 02142*
An International Thomson Publishing Company

Comprehensive Lotus 1-2-3 Release 4 for Windows is published by Course Technology, Inc.

Managing Editor	Marjorie Schlaikjer
Series Consulting Editor	Susan Solomon
Product Manager	Nicole Jones
Developmental Editor	Katherine T. Pinard
Director of Production	Myrna D'Addario
Production Editor	Kathleen Finnegan
Desktop Publishing Supervisor	Debbie Masi
Desktop Publishers	Andrew Giammarco
	Andrea Greitzer
Composition	Gex, Inc.
Production Assistant	Christine Spillett
Copyeditor	Jane Pedicini
Proofreaders	Ellen Grimm
	Joyce Churchill
Product Testing and Support Supervisor	Jeff Goding
Technical Reviewers	Jennifer Schimpf
	Joshua Merritt
	Thomas Kutter
	Mark Vodnik
	Sean Barrett
Manufacturing Manager	Elizabeth Martinez
Prepress Production	Gex, Inc.
Text Designer	Sally Steele
Illustrations	Andrew Giammarco
	Gex, Inc.
	illustrious, inc.
Cover Designer	John Gamache
Indexer	Alexandra Nickerson

Comprehensive Lotus 1-2-3 Release 4 for Windows © 1994 Course Technology, Inc.

Trademarks

Course Technology and the open book logo are registered trademarks of Course Technology, Inc.

Lotus 1-2-3 is a registered trademark of Lotus Development Corporation and Windows is a trademark of Microsoft Corporation.

Some of the product names and company names used in this book have been used for identification purposes only and may be trademarks or registered trademarks of their respective manufacturers and sellers.

Disclaimer

Course Technology, Inc. reserves the right to revise this publication and make changes from time to time in its content without notice.

ISBN 1-56527-143-2 (text)

Printed in the United States of America

10 9 8 7 6 5 4 3

From the Publisher

At Course Technology, Inc., we believe that technology will transform the way that people teach and learn. We are very excited about bringing you, college professors and students, the most practical and affordable technology-related products available.

The Course Technology Development Process

Our development process is unparalleled in the higher education publishing industry. Every product we create goes through an exacting process of design, development, review, and testing.

Reviewers give us direction and insight that shape our manuscripts and bring them up to the latest standards. Every manuscript is quality tested. Students whose backgrounds match the intended audience work through every keystroke, carefully checking for clarity, and pointing out errors in logic and sequence. Together with our own technical reviewers, these testers help us ensure that everything that carries our name is error-free and easy to use.

Course Technology Products

We show both *how* and *why* technology is critical to solving problems in college and in whatever field you choose to teach or pursue. Our time-tested, step-by-step instructions provide unparalleled clarity. Examples and applications are chosen and crafted to motivate students.

The Course Technology Team

This book will suit your needs because it was delivered quickly, efficiently, and affordably. In every aspect of our business, we rely on a commitment to quality and the use of technology. Every employee contributes to this process. The names of all of our employees are listed below:

Tim Ashe, David Backer, Stephen M. Bayle, Josh Bernoff, Ann Marie Buconjic, Jody Buttafoco, Kerry Cannell, Jim Chrysikos, Barbara Clemens, Susan Collins, John M. Connolly, Kim Crowley, Myrna D'Addario, Lisa D'Alessandro, Howard S. Diamond, Kathryn Dinovo, Katie Donovan, Joseph B. Dougherty, MaryJane Dwyer, Chris Elkhill, Don Fabricant, Kate Gallagher, Laura Ganson, Jeff Goding, Laurie Gomes, Eileen Gorham, Andrea Greitzer, Catherine Griffin, Tim Hale, Roslyn Hooley, Nicole Jones, Matt Kenslea, Susannah Lean, Suzanne Licht, Laurie Lindgren, Kim Mai, Elizabeth Martinez, Debbie Masi, Don Maynard, Dan Mayo, Kathleen McCann, Jay McNamara, Mac Mendelsohn, Laurie Michelangelo, Kim Munsell, Amy Oliver, Michael Ormsby, Kristine Otto, Debbie Parlee, Kristin Patrick, Charlie Patsios, Jodi Paulus, Darren Perl, Kevin Phaneuf, George J. Pilla, Cathy Prindle, Nancy Ray, Marjorie Schlaikjer, Christine Spillett, Susan Stroud, Michelle Tucker, David Upton, Mark Valentine, Karen Wadsworth, Anne Marie Walker, Renee Walkup, Donna Whiting, Janet Wilson, Lisa Yameen.

Preface

Course Technology, Inc. is proud to present this new book in its Windows Series. *Comprehensive Lotus 1-2-3 Release 4 for Windows* is designed for a first course on Lotus 1-2-3. This book capitalizes on the energy and enthusiasm students have for Windows-based applications and clearly teaches students how to take full advantage of 1-2-3's power. It assumes no prerequisite knowledge of computers, the Windows environment, or 1-2-3.

Organization and Coverage

Comprehensive Lotus 1-2-3 Release 4 for Windows contains a Guided Tour and ten tutorials that present hands-on instruction. In these tutorials students learn how to plan, build, test, and document 1-2-3 worksheets. Moreover, this book harnesses 1-2-3's power by emphasizing the SmartIcons and other Windows features for calculating, charting and managing data. Using this book, students will learn how to do more advanced tasks sooner than they would using other introductory texts; a perusal of the table of contents affirms this. By the end of the book, students will have learned "advanced" tasks such as analyzing "what-if" alternatives with Version Manager, creating automated solutions executed with macro buttons, producing crosstab reports from databases, performing goal seeking, combining worksheet results, pasting worksheet solutions in other Windows applications, and writing user-defined macro menus. The book also contains four additional case problems, which allow students to apply what they've learned throughout the book to solve realistic business problems. The References section following the Additional Cases contains documentation on 1-2-3 commands, @functions, macro commands, and SmartIcons, providing a valuable resource for students both during and after their 1-2-3 course.

Approach

Comprehensive Lotus 1-2-3 Release 4 for Windows distinguishes itself from other Windows books because of its unique two-pronged approach. First, it motivates students by demonstrating *why* they need to learn the concepts and skills. This book teaches 1-2-3 using a task-driven approach rather than a feature-driven approach. By working through the tutorials—each motivated by a realistic case—students learn how to use 1-2-3 in situations they are likely to encounter in the workplace, rather than learn a list of features one-by-one, out of context. Second, the content, organization, and pedagogy of this book make full use of the Windows environment. What content is presented, when it's presented, and how it's presented capitalize on 1-2-3's power to perform complex analyses, which supports effective decision making more easily than was possible under DOS.

Features

Comprehensive Lotus 1-2-3 Release 4 for Windows is an exceptional textbook also because it contains the following features:

- ■ **"Read This Before You Begin" Page** This page is consistent with Course Technology's unequalled commitment to helping instructors introduce technology into the classroom. Technical considerations and assumptions about hardware, software, and default settings are listed in one place to help instructors save time and eliminate unnecessary aggravation.

■ **Tutorial Case** Each tutorial begins with a spreadsheet-related problem that students could reasonably encounter in business. Thus, the process of solving the problem will be meaningful to students. These cases touch on multicultural, international and ethical issues—so important in today's business curriculum.

■ **Step-by-Step Methodology** The unique Course Technology, Inc. methodology keeps students on track. They click or press keys always within the context of solving the problem posed in the Tutorial Case. The text constantly guides students, letting them know where they are in the process of solving the problem. The numerous screen shots include labels that direct students' attention to what they should look at on the screen.

■ **Page Design** Each *full-color* page is designed to help students easily differentiate between what they are to *do* and what they are to *read*. The steps are easily identified by their color background and numbered bullets. Windows default colors are used in the screen shots so instructors can more easily assure that students' screens look like those in the book.

■ **TROUBLE?** TROUBLE? paragraphs anticipate the mistakes that students are likely to make and help them recover from these mistakes. This feature facilitates independent learning and frees the instructor to focus on substantive conceptual issues rather than common procedural errors.

■ **Reference Windows and Task Reference** Reference Windows provide short, generic summaries of frequently used procedures. The Task Reference appears at the end of the book and summarizes how to accomplish tasks using the buttons/SmartIcons, the menus, and the keyboard. Both of these features are specially designed and written so students can use the book as a reference manual after completing the course.

■ **Questions, Tutorial Assignments, and Case Problems** Each tutorial concludes with meaningful, conceptual Questions that test students' understanding of what they learned in the tutorial. The Questions are followed by Tutorial Assignments, which provide students with additional hands-on practice of the skills they learned in the tutorial. The Tutorial Assignments are followed by three complete Case Problems that have approximately the same scope as the Tutorial Case.

■ **Exploration Exercises** Unlike DOS, the Windows environment allows students to learn by exploring and discovering what they can do. The Exploration Exercises are Questions, Tutorial Assignments, or Case Problems designated by an **E** that encourage students to explore the capabilities of the computing environment they are using and to extend their knowledge using the Windows on-line Help facility and other reference materials.

The CTI WinApps Setup Disk

The CTI WinApps Setup Disk bundled with the instructor's copy of this book contains an innovative Student Disk generating program designed to save instructors time. Once this software is installed on a network or standalone workstation, students can double-click the "Make Lotus 1-2-3 Release 4 Student Disk" icon in the CTI WinApps group window. Double-clicking this icon transfers all the data files students need to complete the tutorials, Tutorial Assignments, and Case Problems to a high-density disk in drive A or B. The Guided Tour provides complete step-by-step instructions for making the Student Disk.

Adopters of this text are granted the right to install the CTI WinApps group window on any standalone computer or network used by students who have purchased this text.

For more information on the CTI WinApps Setup Disk, see the section in this book called, "Read This Before You Begin."

The Supplements

- **Instructor's Manual** The Instructor's Manual is written by the author and is quality assurance tested. It includes:
  - Answers and solutions to all the Questions, Tutorial Assignments, and Case Problems. Suggested solutions are also included for the Exploration Exercises.
  - A disk (3.5-inch or 5.25-inch) containing solutions to all the Questions, Tutorial Assignments, and Case Problems.
  - Tutorial Notes, which contain background information from the author about the Tutorial Case and the instructional progression of the tutorial.
  - Technical Notes, which include troubleshooting tips as well as information on how to customize the students' screens to closely emulate the screen shots in the book.
  - Transparency Masters of key concepts.
- **Test Bank** The Test Bank contains 50 questions per tutorial in true/false, multiple choice, and fill-in-the-blank formats, plus two essay questions. Each question has been quality assurance tested by students to achieve clarity and accuracy.
- **Electronic Test Bank** The Electronic Test Bank allows instructors to edit individual test questions, select questions individually or at random, and print out scrambled versions of the same test to any supported printer.

Acknowledgments

I would like to thank the many individuals who contributed to the successful completion of *Comprehensive Lotus 1-2-3 Release 4 for Windows*.

I am grateful to John Connolly, who created this innovative company and formed a strategic alliance with Lotus Development Corporation. This alliance has made this book possible and continues to integrate technology in education.

Thanks to Joe Dougherty for his support and Susan Solomon for her guidance in formulating the book's content and approach. Nicole Jones and Kitty Pinard performed editing magic. Their combined "spin" on the book's content makes this a truly remarkable book for learning 1-2-3. I want to thank the members of Course Technology's Production Department for turning the manuscript into a colorful, well-designed textbook. And to all the people at Course Technology, Inc. who contributed to the overall success of this project in ways too numerous to recount, I extend my sincere thanks.

I would also like to thank the following reviewers—David Bourque of Middlesex County College, Joseph Ohl of Spokane Community College, Jan Richmond of St. Louis Community College at Merremac, Ken Seal of Robeson Community College, Rick Weible of Marshall University, and Steve Zylstra of Hope College—who offered valuable comments, suggestions, and criticisms, which helped to shape this book.

I am also grateful for the many suggestions and valuable insights provided by my colleagues. Robert Hanson, interim dean of the College of Business Administration, provided motivation in pursuing this project. Peter Smidt, a graduate assistant, contributed in many ways including the development of the case problems and the myriad of repeated screen shots. The faculty and staff in the Office and Information Systems Department encouraged and supported the book's formulation and development in a variety of ways.

And, last but certainly not least, I would like to thank my family. During this project, the book overshadowed many family activities, but their encouragement, support, and most of all, perseverance enabled me to complete this project.

Roger Hayen

Brief Contents

Contents

TUTORIAL 6
Creating and Using Macros

TUTORIAL 7
Creating and Using a
Worksheet Database

TUTORIAL 8
Exploring Advanced What-If
Alternatives

REFERENCE WINDOWS

Microsoft Windows 3.1 Tutorials

1 **Essential Windows Skills**

2 **Effective File Management**

Read This Before You Begin

To the Student

To use this book, you must have a Student Disk. Your instructor will either provide you with a Student Disk or ask you to make your own by following the instructions in the section called "Preparing Your Student Disk" in Windows Tutorial 2. See your instructor or lab manager for further information.

Using Your Own Computer If you are going to work through this book using your own computer, you need:

- The Student Disk. ***You will not be able to complete the tutorials and exercises in this book using your own computer until you have the Student Disk.*** Ask your instructor or lab manager for details on how to get it.

- A computer system running Microsoft Windows 3.1 and DOS.

To the Instructor

Making the Student Disk To complete the tutorials in this book, your students must have a copy of the Student Disk. To relieve you of having to make multiple Student Disks from a single master copy, we provide you with the CTI WinApps Setup Disk, which contains an automatic Student Disk generating program. Once you install the Setup Disk on a network or standalone workstation, students can easily make their own Student Disks by double clicking on the "Make Win 3.1 Student Disk" icon in the CTI WinApps icon group. Double clicking this icon transfers all the data files students will need to complete the tutorials and Tutorial Assignments to a high-density disk in drive A or B. If some of your students will use their own computers to complete the tutorials and exercises in this book, they must first get the Student Disk. The section called "Preparing Your Student Disk" in Windows Tutorial 2 provides complete instructions on how to make the Student Disk.

If you have disk copying resources available, you might choose to use them for making quantities of the Student Disk. The "Make Win 3.1 Student Disk" provides an easy and fast way to make multiple Student Disks.

Installing the CTI WinApps Setup Disk: To install the CTI WinApps icon group from the Setup Disk, follow the instructions inside the disk envelope that was bundled with your book. By adopting this book, you are granted a license to install this software on any computer or computer network used by you or your students.

Readme File: A Readme.txt file located on the Setup Disk provides additional technical notes, troubleshooting advice, and tips for using the CTI WinApps software in your school's computer lab. You can view the Readme file using any word processor you choose.

System Requirements for installing the CTI WinApps Disk The minimum software and hardware requirements your computer system needs to install the CTI WinApps icon group are as follows:

- Microsoft Windows version 3.1 on a local hard drive or on a network drive

- A 286 (or higher) processor with a minimum of 2 MB RAM (4 MB RAM or more is strongly recommended).

- A mouse supported by Windows

- A printer that is supported by Windows 3.1

- A VGA 640 x 480 16-color display is recommended; an 800 x 600 or 1024 x 768 SVGA, VGA monochrome, or EGA display is also acceptable

- 1.5 MB of free hard disk space

- Student workstations with at least 1 high-density disk drive. If you need a 5.25 inch CTI WinApps Setup Disk, contact your CTI sales rep or call customer service at 1-800-648-7450. In Canada call Times Mirror Professional Publishing/Iwin Dorsey at 1-800-268-4178.

- If you wish to install the CTI WinApps Setup Disk on a network drive, your network must support Microsoft Windows.

Essential Windows Skills

Using the Program Manager, CTI WinApps, and Help

CASE

A New Computer, Anywhere, Inc. You're a busy employee without a minute of spare time. But now, to top it all off, a computer technician appears at your office door, introduces himself as Steve Laslow, and begins unpacking your new computer!

You wonder out loud, "How long is it going to take me to learn this?"

Steve explains that your new computer uses Microsoft Windows 3.1 software and that the **interface**—the way you interact with the computer and give it instructions—is very easy to use. He describes the Windows software as a "gooey," a **graphical user interface (GUI)**, which uses pictures of familiar objects such as file folders and documents to represent a desktop on your screen.

Steve unpacks your new computer and begins to connect the components. He talks as he works, commenting on three things he really likes about Microsoft Windows. First, Windows applications have a standard interface, which means that once you learn how to use one Windows application, you are well on your way to understanding how to use others. Second, Windows lets you use more than one application at a time, a capability called **multitasking**, so you can easily switch between applications such as your word processor and your calendar. Third, Windows lets you do more than one task at a time, such as printing a document while you create a pie chart. All in all, Windows makes your computer an effective and easy-to-use productivity tool.

Using the Windows Tutorials Effectively

This tutorial will help you learn about Windows 3.1. Begin by reading the text that explains the concepts. Then when you come to numbered steps on a colored background, follow those steps as you work at your computer. Read each step carefully and completely *before* you try it.

Don't worry if parts of your screen display are different from the figures in the tutorials. The important parts of the screen display are labeled in each figure. Just be sure these parts are on your screen.

Don't worry about making mistakes—that's part of the learning process. TROUBLE? paragraphs identify common problems and explain how to get back on track. Do the steps in the TROUBLE? paragraph *only* if you are having the problem described.

Starting Your Computer and Launching Windows

The process of starting Windows is sometimes referred to as **launching**. If your computer system requires procedures different from those in the steps below, your instructor or technical support person will provide you with step-by-step instructions for turning on your monitor, starting or resetting your computer, logging into a network if you have one, and launching Windows.

To start your computer and launch Windows:
❶   Make sure your disk drives are empty.
❷   Find the power switch for your monitor and turn it on.
❸   Locate the power switch for your computer and turn it on. After a few seconds you should see C:\> or C> on the screen.

   TROUBLE?   If your computer displays a "non-system disk" error message, a floppy disk was left in a disk drive at startup. To continue, remove the disk and press [Enter].

❹   Type **win** to launch Windows. See Figure 1-1.

type win ──────┐
your screen │
shows C:\> ├──►

Figure 1-1
Launching Windows

❺ Press the key labeled **[Enter]**. Soon the Windows 3.1 title screen appears. Next you might notice an hourglass on the screen. This symbol means your computer is busy with a task and you must wait until it has finished.

After a brief wait, the title screen is replaced by one similar to Figure 1-2. Don't worry if your screen is not exactly the same as Figure 1-2. You are ready to continue the Tutorial when you see the Program Manager title at the top of the screen. If you do not see this title, ask your technical support person for assistance.

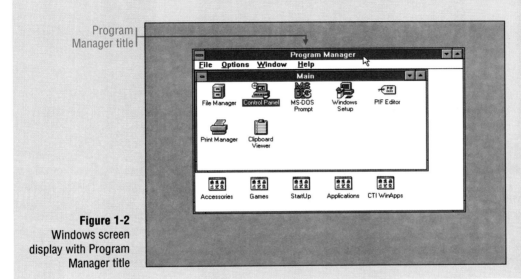

Figure 1-2
Windows screen
display with Program
Manager title

Basic Windows Controls and Concepts

Windows has a variety of **controls** that enable you to communicate with the computer. In this section you'll learn how to use the basic Windows controls.

The Windows Desktop

Look at your screen display and compare it to Figure 1-3 on the following page. Your screen may not be exactly the same as the illustration. You should, however, be able to locate components on your screen similar to those in Figure 1-3 on the following page.

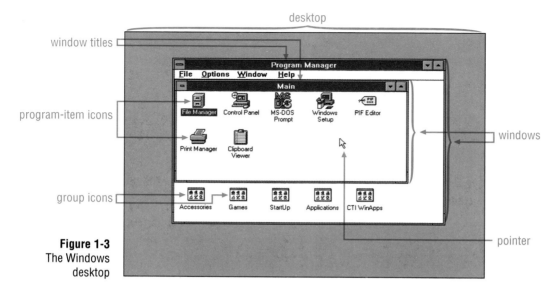

Figure 1-3
The Windows
desktop

The screen represents a **desktop**, a workspace for projects and for the tools that are needed to manipulate those projects. Rectangular **windows** (with a lowercase *w*) define work areas on the desktop. The desktop in Figure 1-3 contains the Program Manager window and the Main window.

Icons are small pictures that represent real objects, such as disk drives, software, and documents. Each icon in the Main window represents an **application**, that is, a computer program. These icons are called **program-item icons**.

Each **group icon** at the bottom of the Program Manager window represents a collection of applications. For example, the CTI WinApps icon represents a collection of tutorial and practice applications, which you can use to learn more about Windows. A group icon expands into a group window that contains program-item icons.

The **pointer** helps you manipulate objects on the Windows desktop. The pointer can assume different shapes, depending on what is happening on the desktop. In Figure 1-3 the pointer is shaped like an arrow.

The Program Manager

When you launch Windows, the Program Manager application starts automatically and continues to run as long as you are working with Windows. Think of the Program Manager as a launching pad for other applications. The **Program Manager** displays icons for the applications on your system. To launch an application, you would select its icon.

Using the Mouse

The **mouse** is a pointing device that helps you interact with the screen-based objects in the Windows environment. As you move the mouse on a flat surface, the pointer on the screen moves in the direction corresponding to the movement of the mouse. You can also control the Windows environment from the keyboard; however, the mouse is much more efficient for most operations, so the tutorials in this book assume you are using one.

Find the arrow-shaped pointer on your screen. If you do not see the pointer, move your mouse until the pointer comes into view. You will begin most Windows-based operations by **pointing**.

To position the pointer:

❶ Position your right index finger over the left mouse button, as shown in Figure 1-4.

   TROUBLE?   If you want to use your mouse with your left hand, ask your technical support person to help you. Be sure you find out how to change back to the right-handed mouse setting, so you can reset the mouse each time you are finished in the lab.

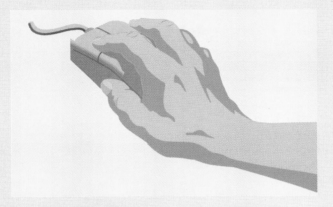

Figure 1-4
How to hold
the mouse

❷ Locate the arrow-shaped pointer on the screen.

❸ Move the mouse and watch the movement of the pointer.

❹ Next, move the mouse to each of the four corners of the screen.

   TROUBLE?   If your mouse runs out of room, lift it, move it into the middle of a clear area on your desk, and then place it back on the table. The pointer does not move when the mouse is not in contact with the tabletop.

❺ Continue experimenting with mouse pointing until you feel comfortable with your "eye-mouse coordination."

Pointing is usually followed by clicking, double-clicking, or dragging. **Clicking** means pressing a mouse button (usually the left button) and then quickly releasing it. Clicking is used to select an object on the desktop. Windows shows you which object is selected by highlighting it.

To click an icon:

❶ Locate the Print Manager icon in the Main window. If you cannot see the Print Manager icon, use any other icon for this activity.

❷ Position the pointer on the icon.

❸ Once the pointer is on the icon, *do not move the mouse*.

❹ Press the left mouse button and then quickly release it. Your icon should have a highlighted title like the one in Figure 1-5 on the following page.

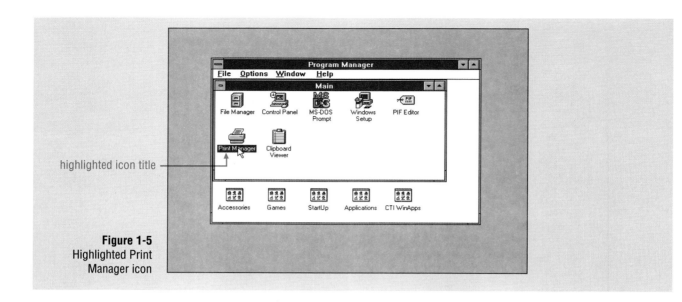

highlighted icon title

Figure 1-5
Highlighted Print
Manager icon

Double-clicking means clicking the mouse button twice in rapid succession. Double-clicking is a shortcut. For example, most Windows users double-click to launch and exit applications.

To double click:
❶ Position the pointer on the Program Manager Control-menu box, as shown in Figure 1-6.

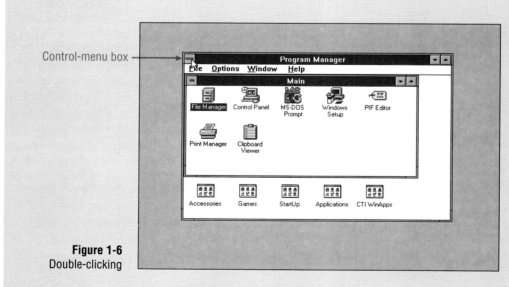

Control-menu box

Figure 1-6
Double-clicking

❷ Click the mouse button twice in rapid succession. If your double-clicking is successful, an Exit Windows box appears on your screen.
❸ Now, single-click the **Cancel button**.

Dragging means moving an object to a new location on the desktop. To drag an object, you would position the pointer on the object, then hold the left mouse button down while you move the mouse. Let's drag one of the icons to a new location.

To drag an icon:

❶ Position the pointer on any icon on the screen, such as on the Clipboard Viewer icon. Figure 1-7 shows you where to put the pointer and what happens on your screen as you carry out the next step.

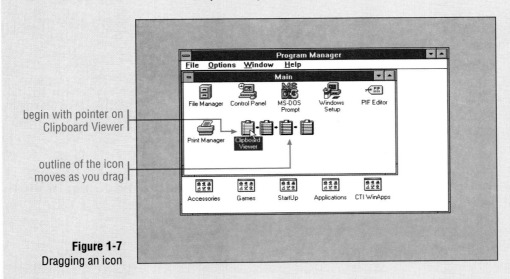

begin with pointer on Clipboard Viewer

outline of the icon moves as you drag

Figure 1-7
Dragging an icon

❷ Hold the left mouse button down while you move the mouse to the right. Notice that an outline of the icon moves as you move the mouse.

❸ Release the mouse button. Now the icon is in a new location.

TROUBLE? If the icon snaps back to its original position, don't worry. Your technical support person probably has instructed Windows to do this. If your icon automatically snapped back to its original position, skip Step 4.

❹ Drag the icon back to its original location.

Using the Keyboard

You use the keyboard to type documents, enter numbers, and activate some commands. You can use the on-screen CTI Keyboard Tutorial to learn the special features of your computer keyboard. To do this, you need to learn how to launch the Keyboard Tutorial and other applications.

Launching Applications

Earlier in this tutorial you launched Windows. Once you have launched Windows, you can launch other Windows applications such as Microsoft Works. When you launch an application, an application window opens. Later, when you have finished using the application, you close the window to exit.

Launching the CTI Keyboard Tutorial

To launch the CTI Keyboard Tutorial, you need to have the CTI WinApps software installed on your computer. If you are working in a computer lab, these applications should already be installed on your computer system. Look on your screen for a group icon or a window labeled "CTI WinApps."

If you don't have anything labeled "CTI WinApps" on your screen's desktop, ask your technical support person for help. If you are using your own computer, you will need to install the CTI WinApps applications yourself. See your technical support person or your instructor for a copy of the Setup Disk and the Installation Instructions that come with it.

To open the CTI Win Apps group window:

❶ Double-click the **CTI WinApps group icon**. Your screen displays a CTI WinApps group window similar to the one in Figure 1-8.

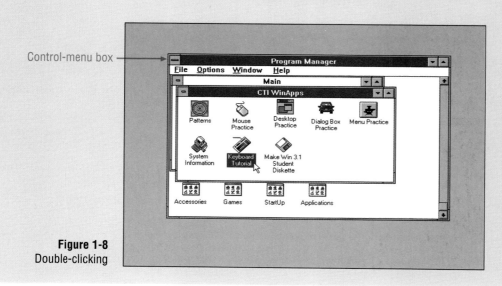

Control-menu box

Figure 1-8
Double-clicking

The CTI WinApps group window contains an icon for each application provided with these tutorials. Right now we want to use the Keyboard Tutorial application.

To launch the Keyboard Tutorial:

❶ Double-click the **Keyboard Tutorial icon**. Within a few seconds, the tutorial begins.

❷ Read the opening screen, then click the **Continue button**. The CTI Keyboard Tutorial window appears. Follow the instructions on your screen to complete the tutorial. See Figure 1-9.

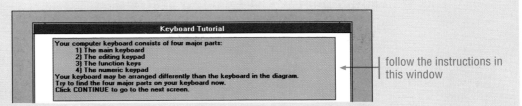

Figure 1-9
Instructions in the
CTI Keyboard
Tutorial window

follow the instructions in
this window

TROUBLE?   Click the Quit button at any time if you want to exit the Tutorial.

❸   When you have completed the Keyboard Tutorial, click the **Quit button**. This takes you back to the Program Manager and CTI WinApps group window.

TROUBLE?   *If you did not have trouble in Step 3, skip this entire paragraph!* If the Program Manager window is not open, look for its icon at the bottom of your screen. Double-click this icon to open the Program Manager window. To prevent this problem from happening again, click the word Options on the Program Manager menu bar, then click Minimize on Use.

Launching the CTI Mouse Practice

To discover how to use the mouse to manipulate Windows controls, you should launch the Mouse Practice.

To launch the Mouse Practice:

❶   Make sure the Program Manager and the CTI WinApps windows are open. It is not a problem if you have additional windows open.

TROUBLE?   If the Program Manager window is not open, look for its icon at the bottom of your screen. Double-click this icon to open the Program Manager window. To prevent this problem from happening again, click the word Options that appears near the top of the Program Manager window, then click Minimize.

❷   Double-click the **Mouse Practice icon**. The Mouse Practice window opens.

TROUBLE?   If you don't see the Mouse Practice icon, try clicking the scroll bar arrow button or see your technical support person.

❸   Click, drag, or double-click the objects on the screen to see what happens. Don't hesitate to experiment.

❹   When you have finished using the Mouse Practice, click the **Exit button** to go back to the Program Manager and continue the tutorial steps.

Organizing Application Windows on the Desktop

The Windows desktop provides you with capabilities similar to your desk; it lets you stack many different items on your screen-based desktop and activate the one you want to use.

There is a problem, though. Like your real desk, your screen-based desktop can become cluttered. That's why you need to learn how to organize the applications on your Windows desktop.

Launching the CTI Desktop Practice

The Desktop Practice application will help you learn the controls for organizing your screen-based desktop.

To Launch the Desktop Practice:
❶ Double-click the **Desktop Practice icon** to open the Desktop Practice window, shown in Figure 1-10. Your windows might be a different size or in a slightly different position. Don't worry. What's important is that you see a window with the title "Desktop Practice."

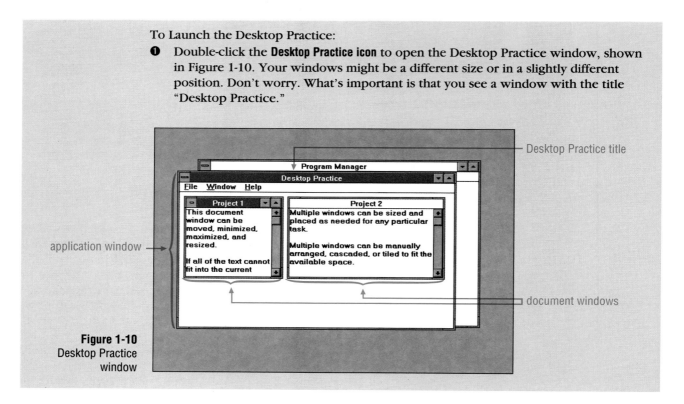

Figure 1-10
Desktop Practice
window

Launching the Desktop Practice application opens three new windows on the desktop: Desktop Practice, Project 1, and Project 2. You might be able to see the edges of the Program Manager window "under" the Desktop Practice window. Essentially, you have stacked one project on top of another on your desktop.

The Desktop Practice window is an **application window**, a window that opens when you launch an application. The Project 1 and Project 2 windows are referred to as **document windows**, because they contain the documents, graphs, and lists you create using the application. Document windows are also referred to as **child windows**, because they belong to and are controlled by a "parent" application window.

The ability to have more than one document window open is one of many useful features of the Windows operating environment. Without this capability, you would have to print the documents that aren't being displayed so you could refer to them.

The Anatomy of a Window

Application windows and document windows are similar in many respects. Take a moment to study the Desktop Practice window on your screen and in Figure 1-11 on the following page to familiarize yourself with the terminology. Notice the location of each component but *don't* activate the controls.

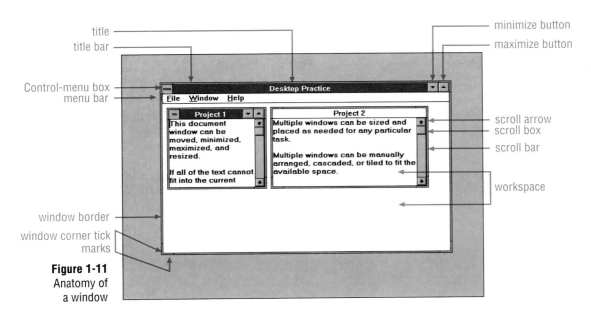

Figure 1-11
Anatomy of
a window

At the top of each window is a **title bar**, which contains the window title. A darkened or highlighted title bar indicates that the application window is active. In Figure 1-11, the Desktop Practice application and the Project 1 document windows are active.

In the upper-right of the application window are two buttons used to change the size of a window. The **minimize button**—a square containing a triangle with the point down—is used to shrink the window. The **maximize button**, with the triangle pointing up, is used to enlarge the window so it fills the screen. When a window is maximized, a **restore button** with two triangles replaces the maximize button. Clicking the restore button reduces a maximized window to its previous size.

The **Control-menu box**, located in the upper-left of the Desktop Practice application window, is used to open the **Control menu**, which allows you to switch between application windows.

The **menu bar** is located just below the title bar on application windows. Notice that child windows do not contain menu bars.

The thin line running around the entire perimeter of the window is called the **window border**. The **window corners** are indicated by tick marks on the border.

The gray bar on the right side of each document window is a **scroll bar**, which you use to view window contents that don't initially fit in the window. Both application windows and document windows can contain scroll bars. Scroll bars can appear on the bottom of a window as well as on the side.

The space inside a window where you type text, design graphics, and so forth is called the **workspace**.

Maximizing and Minimizing Windows

The buttons on the right of the title bar are sometimes referred to as **resizing buttons**. You can use the resizing buttons to **minimize** the window so it shrinks down to an icon, **maximize** the window so it fills the screen, or **restore** the window to its previous size.

Because a minimized program is still running, you have quick access to the materials you're using for the project without taking up space on the desktop. You don't need to launch the program when you want to use it again because it continues to run.

A maximized window is useful when you want to focus your attention on the project in that window without being distracted by other windows and projects.

To maximize, restore, and minimize the Desktop Practice window:

❶ Locate the maximize button (the one with the triangle pointing up) for the Desktop Practice window. You might see a portion of the Program Manager window behind the Desktop Practice window. Be sure you have found the Desktop Practice maximize button. See Figure 1-12.

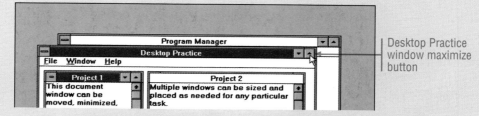

Figure 1-12
Maximizing a window

Desktop Practice window maximize button

❷ Click the **maximize button** to expand the window to fill the screen. Notice that in place of the maximize button there is now a restore button that contains double triangles.

❸ Click the **restore button**. The Desktop Practice window returns to its original size.

❹ Next, click the **minimize button** (the one with the triangle pointing down) to shrink the window to an icon.

❺ Locate the minimized Desktop Practice icon at the bottom of your screen. See Figure 1-13.

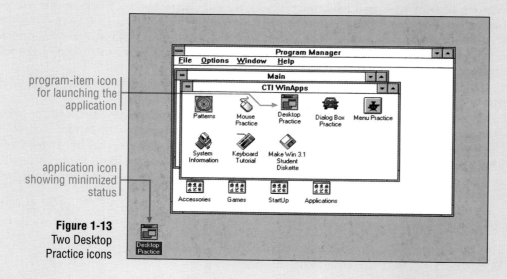

program-item icon for launching the application

application icon showing minimized status

Figure 1-13
Two Desktop Practice icons

TROUBLE?   If you cannot locate the Desktop Practice icon at the bottom of your screen, the Program Manager is probably maximized. To remedy this situation, click the restore button on the Program Manager Window.

When you *close* an application window, you exit the application and it stops running. But when you *minimize* an application, it is still running even though it has been shrunk to an icon. It is important to remember that minimizing a window is not the same as closing it.

The icon for a minimized application is called an **application icon**. As Figure 1-13 illustrates, your screen shows two icons for the Desktop Practice application. The icon at the bottom of your screen is the application icon and represents a program that is currently running even though it is minimized. The other Desktop Practice icon is inside the CTI WinApps window. If you were to double-click this icon, you would launch a second version of the Desktop Practice application. *Don't launch two versions of the same application.* You should restore the Desktop Practice window by double-clicking the minimized icon at the bottom of your screen. Let's do that now.

To restore the Desktop Practice window:

❶ Double-click the minimized **Desktop Practice icon** at the bottom of your screen. The Desktop Practice window opens.

Changing the Dimensions of a Window

Changing the dimensions of a window is useful when you want to arrange more than one project on your desktop. Suppose you want to work with the Desktop Practice application and at the same time view the contents of the Program Manager window. To do this, you will need to change the dimensions of both windows so they don't overlap each other.

To change the dimensions of the Desktop Practice window:

❶ Move the pointer slowly over the top border of the Desktop Practice window until the pointer changes shape to a double-ended arrow. See Figure 1-14.

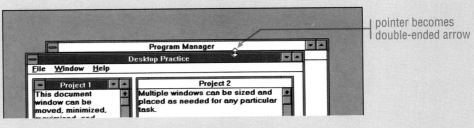

Figure 1-14
Preparing to change the window dimensions

❷ Press the left mouse button and hold it down while you drag the border to the top of the screen. Notice how an outline of the border follows your mouse movement.

❸ Release the mouse button. As a result the window adjusts to the new border.

❹ Drag the left border of the Desktop Practice window to the left edge of the screen.

❺ Move the pointer slowly over the lower-right corner of the Desktop Practice window until the pointer changes shape to a double-ended diagonal arrow. Figure 1-15 on the following page shows you how to do this step and the next one.

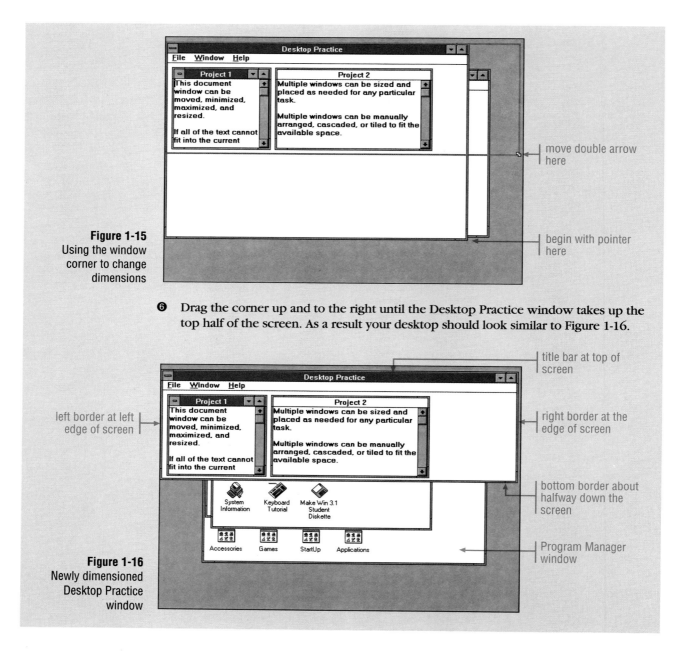

Figure 1-15
Using the window
corner to change
dimensions

move double arrow
here

begin with pointer
here

❻   Drag the corner up and to the right until the Desktop Practice window takes up the
top half of the screen. As a result your desktop should look similar to Figure 1-16.

title bar at top of
screen

left border at left
edge of screen

right border at the
edge of screen

bottom border about
halfway down the
screen

Program Manager
window

Figure 1-16
Newly dimensioned
Desktop Practice
window

Switching Applications

In the preceding steps you arranged the application windows so they were both visible
at the same time. A different approach to organizing windows is to maximize the windows and then switch between them using the **Task List**, which contains a list of all
open applications.

Let's maximize the Desktop Practice window. Then, using the Task List, let's switch
to the Program Manager window, which will be hidden behind it.

To maximize the Desktop Practice window and then switch to the Program Manager:

❶ Click the **maximize button** on the Desktop Practice title bar. As a result the maximized Desktop Practice window hides the Program Manager window.

❷ Click the **Control-menu box** on the left side of the Desktop Practice title bar. Figure 1-17 shows you the location of the Control-menu box and also the Control menu, which appears after you click.

Control-menu box

Control menu

Switch To... command

Figure 1-17
The Control menu

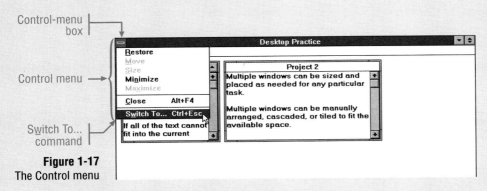

❸ Click **Switch To...** The Task List box appears, as shown in Figure 1-18.

then click Switch To... button

Figure 1-18
Switching applications using the Task List

click Program Manager

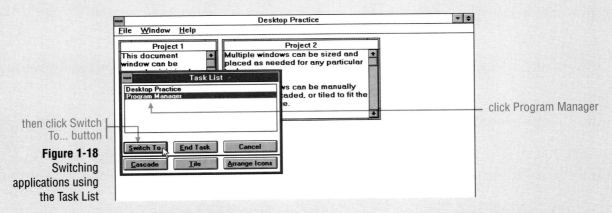

❹ Click the **Program Manager option** from the list, then click the **Switch To button** to select the Program Manager. As a result the Program Manager reappears on the bottom half of your screen.

❺ If it is not already maximized, click the **maximize button** on the Program Manager window so both applications (Program Manager and Desktop Practice) are maximized.

The Program Manager window is active and "on top" of the Desktop Practice window. To view the Desktop Practice window, you will need to switch application windows again. You could switch tasks using the mouse, as we did in the last set of steps, or you can use the keyboard to quickly cycle through the tasks and activate the one you want. Let's use the keyboard method for switching windows this time, instead of using the Task List.

To switch to the Desktop Practice window using the keyboard:

❶ Hold down **[Alt]** and continue holding it down while you press **[Tab]**. Don't release the Alt key yet! On the screen you should see a small rectangle that says "Desktop Practice."

TROUBLE?   Don't worry if you accidentally let go of the Alt key too soon. Try again. Press [Alt][Tab] until the "Desktop Practice" rectangle reappears.

❷ Release the Alt key. Now the maximized Desktop Practice window is open.

When a window is maximized, it is easy to forget what's behind it. If you forget what's on the desktop, call up the Task List using the Control menu or use [Alt][Tab] to cycle through the tasks.

Organizing Document Windows

Think of document windows as subwindows within an application window. Because document windows do not have menu bars, the commands relating to these windows are selected from the menu bar of the application window. For example, you can use the Tile command in the Window menu to arrange windows so they are as large as possible without any overlap. The advantage of tiled windows is that one window won't cover up important information. The disadvantage of tiling is that the more windows you tile, the smaller each tile becomes and the more scrolling you will have to do.

You can use the Cascade command in the Window menu to arrange windows so they are all a standard size, they overlap each other, and all title bars are visible. Cascaded windows are often larger than tiled windows and at least one corner is always accessible so you can activate the window. Try experimenting with tiled and cascading windows. The desktop organizational skills you will learn will help you arrange the applications on your desktop so you can work effectively in the Windows multi-tasking environment.

Closing a Window

You close a window when you have finished working with a document or when you want to exit an application program. The steps you follow to close a document window are the same as those to close an application window. Let's close the Desktop Practice window.

To close the Desktop Practice application window:

❶ Click the **Control-menu box** on the Desktop Practice window.

❷ Click **Close** as shown in Figure 1-19 on the following page. The Desktop Practice window closes and you see the Program Manager window on the desktop.

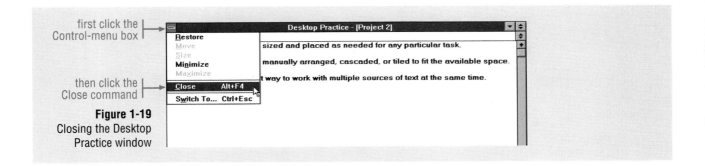

first click the
Control-menu box

then click the
Close command

Figure 1-19
Closing the Desktop
Practice window

Using Windows to Specify Tasks

In Windows, you issue instructions called **commands** to tell the computer what you want it to do. Windows applications provide you with lists of commands called **menus**. Many applications also have a ribbon of icons called a **toolbar**, which provides you with command shortcuts. Let's launch the Menu Practice application to find out how menus and toolbars work.

To launch the Menu Practice application:

❶ If the CTI WinApps window is not open, double-click its group icon at the bottom of the Program Manager window.

❷ Double-click the **Menu Practice** icon to open the Menu Practice window. See Figure 1-20.

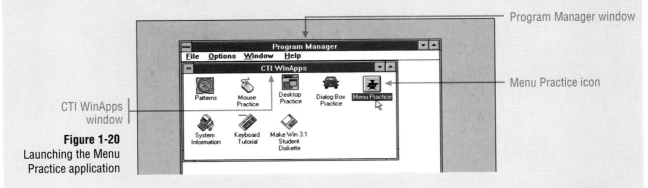

Program Manager window

Menu Practice icon

CTI WinApps
window

Figure 1-20
Launching the Menu
Practice application

❸ Click the **maximize button** (the one with the triangle point up) for the Menu Practice window. The maximized Menu Practice window is shown in Figure 1-21 on the following page.

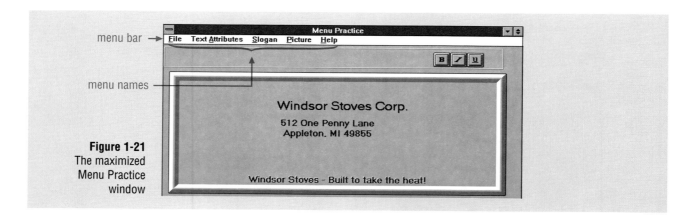

menu bar →

menu names →

Figure 1-21
The maximized
Menu Practice
window

Opening and Closing Menus

Application windows, but not document windows, have menu bars such as the one shown in Figure 1-21. The menu bar contains menu names such as File, Text Attributes, Slogan, Picture, and Help. Let's practice opening and closing menus.

To open a menu:
❶ Click **File**. Figure 1-22 shows you where to click and the menu that appears.

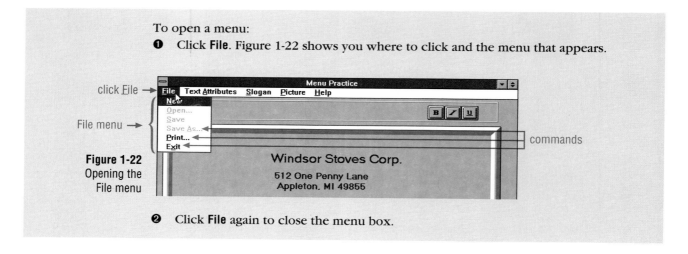

click File →

File menu →

commands

Figure 1-22
Opening the
File menu

❷ Click **File** again to close the menu box.

When you click a menu name, the full menu drops down to display a list of commands. The commands on a menu are sometimes referred to as **menu items**.

Menu Conventions

The commands displayed on the Windows menus often include one or more **menu conventions**, such as check marks, ellipses, shortcut keys, and underlined letters. These menu conventions provide you with additional information about each menu command.

A check mark in front of a menu command indicates that the command is in effect. Clicking a checked command will remove the check mark and deactivate the command. For example, the Windsor Stoves logo currently has no graphic because the Show Picture command is not active. Let's add a picture to the logo by activating the Show Picture command.

To add or remove a check mark from the Show Picture command:

❶ Click **Picture**. Notice that no check mark appears next to the Show Picture command.

❷ Click **Show Picture**. The Picture menu closes, and a picture of a stove appears.

❸ Click **Picture** to open the Picture menu again. Notice that a check mark appears next to the Show Picture command because you activated this command in Step 2.

❹ Click **Show Picture**. This time clicking Show Picture removes the check mark and removes the picture.

Another menu convention is the use of gray, rather than black, type for commands. Commands displayed in gray type are sometimes referred to as **grayed-out commands**. Gray type indicates that a command is not currently available. The command might become available later, when it can be applied to the task. For example, a command that positions a picture on the right or left side of the logo would not apply to a logo without a picture. Therefore, the command for positioning the picture would be grayed out until a picture was included with the logo. Let's explore how this works.

To explore grayed-out commands:

❶ Click **Picture**. Figure 1-23 shows the Picture menu with two grayed-out choices.

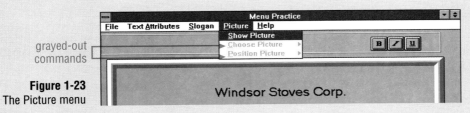

grayed-out
commands

Figure 1-23
The Picture menu

❷ Click the grayed-out command **Position Picture**. Although the highlight moves to this command, nothing else happens because the command is not currently available. You cannot position the picture until a picture is displayed.

❸ Now click **Show Picture**. The Picture menu closes, and a picture is added to the logo.

❹ Click **Picture**. Now that you have opened the Picture menu again, notice that the Choose Picture and Position Picture commands are no longer grayed out.

A **submenu** provides an additional set of command choices. On your screen the Choose Picture and Position Picture commands each have triangles next to them. A triangle is a menu convention that indicates a menu has a submenu. Let's use the submenu of the Position Picture command to move the stove picture to the right of the company name.

To use the position Picture submenu:

❶ Click **Position Picture**. A submenu appears with options for left or right. In Figure 1-24 on the following page, the picture is to the left of the company name.

submenu for the
Position Picture
command

Figure 1-24
Viewing a submenu

❷   Click **Right**. Selecting this submenu command moves the picture to the right of the company name.

Some menu conventions allow you to use the menus without a mouse. It is useful to know how to use these conventions because, even if you have a mouse, in some situations it might be faster to use the keyboard.

One keyboard-related menu convention is the underlined letter in each menu name. If you wanted to open a menu using the keyboard, you would hold down the Alt key and then press the underlined letter. Let's open the Text Attributes menu using the keyboard.

To open the Text Attributes menu this way:
❶   Look at the menu name for the Text Attributes menu. Notice that the A is underlined.
❷   Press **[Alt][A]**. The Text Attributes menu opens.

   TROUBLE?   Remember from the Keyboard Tutorial that the [Alt][A] notation means to hold down the Alt key and press A. Don't type the brackets and don't use the Shift key to capitalize the A.

You can also use the keyboard to highlight and activate commands. On your screen the Bold command is highlighted. You use the arrow keys on the keyboard to move the highlight. You activate highlighted commands by pressing [Enter]. Let's use the keyboard to activate the Underline command.

To choose the Underline command using the keyboard:
❶   Press [↓] two times to highlight the Underline command.
❷   Press **[Enter]** to activate the highlighted command and underline the company name. Now look at the B , I , and U buttons near the upper-right corner of the screen. The U button has been "pressed" or activated. This button is another control for underlining. You'll find out how to use these buttons later.

Previously you used the Alt key in combination with the underlined letter in the menu title to open a menu. You might have noticed that each menu command also has an underlined letter. Once a menu is open, you can activate a command by pressing the underlined letter—there is no need to press the Alt key.

To activate the Italic command using the underlined letter:

❶ Press **[Alt][A]**. This key combination opens the Text Attributes menu. Next, notice which letter is underlined in the Italic command.

❷ Press **[I]** to activate the Italic command. Now the company name is italicized as well as underlined.

Look at the menu in Figure 1-25. Notice the Ctrl+B to the right of the Bold command. This is the key combination, often called a **shortcut key**, that can be used to activate the Bold command even if the menu is not open. The Windows Ctrl+B notation means the same thing as [Ctrl][B] in these tutorials: hold down the Control key and, while holding it down, press the letter B. When you use shortcut keys, don't type the + sign and don't use the Shift key to capitalize. Let's use a shortcut key to boldface the company name.

Figure 1-25
The Text Attributes
menu

To Boldface the company name using a shortcut key:

❶ Press **[Ctrl][B]** and watch the company name appear in boldface type.

The **ellipsis (...)** menu convention means that when you select a command with three dots next to it, a dialog box will appear. A **dialog box** requests additional details about how you want the command carried out. We'll use the dialog box for the Choose Slogan command to change the company slogan.

To use the Choose Slogan dialog box:

❶ Click **Slogan**. Notice that the Choose Slogan command is followed by an ellipsis.

❷ Click **Choose Slogan...** and study the dialog box that appears. See Figure 1-26. Notice that this dialog box contains four sets of controls: the "Use Slogan" text box, the "Slogan in Bold Letters" check box, the "Slogan 3-D Effects" control buttons, and the OK and Cancel buttons. The "Use Slogan" text box displays the current slogan.

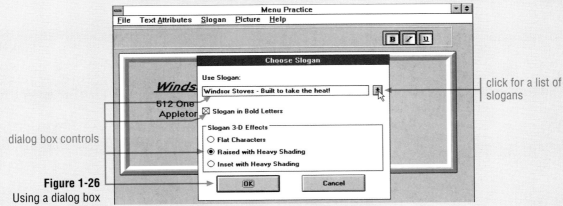

Figure 1-26
Using a dialog box

❸ Click the **down arrow button** on the right of the slogan box to display a list of alternative slogans.

❹ Click the slogan **Windsor Stoves - Built to last for generations!**

❺ Click the **OK button** and watch the new slogan replace the old.

You have used the Menu Practice application to learn how to use Windows menus, and you have learned the meaning of the Windows menu conventions. Next we'll look at dialog box controls.

Dialog Box Controls

Figure 1-27 shows a dialog box with a number of different controls that could be used to specify the requirements for a rental car. **Command buttons** initiate an immediate action. A **text box** is a space for you to type in a command detail. A **list box** displays a list of choices. A drop-down list box appears initially with only one choice; clicking the list box arrow displays additional choices. **Option buttons**, sometimes called radio buttons, allow you to select one option. **Check boxes** allow you to select one or more options. A **spin bar** changes a numeric setting.

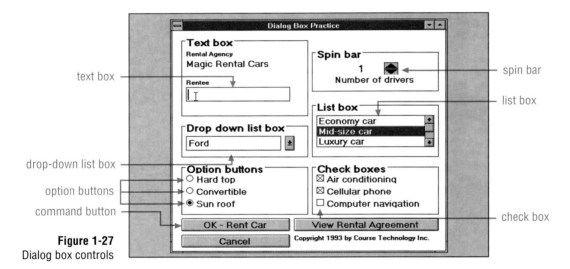

Figure 1-27
Dialog box controls

Windows uses standard dialog boxes for tasks such as printing documents and saving files. Most Windows applications use the standard dialog boxes, so if you learn how to use the Print dialog box for your word processing application, you will be well on your way to knowing how to print in any application. As you may have guessed, the rental car dialog box is not a standard Windows dialog box. It was designed to illustrate the variety of dialog box controls.

Let's see how the dialog box controls work. First, we will use a text box to type text. The Choose Slogan dialog box for the Menu Practice application has a text box that will let us change the slogan on the Windsor Stoves Corp. logo.

To activate the Use Slogan text box:

❶ Click **Slogan** to open the Slogan menu.

❷ Click **Choose Slogan...** and the Choose Slogan dialog box appears.

❸ Move the pointer to the text box and notice that it changes to an **I-bar** shape for text entry. See Figure 1-28.

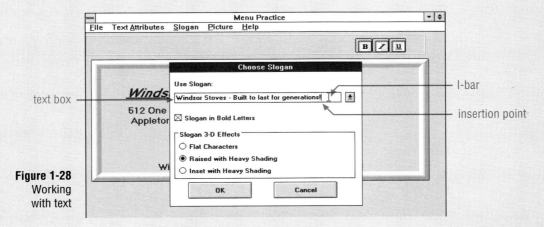

Figure 1-28
Working
with text

❹ Click the **left mouse button** to activate the text box. A blinking bar called an **Insertion point** indicates that you can type text into the box. Also notice that all the text is highlighted.

❺ Press **[Del]** to erase the highlighted text of the old slogan.

When you work with a dialog box, be sure to set all the components the way you want them *before* you press the Enter key or click the OK button. Why? Because the Enter key, like the OK button, tells Windows that you are finished with the entire dialog box. Now let's type a new slogan in the text box and change the slogan 3-D effect.

To type a new slogan in a text box:

❶ Type **Quality is our Trademark!** but don't press [Enter], because while this dialog box is open, you are also going to change the slogan 3-D effect.

TROUBLE?   If you make a typing mistake, press [Backspace] to delete the error, then type the correction.

❷ Look at the Slogan 3-D Effects list. Notice that the current selection is Raised with Heavy Shading.

❸ Click **Inset with Heavy Shading**.

❹ Click the **OK button** and then verify that the slogan and the 3-D effect have changed.

TROUBLE?   If you are working on a monochrome system without the ability to display shade of gray, you may not be able to see the 3-D effect.

Using the Toolbar

A **toolbar** is a collection of icons that provides command shortcuts for mouse users. The icons on the toolbar are sometimes referred to as buttons. Generally the options on the toolbar duplicate menu options, but they are more convenient because they can be activated by a single mouse click. The toolbar for the Menu Practice application shown in Figure 1-29 has three buttons that are shortcuts for the Bold, Italic, and Underline commands. In a previous exercise you underlined, boldfaced, and italicized the company name using the menus. As a result the B, U, and I buttons are activated. Let's see what they look like when we deactivate them.

Figure 1-29
The Menu Practice
toolbar

To change the type style using the toolbar:
❶ Click B to remove the boldface.
❷ Click I to turn off italics.
❸ Click U to turn off underlining.
❹ Click B to turn on boldface again.

You might want to spend a few minutes experimenting with the Menu Practice program to find the best logo design for Windsor Stoves Corp. When you are finished, close the Menu Practice window.

To close the Menu Practice window:
❶ Click the **Control-menu box**.
❷ Click **Close**. The Menu Practice program closes and returns you to Windows Program Manager.

You have now learned about Windows menus, dialog boxes and toolbars. In the next section, you will survey the Paintbrush application, experiment with tools, and access on-line help.

Using Paintbrush to Develop Your Windows Technique

After you have learned the basic Windows controls, you will find that most Windows *applications* contain similar controls. Let's launch the Paintbrush application and discover how to use it.

To launch the Paintbrush application:

❶ Be sure the Program Manager window is open. If it is not open, use the skills you have learned to open it.

❷ You should have an Accessories icon or an Accessories window on the desktop. If you have an Accessories group icon on the desktop, double-click it to open the Accessories group window.

> **TROUBLE?** If you don't see the Accessories icon or window, click the Window menu on the Program Manager menu bar. Look for Accessories in the list. If you find Accessories in this list, click it. If you do not find Accessories, ask your technical support person for help.

❸ Double-click the **Paintbrush icon** to launch the Paintbrush application. Your screen will look similar to the one in Figure 1-30.

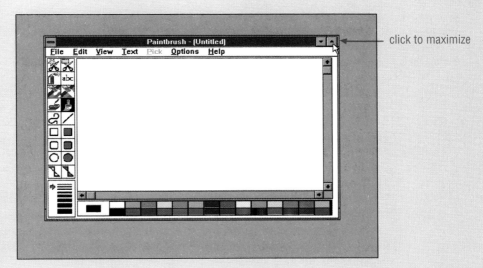

Figure 1-30
The Paintbrush
window

❹ Click the Paintbrush window **maximize button** so you will have a large drawing area.

Surveying the Paintbrush Application Window

Whether you are using a reference manual or experimenting on your own, your first step in learning a new application is to survey the window and familiarize yourself with its components.

Look at the Paintbrush window on your screen and make a list of the components you can identify. If you have not encountered a particular component before, try to guess what it might be.

Now refer to Figure 1-31 on the following page, which labels the Paintbrush window components.

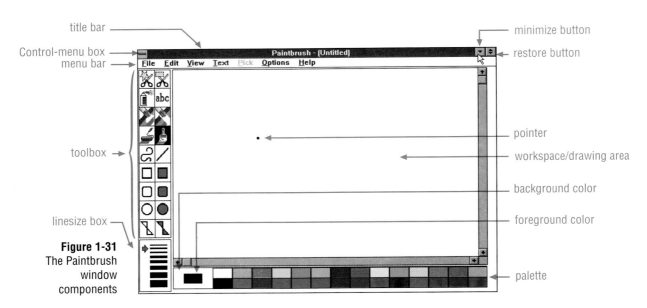

title bar

Control-menu box

menu bar

toolbox ➤

linesize box

minimize button

restore button

pointer

workspace/drawing area

background color

foreground color

palette

Figure 1-31
The Paintbrush
window
components

The darkened title bar shows that the Paintbrush window is activated. The resizing buttons are in the upper-right corner, as usual. Because there is a restore button and because the window takes up the entire screen, you know that the window is maximized. The Control-menu box is in the upper-left corner, and a menu bar lists seven menus.

On the left side of the window are a variety of icons. This looks similar to the toolbar you used when you created the logo, only it has more icons, which are arranged vertically. The Windows manual refers to this set of icons as the **toolbox**.

Under the toolbox is a box containing lines of various widths. This is the **linesize box**, which you use to select the width of the line you draw.

At the bottom of the screen is a color **palette**, which you use to select the foreground and background colors. The currently selected colors for the foreground and background are indicated in the box to the left of the palette.

The rectangular space in the middle of the window is the drawing area. When the pointer is in the drawing area, it will assume a variety of shapes, depending on the tool you are using.

Experimenting with Tools

The icons on toolbars might be some of the easiest Windows controls, but many people are a little mystified by the symbols used for some of the tools. Look at the icons in the Paintbrush toolbox and try to guess their use.

You can often make good guesses, when you know what the application does. For example, you probably guessed that the brush tool shown in Figure 1-32 is used for drawing a picture. However, you might not be able to guess how the brush and the roller tools differ.

paint roller tool

Figure 1-32
The paint roller and
brush icons

brush tool

If you can make some reasonable guess about how a tool works, it's not a bad idea to try it out. Can you write your name using the paintbrush tool? Let's try it.

To use the brush tool:

❶ Locate and click the **brush tool** in the toolbox. The brush tool becomes highlighted, indicating that it is now the selected tool.

❷ Move the pointer to the drawing area. Notice that it changes to a small dot.

❸ Move the pointer to the place where you want to begin writing your name.

When the left mouse button is down, the brush will paint. When you release the mouse button, you can move the pointer without painting.

❹ Use the mouse to control the brush as you write your name. Don't worry if it looks a little rough. Your "John Hancock" might look like the one in Figure 1-33.

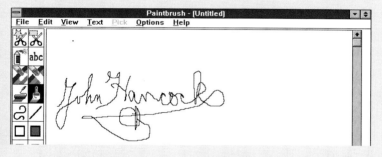

Figure 1-33
Your "John Hancock"

You will recall that we were curious about the difference between the brush and the paint roller. Let's experiment with the paint roller next.

To try the paint roller:

❶ Click the **paint roller** tool.

❷ Position the pointer in the upper-left corner of the drawing area and click. What happened?!

Did you get a strange result? Don't panic. This sort of thing happens when you experiment. Still, we probably should find out a little more about how to control the roller. To do this, we'll use the Paintbrush Help facility.

Using Help

Most Windows applications have an extensive on-line Help facility. A **Help facility** is an electronic reference manual that contains information about an application's menus, tools, and procedures. Some Help facilities also include **tutorials**, which you can use to learn the application.

There are a variety of ways to access Help, so people usually develop their own technique for finding information in it. We'll show you one way that seems to work for many Windows users. Later you can explore on your own and develop your own techniques.

When you use Help, a Help window opens. Usually the Help window overlays your application. If you want to view the problem spot and the Help information at the same time, it is a good idea to organize your desktop so the Help and application windows are side by side.

To access Help and organize the desktop:

❶   Click **Help**. A Help menu lists the Help commands.

❷   Click **Contents** to display a Paintbrush Help window similar to the one in Figure 1-34.

Paintbrush Help window

Paintbrush title bar

Figure 1-34
The Paintbrush
Help window

Help window overlays
Paintbrush windows

❸   If the Paintbrush Help window is not the same size and shape as the one in Figure 1-34, drag the corners of the Help window until it looks like the one in the figure.

The Paintbrush application window is partially covered by the Help window. We need to fix that.

❹   Click the **Paintbrush title bar** to activate the Paintbrush window.

❺   Click the **restore button** to display the window borders and corners.

❻   Drag the corners of the Paintbrush application until your screen resembles the one in Figure 1-35 on the following page.

Paintbrush window ⎯⎯⎯⎯⎯⎯⎯⎯⎯⎯⎯⎯⎯⎯⎯⎯⎯⎯⎯⎯⎯⎯⎯⎯⎯⎯⎯⎯⎯⎯ Help window

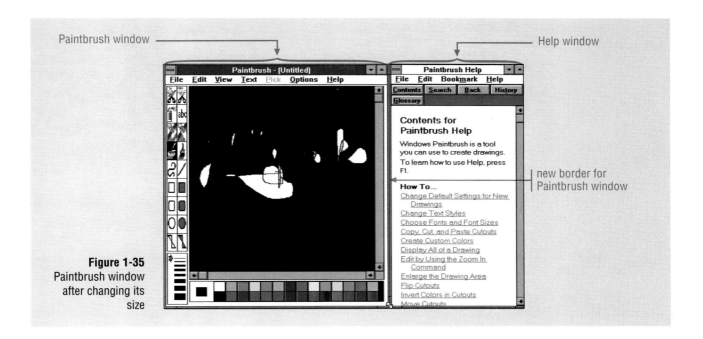

new border for
Paintbrush window

Figure 1-35
Paintbrush window
after changing its
size

Now that the windows are organized, let's find out about the roller tool. The Paintbrush Help window contains a Table of Contents, which is divided into three sections: How To, Tools, and Commands.

The **How To** section is a list of procedures that are explained in the Help facility. Use this section when you want to find out how to do something. The **Tools** section identifies the toolbar icons and explains how to use them. The **Commands** section provides an explanation of the commands that can be accessed from the menu bar.

To find information about the paint roller tool on the Help facility:

❶ Use the scroll box to scroll down the text in the Help window until you see the Tools section heading.

❷ Continue scrolling until the Paint Roller option comes into view.

❸ Position the pointer on the Paint Roller Option. Notice that the pointer changes to a pointing hand, indicating that Paint Roller is a clickable option.

❹ Click the **left mouse button**. The Help window now contains information about the paint roller, as shown in Figure 1-36 on the following page.

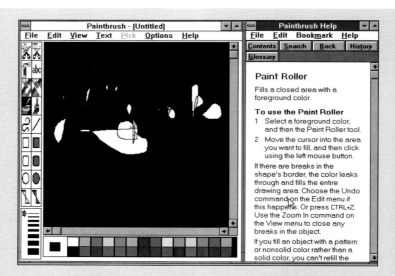

Figure 1-36
Paint Roller Help

❺ Read the information about the Paint Roller, using the scroll bar to view the entire text.

What did you learn about the paint roller? The first item you likely discovered is that the paint roller is used to fill an area. Well, it certainly did that in our experiment. It filled the entire drawing area with the foreground color, black. Next you might have noted that the first step in the procedure for using the paint roller is to select a foreground color. In our experiment, it would have been better if we selected some color other than black for the fill. Let's erase our old experiment so we can try again.

To start a new painting:
❶ Click **File** on the Paintbrush menu bar (not on the Help menu bar) to open the File menu.
❷ Click **New**, because you want to start a new drawing. A dialog box asks, "Do you want to save current changes?"
❸ Click the **No button** to clear the drawing area, because you don't want to save your first experiment.

Now you can paint your name and then use the roller to artistically fill areas. When you have finished experimenting, exit the Paintbrush application.

To exit Paintbrush:
❶ Click the **Control-menu box** and then click **Close**.
❷ In response to the prompt "Do you want to save current changes?" click the **No button**. The Paintbrush window closes, which also automatically closes the Help window.

You've covered a lot of ground. Next, it's time to learn how to exit Windows.

Exiting Windows

You might want to continue directly to the Questions and Tutorial Assignments. If so, stay in Windows until you have completed your work, then follow these instructions for exiting Windows.

To exit Windows:

❶ Click the **Control-menu box** in the upper-left of the Program Manager window.

❷ Click **Close**.

❸ When you see the message "This will end your Windows session," click the **OK button**.

■   ■   ■

Steve congratulates you on your Windows progress. You have learned the terminology associated with the desktop environment and the names of the controls and how to use them. You have developed an understanding about desktop organization and how to arrange the application and document windows so you will use them most effectively. You have also learned to use menus, dialog boxes, toolbars and Help.

Questions

1. GUI is an acronym for _____.
2. A group window contains which of the following?
   a. application icons
   b. document icons
   c. program-item icons
   d. group icons
3. What is one of the main purposes of the Program Manager?
   a. to organize your diskette
   b. to launch applications
   c. to create documents
   d. to provide the Help facility for applications
4. Which mouse function is used as a shortcut for more lengthy mouse or keyboard procedures?
   a. pointing
   b. clicking
   c. dragging
   d. double-clicking
5. To change the focus to an icon, you _____ it.
   a. close
   b. select
   c. drag
   d. launch

6. What is another name for document windows?
   a. child windows
   b. parent windows
   c. application windows
   d. group windows

7. In Figure 1-37 each window component is numbered. Write the name of the component that corresponds to the number.

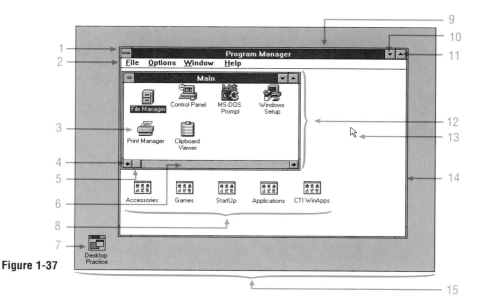

Figure 1-37

8. In Windows terminology you _____ a window when you want to get it out of the way temporarily but leave the application running.

9. You _____ a window when you no longer need to have the application running.

10. The _____ provides you with a way to switch between application windows.
    a. Task List
    b. program-item icon
    c. Window menu
    d. maximize button

11. How would you find out if you had more than one application running on your desktop?

12. _____ refers to the capability of a computer to run more than one application at the same time.

13. Which menu provides the means to switch from one document to another?
    a. the File menu
    b. the Help menu
    c. the Window menu
    d. the Control menu

14. Describe three menu conventions used in Windows menus.

E 15. The flashing vertical bar that marks the place your typing will appear is _____.

E 16. If you have access to a Windows reference manual such as the *Microsoft Windows User's Guide*, look for an explanation of the difference between group icons, program-item icons, and application icons. For your instructor's information, write down the name of the reference, the publisher, and the page(s) on which you found this information. If you were writing a textbook for first-time Windows users, how would you describe the difference between these icons?

E 17. Copy the definition of "metaphor" from any standard dictionary. For your instructor's information, write down the dictionary name, the edition, and the page number. After considering the definition, explain why Windows is said to be a "desktop metaphor."

Tutorial Assignments

If you exited Windows at the end of the tutorial, launch Windows and do Assignments 1 through 15. Write your answers to the questions in Assignments 1, 2, 3, 4, 5, 9, 10, 11, 12, 13, and 15. Also fill out the table in Assignment 7.

1. Close all applications except the Program Manager and shrink all the group windows to icons. What are the names of the group icons on the desktop?
2. Open the Main window. How many program-item icons are in this window?
3. Open the Accessories window. How many program-item icons are in this window?
4. Open, close, and change the dimensions of the windows so your screen looks like Figure 1-38.
   a. How many applications are now on the desktop?
   b. How did you find out how many applications are on the desktop?

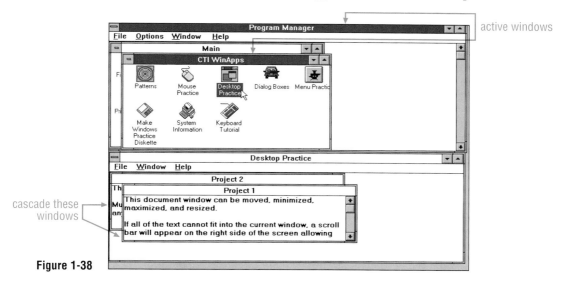

Figure 1-38

5. Open, close, and change the dimensions of the windows so your screen looks like Figure 1-39 on the following page. After you're done, close the Desktop Practice window using the fewest mouse clicks. How did you close the Desktop Practice window?

Open the CTI WinApps window and do Assignments 6 through 8.

Figure 1-39

6. Double-click the System Information icon.
7. Using the information displayed on your screen, fill out the following table:

CPU Type:	
Available Memory:	
Number of Diskette Drives:	
Capacity of Drive A:	
Capacity of Drive B:	
Horizontal Video Resolution:	
Vertical Video Resolution:	
Screen Colors or Shades:	
Network Type:	
DOS Version:	
Windows Version:	
Windows Mode:	
Windows Directory:	
Windows Free Resources:	
Available Drive Letters:	
Hard Drive Capacities:	

8. Click the Exit button to return to the Program Manager.

Launch the Mouse Practice application and do Assignments 9 through 14.

9. What happens when you drag the letter to the file cabinet?
10. What happens when you double-click the mouse icon located in the lower-left corner of the desktop?
11. What happens when you click an empty check box? What happens when you click a check box that contains an "X"?
12. Can you select both option buttons at the same time?
13. What happens when you click "Item Fourteen" from the list?
14. Exit the Mouse Practice.

Launch the Desktop Practice and do Assignments 15 through 17.

15. What is the last sentence of the document in the Project 2 window?
16. Close the Desktop Practice window.
17. Exit Windows.

Effective File Management

Using the File Manager

OBJECTIVES

In this tutorial you will:

- Open and close the File Manager
- Format and make your student disk containing practice files
- Change the current drive
- Identify the components of the File Manager window
- Create directories
- Change the current directory
- Move, rename, delete, and copy files
- Make a disk backup
- Learn how to protect your data from hardware failures

CASE

A Professional Approach to Computing at Narraganset Shipyard   Ruth Sanchez works at the Narraganset Shipyard, a major government defense contractor. On a recent business trip to Washington, DC, Ruth read a magazine article that convinced her she should do a better job of organizing the files on her computer system. The article pointed out that a professional approach to computing includes a plan for maintaining an organized set of disk-based files that can be easily accessed, updated, and secured.

Ruth learns that the Windows File Manager can help to organize her files. Ruth has not used the File Manager very much, so before she begins to make organizational changes to the valuable files on her hard disk, she decides to practice with some sample files on a disk in drive A.

In this Tutorial, you will follow the progress of Ruth's File Manager practice and learn how to use Windows to manage effectively the data stored in your computer.

Files and the File Manager

A **file** is a named collection of data organized for a specific purpose and stored on a floppy disk or a hard disk. The typical computer user has hundreds of files.

The Windows File Manager provides some handy tools for organizing files. Ruth's first step is to launch the File Manager. Let's do the same.

To launch the File Manager:

❶   Launch Windows.

❷   Compare your screen to Figure 2-1. Use the skills you learned in Tutorial 1 to organize your desktop so only the Program Manager window and the Main window are open.

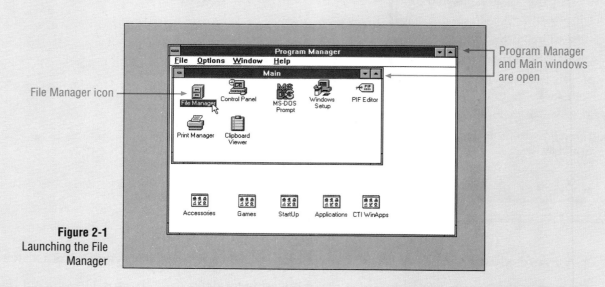

Figure 2-1
Launching the File
Manager

❸   Double-click the **File Manager icon** to launch the File Manager program and open the File Manager window.

❹   If the File Manager window is not maximized, click the **maximize button**.

❺   Click **Window**, then click **Tile**. You should now have one child window on the desktop. See Figure 2-2a on the following page. Don't worry if the title of your child window is not the same as the one in the figure.

your child window
title might be different

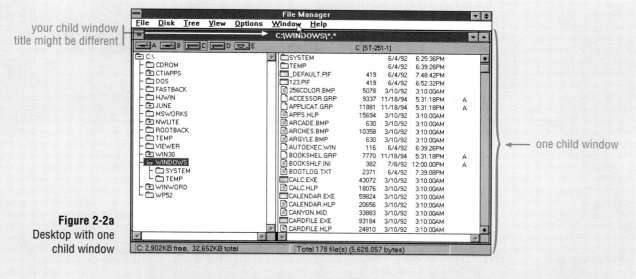

one child window

Figure 2-2a
Desktop with one
child window

TROUBLE? If your desktop contains more than one child window, as in Figure 2-2b, you must double-click the Control-menu box on one of the child windows to close it. Then click the Window menu and click Tile in order to tile the remaining child window.

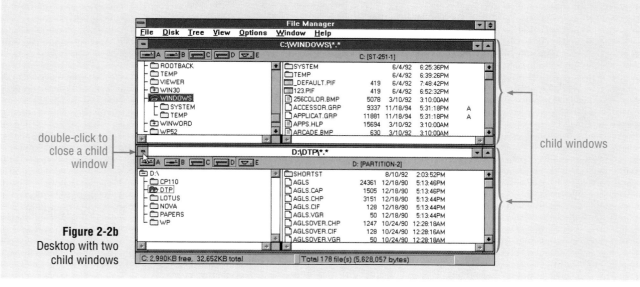

child windows

double-click to
close a child
window

Figure 2-2b
Desktop with two
child windows

Ruth decides to check her File Manager settings, which affect the way information is displayed. By adjusting your File Manager settings to match Ruth's, your computer will display screens and prompts similar to those in the Tutorial. *If you do not finish this tutorial in one session, remember to adjust the settings again when you begin your next session.*

To adjust your File Manager settings:

❶ Click **Tree**. Look at the command "Indicate Expandable Branches." See Figure 2-3. If no check mark appears next to this command, position the pointer on the command and click. If you see the check mark, go to Step 2.

be sure this command is checked

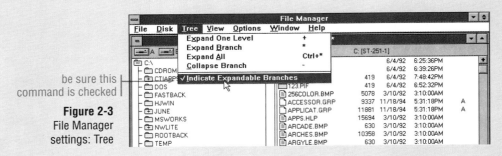

Figure 2-3
File Manager
settings: Tree

❷ Click **View**. Make any adjustments necessary so that the settings are the same as those in Figure 2-4.

be sure these commands are checked

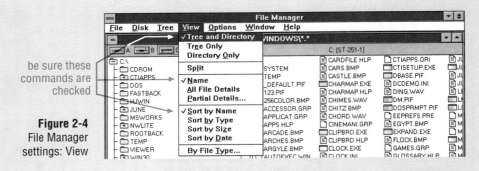

Figure 2-4
File Manager
settings: View

TROUBLE? When you click a command to change the check mark, the menu closes. To change another command in the menu or to confirm your changes, you need to click the View menu again.

❸ Click **Options** and then click **Confirmation....** Referring to Figure 2-5, make any adjustments necessary so that all the check boxes contain an X, then click the **OK button**.

be sure each box contains "X"

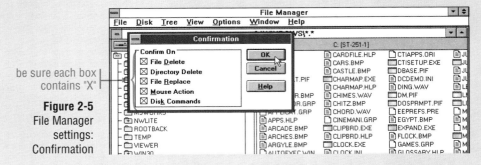

Figure 2-5
File Manager
settings:
Confirmation

❹ Click **Options** again and then click **Font**. Make any adjustments necessary so your font settings match those in Figure 2-6 on the following page. Click the **OK button** whether or not you changed anything in this dialog box.

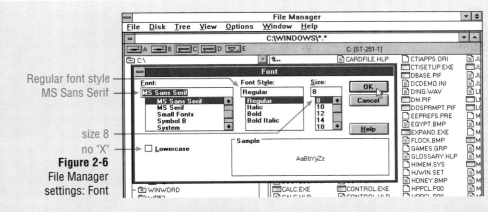

Regular font style
MS Sans Serif

size 8

no "X"

Figure 2-6
File Manager
settings: Font

❺   Click **Options** again. Make any adjustments necessary so that the settings are the same as those in Figure 2-7. If no adjustments are necessary, click **Options** again to close the menu.

only Status Bar
is checked

Figure 2-7
File Manager
settings: Status Bar

Formatting a Disk

Next, Ruth needs to format the disks she will use for her File Manager practice. Disks must be formatted before they can be used to store data. Formatting arranges the magnetic particles on the disks in preparation for storing data. You need to format a disk when:

- you purchase a new disk
- you want to recycle an old disk that you used on a non-IBM-compatible computer
- you want to erase all the old files from a disk

Pay attention when you are formatting disks. *The formatting process erases all the data on the disk.* If you format a disk that already contains data, you will lose all the data. Fortunately, Windows will not let you format the hard disk or network drives using the Format Disk command.

To complete the steps in this Tutorial you need two disks of the same size and density. You may use blank, unformatted disks or disks that contain data you no longer need. *The following steps assume that you will format the disks in drive A. If you want to use drive B for the formatting process, substitute drive B for drive A* in Steps 3, 4, and 6.

To format the first disk:

❶   Make sure your disk is *not* write-protected. On a 5.25-inch disk the write-protect notch should *not* be covered. On a 3.5-inch disk the hole on the left side of the disk should be *closed*.

❷   Write your name, course title, and course meeting time on an adhesive disk label. For the title of the disk, write Student Disk (Source Disk). Apply this label to one of the disks you are going to format. If you are using a 3.5-inch disk, do not stick the label on any of the metal parts.

❸   Put this disk into drive A. If your disk drive has a door or a latch, secure it. See Figure 2-8.

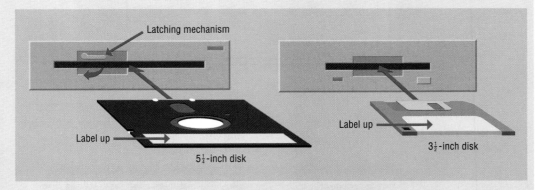

Figure 2-8
Inserting your disk

❹   Click **Disk** and then click **Format Disk....** A Format Disk dialog box appears. See Figure 2-9. If the Disk In box does not indicate Drive A, click the [↓] (down-arrow) button on this box, then click the Drive A option.

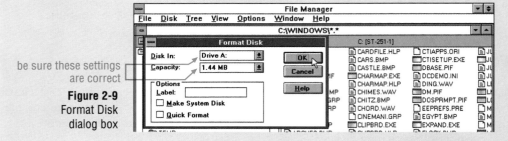

be sure these settings
are correct

Figure 2-9
Format Disk
dialog box

❺   Look at the number displayed in the Capacity box. If you are formatting a disk that cannot store the displayed amount of data, click the [↓] (down-arrow) button at the right side of the Capacity box and then click the correct capacity from the list of options provided.

   TROUBLE? How can you determine the capacity of your disk? The chart in Figure 2-10 (on the next page) will help you. If you still are not sure after looking at the figure, ask your technical support person.

Diskette size	Diskette density	Diskette capacity
51/4-inch	DD	360K
51/4-inch	HD	1.2MB
31/2-inch	DD	720K
31/2-inch	HD	1.44MB

Figure 2-10
Disk capacities

❻ Click the **OK button**. The Confirm Format Disk dialog box appears with a warning. Read it. Look at the drive that is going to carry out the format operation (drive A). Be sure this is the correct drive. Double-check the disk that's in this drive to be sure it is the one you want to format.

❼ Click the **Yes button**. The Formatting Disk dialog box keeps you updated on the progress of the format.

❽ When the format is complete, the Format Complete dialog box reports the results of the format and asks if you'd like to format another disk. See Figure 2-11.

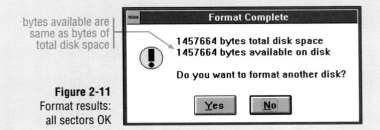

bytes available are same as bytes of total disk space

Figure 2-11
Format results:
all sectors OK

Let's format your second floppy disk:

❶ Click the **Yes button** after you review the formatting results.

❷ Remove your Student disk from drive A.

❸ Write your name, course title, and course meeting time on the label for the second disk. For the title of this disk write Backup (Destination Disk). Apply this label to your second disk and place this disk in drive A.

❹ Be sure the **Disk In box** is set to drive A and the capacity is set to the capacity of your disk. (Remember to substitute B here if you are formatting your disk in drive B.)

❺ Click the **OK button** to accept the settings. When you see the Confirm Format Disk dialog box, check to be sure you have the correct disk in the correct drive.

❻ Click the **Yes button** to confirm that you want to format the disk. When the format is complete, review the format results.

❼ You do not want to format another disk, so click the **No button** when the computer asks if you wish to format another disk.

❽ *Remove the backup disk from drive A.* You will not need this backup disk until later.

Preparing Your Student Disk

Now that Ruth has formatted her disks, she is going to put some files on one of them to use for her file management exploration. To follow Ruth's progress, you must have copies of her files. A collection of files has been prepared for this purpose. You need to transfer them to one of your formatted disks.

To transfer files to your Student Disk:

❶ Place the disk you labeled Student Disk (Source Disk) in drive A.

The File Manager window is open, but you need to go to the Program Manager window to launch the application that will transfer the files.

❷   Hold down [Alt] and continue to press [Tab] until Program Manager appears in the box, then release both keys. Program Manager becomes the active window.

❸   If the CTI WinApps window is not open, double-click the **CTI WinApps group icon**. If the CTI WinApps window is open but is not the active window, click it. Your screen should look similar to Figure 2-12.

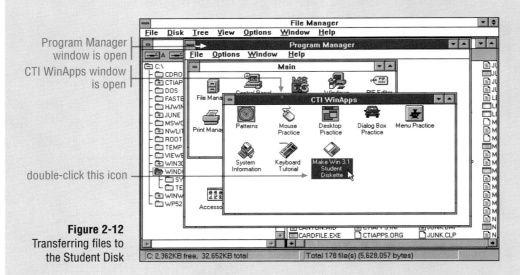

Program Manager
window is open

CTI WinApps window
is open

double-click this icon

Figure 2-12
Transferring files to
the Student Disk

❹   Double-click the **Make Win 3.1 Student Disk icon**. A dialog box appears.

❺   Make sure the drive that is selected in the dialog box corresponds to the drive that contains your disk (drive A or drive B), then click the **OK button**. It will take 30 seconds or so to transfer the files to your disk.

❻   Click the **OK button** when you see the message "24 files copied successfully!"

❼   Double-click on the **CTI WinWorks Apps Control-menu box** to close the window.

Now the data files you need should be on your Student Disk. To continue the Tutorial, you must switch back to the File Manager.

To switch back to the File Manager:
❶   Hold down [Alt] and press [Tab] until a box with File Manager appears. Then release both keys.

Finding Out What's on Your Disks

Ruth learned from the article that the first step toward effective data management is to find out what's stored on her disks. To see what's on your Student Disk, you will need to be sure your computer is referencing the correct disk drive.

Changing the Current Drive

Each drive on your computer system is represented by a **drive icon** that tells you the drive letter and the drive type. Figure 2-13 shows the drive types represented by these icons.

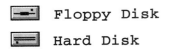

Floppy Disk

Hard Disk

Network Drive

Figure 2-13
Drive icons

CD-ROM Drive

Near the top of the File Manager window, a **drive icon ribbon** indicates the drives on your computer system. See Figure 2-14. Your screen may be different because the drive icon ribbon on your screen reflects your particular hardware configuration.

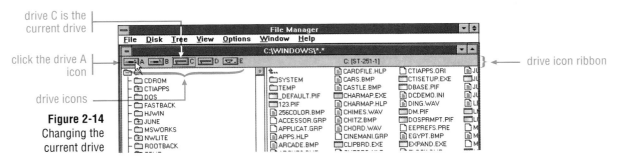

Figure 2-14
Changing the
current drive

Your computer is connected to a number of storage drives or devices, but it can work with only one drive at a time. This drive is referred to as the **current drive** or **default drive**. You must change the current drive whenever you want to use files or programs that are stored on a different drive. The drive icon for the current drive is outlined with a rectangle. In Figure 2-14, the current drive is C.

To work with Ruth's files, you must be sure that the current drive is the one in which you have your Student Disk. *For this Tutorial we'll assume that your Student Disk is in drive A. If it is in drive B, substitute "drive B" for "drive A" in the rest of the steps for this Tutorial.*

Follow the next set of steps to change the current drive, if your current drive is not the one containing your Student Disk.

To change the current drive to A:

❶ Be sure your Student Disk is in drive A.

❷ Click the **drive A icon**. Drive A becomes the current drive. See Figure 2-15 on the following page.

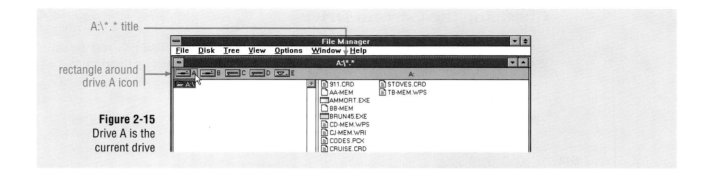

A:*.* title

rectangle around
drive A icon

Figure 2-15
Drive A is the
current drive

After you make drive A the current drive, your screen should look similar to
Figure 2-15. Don't worry if everything is not exactly the same as the figure. Just be
sure you see the A:*.* window title and that there is a rectangle around the drive A
icon (or the drive B icon if drive B contains your floppy disk).

The File Manager Window

The components of the File Manager window are labeled in Figure 2-16. Your screen
should contain similar components.

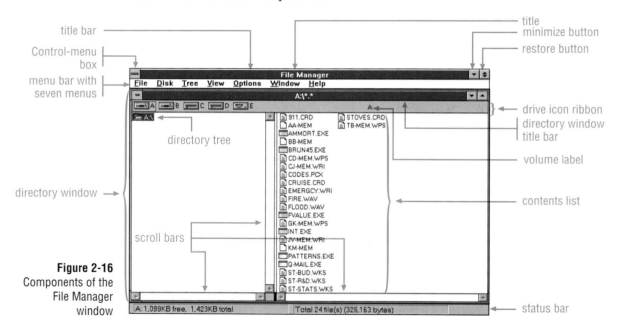

title bar
Control-menu
box
menu bar with
seven menus

directory tree

directory window

scroll bars

title
minimize button
restore button

drive icon ribbon
directory window
title bar

volume label

contents list

status bar

Figure 2-16
Components of the
File Manager
window

The top line of the File Manager window contains the Control-menu box, the title
bar, the title, and the resizing buttons. The File Manager menu bar contains seven menus.
Inside the File Manager window is the **directory window**, which contains information about the current drive. The title bar for this window displays the current drive, in
this case, A:*.*. This window has its own Control-menu box and resizing buttons.
Below the directory window title bar is the drive icon ribbon. On this line, the drive
letter is followed by a volume label, if there is one. **A volume label** is a name you can

assign to your disk during the format process to help you identify the contents of the disk. We did not assign a volume label, so the area after the A: is blank. Why is there a colon after the drive letter? Even though the colon is not displayed on the drive icons, when you type in a drive letter, you must always type a colon after it. The colon is a requirement of the DOS operating system that Windows uses behind the scenes to perform its file management tasks.

At the bottom of the screen, a status bar displays information about disk space. Remember that a byte is one character of data.

Notice that the directory window is split. The left half of the directory window displays the **directory tree**, which illustrates the organization of files on the current drive. The right half of the directory window displays the **contents list**, which lists the files on the current drive. Scroll bars on these windows let you view material that doesn't fit in the current window.

The Directory Tree

A list of files is called a **directory**. Because long lists of files are awkward to work with, directories can be subdivided into smaller lists called **subdirectories**. The organization of these directories and subdirectories is depicted in the directory tree.

Suppose you were using your computer for a small retail business. What information might you have on your disk, and how would it be organized? Figure 2-17 shows the directory tree for a hard disk (drive C) of a typical small business computer system.

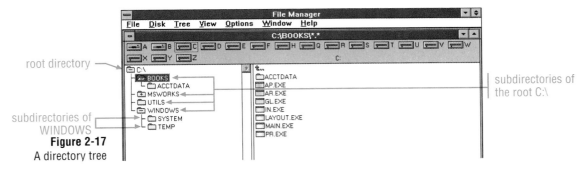

root directory

subdirectories of WINDOWS

Figure 2-17
A directory tree

subdirectories of the root C:\

At the top of the directory tree is the **root directory**, called C:\ . The root directory is created when you format a disk and is indicated by a backslash after the drive letter and colon. Arranged under the root directory are the subdirectories BOOKS, MSWORKS, UTILS, and WINDOWS.

Directories other than the root directory can have subdirectories. In Figure 2-17 you can see that the BOOKS directory has a subdirectory called ACCTDATA. The WINDOWS directory contains two subdirectories, SYSTEM and TEMP. MSWORKS also has some subdirectories, but they are not listed. You'll find out how to expand the directory tree to display subdirectories later in the this tutorial.

Windows uses directory names to construct a path through the directory tree. For example, the path to ACCTDATA would be C:\BOOKS\ACCTDATA. To trace this path on Figure 2-17, begin at the root directory C:\, follow the line leading to the BOOKS directory, then follow the line leading to the ACCTDATA directory.

Each directory in the directory tree has a **file folder icon**, which can be either open or closed. An open file folder icon indicates the **active** or **current directory**. In Figure 2-17 the current directory is BOOKS. Only one directory can be current on a disk at a time.

Now look at the directory tree on your screen. The root directory of your Student Disk is called A:\. The file folder icon for this directory is open, indicating that this is the current directory. Are there any subdirectories on your disk?

The answer is no. A:\ has no subdirectories because its file folder icon does not contain a plus sign or a minus sign. A plus sign on a folder indicates that the directory can be expanded to show its subdirectories. A minus sign indicates that the subdirectories are currently being displayed. A file folder icon without a plus or a minus sign has no subdirectories.

Organizing Your Files

Ruth's disk, like your Student Disk, contains only one directory, and all her files are in that directory. As is typical of a poorly organized disk, files from different projects and programs are jumbled together. As Ruth's disk accumulates more files, she will have an increasingly difficult time finding the files she wants to use.

Ruth needs to organize her disk. First, she needs to make some new directories so she has a good basic structure for her files.

Creating Directories

When you create a directory, you indicate its location on the directory tree and specify the new directory name. The directory you create becomes a subdirectory of the current directory, which is designated by an open file folder. Directory names can be up to eight characters long.

Your Student Disk contains a collection of memos and spreadsheets that Ruth has created for a project code named "Stealth." Right now, all of these files are in the root directory. Ruth decides that to improve the organization of her disk, she should place her memos in one directory and the Stealth spreadsheets in another directory. To do this, she needs to make two new directories, MEMOS and STEALTH.

To make a new directory called MEMOS:

❶ Click the **file folder icon** representing the root directory of drive A. Figure 2-18 shows you where to click. This highlights the root directory A:\, making it the current directory.

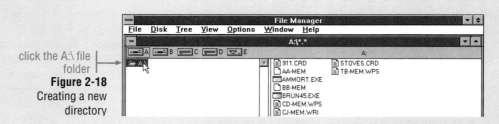

click the A:\ file folder

Figure 2-18
Creating a new directory

❷ Click **File**, then click **Create Directory....** The Create Directory dialog box indicates that the current directory is A:\ and displays a text box for the name of the new directory.

❸ In the text box, type **MEMOS**, then click the **OK button**. It doesn't matter whether you type the directory name in uppercase or lowercase letters.

As a result, your screen should look like Figure 2-19. A new directory folder labeled MEMOS is now a subdirectory of A:\. The A:\ file folder now displays a minus sign to indicate that it has a subdirectory and that the subdirectory is displayed.

A:\ file folder displays minus sign

MEMOS subdirectory

Figure 2-19
The new subdirectory

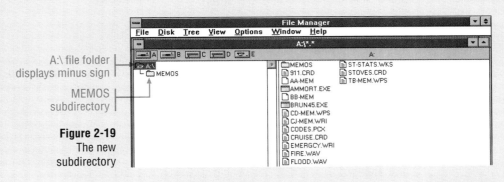

TROUBLE? If you do not see the minus sign on the A:\ file folder, click Tree, then click Indicate Expandable branches.

Next Ruth will make a directory for the spreadsheets. She wants her directory tree to look like the one in Figure 2-20a, not the one in Figure 2-20b.

Figure 2-20a
SHEETS is a subdirectory of A:\

Figure 2-20b
SHEETS is a subdirectory of MEMOS

The spreadsheet directory should be a subdirectory of the root, *not* of MEMOS.

To make a directory for spreadsheets:
❶ Click the **directory folder icon for A:**.
❷ Click **File**, then click **Create Directory….**
❸ In the text box type **SHEETS**, then click the **OK button**.
❹ Make sure that your newly updated directory tree resembles the one in Figure 2-20a. There should be two directories under A:\ — MEMOS and SHEETS.

TROUBLE? If your directory tree is structured like the one in Figure 2-20b, use your mouse to drag the SHEETS directory icon to the A:\ file folder icon.

Now Ruth's disk has a structure she can use to organize her files. It contains three directories: the root A:\, MEMOS, and SHEETS. Each directory can contain a list of files. Ruth is happy with this new structure, but she is not sure what the directories contain. She decides to look in one of the new directories to see what's there.

Changing Directories

When you change directories, you open a different directory folder. If the directory contains files, they will be displayed in the contents list.

First, Ruth wants to look in the MEMOS directory.

To change to the MEMOS directory:

❶   Click the **MEMOS directory file folder icon**.

Notice that the A:\ file folder icon is closed and the MEMOS file folder icon is open, indicating that the MEMOS directory is now current.

Look at the status line at the bottom of your screen. The left side of the status line shows you how much space is left on your disk. The right side of the status line tells you that no files are in the current directory, that is, in the MEMOS directory. This makes sense. You just created the directory, and haven't put anything in it.

❷   Click the **A:\ file folder icon** to change back to the root directory.

Expanding and Collapsing Directories

Notice on your screen that the A:\ file folder icon has a minus sign on it. As you know, the minus sign indicates that A:\ has one or more subdirectories and that those subdirectories are displayed. To look at a simplified directory tree, you would **collapse** the A:\ directory. You would **expand** a directory to redisplay its subdirectories. Ruth wants to practice expanding and collapsing directories.

To expand and then collapse a directory:

❶   Double-click the **A:\ file folder icon** to collapse the directory. As a result the MEMOS and SHEETS branches of the directory tree are removed and a plus sign appears on the A:\ file folder icon.

❷   Double-click the **A:\ file folder icon** again. This time the directory expands, displaying the MEMOS and SHEETS branches. Notice the minus sign on the A:\ file folder icon.

The Contents List

The **contents list** on the right side of the desktop contains the list of files and subdirectories for the current directory. On your screen the directory tree shows that A:\ is the current directory. The status bar shows that this directory contains 26 files and subdirectories. These files are listed in the contents list. Ruth recalls that she had to follow a set of rules when she created the names for these files. Let's find out more about these rules, since you will soon need to create names for your own files.

Filenames and Extensions

A **filename** is a unique set of letters and numbers that identifies a program, document file, directory, or miscellaneous data file. A filename may be followed by an **extension**, which is separated from the filename by a period.

The rules for creating valid filenames are as follows:

- The filename can contain a maximum of eight characters.
- The extension cannot contain more than three characters.
- Use a period only between the filename and the extension.
- Neither the filename nor extension can include any spaces.
- Do not use the following characters: / [ ] ; = " \ : | ,
- Do not use the following names: AUX, COM1, COM2, COM3, COM4, CON, LPT1, LPT2, LPT3, PRN, or NUL.

Ruth used the letters ST at the beginning of her spreadsheet filenames so she could remember that these files contain information on project Stealth. Ruth used the rest of each filename to describe more about the file contents. For example, ST-BUD is the budget for project Stealth, ST-R&D is the research and development cost worksheet for the project, and ST-STATS contains the descriptive statistics for the project. Ruth's memos, on the other hand, begin with the initials of the person who received the memo. She used MEM as part of the filename for all her memos. For example, the file CJMEM.WRI contains a memo to Charles Jackson.

The file extension usually indicates the category of information a file contains. We can divide files into two broad categories, program files and data files. **Program files** contain the programming code for applications and systems software. For example, the computer program that makes your computer run the WordPerfect word processor would be classified as a program file. Program files are sometimes referred to as **executable files** because the computer executes, or performs, the instructions contained in the files. A common filename extension for this type of file is .EXE. Other extensions for program files include .BAT, .SYS, .PIF, and .COM. In the contents list, program files are shown with a **program file icon**, like the one you see next to the file PATTERNS.EXE on your screen and in Figure 2-21.

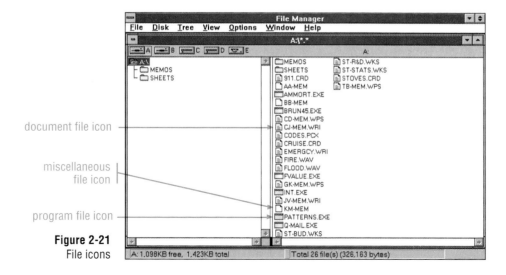

document file icon

miscellaneous file icon

program file icon

Figure 2-21
File icons

The second file category is data files. **Data files** contain the information with which you work: the memos, spreadsheets, reports, and graphs you create using applications such as word processors and spreadsheets. The filename extension for a data file usually indicates which application was used to create the file. For example, the file CD-MEM.WPS was created using the Microsoft Works word processor, which automatically puts the extension .WPS on any file you create with it. The use of .WPS as the standard extension for Works word processing documents creates an association between the application and the documents you create with it. Later, when you want to make modifications to your documents, Works can find them easily by looking for the .WPS extension.

Data files you create using a Windows application installed on your computer are shown in the contents list with a **document file icon** like the one you see next to CD-MEM.WPS on your screen. Data files you create using a non-Windows application or a Windows application that is not installed on your computer are shown in the contents list with a **miscellaneous file icon** like the one you see next to AA-MEM on your screen. AA-MEM was created using a non-Windows word processor.

Now that you have an idea of the contents for each of Ruth's files, you will be able to help her move them into the appropriate directory.

Moving Files

You can move files from one disk to another. You can also move files from one directory to another. When you move a file, the computer copies the file to its new location, then erases it from the original location. The File Manager lets you move files by dragging them on the screen or by using the File Manager menus.

Now that Ruth has created the MEMOS and SHEETS directories, the next step in organizing her disk is to put files in these directories. She begins by moving one of her memo files from the root directory A:\ to the MEMOS subdirectory. She decides to move JV-MEM.WRI first.

To move the file JV-MEM.WRI from A:\ to the MEMOS subdirectory:

❶ Position the pointer on the filename JV-MEM.WRI and click the mouse button to select it. On the left side of the status bar, the message "Selected 1 file(s) (1,408 bytes)" appears.

❷ Press the mouse button and hold it down while you drag the file icon to the MEMOS file folder in the directory tree.

❸ When the icon arrives at its target location, a box appears around the MEMOS file icon. Release the mouse button. Figure 2-22 on the following page illustrates this procedure.

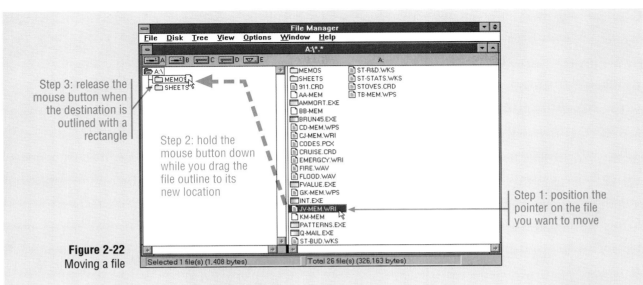

Step 3: release the mouse button when the destination is outlined with a rectangle

Step 2: hold the mouse button down while you drag the file outline to its new location

Step 1: position the pointer on the file you want to move

Figure 2-22
Moving a file

❹ Click the **Yes button** in response to the message "Are you sure you want to move the selected files or directories to A:\MEMOS?" A Moving... dialog box may flash briefly on your screen before the file is moved. Look at the contents list on the right side of the screen. The file JV-MEM.WRI is no longer there.

Ruth wants to confirm that the file was moved.

❺ Single click the **MEMOS file folder icon** in the directory tree on the left side of the screen. The file JV-MEM.WRI should be listed in the contents list on the right side of the screen.

   TROUBLE?   If JV-MEM.WRI is not in the MEMOS subdirectory, you might have moved it inadvertently to the SHEETS directory. You can check this by clicking the SHEETS directory folder. If the file is in SHEETS, drag it to the MEMOS directory folder.

❻ Click the **A:\file folder icon** to display the files in the root directory again.

Ruth sees that several memos are still in the root directory. She could move these memos one at a time to the MEMOS subdirectory, but she knows that it would be more efficient to move them as a group. To do this, she'll first select the files she wants to move. Then, she will drag them to the MEMOS directory.

To select a group of files:
❶ The directory A:\ should be selected on your screen and the files in this directory should be displayed in the right directory window. If this is not the case, click the directory icon for A:\.
❷ Click the filename **CD-MEM.WPS** to select it.
❸ Hold down [Ctrl] while you click the next filename you want to add to the group, **CJMEM.WRI**. Now two files should be selected. Ruth wants to select two more files.
❹ Hold down [Ctrl] while you click **GK-MEM.WPS**.
❺ Hold down [Ctrl] while you click **TB-MEM.WPS**. Release [Ctrl]. When you have finished selecting the files, your screen should look similar to Figure 2-23 on the following page. Notice the status bar message, "Selected 4 file(s) (4,590 bytes)."

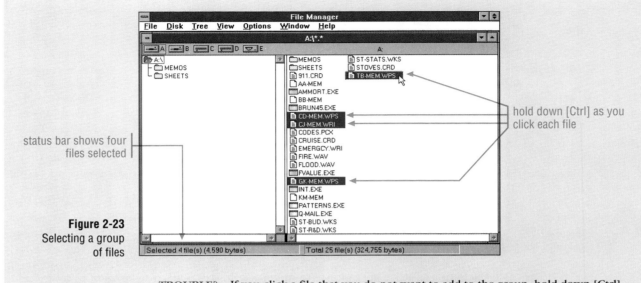

status bar shows four
files selected

hold down [Ctrl] as you
click each file

Figure 2-23
Selecting a group
of files

TROUBLE?   If you click a file that you do not want to add to the group, hold down [Ctrl] and click that filename again. This will deselect that one file and remove the highlighting.

Now that Ruth has selected the files she wants to move, she can drag them to their new location.

To move a group of files:

❶   Position the pointer on any one of the highlighted filenames.

❷   Press the mouse button and drag the pointer, which now is attached to a multiple file icon, to the MEMOS directory icon. See Figure 2-24.

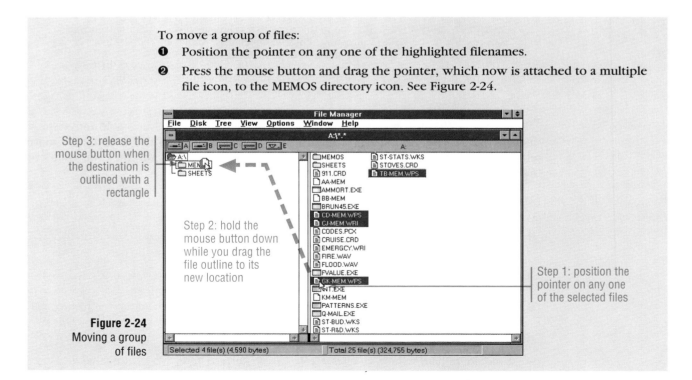

Step 3: release the
mouse button when
the destination is
outlined with a
rectangle

Step 2: hold the
mouse button down
while you drag the
file outline to its
new location

Step 1: position the
pointer on any one
of the selected files

Figure 2-24
Moving a group
of files

❸ When the you move the file icon onto the MEMOS directory, a box will outline the directory icon. Release the mouse button. The Confirm Mouse Operation dialog box appears.

❹ Click the **Yes button** to confirm that you want to move the files. After a brief period of activity on your disk drive, the contents list for the A:\ directory is updated and should no longer include the files you moved.

❺ Click the **MEMOS directory icon** to verify that the group of files arrived in the MEMOS directory.

❻ Click the **A:\ directory icon** to once again display the contents of the root directory.

Renaming Files

You may find it useful to change the name of a file to make it more descriptive of the file contents. Remember that Windows uses file extensions to associate document files with applications and to identify executable programs, so when you rename a file you should not change the extension.

Ruth looks down the list of files and notices ST-BUD.WKS, which contains the 1994 budget for project Stealth. Ruth knows that next week she will begin work on the 1995 budget. She decides that while she is organizing her files, she will change the name of ST-BUD.WKS to ST-BUD94.WKS. When she creates the budget for 1995, she will call it ST-BUD95.WKS so it will be easy to distinguish between the two budget files.

To change the name of ST-BUD.WKS to ST-BUD94.WKS:

❶ Click the filename **ST-BUD.WKS**.

❷ Click **File**, then click **Rename**. See Figure 2-25. The Rename dialog box shows you the current directory and the name of the file you are going to rename. Verify that the dialog box on your screen indicates that the current directory is A:\ and that the file you are going to rename is ST-BUD.WKS.

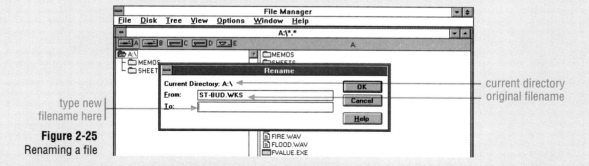

Figure 2-25
Renaming a file

TROUBLE? If the filename is not ST-BUD.WKS, click the Cancel button and go back to Step 1.

❸ In the To text box type **ST-BUD94.WKS** (using either uppercase or lowercase letters.

❹ Click the **OK button**.

❺ Check the file listing for ST-BUD94.WKS to verify that the rename procedure was successful.

Deleting Files

When you no longer need a file, it is good practice to delete it. Deleting a file frees up space on your disk and reduces the size of the directory listing you need to scroll through to find a file. A well-organized disk does not contain files you no longer need.

Ruth decides to delete the ST-STATS.WKS file. Although this file contains some statistics about the Stealth project, Ruth knows by looking at the file's date that those statistics are no longer current. She'll receive a new file from the Statistics department next week.

To delete the file ST-STATS.WKS:

❶ Click the filename **ST-STATS.WKS**.

❷ Click **File**, then click **Delete**. The Delete dialog box shows you that the file scheduled for deletion is in the A:\ directory and is called ST-STATS.WKS. See Figure 2-26.

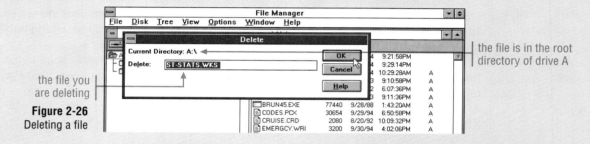

the file you are deleting

the file is in the root directory of drive A

Figure 2-26
Deleting a file

TROUBLE?   If the filename ST-STATS.WKS is not displayed in the Delete dialog box, click the Cancel button and go back to Step 1.

❸ Click the **OK button**. The Confirm File Delete dialog box appears. This is your last chance to change your mind before the file is deleted.

❹ Click the **Yes button** to delete the file. Look at the contents list to verify that the file ST-STATS.WKS has been deleted.

After using a floppy disk in drive A to experiment with the File Manager, Ruth feels more confident that she can use the File Manager to organize her hard disk. However, she feels slightly uncomfortable about something else. Ruth just learned that one of her co-workers lost several days worth of work when his computer had a hardware failure.

Ruth resolves to find out more about the problems that can cause data loss so she can take appropriate steps to protect the data files on her computer.

Data Backup

Ruth's initial research on data loss reveals that there is no totally fail-safe method to protect data from hardware failures, human error, and natural disasters. She does discover, however, some ways to reduce the risk of losing data. Every article Ruth reads emphasizes the importance of regular backups.

A **backup** is a copy of one or more files, made in case the original files are destroyed or become unusable. Ruth learns that Windows provides a Copy command and a Copy Disk command that she can use for data backup. Ruth decides to find out how these commands work, so she refers to the *Microsoft Windows User's Guide* which came with the Microsoft Windows 3.1 software. She quickly discovers that the Copy and Copy Disk commands are in the Windows File Manager.

To prepare the File Manager for data backup:

❶ If you are returning from a break, launch Windows if it is not currently running. Be sure you see the Program Manager window.

❷ Relaunch the File Manager if necessary. Make sure your Student Disk is in drive A.

TROUBLE?   If you want to use drive B instead of drive A, substitute "B" for "A" in any steps when drive A is specified.

❸ Click the File Manager **maximize button** if the File Manager is not already maximized.

❹ If necessary, click the **drive A icon** on the drive ribbon to make drive A the default drive.

❺ Click **View** and be sure that a check mark appears next to All File Details.

❻ Click **Window**, then click **Tile**. As a result, your desktop should look similar to Figure 2-27. Don't worry if your list of directories and files is different from the one shown in the figures.

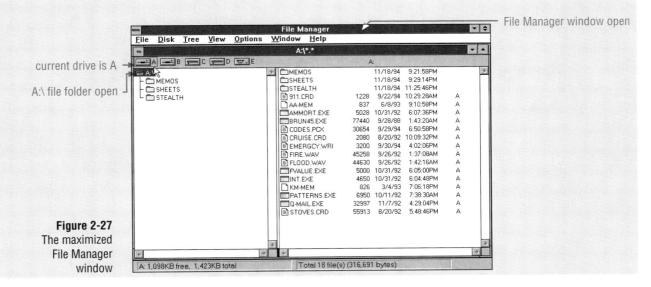

Figure 2-27
The maximized
File Manager
window

Now that Ruth has the File Manager window set-up, she decides to practice with the Copy command first.

The Copy Command

The Copy command duplicates a file in a new location. When the procedure has been completed, you have two files, your original and the copy. The additional copy of the file is useful for backup in case your original file develops a problem and becomes unusable.

The Copy command is different from the Move command, which you used earlier. The Move command deletes the file from its old location after moving it. When the move is completed, you have only one file.

If you understand the terminology associated with copying files, you will be able to achieve the results you want. The original location of a file is referred to as the **source**. The new location of the file is referred to as the **destination** or **target**.

You can copy one file or you can copy a group of files. In this Tutorial you will practice moving one file at a time. You can also copy files from one directory to another or from one disk to another. The disks you copy to and from do not need to be the same size. For backup purposes you would typically copy files from a hard disk to a disk.

Copying Files Using a Single Disk Drive

Ruth has been working on a spreadsheet called ST-BUD94.WKS for an entire week, and the data on this spreadsheet are critical for a presentation she is making tomorrow. The file is currently on a disk in drive A. Ruth will sleep much better tonight if she has an extra copy of this file. But Ruth has only one floppy disk drive. To make a copy of a file from one floppy disk to another, she must use her hard disk as a temporary storage location.

First, she will copy the file ST-BUD94.WKS to her hard disk. Then she will move the file to another floppy disk. Let's see how this procedure works.

To copy the file ST-BUD94.WKS from the source disk to the hard disk:

❶ Make sure your Student Disk is in drive A. Be sure you also have the backup disk you formatted earlier in the tutorial.

❷ Find the file ST-BUD94.WKS. It is in the root directory .

❸ Click the filename **ST-BUD94.WKS**.

❹ Click **File**, then click **Copy**.

TROUBLE? If you see a message that indicates you cannot copy a file to drive C, click the OK button. Your drive C has been write-protected, and you will not be able to copy ST-BUD94.WKS. Read through the copying procedure and resume doing the steps in the section entitled "Making a Disk Backup."

❺ Look at the ribbon of drive icons at the top of your screen. If you have an icon for drive C, type **C:** in the text box of the Copy dialog box. If you do not have an icon for drive C, ask your technical support person which drive you can use for a temporary destination in the file copy process, then type the drive letter.

❻ Confirm that the Copy dialog box settings are similar to those in Figure 2-28, then click the **OK button**. The file is copied to the root directory of drive C (or to the directory your technical support person told you to use).

name of the file you
want to copy

the destination
drive is C:\

Figure 2-28
Copying
ST-BUD94.WKS
to drive C

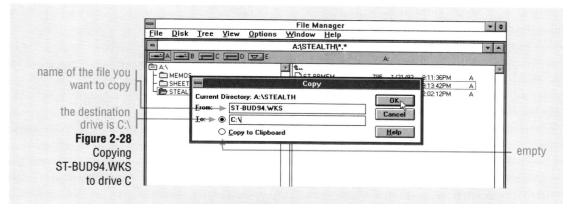

empty

TROUBLE?   If a dialog box appears and prompts you to verify that you want to replace the existing file, click the Yes button. This message appeared because another student left the ST-BUD94.WKS file on the hard disk.

After the file has been copied to the hard disk, Ruth needs to switch disks. She will take her original disk out of drive A and replace it with the disk that will receive the copy of the ST-BUD94.WKS file. After Ruth switches disks, she must tell the File Manager to **refresh** the directory tree and the contents list so they show the files and directories for the disk that is now in the drive.

To switch disks and refresh the contents list:

❶ Remove your Student Disk from drive A.

❷ Put your Backup Disk in drive A.

❸ Click the **drive A icon** on the drive ribbon to refresh the contents list. The directory tree will contain only the A:\ folder, because your backup disk does not have the directories you created for your original Student Disk.

Now let's look for the copy of ST-BUD94.WKS that is on drive C.

To locate the new copy of ST-BUD94.WKS:

❶ Click the **drive C icon** (or the drive your technical support person told you to use).

❷ Click the **C:\ file folder icon** (or the directory your technical support person told you to use).

❸ If necessary, use the scroll bar on the side of the content list to find the file ST-BUD94.WKS in the contents list.

Now you need to move the file from the hard disk to the backup disk in drive A. You must use Move instead of Copy so you don't leave the file on your hard disk.

To move the new file copy to drive A:

❶ Click the filename **ST-BUD94.WKS**.

❷ Click **File**, then click **Move**. (Don't use Copy this time.) A Move dialog box appears.

❸ Type **A:** in the text box.

❹ Click the **OK button**. As a result, ST-BUD94.WKS is moved to the disk in drive A.

❺ Click the **drive A icon** on the drive ribbon to view the contents list for the Backup disk. Verify that the file ST-BUD94.WKS is listed.

❻ Remove the Backup disk from drive A.

❼ Insert the **Student Disk** in drive A and click the **drive A icon** in the drive ribbon to refresh the contents listing.

Now you and Ruth have completed the entire procedure for copying a file from one disk to another on a single floppy disk system. In her research, Ruth also has discovered a Windows command for copying an entire disk. She wants to practice this command next.

Making a Disk Backup

The Windows Copy Disk command makes an exact duplicate of an entire disk. All the files and all the blank sectors of the disk are copied. If you have files on your destination disk, the Copy Disk command will erase them as it makes the copy so that the destination disk will be an exact duplicate of the original disk.

When you use the Copy Disk command, both disks must have the same storage capacity. For example, if your original disk is a 3.5-inch high-density disk, your destination disk also must be 3.5-inch high-density disk. For this reason, you cannot use the Copy Disk command to copy an entire hard disk to a floppy disk. If your computer does not have two disk drives that are the same size and capacity, the Copy Disk command will work with only one disk drive. When you back up the contents of one disk to another disk using only one disk drive, files are copied from the source disk into the random access memory (RAM) of the computer.

RAM is a temporary storage area on your computer's mother board which usually holds data and instructions for the operating system, application programs, and documents you are using. After the files are copied into RAM, you remove the source disk and replace it with the destination disk. The files in RAM are then copied onto the destination disk. If you don't have enough RAM available to hold the entire contents of the disk, only a portion of the source disk contents are copied during the first stage of the process, and the computer must repeat the process for the remaining contents of the disk.

Ruth wants to practice using the Copy Disk command to make a backup of a disk. She is going to make the copy using only one disk drive because she can use this procedure on both her computer at home, which has one disk drive, and her computer at work, which has two different-sized disk drives.

While Ruth makes a copy of her disk, let's make a backup of your Student Disk. After you learn the procedure, you'll be responsible for making regular backups of the work you do for this course. You should back up your disks at least once a week. If you are working on a particularly critical project, such as a term paper or a thesis, you might want to make backups more often.

To make a backup copy of your Student disk:

❶ Be sure your Student Disk is in drive A and that you have the disk you labeled Backup handy. If you want to be very safe, write-protect your source disk before continuing with this procedure. Remember, to write-protect a 5.25-inch disk, you place a tab over the write-protect notch. On a 3.5-inch disk you open the write-protect hole.

❷ Click **Disk**, then click **Copy Disk....** Confirm that the Copy Disk dialog box on your screen looks like the one in Figure 2-29. The dialog box should indicate that "Source In" is A: and "Destination In" is A:. If this is not the case, click the appropriate down-arrow button and select A: from the list. When the dialog box display is correct, click the **OK button**.

both the source and the destination should be A:

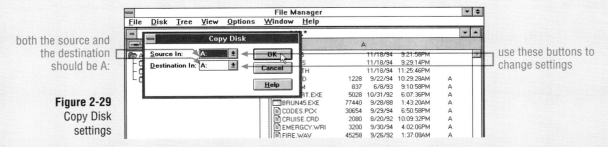

use these buttons to change settings

Figure 2-29
Copy Disk
settings

❸ The Confirm Copy Disk dialog box reminds you that this operation will erase all data from the destination disk. It asks, "Are you sure you want to continue?"

❹ Click the **Yes button**. The next dialog box instructs you to "Insert source disk." Your source disk is the Student Disk and it is already in drive A.

❺ Click the **OK button**.

After a flurry of activity, the computer begins to copy the data from drive A into RAM. The Copying Disk dialog box keeps you posted on its progress.

❻ Eventually another message appears, telling you to "Insert destination disk." Take your Student Disk out of drive A and replace it with the disk you labeled Backup.

❼ Click the **OK button**. The computer copies the files from RAM to the destination disk.

Depending on how much internal memory your computer has, you might be prompted to switch disks twice more. Carefully follow the dialog box prompts, remembering that the *source* disk is your Student Disk and the *destination* disk is your Backup disk.

❽ When the Copy Disk operation is complete, the Copying Disk dialog box closes. If you write-protected your Student Disk in Step 1, you should unprotect it now; otherwise you won't be able to save data to the disk later.

As a result of the Copy Disk command, your Backup disk should be an exact duplicate of your Student Disk.

Ruth has completed her exploration of file management. Now, Ruth decides to finish for the day. If you are not going to proceed directly to the Tutorial Assignments, you should exit the File Manager.

To exit the File Manager:

❶ Click the File Manager **Control-menu box**.

❷ Click **Close**.

❸ If you want to exit Windows, click the **Program Manager Control-menu box**, then click **Close**, and finally click the **OK button**.

Questions

1. Which one of the following is not a characteristic of a file?
   a. It has a name.
   b. It is a collection of data.
   c. It is the smallest unit of data.
   d. It is stored on a device such as a floppy disk or a hard disk.

2. What process arranges the magnetic particles on a disk in preparation for data storage?

3. In which one of the following situations would formatting your disk be the least desirable procedure?
   a. You have purchased a new disk.
   b. You have difficulty doing a spreadsheet assignment, and you want to start over again.
   c. You want to erase all the old files from a disk.
   d. You want to recycle an old disk that was used on a non-IBM-compatible computer.

4. If the label on your 3.5 inch diskette says HD, what is its capacity?
   a. 360K
   b. 720K
   c. 1.2MB
   d. 1.44MB

5. The disk drive that is indicated by a rectangle on the drive ribbon is called the _____ drive or the _____ drive.

6. Refer to the File Manager window in Figure 2-30 on the following page. What is the name of each numbered window component?

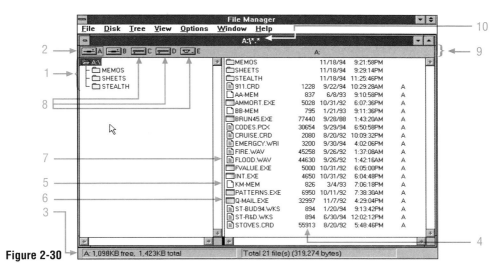

Figure 2-30

7. What is the directory that is automatically created when a disk is formatted?

8. What does a plus sign on a directory file folder icon indicate?
   a. The subdirectories are currently being displayed.
   b. The directory can be expanded.
   c. There are files in the directory.
   d. There are no subdirectories for this directory.

9. Indicate whether each of the following filenames is a valid or not valid Windows filename. If a filename is not valid, explain what is wrong.
   a. EOQ.WKS
   b. STATISTICS.WKS
   c. NUL.DOC
   d. VB-LET.DOC
   e. M
   f. M.M
   g. 92.BUD
   h. LET03/94
   i. CON.BMP
   d. Escape key

Tutorial Assignments

Launch Windows if necessary. Write your answers to Assignments 5, 6, 7, 8, 9, 11, 12, 13, and 14.

1. Move the two Microsoft Works spreadsheet files (.WKS extension) from the root directory to the SHEETS directory of your Student Disk.

2. You have a memo called BB-MEM that is about project Stealth. Now you need to change the filename to reflect the contents of the memo.
   a. Change the name to ST-BBMEM.
   b. Move ST-BBMEM into the MEMOS directory.

3. Create a directory called STEALTH under the root directory of your Student Disk. After you do this, your directory tree should look like Figure 2-30.

4. Now consolidate all the Stealth files.
   a. Move the file ST-BBMEM from the MEMOS directory to the STEALTH directory.

      b. Move the files ST-BUD94.WKS and ST-R&D.WKS from the SHEETS directory to the STEALTH directory.

5. After doing Assignment 4, draw a diagram of your directory tree.
6. Make a list of the files that you now have in the MEMOS directory.
7. Make a list of the files that are in the SHEETS directory.
8. Make a list of the files that are in the STEALTH directory.
9. Describe what happens if you double-click the A:\ file folder icon.

E 10. Click to open the View menu and make sure the All File Details command has a check mark next to it.

E 11. Use the View menu to sort the files by date. What is the oldest file on your disk? (Be sure to look at all directories!)

E 12. Use the View menu to sort the files by type. Using this view, name the last file in your root directory contents list.

E 13. Use the View menu to sort the files by size. What is the name of the largest file on your Student Disk?

E 14. Change the current drive to C:, or, if you are on a network, to one of the network drives.

      a. Draw a diagram of the directory tree for this disk.

      b. List the filename of any files with .SYS, .COM, or .BAT extensions in the root directory of this disk.

      c. Look at the file icons in the contents list of the root directory. How many of the files are program files? Document files? Miscellaneous data files?

      d. Review the file organization tips that were in the article Ruth read. Write a short paragraph evaluating the organizational structure of your hard disk or network drive.

Windows Tutorials Index

TASK	MOUSE	MENU	KEYBOARD
GENERAL / PROGRAM MANAGER			
Change dimensions of a window *WIN 15*	Drag border or corner	Click ▬, <u>S</u>ize	`Alt` `spacebar`, `S`
Click *WIN 7*	Press mouse button, then release it		
Close a window *WIN 18*	Double-click ▬	Click ▬, <u>C</u>lose	`Alt` `spacebar`, `C` or `Alt` `F4`
Double-click *WIN 8*	Click left mouse button twice		
Drag *WIN 9*	Hold left mouse button down while moving mouse		
Exit Windows *WIN 33*	Double-click Program Manager ▬, click `OK`	Click Program Manager ▬, <u>C</u>lose, `OK`	`Alt` `spacebar`, `C`, `Enter`, or `Alt` `F4`, `Enter`
Help *WIN 30*		Click <u>H</u>elp	`F1` or `Alt` `H`
Launch Windows *WIN 4*			Type win and press `Enter`
Maximize a window *WIN 14*	Click ▲	Click ▬, Ma<u>x</u>imize	`Alt` `spacebar`, `X`
Minimize a window *WIN 14*	Click ▼	Click ▬, Mi<u>n</u>imize	`Alt` `spacebar`, `N`
Open a group window *WIN 10*	Double-click group icon	Click icon, click <u>R</u>estore	`Ctrl` `F6` to group icon, `Enter`
Restore a window *WIN 14*	Click ⬍	Click ▬, <u>R</u>estore	`Alt` `spacebar`, `R`
Switch applications *WIN 16*		Click ▬, <u>S</u>witch To...	`Alt` `Tab` or `Ctrl` `Esc`
Switch documents *WIN 28*	Click the document	Click <u>W</u>indow, click name of document	`Alt` `W`, press number of document
FILE MANAGER			
Change current/default drive *WIN 45*	Click ▭ on drive icon ribbon	Click <u>D</u>isk, <u>S</u>elect Drive...	`Alt` `D`, `S` or `Ctrl` [drive letter]
Change current/default directory *WIN 50*	Click 📁		Press arrow key to directory
Collapse a directory *WIN 50*	Double-click 📁	Click <u>T</u>ree, <u>C</u>ollapse Branch	`-`
Copy a file *WIN 58*	Hold `Ctrl` down as you drag the file	Click the filename, click <u>F</u>ile, <u>C</u>opy	`F8`
Create a directory *WIN 48*		Click <u>F</u>ile, Cr<u>e</u>ate Directory	`Alt` `F`, `E`
Delete a file *WIN 56*		Click the filename, click <u>F</u>ile, <u>D</u>elete	Click the filename, press `Del`, `Enter`
Diskette copy/backup *WIN 61*		Click <u>D</u>isk, <u>C</u>opy Disk...	`Alt` `D`, `C`

TASK REFERENCE
BRIEF MICROSOFT WINDOWS 3.1
Italicized page numbers indicate the first discussion of each task.

TASK	MOUSE	MENU	KEYBOARD
FILE MANAGER *(continued)*			
Exit File Manager *WIN 62*	Double-click ▬ File Manager	Click ▬, <u>C</u>lose	`Alt` `F4`
Expand a directory *WIN 50*	Double-click 📁	Click <u>T</u>ree, Expand <u>B</u>ranch	`*`
Format a diskette *WIN 41*		Click <u>D</u>isk, <u>F</u>ormat Disk...	`Alt` `D` , `F`
Launch File Manager *WIN 38*	Double-click File Manager	Press arrow key to File Manager, click <u>F</u>ile, <u>O</u>pen	Press arrow key to File Manager, `Enter`
Make Student Diskette *WIN 43*	Double-click Make Win 3.1 Student Diskette	Press arrow key to Make Win 3.1 Student Diskette , click <u>F</u>ile, <u>O</u>pen	Press arrow key to Make Win 3.1 Student Diskette , `Enter`
Move a file *WIN 52*	Drag file to new directory	Click <u>F</u>ile, <u>M</u>ove	`F7`
Rename a file *WIN 55*		Click <u>F</u>ile, Re<u>n</u>ame	`Alt` `F` , `N`
Select multiple files *WIN 53*	Hold `Ctrl` down and click filenames	Click <u>F</u>ile, <u>S</u>elect Files...	`Alt` `F` , `S`
APPLICATIONS			
Exit application *WIN 33*	Double-click ▬ application	Click ▬, <u>C</u>lose	`Alt` `F4`
Launch application *WIN 10*	Double-click application icon	Press arrow key to icon, click <u>F</u>ile, <u>O</u>pen	Press arrow key to icon, `Enter`

Lotus® 1-2-3® Release 4 for Windows™ Tutorials

A Guided Tour
Fundamentals of Lotus
1-2-3 Release 4 for Windows

1   Creating and Printing Worksheets

2   Modifying a Worksheet

3   Enhancing the Worksheet and
Producing Reports

4   Creating and Printing Charts

5   Preparing and Examining
What-If Alternatives

6   Creating and Using Macros

7   Creating and Using a Worksheet
Database

8   Exploring Advanced What-If
Alternatives

9   Combining and Integrating
Worksheet Applications

10   Developing Advanced Macro
Applications

Additional Cases

Read This Before You Begin

To the Student

To use this book, you must have a Student Disk. Your instructor will either provide you with one or ask you to make your own by following the instructions in the section "Your Student Disk" in the Guided Tour. See your instructor or lab manager for further information. If you are going to work through this book using your own computer, you need a computer system running Microsoft Windows 3.1, Lotus 1-2-3 Release 4 or 4.01 for Windows (commercial or Student Version), and a Student Disk. *You will not be able to complete the tutorials and exercises in this book using your own computer until you have a Student Disk*. The Student Disk also contains SmartIcon palettes created for use with this book. See your instructor or lab manager for instructions on installing the palettes on your own computer.

To the Instructor

Making the Student Disk To complete the tutorials in this book, your students must have a copy of Lotus 1-2-3 Release 4 or 4.01 for Windows and the Student Disk. To relieve you of having to make multiple Student Disks from a single master copy, we provide you with the CTI WinApps Setup Disk, which contains an automatic Student Disk generating program. Once you install the Setup Disk on a network or stand-alone workstation, students can easily make their own Student Disks by double-clicking the "Make 1-2-3 Release 4 Student Disk" icon in the CTI WinApps icon group. Double-clicking this icon transfers all the data files students need to complete the tutorials, Tutorial Assignments, and Case Problems to a high-density disk in drive A or B. If some of your students will use their own computers to complete the tutorials and exercises in this book, they must first get the Student Disk. The section called "Your Student Disk" in the Guided Tour provides complete instructions on how to make the Student Disk.

Installing the CTI WinApps Setup Disk To install the CTI WinApps icon group from the Setup Disk, fol-low the instructions inside the disk envelope that was bundled with your book. By adopting this book, you are granted a license to install this software on any computer or network used by you or your students.

Installing the Predefined SmartIcon Palettes
The SmartIcon palettes for the tutorials are in the *.SMI files in the LOTUS4 directory of the Setup Disk and need to be copied to the hard disk where Lotus 1-2-3 Release 4 for Windows resides. Copy the *.SMI files to the \123R4W\PROGRAMS\SHEETICO directory after installing 1-2-3.

README File A README.TXT file located on the Setup Disk provides additional technical notes, troubleshooting advice, and tips for using the CTI WinApps software in your school's computer lab. You can view the README.TXT file using any word processor you choose, and a printout of the README.TXT file is included with the Instructor's Manual.

System Requirements

The recommended minimum software and hardware requirements are as follows:
- Windows version 3.1 or later on a local hard drive or a network drive and DOS version 3.30 or later.
- A 286 (or higher) processor with a minimum of 4 MB of RAM. (Use on a 286-based computer might require more RAM.)
- A mouse and printer supported by Windows 3.1.
- A VGA 640 x 480 16-color display is recommended; an 800 x 600 or 1024 x 768 SVGA, VGA monochrome, or EGA display is also acceptable.
- 9 MB or more of available disk space. 7.5 MB or more for 1-2-3 and approximately 1.5 MB for the CTI WinApps software.
- Student workstations with at least one high-density 3.5-inch disk drive. If you need a 5.25-inch CTI WinApps Setup Disk, contact your sales rep or call customer service at 1-800-648-7450. In Canada call Times Mirror Professional Publishing/Irwin Dorsey at 1-800-268-4178.
- To install the CTI WinApps Setup Disk on a network drive, your network must support Windows.

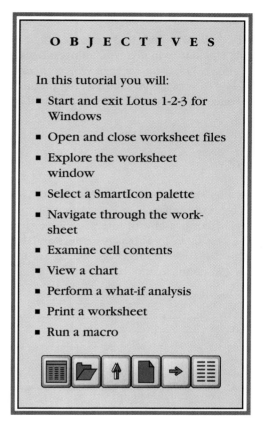

OBJECTIVES

In this tutorial you will:

- Start and exit Lotus 1-2-3 for Windows
- Open and close worksheet files
- Explore the worksheet window
- Select a SmartIcon palette
- Navigate through the worksheet
- Examine cell contents
- View a chart
- Perform a what-if analysis
- Print a worksheet
- Run a macro

Fundamentals of Lotus 1-2-3 Release 4 for Windows

Preparing a Marketing Expense Budget

CASE

SeaJet International Angela Ortega has been working for SeaJet International for almost two years as a marketing analyst. Even before she was hired, she owned a SeaJet personal watercraft, known as a PWC. As an owner she saw how popular PWCs were becoming as recreational vehicles for young and old alike, and so she was particularly excited when she was hired by SeaJet's Marketing Department.

Last month Angela was promoted to assistant marketing manager. In her new job she assists Sharon Romone, vice president of Sales and Marketing. Sharon has been using Lotus 1-2-3 Release 4 for Windows to create the marketing expense budget for the next six months. A **budget** is a plan for managing resources and/or expenditures for a specific amount of time. Sharon has completed the initial draft of her budget and wants to review the worksheet with Angela. As part of her new job assignment, Angela is responsible for monitoring and updating the budget, making sure that the various marketing expenses stay within the planned limits.

On Monday morning, Sharon and Angela meet to review the initial marketing expense budget. Sharon explains that some of the numbers are **projected**, or estimated for the future, so she expects them to change as Angela finalizes the budget. Angela must update the worksheet whenever there is a change. She knows that making changes to the budget will be easy since it was created in Lotus 1-2-3 for Windows. Lotus 1-2-3 for Windows is a powerful tool used in a variety of business settings.

In this Guided Tour, you will preview Lotus 1-2-3 for Windows and examine Sharon's marketing expense budget for SeaJet International. This tour will give you an overview of the many features that you will be learning in this book. *Don't be concerned if you can't remember all the details of this tour.* The purpose is to provide you with a "big picture" overview of Lotus 1-2-3 for Windows. Everything you are introduced to in this tour will be reinforced throughout the tutorials.

What Is Lotus 1-2-3 for Windows?

Lotus 1-2-3 for Windows is a software tool known as an **electronic spreadsheet**. This type of software is designed to help you produce reports similar to an accountant's paper worksheet like the one shown in Figure 1. A **worksheet** is a grid of intersecting vertical columns and horizontal rows that organizes data as a table in an easily understandable way. With this grid organization, data is entered in the appropriate **cells**, which are the intersections of rows and columns. Lotus 1-2-3 has 256 columns and 8192 rows.

SeaJet International Marketing Expense Budget							
	May	June	July	August	September	October	Total
Salaries	$33,600	$33,600	$33,600	$46,800	$46,800	$46,800	$241,200
Benefits	7,392	7,392	7,392	10,296	10.296	10,296	53,064
Commissions	11,320	16,840	15,970	12,320	10,890	9,760	77,100
Advertising and Promotion	24,700	25,194	25,698	32,212	26,800	27,336	161,940
Competitive Sponsorships	6,400	12,800	9,600	9,600	6,400	3,200	48,000
Automobile Expenses	2,638	3,631	3,475	2,818	2,560	2,357	17,478
Dues and Subscriptions	350	350	480	370	340	390	2,280
Contributions	566	842	799	616	545	488	3,855
Insurance	570	570	570	570	570	570	3,420
Entertainment	1,698	2,526	2,396	1,848	1,634	1,464	11,565
Janitorial	390	390	390	390	390	390	2,340
Maintenance	820	820	1,790	1,950	820	820	7,020
Office Equipment	1,140	1,140	4,740	1,140	1,140	1,140	10,440
Postage	1,590	2,240	2,370	1,830	1,590	1,590	11,210
Rents	1,470	1,470	1,470	1,470	1,470	1,470	8,820
Supplies	2,640	2,772	2,911	3,056	3,209	3,369	17,957
Taxes	8,984	10,088	9,914	11,824	11,538	11,312	63,660
Telephone	1,730	1,730	1,730	1,730	1,730	1,730	10,380
Travel	3,700	4,600	5,100	3,200	2,900	2,500	22,000
Utilities	780	780	780	780	780	780	4,680
Miscellaneous	2,100	2,800	3,300	3,200	2,900	2,300	16,600
Total Marketing Expense	$114,579	$132,575	$134,473	$148,020	$135,301	$130,062	$795,009

cell

row →

Figure 1
The SeaJet marketing expense budget on an accountant's paper worksheet

column

With a paper worksheet, you use a calculator and a pencil to calculate totals and write them in the proper cells. Then, if just one number changes, you have to recalculate and rewrite the entire worksheet. With 1-2-3, the computer automatically recalculates for you and displays the revised numbers. Figure 2 shows a printout of the SeaJet marketing expense budget, which Sharon produced after entering all the data in 1-2-3. Some totals might not appear correct due to rounding. However, all totals are correct and you will learn more about rounding in Tutorial 2.

SeaJet International
Marketing Expense Budget

	May	June	July	August	September	October	Total
Salaries	$33,600	$33,600	$33,600	$46,800	$46,800	$46,800	$241,200
Benefits	7,392	7,392	7,392	10,296	10,296	10,296	53,064
Commissions	11,320	16,840	15,970	12,320	10,890	9,760	77,100
Advertising and Promotion	24,700	25,194	25,698	32,212	26,800	27,336	161,940
Competitive Sponsorships	6,400	12,800	9,600	9,600	6,400	3,200	48,000
Automobile Expenses	2,638	3,631	3,475	2,818	2,560	2,357	17,478
Dues and Subscriptions	350	350	480	370	340	390	2,280
Contributions	566	842	799	616	545	488	3,855
Insurance	570	570	570	570	570	570	3,420
Entertainment	1,698	2,526	2,396	1,848	1,634	1,464	11,565
Janitorial	390	390	390	390	390	390	2,340
Maintenance	820	820	1,790	1,950	820	820	7,020
Office Equipment	1,140	1,140	4,740	1,140	1,140	1,140	10,440
Postage	1,590	2,240	2,370	1,830	1,590	1,590	11,210
Rents	1,470	1,470	1,470	1,470	1,470	1,470	8,820
Supplies	2,640	2,772	2,911	3,056	3,209	3,369	17,957
Taxes	8,984	10,088	9,914	11,824	11,538	11,312	63,660
Telephone	1,730	1,730	1,730	1,730	1,730	1,730	10,380
Travel	3,700	4,600	5,100	3,200	2,900	2,500	22,000
Utilities	780	780	780	780	780	780	4,680
Miscellaneous	2,100	2,800	3,300	3,200	2,900	2,300	16,600
Total Marketing Expense	$114,578	$132,575	$134,473	$148,020	$135,301	$130,062	$795,009

Figure 2 Printout of SeaJet marketing expense budget

Lotus 1-2-3 is not only effective at summarizing numerical data and keeping records—it is also a powerful decision-making tool. The spreadsheet's ability to answer the question "What if?" helps business people make sound decisions. For example, what if Sharon's estimated Advertising and Promotion expense for May increases to $28,600—then how much is the total for this expense? A **what-if analysis** occurs whenever you revise a data value and the entire spreadsheet is recalculated so the new results are available immediately for your analysis. After you create a 1-2-3 worksheet, you can perform a series of different what-if analyses quickly and easily.

This what-if capability makes spreadsheet software such as 1-2-3 essential throughout a business organization—in accounting, marketing, finance, manufacturing, and human resources management. The tutorials and case problems in this book provide examples of how 1-2-3 can be used in these business disciplines. You'll also see how to display information in different chart formats, and how to use 1-2-3's database capabilities.

Using the Tutorials Effectively

This book will help you learn about 1-2-3. The book is divided into the Guided Tour and seven tutorials, which are designed to be used at your computer. First read the text that explains the concepts. Then when you come to the numbered steps, which appear on a colored background, follow the steps as you work at your computer. Read each step carefully and completely before you try it.

As you work, compare your screen with the figures to verify your results. Your screen might look slightly different because of the printer or monitor that you are using. The important parts of the screen display are labeled in each figure. Just make sure the labeled parts appear on your screen.

Don't worry about making mistakes—that's part of the learning process. TROUBLE? paragraphs identify common problems and explain how to get back on track. Complete the steps in the TROUBLE? paragraph *only* if you are having the problem described.

After you read the conceptual information and complete the steps, you can do the exercises found at the end of each tutorial in the sections entitled "Questions," "Tutorial Assignments," and "Case Problems." Note that this Guided Tour provides only one Case Problem; the tutorials, however, each include three Case Problems. The exercises are carefully structured to help you review what you learned in the tutorials and apply your knowledge to new situations.

When you are doing the exercises, refer back to the Reference Window boxes. These boxes, which are found throughout the tutorials, provide you with short summaries of frequently used procedures. You can also use the Task Reference at the end of the book; it summarizes how to accomplish tasks using the mouse, the menus, and the keyboard.

Before you begin the Guided Tour and the tutorials, you should know how to use the menus, dialog boxes, Help facility, Program Manager, and File Manager in Microsoft Windows. If you need to learn these concepts or if you just need a refresher, Course Technology, Inc. publishes two excellent texts for learning Windows: *A Guide to Microsoft Windows* and *An Introduction to Microsoft Windows*.

Your Student Disk

To complete the tutorials and exercises in this book, you must have a Student Disk. The Student Disk contains all the practice files you need for the tutorials, the Tutorial Assignments, and the Case Problems. If your instructor or lab manager provides you with your Student Disk, you may skip this section and go to the next section entitled "Launching 1-2-3." If your instructor asks you to make your own Student Disk, you need to follow the steps in this section. To make your Student Disk you need:

- A blank, formatted, high-density 3.5-inch or 5.25-inch disk.
- A computer with Microsoft Windows 3.1, Lotus 1-2-3 Release 4 for Windows, and the CTI WinApps icon group installed on it.

If you are using your own computer, the CTI WinApps icon group will not be installed on it. Before you proceed, you must go to your school's computer lab and find a computer with the CTI WinApps icon group installed on it. Once you have made your own Student Disk, you can use it to complete all the tutorials and exercises in this book on any computer you choose.

To make your Lotus 1-2-3 Student Disk:

❶ Launch Windows and make sure the Program Manager window is open.

TROUBLE? The exact steps you follow to launch Windows might vary depending on how your computer is set up. On many computer systems, type WIN at the DOS prompt and then press [Enter] to launch Windows. If you don't know how to launch Windows, ask your technical support person.

❷ Label your formatted disk "Lotus 1-2-3 Student Disk" and place it in drive A.

TROUBLE? If your computer has more than one disk drive, drive A is usually on top. If your Student Disk does not fit into drive A, then place it in drive B and substitute "drive B" whenever you see "drive A" in the steps.

❸ Look for an icon labeled "CTI WinApps" like the one in Figure 3 or a window labeled "CTI WinApps" like the one in Figure 4.

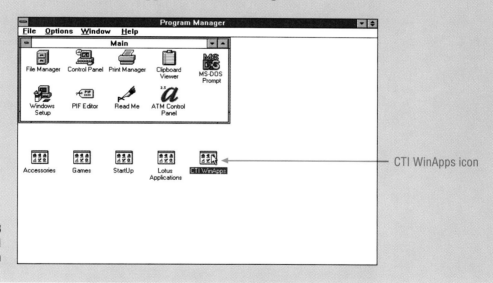

CTI WinApps icon

Figure 3
The CTI
WinApps icon

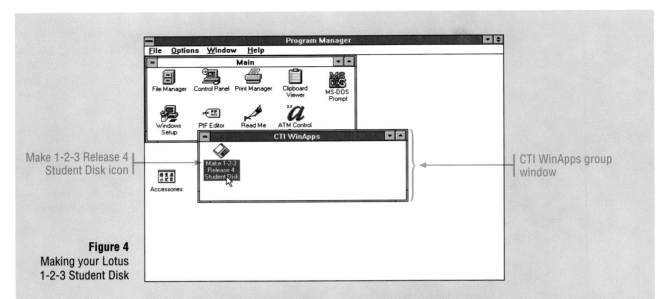

Make 1-2-3 Release 4 Student Disk icon

CTI WinApps group window

Figure 4
Making your Lotus
1-2-3 Student Disk

TROUBLE? If you cannot find anything labeled "CTI WinApps," the CTI software might not be installed on your computer. If you are in a computer lab, ask your technical support person for assistance. If you are using your own computer, you will not be able to make your Student Disk. To make it you need access to the CTI WinApps icon group, which is, most likely, installed on your school's lab computers. Ask your instructor or technical support person for further information on where to locate the CTI WinApps icon group. Once you create your Student Disk, you can use it to complete all the tutorials and exercises in this book on any computer you choose.

❹ If you see an icon labeled "CTI WinApps," double-click it to open the CTI WinApps group window. If the CTI WinApps group window is already open, go to Step 5.

❺ Double-click the icon labeled "Make 1-2-3 Release 4 Student Disk." The Make 1-2-3 Release 4 Student Disk window opens. See Figure 5.

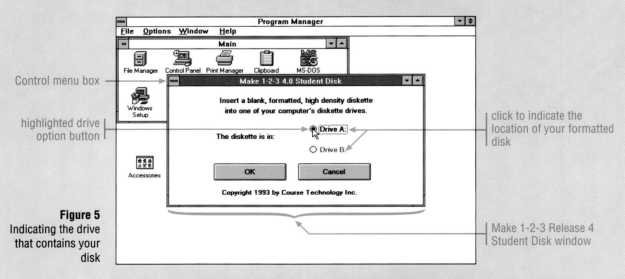

Control menu box

highlighted drive option button

click to indicate the location of your formatted disk

Figure 5
Indicating the drive
that contains your
disk

Make 1-2-3 Release 4 Student Disk window

❻ Make sure the drive that contains your formatted disk corresponds to the drive option button that is highlighted in the dialog box on your screen.

❼ Click the **OK button** to copy the practice files to your formatted disk.

❽ When the copying is complete, a message appears indicating the number of files copied to your disk. Click the **OK button**.

❾ To close the CTI WinApps window, double-click the **Control menu box** on the CTI WinApps window.

Now the files you need to complete the tour, the tutorials, and the exercises are on your Student Disk. Your next step is to launch 1-2-3.

Launching 1-2-3

Launching, or starting, 1-2-3 is similar to starting other Windows applications. When you launch 1-2-3, the Untitled document window appears on the screen. You can use this untitled window to create a new worksheet, or you can open a worksheet that has already been created. Let's launch 1-2-3 and review Sharon's marketing expense budget.

To launch 1-2-3:

❶ Launch Windows.

❷ Look for an icon or window titled "Lotus Applications" or "Lotus 1-2-3 for Windows." See Figure 6.

TROUBLE? If you don't see anything called "Lotus Applications" or "Lotus 1-2-3 for Windows," click Window on the menu bar and, if you find either menu item in the list, click it. If you still can't find anything called "Lotus Applications" or "Lotus 1-2-3 for Windows," ask your technical support person for help on how to start 1-2-3. If you are using your own computer, make sure the 1-2-3 software has been installed.

Lotus 1-2-3 Release 4
for Windows
program-item icon

Lotus Applications
group window

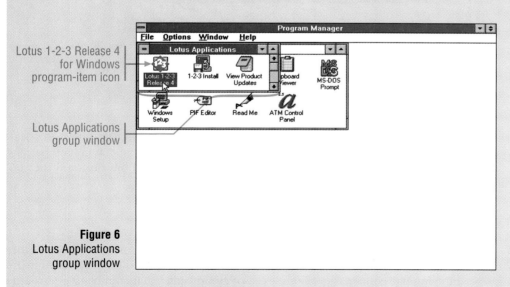

Figure 6
Lotus Applications
group window

❸ If you see the Lotus Applications group icon, double-click the **Lotus Applications group icon** to open the group window. If you see the Lotus Applications *group window* instead of the *group icon*, go to Step 4.

❹ Double-click the **Lotus 1-2-3 Release 4 for Windows program-item icon**. After a short pause, the 1-2-3 copyright information appears in a box and remains on the screen until 1-2-3 is ready for use.

❺ Click the **application window Maximize button** if your Lotus 1-2-3 application window is not maximized.

❻ Click the **worksheet window Maximize button** to maximize the Untitled window, if it is not already maximized. See Figure 7.

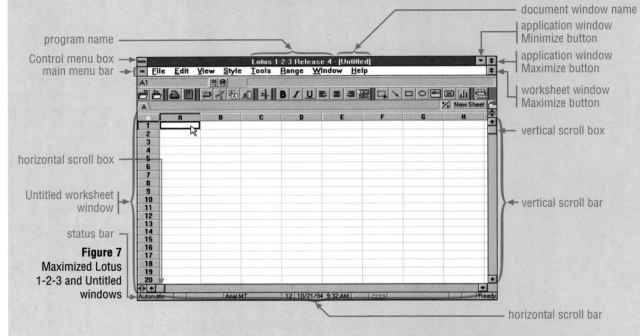

Figure 7
Maximized Lotus
1-2-3 and Untitled
windows

TROUBLE? Your screen might display a little more or a little less of the grid shown in Figure 7. Also, if you are using the Student Version of the software, the words "Student Version" will appear in the title bar of your worksheet window throughout the tutorials. Don't worry if your screen doesn't look exactly the same as Figure 7.

Notice that the 1-2-3 window (Figure 7) contains components common to all Windows applications. Some examples are the Control menu box, the main menu bar, the status bar, the Minimize and Maximize buttons, the scroll bars and buttons, and the program and window name.

Main Menu Bar

The 1-2-3 **main menu bar**, located at the top of the screen, is similar to that of other Windows applications, but it contains commands specifically created for 1-2-3. Each menu on the main menu bar contains a pull-down list of commands. Each command controls an operation of 1-2-3, such as printing a document, saving a file, or changing the appearance of data in the worksheet. The 1-2-3 main menu is **context-sensitive**, which means that menu choices change as you perform different activities. For example, different menu choices appear when you create a 1-2-3 chart.

You can select commands in the main menu bar by using the mouse or the keyboard, including shortcut keys, in the same way as you do for other Windows programs. Because using the mouse is often the most efficient method for choosing commands in 1-2-3, this method is emphasized in this book.

Now that you've successfully launched 1-2-3, you can open Sharon's worksheet file for the marketing budget.

Opening a Worksheet File

When you want to use a worksheet that has already been created, you must first open it. Opening a worksheet means that a copy of the worksheet file is transferred into the random access memory (RAM) of your computer and displayed on your screen. To help you understand what occurs when you open a worksheet file, look at Figure 8. Lotus 1-2-3 *copies* the worksheet file named BUDGET.WK4 from your Student Disk to the computer's memory (RAM). When the worksheet is open, it is both in the computer's memory and stored on your Student Disk. Any changes that are made *affect only the copy in the computer's memory*. The file must be *saved* to your Student Disk before the file on disk is changed. Once you open a worksheet, you can view, edit, print, or save it again on your disk.

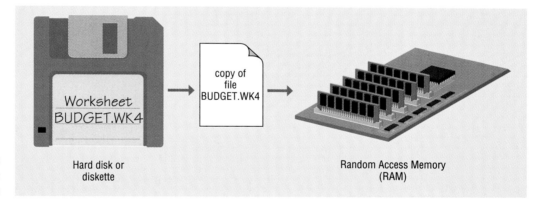

Figure 8
Opening a
worksheet file

Hard disk or
diskette

copy of
file
BUDGET.WK4

Random Access Memory
(RAM)

Worksheet
BUDGET.WK4

REFERENCE WINDOW   **Opening a Worksheet File**

- Click the Open File SmartIcon.

  or

  Click File then click Open.

- Click the Drives drop-down list arrow to display the available disk drives.

- Click the disk drive containing the worksheet file you want to open.

- In the File name list box, double-click the filename of the worksheet you want to open.

Let's open Sharon's worksheet file for the marketing expense budget, which she saved as BUDGET.WK4. The file extension WK4 is added automatically to all 1-2-3 Release 4 for Windows files to identify them as worksheet files.

To open the BUDGET.WK4 worksheet:

❶ Make sure your Student Disk is in the disk drive.

TROUBLE? If you don't have a Student Disk, then you need to get one. Your instructor will either give you one or ask you to make your own by following the steps earlier in this tutorial in the section entitled "Your Student Disk." See your instructor for information.

❷ Click **File** then click **Open** to display the Open File dialog box. See Figure 9.

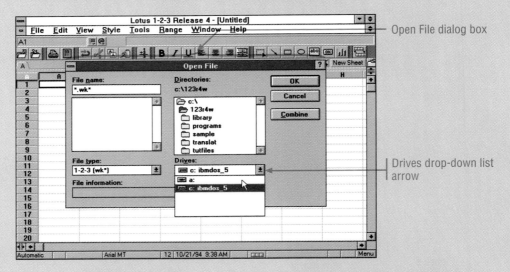

Figure 9
Open File dialog box

❸ Click the **Drives drop-down list arrow** to see the list of available drives (Figure 9).

❹ Click **a:** to choose the drive where your Student Disk is located. (If your disk is in another drive, click that drive.) You might need to scroll the list of drives to find the drive you want.

❺ Click the filename **BUDGET.WK4** in the File name list box. See Figure 10. Your filename list might not match the list in Figure 10.

TROUBLE? If you do not see BUDGET.WK4 in the list, use the scroll bar to display additional filenames.

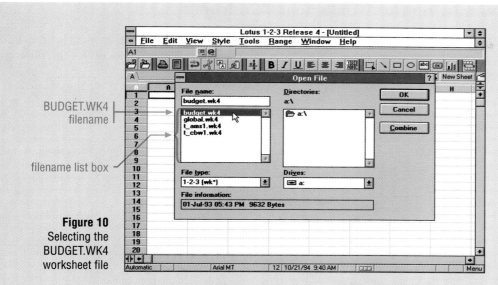

BUDGET.WK4
filename

filename list box

Figure 10
Selecting the
BUDGET.WK4
worksheet file

❻ Click the **OK button** or double-click **BUDGET.WK4**. The file appears in a worksheet window. See Figure 11.

TROUBLE? If you selected the wrong file, click the Control menu box in the main menu bar or the worksheet window title bar, depending on which one is displayed. Then select Close to remove the unwanted worksheet file. Repeat Steps 2 through 6 to select the BUDGET.WK4 worksheet file.

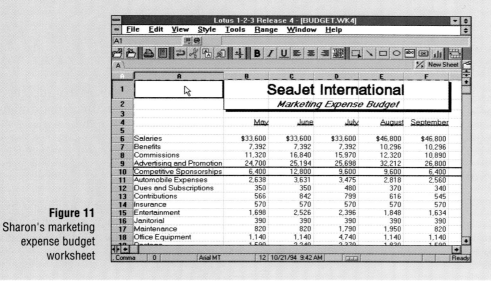

Figure 11
Sharon's marketing
expense budget
worksheet

You have successfully opened Sharon's worksheet. Now, you can look at the components and features of 1-2-3.

Examining the Worksheet Window

Examining Sharon's worksheet will show you the fundamental arrangement of the 1-2-3 window and introduce you to some of its basic features. Figure 12 identifies the different components of the 1-2-3 worksheet window.

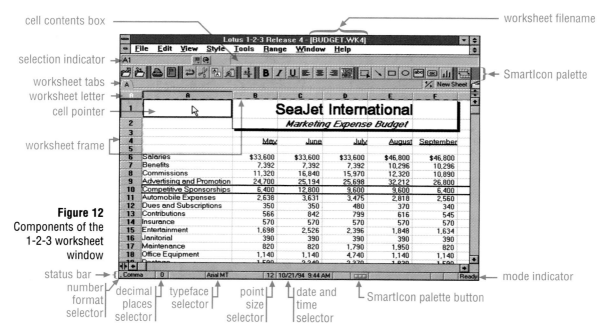

Figure 12
Components of the
1-2-3 worksheet
window

Worksheet Frame

The **worksheet frame** contains the column letters and row numbers that identify cell locations. You should see letters beginning with A across the top of the frame and numbers starting with 1 along the left side of the frame. The actual number of rows and columns that appear depends on your monitor.

Cell Pointer

The **cell pointer** indicates the current cell location. The cell pointer is identified by the rectangular highlight surrounding the cell. The **current cell** is where the cell pointer is and where data you enter is stored. When you first opened the worksheet, the cell pointer was located in cell A1, so A1 is the current cell.

Worksheet Letter

The **worksheet letter** identifies the current worksheet. A 1-2-3 file can contain more than one worksheet. The **current worksheet** is the one in which you are entering data or performing other tasks. The worksheet letter appears in the upper-left corner of the worksheet frame. On your screen, the worksheet letter "A" identifies A as the current worksheet.

Worksheet Tabs

The **worksheet tabs** identify the worksheets contained in a single file. Lotus 1-2-3 automatically names each tab A, B, C, etc. In this case you see only the letter "A," which means that the file BUDGET.WK4 includes only one worksheet. If the file included more than one worksheet, the tab for each worksheet would appear in the worksheet tabs area.

Selection Indicator

The **selection indicator** displays the cell name, or cell address, of the current cell. A **cell name**, or **cell address**, is the worksheet letter, column letter, and row number of a cell. For example, A:C10 is the cell address of the cell in worksheet A at the intersection of column C and row 10. If there is only one worksheet in a file, the A is not used, so the cell address is simply C10.

Cell Contents Box

The **cell contents box** displays the contents of the current cell. A cell's **content** is the data that you enter into a cell. For example, the content of cell A15 is "Entertainment."

Worksheet Filename

The **worksheet filename** indicates the name of the worksheet file displayed in the worksheet window, in this case, BUDGET.WK4.

Status Bar

The **status bar** contains several status indicators that advise you of conditions concerning the content and operation of the worksheet. For example, you should see Arial MT and the number 12 in the middle of the status bar. Arial MT is the name of the **typeface**, the style that the letters and numbers appear in, and 12 indicates the size of the typeface, or point size. The status bar also displays the current date and time from your computer's clock, the SmartIcon palette button, the mode indicator (defined below), and the number format and decimal places selectors. SmartIcons are defined in the next section; formats and decimal places are discussed later in the tour.

Mode Indicator

Located on the right side of the status bar, the **mode indicator** specifies the **mode**, or state, that 1-2-3 is currently in. For example, when 1-2-3 is ready for you to type or select a command, 1-2-3 is in Ready mode. If you make a mistake, 1-2-3 will display the word "Error." The mode indicator changes to show the current type of task you are performing. For example, when you are selecting a menu option, the Menu indicator appears, whereas Wait indicates 1-2-3 is performing a task and wants you to wait until that task is completed. Other mode indicators will be described as they occur throughout the tutorials.

SmartIcons

SmartIcons are pictures that provide you with immediate and easy access to many commonly used 1-2-3 commands, allowing you to perform tasks more quickly. For example, instead of accessing the menu bar or using the shortcut key to open a file, you can click the Open File SmartIcon. A **SmartIcon palette** is a row of SmartIcons that appears at the top of the worksheet window, below the main menu bar. Lotus 1-2-3 provides several SmartIcon palettes. You can also create your own custom arrangements of SmartIcons. In Tutorial 5 you will learn how to customize your own SmartIcon palette. Some palettes have already been created for you; these are called **predefined SmartIcon palettes**. You will use a predefined palette called "Guided Tour" later in this tour.

1-2-3 Classic Menu

The 1-2-3 Classic menu displays commands in the same way as DOS releases of 1-2-3 and gives experienced users of Lotus 1-2-3 for DOS a familiar method for using Lotus 1-2-3 for Windows. Because the real power of 1-2-3 Release 4 comes from using it as a true Windows application, operation of the Classic menu is *not* covered in the tutorials. However, you need to know about the 1-2-3 Classic menu in case you accidentally display it. The Classic menu appears when 1-2-3 is in Ready mode and you press either the slash (/) or less than symbol (<). Let's practice displaying the Classic menu and returning to Ready mode.

To display the 1-2-3 Classic menu:

❶   Press / and the menu appears. See Figure 13.

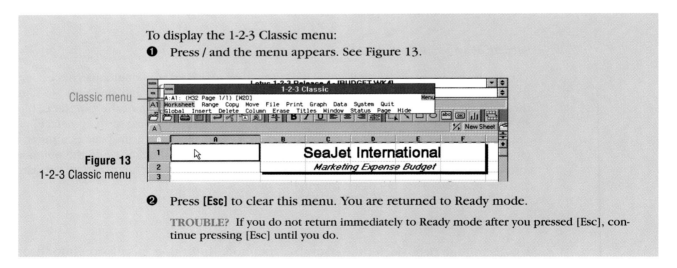

Classic menu

Figure 13
1-2-3 Classic menu

❷   Press **[Esc]** to clear this menu. You are returned to Ready mode.

   TROUBLE? If you do not return immediately to Ready mode after you pressed [Esc], continue pressing [Esc] until you do.

Now that you are more familiar with the 1-2-3 worksheet window, you can select the predefined SmartIcon palette you will use in this tour.

Selecting a Predefined SmartIcon Palette

As mentioned earlier, a predefined SmartIcon palette is a custom arrangement of icons already prepared for you. You select a predefined palette using the SmartIcon palette selector, which appears in the status bar.

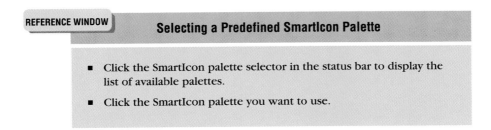

Selecting a Predefined SmartIcon Palette

- Click the SmartIcon palette selector in the status bar to display the list of available palettes.
- Click the SmartIcon palette you want to use.

Let's display the SmartIcon palette that has been created for this Guided Tour.

To display the predefined SmartIcon palette for the tour:

❶ Click the **SmartIcon palette selector** ⌗ in the status bar to display the list of available SmartIcon palettes. See Figure 14.

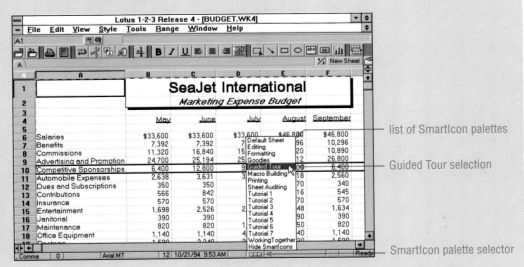

Figure 14
The SmartIcon
palette list

❷ Click **Guided Tour**. The Guided Tour SmartIcon palette is displayed above the worksheet window and you are returned to Ready mode. See Figure 15.

TROUBLE? If "Guided Tour" does not appear in your list of available SmartIcon palettes, then the palette might not be installed with your copy of 1-2-3. If you are in a computer lab, ask your technical support person for assistance. If you are using your own computer, you need to install the Guided Tour palette. See your instructor or technical support person for a copy of the Setup Disk, which contains a README file with instructions for installing the SmartIcon palette.

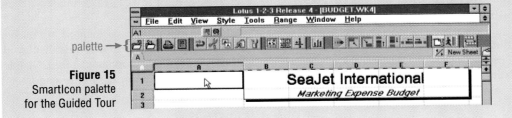

Figure 15
SmartIcon palette
for the Guided Tour

TROUBLE? If your SmartIcons are larger and have different pictures than the ones in Figure 15, the icon size is set to "Large." You need to set the size to Medium to match the icons used in this book. To set the icons to Medium, click the Tools menu, then click SmartIcons, Icon Size, and the Medium option button. Finally, click OK to leave the Icon Size dialog box, and click OK to exit the SmartIcons dialog box.

You can obtain a description of the action of any SmartIcon displayed in the palette. Let's do that, now.

To display the description of the Undo SmartIcon:
❶ Position the mouse pointer on the **Undo SmartIcon** ⮌.
❷ Press and hold the **right mouse button**. Do not press the *left* mouse button—that executes the SmartIcon command. Read the description in the program name area as you continue to keep the right mouse button depressed. See Figure 16. Note that you can use this SmartIcon at any time during this tour if you make a mistake. It will "undo" your last action.

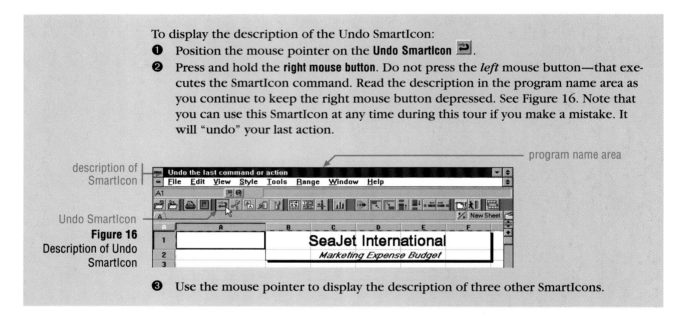

description of SmartIcon

Undo SmartIcon

program name area

Figure 16
Description of Undo SmartIcon

❸ Use the mouse pointer to display the description of three other SmartIcons.

You will learn the operation of many of the SmartIcons in the tutorials. Each SmartIcon will be described when it is first used.

Next, let's learn how to move around the worksheet window.

Navigating Through the Worksheet

Looking at Sharon's worksheet, notice that the entire worksheet is not visible. It is too big to fit the entire budget in the worksheet window. The number of visible rows and columns depends on your particular screen display. Because you can view only one area of the worksheet at a time, you must navigate through the worksheet to see other areas of the worksheet. You do this by clicking specific cells, using the scroll buttons and bars, using the cursor movement keys, and using SmartIcons.

When you initially access Sharon's worksheet, your cell pointer is located at cell A1, the selection indicator displays A1, and the upper-left area of your worksheet is displayed. First, let's practice moving the cell pointer around the part of the worksheet that *is* visible. Then, you can inspect the areas of Sharon's worksheet that do not appear in the window.

To move the cell pointer in the worksheet:

❶ Click cell **C6**, Salaries for June. Notice that the selection indicator confirms the cell location by displaying C6, and the cell contents box displays 33600. See Figure 17.

TROUBLE? If you placed the cell pointer in the wrong location, move the mouse pointer to the correct location and try again.

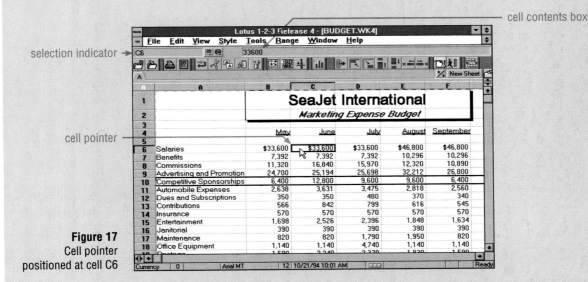

cell contents box

selection indicator →

cell pointer →

Figure 17
Cell pointer
positioned at cell C6

❷ Click **D14** to move the cell pointer to cell D14. The number 570 appears in the cell contents box.

Continue moving the cell pointer to other locations for more practice; then continue with the next section.

Scrolling Using the Keyboard and the Mouse

You can view different areas of the worksheet that aren't visible by scrolling the work-sheet window. **Scrolling** is a way to view other areas of a large worksheet. You scroll by using the mouse with the vertical and horizontal scroll bars or by using the cursor move-ment keys. Figure 18 on the following page lists the most commonly used cursor move-ment keys.

Key	Moves Cell Pointer
[→]	Right one cell
[←]	Left one cell
[↓]	Down one cell
[↑]	Up one cell
[Tab]	Right one screen
[Shift][Tab]	Left one screen
[Ctrl][→]	Right one screen
[Ctrl][←]	Left one screen
[Home]	To cell A1
[PgDn]	Down one screen
[PgUp]	Up one screen

Figure 18
Commonly used cursor
movement keys

Let's look at various areas of Sharon's worksheet by scrolling, using the cursor movement keys and the scroll bars and boxes. You can decide which method you prefer.

To scroll the worksheet window and display different areas:
❶ Press **[Home]**. Your cell pointer moves to cell A1.
❷ Press **[PgDn]** to move one screen down the worksheet. The cell pointer is now located at A20. See Figure 19. You should now see row 28, which wasn't visible before. Notice that you remain in Ready mode when scrolling the worksheet window.

TROUBLE? Don't worry if your cell pointer is not at A20—some screens can hold more or fewer rows than others. Just make sure that the worksheet scrolled down one screen.

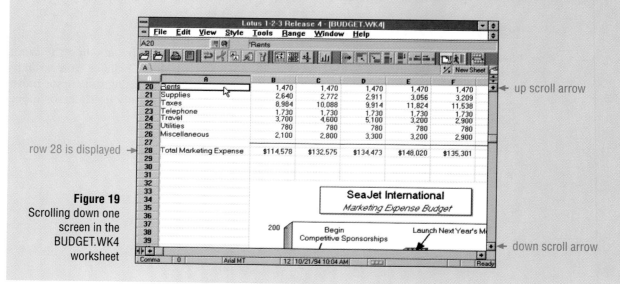

row 28 is displayed →

up scroll arrow →

down scroll arrow →

Figure 19
Scrolling down one
screen in the
BUDGET.WK4
worksheet

❸ Press **[PgUp]** to move one screen up the worksheet. The cell pointer returns to cell A1. You can practice using the other cursor movement keys to scroll around the worksheet.

Now, use the mouse and scroll bars to display areas of the worksheet.

❹ Click the **down scroll arrow** in the vertical scroll bar several times until Total Marketing Expense is displayed and cell A20 is located in the upper-left corner of the worksheet. See Figure 19.

❺ Click the **right scroll arrow** in the horizontal scroll bar to display columns G and H. These columns contain the data for October and Total. Notice that column A has disappeared from the left side of your worksheet window. See Figure 20.

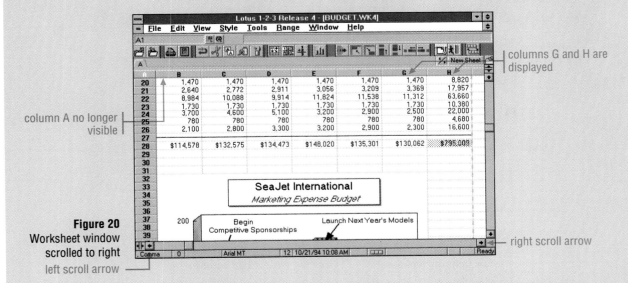

columns G and H are displayed

column A no longer visible

Figure 20
Worksheet window scrolled to right

left scroll arrow

right scroll arrow

You should now see the top of the chart Sharon created. Let's take a closer look.

❻ Drag the **vertical scroll box** to move down the worksheet and drag the **horizontal scroll box** to move to the right or left to display Sharon's marketing expense budget chart. See Figure 21 on the following page.

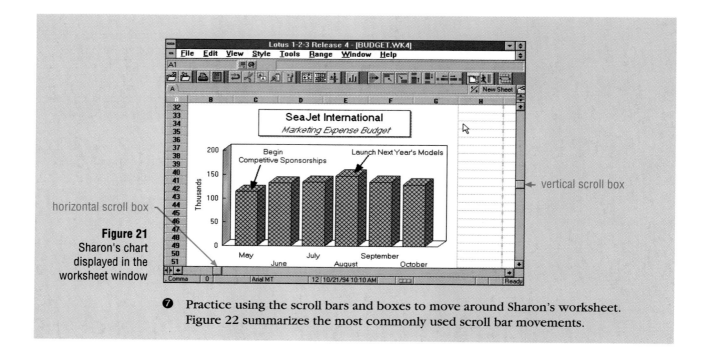

Figure 21
Sharon's chart
displayed in the
worksheet window

horizontal scroll box

vertical scroll box

❼ Practice using the scroll bars and boxes to move around Sharon's worksheet. Figure 22 summarizes the most commonly used scroll bar movements.

To Move Cell Pointer:	Do This:
Up or down one row	Click the up or down scroll arrow
Left or right one column	Click the left or right scroll arrow
Left or right one full screen	Click the horizontal scroll bar to the left or right of the scroll box
Up or down one full screen	Click the vertical scroll bar above or below the scroll box
Left or right to any position	Drag the scroll box in the horizontal scroll bar
Up or down to any position	Drag the scroll box in the vertical scroll bar

Figure 22
Commonly used scroll
bar movements

Scrolling Using SmartIcons

In addition to scroll bars and cursor movement keys, several SmartIcons are available to help you quickly move around the worksheet. Each of these SmartIcons has a corresponding cursor movement key. See Figure 23 for a description of these SmartIcons. Note that the notation [End] + [↑] means that you press the End key and release it and then press [↑]—*do not press both keys at the same time.*

SmartIcon	Corresponding Cursor Movement Keys	Description
	[Home]	Moves cell pointer directly to cell A1
	[F5]	Moves cell pointer directly to a location you specify
	[End] + [↑]	Moves cell pointer up to the first row that contains data
	[End] + [↓]	Moves cell pointer down to the last row that contains data
	[End] + [→]	Moves cell pointer to the last cell on the right that contains data
	[End] + [←]	Moves cell pointer to the last cell on the left that contains data
	[End] + [Home]	Moves cell pointer to bottom right corner of worksheet's active area

Figure 23
Cell pointer movement
SmartIcons

Let's try using the Go To SmartIcon to move the cell pointer to a location you specify. When the Go To dialog box appears, you type the cell address that you want to go to.

To move the cell pointer to H26 using the Go To SmartIcon:
❶ Click the **Go To SmartIcon** . The Go To dialog box appears as shown in Figure 24.

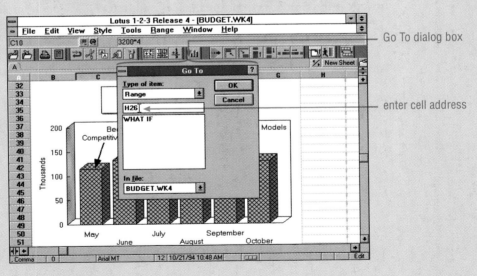

Figure 24
Go To dialog box

❷ Type **H26**.
❸ Click the **OK button** or press **[Enter]** to position the cell pointer at H26. See Figure 25 on the following page.

TROUBLE? If you entered the wrong cell address, click and try again.

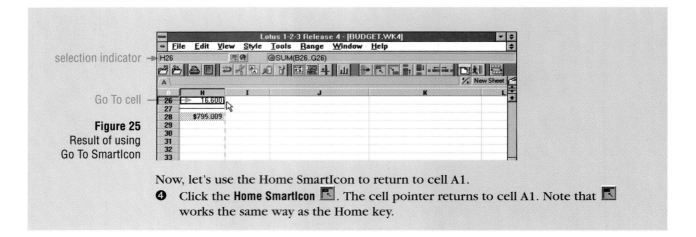

selection indicator →

Go To cell →

Figure 25
Result of using
Go To SmartIcon

Now, let's use the Home SmartIcon to return to cell A1.

❹ Click the **Home SmartIcon** 🔲. The cell pointer returns to cell A1. Note that 🔲 works the same way as the Home key.

It does not matter which method you choose to navigate through the worksheet. You can use the mouse, keyboard, SmartIcons, or a combination of the three. But once the cell pointer is in the cell, your next question might be, what does the cell contain? In the next section, you will explore the various contents of the cells in Sharon's worksheet.

Exploring Cell Contents

The cells in Sharon's worksheet contain labels, values, formulas, and functions. A **label** is any descriptive text, such as a name or address. A **value** is a number, formula, or function. A **formula** is the arithmetic used to calculate numbers displayed in the worksheet. A **function** is a predefined formula that is built into 1-2-3. Functions save you the trouble of creating your own formulas to perform various mathematical tasks. Lotus 1-2-3 classifies a cell's content as either a label or a value.

Let's examine the various labels and values Sharon entered into her worksheet. When you create a worksheet in Tutorial 1, you will enter similar labels and values.

Labels

Sharon's worksheet contains an assortment of labels. These labels describe the rest of the data in the worksheet. Let's look at several of the labels.

To examine cells that contain labels:

❶ Click **A6**. This cell contains the label "Salaries." The apostrophe (') before the letter S in the cell contents box indicates that this cell contains a label. Note that the apostrophe is not displayed in the worksheet. See Figure 26.

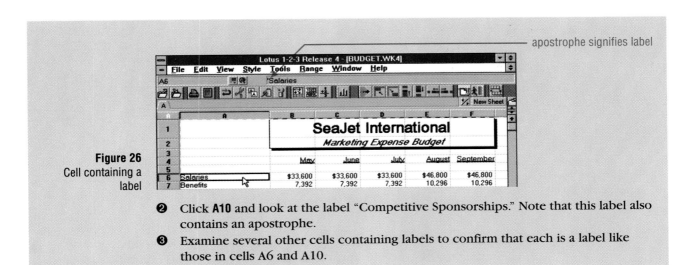

apostrophe signifies label

Figure 26
Cell containing a
label

❷ Click **A10** and look at the label "Competitive Sponsorships." Note that this label also contains an apostrophe.

❸ Examine several other cells containing labels to confirm that each is a label like those in cells A6 and A10.

The apostrophe that precedes the first character of a label is called the **label prefix**. The label prefix appears in the cell contents box but is *not* displayed in the worksheet. The apostrophe before the label in cells A6 and A10 tells 1-2-3 to left-justify the label. A **left-justified** label is flush with the left side of the cell where it has been entered. All labels must begin with one of the four special label prefix characters ' " ^ \. Figure 27 defines each of the label prefixes.

Prefix	Result
'	Left-justifies text
"	Right-justifies text
^	Centers text
\	Fills entire cell with the character immediately following the backslash

Figure 27
Label prefixes

Let's look for labels with different label prefixes in Sharon's worksheet.

To look at labels with other prefixes:
❶ Click **C4** and note the quotation mark (") as the label prefix. The label "June" is right-justified. See Figure 28 on the following page. A *right-justified* label is flush with the right side of the cell where it has been entered. This label is also underlined. Underlining is not displayed in the cell contents box but does appear with the label in the cell in the worksheet. You will learn how to use underlining in Tutorial 2.

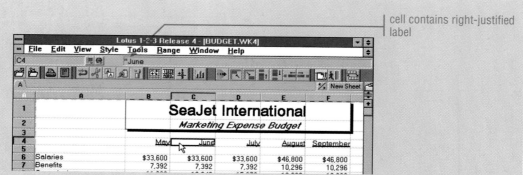

cell contains right-justified label

Figure 28
Right-justified label
with underlining

Next, let's examine centered labels.

❷ Click **D1** and confirm that the cell contents box contains "^SeaJet International." Here the caret (^) specifies that this label is centered. For this report Sharon has centered this heading across columns so it extends to the left and right of column D, where it is located. This label appears in a large, bold typeface. The SeaJet International and Marketing Expense Budget headings are surrounded by an outline and drop shadow box. See Figure 29. You will learn how to center labels across columns and add these special appearance characteristics in several of the tutorials.

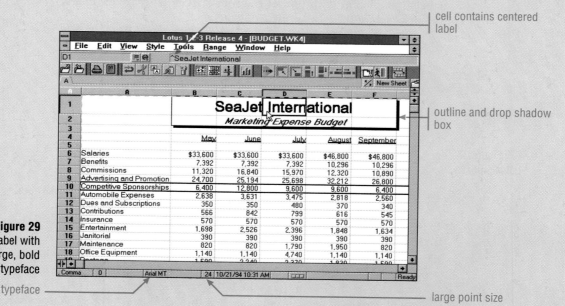

cell contains centered label

outline and drop shadow box

Figure 29
Centered label with
a large, bold
typeface

typeface

large point size

Finally, let's inspect a cell filled with dashes.

❸ Press **[PgDn]** then click **B27** to confirm that the cell contents box contains a backslash followed by a minus sign (\ -). This causes the entire cell to be filled with dashes. Sharon used this label prefix to add an underline above all the total marketing expense data values. See Figure 30.

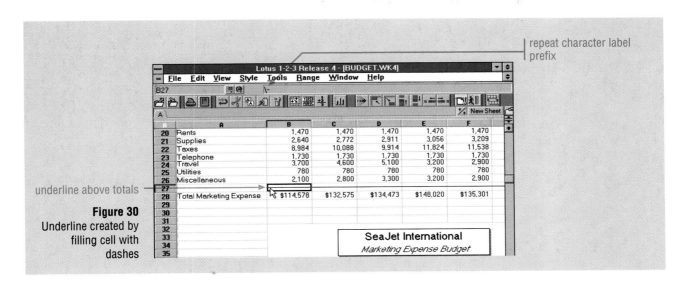

repeat character label prefix

underline above totals

Figure 30
Underline created by
filling cell with
dashes

Values

Values can be numbers, formulas, or functions. You can use numbers in formulas that you create to calculate a value that is displayed. These values can, in turn, be used in formulas in other cells. Lotus 1-2-3 lets you include special **data editing characters**, like the comma (,) and the currency symbol ($) to control how a value is displayed in the worksheet. The manner in which a number is displayed is called the cell's **format**. Let's look at several cells that contain values and examine their contents and format.

To look at cells that contain values and examine their format:

❶ Click the **Home SmartIcon** to position the worksheet area for viewing the cells.

❷ Click **C8**. The number 16840 appears in the cell contents box. See Figure 31 on the following page. Notice that the number in the cell contents box does *not* contain a comma, although a comma is displayed in the worksheet. Also notice that the number format selector in the status bar displays ",Comma" to indicate that this number is displayed using commas.

numeric value in cell
contents box

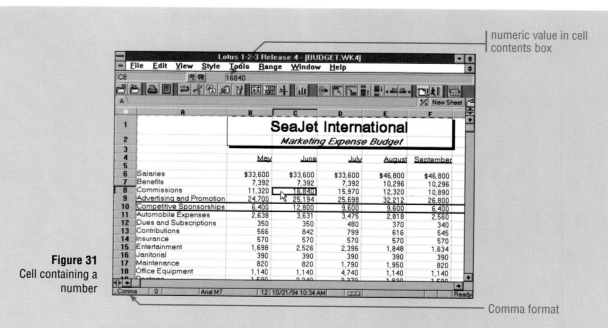

Figure 31
Cell containing a
number

Comma format

Now, let's examine a cell displaying the currency symbol.

❸   Click **B6** to examine the cell contents box for Salaries. See Figure 32. The number
format selector in the status bar displays "Currency" which indicates that this cell
contains the currency symbol ($). The decimal places selector contains 0 (zero),
which specifies that the number is displayed with no places to the right of the
decimal.

numeric value

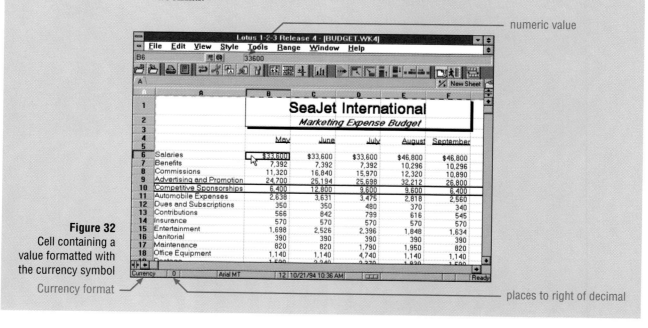

Figure 32
Cell containing a
value formatted with
the currency symbol

Currency format

places to right of decimal

You have examined cells that contain numbers but you have not seen any cells that
contain formulas or functions. Let's look at those next.

Formulas

You use formulas to calculate data values that are displayed in cells. You can take advantage of the power of 1-2-3 by using formulas in your worksheet and letting 1-2-3 calculate the results of all of the formulas for you. If you change one number in the worksheet, 1-2-3 recalculates any formula that is affected by the change. This saves you time reentering calculated values and reduces the possibility of making mistakes.

Formulas are constructed by combining numbers, cell names, and arithmetic operators such as the plus sign (+) and the minus sign (-) to define your calculation. Figure 33 displays the complete list of arithmetic operators.

Symbol	Operation
+	Add
–	Subtract
*	Multiply
/	Divide
^	Exponentiation
( )	Group calculations

Figure 33
Arithmetic
operators used in
formulas

Each formula must begin with an arithmetic operator or a number, followed by a cell address or a number. Including a cell address in a formula is referred to as using a **cell reference**. For example, Sharon knows that at SeaJet the total cost of benefits for each employee is 22% of his or her salary. She entered the value for May's Salaries in cell B6. To calculate the value for Benefits and display it in cell B7, she used the formula +B6*0.22. This formula instructs 1-2-3 to take the value in cell B6, multiply it by 0.22, and display the result in cell B7. Sharon used a formula instead of calculating the result herself, because she knows that the Salaries value might change. By using a formula to calculate Benefits, this data value is recalculated automatically by 1-2-3 whenever the data value for Salaries changes.

When you construct a formula, the cell contents box displays the formula; the result calculated by the formula is displayed in the cell. You can observe this by looking at several numeric values that Sharon calculated using formulas. Let's examine the formulas Sharon used for calculating Benefits and Competitive Sponsorships.

To inspect cells that contain formulas:

❶ Click **B7**. Notice that the value 7,392 appears in the cell, and that the formula +B6*0.22 appears in the cell contents box. See Figure 34 on the following page.

formula with cell reference

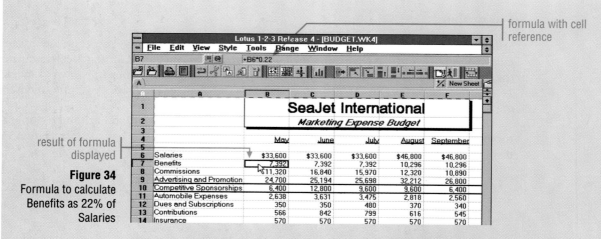

result of formula displayed

Figure 34
Formula to calculate Benefits as 22% of Salaries

Now, let's examine the formula that calculates the data value for the Competitive Sponsorships for June:

❷ Click **C10** and examine the cell contents box. See Figure 35. Here, Sharon entered the formula 3200*4. She could have figured this out on paper and then typed in the answer, but she used this formula to help her remember how the value for June was obtained and to reduce the possibility of making a mistake. This cell and the other cells in row 10 have an outline box surrounding them. You will learn how to create an outline box in Tutorial 3.

formula to calculate value

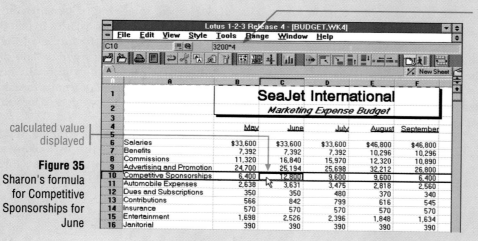

calculated value displayed

Figure 35
Sharon's formula for Competitive Sponsorships for June

Functions

The last type of value you need to examine is a function. As noted earlier, a function is a predefined formula that is built into 1-2-3 as a shortcut means of performing mathematical calculations. For example, H6 contains the formula to calculate the six-month total for Salaries. This can be entered as +B6+C6+D6+E6+F6+G6 or it can be calculated with the @SUM function as @SUM (B6..G6). The **@ symbol** is used to specify a 1-2-3 function. The **@SUM function** adds the numbers you specify. The range of cells to add is enclosed in parentheses and indicated with two points, as in (B6..G6).

Let's look at how Sharon used the @SUM function in her budget worksheet.

To inspect cells that contain the @SUM function:

❶ Scroll your worksheet to the right then click **H8**. The value 77100 displayed in this cell was calculated using the @SUM function. See Figure 36. The function added the values in the range of cells from B8 to G8. As with formulas, the result of the calculation appears in the cell, but the function appears in the cell contents box.

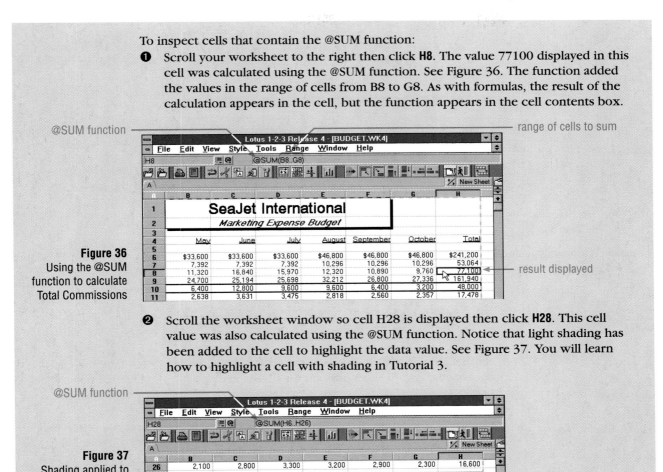

Figure 36
Using the @SUM function to calculate Total Commissions

❷ Scroll the worksheet window so cell H28 is displayed then click **H28**. This cell value was also calculated using the @SUM function. Notice that light shading has been added to the cell to highlight the data value. See Figure 37. You will learn how to highlight a cell with shading in Tutorial 3.

Figure 37
Shading applied to the result of an @SUM function

You'll learn more about the @SUM function and other 1-2-3 functions in the tutorials.

After Sharon entered all the data into her worksheet, she reviewed it to make sure all the calculations were correct. She then decided to use another 1-2-3 feature that allows her to make better business decisions and increases the effectiveness of her worksheet—she added a chart to her worksheet.

Examining a Chart

Sharon created a chart of the Total Marketing Expense. A **chart** is a tool for illustrating the relationship between numbers included in a 1-2-3 worksheet. Charts let you *visually communicate* the numbers displayed in a worksheet. They often convey messages about the numbers more quickly, dramatically, and effectively than a worksheet. A visual presentation makes it easier for Sharon and Angela to compare the expenses for each month and to spot any irregularities or trends. Let's take a closer look at Sharon's chart.

To examine the marketing expense budget chart:

❶ Scroll the worksheet window so the marketing expense budget chart is displayed. See Figure 38.

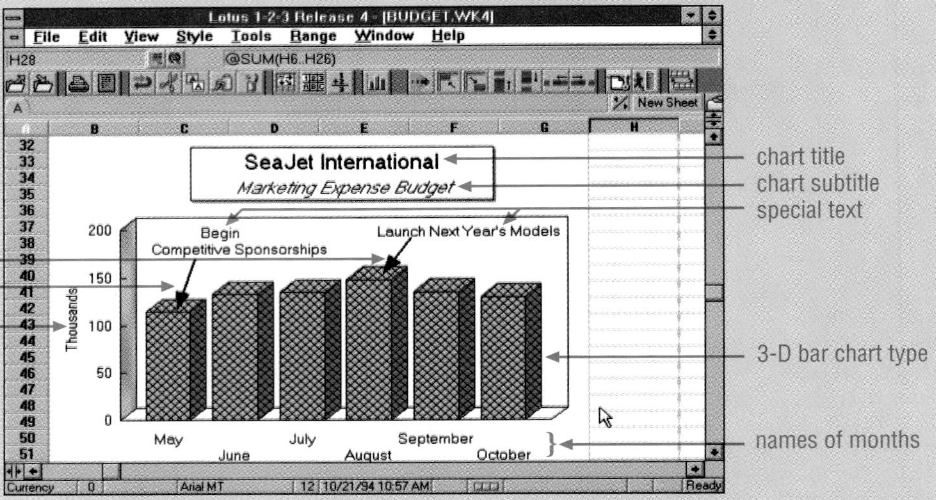

Figure 38
Sharon's chart displayed in the worksheet

❷ Click **B32**, the upper-left corner of the chart. This is the location where the chart appears on the worksheet both on the screen and in a printout. Notice that the context-sensitive SmartIcon palette changes to a palette used for working with charts.

❸ Make sure the entire chart is displayed in your worksheet window and observe its characteristics. Depending on your monitor, you might need to scroll to see the entire chart.

Notice that the chart has a title and a subtitle. The vertical axis displays dollars in thousands. The horizontal axis displays the names of the months. The numeric values are obtained from the Total Marketing Expense in row 28 in the worksheet and are displayed using a 3-D bar chart type. The words "Begin Competitive Sponsorships" and "Launch Next Year's Models" are explanatory comments. Sharon added the arrows to enhance the chart's appearance. You will learn about many of the different types of charts and how to construct them in Tutorial 4.

Performing a What-If Analysis

Another powerful feature of 1-2-3 that can be used to make better business decisions is the what-if analysis. As noted earlier in this tour, a **what-if analysis** is when you revise one or more cells in a worksheet and observe the affect this change has on other cells in the worksheet.

Sharon can change the values in her worksheet to see how new values would affect the results. For example, what if the Advertising and Promotion expense for May increased? How would that affect the Total Marketing Expense? Because Sharon set up her worksheet using formulas to calculate many of the numeric values, she knows that if she enters a new amount for the Advertising and Promotion expense, 1-2-3 will recalculate her entire worksheet.

REFERENCE WINDOW

Performing a What-If Analysis

- Position the cell pointer at the cell that contains the value you want to change.
- Enter the new value for the what-if analysis.
- Review the recalculated results.

Let's evaluate Sharon's what-if analysis by entering the new value 28,600 in cell B9 for the Advertising and Promotion expense amount for May.

To perform a what-if analysis:

❶ Click anywhere in the worksheet other than on the chart.

❷ Click the **Home SmartIcon** to move back to the top of the worksheet.

❸ Click **B9**. This is the value you want to change. *Your cell pointer must be located at the cell containing the value that you want to change.*

❹ Type **28600** then press **[Enter]**. This is the alternative value for the what-if analysis. Notice that the mode indicator displays "Value" while you are entering the number.

TROUBLE? If you enter the wrong value or place the value in the wrong cell, click the Undo SmartIcon and repeat Steps 2 and 3.

The new value affects the Advertising and Promotion expenses for June and July because the formulas in those cells reference cell B9. Note the changes in the Advertising and Promotion expense amounts. See Figure 39.

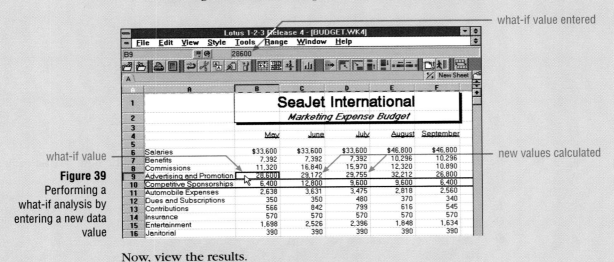

Figure 39
Performing a what-if analysis by entering a new data value

Now, view the results.

❺ Position the worksheet area so you can view the Total Marketing Expense and notice how these data values were also recalculated for the what-if analysis. See Figure 40.

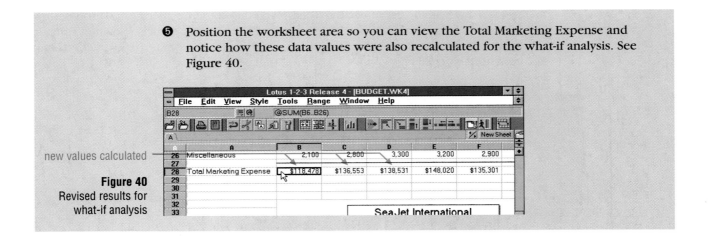

new values calculated ──

Figure 40
Revised results for
what-if analysis

At this point, Sharon could make a decision about this what-if analysis. She should ask herself if this is an acceptable increase in the Total Marketing Expense. If it is not, she can easily change the worksheet back to the way it was. She decides to print this version of her worksheet so she can better evaluate the results.

Printing a Worksheet

The first time you print a worksheet, you need to select the Print command and specify the area of the worksheet, or range of cells, you want to print. After that, you can use the Print SmartIcon because 1-2-3 remembers the area that you want to print—even after you close the worksheet and exit 1-2-3. Because Sharon has already printed the worksheet once before, you can now use the Print SmartIcon to print it with the new what-if values. You'll learn how to specify the worksheet area to be printed in the next tutorial.

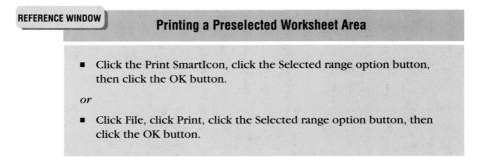

REFERENCE WINDOW

Printing a Preselected Worksheet Area

- Click the Print SmartIcon, click the Selected range option button, then click the OK button.

or

- Click File, click Print, click the Selected range option button, then click the OK button.

Let's use the Print SmartIcon to print Sharon's worksheet with the new what-if values.

To print Sharon's marketing expense budget:
❶ Make sure your printer is turned on and contains paper.
❷ Press **[Home]** to position your worksheet so the report title is displayed while you are printing.
❸ Click the **Print SmartIcon** 🖨 to display the Print dialog box. See Figure 41.

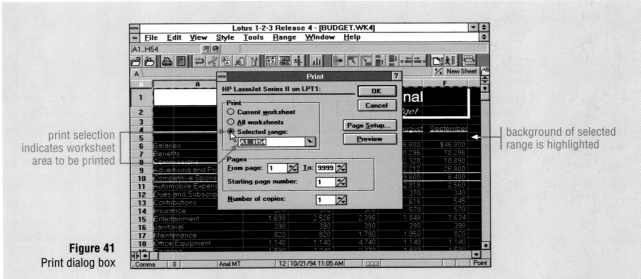

Figure 41
Print dialog box

print selection
indicates worksheet
area to be printed

background of selected
range is highlighted

❹   Click the **Selected range option button** to request Sharon's previously printed cell range.

TROUBLE? If the Selected range option does not appear in the Print dialog box, click Cancel to return to Ready mode. Click any cell in the worksheet area *except* the chart. Redisplay the Print dialog box using 🖨 and continue with Step 4.

❺   Click the **OK button** to print the selected range. Notice that a dialog box is displayed while the worksheet is being printed so that you can cancel this activity before it is completed, if necessary. See Figure 42. The mode indicator displays "Wait."

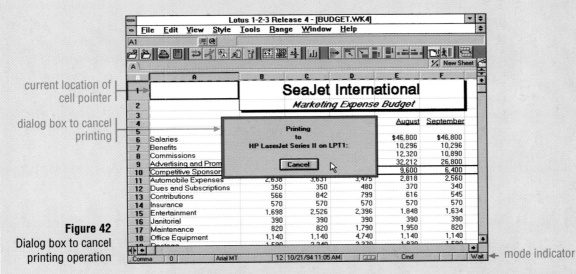

Figure 42
Dialog box to cancel
printing operation

current location of
cell pointer

dialog box to cancel
printing

mode indicator

❻   Wait while the report is printed. This may take a minute or two, depending on your computer hardware configuration. Your printed worksheet should look like the worksheet in Figure 2. Note that your printout will also include the chart. If you are using the Student Version of the software, your printout will also include additional text inserted by 1-2-3 at the bottom of the page.

TROUBLE? If the worksheet doesn't print, check to make sure that your printer is on and that it contains paper. If it still doesn't print, ask your technical support person for assistance.

Next, you will examine a feature of 1-2-3 that can make working with your spreadsheet easier and more efficient.

Running a Macro

In 1-2-3, you can create and store sets of commands and keystrokes called **macro instructions,** or **macros** for short. When executed, a macro automatically carries out the sequence of stored commands. You create macros to automate the 1-2-3 tasks that you perform frequently and that require a series of steps.

You have already used macros in this tour of 1-2-3; SmartIcons are a type of macro. For example, when you click the Open File SmartIcon, 1-2-3 executes a recorded set of steps that opens the file you select.

Sharon expects that Angela will have to revise the Competitive Sponsorships amounts frequently as she monitors the budget. For this reason, she created a macro that makes it easier for Angela to enter the updated expenses. When you **run,** or execute, Sharon's macro, three actions occur:

• The worksheet is displayed so that the Competitive Sponsorships row is visible.
• The cell pointer is positioned on Competitive Sponsorships for May, waiting for a new value to be entered.
• The cell pointer moves to each of the other months and waits for a new value to be entered.

Let's run Sharon's data entry macro to update the Competitive Sponsorships expense. To run a macro, you click a button—similar to clicking a SmartIcon. Macros can also be executed by using the keyboard.

To run the data entry macro:
❶ Click the **Go To SmartIcon** then type **A55** to position the worksheet and display Sharon's macro button. See Figure 43. A macro button can be placed at any convenient location on the worksheet.

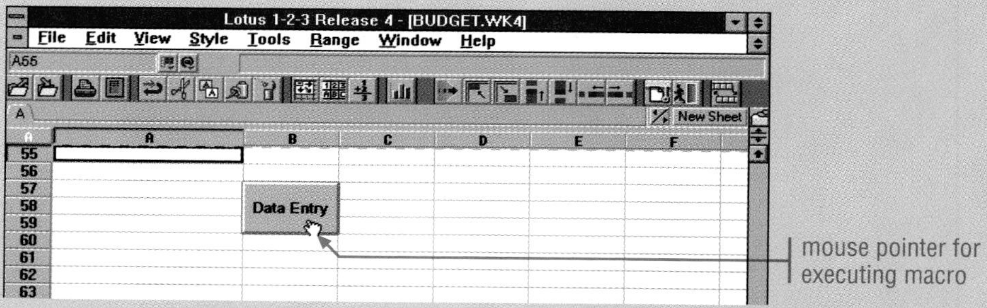

Figure 43
Sharon's Data Entry
macro button

mouse pointer for
executing macro

❷ Click the **Data Entry macro button.** The pointer changes to 🖑 when it is positioned on the button for the selection. See Figure 43. Notice that "Cmd" appears in the status bar to indicate that a macro (command) is being executed. See Figure 44.

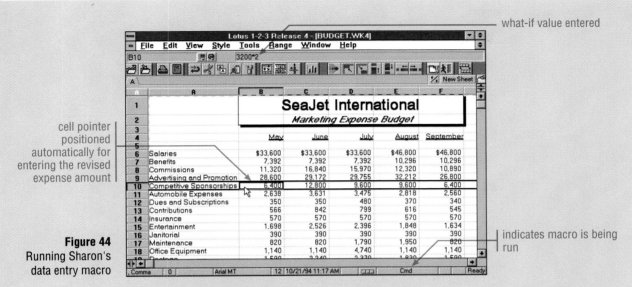

Figure 44
Running Sharon's
data entry macro

cell pointer
positioned
automatically for
entering the revised
expense amount

what-if value entered

indicates macro is being
run

❸ In cell B10, type **2022*2** then press **[Enter]**. This is the new, updated expense
amount multiplied by the number of events scheduled for that month. Do *not*
include a comma when you enter the number.

❹ Because the cell pointer is automatically positioned by the macro at the appropriate cell location, continue entering values in the cell for each of the other months
as follows:

Month	Value
June	2022*4
July	2022*3
August	2022*3
September	2022*2
October	2022

TROUBLE? If you accidentally type the wrong value in one of the cells, finish entering the
values to complete the macro, go back to Step 1, and start the macro over again.

❺ Inspect the revised results for the Competitive Sponsorships. Notice that Cmd is
no longer displayed in the status bar because the macro's execution is completed.

From this sample macro execution, you should see that macros like Sharon's can be
easily used by someone with little prior knowledge of 1-2-3. This, combined with the fact
that macros save you time and effort, makes them a powerful feature of 1-2-3. You will
learn how to create your own macros in Tutorial 6.

Closing the Worksheet

Congratulations on completing the Guided Tour! You have finished exploring Sharon's
worksheet, so you need to close it. This removes it from the worksheet window and from
RAM, but the file remains stored on your Student Disk.

Closing a Worksheet

- Click the Control menu box located at the left side of the main menu bar or in the worksheet window title bar, depending on whether the worksheet is maximized.

- Click Close.

- When the Close dialog box appears, select the desired action for saving the file before closing it.

Let's close the BUDGET.WK4 worksheet.

To close the BUDGET.WK4 worksheet file:

❶ Click the **Control menu box** located at the left side of the main menu bar.

❷ Click **Close**.

❸ When the Close dialog box appears, as shown in Figure 45, click **No** because you do *not* want to save your changes. (When you create other worksheets and *do* want to save the changes, you should click Yes.)

TROUBLE? The Close dialog box might not appear if the automatic save option is turned on for your installation of 1-2-3. In this situation, you are returned to the Untitled worksheet. Just continue with the next task of exiting from 1-2-3.

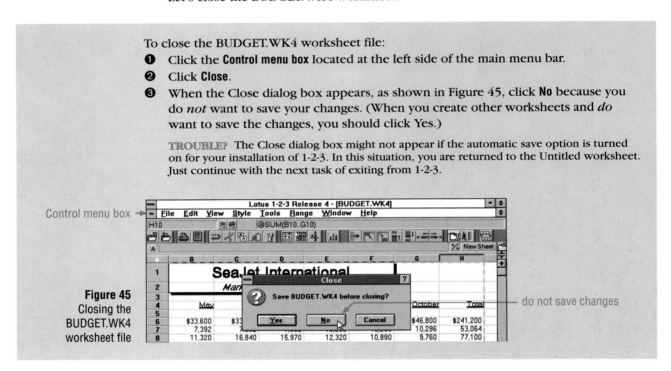

Control menu box →

do not save changes

Figure 45
Closing the
BUDGET.WK4
worksheet file

Exiting 1-2-3

You can now exit from 1-2-3 and, if you want, turn off your computer. When you want to complete the exercises at the end of this tour, you will need to start 1-2-3 again.

REFERENCE WINDOW　　　　　　　　　　**Exiting 1-2-3**

- Click the End 1-2-3 SmartIcon.

or

- Click the Control menu box located at the left side of the title bar and then select Close.

Let's exit from 1-2-3.

To exit from 1-2-3:

❶ Click the **End 1-2-3 SmartIcon** to exit from 1-2-3 and return to the Program Manager.

Now you have a better understanding of Lotus 1-2-3 for Windows, and you are familiar with Sharon's preliminary marketing expense budget. In Tutorial 1, you will follow along with Angela as she creates her own worksheet based on this data.

Questions

1. Identify each of the lettered components of the 1-2-3 window shown in Figure 46.

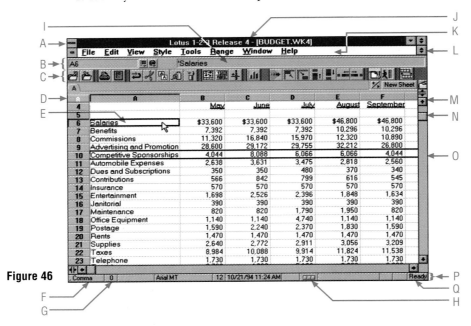

Figure 46

2. Is a cell's content a value or a label when it contains the following data items? Why?
   a. 49 (number of units on hand)
   b. 3.19 (price per unit)
   c. Angela Ortega (name)
   d. Beginning Inventory (planning item name)
   e. 3426 Splash Boulevard (street address)
   f. (800) 456-7890 (phone number)
   g. 123-456-7890 (identification number)

3. Which one of the following mode indicators advises you that 1-2-3 is ready for you to enter data, locate the cell pointer, or select a command:
   a. Edit
   b. Menu
   c. Wait
   d. Ready

4. The content of cell B7 is 200 and the content of cell B8 is 4. If the cell content of B9 is entered as follows, what result is displayed in cell B9?
   a. +B7+B8
   b. +B7/B8
   c. +B8*B7
   d. 2*B8+B7

5. This cursor movement key positions the cell pointer to the right by one entire screen:
   a. [→]
   b. [Tab]
   c. [Home]
   d. [Ctrl]+[←]

6. Using your 1-2-3 worksheet to prepare several different alternatives by revising input data values is known as performing a(n):
   a. Report projection
   b. What-if analysis
   c. Extrapolation analysis
   d. Extended review

7. This label prefix causes a specified character to fill the entire cell:
   a. " (quotation mark)
   b. ^ (caret)
   c. \ (backslash)
   d. + (plus sign)

8. This feature of 1-2-3 lets you automatically execute a set of stored 1-2-3 commands:
   a. Solver
   b. Macro
   c. What-if
   d. Commander

9. This 1-2-3 SmartIcon always moves the cell pointer directly to cell A1:
   a.
   b.
   c.
   d.

Tutorial Assignments

Make sure your Student Disk is in the disk drive, then start 1-2-3 and open the T_AMS1.WK4 worksheet file for Associated Medical Supply. Review this worksheet and do the following:

1. Maximize your worksheet window, if necessary, then position your cell pointer at the cell containing Employee Name. What is this cell's address? Does this cell contain a label? Why? If it contains a label, what is the label prefix?

2. Move your cell pointer to the cell containing 3rd Qtr. Is this a label? If so, what is the label prefix? What is the action of the label prefix?

3. Move to cell A7. What is the content of this cell? Is this a label? Why? What is the action of any label prefix included in this cell?

4. Move to cell B9. Does this cell contain a label or a value? Why?

5. Move to cell F15. What is the formula in this cell? What special formatting is used with this cell? Does this formatting draw your attention to the number displayed in the cell?

6. Use [PgDn] or the vertical scroll bar to look at the 3-D bar chart of the Third Quarter Sales and the pie chart of the Commission Comparison. What are the x-axis labels? What are the y-axis labels? Position the cell pointer at A1 and produce a hard copy of this worksheet using the Print SmartIcon.

7. Use the scroll bars to move around the worksheet and look at the contents of several other cells. Examine at least four more cells. Write down each cell's address and its content. Identify the content of each cell as either a label or value. If a cell contains a label, indicate its label prefix.

8. Perform a what-if analysis by moving the cell pointer to cell D8 and entering 396000. Position the worksheet so you can look at the 3-D bar chart of Third Quarter Sales. Did this graph change when you entered the what-if value? With the cell pointer at A1, print a hard copy of the result of this what-if analysis. If you want, exit from 1-2-3, but do *not* save any changes to the worksheet file.

Make sure your Student Disk is in the disk drive, then start 1-2-3 and open the T_CBW1.WK4 worksheet file for preparing a damage repair estimate at the Classic Body Works. Review this worksheet and do the following:

9. Maximize your worksheet window, if necessary, then position your cell pointer at the cell containing Body Type. What is this cell's address? Does this cell contain a label? Why? If it contains a label, what is the label prefix?

10. Move your cell pointer to the cell containing 4 door - Cavalier. Is this a label? If so, what is the label prefix? What is the action of the label prefix?

11. Move to cell B13. What is the content of this cell? Is this a label? Why? What is the action of any label prefix included in this cell?

12. Move to cell A9. Does this cell contain a label or value? Why?

13. Examine the contents of cells D31 and D34. What are the formulas in these cells? What special formatting is used with each cell? Does the formatting draw your attention to the number displayed in the cell?

E   14. Use [PgDn] or the vertical scroll bar to look at the pie chart and the 3-D bar chart of the Cost Comparison. Identify the problem with the placement of the 3-D bar chart. Print the worksheet.

15. Use the scroll bars to move around the worksheet and look at the contents of several other cells. Examine at least four more cells. Write down each cell's address and its content. Identify the content of each cell as either a label or value. If a cell contains a label, indicate its label prefix.

16. Perform a what-if analysis by moving the cell pointer to cell E16 and entering 6.2. Position the worksheet so you can look at the pie chart and 3-D bar chart of the Cost Comparison. Did these change when you entered the what-if value? Position the cell pointer at A1 and print a hard copy of the result for this what-if analysis. If you want, exit from 1-2-3, but do *not* save any changes to the worksheet file.

Case Problems

1. Global Entertainment Enterprises

Global Entertainment Enterprises is a diversified services company that provides entertainment through films, theme parks, and consumer products. Global is among the most profitable companies in the travel and leisure industry. The company reports financial results for each of its three major business units.

Dawn Bucilli, an accounting associate, works with Richard Nanula, Global's chief financial officer. Richard assigned Dawn the responsibility of preparing Global's quarterly financial statements for his review and final approval before they are presented to the company's board of directors and published in the quarterly report to shareholders. Dawn used 1-2-3 to prepare the financial statements for Richard's review, and to print a copy for his approval. To increase your understanding of 1-2-3 and its use in preparing business reports, such as Dawn's Statement of Income for Global Entertainment Enterprises, you will review this worksheet and do the following:

1. Make sure your Student Disk is in the disk drive.

2. Start 1-2-3, maximize the worksheet window, and then open the GLOBAL.WK4 worksheet file.

3. Examine the contents of cells A5, A7, B5, B1, D6, C8, D12, C19, B22, C31, B38 and B41. As you examine each cell, ask yourself the following questions: Does the cell contain a label or value? How do you know? If it contains a label, what is the label prefix and the result of that prefix? If it contains a formula, what is the first character that indicates it is a formula? Which of these cells contain numbers? Do they have a label prefix?

4. Using the Print SmartIcon, print Dawn's Statement of Income, including the charts.

5. Dawn often gets several different sets of numbers for the theme parks and resorts while the results for the current reporting period are being finalized. She developed a macro that guides her data entry for making these changes. She assigned the macro to the Theme Parks macro button, located below the charts. Find the macro button and run the macro, entering the following data for the theme parks:

Revenues	2864.7
Costs and Expenses	2275.6

6. Print the revised report.

7. Close the worksheet file, but do *not* save the changes. If you want, exit from 1-2-3.

E

8. Compare the results of Dawn's preliminary report (Problem 4) with the results of the revised report (Problem 5). Did the revised numbers have a significant impact on Net Income? Is one of Global's business units more profitable than the others? Explain your answers.

Creating and Printing Worksheets

Producing a Detailed Expense Schedule

CASE

Hot Water Tour In the Guided Tour, you examined Sharon's marketing expense budget for SeaJet International. Sharon and Angela have reviewed the budget to make sure Angela understands her new assignment. Angela's assignment is to monitor the projected expenses to make sure they stay within the budget.

Sharon advises Angela to pay close attention to Competitive Sponsorships because Sharon is worried that this expense could go over budget. To monitor the budget for Competitive Sponsorships, Angela needs to develop a detailed expense schedule. A **detailed expense schedule** is a list of all the expenses for each budget item. For example, in Sharon's worksheet, Competitive Sponsorships for June is budgeted at a total of $12,800. The detailed expense schedule for Competitive Sponsorships will list all of the individual expenses that add up to $12,800.

The Hot Water Tour is the only Competitive Sponsorship event in June. It is a popular tour consisting of 15 races, the first of which occurs this weekend at Lake Havasu. Each year SeaJet sponsors two athletes in the 15 competitive events of the Hot Water Tour. This year SeaJet will sponsor Tera Laho and Minoru Kanamori, both veteran racers of PWCs. Sharon asks Angela to meet with Tera and Minoru to help them estimate how much money she should budget for this weekend's event. Once Angela has a budget for this weekend's event, she can multiply the number by four (four weekend events in June) to estimate the total June budget for Competitive Sponsorships. Then, she can compare that value to June's budget of $12,800 to see if the budget is on track.

Angela telephones Minoru and asks him if he and Tera could **itemize**, or list in detail, their estimated expenses for this weekend. She explains that she is monitoring the budget, making sure it is on target for the month of June. Minoru says he will call her back before the end of the day with the necessary information. Later that afternoon, Minoru phones Angela to give her the necessary data (Figure 1-1). Now, Angela has all the information she needs to create her detailed expense schedule worksheet.

Figure 1-1
Expense data that Minoru dictates to Angela

In this tutorial you will work with Angela as she creates a detailed expense schedule worksheet for the Hot Water Tour at Lake Havasu. This worksheet will provide an updated estimate of the Competitive Sponsorships budget, making sure the budget is on target for the month of June. Angela knows that to create an effective worksheet she needs to plan, design, build, and review the worksheet.

Creating a Worksheet

A well-designed worksheet should clearly identify the overall goal of the worksheet, present information in a clear and well-organized format, include all the necessary data, and produce the results that address the goal. You can divide the process of creating a worksheet into four activities:

- planning the worksheet
- designing the worksheet
- building the worksheet
- reviewing the worksheet

Planning the Worksheet

When you plan a worksheet, you analyze the problem you are trying to solve. By analyzing the problem, you define the overall goal of the worksheet and determine the information you need to include in it. This information is the data and the calculations you need to gather and enter in the worksheet to produce the results you want to see.

Sharon has already defined the problem for Angela. Angela knows the overall goal is to create a detailed expense schedule for all four June events based on the upcoming Hot Water Tour. In her phone conversation with Minoru, Angela collected all of the data she needs, as illustrated in Figure 1-1. Tera and Minoru knew the exact totals for entry fees, gas and oil for running the PWCs, lodging, and mileage, but they had to estimate the cost of meals and decide on the mileage reimbursement.

Once Angela gathered the necessary information, she created a planning analysis sheet. A **planning analysis sheet** answers the following four questions:

1. What is the goal of the worksheet? The goal defines the problem you need to solve.
2. What results do I want to see? This information is the output, the information that solves the problem you have defined.
3. What information do I need to build the worksheet to produce the results I want to see? This information is the input, the data you enter into the worksheet to solve the problem.
4. What calculations will I need to perform to produce the output? These calculations are the formulas you use in your worksheet.

Angela's completed planning analysis sheet is shown in Figure 1-2.

Planning Analysis Sheet

<u>My goal:</u>
Develop a worksheet for the detailed expense items of one Hot Water Tour event by day and compare to original budget amount of $12,800 for June

<u>What results do I want to see?</u>
Detailed expense items by day with a total for each expense item and a total for all four events for June

<u>What information do I need?</u>
Columns are Saturday, Sunday, Total
Entry fees for each day (400 for Saturday; 25% of 400 for Sunday)
Gas and oil for each day (125)
Meals for each day (half of one day's lodging)
Lodging room rate per day (95)
Number of rooms (2)
Miles driven each day (540)
Mileage rate (0.65 per mile)

<u>What calculations will I perform?</u>
Entry fees [Sunday] = 0.25 * entry fees [Saturday]
Meals = Lodging / 2
Lodging = 95 * 2
Mileage allowance = 540 * 0.65
Total = Add each detailed expense item together for the two days
Total Expenses = Add the daily expenses together
Competitive Sponsorships = Total expenses for both days * 4

Figure 1-2
Angela's planning
analysis sheet

Angela can begin designing the worksheet based on her completed planning analysis sheet.

Designing the Worksheet

On a piece of paper Angela sketches what she thinks the worksheet should look like (Figure 1-3 on the following page). First, she identifies the worksheet titles, column headings, and expense item names. Then, she adds the data values and specifies formulas to complete her worksheet sketch. Finally, Angela examines her sketch to make sure she has included all the required information.

	A	B	C	D
1	Hot Water Tour			
2	Lake Havasu Event			
3	Detailed Expense Schedule			
4				
5		Saturday	Sunday	Total
6	Entry Fees	400	25% of Sat.	Sat. + Sun.
7	Gas and Oil	125	125	Sat. + Sun.
8	Meals	Lodging/2	Lodging/2	Sat. + Sun.
9	Lodging	2*95	2*95	Sat. + Sun.
10	Mileage Allowance	540*.65	540*.65	Sat. + Sun.
11				
12	Total Expenses	add Saturday's expenses	add Sunday's expenses	add expenses for both days
13				
14	Competitive Sponsorships			Total for both days*4

Figure 1-3
Angela's sketch of
her worksheet

Angela is now ready to build the worksheet using 1-2-3.

Building the Worksheet

Angela will use her rough sketch in Figure 1-3 to create the worksheet shown in Figure 1-4. As you work with Angela, you will learn how to enter labels, values, and formulas into cells.

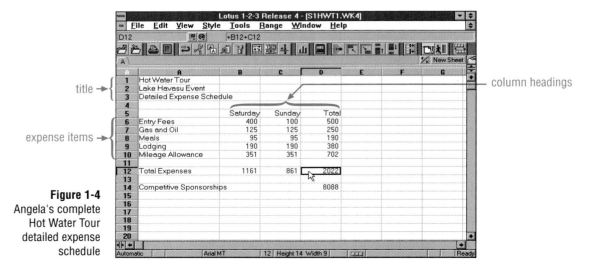

Figure 1-4
Angela's complete
Hot Water Tour
detailed expense
schedule

Let's launch 1-2-3 and display the Untitled worksheet window. This is the window Angela will use to build her worksheet.

To launch 1-2-3 and display the Untitled worksheet window in Ready mode:
❶ Launch 1-2-3. The Untitled window appears.
❷ Make sure 1-2-3 is in Ready mode.

TROUBLE? If 1-2-3 is not in Ready mode, press [Esc] until Ready is displayed on the status bar.

A SmartIcon palette has been created for you to use with each of the tutorials. Let's select the SmartIcon palette designed for Tutorial 1.

To select the predefined SmartIcon palette for Tutorial 1:
❶ Click the **SmartIcon palette selector** ▭ in the status bar.
❷ Click **Tutorial 1** from the pop-up menu. The predefined SmartIcon palette for Tutorial 1 is displayed at the top of the worksheet window, and you are returned to Ready mode. See Figure 1-5.

TROUBLE? If "Tutorial 1" does not appear in the pop-up menu of SmartIcon palette choices, then the palette might not be installed with your copy of 1-2-3. If you are in a computer lab, ask your technical support person for assistance. If you are using your own computer, you need to install the Tutorial 1 palette. See your instructor for assistance.

Figure 1-5
SmartIcon palette
for Tutorial 1

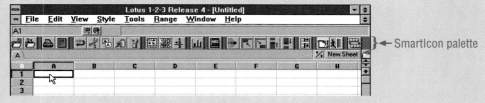

Now, you are ready to enter the information for Angela's detailed expense schedule.

Entering Labels

It is a good practice to enter identifying labels *before* any other data. These labels help you identify the data values that you need to enter in the worksheet. When you enter a label into a cell you have three ways to complete your entry: you can click the Confirm button (✔), you can press [Enter], or you can click in another cell. If you make a mistake you can click the Cancel button (X) to cancel your entry and try again.

REFERENCE WINDOW

Entering Labels

- Click the cell where you want the label to appear.
- Type the label.
- Press [Enter] or click the Confirm button to enter (or confirm) the label in the cell.

  or

  Click another cell to finish the cell entry and move the pointer to another cell.

Let's enter the labels for Angela's worksheet according to her sketch in Figure 1-3.

To enter the Hot Water Tour worksheet title:

❶ Make sure that the cell pointer is located at cell A1. If it is not at that location, then click **A1**.

❷ Type **H**.

Note that the mode indicator now displays "Label." Also notice that the "H" appears in both the cell contents box and in cell A1, and that the Cancel button (X) and Confirm button (✔) appear to the left of the cell contents box. See Figure 1-6. Lotus 1-2-3 detects that you are entering a label or value based on the first character you type.

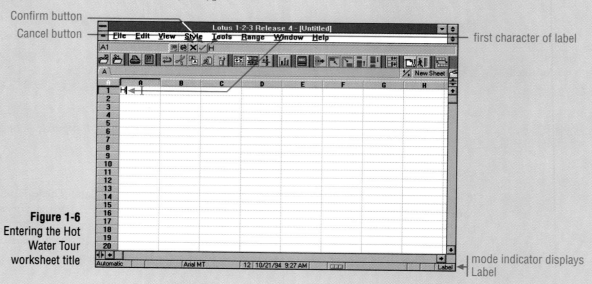

Figure 1-6
Entering the Hot
Water Tour
worksheet title

❸ Type **ot Water Tour**.

❹ Press **[Enter]** or click the **Confirm button** to finish entering this label in cell A1. Note that the label "Hot Water Tour" appears in cell A1 and that 1-2-3 inserted an apostrophe (') to the left of the "H" in the cell contents box. See Figure 1-7. Remember from the Guided Tour that this apostrophe is called a label prefix.

TROUBLE? If you make a mistake in entering the Hot Water Tour label, click A1 and repeat Steps 2, 3, and 4. You will learn how to edit the contents of a cell later in this tutorial.

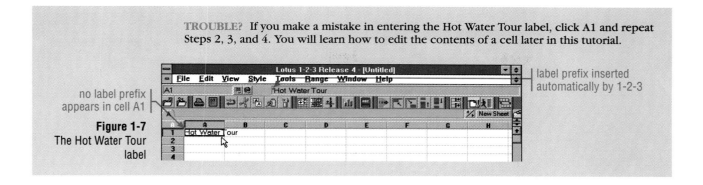

no label prefix appears in cell A1

Figure 1-7
The Hot Water Tour label

label prefix inserted automatically by 1-2-3

Now let's enter the other worksheet titles and all the expense item labels for Angela's worksheet.

To continue entering the labels in the detailed expense schedule:
❶ Click **A2** or press [↓] to position the cell pointer for the next label.
❷ Type **Lake Havasu Event**.
❸ Click **A3** to complete entering the data in cell A2 and move the cell pointer. When entering data in a cell, you can both finish the cell entry and move the cell pointer by clicking the next cell where you want the pointer.
❹ Type **Detailed Expense Schedule** then press **[Enter]**.
❺ Refer to Figure 1-3 as needed and enter the labels for cells A6 through A14.

According to Angela's sketch, the column headings are right-justified within each cell, so she needs to include the quotation mark (") as the label prefix when entering the column headings.

To enter the right-justified column headings:
❶ Click **B5**.
❷ Type **"Saturday** then press **[Enter]**.

Note that the "y" in Saturday is flush against the right side of column B.

TROUBLE? If the "y" is not flush against the right side of column B, you need to type the correct label prefix. Repeat Steps 1 and 2.

❸ Click **C5**.
❹ Type **"Sunday** then press **[Enter]**.
❺ In cell D5 type **"Total** then press **[Enter]**. Make sure your labels match those shown in Figure 1-8 on the following page.

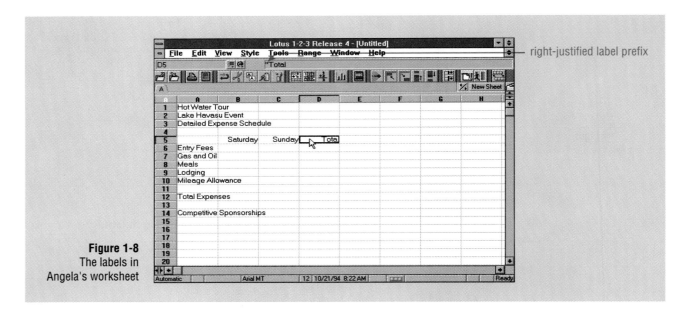

Figure 1-8
The labels in
Angela's worksheet

Entering Values

The next step in building the worksheet is entering the values in the appropriate cells. Remember that values can be numbers, formulas, or functions. In this set of steps, you will enter all the numbers, or numeric values. Then, in the next set of steps you will enter formulas. There are no functions in Angela's worksheet.

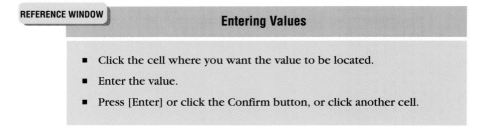

REFERENCE WINDOW

Entering Values

- Click the cell where you want the value to be located.
- Enter the value.
- Press [Enter] or click the Confirm button, or click another cell.

Let's begin by entering the value for Entry Fees for Saturday.

To enter the value for Entry Fees for Saturday:
① Click **B6**.
② Type **4** and note that 1-2-3 is in Value mode. See Figure 1-9. Lotus 1-2-3 detects that you are entering a value based on the number 4.

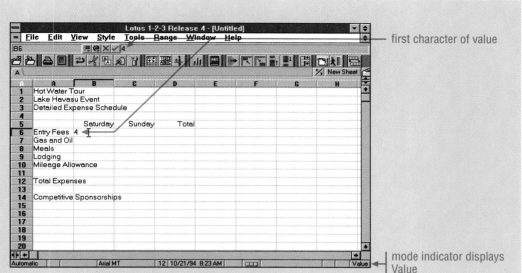

first character of value

mode indicator displays
Value

Figure 1-9
Entering a numeric
value

❸ Type **00** to complete the number. Make sure to type the number zero and not the letter "O."

❹ Press **[Enter]** or click the **Confirm button** to finish entering this value in cell B6. Note that 1-2-3 did not place an apostrophe before the numeric value 400. Remember from the Guided Tour that values are not preceded by apostrophes.

Now, let's enter the data values for Gas and Oil.

❺ Enter the values for Gas and Oil in cells B7 and C7 according to Angela's sketch, as shown in Figure 1-3. Observe the mode indicator as you enter this data.

You are finished entering the numeric values in Angela's worksheet. All the remaining values are formulas. Let's enter those next.

Entering Formulas

In the Guided Tour you learned that a formula is a mathematical expression that can include numbers, cell addresses, arithmetic operators, and parentheses. In 1-2-3, you use formulas to calculate values using other values you have entered in your worksheet. If you change a value used in a formula, 1-2-3 automatically recalculates the result.

Let's enter the formula for calculating the entry fees for Sunday. Recall from Minoru's note that Sunday's entry fees are 25% of Saturday's entry fees or, in other words, the value in cell B6 * .25.

To enter the entry fees formula for Sunday:

❶ Click **C6**.

❷ Type the formula **+B6*.25** then press **[Enter]**. Make sure you type the formula exactly as it appears. Note that 100 is displayed in cell C6. See Figure 1-10 on the following page. Remember that when a formula is used to calculate a value, the result of the calculation is displayed in the cell, and the formula is displayed in the cell contents box.

TROUBLE? If the formula is displayed in the cell instead of the calculated result, make sure you included the arithmetic operator—in this case, the plus sign (+)—before the cell name. If you forgot to include the arithmetic operator, repeat Steps 1 and 2.

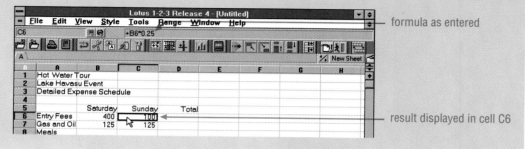

Figure 1-10
Entering the formula for Sunday's entry fees

Next, let's enter the formula for the total entry fees. This is the sum of the fees for Saturday and Sunday. In the next set of steps, you'll intentionally enter the formula incorrectly so you can see what happens when you omit the arithmetic operator. Then you'll correct the error by retyping the formula.

To enter the formula for the total entry fees:

❶ Click **D6**.

❷ Type the formula **B6+C6** then press **[Enter]**. Note that the formula appears in the worksheet area instead of the calculated result. See Figure 1-11. This occurred because when you typed the letter B first, 1-2-3 determined that you were entering a label and not a value. Notice the apostrophe in the cell contents box, which indicates this is a label. When you are entering a formula that begins with a cell name, you must precede the cell name with an arithmetic operator to indicate that it is a formula.

Figure 1-11
Formula incorrectly entered as a label

Let's correct this error by retyping the cell formula.

❸ Type **+B6+C6** then press **[Enter]**.

A formula must begin with a number or one of the characters shown in Figure 1-12. Otherwise, 1-2-3 will treat it as a label and your worksheet will not calculate correctly.

First Character	Example	Explanation
number	8*C11	multiply the value in cell C11 by 8
+ (plus sign)	+D5*0.68	multiply the positive value in cell D5 by 0.68
− (minus sign)	−C12+25	add the negative value in cell C12 to 25
. (period)	.68*D5	multiply the value in cell D5 by .68
@ (at sign)	@SUM(B5..D5)	sum the values in cells B5 through D5
((open parenthesis)	(C17+D17)/2	divide the sum of the values in cells C17 and D17 by 2

Figure 1-12
First characters that specify a formula in a cell

Let's finish entering the formulas in Angela's worksheet.

To enter the remaining formulas:

❶ To enter the formulas for Meals in row 8, click **B8** and type **+B9/2**. Then click **C8** and type **+C9/2**. Notice that zeros appear in the cells. See Figure 1-13. Why has this occurred? This occurs because the formulas use the values in row 9 to perform the calculations and you have *not* entered those values yet. When you enter those values, the correct calculated results will appear in row 8. This is called *natural order*. It doesn't matter which formulas you enter first in your worksheet; 1-2-3 will calculate the results as soon as you enter the values.

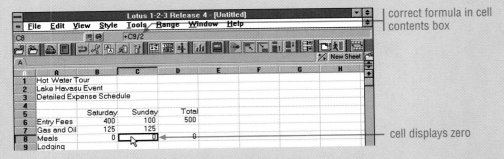

correct formula in cell contents box

cell displays zero

Figure 1-13
Formula references a blank cell

❷ Enter all of the remaining formulas as shown below:

B9	**2*95**
C9	**2*95**
B10	**540*.65**
C10	**540*.65**
B12	**+B6+B7+B8+B9+B10**
C12	**+C6+C7+C8+C9+C10**
D12	**+B12+C12**
D14	**+D12*4**

When you enter the formula for Mileage Allowance in cell B10, only "Mileage Allo" will be displayed in cell A10. See Figure 1-14 on the following page. This occurs because the label 'Mileage Allowance is wider than the cell, and there is now a value in the cell *immediately to the right* so the label can't spill over into the next cell. You will correct this situation later in this tutorial when you review the worksheet.

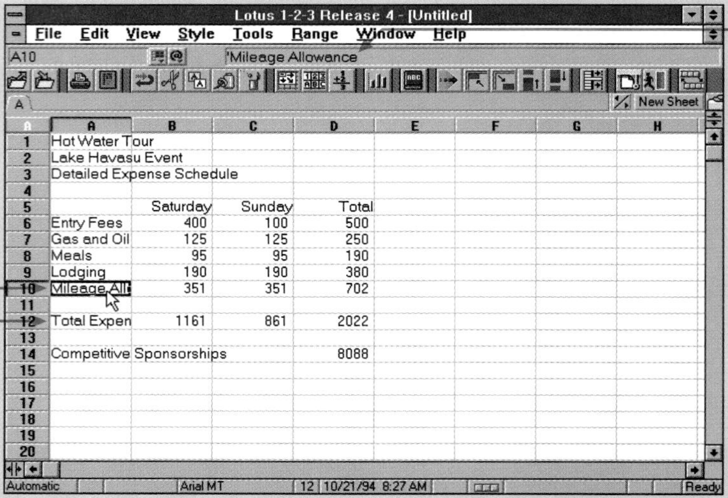

cell contains entire label

labels cut off

Figure 1-14
Display of Mileage
Allowance and Total
Expenses labels

You learned in the Guided Tour that when you enter a formula into your worksheet, Lotus 1-2-3 calculates the result for you and updates the result automatically if any of the data values change. There are a few rules you should know when using formulas in your worksheet. Knowing the rules will help you to create more accurate formulas, resulting in fewer errors.

Rules of Arithmetic Precedence

When calculating a formula, 1-2-3 can perform only one operation at a time. If a formula contains two or more arithmetic operators, as in 1+.07*100, 1-2-3 performs the calculation in a particular sequence. This sequence is called the **order of precedence**. Figure 1-15 shows the order of precedence.

Order	Operator	Description
1.	( )	parentheses
2.	∧	exponentiation
3.	* /	multiplication or division
4.	+ -	addition or subtraction
5.	= <> > < >= <=	comparison

Figure 1-15
Order of precedence

For example, consider the formula 1+.07*100. The following steps show how 1-2-3 calculates this formula:
1. 07*100=7
2. 1+7=8

Left-to-Right Rule

When a formula contains two or more arithmetic operators of equal precedence, the operations with the same precedence are calculated in order from left to right. The rules of arithmetic precedence are also still in effect. For example, consider the formula 1+107-200/2. The following steps show how 1-2-3 calculates this formula:

1. 200/2 = 100
2. 1 + 107 = 108
3. 108 – 100 = 8

Use of Parentheses

Sometimes you want the arithmetic operations in your formulas done in a sequence different from that determined by the order of precedence and left-to-right rules. By using parentheses, you can override these rules. The operations *inside* the parentheses are calculated before the operations *outside* the parentheses.

For example, suppose you want to calculate the average daily entry fees. You'd write the formula as 400+.25*400/2—the fees for Saturday plus the fees for Sunday divided by 2. Lotus 1-2-3 gives you an *incorrect* answer of 450 because the formula is calculated as shown in the following steps:

1. .25*400 = 100
2. 100/2 = 50
3. 400+50 = 450

By using parentheses in the formula, you can control the sequence of the arithmetic operations to ensure that 1-2-3 calculates the correct result. You'd rewrite the formula as (400+.25*400)/2 so the daily entry fees are added before the division is performed in order to calculate the average. The following steps show the correct order of calculations:

1. .25*400 = 100
2. 400 + 100 = 500
3. 500/2 = 250

Now you have finished entering all the labels, values, and formulas needed to build Angela's worksheet. Your next step is to save the worksheet onto your Student Disk.

Saving a Worksheet

Saving a worksheet gives you access to the worksheet even after you end your 1-2-3 session. It is important to save your work frequently. When you are building the worksheet it is stored in RAM, which is volatile. If there is a power surge or if your computer stops working, you might lose all the information you included since the last time you saved. Figure 1-16 on the following page illustrates the process that occurs when you save a worksheet.

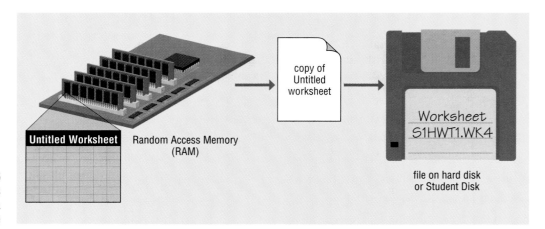

Figure 1-16
The process
of saving a
worksheet file

There are two ways to save a worksheet—you can use the Save command or the Save As command. The Save command copies the worksheet to the disk using the current filename. You use the Save command to update the current file with changes you have made. If the worksheet does not have a filename or if you want to give it a different filename, you use the Save As command. Because you created the worksheet in the Untitled worksheet window, you need to give this worksheet a filename. Later in this tutorial you will update the worksheet using the Save command. Because you update your files frequently using the Save command, the Save File SmartIcon is provided for you. Figure 1-17 shows the decision process that occurs when you want to save a file.

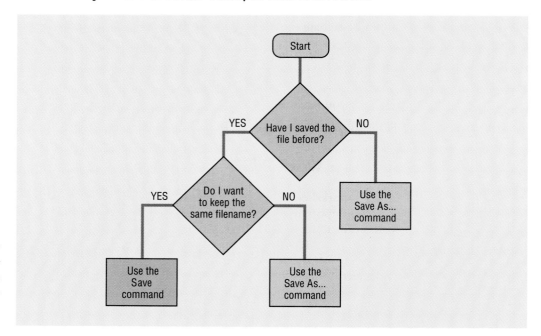

Figure 1-17
Deciding whether
to use the Save
command or the
Save As...
command

Using Save As to Save a Worksheet

- Click File then click Save As.
- In the File name text box, type the filename you want for the worksheet.
- Make sure the Drives box displays the drive in which you want to save your worksheet.
- Click the OK button.

Now that you know what command to use, you are ready to save your worksheet file.

To save a worksheet file using Save As:

❶   Click **File**.

❷   Click **Save As**.

Note that the File name text box contains the default filename "file0001.wk4." This is the filename 1-2-3 gives the file until you give it a different name. See Figure 1-18.

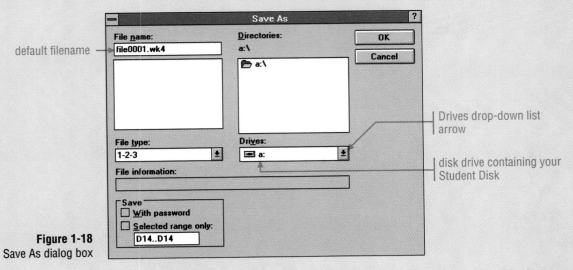

Figure 1-18
Save As dialog box

❸   In the File name text box, type **S1HWT1**. The naming convention for files used in this book is explained in the next section, "Worksheet Filenames for the Tutorials."

   TROUBLE? If the filename you type doesn't replace the default filename, double-click in the File name text box and repeat Step 3.

❹   Make sure the selected drive is the drive in which your Student Disk is located.

   TROUBLE? If the selected drive is not the one for your Student Disk, then click the Drives drop-down list arrow and select the appropriate disk drive.

❺   Click the **OK button** to accept the filename and save it to your Student Disk. Notice that S1HWT1.WK4 now appears as the filename at the top of the worksheet window. See Figure 1-19. Note that 1-2-3 automatically adds the WK4 file extension to the filename.

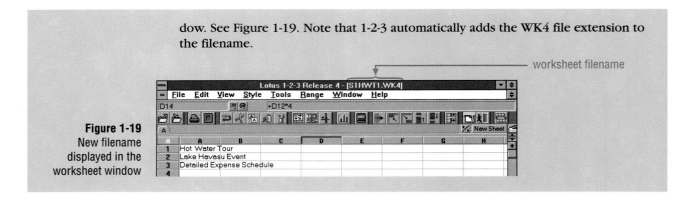

Figure 1-19
New filename displayed in the worksheet window

Worksheet Filenames for the Tutorials

When saving files, you should use descriptive names that identify the contents of your worksheet files. Worksheet filenames can contain up to eight characters. These characters can be letters, numbers, and all symbols except for spaces, commas, colons, and asterisks. Remember that 1-2-3 automatically adds the WK4 file extension to the filename. Although eight characters do not often allow you to use descriptive names, you can create meaningful abbreviations. For example, the files on your Student Disk are named and categorized using the first letter of the filename, as shown in Figure 1-20.

First Letter	File Category	Description of File Category
C	Tutorial Cases	The files you open to use with each tutorial
T	Tutorial Assignments	The files that contain the worksheets you need to complete the Tutorial Assignments at the end of each tutorial
P	Case Problems	The files that contain the worksheets you need to complete the Case Problems at the end of each tutorial
S	Saved Worksheets	Any worksheet file that you have saved

Figure 1-20
Categories of files on the Student Disk

The second character in the filenames on your Student Disk indicates the tutorial in which the file is created or used. In this case, S1 indicates the worksheet you saved in Tutorial 1. The next three characters identify the name assigned to the specific worksheet, Hot Water Tour. The last number indicates a version number. For example, a file named S1HWT2 is the second version of a saved file from Tutorial 1. This naming convention continues throughout these tutorials.

If you want to take a break and resume the tutorial at a later time, close your worksheet and exit 1-2-3 according to the steps you learned in the Guided Tour. Make sure you remove your Student Disk from the disk drive. When you want to resume the tutorial, launch 1-2-3 and place your Student Disk in the disk drive. Open the S1HWT1.WK4 worksheet, select the Tutorial 1 SmartIcon palette, and continue with the tutorial.

■   ■   ■

Reviewing the Worksheet

You are now ready for the fourth and final activity in the process of creating a worksheet—reviewing the worksheet. This is when you look closely at your worksheet. Are all the calculations correct? Is anything misspelled? How does it look? In the following sections you will make changes to improve Angela's worksheet.

Editing Labels and Values

Based on a conversation with Sharon, Angela decides that a mileage reimbursement of $.65 per mile is too much. Angela knows that Minoru and Tera will be driving a truck and towing the PWCs, which reduces gas mileage, but she and Sharon feel that $.50 per mile is more appropriate. In reviewing her worksheet, Angela realizes that she needs to make this change.

You can change the contents of a cell by either replacing or editing the contents. You have already learned how to replace a cell's content. In this section you will learn how to edit a cell's content. Lotus 1-2-3 uses a method of entering and revising a cell's content known as in-cell editing. With **in-cell editing**, the edit cursor appears in the cell whose contents you are editing, and any edit changes you make to the cell's content are displayed both in the worksheet cell *and* in the cell contents box. Remember that before you can edit a cell's content, you must position the cell pointer in the cell you want to edit.

REFERENCE WINDOW

Editing Labels and Values

- Click the cell containing the label or value you want to change.

- Double-click the cell or press [F2] to enter Edit mode.

- Move the edit cursor to where you want to remove or insert characters.

- Use either [Backspace] or [Delete] to remove unwanted characters; then type the appropriate characters if necessary.

Let's practice editing a cell's content by revising the mileage allowance calculation for Saturday in Angela's worksheet.

To edit the contents of cell B10:

❶ Click **B10**.

❷ Double-click **B10** or press **[F2]** to initiate editing. Notice the mode indicator now displays Edit, and the edit cursor appears as a vertical bar (|) indicating that 1-2-3 is ready for in-cell editing. See Figure 1-21. The pointer changes to I, which you drag to highlight the characters you want to delete or replace.

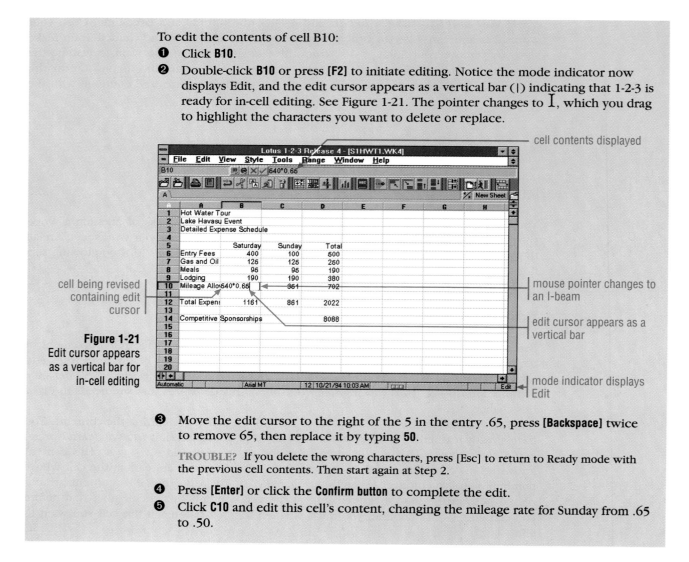

cell contents displayed

cell being revised containing edit cursor

mouse pointer changes to an I-beam

edit cursor appears as a vertical bar

mode indicator displays Edit

Figure 1-21
Edit cursor appears as a vertical bar for in-cell editing

❸ Move the edit cursor to the right of the 5 in the entry .65, press **[Backspace]** twice to remove 65, then replace it by typing **50**.

TROUBLE? If you delete the wrong characters, press [Esc] to return to Ready mode with the previous cell contents. Then start again at Step 2.

❹ Press **[Enter]** or click the **Confirm button** to complete the edit.

❺ Click **C10** and edit this cell's content, changing the mileage rate for Sunday from .65 to .50.

Angela's calculations are now correct. Her next step in reviewing the worksheet is to check the spelling.

Spell Checking the Worksheet

Angela knows that spelling errors make a worksheet look very unprofessional. Checking the spelling of your worksheet should always be part of the review process.

The commercial edition of Lotus 1-2-3 Release 4 for Windows provides a spell check feature, but the Student Version does not. If you are using the Student Version of this software, read this section but do not attempt to complete the steps. You should review the worksheet yourself by carefully looking for spelling errors.

REFERENCE WINDOW

Spell Checking the Worksheet

- Click the Spell Check SmartIcon to display the Spell Check dialog box.

  or

  Click Tools then click Spell Check.
- Make sure that the Entire File option is selected.
- Correct any potentially misspelled words as they are displayed and underlined in the Spell Check dialog box by clicking the appropriate Alternative or by clicking Skip to accept your spelling.
- Click the OK button to acknowledge completion of the spell check.

If you are using the commercial edition of the software and have spell check installed, you can complete the following steps.

To spell check the worksheet:

❶ Click the **Spell Check SmartIcon** [ABC] .

> TROUBLE? If you get an information box with the error message, "You did not install Spell Check ..." you need to run the Lotus 1-2-3 Customized Installation to install this feature. If you are using the Student Version, this feature is not available.

❷ When the Spell Check dialog box appears with the unknown word "Havasu," click **Skip** because this word is spelled correctly but is not recognized by 1-2-3. See Figure 1-22.

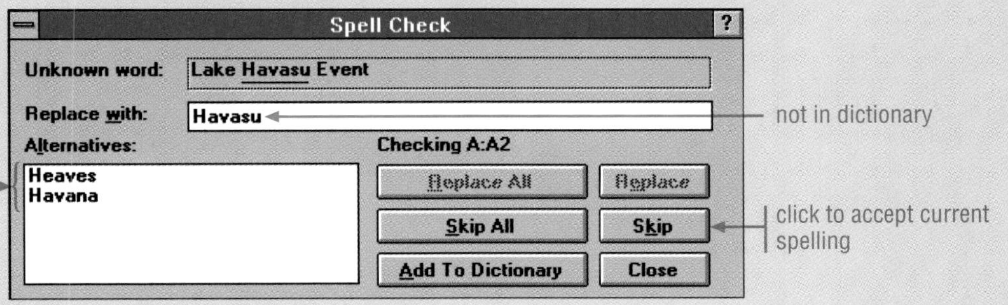

list of suggested alternatives

Figure 1-22
Spell Check dialog box with an unknown word

Spell Check

Unknown word: Lake Havasu Event

Replace with: Havasu ◄────── not in dictionary

Alternatives: Checking A:A2

Heaves
Havana

Replace All   Replace
Skip All   Skip ──── click to accept current spelling
Add To Dictionary   Close

❸ If any other words appear in the Spell Check dialog box, use the appropriate buttons to make your changes.

❹ Click the **OK button** when the "Spell check complete" message appears.

As she reviews the worksheet, Angela notices that column A is too narrow. She needs to widen the column but forgets how to do this. She decides to use 1-2-3's Help feature to refresh her memory.

Using Help

Lotus 1-2-3 has an on-line Help feature that displays information in a separate Help window. You use Help to answer your questions on various commands and activities that are available for creating worksheets and charts.

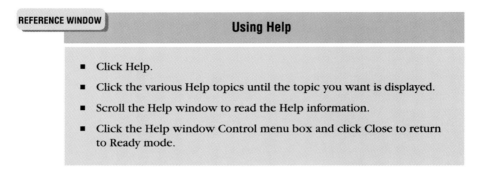

REFERENCE WINDOW

Using Help

- Click Help.
- Click the various Help topics until the topic you want is displayed.
- Scroll the Help window to read the Help information.
- Click the Help window Control menu box and click Close to return to Ready mode.

Angela needs help remembering how to widen a column in her worksheet. Let's explore the use of the Help feature and learn how to widen a column.

To access 1-2-3's on-line Help:

❶ Click **Help**.

❷ Click **Contents** to view the Help Contents. See Figure 1-23. The Help Contents is a listing of topics available with the 1-2-3 Help feature.

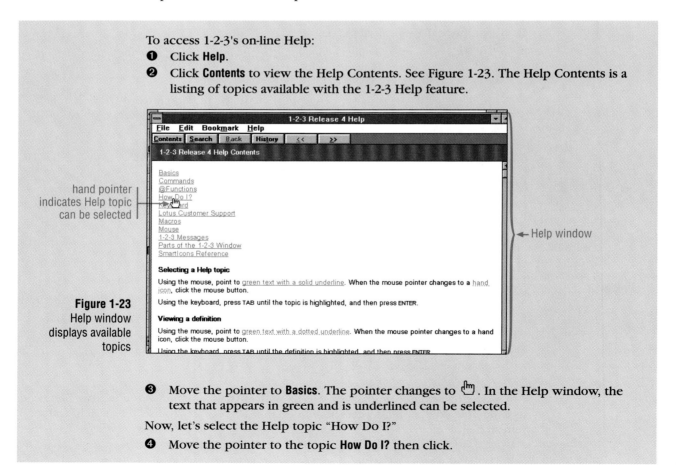

hand pointer
indicates Help topic
can be selected

Figure 1-23
Help window
displays available
topics

Help window

❸ Move the pointer to **Basics**. The pointer changes to 👆. In the Help window, the text that appears in green and is underlined can be selected.

Now, let's select the Help topic "How Do I?"

❹ Move the pointer to the topic **How Do I?** then click.

❺ Scroll down the Help Window and click **Change the Worksheet display and characteristics.**

❻ Click **Style Column Width** and read the Help screen. Use the scroll bars to move forward and backward through this Help information. Make sure you read the description for using a mouse and for the "Related SmartIcons."

TROUBLE? If you selected the wrong Help topic, click Back to back up one screen and click the desired topic.

You can use Help to find out more about any topic. After you get the information you need, you can exit from Help and return to Ready mode.

To exit from Help:

❶ Click the Help window **Control menu box.**

❷ Click **Close** to close the Help window and return to the worksheet window.

Thanks to the 1-2-3 Help feature, Angela now knows how to widen a column. Let's do that next.

Changing Column Width

Changing column width is one way to improve the appearance of the worksheet, making it easier to read and interpret data. Angela wants to increase the width of column A so the entire "Mileage Allowance" label appears in the cell.

REFERENCE WINDOW
Changing Column Width

- Click the column letter in the worksheet border to size the column to accommodate the widest cell in the column, or click the cell whose content is to be used to determine the column width.
- Click the Size Column SmartIcon.

or

- Move the pointer to the worksheet frame and point to the line that separates the column you want to change from the next column. The pointer changes to ✛.
- Drag the pointer left to narrow the column or right to widen it.
- Release the mouse button when the column width is correct.
- Click any cell to unselect the column.

Let's change the width of column A using the Size Column SmartIcon. The Size Column SmartIcon adjusts the size of the column to accommodate the longest label.

To change the width of column A:

❶ Click the column letter **A** in the worksheet border to select the column.

❷ Click the **Size Column SmartIcon** 📊 . The column automatically adjusts to accommodate the longest label in the column—in this case, "Detailed Expense Schedule." Detailed Expense Schedule is the longest label (21 character positions), but because there wasn't anything in the column next to it, the label spilled over into the adjacent cell.

Now, there is too much space between the labels in column A and the values in column B. Angela wants to adjust the column width to reduce the white space between the expense items and the data for Saturday. Let's resize column A so it is only 18 characters wide.

To resize a column to a desired width:

❶ Check the status bar to determine the height and width of the column. The width is currently set at 21 characters.

TROUBLE? If the date and time are displayed instead of the height and width, click the Date and Time selector to display the height and width. This is a toggle button. A *toggle button* switches back and forth between two choices.

❷ Move the pointer to the line that separates column A from column B in the worksheet frame. The pointer changes to ✛ . See Figure 1-24.

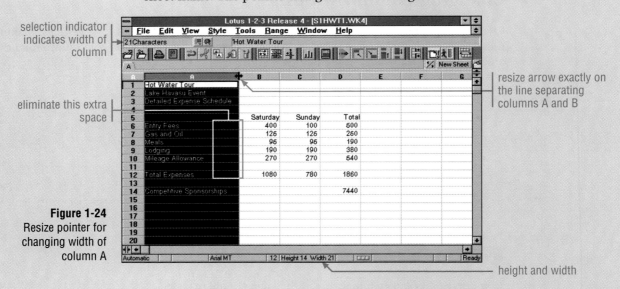

selection indicator indicates width of column

eliminate this extra space

resize arrow exactly on the line separating columns A and B

height and width

Figure 1-24
Resize pointer for changing width of column A

❸ Drag the pointer to the left to decrease the width of the column to 18 characters as indicated in the selection indicator. The status bar displays the new column width.

TROUBLE? If the column is too narrow or too wide, repeat Steps 2 and 3 until the column is 18 characters wide in the selection indicator.

❹ Click any cell in column A to unselect the column.

In reviewing your worksheet, you have made important changes since you last saved. You edited a formula, performed a spell check, and widened a column. Let's save these changes.

Using Save to Save the Worksheet

As mentioned earlier, you can use the Save command or the Save File SmartIcon to save the changes you have made to your worksheet, using the same filename. Saving the new, edited version of your worksheet *replaces* the old version (Figure 1-25). Use the Save command if you do *not* want to keep a copy of the old version of the worksheet.

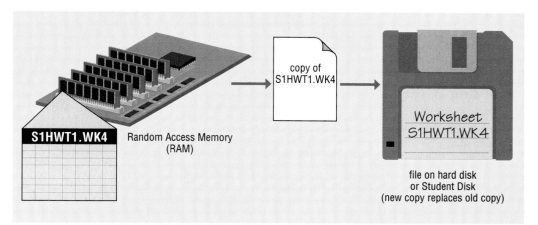

Figure 1-25
Save replaces
previous copy of
worksheet

To save the worksheet using the Save File SmartIcon:
❶ Make sure 1-2-3 is in Ready mode.
❷ Click the **Save File SmartIcon** 🖫. Note that 1-2-3 is in Wait mode while the file is being saved to your Student Disk, and it returns to Ready mode when the save is complete.

Angela has completed the four activities in creating a worksheet—planning, designing, building, and reviewing. She is pleased with her work and wants to print out the detailed expense schedule worksheet and show it to Sharon.

Specifying Cell Ranges

Before printing a worksheet, you need to specify the range of cells that you want to print. A **range** is a rectangular group of cells. For example, because Angela's worksheet does not use all 256 columns and 8192 rows of the 1-2-3 worksheet, you want to print only the range that contains the detailed expense schedule.

When using ranges you must follow two simple rules. First, ranges must be rectangular. Second, you identify a range of cells by specifying the upper-left corner of the range and the lower-right corner of the range. Lotus 1-2-3 automatically adds two points (..) to separate the cells. For example, range A5..C10 specifies cells A5 through C10. Examples of valid and invalid cell ranges appear in Figure 1-26.

Range Identification	Shape of Range	Example
C6..C6	a single cell	
A5..D5	a single row of cells	
B5..B12	a single column of cells	
A5..C10	a rectangular block of cells	
	any other shape is not considered a valid range	

Figure 1-26
Valid and invalid
cell ranges

Let's select the range A5..C10.

To select the range A5..C10:

❶ Click and hold the mouse button at cell **A5**. This will be the upper-left corner of the cell range. The pointer changes to ▦.

TROUBLE? If the pointer changes to ✋ you will accidentally move the cell's contents rather than select a cell range. Release the mouse button and click the Undo SmartIcon ▦. Then repeat Step 1.

❷ Drag the pointer to **C10** to specify the lower-right corner of the range. When you select a range, the first cell in the range, cell A5 in this example, is outlined and the other cells in the range are highlighted. While you are dragging the pointer to specify the cell range, 1-2-3 is in Point mode. See Figure 1-27.

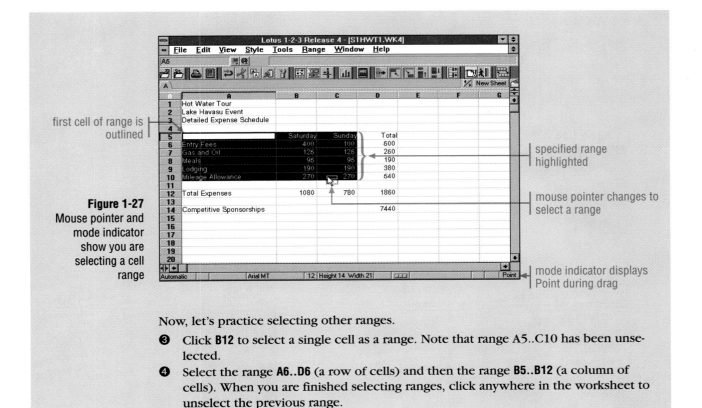

first cell of range is outlined

specified range highlighted

mouse pointer changes to select a range

Figure 1-27
Mouse pointer and mode indicator show you are selecting a cell range

mode indicator displays Point during drag

Now, let's practice selecting other ranges.

❸ Click **B12** to select a single cell as a range. Note that range A5..C10 has been unselected.

❹ Select the range **A6..D6** (a row of cells) and then the range **B5..B12** (a column of cells). When you are finished selecting ranges, click anywhere in the worksheet to unselect the previous range.

You will frequently select cell ranges as you build, modify, and print worksheets.

Printing the Worksheet

Before Angela prints her worksheet, she wants to preview it on the screen to check its overall layout. If it isn't what she wants, she can change the worksheet before she prints it. Let's preview and then print Angela's worksheet.

To preview and print the worksheet:

❶ Select the range **A1..D14**. Remember do not move the mouse if the pointer changes to 🖑—this will move the data in cell A1 instead of selecting the range.

❷ Click the **Preview SmartIcon** 🖳 to display the Print Preview dialog box. See Figure 1-28 on the following page.

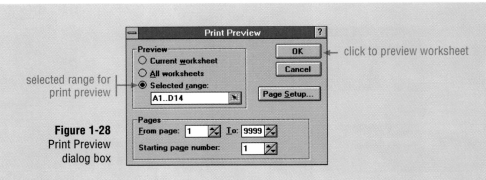

selected range for
print preview

Figure 1-28
Print Preview
dialog box

click to preview worksheet

❸   Click the **OK button** to preview the worksheet on your screen. See Figure 1-29.
    Don't worry if the preview isn't readable. It's intended only to show you the layout
    of the worksheet and how the worksheet will fit on a piece of paper.

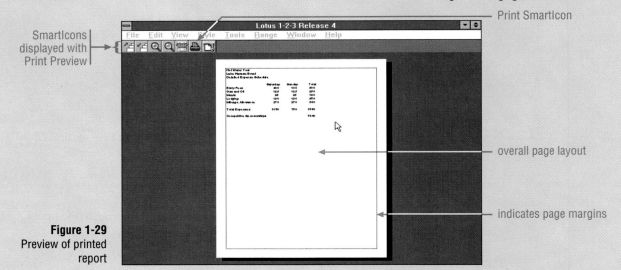

Print SmartIcon

SmartIcons
displayed with
Print Preview

overall page layout

indicates page margins

Figure 1-29
Preview of printed
report

The layout of the worksheet is fine. Let's print the worksheet.

❹   Make sure your printer is turned on.
❺   Click the **Print SmartIcon** 🖨 to display the Print dialog box.
❻   Click the **OK button**. Notice that a Cancel Printing dialog box appears. In 1-2-3,
    you can cancel printing at any time, if necessary. Your printout should look like
    Figure 1-30.

```
Hot Water Tour
Lake Havasu Event
Detailed Expense Schedule

                        Saturday    Sunday      Total
Entry Fees                  400        100        500
Gas and Oil                 125        125        250
Meals                        95         95        190
Lodging                     190        190        380
Mileage Allowance           270        270        540

Total Expenses             1080        780       1860

Competitive Sponsorships                          7440
```

Figure 1-30
Printout of the
detailed expense
schedule

Angela removes her printed worksheet from the printer and meets with Sharon to get her opinion. They are both happy to see that the total expense for Competitive Sponsorships for June is well below the original budget of $12,800. Now they know that they are on target for the month of June. Sharon is impressed with Angela's worksheet but suggests adding one thing—a chart. Sharon explains that a chart will help her spot any inconsistencies in the expenses quickly, without having to look closely at the dollar amounts. Angela goes back to her computer and creates the chart.

If you want to take a break and resume the tutorial at a later time, close your worksheet and exit 1-2-3. Make sure you remove your Student Disk from the disk drive. When you resume the tutorial, launch 1-2-3 and place your Student Disk in the disk drive. Open the S1HWT1.WK4 worksheet, select the Tutorial 1 SmartIcon palette, and then continue with the tutorial.

Creating a Chart

Angela needs to create a chart of the detailed expense schedule for the Competitive Sponsorships budget. Ideally, she should have included this chart in her planning analysis sheet, but 1-2-3 makes it easy to add a chart to a worksheet at any time. Angela knows that the chart needs to compare the expenses, making it easy to spot inconsistencies or trends. She sketches a bar chart, as shown in Figure 1-31. A **bar chart** is a type of chart that shows comparisons between the data represented by the height of each bar.

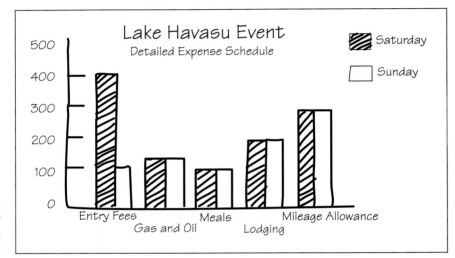

Figure 1-31
Angela's chart to accompany her detailed expense schedule

With 1-2-3 Release 4, you specify the data to be illustrated in the chart, including the titles, column headings, and labels that you want to appear on your chart. Next, you decide where you want the chart to appear in the worksheet. Lotus 1-2-3 does the rest.

REFERENCE WINDOW

Creating a Chart

- Select the range that contains the values and labels you want to appear in the chart.
- Click the Chart SmartIcon.
- Click the cell that will be the upper-left corner of the chart.

Let's create the chart Angela has planned.

To create the chart:
❶ Select the range A2..C10. Remember you must specify a valid range. Notice how the expense names are located in the left-most column of the range and the headings are above the data for the chart. Lotus 1-2-3 expects this arrangement of the data for this type of chart. The default chart type is the bar chart.
❷ Click the **Chart SmartIcon**. Notice that the pointer changes to when you move it into the worksheet area. See Figure 1-32.

range selected for chart

chart pointer

Figure 1-32
Chart pointer for specifying location of chart

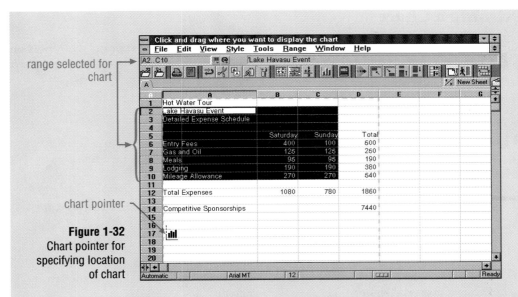

❸ Move the pointer to cell A17. This will be the upper-left corner of the chart.

❹ Click **A17**. See Figure 1-33. Note that the SmartIcon palette changes to a palette specifically designed for creating charts. Lotus 1-2-3 switches to this palette automatically whenever you work with a chart.

TROUBLE? If your bar chart contains the wrong data, click Edit then click Clear to remove the unwanted chart. Repeat Steps 1 through 4.

default SmartIcon palette for charts

chart placed in range A17..C29 of worksheet

Figure 1-33
Bar chart

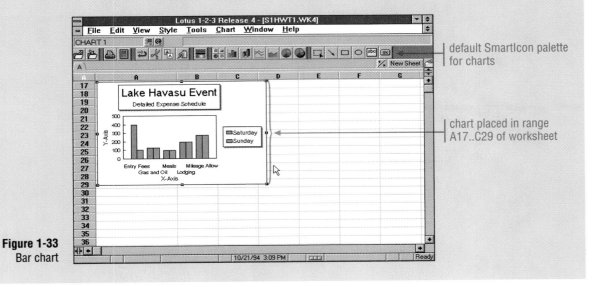

You can specify many options for a chart. In Angela's chart, the y-axis displays the scale for the dollar amount of each expense, whereas the x-axis identifies the bar for these expenses. The legend on the right side of the chart distinguishes the bars for Saturday and Sunday. Lotus 1-2-3 assigns these chart elements automatically based on the data in the selected range. You will learn more about 1-2-3 charts and how to enhance them in Tutorial 4.

Printing a Chart

Angela wants the worksheet and chart to appear as one report. If she prints the report on one page, she can look it over easily with Sharon. To make sure the worksheet and chart fit on one page, Angela wants to preview the report before printing it.

To preview and print the report:

❶ Click any cell not covered by the chart to redisplay the worksheet SmartIcons. Remember that when you selected the chart, the SmartIcons changed to a chart-specific palette.

❷ Click the **Home SmartIcon** 🔲.

❸ Select range A1..F32. This range contains the area of the worksheet that you want to print.

　　TROUBLE? If you accidentally release the mouse button, repeat Steps 2 and 3. The unwanted range is unselected when you click 🔲.

❹ Click the **Preview SmartIcon** 🔲 then click the **OK button** for a quick look at the layout of your report. See Figure 1-34.

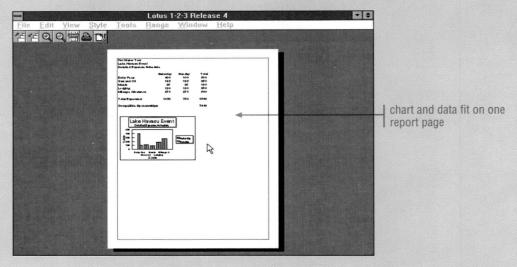

chart and data fit on one report page

Figure 1-34
Preview of the
report with chart
and data

❺ Click the **Print SmartIcon** 🖨 then click the **OK button**. Your report should look similar to the printed report. See Figure 1-35.

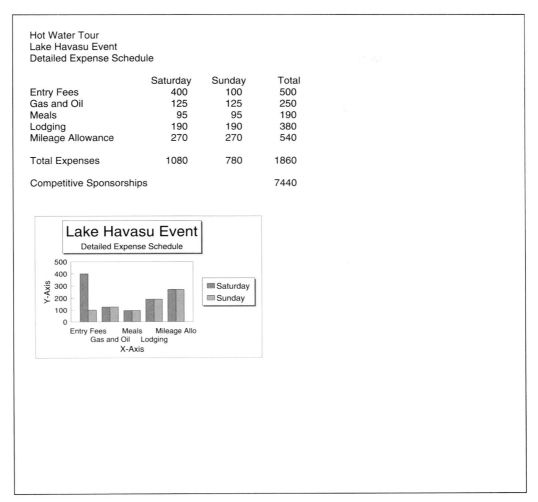

Figure 1-35
Angela's detailed expense schedule report

Angela has made several changes to her worksheet since she last saved so she wants to save it again. When you save your 1-2-3 worksheet file, any charts that you have created will be saved in the same worksheet file. Angela wants to keep a copy of her worksheet without the chart in it. Therefore, she has to save this worksheet with another name using the Save As command. If she used the Save command, the previous version of her worksheet would be replaced with her new version.

Let's save Angela's worksheet and chart as S1HWT2.WK4. As noted earlier in this tutorial, the number 2 tells you that this is the second version of the Hot Water Tour file.

To save the worksheet file with a new filename:

❶ Click **File**.

❷ Click **Save As**.

❸ Make sure the Drives box shows the drive containing your Student Disk.

❹ Type the new filename **S1HWT2**.

❺ Click the **OK button**.

■   ■   ■

You have successfully completed the detailed expense schedule worksheet and chart. If you want, you can continue with the exercises or you can exit from 1-2-3.

Questions

1. In which activity of your worksheet-creating process should you determine your input data values and cell formulas:
   a. planning
   b. designing
   c. building
   d. reviewing

2. Lotus 1-2-3 has a feature that lets you enter numbers and formulas in your worksheet in the order that you want them to appear in your worksheet, rather than the order in which they must be calculated. The name of this feature is:
   a. report ordering
   b. random calculation
   c. natural order
   d. alternate calculating

3. If each of the following formulas is entered in a cell, what results would 1-2-3 calculate:
   a. 100*.05+4/2
   b. 200+50/5*4-20
   c. 100*(25/50-.2)
   d. ((150-100/2)*.08+12)/2

4. If the cell content of D9 is entered as follows, which of these are formulas? Why?
   a. 260+B8
   b. +F7/G11
   c. D5*3+B11
   d. .2*C16+B7

5. Which one of these activities *must* be performed *before* you can print a report:
   a. save the worksheet file
   b. preview the report
   c. copy the range of cells to be printed to the clipboard
   d. specify the range of cells to be printed

6. Which function key is used to access the 1-2-3 Help feature?
   a. [F1]
   b. [F2]
   c. [F3]
   d. [F5]

7. To completely remove or erase the contents of a cell, you should position the cell pointer on the cell and then press:
   a. [Backspace]
   b. [Enter]
   c. [Esc]
   d. [Delete]

8. Which of the following groups of cells specify a valid cell range? Explain why each case is valid or not.
   a. G24..R24
   b. A:A10..A:F45
   c. E10..E21
   d. A:C15..A:C29

E 9. Using the Task Reference located at the end of the book, determine the number of different ways you can do the same task as those performed with the following SmartIcons. Write down at least one other method for each SmartIcon:

   a.
   b.
   c.
   d.

Tutorial Assignments

Launch 1-2-3, if necessary, and insert your Student Disk in the disk drive. Open T1BPC1.WK4, the Profit Plan for Berber Products Company. Familiarize yourself with the worksheet by scrolling through it, then do the following:

1. Click the cell containing "1st Quarter." Why is there an apostrophe before the 1?
2. Enter the column heading "2nd Quarter" in cell C4.
3. Why is there a zero displayed for the Gross Profit in the 1st Quarter? Correct this error. What is the Gross Profit in the 1st Quarter?
4. In column C, enter the formulas to calculate the three planning items: Sales, Cost of Sales, and Gross Profit. What is the Gross Profit in the 2nd Quarter? (Note that these formulas are similar to those in column B with the calculations performed as defined by the comments in column F.)
5. In column D, enter the formulas to calculate the six-month totals for the planning items: Sales, Cost of Sales, and Gross Profit. What is the Gross Profit for Six Months?
6. What's wrong with the width of column A? Change the column width so the entire expense item names are visible.
7. Save the worksheet as S1BPC1.WK4. Preview and print the worksheet. Your report should contain the range A1..D10.
8. Perform a what-if analysis by changing the Price Per Unit to 3.29 in the 1st Quarter and 3.39 in the 2nd Quarter. Print this what-if analysis. For this analysis, what is the new Gross Profit for Six Months?
9. Prepare a bar chart of Units Sold for the 1st Quarter and 2nd Quarter. Add this to your worksheet at cell A12. Save this version of your worksheet as S1BPC2.WK4. Preview and print a report containing both the Profit Plan and the chart.

Next, open T1HWT1.WK4, the detailed expense schedule for the Hot Water Tour sponsored by SeaJet International. Review the cell locations of the expense items and formulas. Note the rows Angela added below the mileage allowance for new anticipated expenses. She added these after reviewing the detailed expense schedule for the Lake Havasu Event with Sharon, Tara, and Minoru. They all agreed that the schedule should include these additional expenses for Parts, Repairs (Labor x Parts), and Telephone. These expenses are as follows:

	Saturday	Sunday
Parts	430	240
Repairs	0.6 * Parts	0.6 * Parts
Telephone	55	40

E   10. Complete Angela's worksheet sketch in Figure 1-36 by specifying the row numbers and writing out the cell formulas for Repairs, Total Expenses, and the Total column (column D).

Worksheet Planning Sketch

Row	A	B	C	D
——	Parts			
——	Repairs			
——	Telephone			
——				
——	Total Expenses			

Figure 1-36

E   11. Using your sketch, enter the new labels, values, and formulas for the additional expenses.

E   12. You need to edit the formulas for the Total Expenses row to include the new expenses. Use Help to learn the various methods for editing cell contents. Select "How Do I?" from the list of Help topics and then read about the various editing keys under the "Correct Mistakes" subtopic. Close the Help window and make the changes to the Total Expenses formulas. Which editing method did you choose?

13. Save the worksheet as S1HWT3.WK4. Preview and print this report. What are the total expenses for the Lake Havasu Event? Is the Competitive Sponsorships amount still within budget for June?

14. Prepare a bar chart containing the individual expense items for Saturday and Sunday. Add this chart to your worksheet below the Total Expenses row.

15. Save the worksheet as S1HWT4.WK4. Preview and print the report containing both the expense schedule and the chart.

E   16. Open Sharon's marketing expense budget, BUDGET.WK4. Run the Data Entry macro for the Competitive Sponsorships. Multiply the number of events each month by the Total Expenses amount you found in Assignment 13. Print a report of both the updated expenses and the chart. Save the worksheet as S1SJI2.WK4. Now, what is the total Competitive Sponsorships and the total Marketing Expense?

Case Problems

1. Conducting an Audit for Grant Donnelly & Company

Grant Donnelly & Company (GDC) is an international public accounting firm that often performs accounting audits for their clients. An audit is an independent examination of the client's business records to provide an expert opinion about the client's financial statements. The purpose of an audit is to determine whether the company's financial statements have been presented to shareholders and other concerned parties following generally accepted accounting principles.

Jorge Chavez, an auditing manager in the Seattle office, is the team leader for conducting the audit at WestCoast Energy Inc. WestCoast Energy is a large gas distribution utility with over a million industrial, commercial, and residential customers. Jorge's responsibilities include reviewing and approving the information his team collects during the audit, commonly called workpapers.

Crystal Gamble, a recent college graduate, is the audit associate who will use 1-2-3 to turn her workpapers into a Statement of Earnings for WestCoast Energy. She has a progress meeting with Jorge tomorrow and has to bring the first draft of her workpapers. She has been examining WestCoast's records and gathering information about the company's operations, such as Cost of Sales and Marketing expenses. She has included this information in her worksheet planning sketch in preparation for her meeting with Jorge (Figure 1-37).

	A	B	C	D
1				
2		'WestCoast Energy Inc.		
3		'STATEMENT OF EARNINGS		
4		'(Dollars in thousands)		
5				
6		"1996	"1995	"Increase
7		"------	"------	"------
8	'Net Sales	807582	678926	+B8–C8
9	'Cost of Sales	552455	462959	+B9–C9
10		"------	"------	"------
11	' Gross Profit	+B8–B9	+C8–C9	+B11–C11
12	'Operating Expenses			
13	' Marketing	107748	91995	+B13–C13
14	' Research and Development	23734	16802	+B14–C14
15	' Administrative	58536	49279	+B15–C15
16		"------	"------	"------
17	' Operating Profit	+B11–(B13+B14+B15)	+C11–(C13+C14+C15)	+B17–C17
18	'Other Income	12514	4356	+B18–C18
19	' Earnings Before Tax	+B17+B18	+C17+C18	+B19–C19
20	'Income Tax	20189	17532	+B20–C20
21		"------	"------	"------
22	' Net Earnings	+B19–B20	+C19–C20	+B22–C22

Figure 1-37

In this sketch, the dollar amounts are data that Crystal collected, and the formulas are generic accounting equations used in calculating the other financial statement accounts. After reviewing Crystal's workpapers and worksheet sketch, Jorge gives his approval and Crystal is ready to build her worksheet.

1. Launch 1-2-3. In the Untitled worksheet window, resize column A to a width of 25 characters so all the account names will fit.
2. Build Crystal's audit worksheet by entering the labels, numbers, and formulas from her sketch. (*Hint:* If Net Earnings [Increase] equals 12719, you have entered the data and formulas correctly.) If you are using the commercial version of Lotus 1-2-3 Release 4 for Windows, spell check the worksheet. (If you are using the Student Version of the software, this feature is not available.) Did you skip any unknown words? Which ones? Save the worksheet as S1WCE1.WK4. Preview and print this report.

3. Produce a bar chart of the Marketing, Research and Development, and Administrative expenses for 1995 and 1996. Add this chart to your worksheet at cell A24. Save the worksheet as S1WCE2.WK4. Preview and print an audit report containing both the Statement of Earnings and the chart.

4. Review your audit report and draw a circle around the operating expense that increased the most.

2. Recruiting Personnel for Grand Cayman Cruises

Grand Cayman Cruises (GCC) has grown rapidly in the last four years—expanding from three to twelve pleasure cruise ships. GCC's Human Resource (HR) Department recruits the crews for all of GCC's cruise ships. Many of the service and support crew members are recruited from college campuses.

Carol Zahn is a campus relations representative for GCC, and she monitors the number of interviews conducted by recruitment staff to help her plan recruiting activities. Carol uses three methods to establish contact with prospective employees: campus visits, college newspaper advertisements, and radio announcements. She wants to know which source yields the most hires and the average cost per hire. She will use this information to plan future recruiting activities by quarter. Carol analyzed her information requirements and sketched a worksheet to help her track the information she collects (Figure 1-38).

Worksheet Planning Sketch

	A	B	C	D
1	Grand Cayman Cruises			
2	Recruitment Planning			
3	Quarterly Yield Analysis			
4				
5		Campus	Magazine	Radio
6	Interviews	421	501	361
7	Offers	157	121	79
8	Hires	121	81	46
9	Total Cost	34760	42520	16480
10				
11	Percent Offers			
12	Yield Ratio			
13	Cost/Interview			
14	Cost/Hire			

Figure 1-38

She also made some notes to help her calculate each of her yield performance measurements (Figure 1-39). These yield performance measurements are the same for each source (campus, newspaper, and radio) and indicate recruiting efficiency based on the number of individuals interviewed and hired, such as the percentage of those interviewed that were hired.

Figure 1-39

```
Percent Offers    =    Offers / Interviews
Yield Ratio       =    Hires / Interviews
Cost/Interview    =    Total Cost / Interviews
Cost/Hire         =    Total Cost / Hires
```

You will complete the sketch of Carol's quarterly recruiting analysis and build her 1-2-3 worksheet.

1. Refer to Figure 1-38 and complete Carol's design by determining the formulas for her performance measures of Percent Offers, Yield Ratio, Cost/Interview, and Cost/Hire. Then launch 1-2-3 and build this worksheet by entering the labels, numbers, and formulas from the completed sketch. (*Hint:* Let 1-2-3 control the number of decimal places displayed with each of these formulas. You will learn how to control this in the next tutorial.) Widen the columns as necessary to accommodate the labels. Save the worksheet as S1GCC1.WK4, then preview and print this report. (*Hint:* If the Yield Ratio [Radio] equals 0.127, you have entered the data and formulas correctly.)

2. Create a bar chart of Cost/Interview and Cost/Hire. Add this chart to your worksheet in cell A17. Save the worksheet as S1GCC2.WK4. Preview and print a report containing both the performance measures and the chart.

3. Review the quarterly yield analysis. Circle the highest Yield Ratio. Which recruiting method resulted in the lowest cost per hire?

E 4. Carol wants to make a backup copy of her worksheet—a copy that has the same filename but a different extension. In the future, if she makes changes to her worksheet that she doesn't want or if there is a problem with the file, she can retrieve the backup copy of her worksheet. Use the "How Do I?" topic in Help to find out how to make a 1-2-3 backup copy of her worksheet. The information you need is in the subtopic "Save or retrieve work." Read the description for making a backup of your work, close the Help window, and then make a backup copy of the worksheet S1GCC2.

3. Planning a Store Size for Pizza Delight

Nick DiPietro and Lynne Feraldi recently graduated from college with degrees in general business. While in college, Nick and Lynne dreamed about owning their own restaurant. As soon as they saved enough money, they planned to open a pizza restaurant near a college or university and call it Pizza Delight.

A pizza restaurant was a natural choice for Nick and Lynne. Nick knows his mother's secret recipe for making pizza and believes that hers is the best pizza he has ever eaten. Lynne worked as an assistant manager at a pizza restaurant during college, and is familiar with many of the daily operating tasks.

After three years of saving, they have enough money and are ready to put their plan into action. The first step is to find a building to lease near a college or university. Lynne found three locations that would be suitable for Pizza Delight. The only difference among the three locations is their size. One has 950 square feet, another has 1,200 square feet, and the third has 1,500 square feet. A larger building is more expensive to lease but it could produce more sales. Lynne suggests they build a 1-2-3 worksheet to help them determine the most profitable size building for Pizza Delight. This worksheet needs to project weekly performance goals for pizza sales, salad sales, and drink sales, as well as the costs that pertain to those sales.

Your task is to finish creating the worksheet that Nick and Lynne started. To finish the worksheet, perform the following activities:

1. Launch 1-2-3 and open P1PDL1.WK4. Review this worksheet, which Nick and Lynne have already started. The formulas for the small and medium store sizes have already been entered. What is the Store Profit for the medium store size?

E 2. Why are zeros displayed for the calculations of the small store size? Correct this error and any other errors for the small store size. What is the Store Profit for this size store? What is the Sales per Hour amount for this size store?

E 3. Enter formulas for the large store size:
Pizza Costs = 65% of Pizza Sales
Salad Sales = 20% of Pizza Sales
Salad Costs = 30% of Salad Sales
Drink Sales = 20% of Pizza Sales
Drink Costs = 10% of Drink Sales
Enter the formulas for calculating the Sales per Hour and Profit per Hour. What is the Store Profit, Sales per Hour, and Profit per Hour for the large store size?

4. Save this worksheet as S1PDL2.WK4 and preview and print the Weekly Performance Goal report. Which store size would be the best size for Nick and Lynne? Why?

5. Prepare a bar chart of Store Sales, Store Costs, and Store Profits for the three store sizes. This chart has only one row for the heading. Add this chart to your worksheet. If you are using the commercial version of Lotus 1-2-3 Release 4 for Windows, spell check the worksheet. (If you are using the Student Version of the software, this feature is not available.) Did 1-2-3 check the spelling in the chart? Save the worksheet as S1PDL2.WK4, then preview and print the report including the bar chart.

6. Prepare a second bar chart of Sales per Hour and Profit per Hour for the three store sizes. Your selected range will not include any rows with headings, only the two rows containing the data. You learned in the tutorial that you should include the title of the worksheet in the range you want to chart. Sometimes, as in this case, that isn't possible because the title is not part of the range you want to chart. You will learn how to correct this situation in Tutorial 4. Add this chart to your worksheet and examine its contents. What is missing? Save this version of your worksheet as S1PDL3.WK4. Preview and print a report containing the Performance Goal numbers and the two charts.

E 7. Costs usually go down if you buy in bulk. What if the Pizza Costs for the large store decreases by 7%? How would this affect the large store's potential profit? Perform a what-if analysis by revising the Pizza Costs for the large store. (*Hint:* You will need to edit a formula to perform this what-if analysis.) Print the same report as the report you printed in Problem 6.

E 8. Compare the bar charts of the Profit per Hour in Problems 6 and 7. Notice how your charts were automatically updated when you performed the what-if analysis. Does the what-if value change the outcome of which store size Nick and Lynne should choose? If so, why? What else might Nick and Lynne need to consider when deciding what store size to choose? Explain your answer.

Modifying a Worksheet

OBJECTIVES

In this tutorial you will:

- Complete a sequence of column headings
- Use the pointing method to build formulas
- Copy formulas
- Understand relative and absolute references
- Use the @SUM and @ROUND functions
- Format the numbers in a worksheet
- Underline labels and values

Developing a Personnel Plan

CASE

Interim Personnel Services Interim Personnel Services (IPS) is an employment contractor providing temporary help to a variety of businesses, such as banks, insurance companies, medical offices, manufacturing companies, and government offices. IPS's specialized services are grouped in four major categories as follows:

- Office—clerical staff, secretarial staff, word processors
- Industrial—light manufacturers, laborers
- Marketing—sales clerks, product demonstrators, telemarketers
- Computer—data entry clerks, systems analysts, data processing operators

For many workers just entering the job market, IPS provides the opportunity to obtain the valuable one to two years of job experience that many employers seek when they hire full-time employees. For other workers, the variety of job assignments and the ability to juggle part-time employment around their busy personal schedules make IPS an attractive career choice.

IPS has grown dramatically as a result of recent corporate restructurings and a greater reliance on temporary workers. IPS management expects the growth to continue at a rate of nearly 20% per year for the next three years. The vice president of human resources, Ricardo Resio, is responsible for coordinating staff planning for the entire firm. Ricardo recently hired Julie Del Greco to assist him with staff planning. Ricardo assigned Julie the task of preparing the personnel plan for the coming year to support IPS's anticipated growth. Because the size of the pool of talented temporaries determines the company's ability to grow, this planning is extremely important for IPS.

Julie is excited about her new position and wants to prepare the best possible plan. She meets with Ricardo to define the requirements of the personnel plan. Her goal is to create a personnel plan for next year that will include the number of temporaries they need to hire each quarter with a summary for the year. To determine the number of temporaries for each quarter, she needs to determine the beginning staff level for the first quarter; the **turnover**, or losses, of staff for the first quarter; the turnover growth rate for the other quarters; the retirement rate by quarter; and the new hire rate by quarter. To create the summary for the year, she will take the beginning staff level for the first quarter, add the growth for all four quarters, subtract the losses for all four quarters, and the result will be the ending staff level in Quarter 4—what IPS started the year with and ended the year with. Ricardo helps her plan the calculations.

Using personnel records, Julie verifies that IPS's current staffing level of temporaries is 1100. This is the starting point for the personnel plan.

With Ricardo's help, Julie calculates the turnover for the first quarter (32) and estimates the turnover growth rate (12%) for the next three quarters. The turnover **growth rate** is the amount of increase in staff turnover from a prior time period, such as the previous quarter. Another common use for a growth rate is a sales growth rate from quarter to quarter or from year to year. The general formula for a growth rate is:

prior value x (1 + growth rate as a decimal)

Because the growth rate is an increase in a prior amount, the 1 is required in the formula to obtain the prior amount and is then increased by the growth rate. A growth rate can also be negative when a decrease occurs.

By analyzing last year's data, Julie determines the quarterly retirement rate to be 1%. Finally, using IPS's corporate plan, Ricardo estimates the quarterly new hire rate for Julie's use in their personnel plan. He believes that a hire rate of 8% is necessary to support the company's anticipated growth.

With this data collected, Julie develops her planning analysis sheet, as shown in Figure 2-1, and sketches her worksheet, as shown in Figure 2-2.

Planning Analysis Sheet

My goal:
Develop a worksheet for recruitment planning by quarter for next year

What results do I want to see?
Recruitment information by quarter with a total for the year

What information do I need?
Beginning staff level for the first quarter (1100)
Turnover for the first quarter (32)
Turnover growth rate by quarter for the next three quarters (12%)
Retirement rate by quarter (1%)
New hire rate by quarter (8%)

What calculations will I perform?
Beginning staff level [Qtr 1] = 1100, Beginning staff level for next quarter = ending staff
 level for previous quarter (for each quarter), Beginning staff level for the year = [Qtr 1]
Retirements = beginning staff level * .01 for four columns, four quarter total
Turnover = 32, previous turnover * 1.12 for three columns, four quarter total
New hires = (beginning staff level - retirements) * .08 for four columns, four quarter total
Ending staff level = beginning staff level - retirements - turnover + new hires for four
 columns, ending staff level [Qtr 4]

Figure 2-1
Julie's planning
analysis sheet

	A	B	C	D	E	F
1		QTR1	QTR2	QTR3	QTR4	YEAR
2						
3	Beginning Staff Level	1100	Ending Staff Level QTR1	Ending Staff Level QTR2	Ending Staff Level QTR3	Beginning Staff Level QTR1
4	Retirements	Beginning Staff Level QTR1 *.01	Beginning Staff Level QTR2 *.01	Beginning Staff Level QTR3 *.01	Beginning Staff Level QTR4 *.01	Add Cells B4..E4
5	Turnover	32	Turnover QTR1 * (1 + .12)	Turnover QTR2 * (1 + .12)	Turnover QTR3 * (1 +.12)	Add Cells B5..E5
6	New Hires	(Beginning Staff Level QTR1 - Retirements QTR1) *.08	(Beginning Staff Level QTR2 - Retirements QTR2) *.08	(Beginning Staff Level QTR3 - Retirements QTR3) *.08	(Beginning Staff Level QTR4 - Retirements QTR4) *.08	Add Cells B6..E6
7						
8	Ending Staff Level	B3-B4-B5+B6	C3-C4-C5+C6	D3-D4-D5+D6	E3-E4-E5+E6	Ending Staff Level QTR4

Figure 2-2
Julie's worksheet sketch

Julie meets with Ricardo to determine if her worksheet satisfies the information requirements for their personnel plan. Ricardo is pleased with Julie's analysis, and he gives his approval. Julie returns to her desk, ready to build the worksheet.

When Julie finishes building the IPS personnel plan by entering the various labels, numeric constants, and formulas, her completed first draft worksheet will look similar to Figure 2-3. In this tutorial you will complete Julie's personnel plan and learn how to build formulas by pointing, to copy cell contents, to use the @SUM and @ROUND functions, and to improve the appearance of your worksheet.

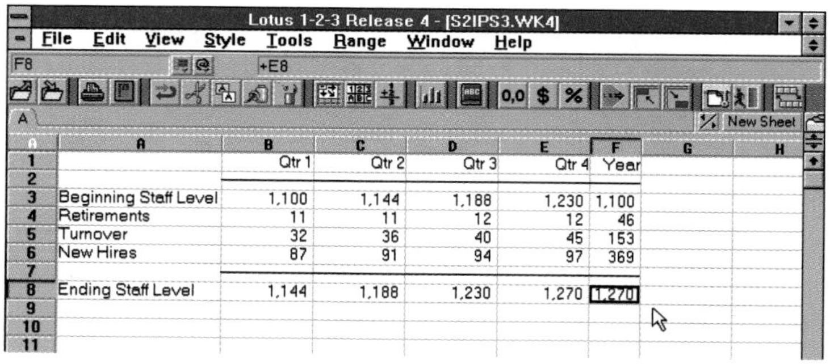

Figure 2-3
Julie's completed
personnel plan

Retrieving the Worksheet

In this tutorial you need to select the SmartIcon palette created for Tutorial 2, then retrieve the worksheet that Julie has started based on Ricardo's requirements. First, let's launch 1-2-3.

To launch 1-2-3, select the SmartIcon palette for Tutorial 2, then retrieve the C2IPS1.WK4 worksheet:

❶ Launch 1-2-3 and place your Student Disk in the disk drive.

❷ Select the Tutorial 2 SmartIcon palette using the SmartIcon palette selector 🔲 in the status bar.

   TROUBLE? If "Tutorial 2" is not one of the choices, this icon palette needs to be installed. See your instructor or technical support person for assistance. If you are using your own computer, you need to install the Tutorial 2 palette. See your instructor for assistance.

❸ Click the **Open File SmartIcon** 📂 to open Julie's C2IPS1.WK4 worksheet file on your Student Disk. The opened worksheet appears. See Figure 2-4.

   TROUBLE? If the File Name list box does not display the list of files on your Student Disk, make sure you have selected the correct disk drive in the Drives drop-down list box.

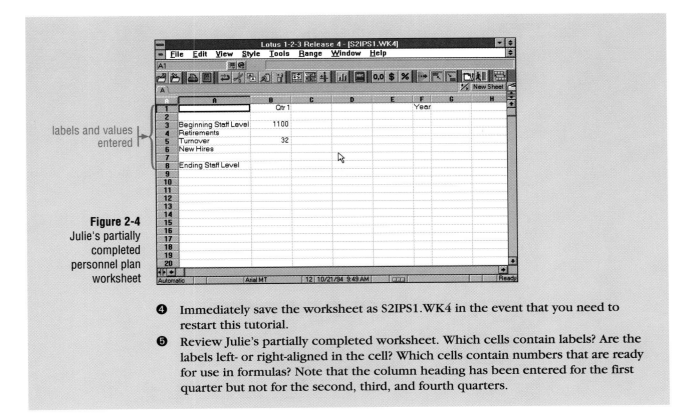

labels and values
entered

Figure 2-4
Julie's partially
completed
personnel plan
worksheet

❹ Immediately save the worksheet as S2IPS1.WK4 in the event that you need to restart this tutorial.

❺ Review Julie's partially completed worksheet. Which cells contain labels? Are the labels left- or right-aligned in the cell? Which cells contain numbers that are ready for use in formulas? Note that the column heading has been entered for the first quarter but not for the second, third, and fourth quarters.

You learned in Tutorial 1 that the first step in building a worksheet is entering the identifying labels. According to Julie's sketch, three of the column headings are missing. Let's enter the missing column headings first.

Completing a Sequence of Column Headings

Before Julie enters the formulas for calculating the staffing requirements, she wants to enter the missing column headings to help her identify where the numbers and formulas will be entered. Although Julie could type the column headings for the second, third, and fourth quarters, 1-2-3 provides a convenient method for completing a sequence of data in a specified cell range, called **Fill by Example**. The sequence can be numbered quarters like Julie's, or it can be a numeric or alphabetical series. For example, if you have the headings January, February, and so forth in your worksheet, you can use Fill by Example to fill in the month names for the entire year. You start the sequence by entering the beginning data, which serves as the example, in the first cell.

> **REFERENCE WINDOW**
>
> ### Filling Cells by Example
>
> - Enter the beginning, or example, data in the first cell.
> - Select the cell range to be filled, including the example cell.
> - Click the Complete Sequence SmartIcon.

Let's complete the column headings for the second, third, and fourth quarters of Julie's report using Fill by Example.

To complete the sequence of column headings using Fill by Example:

❶ Select the range B1..E1. See Figure 2-5. The label in cell B1 is the beginning of the sequence. Note that the mode indicator changes to Point when you are selecting a range.

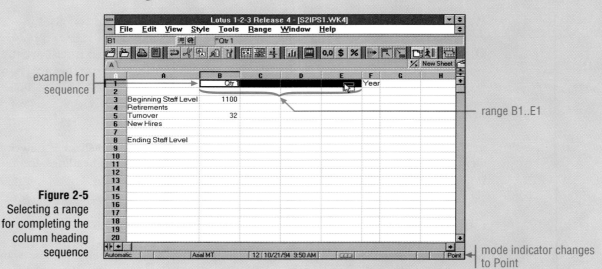

Figure 2-5
Selecting a range for completing the column heading sequence

❷ Click the **Complete Sequence SmartIcon** to place the appropriate labels in cells C1, D1, and E1. See Figure 2-6.

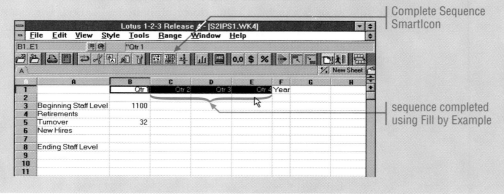

Figure 2-6
Using Fill by Example to complete a column heading sequence

Now, Julie has all the rows and columns identified in the worksheet. She is ready to enter the formulas for calculating the staffing requirements.

Building Formulas by Pointing

Lotus 1-2-3 lets you create formulas by either typing them, as you have done so far, or by pointing to the cell addresses you want to enter in the formulas. Pointing is the preferred method for building formulas because it is quicker and reduces your chances of making a mistake. For example, it is very easy to type E32 when you mean E23. It is more difficult to point to the wrong cell. You will be able to enter seven of Julie's cell formulas using the pointing method at the locations indicated in Figure 2-7. The remaining cell formulas are similar to these, and you can enter them using a copy operation you will learn later in this tutorial.

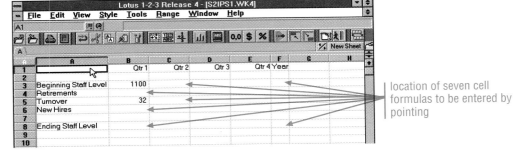

Figure 2-7
Location of cell formulas to be entered by pointing

location of seven cell formulas to be entered by pointing

REFERENCE WINDOW   **Building a Formula by Pointing**

- Click the cell where you want to enter the formula.
- Type an arithmetic operator.
- Click the cell to be included in the formula.
- Repeat typing arithmetic operators and clicking cells until the formula is complete.
- Click the Confirm button or press [Enter] to finish entering the formula.

The first formula you need to enter according to Julie's planning analysis sheet (Figure 2-1) and worksheet sketch (Figure 2-2) is in cell B4, which calculates Retirements as 1% of the Beginning Staff Level or, in other words +B3*.01. Let's enter this formula using the pointing method.

To enter the formula by pointing:
❶ Click **B4**. Before entering a formula by pointing, make sure the cell pointer is located in the cell where you want the completed formula.

❷   Type **+** (plus sign) to begin the formula. Remember from Tutorial 1 that any formula that starts with a cell address must have an arithmetic operator before it. The mode indicator displays "Value," verifying that a formula is being entered.

❸   Click **B3**. This is pointing to cell B3. Notice that the mode indicator displays "Point." The cell address appears in the formula you are entering in cell B4. See Figure 2-8. Note that instead of clicking cell B3, you could also use the cursor movement keys to point to the cell address. However, using the mouse is more efficient, and this method is used throughout this book.

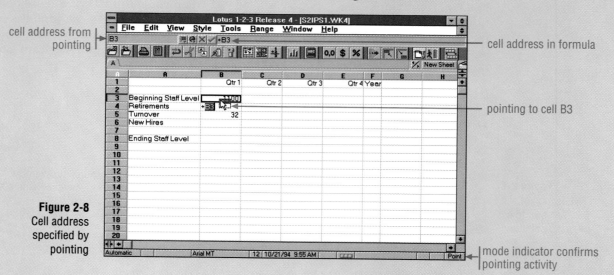

Figure 2-8
Cell address specified by pointing

❹   Type * (asterisk) to specify the multiplication arithmetic operator.

❺   Type **.01** to include the numeric constant used in this formula.

TROUBLE? If you make a typing error when entering the formula, use [Backspace] (or [Del]) to correct it, or click the Cancel button and repeat Steps 1 through 5.

❻   Press **[Enter]** or click the **Confirm button** to complete the formula. The formula is displayed in the cell contents box while the result, 11, is displayed in the worksheet in cell B4. The value 11 is displayed in the worksheet because 1-2-3 calculates it as an integer with no decimal places. For now, accept the number of decimal places as displayed by 1-2-3. You will change the number of decimal places displayed in the worksheet when you review Julie's worksheet. Note that the worksheet letter is not included in the completed formula, because the cell referenced in the formula is on the same worksheet as the cell location of the formula. See Figure 2-9.

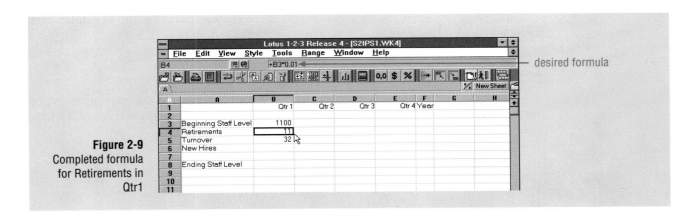

Figure 2-9
Completed formula
for Retirements in
Qtr1

Enter the next six formulas according to Julie's sketch in Figure 2-2 using the pointing method.

To enter the next six formulas by pointing:

❶ Place the cell pointer in the appropriate cells and enter the following formulas. Make sure you enter the formulas exactly as they appear. Don't forget the arithmetic operators, including parentheses.

Cell	Formula
B6	(B3-B4)*.08
B8	+B3-B4-B5+B6
C3	+B8
C5	+B5*(1+.12)
F3	+B3
F8	+E8

After you enter all the formulas, your worksheet should look like Figure 2-10. Cell F8 displays a zero for the calculated result because the formula references cell E8, which is currently empty. As soon as you enter a value in cell E8, 1-2-3 can calculate the correct result for the formula in cell F8. Notice that asterisks appear in cell F3.

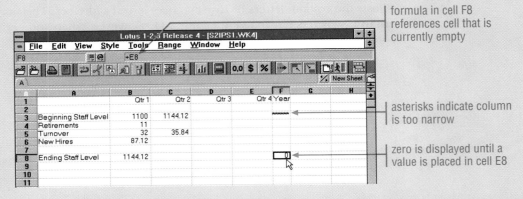

Figure 2-10
Formulas entered by
pointing

❷ Click **F3** to check that this cell contains the correct formula +B3. Although the cell contents box displays the right formula, the asterisks indicate that the value is too large to fit in the space available with the current column width.

You need to widen the Year column so the complete value for the Beginning Staff Level will be displayed.

Correcting Cells Filled with Asterisks

When asterisks fill a cell, they indicate that the width of the cell is too narrow to display the cell's current value. As you learned in Tutorial 1, you can increase the width of the column containing the cell whose value does not display correctly.

Let's correct cell F3 by changing the width of column F.

To correct the cell filled with asterisks by changing the width of column F:

❶ Place the cell pointer at F3 where the asterisks appear.

❷ Resize the column using the pointer ✛ in the worksheet frame as described in Tutorial 1. Increase the column width so the asterisks disappear and the number is displayed.

Now that you have made changes, you should save your worksheet.

❸ Click the **Save File Smartlcon** to save the worksheet with these newly entered formulas as S2IPS1.WK4.

Next, you will continue to build the personnel plan by copying the remaining formulas in Julie's worksheet.

Copying Formulas Using Relative References

Although you could enter the remaining formulas either by typing or by pointing, a more efficient solution is to copy them. Once you enter a label or a value into a cell, you can copy it into any other cell. Julie's personnel plan worksheet contains several formulas that can be copied to other cells. For example, the formula in cell C3 can be copied to cells D3 and E3. From Julie's sketch (Figure 2-3), you can see that the formulas to be copied are nearly identical to the formulas already entered in each row; the only difference is the column letters. When you copy a formula from one cell to another, 1-2-3 automatically adjusts the column letters or row numbers in cell addresses. This is called **relative referencing**, which is illustrated in Figure 2-11. However, when you copy labels and numeric constants, *exact duplicates* are placed in the other cells.

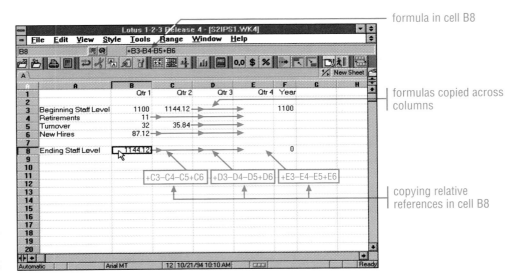

formula in cell B8

formulas copied across columns

copying relative references in cell B8

Figure 2-11
Arrangement for copying formulas in Julie's worksheet

Lotus 1-2-3 provides several methods for copying, depending on the number of cells you want to copy at one time and whether the range you're copying from is the same shape as the range you're copying to. Let's explore these methods next by copying the formulas in Julie's worksheet.

REFERENCE WINDOW

Copying Cells to a Range of the Same Shape

- Select the cells to copy.
- Position the mouse pointer on the edge of the range so the pointer changes to 🖑.
- Press and hold [Ctrl], then press and hold the mouse button. The pointer changes to ⊕.
- Drag the pointer and dotted outline of the range to the location you want.
- Release the mouse button and [Ctrl] to copy the cell contents to this location.

Let's copy the formula for the Beginning Staff Level for the third and fourth quarters using the mouse pointer. The range you are copying from is the same shape as the range you are copying to.

To copy the Beginning Staff Level formula using the mouse pointer:
❶ Click **C3** to select this cell as the range to be copied. The formula in cell C3 will be copied to cell D3.
❷ Move the mouse pointer to any edge of the cell until it changes to 🖑.

❸ Press and hold **[Ctrl]**, then press and hold the mouse button. The pointer changes again, this time to ✥ to indicate a copy is being performed. Move this pointer to cell D3, then release both the mouse button and [Ctrl]. The copy is completed. See Figure 2-12. Because this formula references a cell that is currently blank, a zero is displayed. Once the other formulas are copied, the correct value will appear.

TROUBLE? If you move the pointer when it is shaped like ✋, you will move the contents in cell C3 rather than copy the contents. Use the Undo SmartIcon 🔁 to undo the move operation, then repeat Step 3.

formula copied from cell
C3 to cell D3

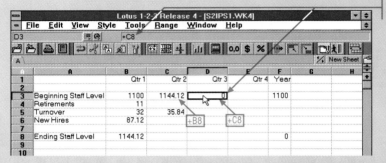

Figure 2-12
Formula copied to
cell D3

❹ Repeat the copy procedure to copy the contents of cell D3 to cell E3.

❺ Inspect the formulas in cells D3 and E3 by moving the cell pointer to each cell. Observe how 1-2-3 adjusted the column letters automatically as the copies were performed. Zeros are displayed in both cells because the formulas reference cells that are currently empty.

To copy the contents of a single cell to several cells at one time, you can use the Copy Current Cell SmartIcon.

REFERENCE WINDOW

Copying a Single Cell to Several Cells Using the Copy Current Cell SmartIcon

- Select the range for the copy with the single cell to be copied in the upper-left corner of the range.

- Click the Copy Current Cell SmartIcon to copy the contents of the single cell to all the other cells in the range.

Let's copy the formulas for Retirements and Turnover across the row using the Copy Current Cell SmartIcon.

To copy the Retirements and Turnover formulas using the Copy Current Cell SmartIcon:

❶ Select the range B4..E4. See Figure 2-13. The formula in cell B4 will be copied into the other cells in the range.

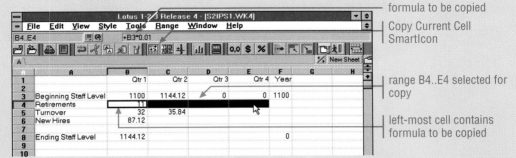

Figure 2-13
Selected range for use with Copy Current Cell SmartIcon

formula to be copied

Copy Current Cell SmartIcon

range B4..E4 selected for copy

left-most cell contains formula to be copied

❷ Click the **Copy Current Cell SmartIcon** 🔲. Lotus 1-2-3 uses this SmartIcon to copy the contents of one cell to the other cells in the range.

TROUBLE? If the values for the formula do not appear in the cells in row 4, you did not select the correct range. Click the Undo SmartIcon 🔲 to delete the contents of the cells and repeat Steps 1 and 2.

❸ Inspect the formulas in cells C4, D4, and E4 by moving the cell pointer to each cell. Again, observe how the column letters were adjusted automatically by 1-2-3. See Figure 2-14. Zeros appear for the formulas that reference blank cells.

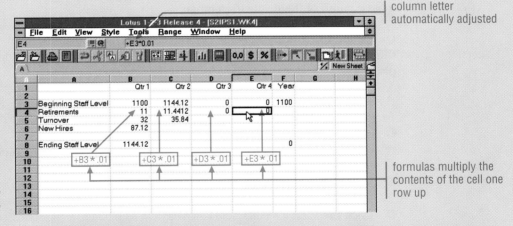

Figure 2-14
Column letters in formulas adjusted automatically by 1-2-3 with copy

column letter automatically adjusted

formulas multiply the contents of the cell one row up

❹ Select the range C5..E5 then click 🔲 to copy the formulas for Turnover. Check your formulas and make sure that they are the same except for the column letters before you continue.

You can copy Julie's formulas for New Hires and Ending Staff Level at the same time by using 1-2-3's clipboard. The **clipboard** is a Windows area used to temporarily store data that you copy so you can paste that same data elsewhere. You need to use the clipboard because the range you will copy from is a different shape from the range you are copying to.

Copying Cells to a Range of a Different Shape

- Select the range of cells you want to copy.

- Click the Copy to Clipboard SmartIcon to copy the cell contents to the clipboard.

  or

  Click the right mouse button to display the Quick menu, then click Copy to copy the cell contents to the clipboard.

- Select the range to which you want to copy the clipboard contents.

- Click the Paste from Clipboard SmartIcon to place the clipboard contents in the selected range.

  or

  Click the right mouse button to display the Quick menu, then click Paste to place the clipboard contents in the selected range.

Now let's copy Julie's formulas for New Hires and Ending Staff Level using the clipboard. When you copy a range of cells, you select the entire range you want copied, but you do not have to select the entire destination range. To copy a column you specify only the top row of the destination range. Similarly, to copy a row you specify only the left-most column of the destination range.

You can use the Copy to and Paste from Clipboard SmartIcons or you can use 1-2-3's Quick menu to copy several cells at a time. Let's use the Copy to and Paste from Clipboard SmartIcons—they are included in the predefined SmartIcon palette and are simple to use.

To copy the formulas for New Hires and Ending Staff Level using the SmartIcons:
1. Select the range B6..B8, the range to be copied.
2. Click the **Copy to Clipboard SmartIcon** to place a copy of the contents of this range in the clipboard.
3. Select the range C6..E6, which is the top row of the destination range. Remember, when a column is copied, you specify only the top row of the destination range.
4. Click the **Paste from Clipboard SmartIcon** to place the clipboard contents in the selected destination range. The worksheet with all the formulas copied appears, as shown in Figure 2-15.

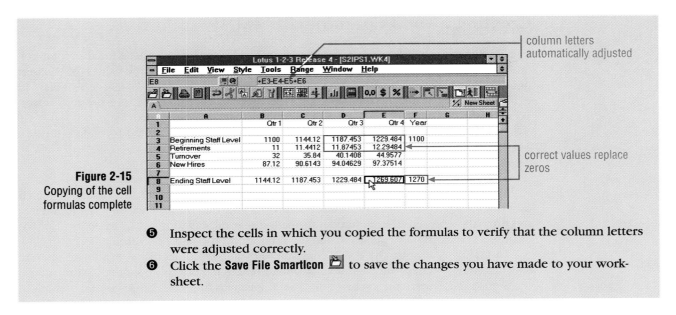

column letters
automatically adjusted

correct values replace
zeros

Figure 2-15
Copying of the cell
formulas complete

⑤ Inspect the cells in which you copied the formulas to verify that the column letters were adjusted correctly.

⑥ Click the **Save File SmartIcon** 📁 to save the changes you have made to your worksheet.

Relative and Absolute References

When you copied Julie's formulas for the Beginning Staff Level, Retirements, Turnover, New Hires, and Ending Staff Level, the column letters were adjusted automatically as the copy was carried out, because the cell addresses in these formulas are relative references. A relative reference tells 1-2-3 which cell to use based on its location relative to the cell containing the formula. When you copy a formula that contains a relative reference, 1-2-3 changes the cell references so they refer to cells located in the same position relative to the cell that contains the new copy of the formula, as shown previously in Figure 2-14.

All references in formulas are relative references unless you specify otherwise. Most of the time, you will want to use relative references because you can then copy formulas easily for use in different cells in your worksheet.

From time to time, you might need to create a formula that refers to a cell in a fixed location on the worksheet. A reference that always specifies the same cell when it is copied is an **absolute reference**. Absolute references contain a dollar sign before the column letter and/or the row number. Examples of absolute references include A4 and C27. You will learn more about using absolute references in Tutorial 3.

If you want to take a break and resume the tutorial at a later time, close your worksheet and exit 1-2-3. Make sure you remove your Student Disk from the disk drive. When you want to resume the tutorial, launch 1-2-3 and place your Student Disk in the disk drive. Select the Tutorial 2 SmartIcon palette, open the S2IPS1.WK4 worksheet, and continue with the tutorial.

Creating a Total Column with @SUM

The final step in building the personnel plan is entering the formulas for the Total column. For Retirements, Turnover, and New Hires, Julie needs to add the values for the four quarters to obtain the total for the year. She could enter the formula +B4+C4+D4+E4 in cell F4, but this would be tedious and, even by using pointing, is more prone to error. When you add a range of cells, the @SUM function is your best choice.

Remember from the Guided Tour that a function is a predefined formula built into 1-2-3 with the following format:

@FUNCTION (arguments)

Functions begin with an at sign (@) followed by the name of the function, which describes its purpose. In parentheses following the function name are the arguments. **Arguments** represent the required information that the function needs to do its task. For example, @SUM (B4..E4) means to add the numbers in the range B4 through E4.

In 1-2-3, you can use the @SUM function to create a formula that adds the cells in one specified range. When you have several similar ranges of cells to be summed, you can use the Sum Range SmartIcon to create the @SUM formulas for these ranges in one operation. If you use the Sum Range SmartIcon to create several formulas, you must include a blank cell to the right of or below the range of cells that you want to sum. Lotus 1-2-3 places the @SUM formulas in the blank cells when you use the Sum Range SmartIcon. When you enter a formula that includes the @SUM function in an individual cell, no additional blank cell is required.

Using the Sum Range SmartIcon

You use the Sum Range SmartIcon when you want to sum several ranges in rows or columns at one time. Remember to leave blank cells to the right of or below the ranges containing the cells to be summed. This is a quick method for entering several @SUM functions in a worksheet at one time.

REFERENCE WINDOW

Using the Sum Range SmartIcon

- Select the ranges you want to sum, including the blank cells to the right of *or* below the ranges.
- Click the Sum Range SmartIcon.

Let's enter the @SUM formulas for the four quarter totals for Retirements and Turnover at one time using the Sum Range SmartIcon.

To total the values in rows 4 and 5 using the Sum Range SmartIcon:

❶ Select the range B4..F5, which includes the rows to be summed and the blank cells to the right of the range. See Figure 2-16.

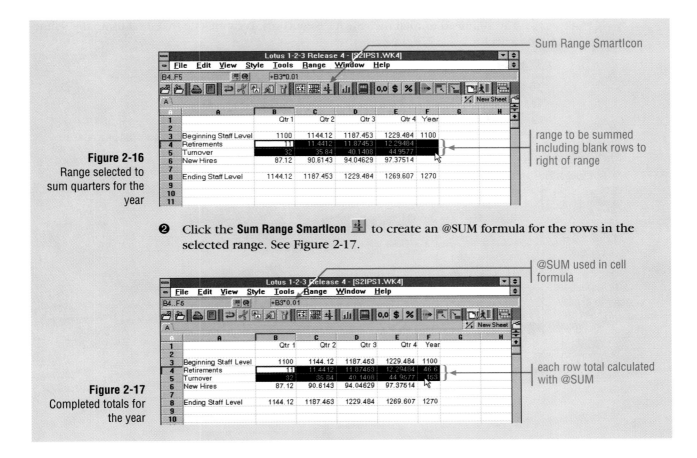

Figure 2-16
Range selected to
sum quarters for the
year

Figure 2-17
Completed totals for
the year

❷ Click the **Sum Range SmartIcon** to create an @SUM formula for the rows in the selected range. See Figure 2-17.

Using the @function Selector

The **@function selector** provides a list of frequently used 1-2-3 functions. This is another method for entering an @SUM formula but does not require a blank cell to the right of or below the range being summed. With this method, you can place the @SUM function anywhere in the worksheet.

You still need to total the row for New Hires. Let's include that total using the @function selector.

To total the values in row 6 using the @function selector:

❶ Click **F6**, the location for the total formula.

❷ Click the **@function selector** ▣ to display a list of 1-2-3 functions. See Figure 2-18. This list contains the more frequently used functions, but you can customize it to include the functions you use the most.

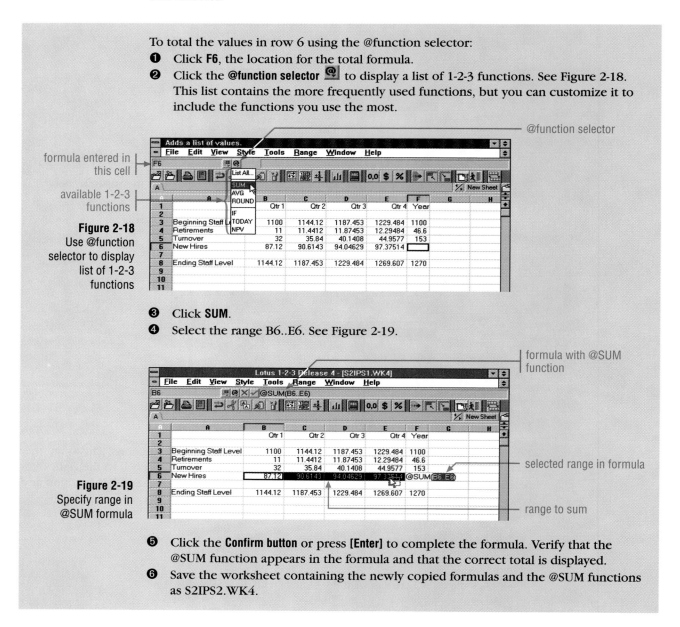

Figure 2-18
Use @function selector to display list of 1-2-3 functions

❸ Click **SUM**.

❹ Select the range B6..E6. See Figure 2-19.

Figure 2-19
Specify range in @SUM formula

❺ Click the **Confirm button** or press **[Enter]** to complete the formula. Verify that the @SUM function appears in the formula and that the correct total is displayed.

❻ Save the worksheet containing the newly copied formulas and the @SUM functions as S2IPS2.WK4.

Next, you need to review your completed worksheet.

Reviewing the Worksheet

Although Julie has completed the calculations for her personnel plan, she is not pleased with the appearance of the worksheet. For instance, the numbers don't include commas and the decimal places should be eliminated. Also, Julie doesn't think the column headings stand out enough from the values.

In this section of the tutorial, you will learn how to improve your worksheet's appearance. Figure 2-20 shows how the worksheet will look when you are finished.

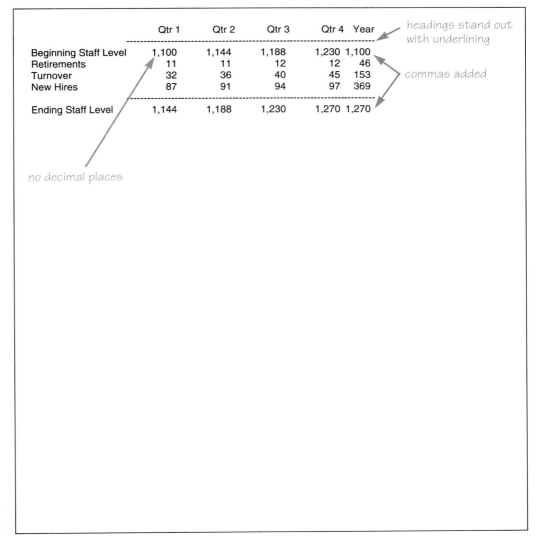

Figure 2-20
Final version of
Julie's worksheet

Changing Appearance with Number Formats

The way in which a number is displayed in a cell is called the cell's **format**. You change how 1-2-3 displays numbers by using the Number Format command or by typing special data editing characters, such as commas and currency symbols, as you enter the numbers.

Unless you specify otherwise, 1-2-3 displays numbers with the **General format**, which uses a minus sign for negative values, no thousands separator, and no trailing zeros to the right of the decimal point. The number of decimals displayed is determined by 1-2-3 depending on the value in a cell and the column width. Lotus 1-2-3 provides several formats that change the appearance of numbers in the worksheet. Figure 2-21 describes the number formats available in 1-2-3 with examples of these formats for both positive and negative numbers. These examples illustrate the display of negative numbers, thousands separators, currency symbols, percent symbols, dates, and times when the number 1234.5678 is entered in a cell.

Format Type (decimals specified)	Cell Display	Description
General	1234.5678 –1234.5678	Displays numbers with a minus sign for negatives, no commas to separate thousands, and no trailing zeros to the right of the decimal point. Decimal places selected automatically depending on value and column width.
Fixed (2)	1234.57 –1234.57	Displays numbers with two places to the right of the decimal, a minus sign for negatives, and a leading zero for decimal values.
, Comma (2)	1,234.57 (1,234.57)	Displays numbers with commas to separate thousands, two places to the right of the decimal, and parentheses for negatives.
Currency (2)	$1,234.57 ($1,234.57)	Displays numbers with a currency symbol, commas to separate thousands, two places to the right of the decimal, and parentheses for negatives.
Percent (1)	123456.8% –123456.8%	Multiplies a number by 100, then displays it with the percent sign and one place to the right of the decimal.
Scientific (2)	1.23E+03 –1.23E+03	Displays numbers as a power of 10 with one place to the left of the decimal. "E" is used to indicate the power of 10.
Hidden	value not displayed	Does not display data in the worksheet area, but the data does exist in the cell.
Text	+B1	Displays the formula rather than the calculated results.
Date	21-Dec-94	Displays the date in one of five different available formats.
Time	11:59 AM	Displays the time in one of four different available formats.
Automatic	When $1234 is entered, Currency is assigned, while 10/26/94 is recognized as a date format	Default 1-2-3 format that displays a number in a format you enter it in. Lotus 1-2-3 determines the format as General, Comma, Currency, Percent, Scientific, Date, or Time depending on how you enter the number.
Reset	default format selected	Returns the format to the default worksheet setting.

Figure 2-21
Selected 1-2-3
number formats

Lotus 1-2-3's initial default format for numbers is the Automatic format. The **Automatic format** is different from the other format types available in 1-2-3 because the determination of how a number is displayed depends on the way you enter the number into a cell. Lotus 1-2-3 automatically assigns a format to a number depending on the data editing characters you type. For example, typing a comma in a number as you enter it will assign the cell the Comma format. If you don't use any data editing characters, then the cell is displayed using the General format.

You can change the way numbers are displayed in Julie's worksheet. Because commas would make the numbers more legible, you can apply the Comma format to the numbers in the worksheet.

Formatting Numbers in Cells

- Click the cell or select the range of cells to be formatted.
- Click the Comma format, Currency format, or Percent format SmartIcon.

or

Click the number format selector in the status bar and select the format you want.

or

Click the right mouse button to display the Quick menu, click Number Format, then choose one of the available formatting options.

Adding the Comma Format

Let's improve the appearance of Julie's personnel plan by applying the Comma format to the values in her worksheet using the Comma Format SmartIcon.

To apply the Comma format using the Comma Format SmartIcon:

❶ Select the range B3..F8 to indicate the cells you want to format.

❷ Click the **Comma Format SmartIcon** [0,0] . The numbers are displayed with commas and no decimal places. See Figure 2-22. Notice that the comma appears in the worksheet but not in the cell contents box. Number formats do not change a cell's content or how its value is used in any calculations; number formats only affect how a number is displayed in the worksheet.

number containing data editing character

decimal places selector

number format selector

Figure 2-22
Numbers displayed with Comma format

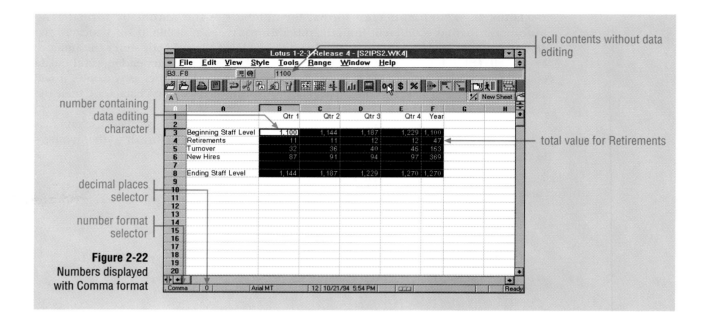

cell contents without data editing

total value for Retirements

Julie notices that the total value for Retirements is off by one. The numbers displayed for each of the four quarters should add to a total of 46, *not* 47 as displayed (see Figure 2-22). This apparent error stems from how numbers are rounded by 1-2-3 when they are displayed. Julie wants to take a closer look at the values used in calculating the year total by displaying the values for the retirements with two decimal places. To do this, she needs to use the decimal places selector (see Figure 2-22).

REFERENCE WINDOW

Formatting the Number of Decimal Places

- Select the range you want to format.
- Click the decimal places selector in the status bar.
- Select the appropriate number of decimal places from the list.

Let's use the decimal places selector in the status bar to change the number of decimal places displayed for the Retirements values.

To change the number of decimal places displayed for Retirements:
❶ Select the range B4..F4 to indicate the cells you want to format.
❷ Click the **decimal places selector** to display the list of available options. See Figure 2-23.

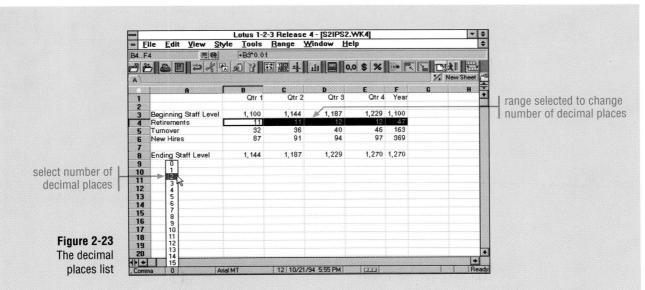

range selected to change
number of decimal places

select number of
decimal places

Figure 2-23
The decimal
places list

❸ Click **2**. The Retirements values are displayed with two decimals, and in the status
bar the decimal places selector displays "2." See Figure 2-24. Notice how the number of decimal places for the quarterly retirement values affects the number calculated for the year. When these values were displayed as integers, 1-2-3 rounded the
values up to 47, causing the rounding error.

TROUBLE? If you accidentally select the wrong number of decimal places, repeat Steps 2
and 3.

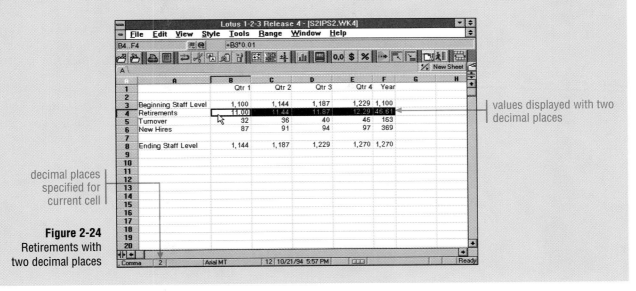

values displayed with two
decimal places

decimal places
specified for
current cell

Figure 2-24
Retirements with
two decimal places

Just as the commas didn't affect the cells' contents, the number of decimal places displayed does not affect the calculations in your worksheet. Number formats do not alter a
cell's content, *only* its appearance. However, Julie's numbers for Retirements were displayed initially as integers, which the Comma format appeared to add incorrectly.

Julie isn't happy with the number of decimal places for Retirements. It doesn't make sense to have 11.44 people. She wants these numbers displayed as integers, without any decimal places. Let's use the decimal places selector to return the Retirements values to integers.

To display the Retirements values as integers:
❶ Select the range B4..F4 to indicate the cells you want to format.
❷ Click the **decimal places selector** to display the list of available options, then click **0**.

The numbers in Julie's worksheet are displayed as integers with the Comma format and no decimals. But the rounding problem still causes an error in the total Retirements for the year. Julie wants to correct the problem so that the integers displayed for the Retirements are the values that are added for the year's total.

Rounding Results

The rounding problem Julie experienced is not unique to 1-2-3 or other spreadsheet programs. It occurs throughout all computing applications. The @ROUND function in 1-2-3 is a convenient method for fixing this problem, so that the displayed results are the same as those used in other calculations. The syntax of the @ROUND function is:

@ROUND(*formula to be calculated, places to right of decimal*)

In general, the @ROUND function has two arguments—a formula to be calculated and the number of decimal places.

You should consider using the @ROUND function with a formula whenever you want to control the calculated number of decimal places, and the formula contains (1) multiplication by a fraction, (2) a division, (3) an exponentiation, or (4) another function that might calculate a fractional result.

You can fix the rounding problem in Julie's worksheet by adding the @ROUND function to the formulas in cells B4 through E4. You can include the @ROUND function in a cell formula by entering it when you initially create the formula or by editing an existing formula to add this function. Let's reenter the formula in cell B4 so it includes rounding.

To reenter the formula in cell **B4** with the @ROUND function:
❶ Click **B4**, which is the cell where you want to enter the formula with the @ROUND function.
❷ Click the **@function selector** 🔳 to display the list of available functions.
❸ Click **ROUND**.
❹ Click **B3** to include the cell in the formula.
❺ Type ***.01,** (the arithmetic operator and numeric constant needed to complete the formula to be calculated).
❻ Move the edit cursor to the "n," which is the temporary argument for the number of decimal places, press **[Del]**, then type **0** to indicate no decimal places.
❼ Press **[Enter]** or click the **Confirm button** to complete the formula. The formula now appears in the cell contents box as @ROUND(B3*.01,0).

When you include rounding for cell B4, is this rounding automatically applied to the formulas in cells C4 through E4, which were previously copied from cell B4? No; once a copy is complete, 1-2-3 does *not* remember that a formula was copied to a cell. As a result, Julie's formula with rounding needs to be copied from cell B4 to the range C4..E4. Let's fix the other formulas for Retirements by copying the formula with the @ROUND function to cells C4 through E4.

To copy the formula with rounding to the other cells:
❶ Select the range B4..E4 in preparation for using the Copy Current Cell SmartIcon because a single cell is being copied.
❷ Click the **Copy Current Cell SmartIcon** 📊. The rounded Retirements values for the four quarters are calculated and displayed. See Figure 2-25.

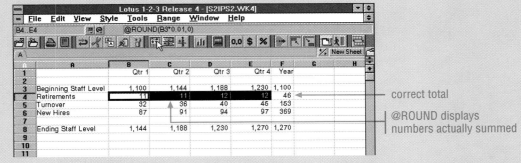

Figure 2-25
Results displayed using @ROUND function

Now Julie's worksheet displays the correctly formatted results she wants.
❸ Save the worksheet as S2IPS3.WK4.

Julie has the results she wants. With the rounding problem fixed, the numbers displayed are the ones actually used in the other calculations. Whenever you need to make the number of decimal places displayed match the number used in other calculations, you should consider using the @ROUND function.

Adding Underlining

Julie wants to underline the column headings and the values above the Ending Staff Level to make her worksheet more legible. Lotus 1-2-3 provides several methods of underlining. You can place the underline in a separate row using the minus sign, or you can include the underline in the same cell as the label or value. In Tutorial 3, you will underline within the cell. Here, let's create an underline in a separate cell.

REFERENCE WINDOW   **Adding Underlining**

- Click the cell where you want the underlining.
- Type a backslash followed by a minus sign (\-).
- Select the other cells in the row where you want the underlining.
- Click the Copy Current Cell SmartIcon to complete the underlining.

Let's complete Julie's worksheet by adding this underlining as specified in her sketch (Figure 2-2).

To add underlining below the column headings and above the values for **Ending Staff Level**:

❶ Click **B2**.

❷ Type \- to fill the cell with the minus sign and create the underline for the column headings. See Figure 2-26.

TROUBLE? If you place the underline in the wrong row, use the Undo SmartIcon 🔄 to reverse this action then repeat Steps 1 and 2.

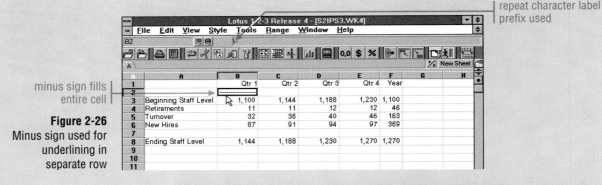

Figure 2-26
Minus sign used for underlining in separate row

❸ Copy the contents of cell B2 to C2..F2 to complete the column heading underlining.

❹ Copy the contents of the range B2..F2 to cell B7 to create the underline above the Ending Staff Level values. See Figure 2-27. This completes Julie's personnel plan worksheet as specified by her design.

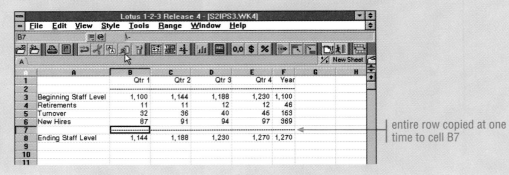

Figure 2-27
Julie's completed personnel plan worksheet

You have built a worksheet and improved its appearance. Now, to complete your work, you can preview the worksheet, print it, and save it.

To preview, print, and save the personnel planning worksheet:
❶ Preview and print the worksheet.
❷ Save the worksheet as S2IPS4.WK4.

■   ■   ■

Julie meets with Ricardo to discuss the completed personnel plan for IPS. Ricardo is impressed with her work and approves the worksheet. IPS now has a plan for hiring temporaries during the next four quarters.

Questions

1. Which SmartIcon lets you complete a sequence of numbers or month names in a specified cell range?
   a. [icon]
   b. [icon]
   c. [icon]
   d. [icon]

2. This is a preferred method of entering formulas because it usually reduces your chances of making a mistake:
   a. typing
   b. pointing
   c. editing
   d. formatting

3. Suppose you place the cell pointer in cell D9, which is empty. The format selector in the status bar displays "Automatic." If you enter $1,234.53 in this cell, what format does 1-2-3 assign to this cell?
   a. Comma
   b. General
   c. Percent
   d. Currency

4. You want to use the Sum Range SmartIcon to place the @SUM function in cell C16, which totals the data values in the range C8..C15. Which cell or cells need to be empty in order for you to use this SmartIcon?
   a. C16
   b. C7
   c. D8..D15
   d. D16

5. The number -2345.678 is displayed in the cell contents box for cell H21. The format and decimal place selectors show the current format as Fixed with 2 decimal places. What appears in cell H21?
   a. 2345.678
   b. -2,345.68
   c. ($2,345.68)
   d. -2345.68

6. If you enter the number 1009.276 in cell E19, what is the cell's format if the following appears in cell E19 in the worksheet?
   a. 100927.6%
   b. $1,009
   c. 1,009.28
   d. 1009.3

7. Which of these formulas adds five cells in row 4?
   a. +D3+D4+D5+D6+D7
   b. @SUM(B3..E3)
   c. @SUM(C4..C8)
   d. +J4+K4+L4+M4+N4

8. You just opened your worksheet file, and asterisks appear in all the cells in column B, which contains numeric values and formulas. Which is the most appropriate action for you to take?
   a. Exit from 1-2-3, relaunch 1-2-3, and reopen the file.
   b. Use the resize pointer to increase the column width to display values for these cells.
   c. Select the column, then change the format to Currency with 5 decimal places.
   d. Select the column, then delete the current cell contents.

E

9. Using the Task Reference, determine the number of different ways that you can do the same task as those performed with the following SmartIcons. Write down at least one other method for each SmartIcon:
   a.
   b. 0,0
   c.
   d.

Tutorial Assignments

Launch 1-2-3, if necessary, and insert your Student Disk in the disk drive. Open the T2RCL1.WK4 worksheet for Royal Coach Limousine. Review this worksheet, then do the following.

1. Complete the sequence of column titles for the four quarters of the year in row 5.

2. Trips are expected to grow by 8% per quarter. Using the pointing method, enter the formula that calculates trips for the second quarter.

3. The fare per trip is expected to increase by $6 each quarter. Use pointing to enter the formula that calculates the fare per trip for the second quarter.

4. The formulas that calculate revenues, expenses, and gross profit are:

   Revenues = Trips * Fare per Trip
   Expenses = Revenues * .85
   Gross profit = Revenues - Expenses

   Use pointing to enter these formulas for the first quarter and include the @ROUND function to round to 0 decimal places in calculating the expenses. Why is it a good idea to use rounding for the expense calculation?

5. Copy the formulas for trips and fare per trip from the second quarter to the other two quarters.
6. Copy the formulas for revenues, expenses, and gross profit from the first quarter to the other three quarters using the Quick menu.
7. Place a formula in the Total column to sum each of the trips, revenues, expenses, and gross profit planning items. (*Hint:* If the total gross profit is $12,885, you have entered the formulas correctly.)
8. Use pointing to enter a formula that calculates the average fare per trip in the total column. You want the average instead of the sum of the data for four quarters, because summing the fare per trip has little meaning and a different number of trips occurs in each quarter at a different fare per trip. The average is calculated by dividing the total revenues by the total trips. (*Hint:* If the total fare per trip equals 60, you have entered the formula correctly.)
9. Format the planning item data values as follows:

	Format	Decimals
Trips	Fixed	0
Fare per Trip	Fixed	0
Revenues	Currency	0
Expenses	Comma	0
Gross Profit	Currency	0

10. Place underlining in the row below the column headings and in the row above the gross profit amounts.
11. Preview and print the Projected Income report. Save the worksheet as S2RCL2.WK4.
12. What if the number of trips in the first quarter increases to 360 while the fare per trip goes up to $54? What is the total gross profit? Print a copy of this what-if analysis and draw a circle around the total gross profit amount. Is this a significant increase in gross profit? Explain your answer.

E 13. What if the trips and fare per trip remain at the what-if values from Assignment 12, and the expenses ratio changes from .85 to .81 for all four quarters? What is the total gross profit? Edit the formula for expenses in the first quarter to change the expense ratio, then copy this formula to the other three quarters. Print a copy of this what-if analysis, and draw a circle around the total gross profit. Explain the change in total gross profit.

Next, open the file S2IPS4.WK4. (If you did not build this worksheet by completing the steps in this tutorial, you need to build it before you continue with this Assignment.) Review the formulas for Retirements, Turnover, and New Hires, which contain the growth rate and ratios data values that need to be changed in preparing the what-if analysis.

E 14. Edit the Retirements formula in cell B4 and enter a new Retirements rate of 2%. When you complete editing this cell, are the formulas automatically changed in columns C, D, and E? Explain your answer.
15. If necessary, copy the revised formula from cell B4 to the other three columns.
16. Using editing and copying, change the formula for Turnover to include a growth rate of 14% and change the New Hires ratio to 10%. Be careful not to destroy the data value in cell B5.

E 17. Turnover and New Hires consist of formulas that benefit from the use of the @ROUND function. For these two planning items, which formulas should have rounding included? Why? Using editing and copying, revise these formulas. By adding rounding, are any results changed? Which ones?
18. Preview and print Julie's what-if analysis of the personnel plan. Save the worksheet as S2IPS5.WK4.
19. Compare the results of the what-if analysis to the results from the original plan. Circle the Ending Staff Level for the year on both plans.

E 20. If the Ending Staff Level for the what-if analysis is greater than the level indicated on the original plan, then the revised personnel plan meets the needs of IPS for their continued growth. Does the what-if revision meet this need?

Case Problems

1. New Venture Planning for Paradise Hills Golf Club

Paradise Hills Golf Club (PHG) is a public golf course in the northwest region of North Carolina. Paradise Hills offers championship-quality golf at a moderate cost. Over its 40 years of existence, PHG has hosted five Professional Golf Association and Ladies Professional Golf Association events. The attracting feature of PHG is that the golf course can be enjoyed by all levels of golfers, whether they are beginners or professionals.

Jerry Tate is part-owner and club professional at PHG. Jerry has just recently returned from a business trip to Scottsdale, Arizona where he met with a group of golf course designers. Jerry and the other owners of PHG would like to build a second, more challenging 18-hole course to attract more golfers to PHG. The golf course designers stressed to Jerry that they would like to have at least 50% of the projected $3 million building cost before they start building the new course next November. Jerry and his partners would like to finance this up-front cost through the upcoming season's operating income. In order to give the designers the approval to start the preliminary sketches, Jerry and the other PHG owners need to find out if they will be able to generate enough income to pay the $1.5 million up-front costs.

Jerry asks Tonya Mills, the bookkeeper at PHG, to build a worksheet in 1-2-3 to forecast this season's revenues and expenses. Tonya begins by sketching the Forecasted Operating Income worksheet shown in Figure 2-28.

	A	B	C	D	...	G	H
4		May	Jun	Jul	...	Oct	Season
5					...		
6	Rounds	4500	5100	5400	...	3300	@SUM(B6..G6)
7	Fee Per Round	32	+B7	+C7	...	+F7	@SUM(B7..G7)
8					...		
9	Revenues				...		
10	Greens Fees	+B6*B7	+C6*C7	+D6*D7	...	+G6*G7	@SUM(B10..G10)
11	Pro Shop Sales	+B10*0.56	+C10*0.56	+D10*0.56	...	+G10*0.56	@SUM(B11..G11)
12	Club House Revenue	+B10*0.77	+C10*0.77	+D10*0.77	...	+G10*0.77	@SUM(B12..G12)
13	Total Revenues	@SUM(B10..B12)	@SUM(C10..C12)	@SUM(D10..D12)	...	@SUM(G10..G12)	@SUM(B13..G13)
14					...		
15	Expenses				...		
16	Grounds Care	28000	+B16	+C16	...	+F16	@SUM(B16..G16)
17	Pro Shop Costs	+B11*0.6	+C11*0.6	+D11*0.6	...	+G11*0.6	@SUM(B17..G17)
18	Food & Beverages	+B12*0.4	+C12*0.4	+D12*0.4	...	+G12*0.4	@SUM(B18..G18)
19	Total Expenses	@SUM(B16..B18)	@SUM(C16..C18)	@SUM(D16..D18)	...	@SUM(G16..G18)	@SUM(B19..G19)
20					...		
21	Operating Income	+B13–B19	+C13–C19	+D13–D19	...	+G13–G19	@SUM(B21..G21)
22					...		

Figure 2-28

Retrieve Tonya's worksheet and perform the following:

1. Launch 1-2-3 and open the P2PHG1.WK4 worksheet file. Review the worksheet Tonya started by looking at the planning items, column headings, and numeric constants. Study the rough sketch design and notice that columns E and F are calculated using formulas that do the same arithmetic as those for June, July, and October.

2 Plan the work you will do.
   a. List the cell addresses of the formulas you will enter by pointing.
   b. List the cell addresses of the formulas you will place in the worksheet by copying.
   c. List the cell addresses of the formulas you will enter in the worksheet using the @SUM function.

3. Complete the Forecasted Operating Income worksheet by adding the formulas and underlines from Figure 2-28. Complete the sequence of column headings for six months in row 4. Use pointing to enter the formulas you listed in Problem 2-a. Copy the formulas you listed in Problem 2-b into the appropriate cells. Enter the @SUM formulas that calculate the desired totals. Add underlining to the worksheet as specified by the sketch. (*Hint:* Operating income for the season is 1,304,890.)

4. Format all the numeric constants using the Comma format with no decimals. Change the format for the greens fees and operating income items so they include the currency symbol. If necessary, increase the width of column H to display the total for the season.

5. Which formulas should include the @ROUND function? Why? Modify these formulas to include rounding in their calculations.

6. Save the worksheet as S2PHG2.WK4. Preview and print the Forecasted Operating Income report.

7. Using the current forecasts, will PHG earn enough to pay the up-front cost of building an additional 18 holes?

8. Prepare a what-if analysis where the rounds in August and September each increase by 400. Print a copy of this what-if analysis. Does this meet the requirements for PHG's owners?

E 9. Perform a what-if analysis adjusting the fee per round until PHG's requirements are met. Save the worksheet as S2PHG3.WK4. Print the report. What is the fee per round?

E 10. Compare the results of both what-if analyses. Which change had a bigger effect on operating income, rounds or fee per round, and why? At a fee per round of $35, would PHG earn enough to pay the up-front cost?

2. Budget Variance Analysis for Safety-Lite Industries

Safety-Lite Industries (SLI) is a leading manufacturer of automotive sealed-beam head lamps, tail-lamp assemblies, and related plastic molded parts. One example of SLI's products is the rear deck stop and turn signal for the Ford Escort. SLI's advanced plastic molding processes allow them to use nearly 50% of recycled plastics in the parts they manufacture while maintaining their high-quality production standards.

Travis Walker, vice president of Marketing for SLI, is concerned with monitoring SLI's marketing expenses. He received a worksheet from SLI's Accounting Department containing the budget and actual expenses for last year. The Accounting Department staff prepared the summary worksheet by extracting the data from their general ledger system and creating the 1-2-3 worksheet file. Travis wants a variance analysis included as part of the expense report to determine those accounts that require further investigation. A variance analysis is the difference between the estimated budget costs and the recorded actual costs. He asks Bridget Sheehan, a newly hired marketing analyst in his department, to prepare the variance report from the worksheet received from the

Accounting Department. Bridget is familiar with using 1-2-3 to prepare special reports like the one Travis wants. She discusses the details of the report with Travis. For each account he wants to see the variance as a dollar amount and as a percent of budget. These are calculated as follows:

Variance = Budget – Actual
Percent Variance = Variance / Budget

Complete the variance report for Travis using the formulas specified by Bridget.

1. Launch 1-2-3 and open the worksheet P2SLI1.WK4, which contains the data obtained from the Accounting Department. Review the content and arrangement of data in the worksheet.
2. Use pointing to enter the formulas to calculate the variance and percent variance for the first expense in the worksheet, which is located in row 9.
3. Copy these formulas down the rows for each of the other expense items including the total marketing expenses. Rows that do not contain an expense item should not include a formula. If you happen to copy formulas to these rows, delete the unwanted formulas.
4. Use the @SUM function and pointing to enter formulas for each of the following expense category totals: Total Salaries, Total Other Expenses, and Total Taxes. Enter these formulas in the Budget column and then copy them into the Actual and Variance columns.

E
5. Use pointing to enter the formula for the total marketing expenses, which is the sum of the total salaries, total other expenses, and total taxes. Why can't you use the @SUM function with a cell range for this calculation?
6. Format the Budget, Actual, and Variance columns using the Comma format with no decimals.
7. Format the first expense item and total marketing expenses using the Currency format with no decimal places in the Budget, Actual, and Variance columns. Now, the currency symbol, which Travis requested, appears.
8. Format the Percent Variance column using the Percent format with one decimal place for all expense items.
9. Place an underline in the row between total taxes and total marketing expenses.
10. Preview and print the variance report for Travis. Save the worksheet as S2SLI2.WK4.
11. Mary Lou from the Accounting Department just phoned to advise you of an adjustment in the actual amount of advertising and promotion. This value should be 81932. Perform a what-if analysis by changing this value. Print the revised worksheet. Were all the cells affected by the adjusted advertising and promotion expense recalculated? What effect does the change have on the marketing expense variance and percent variance?
12. Review the variance report. Which three accounts have the largest variance and which have the largest percent variance? Circle these six values on the printed copy of the report.

E
13. Is a positive variance good or bad? Why? Using Total Salaries and Automobile Expenses as examples, write a paragraph explaining your answer.

3. Capacity Planning for Mobile One Industries

Mobile One Industries (MOI) produces technologically enhanced wheelchairs for the mobility-impaired. By combining space-age materials with advanced manufacturing processes, MOI products are more affordable. MOI manufactures three different models that are ergonomically designed to provide the best mobility and comfort:

- Generalwheels—a basic utility model designed for all around use
- Execuwheels—a luxury model designed for office use
- Sportswheels—a lightweight, stripped-down model designed for road-race competition

MOI produces all three models in a manufacturing plant that is designed to accommodate the needs of the physically challenged workers they employ.

MOI is experiencing explosive growth as the number of orders increases each quarter. Melissa Pei, manager of Manufacturing Operations, is concerned with MOI's ability to handle the increasing number of orders. She is responsible for organizing operations into two manufacturing cells—fabrication and assembly. A manufacturing cell consists of a work team that turns out complete units. The fabrication cell does plastic molding and metal shaping, whereas the assembly cell does the final assembly of each chair. Melissa needs to know when the design capacity of the current manufacturing cells will be exceeded so she can plan to upgrade their production equipment.

Gary Shibata just completed his first year with MOI as an intern in the Human Resources Department, where he gained experience with 1-2-3 and accepted the job offer as a production planner. Melissa is looking forward to working with Gary. He won last year's Seaway Race and thoroughly tested MOI's Sportswheels. While working with Melissa, Gary made notes on the definitions of their planning items (Figure 2-29). When finished with that, he sketched their manufacturing capacity planning worksheet (Figure 2-30 on the following page). In Figure 2-30, columns E, F, G, and H are calculated using formulas that do the same arithmetic as those for columns C, D, and I.

Assoc hours per month—8 hours per day, 22 days per month, 25% allowance for personal time
Standard hours per order—the usual number of hours to complete the production operations in the manufacturing work cell
Design capacity—the number of orders the manufacturing work cell is designed to produce under normal circumstances
Capacity used—the current number of orders produced by the manufacturing work cell
Capacity cushion—the unused capacity of the manufacturing work cell, calculated as the difference between the design capacity and the capacity used
Capacity utilization—a measure of the extent to which the capacity is actually used, calculated by dividing the capacity used by the design capacity
Associates—the number of employees needed to staff the manufacturing work cell with monthly hours converted to the number of hours per employee per quarter

Figure 2-29

	A	B	C	D	⋯	I	J
4	ASSUMPTIONS						
5	Order growth rate	0.06	+B5	+C5	⋯	+H5	
6	Assoc hours per month	8*22*0.75	+B6	+C6	⋯	+H6	
7					⋯		
8	PROJECTIONS	|------------------------------- Year 1 -------------------------|			⋯		
9		Qtr 1	Qtr 2	Qtr 3	⋯	Qtr 4	Total
10		---					
11	Number of orders	1800	+B11*(1+C5)	+C11*(1+D5)	⋯	+H11*(1+I5)	@SUM(B11..I11)
12					⋯		
13	Fabrication (Mfg cell 1)				⋯		
14	Standard hours per order	3.5	+B14	+C14	⋯	+H14	
15	Design capacity	2100	2100	2100	⋯	2100	
16	Capacity used	+B11	+C11	+D11	⋯	+I11	
17	Capacity cushion	+B15–B16	+C15–C16	+D15–D16	⋯	+I15–I16	
18	Capacity utilization	+B16/B15	+C16/C15	+D16/D15	⋯	+I16/I15	
19	Associates	+B16/(B6*3/B14)	+C16/(C6*3/C14)	+D16/(D6*3/D14)	⋯	+I16/(I6*3/I14)	+I19
20					⋯		
21	Assembly (Mfg cell 2)				⋯		
22	Standard hours per order	1.2	+B22	+C22	⋯	+H22	
23	Design capacity	2500	2500	2500	⋯	2500	
24	Capacity used	+B11	+C11	+D11	⋯	+I11	
25	Capacity cushion	+B23–B24	+C23–C24	+D23–D24	⋯	+I23–I24	
26	Capacity utilization	+B24/B23	+C24/C23	+D24/D23	⋯	+I24/I23	
27	Associates	+B24/(B6*3/B22)	+C24/(C6*3/C22)	+D24/(D6*3/D22)	⋯	+I24/(I6*3/I22)	+I27
28					⋯		
29	Total Associates	+B19+B27	+C19+C27	+D19+D27	⋯	+I19+I27	+I29
30					⋯		

Figure 2-30

With Melissa's approval, Gary started creating the P2MOI1.WK4 worksheet, which is arranged with separate areas for assumptions and projections. Gary entered the labels and data values for the eight-quarter plan. Complete the manufacturing capacity planning worksheet by performing the following:

1. Launch 1-2-3 and open the worksheet P2MOI1.WK4, which contains the Manufacturing Capacity Plan. Review the content and organization of the data in this worksheet.
2. Plan the work you need to do. On a piece of paper, list the cell addresses of the formulas you will enter by pointing. Then list the cell addresses of the formulas you will place in the worksheet by copying.
3. Complete the sequence of column headings for the eight quarters in row 9. Which headings appear for the second year?
4. Use pointing to enter the formulas you listed in Problem 2.
5. Copy the formulas listed in Problem 2 into the appropriate cells. (*Hint:* Total associates for the Total column is 32.1.)
6. Enter the @SUM function in the Total column.
7. Add underlining to the worksheet as indicated by the sketch.
8. Format the worksheet as follows:
    Percent 0—Order Growth Rate, Capacity Utilization
    Fixed 1—Standard Hours per Order, Associates, Total Associates
    Comma 0—Number of Orders, Design Capacity, Capacity Used, Capacity Cushion

9. Preview and print the Manufacturing Capacity Plan. Save the worksheet as S2MOI2.WK4.

E   10. Review the results.

  a. Is additional production capacity required?

  b. How do you know that additional capacity is needed?

  c. In which manufacturing cell is additional capacity needed? When will it be needed?

  d. Circle the capacity cushion and capacity utilization items in the quarter in which additional capacity is required.

E   11. Prepare a what-if analysis where the order growth rate is changed to 9%. In this worksheet, when you change the growth rate percentage in column B, it is changed automatically in the other seven quarters. Why? Print a copy of this what-if analysis. Now, when is additional capacity needed in each of the manufacturing cells? Circle the results as you did in Problem 10.

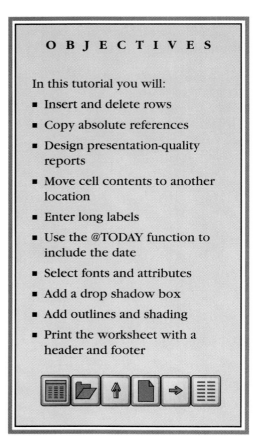

OBJECTIVES

In this tutorial you will:

- Insert and delete rows
- Copy absolute references
- Design presentation-quality reports
- Move cell contents to another location
- Enter long labels
- Use the @TODAY function to include the date
- Select fonts and attributes
- Add a drop shadow box
- Add outlines and shading
- Print the worksheet with a header and footer

Enhancing the Worksheet and Producing Reports

Creating a Five-Year Plan

CASE **Michigan Special Olympics** Each year several thousand athletes converge on the campus of Central Michigan University for the Summer Games of the Michigan Special Olympics. To commemorate the Special Olympics' 25th year, Jeremy Farnan is the Michigan Special Olympics Inspirational Athlete of the Year and is pictured on Wheaties* cereal boxes. His smile is a powerful message to all special Olympians and their supporters.

Lisa Russo is one such supporter. She recently accepted a position with the Michigan Special Olympics (MSO) as an accounting associate. It was important for her to become a part of this organization because her younger brother participates in the games each year and she values what the organization stands for. In her new job, Lisa assists Mary Williams, the executive director, with the preparation of the budget.

In the Guided Tour you learned that a budget is a plan for managing revenues and expenditures for a specific amount of time. **Revenues** are a source of income, whereas **expenditures** are outlays of

---

* Wheaties is a registered trademark of General Mills, Inc.

money. By subtracting expenditures from revenues, you discover the **bottom line**, or the line at the bottom of a financial statement that indicates the company's financial condition. A **surplus** exists when revenues are greater than expenditures, whereas a **deficit** occurs when expenditures are larger than revenues. Lisa and Mary meet to discuss the requirements for the budget. Mary explains that she wants to prepare a five-year plan. Although the budget for the upcoming year is of most concern, Mary wants to develop a plan for the future as she prepares for this year's games. That way she can make arrangements for future commitments while she secures the support for this year's activities.

Mary explains to Lisa how revenues for MSO are obtained from the sponsors, participant fees, and donations from fund-raiser activities. Athletes and their chaperones each pay a $45 participation fee for the Summer Games. There are usually two chaperones for every five athletes. That is, the number of participants involved in the games is about 1.4 times the number of athletes. The single largest expenditure for the game events is for the meals and lodging for the athletes and their chaperones. The other expenditures are typical business expenses.

After collecting the necessary data for the revenues and expenditures in this year's budget, Lisa and Mary discuss the expected changes for the next four years. Lisa returns to her office and prepares her planning analysis sheet and worksheet sketch for the five-year plan. Using her planning analysis sheet and sketch, Lisa prepares a first draft of the plan (Figure 3-1), which she will present at tomorrow's meeting with Mary.

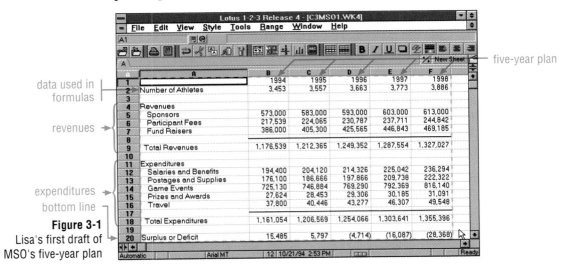

Figure 3-1
Lisa's first draft of MSO's five-year plan

Mary is pleased with Lisa's plan. However, she has new information that Lisa needs to add to the worksheet. Mary explains that MSO will begin receiving telephone marketing revenues from DialAmerica Marketing. For every magazine subscription DialAmerica sells, a percentage of the subscription cost goes to MSO. Mary plans to use these revenues to fund special events during the year that help prepare athletes for the Summer Games. Mary gives Lisa the additional data for the telemarketing revenues and special events expenditures.

After the meeting, Lisa returns to her office and thinks about revising the worksheet. She needs to add the telemarketing and special events data. However, she knows that Mary wants to explore what-if alternatives for these values for the next four years. If Lisa uses these values in formulas, she will have to edit the formulas each time Mary tries a different what-if analysis. Therefore, Lisa wants to add some of the data to the key assumption area in her worksheet. The **key assumption area** is a section of the worksheet that contains data values that are referenced in formulas rather than referencing numeric constants. For example, Lisa has already entered the number of athletes for the next five years—this is considered key assumption data (Figure 3-1). From the meeting, Lisa knows that Mary assumes the growth rate for the telemarketing revenues will be 4% and Lisa has estimated the special events fee per athlete for the next four years. Because this information can change, Lisa wants to separate it from the rest of the worksheet.

Lisa begins the revision by editing her original planning analysis sheet (Figure 3-2) and adding only the new information to her worksheet sketch (Figure 3-3). Let's review Lisa's changes.

Planning Analysis Sheet

My goal:
Develop a five-year plan of expected revenues and expenditures

What results do I want to see?
Each revenue and expenditure for the next five years

What information do I need?
Columns are 1994, 1995, 1996, 1997, 1998
Number of athletes for 1994 (3,453)
Sponsors revenues for 1994 (573,000)
Fee per participant (45)
Fund raisers revenues for 1994 (386,000)
Telemarketing for 1994 (147840)
Salaries and benefits for 1994 (194400)
Postage and supplies for 1994 (176100)
Game cost per participant (145)
Prizes and awards per athlete (8)
Travel for 1994 (37800)
Annual growth rate in athletes (3%)
Annual increase in sponsors revenues (10000)
Annual growth rate in fund raisers revenues (5%)
Annual growth rate in telemarketing (4%)
Annual growth rate in postage and supplies (6%)
Special events fee per athlete by year (34, 35, 37, 38, 41)
Annual growth rate in travel (7%)

What calculations will I perform?
Number of athletes = 3453, previous year value * (1 + .03)
Sponsors = 673000, previous year value + 10000
Participant fees = number of athletes * 1.4 * 45
Fund raisers = 386000, previous year value * (1 + .05)
Telemarketing = 147840, previous year value * (1 + telemarketing growth rate)
Total revenue = sum of revenues
Salaries and benefits = 194400, previous year value * (1 + .05)
Postage and supplies = 176100, previous year value * (1 + .06)
Games events = number of athletes * 1.4 * 145
Prizes and awards = number of athletes * 8
Special events = number of athletes * special event fee per athlete
Travel = 37800, previous year value * (1 + .07)
Total expenditures = sum of expenditures
Surplus or deficit = total revenues - total expenditures

Figure 3-2
Changes to Lisa's planning analysis sheet

	1994	1995	1996	1997	1998
Key Assumptions:					

Telemarketing Growth Rate	0.04				
Special Events Fee per Athlete	34	35	37	38	41
Number of Athletes	XXX,XXX	XXX,XXX	XXX,XXX	XXX,XXX	XXX,XXX
Revenues					
Sponsors	XXX,XXX	XXX,XXX	XXX,XXX	XXX,XXX	XXX,XXX
Participant Fees	XXX,XXX	XXX,XXX	XXX,XXX	XXX,XXX	XXX,XXX
Fund Raisers	XXX,XXX	XXX,XXX	XXX,XXX	XXX,XXX	XXX,XXX
Telemarketing	147840	XXX,XXX	XXX,XXX	XXX,XXX	XXX,XXX
	-------	-------	-------	-------	-------
Total Revenue	XXX,XXX	XXX,XXX	XXX,XXX	XXX,XXX	XXX,XXX
Expenditures					
Salaries and Benefits	XXX,XXX	XXX,XXX	XXX,XXX	XXX,XXX	XXX,XXX
Postages and Supplies	XXX,XXX	XXX,XXX	XXX,XXX	XXX,XXX	XXX,XXX
Game Events	XXX,XXX	XXX,XXX	XXX,XXX	XXX,XXX	XXX,XXX
Prizes and Awards	XXX,XXX	XXX,XXX	XXX,XXX	XXX,XXX	XXX,XXX
Special Events	XXX,XXX	XXX,XXX	XXX,XXX	XXX,XXX	XXX,XXX
Travel	XXX,XXX	XXX,XXX	XXX,XXX	XXX,XXX	XXX,XXX
	-------	-------	-------	-------	-------
Total Expenditures	XXX,XXX	XXX,XXX	XXX,XXX	XXX,XXX	XXX,XXX
Surplus or Deficit	(XXX,XXX)	(XXX,XXX)	(XXX,XXX)	(XXX,XXX)	(XXX,XXX)

Figure 3-3
Lisa's revised worksheet sketch

Now Lisa is ready to include these revisions in her budget worksheet as she prepares the report for this month's meeting of the MSO Board of Directors.

Retrieving the Worksheet

In this tutorial you need to select the SmartIcon palette for Tutorial 3, then retrieve and review Lisa's worksheet before she begins the revisions.

To install the Tutorial 3 SmartIcon palette and retrieve the worksheet:

1. Launch 1-2-3.
2. Select the Tutorial 3 SmartIcon palette using the SmartIcon palette selector in the status bar.
3. Open Lisa's worksheet named C3MSO1.WK4 located on your Student Disk. The opened worksheet appears, as shown previously in Figure 3-1.
4. Immediately save the worksheet as S3MSO1.WK4 in the event you want to restart this tutorial.
5. Review Lisa's first draft worksheet. Look at the formulas used to calculate the revenues and expenditures. Which cells contain formulas that are calculated using a growth rate? What formatting is used for the numeric data displayed in the worksheet?

Adding Rows to the Worksheet

The special events fee per athlete and the telemarketing growth rate are key assumptions that Lisa needs to add to her worksheet. To do this, Lisa will insert four rows at the top of the worksheet between the column headings and the Number of Athletes label, then add the labels and values.

To insert rows into a worksheet, you select a range of cells that specifies the number of rows to be added. The rows are inserted immediately *above* the selected range. By clicking a single cell, you select a range that is just one row. When you insert rows, 1-2-3 automatically adjusts the row numbers in formulas that reference cells *below* the inserted rows. However, it is important to check all existing formulas in the worksheet to make sure they are adjusted for the newly inserted rows.

REFERENCE WINDOW

Inserting Rows and Columns

- Click any cell in the row above which you want to insert the rows; or click in the column to the left of where you want to insert columns.

- Select a range of cells to specify the number of rows or columns to be inserted.

- Click the Insert Row SmartIcon to insert the rows; or click the Insert Column SmartIcon to insert the columns.

or

Click the row number or column letter in the worksheet frame, then press [Ctrl][+ (on the numeric keypad)].

Let's insert the four rows for the key assumptions as indicated by Lisa's sketch (Figure 3-3).

To insert the rows into the worksheet:
1. Select the range A2..A5 to insert four rows above row 2. You could have also selected range B2..B5. It doesn't matter which column the cell pointer is in, providing it is in the row above which you want to insert the rows.
2. Click the **Insert Row SmartIcon** to insert the four blank rows. See Figure 3-4.

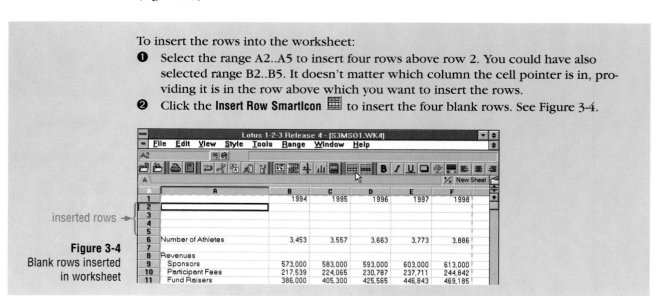

Figure 3-4
Blank rows inserted in worksheet

inserted rows →

❸ Press **[PgDn]** or scroll the worksheet down until row 24 appears, then click **B24**. Review the cell formula displayed in the cell contents box. Notice that the row numbers of the cell addresses in the formula were adjusted automatically to reflect the new location of these cells in the worksheet. Row numbers of all the cell formulas in the rows below row 5 were adjusted automatically for the newly inserted rows.

Now, let's enter the labels and values in the inserted rows as indicated in Lisa's sketch (Figure 3-3).

To add labels and values in the inserted rows:

❶ Scroll the worksheet, click **A2**, then enter the label **Key Assumptions:** *(don't forget the colon)*.

❷ Using Lisa's sketch enter the labels for rows 3, 4, and 5.

❸ Enter the data values in rows 4 and 5 as specified in Lisa's sketch. See Figure 3-5.

labels and values entered

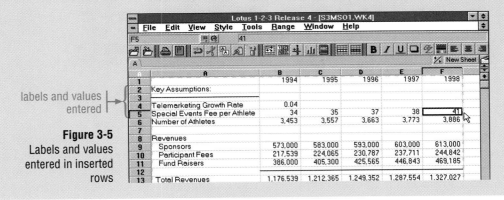

Figure 3-5
Labels and values entered in inserted rows

With the values for the key assumptions entered in her report, Lisa is ready to add the new revenue and expenditure items to the worksheet. She will add two new rows, one in the Revenues section and one in the Expenditures section. Because these new rows are included in calculations totaling revenues and expenditures, Lisa will make sure the formulas include the newly inserted rows.

Let's insert a row for Telemarketing below the row containing the Fund Raisers revenues.

To insert one row for Telemarketing:

❶ Click **B12**. Remember, the row will be inserted immediately *above* the selected cell.

❷ Click the **Insert Row SmartIcon** ▦ to insert a blank row in the worksheet. See Figure 3-6 on the following page.

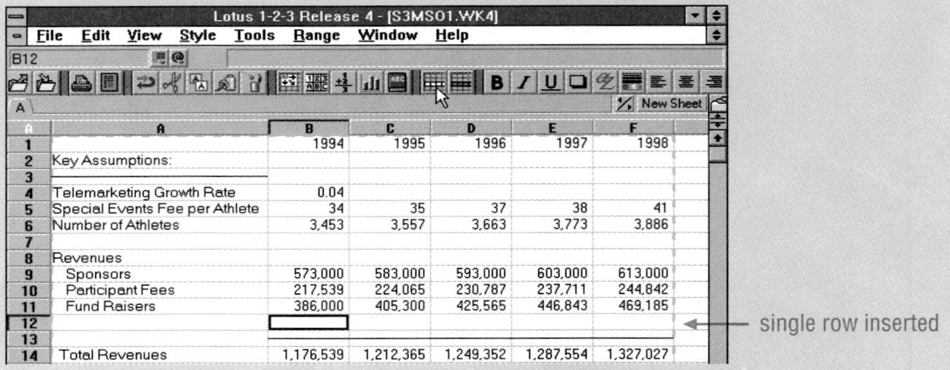

Figure 3-6
Blank row inserted
in worksheet

single row inserted →

TROUBLE? If you accidentally delete the row by clicking the wrong SmartIcon, use the Undo SmartIcon ⮌ to reverse this action, then repeat Steps 1 and 2.

❸ Enter the label **Telemarketing** and the data value for 1994 as shown in Lisa's sketch (Figure 3-3). Make sure you include spaces in front of the "T" in "Telemarketing" to indent the line item. Don't worry about the values for 1995 through 1998—you will insert those values using a copying procedure later in the tutorial.

❹ Click **B14** and look at the @SUM formula displayed in the cell contents box. The formula @SUM(B9..B11) does *not* include the amount for Telemarketing in the new row 12.

Because the new row was inserted *below* the last row of the range specified in the @SUM formula, the range does *not* include the new row. Therefore, the Telemarketing revenue is not included in the sum of total revenues. Whenever you add a row or column to the *end* of a range specified in an @SUM formula, 1-2-3 does not automatically include it in the corresponding formula. If you add a row or column to the *middle* of a range, 1-2-3 does automatically include it in any corresponding formulas. Let's correct this error.

To revise the formula in row 14 to include the newly inserted row:
❶ Click **B14**, then edit the @SUM formula to include row 12.
❷ Copy the formula from cell B14 into the other cells in row 14 so they also include row 12 in calculating total revenues. See Figure 3-7.

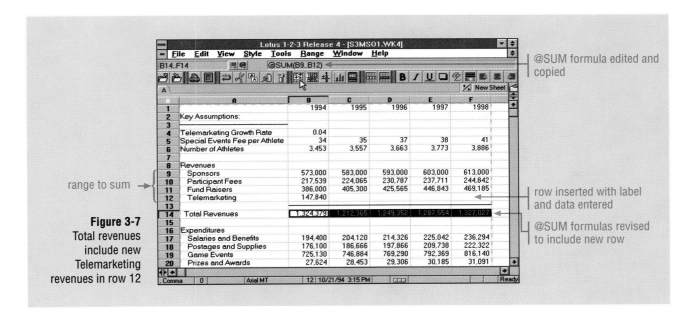

Figure 3-7
Total revenues
include new
Telemarketing
revenues in row 12

Next, let's insert a row for Special Events, then enter its label before entering the formula for this expenditure.

To add the Special Events expenditure to the worksheet:

➊ Click any cell in row 21 so you can insert a row above the Travel expenditure.

➋ Click the **Insert Row SmartIcon** .

TROUBLE? If you insert the row in the wrong location, use the Undo SmartIcon to reverse this action, then repeat Steps 1 and 2.

➌ Enter the label **Special Events**. Make sure you include spaces in front of the "S" in "Special Events" to indent the line item.

➍ Click **B24**, then look at the @SUM formula displayed in the cell contents box. The @SUM formula includes the new row because the row was inserted in the middle of the formula range. See Figure 3-8 on the following page.

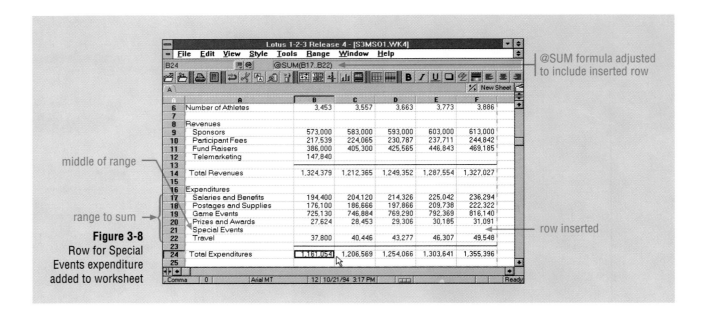

middle of range

range to sum

Figure 3-8
Row for Special
Events expenditure
added to worksheet

@SUM formula adjusted
to include inserted row

row inserted

Now that the row has been inserted, you can enter the formula for Special Events. This formula multiplies the Special Events Fee per Athlete by the Number of Athletes for each year.

To enter the formula for Special Events in cell B21, then copy it to the range C21..F21:
❶ Click **B21**, then use pointing to enter the formula **+B5*B6**.
❷ Copy the formula from cell B21 to the range C21..F21.
❸ Examine the formulas in cells C21 through F21 and click **F21**. Notice that the cell addresses of the formulas in range C21..F21 were adjusted automatically. Remember from Tutorial 2 that this is called relative referencing. See Figure 3-9.

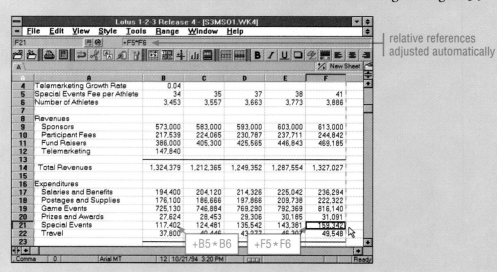

Figure 3-9
Column letters of
relative references
adjusted
automatically when
copied

relative references
adjusted automatically

Now, Lisa needs to go back and enter the formula for calculating Telemarketing, then copy it across row 12.

Using Absolute References

The formula for Telemarketing shown in Lisa's sketch as "previous year value * (1 + telemarketing growth rate)" is different from the formula for Special Events. It references the *same* value for the telemarketing growth rate in cell B4 for all four columns. For this reason, you do *not* want to copy the formula in the same way you copied the formula for Special Events. You don't want the cell reference to B4 to be adjusted for each column. For example, the formula you need to enter in cell C12 is +B12*(1+B4). If you copy this formula to cell D12 using relative referencing, the formula will automatically adjust to +C12*(1+C4). This formula is incorrect—there is no value in cell C4.

To copy the formula correctly, you need to include an absolute reference. An **absolute reference** is a cell address that is *not* adjusted automatically when it is copied to another location in the worksheet—it always references the same cell no matter where it is copied to. You indicate an absolute reference by preceding the column letter and/or row number by a dollar sign. For example, B4 is an absolute reference, whereas B4 is a relative reference. In some situations a cell might have a mixed reference such as $B4. In this case, when the formula is copied, the row number changes but the column letter does not. Similarly, copying B$4 changes the column letter but not the row number. Absolute references, mixed references, and relative references *only make a difference when formulas are copied to different cells*.

REFERENCE WINDOW

Entering Absolute or Mixed References

- Type $ (dollar sign) as you enter a formula to indicate an absolute or mixed reference.

or

- Type the formula.
- Place the edit cursor on or immediately to the right of the cell address that you want to make an absolute reference.
- Press [F4] (ABS) once to indicate an absolute reference, twice to indicate a mixed reference with the column letter absolute, or three times to indicate a mixed reference with the row number absolute.

Now let's enter the Telemarketing formula using an absolute reference.

To enter the Telemarketing formula with an absolute reference:
1. Click **C12**.
2. Type **+** to begin the formula, then point to **B12**.
3. Type ***(1+** then point to **B4** to include this cell address in the formula.
4. Press **[F4]** (ABS) once to indicate an absolute reference. Lotus 1-2-3 automatically inserts the dollar sign ($) into the cell address.

❺ Type **)** then press **[Enter]** or click the **Confirm button** to complete the formula. See Figure 3-10. This cell contains the formula, +B12*(1+B4). Note that B12 is a relative reference and B4 is an absolute reference.

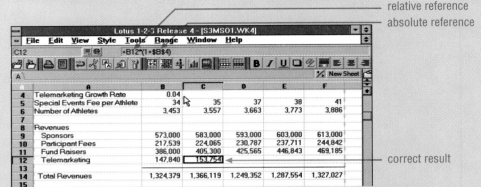

relative reference
absolute reference

correct result

Figure 3-10
Formula including an absolute reference

TROUBLE? If the formula in cell C12 is incorrect because you pointed to the wrong cell or pressed [F4] (ABS) too many times, use [F2] (EDIT) to edit the cell's content and make the necessary corrections.

Now you can copy this formula containing relative and absolute references into the cells that calculate the Telemarketing revenues for the next four years.

To copy the formula containing absolute and relative references:

❶ Click **C12**.

❷ Copy the formula from C12 to the range D12..F12.

❸ Examine the formulas in cells D12 through F12 and click **F12**. See Figure 3-11. Note that the relative references were adjusted automatically but the absolute references were not.

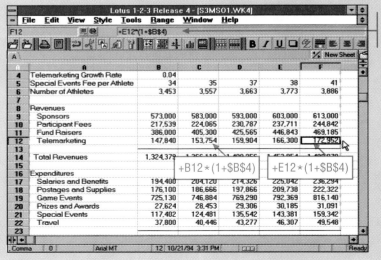

relative reference adjusted when copied; absolute reference not adjusted

Figure 3-11
Absolute and relative references copied across row 12

You are finished including the new information in Lisa's worksheet. Lisa wants to review the worksheet with Mary. Before she does, she wants to check the spelling, save this last revision, then preview and print the worksheet. Let's do that next.

To check the spelling and save, preview, then print the worksheet:
❶ If you are using the commercial edition of the software, click the **Spell Check SmartIcon** ⬛ to spell check your worksheet. If you are using the Student Edition, this feature is not available and you will have to check the spelling yourself. Review the worksheet closely and edit any spelling errors you find.
❷ Save your revised worksheet as S3MSO2.WK4.
❸ Preview and print this modified version of MSO's five-year plan.

If you want to take a break and resume the tutorial at a later time, you can exit 1-2-3 by double-clicking the Control menu box in the upper-left corner of your screen. When you resume the tutorial, launch 1-2-3 and place your Student Disk in the disk drive. Open the file S3MSO2.WK4, select the Tutorial 3 SmartIcon palette, and then continue with the tutorial.

Designing a Presentation-Quality Report

After she prints the updated MSO five-year plan, Lisa shows it to Mary. They both review it to make sure that the formulas and all corresponding results are correct, that there aren't any spelling errors, and that all the information Mary wanted is included. Mary asks Lisa to enhance the report's appearance before presenting it to the Board of Directors. She suggests moving the key assumptions, adding a report title, including the date, and applying spreadsheet publishing features such as boldface, italics, outlines, and shading. Also, she wants specific information printed at the top and bottom of the page. Mary's suggestions for improving the worksheet appear in red in Figure 3-12 on the following page.

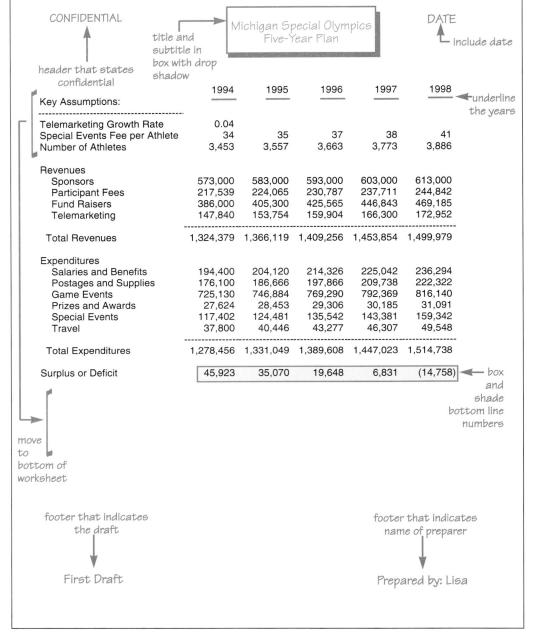

Figure 3-12
Mary's suggestions for improving the appearance of Lisa's worksheet

You will incorporate Mary's suggestions into the worksheet and, in so doing, turn Lisa's basic 1-2-3 worksheet into a more professional-looking document.

Moving Cell Contents

Mary wants Lisa to move the key assumptions to the bottom of the report. This makes the key assumptions available for review, but separates them from the main body of the report.

To move the contents of a single cell or a range of cells to a new location, you simply select the cell range you want to move and use the pointer ✍ to move the contents to the desired location. When cells are moved, the column letters and/or row numbers of both absolute and relative references are adjusted automatically. For example, if a formula references cell B4 and you move the contents of cell B4 to cell B31, 1-2-3 will automatically replace B4 with B31. A cell address remains a relative reference, mixed reference, or absolute reference no matter where you move the cell contents to.

REFERENCE WINDOW   **Moving Cell Contents**

- Select the range to be moved.
- Move the pointer to the bottom of the range until it changes to ✍.
- Click and drag the range to the new location.
- Release the mouse button when the range is in its new location.

Now let's move the key assumptions to the bottom of Lisa's report.

To move the key assumptions to another location:

❶ Select the range A2..F6, which contains the key assumptions data.

❷ Slowly move the pointer to the edge of the selected range until it changes to ✍. See Figure 3-13.

select range to be moved

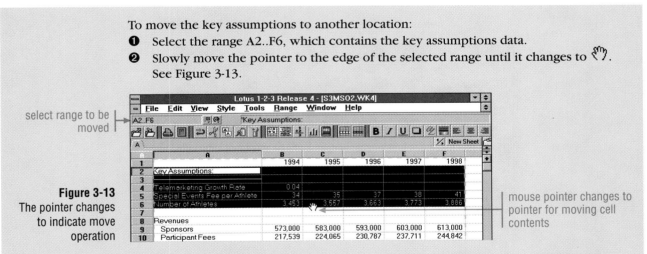

Figure 3-13
The pointer changes to indicate move operation

mouse pointer changes to pointer for moving cell contents

❸ Click and drag the range until the upper-left corner of the range is located at cell A29, then release the mouse button. Do not release the mouse button until the upper-left corner of the range is in cell A29. Your screen will scroll automatically as you drag the range down the screen towards cell A29. Notice that the pointer changes to ✍ as you move the range. See Figure 3-14 on the following page.

TROUBLE? If you release the mouse button too soon and the range is moved to the wrong location, use the Undo SmartIcon ↩ to reverse this action, then repeat Steps 1 through 3.

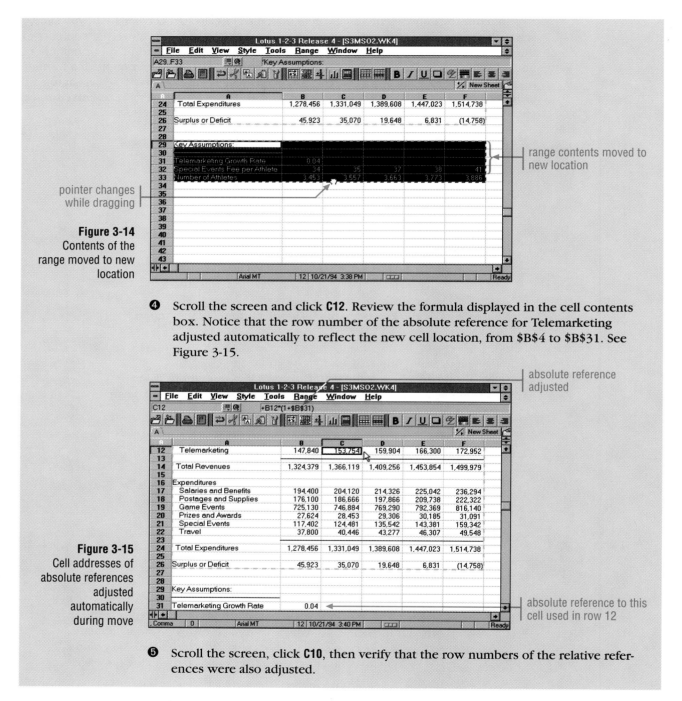

pointer changes while dragging

range contents moved to new location

Figure 3-14
Contents of the range moved to new location

❹ Scroll the screen and click **C12**. Review the formula displayed in the cell contents box. Notice that the row number of the absolute reference for Telemarketing adjusted automatically to reflect the new cell location, from B4 to B31. See Figure 3-15.

absolute reference adjusted

Figure 3-15
Cell addresses of absolute references adjusted automatically during move

absolute reference to this cell used in row 12

❺ Scroll the screen, click **C10**, then verify that the row numbers of the relative references were also adjusted.

Deleting Rows from the Worksheet

Now that you have moved the key assumptions data to the bottom of the worksheet, you can delete the rows that no longer contain data. The procedure for deleting rows is similar to that for adding rows. You select the range you want to delete, indicating the number of rows to be deleted. It doesn't matter which column your cell pointer is in when you select the range of rows for deletion.

Deleting Rows and Columns

- Select the rows or columns to be deleted.
- Click the Delete Row or Delete Column SmartIcon.

  or

  Click the row number or column letter in the worksheet frame, then press [Ctrl][- (on the numeric keypad)].

Let's delete the unwanted rows from Lisa's worksheet.

To delete the rows that no longer contain data:
❶ Select the range C2..C7. See Figure 3-16.

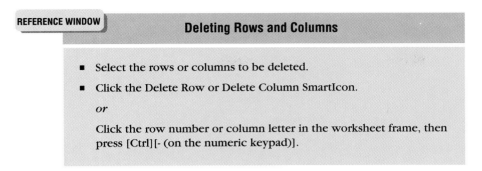

Figure 3-16
Highlighted range specifies rows for deletion

selected rows to be deleted

❷ Click the **Delete Row SmartIcon** 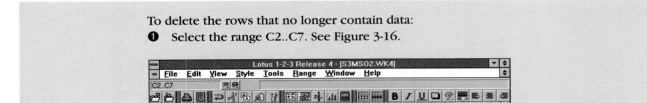 to delete the rows from the worksheet.

❸ Verify that the absolute and relative references in the formulas calculating Participant Fees, Game Events, Telemarketing, and Special Events were adjusted to reflect the new cell addresses. See Figure 3-17 on the following page.

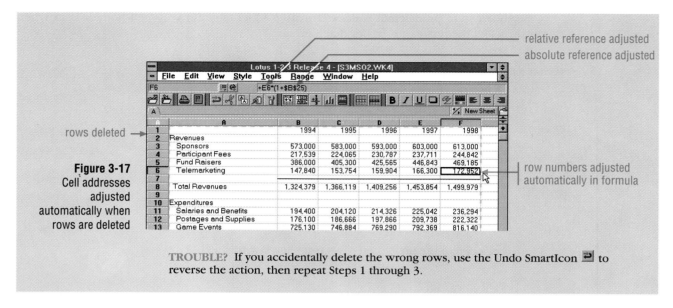

Figure 3-17
Cell addresses
adjusted
automatically when
rows are deleted

rows deleted →

relative reference adjusted
absolute reference adjusted

row numbers adjusted
automatically in formula

TROUBLE? If you accidentally delete the wrong rows, use the Undo SmartIcon to reverse the action, then repeat Steps 1 through 3.

Entering Long Labels in the Worksheet

Lisa needs to add the title "Michigan Special Olympics" and the subtitle "Five-Year Plan" as suggested by Mary. A title will immediately tell the Board of Directors which report they are looking at. Because Mary wants the report title above the column headings, Lisa needs to insert blank rows before she can enter the title and subtitle.

The title and subtitle are considered **long labels** because the number of characters in each label exceeds the current column width. According to Mary's suggestions, Lisa also needs to center the titles. To do this, she will enter the long labels in column C, and use the Center Data SmartIcon to center the titles over columns B through D. This SmartIcon inserts the ^ label prefix, which centers labels. When a long label is used in 1-2-3, the label prefix not only controls the location of a label *within* a cell, it also affects the location of the label *across* adjacent columns. Let's add these centered long labels to Lisa's worksheet.

To insert rows in the worksheet, then enter a centered report title:

❶ Insert four blank rows above the column headings, which are currently located in row 1.

❷ Enter the title and subtitle as long labels in cells C2 and C3. Remember that 1-2-3 automatically left-aligns labels. See Figure 3-18.

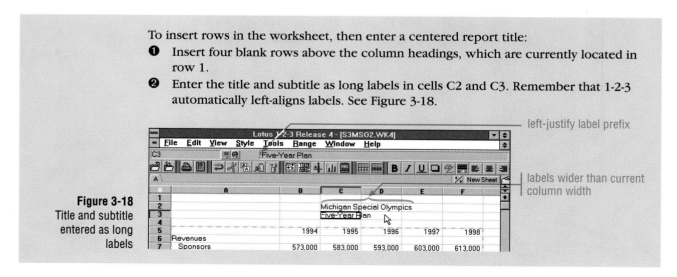

Figure 3-18
Title and subtitle
entered as long
labels

left-justify label prefix

labels wider than current
column width

❸ Select the range C2..C3, which contains the long labels you want centered across the columns.

❹ Click the **Center Data SmartIcon** to change the label prefix and center the long labels. See Figure 3-19.

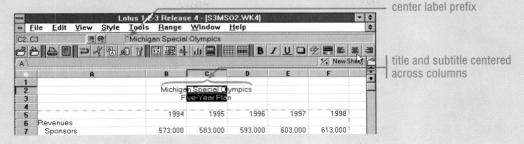

Figure 3-19
Long labels
centered across
columns

If the cells on either side of the long labels were not blank, the labels would be truncated—only the characters that fit into the current column width would appear. Remember this when you add long labels to your worksheet.

Including the Date Using the @TODAY Function

Mary also wants the date on the report so that when she and Lisa revise the report they will know which report is the most current. In 1-2-3, you use the @TODAY function to obtain the current date from your computer's clock. The date appears as an integer because 1-2-3 calculates the date as the number of days since the beginning of the century. To display the number as a date, you apply a format from the list of available date formats. Let's add the current date to Lisa's worksheet using the @TODAY function.

To add the current date to the report using the @TODAY function:

❶ Click **F1**, which is where you want the date to appear.

❷ Click the **@function selector**, click **TODAY** in the list, then click the **Confirm button** or press [Enter].The current date appears as a number. See Figure 3-20. Your number will be different because it is the current date from your computer's clock.

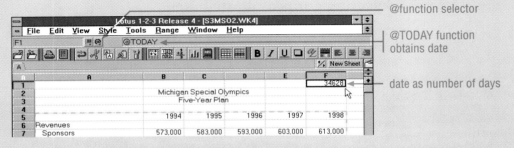

Figure 3-20
Date obtained from
computer's clock

❸ Click the **number format selector** to display the list of available date formats, then click **31-Dec-93**. See Figure 3-21 on the following page.

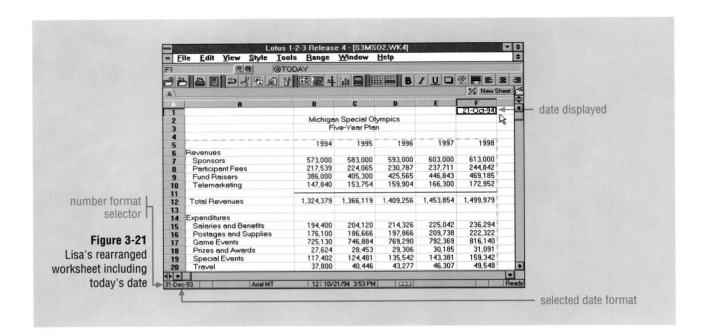

Figure 3-21
Lisa's rearranged worksheet including today's date

number format selector — (pointing to spreadsheet)

date displayed —

selected date format —

This completes the rearrangement of Lisa's report—all of the information is where she wants it. Next, she will enhance the appearance of her worksheet.

Enhancing the Appearance of a Worksheet

By using **spreadsheet publishing features** such as boldface, italics, underlining, outlining, and shading, you can enhance the appearance of your worksheet. Lisa will use these features to turn her basic worksheet in Figure 3-21 into a more professional-looking, presentation-quality report. In 1-2-3, appearance enhancements change only the *look* of data in a worksheet; they do not affect the cell contents. It is best to make sure that the formulas in your worksheet produce the correct results before you begin enhancing the worksheet.

Selecting Fonts and Attributes

One of the most common enhancements to a worksheet is to change the fonts used in displaying and printing the results. A **font** is a set of letters, numbers, and symbols. Fonts are distinguished by their typeface, point size, and attributes.

A **typeface** is a particular graphical design of characters. Each character in the typeface shares the common design. A list of the typefaces included with Lotus 1-2-3 Release 4 for Windows is shown in Figure 3-22. Note that the Wingdings typeface is different because it is a collection of special symbols available with 1-2-3.

Typeface	Example
ARIAL	ABCDEFGH abcdefgh 12345
ARIAL MT	ABCDEFGH abcdefgh 12345
BODONI BOLD CONDENSED	**ABCDEFGH abcdefgh 12345**
BRUSHSCRIPT	*ABCDEFGH abcdefgh 12345*
COURIER	ABCDEFGH abcdefgh 12345
COURIER NEW	ABCDEFGH abcdefgh 12345
DOMCASUAL	**ABCDEFGH abcdefgh 12345**
HELV	ABCDEFGH abcdefgh 12345
LETTERGOTHIC	ABCDEFGH abcdefgh 12345
LINEPRINTER	ABCDEFGH abcdefgh 12345
NEWSGOTHIC	ABCDEFGH abcdefgh 12345
PERPETUA	ABCDEFGH abcdefgh 12345
Symbol	ΑΒΧΔΕΦΓΗ αβχδεφγη 12345
TIMES NEW ROMAN	ABCDEFGH abcdefgh 12345
TIME NEW ROMAN PS	ABCDEFGH abcdefgh 12345
TMS RMN	ABCDEFGH abcdefgh 12345
Wingdings	(symbols)

Figure 3-22
Common 1-2-3
typefaces

The **point size** is the measurement of the height of a character, which is usually specified in points where a **point** is approximately $1/72$ of an inch. Boldface, italics, and underlining are **attributes**, which you can apply to the characters, resulting in alternative versions of the font.

For example, 14-point boldface italics Arial is a specific font. Its typeface is Arial, its point size is 14, and its attributes are boldface and italics. Unless you change it, Arial MT 12 point is the 1-2-3 default font. Besides the available fonts listed in Figure 3-22, you can purchase other fonts, then use them with 1-2-3; however, this book uses the standard fonts provided by Lotus Development Corporation with Lotus 1-2-3 Release 4 for Windows.

When you add these enhancements to your worksheets, be careful not to overdo. Adding enhancements should make the information clearer and more readable, not muddled and confusing. A common practice is to limit the number of typefaces to three or four, rather than trying to use all the available typefaces within a single worksheet.

REFERENCE WINDOW

Selecting Attributes

- Select the range you want to enhance.

- Click the Bold, Italics, and/or Underline SmartIcon(s) to apply the attribute(s) to the selected range.

or

Use the Quick menu or the Fonts and Attributes SmartIcon to display the Fonts and Attributes dialog box; select the typeface, point size, and attributes you want to apply to the selected range; then click the OK button.

Mary has suggested various fonts and attributes to improve the worksheet's appearance and readability. Let's add these enhancements to Lisa's worksheet using the available

SmartIcons. These SmartIcons act like toggle buttons: click once to add the attribute, click again to remove it.

To italicize the Key Assumptions label:
❶ Click **A27**, the cell that contains the label.
❷ Click the **Italics SmartIcon** *I* to apply this attribute to the display of the cell's content. See Figure 3-23.

   TROUBLE? If you accidentally click the Italics SmartIcon twice, you will remove the attribute. Simply click *I* once more to add the attribute.

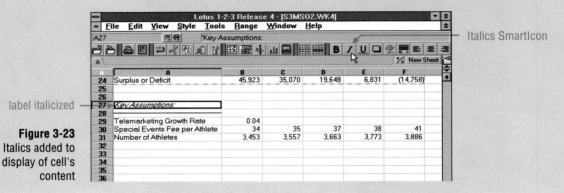

label italicized

Figure 3-23
Italics added to
display of cell's
content

Next, Lisa needs to bold the title.

To bold the title:
❶ Click **C2**, the cell that contains the first title.
❷ Click the **Bold SmartIcon** **B** and the title appears in boldface.

As Mary suggested, let's bold and italicize the subtitle of the report.

To bold and italicize the subtitle:
❶ Click **C3**, the cell that contains the subtitle.
❷ Click the **Bold SmartIcon** **B** to add boldface.
❸ Click the **Italics SmartIcon** *I* to add italics to the bolded subtitle.

Lisa also wants to change the typeface from the default of Arial MT to Times Roman (Tms Rmn) for both the title and subtitle.

REFERENCE WINDOW

Selecting a Typeface

- Select the range you want to modify.

- Click the typeface selector in the status bar to display the list of available typefaces, then select the typeface you want to apply to the selected range.

  or

  Use the Quick menu or the Fonts and Attributes SmartIcon to display the Fonts and Attributes dialog box; select the typeface you want to apply to the selected range; then click the OK button.

Let's change the typeface for the report titles.

To change the typeface of the title and subtitle:
1. Select the range C2..C3, which contains the title and subtitle.
2. Click the **typeface selector** in the status bar, which displays the current typeface of Arial MT. The list of available typefaces appears. See Figure 3-24.

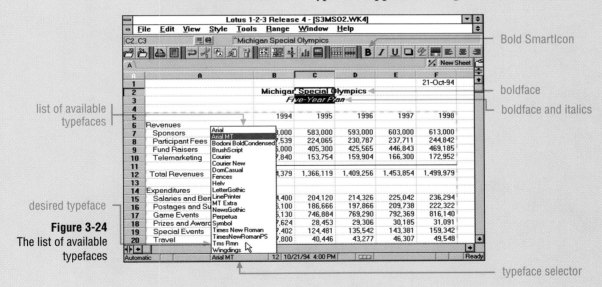

list of available typefaces

desired typeface

Figure 3-24
The list of available typefaces

Bold SmartIcon

boldface

boldface and italics

typeface selector

3. Click **Tms Rmn** (Times Roman).

   TROUBLE? If your list of available typefaces does not include Tms Rmn, select another typeface such as Times New Roman instead. Your screens will be slightly different from the screens in this section.

Now the titles are too small and don't stand out very well, so Lisa wants to increase the point size from 12 to 14 points.

REFERENCE WINDOW

Selecting a Point Size

- Select the range you want to modify.

- Click the point size selector in the status bar to display the list of available point sizes, then select the point size you want to apply to the selected range.

  or

  Use the Quick menu or the Fonts and Attributes SmartIcon to display the Fonts and Attributes dialog box; select the point size you want to apply to the selected range; then click the OK button.

Let's use the point size selector to increase the point size.

To change the point size of the title and subtitle:

❶ Verify that the range C2..C3 containing the two report titles is still selected. If not, select it.

❷ Click the **point size selector** in the status bar, which displays the current point size of 12, to obtain the list of available point sizes. See Figure 3-25.

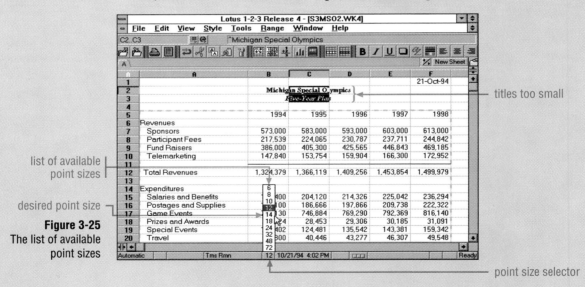

Figure 3-25
The list of available point sizes

❸ Click **14**. Now the titles are larger and more readable.

Adding a Drop Shadow Box

To make the title and subtitle stand out even more, Mary wants Lisa to draw a drop shadow box around the title and subtitle. Let's add this enhancement to her report.

To place a drop shadow box around the title and subtitle:

❶ Select the range B2..D3. This will be the frame of the box.

❷ Click the **Drop Shadow SmartIcon** 🖳. The drop shadow box surrounds the report title.

❸ Click anywhere on the worksheet except in the drop shadow box to unselect the range. See Figure 3-26.

TROUBLE? If you place the drop shadow box around the wrong range, click 🖳 again to remove the attribute, then repeat Steps 1 through 3.

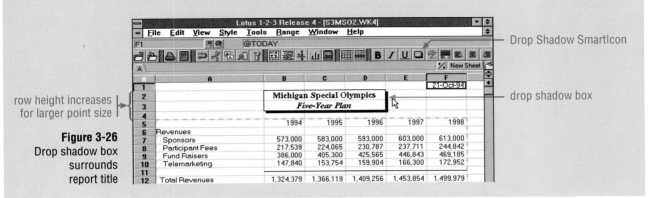

Figure 3-26
Drop shadow box
surrounds
report title

row height increases
for larger point size

Drop Shadow SmartIcon

drop shadow box

Underlining Text Within a Cell

Lisa likes how professional her report titles look. Now she wants to improve the appearance of the column headings. Let's do this by underlining them. Rather than using a separate row of cells containing minus signs as you did in Tutorial 2, you will underline the column headings right in their cells.

To underline the column headings within the cells:

❶ Select the range B5..F5, which contains the column headings.

❷ Click the **Underline SmartIcon** 🔲 to place an underline in each cell of the range.

❸ Click **A5** to clearly see the underline. See Figure 3-27.

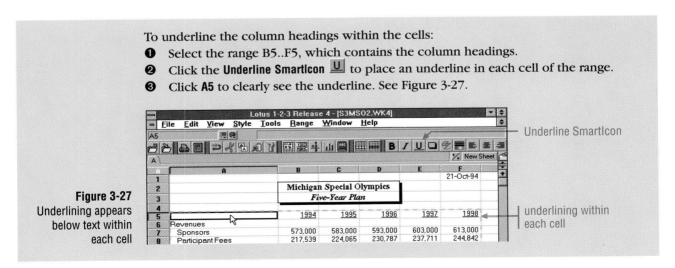

Figure 3-27
Underlining appears
below text within
each cell

Underline SmartIcon

underlining within
each cell

Adding Outlines and Shading

Mary knows the Board of Directors will be particularly interested in the bottom line projections in this report. Therefore, she asks Lisa to outline the cells that contain the Surplus or Deficit data. An **outline** is a border around the edges of a cell or a range of cells.

REFERENCE WINDOW

Adding an Outline to a Range

- Select the range that you want to outline.

- Click the Color and Pattern SmartIcon to display the Lines & Color dialog box.

  or

  Click the right mouse button to display the Quick menu, then click Lines & Color... to display this dialog box.

- Click the Outline check box in the Border box.

- Click the OK button to add an outline to the selected range.

Lisa knows that she can draw a reader's attention even closer to important data by shading a range of cells. **Shading** is a background pattern that you add to a cell or range of cells. Figure 3-28 shows the shading patterns available in 1-2-3.

Figure 3-28
Palette of available
shading patterns

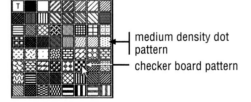

medium density dot
pattern
checker board pattern

REFERENCE WINDOW

Adding a Pattern to a Range

- Select the range that you want to shade.

- Click the Color and Pattern SmartIcon to display the Lines & Color dialog box.

  or

  Click the right mouse button to display the Quick menu, then click Lines & Color... to display this dialog box.

- Click the Pattern drop-down list arrow to display the pattern palette.

- Click a pattern.

- Click the OK button to add the pattern to the selected range.

Let's add these attributes to draw the reader's attention to the bottom line Surplus or Deficit item in the MSO five-year plan.

To outline and shade the Surplus or Deficit amounts:

❶ Select the range B24..F24, which displays the Surplus or Deficit amounts.

❷ Click the **Color and Pattern SmartIcon** to display the Lines & Color dialog box. See Figure 3-29 for the available options.

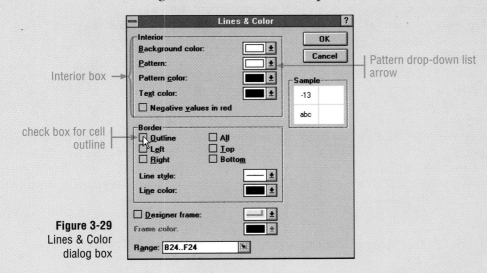

Interior box →

check box for cell outline

Pattern drop-down list arrow

Figure 3-29
Lines & Color
dialog box

❸ Click the **Outline check box** in the Border box to place an outline around the cells.

❹ Click the **Pattern drop-down list arrow** in the Interior box to display the available shading patterns, as shown previously in Figure 3-28.

❺ Click the checker board pattern to select this shading pattern.

❻ Click the **OK button** to apply these attributes to the range.

❼ Move the cell pointer out of the way so you can view the attributes applied to the range. See Figure 3-30.

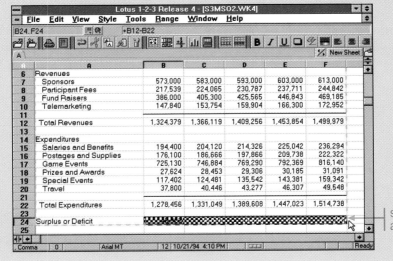

Figure 3-30
Shading and outline
highlight critical
bottom line factor

shading and outline
applied to range of cells

Mary and Lisa are *not* pleased with this shading pattern because they cannot read the numbers. Some patterns are darker and more complicated than others, making them unsuitable for shading values and labels. However, they are ideal for use with charts, as described in the next tutorial. Shading a cell or range of cells sometimes requires several tries before you're satisfied with the results. Let's choose a different shading pattern.

To change the shading pattern:
- ❶ Verify that the range B24..F24 is still selected. If not, select it.
- ❷ Click the **Color and Pattern SmartIcon** ▦ to display the Lines & Color dialog box.
- ❸ Click the **Pattern drop-down list arrow**, then click the medium density dot pattern as shown in Figure 3-28.
- ❹ Click the **OK button** to apply this pattern to the range, then move the cell pointer out of the way so you can view this shading pattern.

Lisa and Mary like the way this shading looks—it draws attention to the numbers without blurring them. Looking back at Mary's suggestions, Lisa has included all of them except the specific information Mary wants printed at the top and bottom of the page. She will add this information by specifying a header and footer when she prints the report.

Printing the Worksheet with a Header and Footer

Lisa can add identifying information to the top and bottom of the page by specifying a header and a footer. A **header** is text that is printed at the top of every page. A **footer** is text that is printed at the bottom of every page. You do not add these enhancements to the cells in the worksheet, but instead you specify this information in the Page Setup dialog box when you print the report.

Lisa also wants to change the margins when she prints the report. When she printed the worksheet earlier, she noticed that the default settings for the margins did not provide enough white space around the worksheet. To correct this, she wants a 1-inch margin for the top and bottom of the page, and a 0.75-inch margin for the left and right sides.

Let's print Lisa's report and specify these printing options. If you are using the Student Version of the software, you can set the margins but you cannot specify the header and/or footer. Lotus 1-2-3 automatically adds the footer, "Printed with the Student Version of 1-2-3 Release 4 for Windows." Skip Step 5 in the following set of steps.

To set the margins, then print the report with a header and footer:
- ❶ Select the range A1..F32 for printing.
- ❷ Click the **Print SmartIcon** 🖨 to display the Print dialog box.
- ❸ Click the **Page Setup... button** to display the Page Setup dialog box. See Figure 3-31.

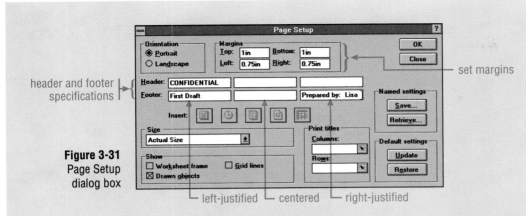

header and footer
specifications

Figure 3-31
Page Setup
dialog box

left-justified   centered   right-justified

❹ Set the margins by typing the numbers as indicated in Figure 3-31. Press [Tab] to move between margin settings. It is optional to include the "in" for inches when entering the settings.

❺ If you are using the commercial version of the software, specify the header and footer by typing the entries as indicated in Figure 3-31. If you are using the Student Version of the software, skip this step. Each header and footer has three text boxes—one for left-justified, one for centered, and one for right-justified text. You enter the text in the box that indicates where you want the information to appear on the page.

Now that all the page formatting options are entered, Lisa can print the report.

❻ Click the **OK button** to complete the page setup specifications and return to the Print dialog box.

❼ Click the **OK button** on the Print dialog box to print the report. See Figure 3-32 on the following page.

CONFIDENTIAL

21-Oct-94

Michigan Special Olympics
Five-Year Plan

	1994	1995	1996	1997	1998
Revenues					
Sponsors	573,000	583,000	593,000	603,000	613,000
Participant Fees	217,539	224,065	230,787	237,711	244,842
Fund Raisers	386,000	405,300	425,565	446,843	469,185
Telemarketing	147,840	153,754	159,904	166,300	172,952
Total Revenues	1,324,379	1,366,119	1,409,256	1,453,854	1,499,979
Expenditures					
Salaries and Benefits	194,400	204,120	214,326	225,042	236,294
Postages and Supplies	176,100	186,666	197,866	209,738	222,322
Game Events	725,130	746,884	769,290	792,369	816,140
Prizes and Awards	27,624	28,453	29,306	30,185	31,091
Special Events	117,402	124,481	135,542	143,381	159,342
Travel	37,800	40,446	43,277	46,307	49,548
Total Expenditures	1,278,456	1,331,049	1,389,608	1,447,023	1,514,738
Surplus or Deficit	45,923	35,070	19,648	6,831	(14,758)

Key Assumptions:

Telemarketing Growth Rate	0.04				
Special Events Fee per Athlete	34	35	37	38	41
Number of Athletes	3,453	3,557	3,663	3,773	3,886

First Draft   Prepared by: Lisa

Figure 3-32
MSO report with
appearance
enhancements

You can also use the Page Setup dialog box to specify the **orientation**—how the worksheet will be printed on a page—as either portrait or landscape. The **portrait** orientation prints the worksheet upright on the page. The **landscape** orientation prints the worksheet sideways on the page. You can also have the worksheet frame and grid lines printed on each page. If you want, you can explore these characteristics by selecting them and previewing the worksheet.

Now that you are aware of the various appearance enhancements available in 1-2-3, you can include them in your worksheets. Let's save the final version of Lisa's worksheet.

To save the final version of Lisa's worksheet:

❶ Review the worksheet one last time. If any corrections are necessary, make those changes, then save the worksheet as S3MSO3.WK4.

❷ If you want, exit from 1-2-3 since you have completed the five-year plan for MSO or continue with the exercises.

The Michigan Special Olympics five-year plan is ready for the Board of Directors' meeting. Lisa and Mary are impressed with its appearance.

Questions

1. Cell C12 contains the formula +B12*(1+B6). After you copy this formula to cells D12 and E12, what is the formula in cell E12?
   a. +B12*(1+B6)
   b. +B12*(1+E6)
   c. +E12*(1+B6)
   d. +D12*(1+D6)
2. Cell B24 contains the formula +B12*1.5*B7. After you copy this formula to cells C24, D24, and E24, what is the formula in cell D24?
   a. +B12*1.5*D7
   b. +B12*1.5*B7
   c. +D12*1.5*B7
   d. +D12*3.5*D7
3. Cell D20 contains the formula @SUM(D11..D19). After you insert a row above row 15, what is the formula in cell D21? Why?
   a. @SUM(D11..D19)
   b. @SUM(D10..D19)
   c. @SUM(D11..D20)
   d. @SUM(D10..D21)
4. When absolute references are used in formulas, which one of these activities would not cause a change in the column letters and row numbers of cell names:
   a. inserting rows
   b. deleting rows
   c. copying cell contents
   d. moving cell contents
5. This function obtains the current date from the computer's clock as the number of days since the beginning of the century:
   a. @SUM
   b. @TODAY
   c. @CLOCK
   d. @WHEN

6. Which of the following is *not* an attribute or font characteristic that you apply to the display of cell contents to enhance the appearance of your worksheet report:
   a. typeface
   b. prefix
   c. point size
   d. italics
7. Which of the following enhancements does *not* appear with your worksheet display but is printed with your report:
   a. footers
   b. column headings
   c. underlines
   d. shading patterns
8. Which of the following SmartIcons is *not* a toggle button—that is, which does not apply the attribute when clicked the first time and remove the attribute when clicked again:
   a. Bold
   b. Right-align
   c. Italics
   d. Underline
9. Using the Task Reference, write down at least one other method of performing the same task as each of the following SmartIcons:
   a.
   b.
   c.
   d.

Tutorial Assignments

Launch 1-2-3, then open the T3KCP1.WK4 worksheet, which contains the annual employee turnover report for King Coil Products. Review this worksheet, then prepare a planning analysis sheet for Assignments 1 through 4 to complete the worksheet. After planning the worksheet, perform the following:
1. Add the formula to calculate the Total Number of Employees in the company.
2. Add the formula to calculate the Total Number of Terminations (employees who left the company).
3. Add formulas in column D to calculate the Department Turnover percentage. This is the number of employees in each department who left the company compared to the number of employees in the department. Use this formula for each department and for the Total:

$$\text{Department Turnover \%} = \frac{\text{number of terminations in each department}}{\text{number of employees in each department}}$$

Do you need to use relative or absolute referencing with these formulas?

4. Add formulas in column E to calculate the Company Turnover percentage. This is the number of employees in each department who left the company compared to the total number of employees in the company. Use this formula for each department and for the Total:

$$\text{Company Turnover \%} = \frac{\text{number of terminations in each department}}{\text{number of employees in company}}$$

Do you need to use relative or absolute referencing with these formulas? (*Hint:* Total Company Turnover % = 16.1%.)

E 5. Why are two of the department names in column A truncated? Correct this situation.

6. Format the Department Turnover percentage and the Company Turnover percentage columns as a percent with one decimal.

7. Are the totals for the Department Turnover and the Company Turnover percentages the same? Why? If they are the same, how is this calculation of both values useful?

8. Place the following title and subtitle at the top of the worksheet in column C:

> King Coil Products
> Annual Employee Turnover Analysis

Center the titles as long labels, which extend into the adjacent columns. Leave a blank row between the subtitle and the column headings.

9. To enhance the appearance of the report title and subtitle:
   a. Bold both titles.
   b. Italicize the subtitle.
   c. Choose another typeface for both titles.
   d. Increase the point size of both titles to 14.
   e. Place a drop shadow around both titles in columns B, C, and D.

10. Add the date from the computer's clock in cell E1, then format it as "31-Dec-93."

11. Underline the column headings using underlining within the cells.

E 12. Add an outline and a shading pattern to the Total Company Turnover % column. Try several different patterns and pick the best one.

13. Preview and print this turnover analysis report. Save the worksheet as S3KCP2.WK4.

Launch 1-2-3, then open the S3MSO3.WK4 worksheet. (If you did not build this worksheet by completing the steps in this tutorial, you need to build it before you continue with these Assignments.) Mary is considering increasing revenues through the direct-mail marketing of t-shirts and related sports apparel. She expects this to generate direct-mail revenue of $52,300 in the first year, which will increase at the rate of 7% each year after that. Revise the plan for MSO by performing the following:

14. Review the growth rate formulas for Telemarketing, which are similar to those for Direct Mail, then examine the Participant Fees, which contain the fee per participant data; this data will change when you revise the plan. Prepare a revised worksheet sketch that includes the changes to the five-year plan by printing a copy of the current worksheet and marking it up with the changes described in Assignments 15 through 17.

15. Add the Direct Mail label to the Revenues section, placing it below the Telemarketing label. Include the Direct Mail Growth Rate label in the key assumptions area, placing it below the Telemarketing Growth Rate label. Create the formulas for this new Direct Mail revenue item, which are similar to those for Telemarketing, then revise any other formulas affected by this change.

16. Place the Participant Fee per Athlete label in the row above Special Events Fee per Athlete. Enter the value $35 for this fee because the members of the Board feel that the additional revenue from direct mail will enable them to reduce the original fee of $45. Modify the formula for the Participant Fees revenue item so it is calculated using the new Participant Fee per Athlete value located in the key assumptions area.

E 17. Add the label Accumulated Surplus or Deficit between the Surplus or Deficit label and the key assumptions area. Then enter the formulas that calculate the accumulated surplus or deficit. Specify the display of any negative values in red in this row. Use the Help system to explore how to change the appearance (color) of data.

E 18. Perform several what-if analyses on the Participant Fee per Athlete item by trying different values to determine, to the nearest dollar, the fee that results in a balanced budget at the end of 1998. That is, the accumulated surplus or deficit is as close as possible to zero, but is still positive.

E 19. Mary feels that the outline and shading in the Surplus or Deficit line are not necessary. To learn how to clear these enhancements, use the Help system to explore how to change and clear the appearance of data. After reading the Help information, remove the outline and shading.

20. Save this file as S3MSO4.WK4. Preview and print the what-if analysis for MSO's five-year plan.

21. Review the results of the what-if analysis. Circle the accumulated surplus or deficit for 1998 and the participant fee per athlete. Has the Board reached its goal for reducing the participant fee per athlete to $35?

Case Problems

1. Analyzing Sales for WeCycle Industries

WeCycle Industries (WCI) has been on the cutting edge of the recycling revolution since the early 1980s when the problems of waste management began to surface worldwide. WeCycle was one of the first to offer recycling services for both residential and commercial customers. When WCI first began operations, it was involved in both the pickup and processing of recycled materials. WeCycle's processing plant was set up to process aluminum, glass, and plastics. After the recyclable materials were processed, WCI would then sell them back to their respective producers. As WCI began to invest more heavily into processing machinery, it sold off the pickup services to another company. WeCycle has now set its sights on being the leader in recycling in the 21st century.

Naoki Kanno has been in charge of developing the recycling process since WCI first began operations. Naoki was largely responsible for WCI's transition towards processing recyclable materials and away from pickup services. Naoki's latest project is the possible addition of paper to WeCycle's recycling capabilities. Naoki feels that with the additional capacity for paper, WeCycle will position itself as the leader in recycling. In order for Naoki to complete this project, she wants to develop a sales revenue analysis report for all recycled materials, including paper. This report should calculate the annual revenues with a contribution analysis of each recycled material. This contribution analysis shows the percentage each material is of the total. Naoki has started to create the sales revenue analysis report. Complete the report by performing the following:

1. Launch 1-2-3, then open the P3WCI1.WK4 worksheet, which contains Naoki's sales revenue analysis by quarter. Review this worksheet, then print a copy to use as your planning analysis sheet for Assignments 2 through 5.

2. Add Paper to the other recycled materials by placing it between Glass and Plastics. The expected sales revenues are:

	Qtr 1	Qtr 2	Qtr 3	Qtr 4
Paper	808	911	944	968

3. Create formulas that calculate the Total Sales by Recycled Material and for the Totals line, which calculates the total of the sales revenue for all four quarters.

E 4. Using the total sales revenue for all four materials, create formulas in column G that calculate the contribution as the percentage of sales by recycled material. This is the total sales for each material divided by the total for all materials. Format these cells as a percentage with one decimal. How are absolute references used in these formulas?

5. Using the total sales revenue for all quarters, create formulas in row 12 that calculate the percentage of sales by quarter. This is the total sales for each quarter divided by the total for all materials for the year. Format these cells as a percentage with one decimal.

6. Save the worksheet as S3WCI2.WK4. Preview and print this sales revenue analysis report. What recycled material makes up the largest percentage of sales? This is the one that makes the largest contribution to sales.

7. Add a title and a subtitle centered across all columns of the report at the top of the worksheet. Use "WeCycle Industries" for the title and "Sales Revenue Analysis" as the subtitle. Then place "(Dollars in thousands)" below the report titles and above the column headings. Place a blank line between the subtitle and "(Dollars in thousands)" and above the column headings.

E 8. Add a row above the report titles then place the date from the computer's clock in the upper-right corner of the report. Select a format that displays only the month and day.

9. Enhance the appearance of the report title by selecting appropriate fonts and attributes. Why did you select these enhancements?

10. Add an outline with a light shading pattern to the percentage of sales for each of the recycled materials.

11. Underline each column heading using underlining within the cells.

E 12. To contrast paper with the other recycled materials, change the color of all the cells in the row containing Paper to red. To learn how to change a color, use the Help system to explore how to change the appearance (color) of data.

13. Preview and print this enhanced sales revenue analysis report. Include an appropriate header and/or footer for this report. Save the worksheet as S3WCI3.WK4.

E 14. Consider other enhancement features to further improve the appearance of the report. Explain how each feature could be used.

2. Budgeting for the Village of Suttons Bay

Suttons Bay, Oregon, is a popular resort and retirement community with a population of about 40,000. Day-to-day activities are run by Sue Talbot, the village manager, who serves under the direction of the village's mayor and council. Following last month's village council meeting, Sue hired Geoff Finch, a recent graduate of Middle State University. Because of his experience in budgeting, Sue assigned Geoff the task of developing the village budget for the next fiscal year. Sue wants the budget completed by next month's council meeting.

Geoff and Sue meet to review this year's budget and to start planning for next year. Sue explains how Suttons Bay's revenues are generated from property taxes, which are charged at the rate of $0.0281 per dollar of assessed property value and are paid by property owners throughout the year. She arranges for Geoff to meet with the managers of the five departments (Public Safety, Public Works, Parks, Housing, and Libraries) so he can work with them to determine their expected expenditures for next year.

Geoff collects data for next year's budget and prepares a first draft of his worksheet with the revenue and expenditure amounts entered as dollars in thousands. Geoff reviews his first draft of the budget with Sue, and she says it looks good but he needs to make some changes. She explains that Suttons Bay will start collecting sales tax revenues next year to support the Parks Department and the operations of their newly opened library. Sue asks Geoff to add these items to his worksheet.

Geoff returns to his office to revise the budget. He begins by making changes to his planning analysis sheet (Figure 3-33) and worksheet sketch (Figure 3-34). Then Geoff collects the additional data he needs for the Parks and Library expenditures. He's ready to modify his budget worksheet to include these revisions as he prepares the report for this month's meeting of the village council.

Planning Analysis Sheet

My goal:
Develop budget of expected revenues and expenditures by quarter

What results do I want to see?
Each revenue source and each department's expenditures by quarter with a total for the year

What information do I need?
Columns are Qtr 1, Qtr 2, Qtr 3, Qtr 4, Annual
Property values (723764)
Property tax rate (0.0281)
Property tax collection percent (40%, 30%, 20%, 10% by quarter)
Retail sales—annual (239441)
Sales tax rate (1.5%)
Retail sales percent (18%, 23%, 27%, 32% by quarter)
Permits (157, 259, 201, 124 by quarter)
Recycling grant (0, 208, 54, 0 by quarter)
City government (924, 924, 924, 924 by quarter)
Public safety (1761, 1924, 2034, 1748 by quarter)
Public works (437, 467, 486, 451 by quarter)
Housing (863, 863, 863, 863 by quarter)
Parks (312, 486, 511, 336 by quarter)
Library (383, 387, 376, 359 by quarter)
Miscellaneous (348, 427, 411, 396 by quarter)

What calculations will I perform?
Sales tax = retail sales * sales tax rate * retail sales percent
Property tax = property values * property tax rate * property tax collection percent
Total revenues=sum of revenues
Benefits = (sum of village government, public safety, public works, parks, housing) * 0.2 (1+0.2)
Total expenditures = sum of expenditures
Surplus or deficit = total revenues − total expenditures

Figure 3-33

Figure 3-34

	QTR 1	QTR 2	QTR 3	QTR 4	YEAR
Key Assumptions:					

Property Values (000's)	*72376400* XXX,XXX				
Property Tax Rate	X.XXXX	*30%*	*20%*	*10%*	
Property Tax Collection	XXX%	XXX%	XXX%	XXX%	
Retail Sales (000's)	*239,441 000*				
Sales Tax Rate	1.5%				
Retail Sales Percent	18%	23%	27%	32%	
Revenues (000's)					
Property Tax	XXX,XXX *8135.11*	XXX,XXX *6101.33*	XXX,XXX *4067.55*	XXX,XXX *2033.7*	XXX,XXX *20337.77*
Sales Tax	XXX,XXX *646,99*	XXX,XXX *826.07*	XXX,XXX *969.78*	XXX,XXX *1149.32*	XXX,XXX *3591.62*
Permits	XXX,XXX *157*	XXX,XXX *25~*	XXX,XXX *201*	XXX,XXX *124*	XXX,XXX *741*
Recycling Grant	XXX,XXX *0*	XXX,XXX *208*	XXX,XXX *54*	XXX,XXX *0*	XXX,XXX *262*
	--------------				----------
Total Revenues	XXX,XXX *8938.6*	XXX,XXX *7394.9*	XXX,XXX *5292.38*	XXX,XXX *3307.0*	XXX,XXX *24932.39*
Expenditures (000's)					
Village Government	XXX,XXX *924*	XXX,XXX *924*	XXX,XXX *924*	XXX,XXX *924*	XXX,XXX *3696*
Public Safety	XXX,XXX *1761*	XXX,XXX *1924*	XXX,XXX *2034*	XXX,XXX *1748*	XXX,XXX *7467*
Public Works	XXX,XXX *437*	XXX,XXX *467*	XXX,XXX *486*	XXX,XXX *451*	XXX,XXX *1841*
Parks	312	486	511	336	XXX,XXX *1645*
Housing	XXX,XXX *863*	XXX,XXX *863*	XXX,XXX *863*	XXX,XXX *863*	XXX,XXX *3452*
Benefits	XXX,XXX *5156.4*	XXX,XXX *5576.8*	XXX,XXX *5781.6*	XXX,XXX *5186.9*	XXX,XXX *21721.2*
Library	383	387	376	359	XXX,XXX *1505*
Miscellaneous	XXX,XXX *348*	XXX,XXX *427*	XXX,XXX *411*	XXX,XXX *396*	XXX,XXX *1582*
	--------------				----------
Total Expenditures	XXX,XXX *5887.4*	XXX,XXX *6410.8*	XXX,XXX *6568.6*	XXX,XXX *5941.4*	XXX,XXX *24808.2*
Surplus or Deficit	(XXX,XXX) *3051.2*	(XXX,XXX) *984.1*	(XXX,XXX) *-1276.2*	(XXX,XXX) *2634.3*	(XXX,XXX) *124.19*

row 34.

Complete the revisions to Geoff's first draft of his worksheet.

1. Launch 1-2-3, then open the P3VSB1.WK4 worksheet, which contains Geoff's first draft of the village budget.
2. Review the worksheet formulas. Why is absolute referencing used in the formulas for property tax?

E
3. Insert rows for the additional key assumptions data as specified by Geoff's sketch. Enter the labels and values used in calculating the sales tax. What number format is assigned to the cells in the newly inserted rows? Which ones do you need to revise to match Geoff's sketch?
4. Insert a row for the Sales Tax revenues between the Property Tax and Permits items. Add the label and formulas for the Sales Tax revenues as indicated by Geoff's design. Sum the four quarters for the annual total.
5. Verify that Sales Tax revenues are added into the total revenues. How do you know this amount is added? If the sales tax amount is not included, modify the formula for total revenues so it includes the sales tax.
6. Insert the Parks expenditures between the Public Works and Housing items. Then place the Library expenditures between the Benefits and Miscellaneous items. Enter the Annual total for the four quarters. Are these new expenditures included in the total expenditures? (*Hint*: The annual surplus or deficit = 124.)
7. Preview and print this version of the budget. Save the worksheet as S3VSB2.WK4.
8. Rearrange the key assumptions by moving them to row 34 so they are at the bottom of the report. Then delete the blank rows from which the key assumptions were moved.

9. Place the following title and subtitle at the top of the worksheet in column C:

   Bold   Village of Suttons Bay

   Italicize Proposed Budget

   After you enter these titles, center them as long labels. Leave one blank line between the subtitle and the column headings.

10. To enhance the appearance of the report title and subtitle:

    a. Bold both titles.

    b. Italicize the subtitle.

    c. Change the typeface of both titles.

    d. Increase the point size of both titles to 14.

    e. Place a drop shadow around both titles in columns B, C, and D.

11. Add the date from the computer's clock in cell F1, then format the number as "31-Dec-93."

12. Underline each column heading using underlining within the cells.

13. Italicize the Key Assumptions label, then add boldface and italics to the Surplus or Deficit label.

14. Add an outline and a shading pattern to the Surplus or Deficit data values by trying different patterns, then selecting one that is appropriate. Describe the other patterns that you tried.

15. Preview and print this copy of the budget report. Include an appropriate header and/or footer for this report. Save the worksheet as S3VSB3.WK4.

E 16. Remove the shading pattern from the Surplus or Deficit data values and have the negative values displayed in red. Which dialog box did you use for this specification? Use the Help system to explore how to change the appearance (color) of data.

17. Sue wants to test a what-if value. What if the sales tax rate is increased to 2% while the property tax rate is reduced to .026? In this alternative, a sales tax increase is used to fund a property tax reduction. What is the surplus or deficit from this alternative? Preview and print this budget alternative, then circle the cell used to evaluate the overall budget result.

3. Controlling Quality for Green & Able Products

Green & Able Products (GAP) is a worldwide manufacturer and distributor of household appliances, such as toasters, mixers, and coffee makers. GAP designs and manufactures appliances that are user- and environmental-friendly. Nearly all of their products contain parts that are manufactured from recycled materials, and each product is easily recycled when the product is worn out. However, GAP is careful to ensure that these products are of the highest quality, regardless of the source of their raw materials.

Kristi Hernandez is the manager of small appliance manufacturing and is responsible for monitoring GAP's quality control systems. She recently hired Dean Sabo to help her manage these activities. Each month she wants him to prepare a manufacturing quality cost report that monitors all the costs attributable to quality control. Kristi classifies these costs into four types:

- Appraisal—costs of inspecting and testing
- Prevention—costs of identifying the causes of defects and implementing corrective action, of training personnel, and of redesigning the product or manufacturing system
- Internal failure—costs incurred within the manufacturing process for scrap, rework, and repair
- External failure—costs incurred after the customer purchases the product including warranty repair or replacement

Dean meets with Kristi to design the new monthly manufacturing quality cost report that summarizes the cost of performing their quality control activities. Dean prepares a sketch showing the layout of the report (Figure 3-35). Kristi and Dean are familiar with the industry guideline "for every dollar spent in prevention, ten dollars are saved in failure and appraisal costs" and want to compare their costs for prevention with those for appraisal and failure. The design shows the dollar amount for each cost, the percentage of total cost by type, and the percentage of overall total quality cost. In his design, Dean includes the "100.0%" values to help specify how the total percentage costs are calculated. Kristi wants the percentages calculated to help her spot those quality control activities that are the most costly.

	Current Month's Cost	Percent of Total by Type	Percent of Total Quality Costs
Appraisal Costs:			
Materials Inspection	XXX,XXX	XXX.X%	XXX.X%
Laboratory	XXX,XXX	XXX.X%	XXX.X%
Total Appraisal	XXX,XXX	100.0%	XXX.X%
Internal Failure Costs:			
Scrap	XXX,XXX	XXX.X%	XXX.X%
Repair and Rework	XXX,XXX	XXX.X%	XXX.X%
Total Internal Failure	XXX,XXX	100.0%	XXX.X%
External Failure Costs:			
Warranty Costs	XXX,XXX	XXX.X%	XXX.X%
Out-of-Warranty Repairs	XXX,XXX	XXX.X%	XXX.X%
Product Liability	XXX,XXX	XXX.X%	XXX.X%
Transportation	XXX,XXX	XXX.X%	XXX.X%
Total External Failure	XXX,XXX	100.0%	XXX.X%
Prevention Costs:			
Reliability Engineering	XXX,XXX	XXX.X%	XXX.X%
Systems Development	XXX,XXX	XXX.X%	XXX.X%
Total Prevention	XXX,XXX	100.0%	XXX.X%
Total Quality Costs	XXX,XXX		100.0%

Figure 3-35

Complete GAP's manufacturing quality cost report, which Dean started to develop, by performing the following:
1. Launch 1-2-3, then open the P3GAP1.WK4 worksheet, which contains Dean's first draft of the quality cost report.
2. Review the worksheet formulas. Which cells are calculated using the @SUM function?
3. After reviewing the first draft, Kristi wants these costs added to the worksheet:

Type	Cost	Amount
Appraisal	Supplies Inspection	2,400
Internal Failure	Downtime	8,300
External Failure	Customer Complaints	5,700
Prevention	Quality Training	2,200

Enter Supplies Inspection immediately below Materials Inspection. Place Downtime immediately below Repair and Rework. Customer Complaints goes immediately below Out-of-Warranty Repairs, and Quality Training goes immediately above Reliability Engineering. As necessary, revise any summations to include the new costs that you added to the worksheet. (*Hint*: The Total Quality Costs = 146,730.)

4. Add the formulas in column C that calculate the Percent of Total by Type. Format these cells as a percentage with one decimal. Use this formula for each quality control cost and for the total for the type:

$$\text{Percent of Total by Type} = \frac{\text{Individual Cost}}{\text{Total Costs by Type}}$$

Do you need to use relative or absolute referencing with these formulas? Make sure you enter the formulas that calculate those cells where Dean included the "100.0%" in his design. Of course, your calculated result in these cells should then be the 100.0%.

5. Add the formulas in column D that calculate the Percent of Total Quality Costs. Also, format these cells as a percentage with one decimal. Use this formula for each quality control cost and for the Total Quality Costs:

$$\text{Percent of Total Quality Costs} = \frac{\text{Individual Cost}}{\text{Total Quality Costs}}$$

E
6. Include underlining as shown in Dean's sketch. Preview and print this version of the quality cost report. Save the worksheet as S3GAP2.WK4. Write a short paragraph that compares the prevention costs to the other costs. Do you think the prevention costs are too high or too low? Why?

7. Because of the importance of prevention and the potential for financial savings through strong prevention activities, Kristi wants to emphasize this by placing Prevention Costs as the first cost type in the report. Rearrange the report and, as necessary, revise any formulas for this change. Did you need to edit any of the cell references?

E
8. Place the following title and subtitle at the top of the worksheet in column A:
   Green & Able Products
   Manufacturing Quality Costs
   After entering these titles, specify the alignment as centered across columns A through D. How does this compare to using centered long labels? Make sure you leave one blank line between the subtitle and the column headings.

9. Enhance the appearance of the report title by using the attributes and fonts you think give the report a professional look.

10. At the top of the report in a separate line above the title, add the date from the computer's clock, then select the month and day format.

11. Underline each column heading using underlining within the cells.

12. Select at least three other cells and change their attributes to draw the reader's attention to these items. Use an outline and shading pattern for at least one cell. Try several different patterns, then pick the best one. Describe the patterns you tried.

13. Preview and print a copy of the manufacturing quality cost report. Include an appropriate header and footer on the report. Save the worksheet as S3GAP3.WK4. Review this report, then draw a circle around the largest total quality cost percent.

14. Kristi is considering expanding training in quality control methods to increase GAP's prevention efforts. If she increases the Quality Training costs by $500 and the Warranty costs are reduced by $10 for each $1 of increase in Quality Training, what will be the Total Quality Costs, assuming all other costs remain the same? Preview and print this report.

15. Produce a chart of the Prevention costs for the what-if analysis in Problem 14. Preview and print a report containing both the manufacturing quality cost report and this chart. Save the worksheet as S3GAP4.WK4.

Creating and Printing Charts

Preparing a Market Segment Analysis

CASE

Yamasuka Chemical Company

Brian Thomson recently graduated from college with a major in International Business. In addition to his business courses, he studied Japanese because he thought that learning a second language would help him find a job. His hard work paid off. Brian was hired as an assistant in the Marketing Department of Yamasuka Chemical Company (YCC)—a leading Japanese chemical company with North American headquarters in San Francisco. "Chemistry at work with the environment" is the best way to describe YCC's products. YCC's diversified product groups include basic chemicals, industrial products, and consumer products. Polyethylene is an example of a basic chemical that is used in a variety of products such as recyclable milk containers. An example of an industrial product is Enviroboard, YCC's leading brand of rigid plastic foam insulation material. Enviroloc plastic bags and plastic food wrap are examples of consumer products, designed specifically for recycling. YCC focuses on the development of new and innovative products that will propel their company ahead of the competition and into the 21st century.

Brian works with Migiwa Kamada, a senior market analyst for North American Operations. Migiwa is responsible for coordinating the market planning activities for YCC's three product groups. She has an upcoming meeting scheduled with YCC's Management Committee to review current performance and long-term strategic market growth. YCC's North American Operations' long-term strategy is for balanced operations with equal sales coming from each of the three strategic market sectors—basics, industrials, and consumers (Figure 4-1). With a balanced focus on market sectors, YCC hopes to minimize its variation in sales due to changing economic conditions. Migiwa is making a presentation at the meeting; her presentation needs to show the Management Committee that YCC is on its way to achieving its goal.

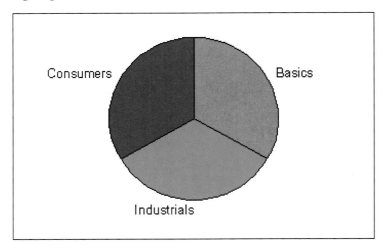

Figure 4-1
YCC's goal for
balanced operations

First, Migiwa asks Brian to develop a worksheet that reports the projected sales and operating income of the three market sectors for the years 1995 through 1999 based on last year's sales and operating income and the information she collected on YCC's expected future direction. Brian returns to his office and spends the rest of the day preparing the worksheet for his report (Figure 4-2).

Figure 4-2
Brian's strategic
sector analysis
worksheet

The next morning Brian shows his worksheet to Migiwa. She looks it over and tells him that the worksheet is excellent, but it isn't enough for her presentation. She wants Brian to create a chart that will help her explain the data in the worksheet. They agree that a chart is an effective way to clarify the abstract data in a worksheet, and a chart helps the audience visualize relationships between that data. A chart is an attention-getting display you use to present data. Brian and Migiwa discuss the different types of charts they could use, and agree the charts should be accurate, clearly labeled, attractive, and able to create a strong impression. Migiwa asks Brian to create at least two charts for her presentation. Brian is excited about his new assignment and returns to his desk to develop his planning analysis sheet for creating the charts (Figure 4-3).

Planning Analysis Sheet

My goal:
Prepare charts showing market share and trends for the three strategic sectors from 1995 to 1999

What results do I want to see?
Comparative stacked bar chart of sales by sector from 1995 to 1999
Pie chart of operating income by sector for 1997

What information do I need?
Expected sales and operating income by strategic sector for 1995 through 1999

Figure 4-3
Brian's planning analysis sheet

After looking over his notes, Brian sketches the two charts he thinks would most effectively represent the data (Figure 4-4). From his discussion with Migiwa, Brian knows he needs to present the data values for 1997 since this is the middle of their projected time frame. Brian decides to create a pie chart because it can effectively display the data for a single year. Now, he is ready to create the charts.

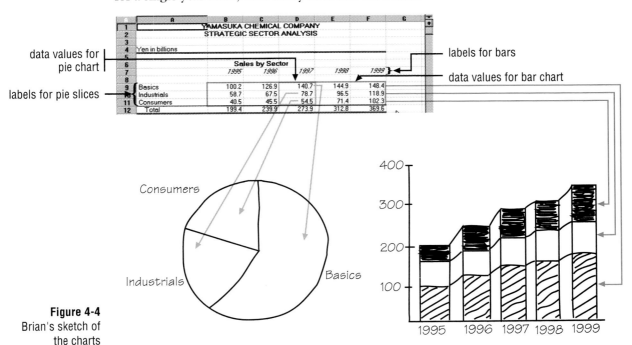

Figure 4-4
Brian's sketch of the charts

In this tutorial you will create Brian's charts for Migiwa's presentation to YCC's Management Committee. You will learn how to construct charts and to determine the type of chart that is best suited to communicate your data.

Introduction to Charts

Charts are used to present data in a visually appealing and easily understood format. Presentations that include charts are more effective and persuasive than presentations without charts. Some examples of what a chart can do for you are:

- Make your message more powerful, clear, and persuasive
- Help viewers grasp your point of view faster and remember it longer
- Summarize large quantities of complex data
- Discover new relationships among data

Once you create a worksheet, you can chart any data that the worksheet contains. Each single set of data that you chart is known as a **data series**. For example, in Tutorial 1 you charted the expense items for Saturday and Sunday. Each expense item, such as "Entry Fees" and "Gas and Oil," is a data series. In a chart a data series can be represented by a line, a bar, or a slice of pie. In Tutorial 1 each data series was represented by a bar.

Once you know what data you want to chart, you have to determine the relationship you want to see between the various data series. The charts used in business often deal with three basic situations:

- Showing trends (How do conditions change over time?)
- Comparing components and relative amounts (What proportion is each individual component to the total amount?)
- Showing the relationship between two variables (How are the two variables related?)

The type of relationship you want your chart to illustrate determines the chart type you need to use. Lotus 1-2-3 includes a variety of chart types: bar charts, line charts, stacked bar charts, pie charts, XY charts, and mixed charts. Figure 4-5 summarizes the application of charts to typical situations.

Situation	Chart Type
Showing trends	Bar chart, line chart, mixed chart
Comparing components	Pie chart, exploded pie chart, stacked bar chart
Showing relationships	XY chart

Figure 4-5
Selecting a chart type

1-2-3 Charts

As you learned in Tutorial 1, it is easy to graphically represent your worksheet data with a chart. Figure 4-6 lists the chart types and their SmartIcons, and explains the purpose of each chart. Of these 15 chart types, 11 produce two-dimensional (2-D) charts and four chart types produce three-dimensional (3-D) charts.

Chart Icon	Chart Type	Purpose
	Area	Shows the magnitude of change over time.
	Vertical Bar	Shows comparisons among the data series represented by vertical bars. Most useful with a limited number of data series.
	Horizontal Bar	Shows comparisons among the data series represented by horizontal bars. Most useful with a limited number of data series.
	HLCO	Shows the high-low-close-open values, such as the changes in the price of stock market data over time.
	Line	Shows trends or changes over time. Most useful for showing trends with many data values in each data series.
	Mixed	Shows how one data series corresponds to another data series by combining parts from a line, bar, or area chart.
	Pie	Shows the proportion of parts to a whole for a single data series.
	Radar	Shows the symmetry or uniformity of data as a function of distance from a central point.
	Stacked Bar	Shows totals in addition to comparing individual data values for each vertical bar segment. Overall height of bar shows the total of the components that make up the data series.
	Horizontal Stacked Bar	Shows totals in addition to comparing individual data values for each horizontal bar segment. Overall length of bar shows the total of the components that make up the data series.
	XY	Shows the pattern or relationship between sets of (x,y) data points. Most useful when the x-axis data series is *not* units of time.
	3-D Area	Shows the magnitude of each data series as a solid three-dimensional shape.
	3-D Bar	Similar to a 2-D bar chart, but bars appear three-dimensional.
	3-D Line	Shows each line as a ribbon within a three-dimensional space.
	3-D Pie	Shows the proportion of parts to a whole, with emphasis on the data values in the front wedges, for a single data series.

Figure 4-6
1-2-3 chart types

Each chart type has several predefined chart formats that specify such format characteristics as the arrangement of data displayed in the chart. The side-by-side or stacked arrangement, like that for the bar charts, is a format selection. For example, there are three format icons for bar charts displayed in the Type dialog box, as shown in Figure 4-7.

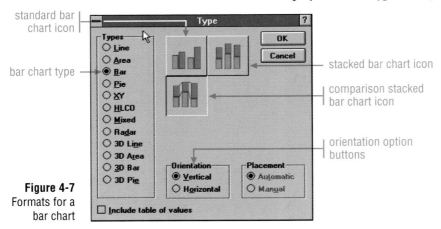

standard bar chart icon

bar chart type

stacked bar chart icon

comparison stacked bar chart icon

orientation option buttons

Figure 4-7
Formats for a bar chart

Like bar charts, many of the other chart types can be displayed in either a vertical or horizontal orientation. This choice is specified as an option in the Type dialog box when it is appropriate to change the orientation of a chart (Figure 4-7).

Examining a 1-2-3 Chart

Figure 4-8 shows the elements of a typical 1-2-3 chart. It is important to understand 1-2-3 chart terminology so you can successfully construct and edit charts. Let's examine the elements of Brian's completed comparison stacked bar chart.

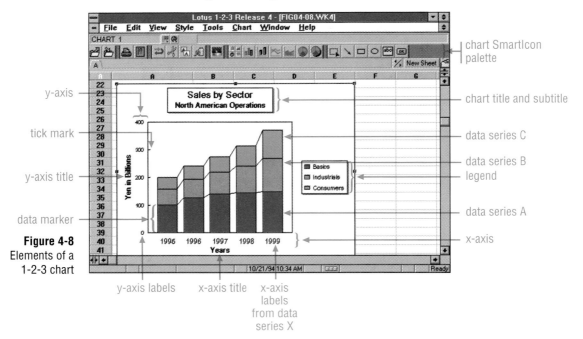

y-axis

tick mark

y-axis title

data marker

Figure 4-8
Elements of a 1-2-3 chart

chart SmartIcon palette

chart title and subtitle

data series C

data series B

legend

data series A

x-axis

y-axis labels

x-axis title

x-axis labels from data series X

The **chart title** identifies the chart. This can be combined with an optional **subtitle** when two lines are needed for identification. The horizontal axis of the chart is referred to as the **x-axis**. The vertical axis is referred to as the **y-axis**. Each axis on a chart can have a title that identifies the scale or categories of the chart data. For example, in Figure 4-8 the x-axis title is "Years" and the y-axis title is "Yen in Billions."

The **y-axis labels** show the scale for the y-axis. A **tick mark** indicates the location for each value on the scale. Lotus 1-2-3 automatically generates this scale based on the values selected for the chart. The **x-axis labels** correspond to the labels you use for the worksheet data to identify this data.

A **data point** is a single data value in a cell in the worksheet. For example, the value 100.2 in cell B9 of Brian's worksheet is a data point (Figure 4-2). A **data marker** is a bar, area, slice, or symbol that marks a single data point on a chart. Each segment of a bar in Figure 4-8 is a data marker. With a line chart, a symbol such as a small square is used as a data marker.

A **data series** is a group of related data points from a range of cells, such as the industrial sales by sector shown in cells B10 through F10 on Brian's worksheet (Figure 4-2). On a chart such as the one in Figure 4-8, a data series is shown as a set of data markers for one segment of each stacked bar. In 1-2-3 each data series is identified as a range for the chart. A chart can contain up to 23 data series, which are identified by a letter from A to W. In addition, the data series X is used to specify values for the x-axis of a chart, and in Figure 4-8 the data series X provides the labels for the x-axis.

When you have more than one data series, your chart will contain more than one set of data markers. For example, each stacked bar in Figure 4-8 has three segments, each representing one of the three data series. When you show more than one data series on a chart, it is a good idea to use a **legend** to identify which data markers represent each data series.

Arranging Data Series for Charts

Data series for 1-2-3 charts are located in ranges of cells that are organized either *by rows* or *by columns* with the same number of data values in each data series. All the data series in one chart should have the same row or column arrangement with each individual data series located in only one row or column. When you create a chart, 1-2-3 automatically plots the data series following several rules that depend on how the data is arranged in the worksheet. When Brian creates his chart, he will select the range A6..F11, as shown in Figure 4-9. Because this selected range contains *more columns of data than rows of data*, 1-2-3 will plot the data series *by rows* as indicated in Figure 4-9. As 1-2-3 examines the range, it will detect the label "Sales by Sector" in row 6; since there are no other data values in the other columns of this row, 1-2-3 will assign this label as the chart title. The data values in the range B7..F7 will be assigned to data series X. Row 8, which is blank, will be ignored, whereas row 9 containing the data values for "Basics" will be detected and assigned to data series A. When the selected range contains blank rows or columns, 1-2-3 ignores them when plotting the data series. The other two rows in this selected range will be assigned to data series B and C of the chart, respectively.

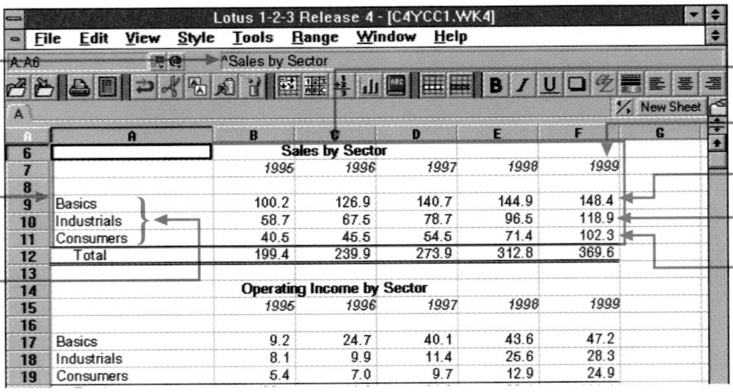

Figure 4-9
Data series
arranged by row

Labels pointing to the figure: label in selected range, range A6..F11, labels for legend, title, data series X for x-axis label, data series A, data series B, data series C

If 1-2-3 detects that the selected range for the chart contains *more rows of data than columns of data*, then the data series are plotted *by columns* with the X range residing in the left-most column of the selected range. If the selected range does *not* include rows with labels at the top of the range, then 1-2-3 creates a chart with a default title, which you can edit after the chart is initially created. You can override 1-2-3's automatic selection of data arranged by rows or by columns if you use the Assign ranges list box in the Ranges dialog box. (To display the Ranges dialog box, click Chart, then click Ranges.... This option is not covered in this tutorial.)

Creating a Comparison Stacked Bar Chart

Brian plans to create a comparison stacked bar chart, and then a pie chart. Now let's retrieve Brian's worksheet, which contains the strategic market sector data for 1995 through 1999 needed for creating his comparison stacked bar chart. You will also need to select the SmartIcon palette created for Tutorial 4.

To open the worksheet and select the predefined SmartIcon palette:

❶ Launch 1-2-3.
❷ Click the **Open File SmartIcon** 📂 to open Brian's worksheet, C4YCC1.WK4, located on your Student Disk. Then save the worksheet as S4YCC1.WK4 in case you need to restart this tutorial. The opened worksheet appears, as shown previously in Figure 4-2.
❸ Select the Tutorial 4 SmartIcon palette by using the SmartIcon palette selector ▦ in the status bar.
❹ Review Brian's worksheet. Observe the rows containing the three data series—Basics, Industrials, and Consumers. The rows are adjacent to one another in a single range.

According to Brian's sketch in Figure 4-4, one of the charts he wants to create is a comparison stacked bar chart comparing expected sales by market sector for the years 1995 through 1999. He chose this type of chart because it is useful for showing comparisons. He wants to place his chart close to the data so he can print both the worksheet and the chart in the same report. Remember from Tutorial 1 that to create a chart you select the range of data you want to chart, and then you specify where you want the chart to appear on the worksheet. Lotus 1-2-3 then uses the default bar chart to chart your data. Depending on the data you are charting, you might want to select a different chart type. You can also add and/or modify headings, titles, fonts, and attributes. Let's use the procedure you learned in Tutorial 1, combined with your new knowledge of chart types, to create Brian's comparison stacked bar chart.

To create the comparison stacked bar chart:

❶ Select the range A6..F11, which contains the three data series arranged by rows that Brian wants to chart. See Figure 4-10.

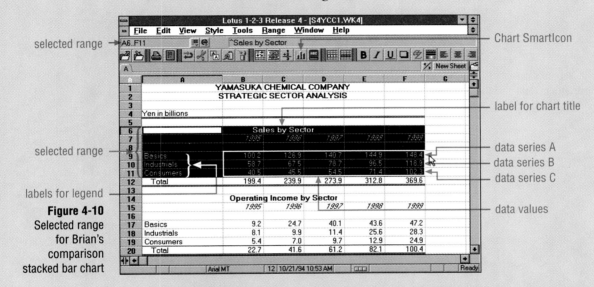

Figure 4-10
Selected range for Brian's comparison stacked bar chart

❷ Scroll the worksheet window until cell A22 is positioned in the upper-left corner of the window. This is the location for the upper-left corner of the chart. *Do not click the mouse*, or you will unselect the range you want to chart.

TROUBLE? If you click A22 by mistake, repeat Steps 1 and 2.

❸ Click the **Chart SmartIcon** ▮▮▮. The pointer changes to ▮▮▮ to indicate 1-2-3 is ready for you to specify the location and size of your new chart.

❹ Move the pointer to cell A22.

❺ Click and drag the pointer over the range A22..E42 to indicate the location and size of the chart. As you drag the pointer, a dotted outline indicates the area the chart will fill.

❻ Release the mouse button when the area is large enough for the chart. When you release the mouse button, a default standard bar chart like the one you used in Tutorial 1 appears, as shown in Figure 4-11.

TROUBLE? If you select the wrong data series, use the Undo SmartIcon ▭ to remove the chart, then repeat Steps 1 through 6.

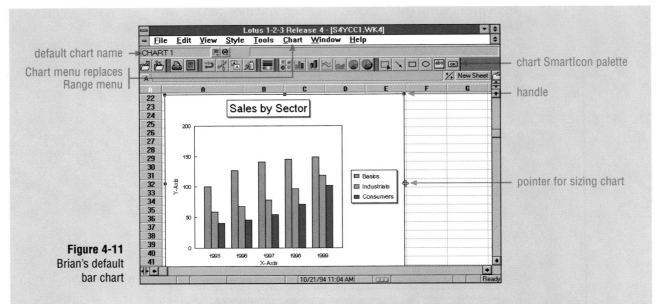

Figure 4-11
Brian's default
bar chart

(callouts on figure:) default chart name → CHART 1 ; Chart menu replaces Range menu ; chart SmartIcon palette ; handle ; pointer for sizing chart

Notice the set of small squares located at the edges of the chart. These squares are called *handles*. Handles appear at the corners, mid-points, and end of objects—a chart is considered an *object*. The handles indicate that the object is *selected*. Once you select an object, you can resize, move, copy, edit, or delete it. You will learn more about objects and about selecting them later in this tutorial.

Also notice that the Chart menu replaces the Range menu; the SmartIcon palette, which is context-sensitive, changes to the default palette for working with charts; and 1-2-3 automatically assigns the chart the default name "CHART 1" so you can work with the chart in the future—for example, when you want to print the chart.

Selecting a Chart Type

After 1-2-3 charts the data you want using the default bar chart, you can select another chart type from the SmartIcon palette or from the Type dialog box. You might have to experiment with different chart types to find the one that best represents your data. Sometimes the chart you planned isn't the right chart type for the information you want to plot. As you work through this tutorial, you will find that changing from one chart type to another is an easy procedure.

REFERENCE WINDOW   **Selecting a Chart Type**

- Click the SmartIcon for the chart type you want if the type is available on the SmartIcon palette.

or

- Click the Chart Type SmartIcon to display the Type dialog box.

  or

  Double-click the default chart to display the Type dialog box.

- Select the chart type from the list of available chart types.

Brian needs to change the default bar chart to the comparison stacked bar chart. Let's change the chart type.

To change the chart to the comparison stacked bar type:
❶ Click the **Chart Type SmartIcon** to display the Type dialog box. See Figure 4-12.

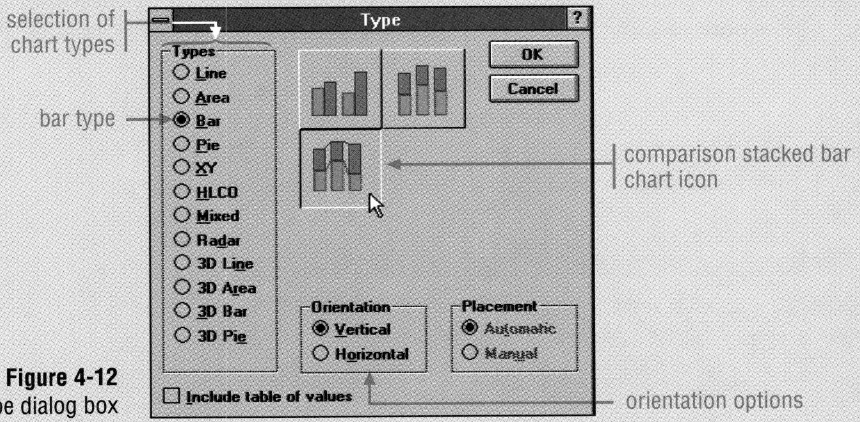

selection of chart types

bar type

comparison stacked bar chart icon

orientation options

Figure 4-12
Type dialog box

❷ Double-click the **comparison stacked bar chart icon** in the Type dialog box. This selects this chart type and returns you to the chart. See Figure 4-13. Note that double-clicking the icon is equivalent to clicking the icon, then clicking the OK button. You can use either method. Notice that 1-2-3 automatically adds x-axis and y-axis titles, and scales the y-axis.

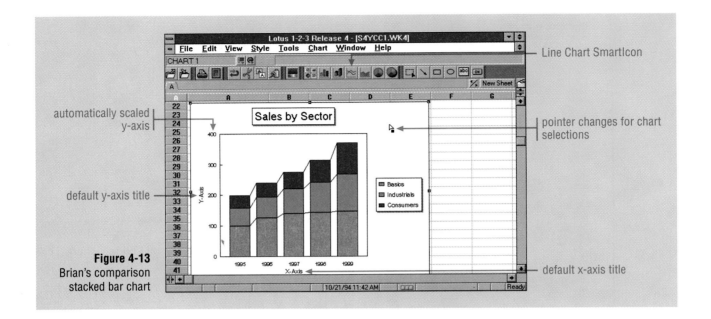

Figure 4-13
Brian's comparison
stacked bar chart

Brian thinks his chart looks good, but now that he sees all of the other chart type options, he wonders how his data would look as a line chart. Let's change Brian's bar chart to a line chart to see what this arrangement of the data looks like.

To change the chart to a line chart using a SmartIcon:

❶ Click the **Line Chart SmartIcon** ☒ . The bar chart changes to a line chart. See Figure 4-14.

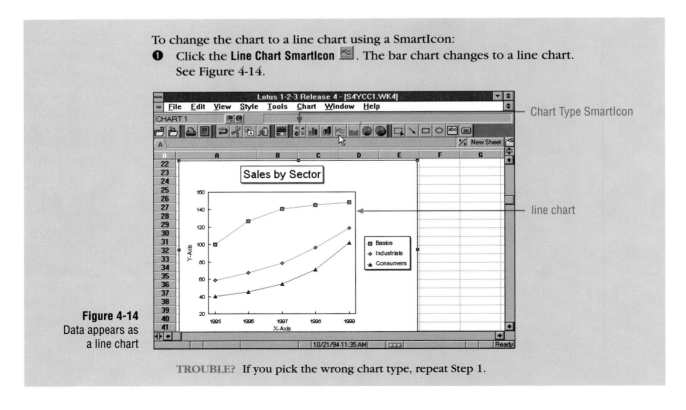

Figure 4-14
Data appears as
a line chart

TROUBLE? If you pick the wrong chart type, repeat Step 1.

Although this line chart is effective at showing the trend from year to year, it is not as good as the comparison stacked bar chart in showing the comparison between the three different components. Let's change it back.

❷ Click the **Chart Type SmartIcon** to display the Type dialog box.

❸ Click the **Bar option button**.

❹ Double-click the **comparison stacked bar chart icon**.

Brian wonders if a horizontal arrangement of the bars in the stacked bar chart might better represent the data than a vertical arrangement. Let's change the orientation of the chart from vertical to horizontal.

To change the orientation of the chart to horizontal:

❶ Double-click near the frame or border of the chart to display the Type dialog box. Notice that handles appear indicating the entire chart is selected.

> TROUBLE? If you select an element of the chart such as the title and the wrong dialog box appears, click the Cancel button in the dialog box, then repeat Step 1.

❷ Click the **Horizontal option button** in the Orientation box.

❸ Click the **OK button** to display the chart with horizontal bars. See Figure 4-15.

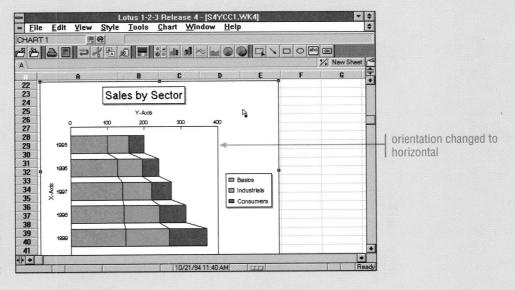

Figure 4-15
Horizontal
orientation of
comparison
stacked bar chart

orientation changed to horizontal

Brian examines the chart and decides that the horizontal bars are confusing so he wants to change the orientation back to vertical.

❹ Double-click the chart to redisplay the Type dialog box, click the **Vertical option button**, then click the **OK button** to display the desired chart.

Brian's comparison stacked bar chart is complete. He wants to save his work and print the chart so he can review it with Migiwa.

Saving and Printing Charts

When you print charts, you can print them alone or you can print the worksheet and chart as one report. Brian wants to print the worksheet with the chart so Migiwa can look at the entire report, making sure that the chart represents the data well. He also wants a printout of just the chart so she can concentrate on the individual elements of the chart.

Let's save the worksheet with this newly created chart, then print just the chart first.

To save the worksheet and print only the chart:

❶ Save the worksheet with the newly created chart as S4YCC2.WK4.

❷ Select the chart by clicking its frame or near its border. When you see the handles in the frame surrounding the chart, you know it is selected.

❸ Click the **Print SmartIcon** 🖨 to display the Print dialog box. See Figure 4-16.

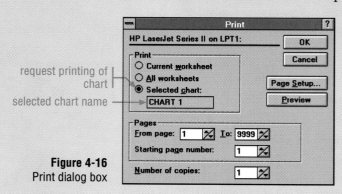

request printing of chart

selected chart name

Figure 4-16
Print dialog box

❹ Make sure the Selected chart option is selected, then click the **OK button** to print only the chart.

Now let's print the chart *and* the worksheet.

To print the chart and worksheet as one report:

❶ Click anywhere in the worksheet other than the chart area.

❷ Click the **Preview SmartIcon** 🖼 to display the Print Preview dialog box.

❸ Make sure the Current worksheet option is selected, then click the **OK button** to preview the worksheet area to be printed.

❹ If the layout is acceptable, click the **Print SmartIcon** 🖨 to display the Print dialog box.

❺ Click the **OK button** to print the worksheet and chart.

With his two printouts in hand, Brian is ready to review the chart with Migiwa.

If you want to take a break and resume the tutorial at a later time, exit 1-2-3 by double-clicking the Control menu box. When you resume the tutorial, launch 1-2-3 and place your Student Disk in the appropriate disk drive. Open the S4YCC2.WK4 worksheet, select the Tutorial 4 SmartIcon palette, then continue with the tutorial.

Enhancing the Chart

Migiwa thinks Brian's chart does a good job of comparing the sales of each sector—Basics, Industrials, and Consumers—over the five-year period. However, she does notice a few things that need to be changed. First, she asks Brian to add the subtitle "North American Operations." She also thinks the title is too large, but wants the subtitle to be smaller than the title. Then, she asks him to add the specific titles to the x- and y-axes: "Years" for the x-axis and "Yen in Billions" for the y-axis. Next, she explains that she will need to make copies of this chart for the managers, and because of YCC's one-color printer and copier, Brian will need to modify the chart. He will have to create a black-and-white copy of the chart with different patterns for the three sectors rather than three different colors. Finally, she asks him to add a note that points to the 1999 values to emphasize that YCC is on track in meeting its goal. Brian understands what he needs to do and gets right to work. Migiwa's suggestions appear in red in Figure 4-17.

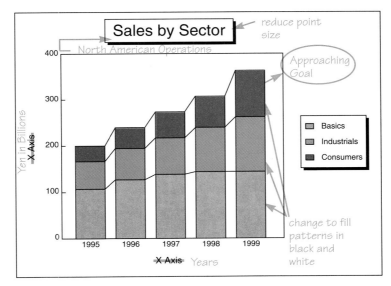

Figure 4-17
Migiwa's suggested changes to the comparison stacked bar chart

Selecting Chart Objects

First, Brian plans to add the subtitle for the chart, and then modify both the x- and y-axis labels.

As mentioned earlier, before you can make a change to an object in a chart—edit, move, resize, rotate, delete, or copy—you need to select the object. An object is automatically selected when it is created, as indicated by the appearance of handles. After that, you need to click it to select it. The pointer changes shape as you move it over the various objects in the chart, which you can select. Each change in pointer shape helps indicate the type of object that you can select.

Selecting Chart Objects

- Move the pointer to the object you want to select and notice that the pointer changes shape to indicate the type of object you are selecting.
- Click the object to select it.

Let's practice moving the pointer to several objects, observing the changes in the pointer shape, and selecting objects in preparation for modifying Brian's chart. You can use this method to select a chart or any item on the chart, including the frame that surrounds the title, text items, any of the data series, x-axis or y-axis text, x-axis or y-axis scales, legend frame, or fill patterns.

To practice selecting objects:

❶ Move the pointer to the frame that surrounds the Sales by Sector title and notice that its shape changes to ⌐⊡.

❷ Click to select this object. Note that handles appear indicating that the frame is selected. See Figure 4-18.

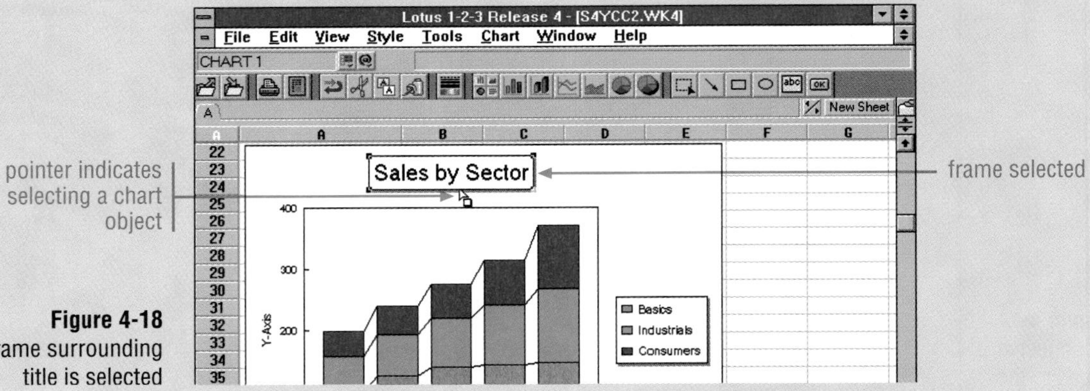

pointer indicates selecting a chart object

frame selected

Figure 4-18
Frame surrounding title is selected

Now let's select a text object.

❸ Move the pointer on top of the words "Sales by Sector" and note that the pointer changes to ⌐Ⓐ. The "A" indicates that alphanumeric text can be selected.

❹ Click the mouse button to select this object. See Figure 4-19. Note also that by selecting one object you unselect the other.

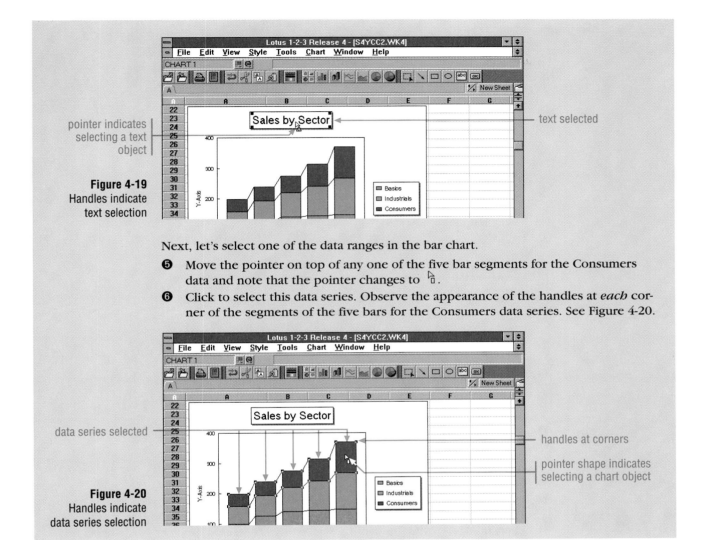

Figure 4-19
Handles indicate
text selection

Next, let's select one of the data ranges in the bar chart.

❺ Move the pointer on top of any one of the five bar segments for the Consumers data and note that the pointer changes to ⬈.

❻ Click to select this data series. Observe the appearance of the handles at *each* corner of the segments of the five bars for the Consumers data series. See Figure 4-20.

Figure 4-20
Handles indicate
data series selection

Now you are ready to select objects in Brian's comparison stacked bar chart and make the necessary changes to them.

Adding Titles

The first change Brian needs to make is to add the subtitle to the chart. A title can come from a cell in the worksheet or you can enter a title manually. You will also change the point size of the title and subtitle to improve their appearance.

REFERENCE WINDOW

Adding Chart Titles

- Click the title, which is a text object, to select it.
- Double-click the selected text object to display the Headings dialog box.
- In the Line 1 text box, enter the title you want for the chart.

  or

  In the Line 1 text box, enter the cell address that contains the label you want to use as the title, then click the Cell check box.
- In the Line 2 text box, enter the subtitle you want for the chart. This step is optional.

  or

  In the Line 2 text box, enter the cell address that contains the label you want to use as the subtitle, then click the Cell check box. This step is optional.
- Click the OK button to add the title(s).

First let's add the subtitle "North American Operations."

To add a subtitle line to the chart's title:

❶ Click the **Sales by Sector title** to select it. Handles appear around the text.

   TROUBLE? If the handles appear at the corners of the frame surrounding the title, you have selected the wrong object. Move the pointer over the title. When the pointer changes to ▲, repeat Step 1.

❷ Double-click the **Sales by Sector title** to display the Headings dialog box. See Figure 4-21. With this dialog box, you can specify both Line 1 and Line 2 of the chart title. Note that the Sales by Sector title is obtained from cell A6. When a title is taken from a cell in the worksheet, the cell address appears in the Line 1 text box—if the cell is part of the selected range. Note also that the Cell check box to the right contains an "X." If you want to change the title, you type the text in the Line 1 text box or enter a different cell address, then make sure the Cell check box is marked appropriately.

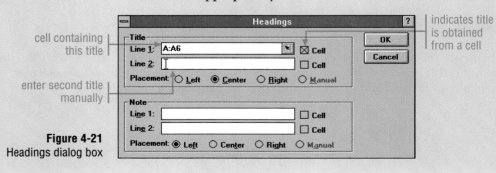

Figure 4-21
Headings dialog box

cell containing this title

enter second title manually

indicates title is obtained from a cell

❸ Click the Line 2 text box to position the cursor for entering the subtitle.

❹ Type **North American Operations**. You need to enter this title manually because it is not located in a cell in the worksheet. If it were, you could enter the cell address in the Line 2 text box, then click the Cell check box.

❺ Click the **OK button** to complete entering the chart title.

TROUBLE? If you click the OK button before completing Line 2, repeat Steps 2 through 5.

Changing Point Sizes and Fonts

Changing point sizes and fonts for text on a chart is the same as changing it for cells in the worksheet—you select the text that you want to format, and then select the desired formatting option.

Brian wants the size of the chart title to be 14 points so it still stands out, but it more closely matches the other text in his report. The current size of the title is 18 points. He also wants to make the subtitle a little larger. Let's make these changes.

To change the point size of the chart titles:

❶ Select the Sales by Sector title on the chart.

❷ Click the **point size selector** in the status bar. See Figure 4-22.

❸ Click **14**, the new point size.

Next, let's change the point size of the subtitle from 10 points to 12 points.

❹ Select the North American Operations subtitle.

❺ Click the right mouse button to display the Quick menu. See Figure 4-22. Remember, this is a context-sensitive menu; it displays only those commands relating to the object selected.

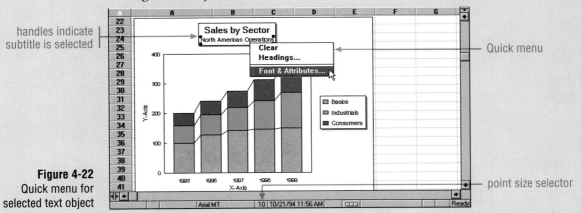

handles indicate subtitle is selected

Quick menu

point size selector

Figure 4-22
Quick menu for selected text object

❻ Click **Font & Attributes** to display this dialog box. See Figure 4-23. This is the same dialog box that you used in Tutorial 3 to change fonts and attributes of cells in the worksheet. The fonts available in your dialog box might be different.

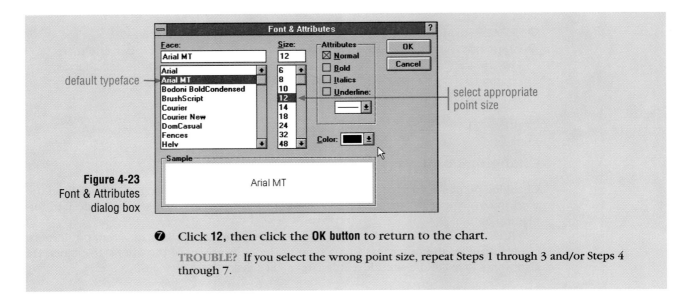

default typeface

select appropriate point size

Figure 4-23
Font & Attributes
dialog box

❼ Click **12**, then click the **OK button** to return to the chart.

TROUBLE? If you select the wrong point size, repeat Steps 1 through 3 and/or Steps 4 through 7.

You can change the appearance of any text object on your chart using these same steps.

Adding Axis Titles

Now that the chart title is complete, Brian needs to add the x-axis and y-axis titles.

When you create a chart, 1-2-3 provides generic titles for the x-axis and y-axis, which you can subsequently modify or delete. As the next step, let's add the y-axis title "Yen in Billions" to Brian's chart.

To add the y-axis title:
❶ Select the default y-axis title on the chart. Make sure the handles appear.
❷ Double-click the **Y-Axis** title to display the Y-Axis dialog box. See Figure 4-24. Note the other y-axis characteristics that you can specify using this dialog box. The 1-2-3 default is to scale the y-axis automatically. However, you can manually control the y-axis scale from this dialog box.

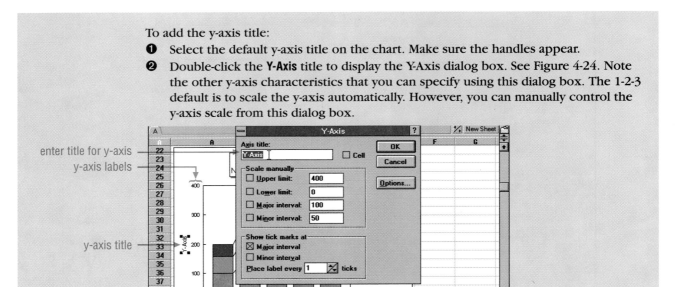

enter title for y-axis

y-axis labels

y-axis title

Figure 4-24
Y-Axis dialog box

❸ Type **Yen in Billions** in the Axis title text box.

❹ Click the **OK button** to return to the chart.

Brian thinks the title he just added and the y-axis labels are too small. Let's change the y-axis title and labels to a point size of 12.

❺ Select the y-axis title, then change the point size to 12 by using the point size selector in the status bar.

❻ Select the y-axis labels, then change the point size from the default of 9 to 12 using the point size selector.

In a similar manner, Brian needs to add the x-axis title "Years." Let's add this title, change its point size, and bold it. The x-axis labels do not need to be adjusted.

To add the x-axis title:

❶ Double-click the **X-Axis** title to display the X-Axis dialog box. See Figure 4-25. Notice that it is similar to the Y-Axis dialog box.

enter title for x-axis

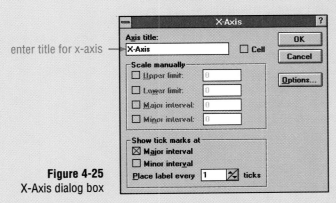

Figure 4-25
X-Axis dialog box

❷ Type **Years** in the Axis title text box, then click the **OK button**.

Now change the point size to 12 and add the boldface attribute.

❸ Position the pointer on the Years title, then click the right mouse button to display the Quick menu.

❹ Click **Font & Attributes** to display this dialog box.

❺ Click **12**, then click the **Bold** check box. Click the **OK button** to complete this specification and return to the chart.

Controlling Colors and Fill Patterns

Brian's comparison stacked bar chart is nearly complete. Because Migiwa wants to distribute paper copies of her presentation, she wants Brian to change the colors of the chart to black and white so they can be copied more readily. To do this, Brian must select three fill patterns to replace the three different colors assigned to each data series. A **fill pattern** is a design used to fill an area of a chart to differentiate it from another area of the chart. This will allow the managers to recognize the difference between the three data series.

REFERENCE WINDOW
                                Changing Fill Patterns

Use these instructions to change background colors or pattern colors by clicking the appropriate drop-down list arrow.

- Select the object you want to fill with a pattern.
- Click the Color SmartIcon to display the Lines & Color dialog box.
- Click the Pattern drop-down list arrow to display the palette of available patterns.
- Select the pattern you want.
- Click the OK button.

Brian wants the Basics bar to have a white background with a black fill pattern; the Industrials bar to have a white background with no fill pattern; and the Consumers bar to have a black background with no fill pattern. Let's change the color and fill pattern for the three data series included in Brian's comparison stacked bar chart.

To change the color and fill pattern for each data series:

❶ Select the Basics data series by clicking any one of the five bars in the series.

❷ Click the **Color SmartIcon** ▣ to display the Lines & Color dialog box. See Figure 4-26. Notice that this is the same dialog box you used in Tutorial 3 to specify the shading pattern for a cell and to add underlining.

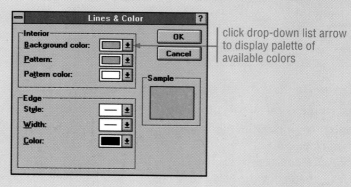

Figure 4-26
Lines & Color
dialog box

❸ Click the **Background color drop-down list arrow** to display the palette of available colors. See Figure 4-27. Note that the current selected color is blinking.

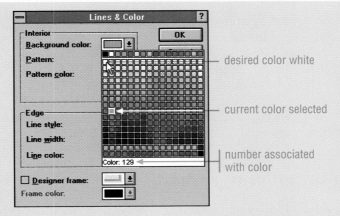

desired color white

current color selected

number associated
with color

Figure 4-27
Background color
palette

❹ Click **White** (Color: 0) to change the background color of this bar segment. Note
   that the selected color appears in the Background color list box.

   TROUBLE? If you select the wrong background color, repeat Steps 3 and 4.

❺ Click the **Pattern color drop-down list arrow** to redisplay the palette of available colors,
   then click **Black** (Color: 255). The selected color appears in the Pattern color list
   box.

❻ Click the **Pattern drop-down list arrow** to display the fill pattern choices. See
   Figure 4-28.

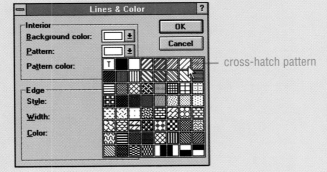

cross-hatch pattern

Figure 4-28
Palette of available
fill patterns

❼ Select the **cross-hatch pattern**, as indicated in Figure 4-28. Note that the selected pattern appears in the Pattern list box, and the pattern is displayed in the color
   selected in Step 5.

   TROUBLE? If you select the wrong fill pattern, repeat Steps 6 and 7.

❽ Click the **OK button** to complete the specifications for the Basics data series.

Brian needs to change only the background colors for the Industrials and Consumers
data series. He doesn't want to add a fill pattern to these bars. Let's do that next.

To change the background colors for the Industrials and Consumers data series:
❶ Select the Industrials data series, then select white as the background color. Do not
   change the pattern.

❷ Click the **OK button** to complete specifying this color.

❸ Select the Consumers data series, then select black as the background color. Do not change the pattern.

❹ Click the **OK button** to complete specifying this color.

Brian's comparison stacked bar chart is almost complete. He still needs to add the note that Migiwa suggested.

Adding Graphics to a Chart

Migiwa suggests one more enhancement that will help her with her presentation—adding graphics to the chart. **Graphics** are **drawn objects**, such as lines, arrows, shapes, and text, used to enhance charts. Figure 4-29 shows a variety of drawn objects. Drawn objects are *added on top* of the worksheet or chart, which means they can sometimes cover important information unless they are carefully placed on the worksheet or chart. Note that charts and chart elements are considered graphics and objects as well.

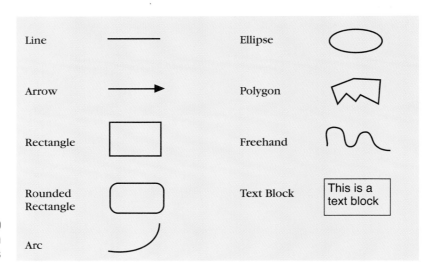

Figure 4-29
Common drawn objects

According to Migiwa's suggestions (Figure 4-17), Brian needs to add a note pointing to the stacked bars for 1999, then circle it to show that YCC is making progress in meeting its goal of equal sales in each sector. To add a note to the chart, Brian will add a text block. A **text block** is like a note you stick on a page to add comments or emphasize important information. When you add a note using a text block, the text is surrounded by a box, which serves as a frame. You can delete this frame and add another drawn object—like an ellipse—to set off the text. You can also add other objects such as arrows, as Brian will, to help draw a relationship between the note and the chart.

Adding a Text Block

- Click the Text Block SmartIcon.
- Position the pointer at the location of one corner of the text block, then drag it to the opposite corner to specify the size of the text block.
- Type the text you want to add.
- Click the worksheet or chart anywhere outside the text block to add it to the chart.

First, let's add the note "Approaching Goal" as a text block.

To add the text block to the chart:

❶ Position the worksheet so the chart is displayed and select the chart, if necessary.

❷ Click the **Text Block SmartIcon** 📄 , then notice that the pointer changes to ⁻ᵢ⁻ for specifying the location and size of the text block.

❸ Move the pointer to the location of the upper-left corner of the text block. Drag the pointer to the opposite corner to specify the size of the text block, then release the mouse button. See Figure 4-30 for the approximate size and location of the text block. Note that the insertion point is blinking, ready for you to type the text. Note also that the SmartIcon palette changed for working with drawn objects.

❹ Type **Approaching Goal**.

❺ Click anywhere in the chart or worksheet, other than the text block, to finishing entering the text block. See Figure 4-30.

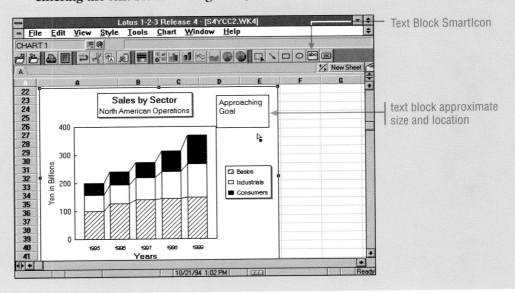

Figure 4-30
Text block object
added to chart

Brian wants to make sure that the text is aligned properly within the text block. Let's center the two lines of text in the text block.

To center the text in the text block:

❶ Select the text block and notice that the pointer changes to I when it is positioned in the text block. Note that the SmartIcon changes again to display the palette for drawn objects.

❷ Click the right mouse button to display the Quick menu.

❸ Click **Alignment** to display this dialog box.

❹ Click the **Center option button**, then click the **OK button** to center the text within the block. See Figure 4-31. Lotus 1-2-3 assigns the text block the default name "Text 1" for future reference.

default name of selected drawn object

SmartIcons for drawn objects

text block selected
selected text centered

Figure 4-31
Text centered in text block

Now Brian needs to circle the note. To do this, he must remove the text block frame, then add the drawn object he wants—which in this case is an ellipse. Before adding the ellipse, you might find it necessary to resize the text block, so the area around the text is proportioned correctly. As mentioned earlier, you can select objects and resize them. When you resize an object, you can change both its size and proportions, as described in Figure 4-32.

To Resize Objects	Do This
Change the width	Drag a middle handle on the left or right side of the object
Change the height	Drag a middle handle on the top or bottom of the object
Change both the height and width	Drag a corner handle
Change size *without* changing the proportions	Drag a corner handle while holding down the Shift key

Figure 4-32
Handles used for resizing an object

REFERENCE WINDOW

Resizing an Object

- Select the object to be resized.
- Move the pointer to the handle you need to resize the selected object and notice that the pointer changes to ⊕.
- Click and drag the pointer to size the object.
- Release the mouse button when the object is the size you want.

When you resize an object or when you first create an object, you might need to change its position. Again, as explained earlier in this tutorial, you can move a selected object.

REFERENCE WINDOW

Moving an Object

- Select the object to be moved.
- Move the pointer over the object, but not to a handle, until the pointer changes shape. The shape depends on what kind of object has been selected.
- Click and drag the pointer, which changes to 🖑.
- Release the mouse button.

Let's resize the text block, remove the rectangular frame, then add an ellipse.

To resize the text block and remove its border:
❶ Make sure the text block is selected.
❷ If necessary, resize the text block by dragging the handle in the lower-right corner until the text is centered better within the frame. Notice that the pointer changes to ⊕ when you place it on the handle. If your first attempt does not produce the desired result, try again. See Figure 4-33.

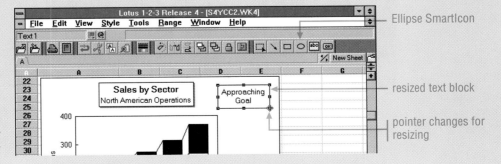

Figure 4-33
Text block sized for better display

TROUBLE? If your text block is not in the location you want, position the pointer inside the text block and drag it to where you want it.

❸ Click the **Color SmartIcon** 🔳 to display the Lines & Color dialog box.

❹ Click the **Line style drop-down list arrow**, click **None** to remove the line surrounding the text block, then click the **OK button**.

Next let's add the ellipse to surround the text block.

❺ Click the **Ellipse SmartIcon** 🔘 and notice that the pointer changes to ⁻¦⁻. You use the pointer to specify the size and location of the ellipse.

❻ Position the pointer at the corner where you want the ellipse to begin.

❼ Click and drag the pointer to the opposite corner to size the ellipse. As you drag the pointer, 1-2-3 displays the outline of the ellipse as a dotted line. When you release the mouse button, a completed ellipse surrounds the text that you entered previously. See Figure 4-34. Note that 1-2-3 automatically assigns the name "Ellipse 1" to this selected drawn object.

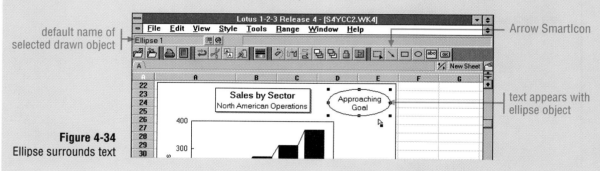

default name of selected drawn object

Arrow SmartIcon

text appears with ellipse object

Figure 4-34
Ellipse surrounds text

When you add drawn objects, 1-2-3 automatically fills them with a default fill pattern of transparent. The **transparent fill pattern** is abbreviated as "T" on the list of available patterns and allows you to see anything that might be underneath the drawn object, in this case the text block.

The changes to Brian's chart will be complete when he adds an arrow that points from the 1999 stacked bars to the ellipse. Let's add this arrow now.

To add an arrow object to the chart:

❶ Click the **Arrow SmartIcon** 🔲 and notice that the pointer changes to ⁻¦⁻ for specifying the location and size of the arrow.

❷ Position the pointer on the edge of the Consumers segment of the 1999 stack bar. This will be the tail of the arrow. See Figure 4-35 for the approximate positioning of the tail of the arrow.

❸ Drag the pointer until it just touches the ellipse; this is the location of the arrowhead. As you drag the pointer, 1-2-3 displays a dotted line. When you release the mouse button, the arrow appears and is selected. See Figure 4-35. Note that 1-2-3 assigns the default name "Line 1" to this selected drawn object.

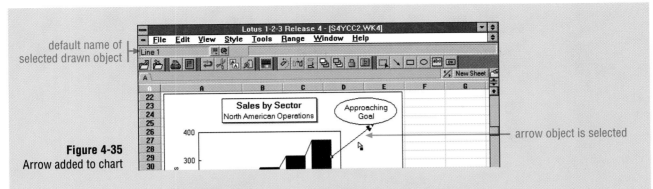

default name of selected drawn object

arrow object is selected

Figure 4-35
Arrow added to chart

Brian wants the line of the arrow to be a little thicker.

❹ Increase the width of the Line 1 size by displaying the Lines & Color dialog box, then clicking the **Line Width drop-down list arrow** and selecting the second line in the list of available widths. Click the **OK button**.

Arranging Drawn Objects

After Brian adds the arrow to the chart (Figure 4-35), he realizes the arrow should point to the stacked bar rather than to the ellipse. A drawn object like the arrow can be rearranged by flipping it either horizontally or vertically. **Flipping** an object *horizontally* turns the object backward, whereas flipping it *vertically* turns the object upside down. By using both flips, Brian's arrow can be rearranged to point towards the bar in his chart.

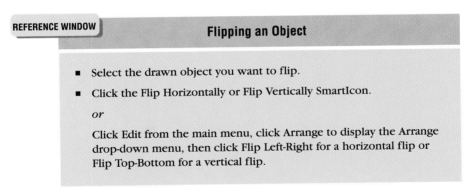

REFERENCE WINDOW

Flipping an Object

- Select the drawn object you want to flip.
- Click the Flip Horizontally or Flip Vertically SmartIcon.

  or

  Click Edit from the main menu, click Arrange to display the Arrange drop-down menu, then click Flip Left-Right for a horizontal flip or Flip Top-Bottom for a vertical flip.

Let's change the direction of Brian's arrow by flipping it both horizontally and vertically, so it points to the bar in the chart.

To flip the arrow:
❶ Select the arrow.
❷ Click the **Flip Horizontally SmartIcon** . Note that the arrow appears misplaced because it doesn't seem to point to anything, but the next step corrects this.
❸ Click the **Flip Vertically SmartIcon** . Now the arrow points towards the bar in the chart, but it is positioned so it no longer touches the ellipse.
❹ Move the arrow so it touches both the bar in the chart and the ellipse. See Figure 4-36.

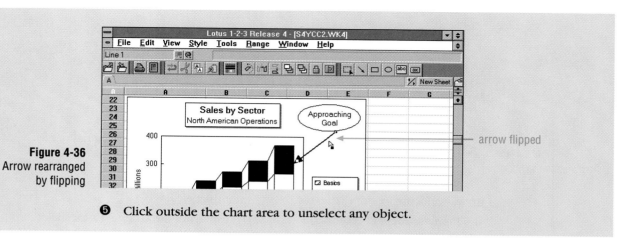

Figure 4-36
Arrow rearranged
by flipping

❺   Click outside the chart area to unselect any object.

Saving and Printing Graphics

Now that he has completed the work for Migiwa, Brian wants to save and print his work-sheet. When you save a worksheet, the worksheet, its charts, and its drawn objects are saved as a single file. Let's save the worksheet, then print the modified comparison stacked bar chart.

To save the worksheet, then preview and print the chart:

❶   Save the worksheet as S4YCC3.WK4.
❷   Select the chart by clicking its frame.
❸   Click the **Print Preview SmartIcon** ▦ and preview the chart. See Figure 4-37. Notice that only the chart appears in the preview and not the drawn objects (arrow, ellipse, and text). This is because the chart was selected to preview and not the range that includes all of the graphic objects. To preview and print the chart with all of the graphic objects, you need to select the range before printing.

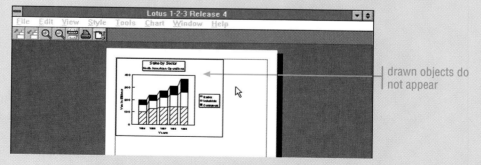

Figure 4-37
Preview of Brian's
chart without
drawn objects

❹   Click the **Close Preview SmartIcon** ▤ to return to Ready mode.
❺   Select the range A22..F43, which contains the chart and the drawn objects. Start this range selection in cell F43 because cell A22 is covered by your chart. If you start selecting the range at cell A22, you might move or resize the chart rather than select the correct range.

   TROUBLE?   If you move or resize the chart, click the Undo SmartIcon ↩ to return the chart to its previous location or size, then repeat Step 5.

❻ Preview the selected range. Now the drawn objects are displayed with the chart.

❼ Print the chart using the **Print SmartIcon** 🖨 with the Selected range option selected. Because the worksheet didn't change, Brian needs a printout of the chart only.

If you want to take a break and resume the tutorial at a later time, you can exit 1-2-3 by double-clicking the Control menu box. When you resume the tutorial, launch 1-2-3 and place your Student Disk in the appropriate disk drive. Open the S4YCC3.WK4 worksheet, select the Tutorial 4 SmartIcon palette, and then continue with this tutorial.

Creating a Pie Chart

According to Brian's worksheet sketch in Figure 4-4, he needs to create a pie chart to display the operating income by sector for 1997. He will create this chart using similar steps to the ones he used when he created the comparison stacked bar chart. However, unlike the comparison stacked bar chart, which has three data series, the pie chart has only *one* data series—the values for the three sectors for 1997. Because the 1997 data values (column D) aren't located in the column next to the sector labels on the worksheet (column A), the range Brian needs to select for the chart is in two parts. For Brian's pie chart, the data series are arranged by columns because there are more rows than columns of data values, with the x-axis labels located in column A and the data series A in column D. Because these columns are not adjacent to one another, Brian will need to specify a collection of columns for the chart instead of just one range. A **collection** of columns and/or rows consists of two or more separate cell ranges that are selected at one time. For example, in Brian's worksheet, the collection of columns that makes up the single data series he needs to chart is A17..A19 and D17..D19.

REFERENCE WINDOW | **Selecting a Collection**

- Select the first range of the data series.

- Move the pointer to the next range.

- Press and hold [Ctrl] while you select the second range.

- Repeat selecting ranges using [Ctrl] for as many additional ranges as you need.

Let's select the collection of columns that make up the data series in Brian's pie chart.

To select the collection of columns for the pie chart:

❶ Press **[Home]** to position the pointer in the worksheet for selecting the data series.

❷ Select the range A17..A19 as the X data series used to label the slices of the pie.

❸ Move the pointer to cell D17, *but do not click.*

   TROUBLE? If you click D17, you will unselect the first range. Repeat Steps 1, 2, and 3 to correct this mistake.

❹ Press and hold **[Ctrl]** while you click **D17**, then drag the pointer to cell D19 and release the mouse button. This range is added to the collection and is the single data series for the pie chart. See Figure 4-38.

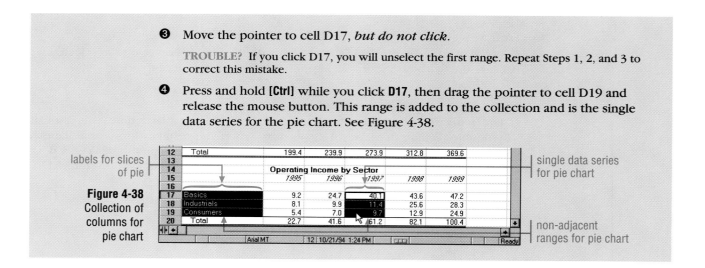

labels for slices of pie

Figure 4-38
Collection of columns for pie chart

single data series for pie chart

non-adjacent ranges for pie chart

With the data for the pie chart selected, the next step is to create the chart.

To create the pie chart with the data series selected as a collection of columns:

❶ Scroll the worksheet window so cell A44 is in the upper-left corner. This is where the pie chart will be placed on the worksheet.

❷ Click the **Chart SmartIcon** 📊. The pointer changes to 📊 to indicate 1-2-3 is ready for you to specify the location and size of this new chart.

❸ Move the pointer to cell A44 and click the mouse button. The default bar chart appears. See Figure 4-39. The pointer automatically changes to ✛ so you can size the chart.

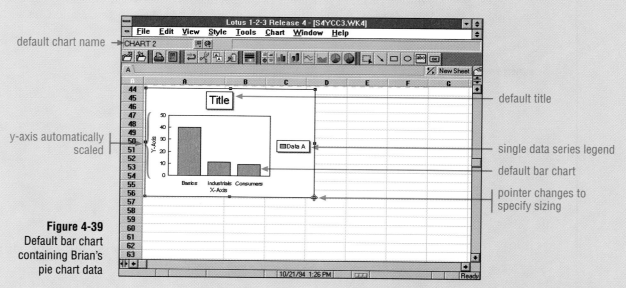

default chart name

y-axis automatically scaled

Figure 4-39
Default bar chart containing Brian's pie chart data

default title

single data series legend

default bar chart

pointer changes to specify sizing

❹ Double-click anywhere on the chart to display the Type dialog box, click **Pie**, then click the **clockwise pie chart icon**, as specified in Brian's sketch. See Figure 4-40.

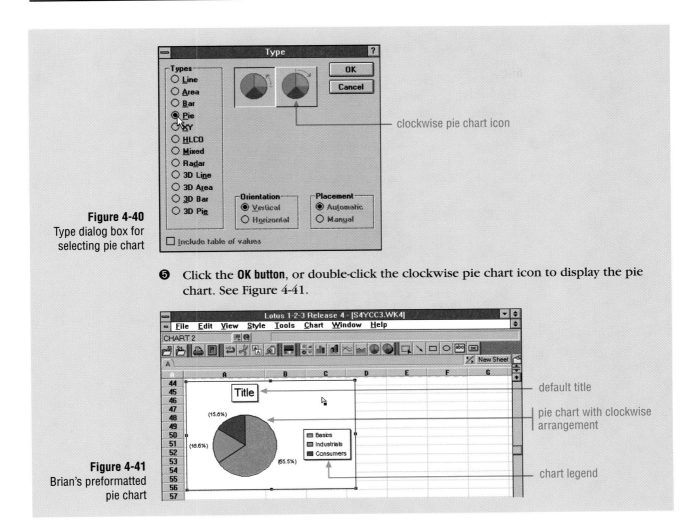

Figure 4-40
Type dialog box for selecting pie chart

clockwise pie chart icon

❺   Click the **OK button**, or double-click the clockwise pie chart icon to display the pie chart. See Figure 4-41.

Figure 4-41
Brian's preformatted pie chart

default title

pie chart with clockwise arrangement

chart legend

Brian reviews the chart to see if it is accurate and clear. He will accept the default colors because Migiwa plans to use this chart as an overhead only, not as a handout. However, he finds several things that he wants to change before he shows it to Migiwa for her approval. First, he will edit the chart's title, and then remove the legend and label the pie slices.

Changing Default Chart Titles

As soon as Brian saw the default chart title "Title," he realized he did not specify a title when he was selecting the ranges to be charted. Because the pie chart's data series are arranged as a collection of columns, the cell containing "Operating Income by Sector" (the title he wants for the pie chart) could *not* be included in the collection. Now Brian needs to add the title separately. Brian also decides to add the subtitle "1997" beneath the title. He can get the subtitle from a cell in the worksheet. He wants to make the titles of the pie chart consistent with the titles of his other chart, making sure they are the correct point size.

To replace the default title of the chart, add the subtitle, then change the point size of the two titles:

❶ Click **Title**, which is the default title 1-2-3 uses until you specify another.

❷ Double-click **Title** to display pie Headings dialog box.

❸ Type the cell address **A14** in the Line 1 text box, then click the **Cell check box** to designate the cell's content, Operating Income by Sector, as the title.

❹ Type the cell address **D15** in the Line 2 text box, then click the **Cell check box** to designate the cell's content, 1997, as the subtitle.

❺ Click the **OK button** to add the titles and return to the chart. The new titles appear. See Figure 4-42.

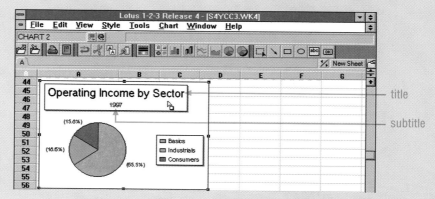

Figure 4-42
Title and subtitle of
Brian's pie chart

TROUBLE? If the chart is not positioned as it was before, use the scroll bars to reposition it.

Now Brian wants to change the point size of the two titles to match the sizes of the titles on the comparison stacked bar chart.

❻ Change the size of the title "Operating Income by Sector" to 14 points and the size of "1997" to 12 points using the point size selector in the status bar.

Labeling a Pie Chart

Next Brian wants to label each slice of the pie chart and display the correct percentage for each slice. These data labels, which describe each data value in the data series, are obtained from the X data series, which is the left-most data series in a collection arranged *by column*. For a collection arranged *by row*, this is the top-most data series in the collection. You can add data labels to other types of charts, including bar charts and line charts.

REFERENCE WINDOW

Labeling Pie Chart Data

- Click Chart in the main menu bar.
- Click Data Labels... to display this dialog box.
- Click the Contents of X data range check box in the Show box.
- Click the Percentages check box in the Show box.
- Click the OK button to complete the specification.

Let's add the data labels with the percentages to each slice of Brian's pie chart to clearly identify the data included in the chart. When the labels are displayed with the percentages for each slice of the pie, the legend is automatically removed by 1-2-3.

To add data labels and percentages to each slice of the pie chart:

❶ Click **Chart** in the main menu bar to display the Chart drop-down menu.

❷ Click **Data Labels...** to display the Data Labels dialog box so you can label each slice of the pie chart. This dialog box is context-sensitive and currently displays options for a pie chart. See Figure 4-43. Note that this dialog box contains options for showing data labels and exploding slices of the pie chart.

options for labeling pie chart

options for exploding slices of pie

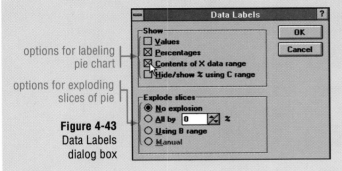

Figure 4-43
Data Labels
dialog box

❸ Make sure the Percentages check box is selected for displaying this characteristic on the chart.

❹ Click the **Contents of X data range check box** to show the labels from the X data series, or range, on the chart.

❺ Click the **OK button** to complete specifying the data labels and return to the worksheet. See Figure 4-44. Notice that the legend is removed automatically.

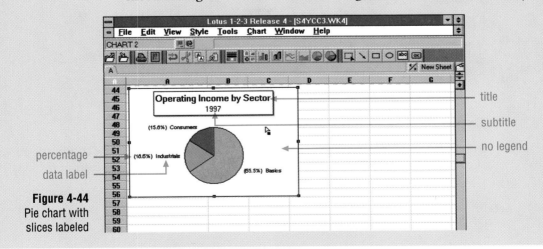

percentage

data label

Figure 4-44
Pie chart with
slices labeled

Brian reviews the pie chart with Migiwa, and they compare it to the comparison stacked bar chart he created and printed previously. Brian notices that the pie chart is smaller than the other chart. Because Migiwa will be using both charts during her presentation, Migiwa and Brian decide the charts should be the same size.

Changing the Size of a Chart

Brian needs to make the pie chart larger so it will be similar in size to the other chart. As mentioned earlier, a chart is considered an object and, like other objects, a chart can be resized, moved, copied, and deleted once you select it. Let's increase the size of Brian's pie chart to match the size of his other chart.

To change the size of the chart:

❶ Click the frame surrounding the entire pie chart to select it. Note that eight handles appear.

❷ Move the pointer to the handle at the lower-right corner of the chart frame and notice that the pointer changes to ⊕, which indicates you can resize the object.

❸ Click and drag the pointer to the bottom right edge of cell E62. A dotted line indicates the suggested size.

❹ Release the mouse button when the chart is the size you want. See Figure 4-45.

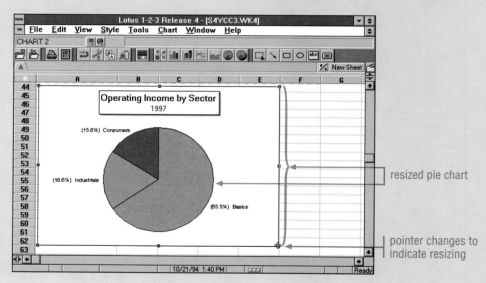

Figure 4-45
Brian's resized
pie chart

resized pie chart

pointer changes to
indicate resizing

Exploding Selected Pie Chart Slices

In reviewing the pie chart with Brian, Migiwa decides to address the size of the Basics pie slice in her presentation. She asks Brian to **explode**, or separate, it from the rest of the chart to call attention to it.

Exploding Pie Chart Slices

- Click and drag the slice you want to explode away from the rest of the pie.

or

- Select the slice you want to explode.
- Click Chart in the main menu bar and then click Data Labels... to display this dialog box.
- Click the All by option button in the Explode slices box, then type the percentage you want to specify for the explosion.
- Click the OK button to complete the specification.

Let's explode the Basics pie slice using the easiest method for exploding pie slices. You simply select the desired slice of the pie chart and drag it to the preferred location.

To explode the Basics pie slice:

❶ Select the Basics pie slice.

❷ Click and drag the slice away from the rest of the pie, as shown in Figure 4-46.

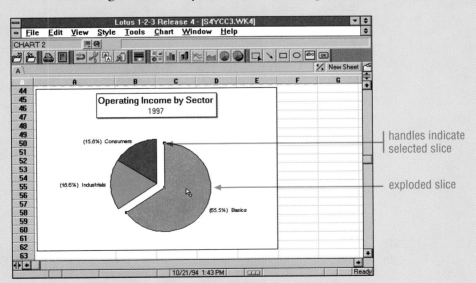

Figure 4-46
Pie chart with
exploded slice

Next, let's save the worksheet, then print this pie chart.

❸ Save the worksheet with the comparison stacked bar chart and pie chart as S4YCC4.WK4.

❹ Print only the pie chart by selecting this chart, then clicking the **Print SmartIcon** 🖨 and clicking the **OK button**.

Performing a What-If Analysis with Charts

Migiwa has been analyzing the operating income by sector for the Basics sector. Her analysis indicates that if new marketing strategies are pursued, the value for 1997 might be reduced to 31.2 billion rather than the original estimate of 40.1 billion. Because she will be presenting this alternative to YCC's Management Committee, she wants Brian to perform this what-if analysis and print the report. In 1-2-3, when a data value that is used in a chart is changed in the worksheet, the chart is automatically updated.

Splitting the Worksheet Window

To see the changes in the chart when you modify the worksheet, you can split the worksheet window. **Splitting** a worksheet window allows you to view two separate areas, or **panes**, of the *same* worksheet at one time. You can split the worksheet window either horizontally or vertically by using the horizontal or vertical splitter. After you split the worksheet, you have two windows, which means two sets of scroll bars and buttons, and two sets of row numbers and column letters. You also have to make sure you select the section of the worksheet that you want to work with. When you want to unsplit the window, you move the splitter back to its original position.

REFERENCE WINDOW

Splitting the Worksheet Window

- Move the pointer to the top of the vertical scroll bar to split the window horizontally and notice that the pointer changes to ✚.

  or

  Move the pointer to the left of the horizontal scroll bar to split the window vertically and notice that the pointer changes to ✚.

- Drag the horizontal or vertical splitter to the position in the window where you want to split it.

- Release the mouse button.

You can unsplit the window by dragging the horizontal or vertical splitter back to its original position.

Let's split the worksheet window horizontally so Brian's operating income by sector data is displayed in the top pane of the worksheet area while the pie chart is displayed in the bottom pane.

To split the worksheet window horizontally:

❶ Position the worksheet so cell A43 is in the upper-left corner. The Operating Income by Sector pie chart is displayed in the worksheet area.

❷ Move the pointer to the top of the vertical scroll bar and notice the pointer changes to ✚.

❸ Drag the **horizontal splitter** to the bottom of row 50.

❹ Release the mouse button. When you release the mouse button, the worksheet window is split. The top worksheet pane displays some of the worksheet, and the bottom pane displays the pie chart. See Figure 4-47.

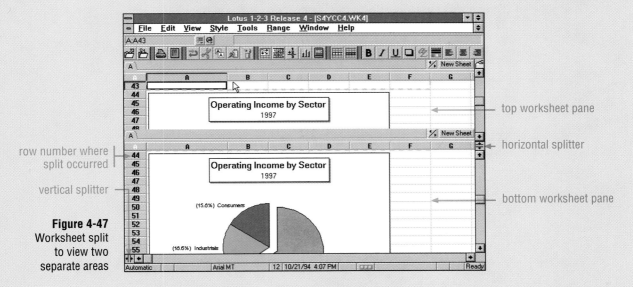

row number where
split occurred

vertical splitter

Figure 4-47
Worksheet split
to view two
separate areas

top worksheet pane

horizontal splitter

bottom worksheet pane

TROUBLE? If the top worksheet pane displays a different area of the worksheet, verify the row number where the split occurred. If it is row 44, you performed the split correctly—your monitor might display either more or fewer rows than the screens in this text. If the worksheet splits at a row other than 44, click the Undo SmartIcon ↩ then repeat Steps 1 through 4.

❺ Scroll the top worksheet pane to display the operating income by sector data, and scroll the bottom worksheet pane to display the pie chart. See Figure 4-48.

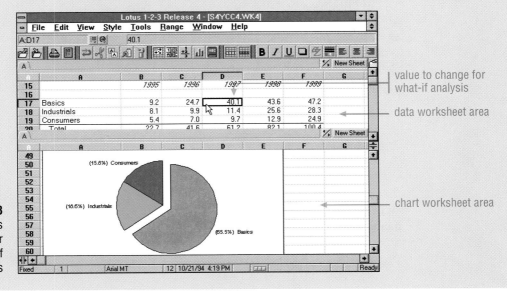

value to change for
what-if analysis

data worksheet area

chart worksheet area

Figure 4-48
Worksheet areas
displayed for
performing a what-if
analysis

Now you are ready to perform Migiwa's what-if analysis by revising the 1997 Basics data. Let's enter this what-if value and watch the effect on the pie chart.

To enter the what-if value and observe the effect on the chart:

❶   Click **D17** for the what-if value.

❷   Enter **31.2** and observe the immediate and automatic updating of the pie chart, including the recalculating of the percentages. See Figure 4-49.

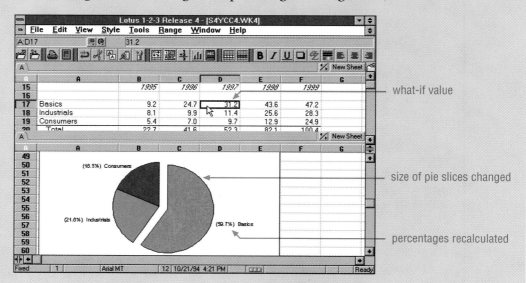

Figure 4-49
Chart automatically updated with what-if value

Now let's save the worksheet, then print the pie chart with the what-if value.

❸   Click the **Save File SmartIcon** 🖫 to save the worksheet file with both the pie chart and the stacked bar chart as S4YCC4.WK4.

❹   Select and print the pie chart.

❺   Change the what-if value back to the original amount of 40.1 billion, then save the worksheet with this value in the same S4YCC4.WK4 file.

❻   Unsplit the worksheet by dragging the horizontal splitter back to the top of the worksheet window.

◾   ◾   ◾

Brian has finished Migiwa's charts for her meeting next Tuesday with YCC's Management Committee. The charts match Brian's design and meet Migiwa's requirements. Brian is certain the charts will help Migiwa to make an impressive and informative presentation.

Questions

1. Which chart is most suitable for displaying weekly sales data on five different products for last year to show how sales varied during the year:
   a. bar chart
   b. line chart
   c. xy chart
   d. radar chart
2. Use Figure 4-50 to identify the following components of a chart:
   a. type of chart
   b. x-axis labels
   c. y-axis title
   d. chart title
   e. data series for actual sales

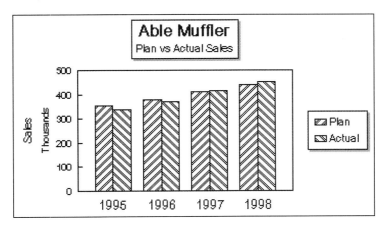

Figure 4-50

3. What appears with an object to indicate the object is selected:
   a. frame
   b. handles
   c.
   d.
4. You created a bar chart and want to change the pattern used with each of the data series. Which of the following dialog boxes do you use to change this chart characteristic?
   a. Lines & Color
   b. Font & Attributes
   c. Ranges
   d. Legend
5. When you select several separate cell ranges to create a chart, the ranges are called a:
   a. column
   b. group
   c. collection
   d. stack

6. When one or more slices of a pie chart are separated from the rest of the pie, this is known as:
   a. zoning
   b. segmenting
   c. dicing
   d. exploding

7. You can view two separate areas of the same worksheet at one time by doing this to the worksheet window:
   a. flashing
   b. sighting
   c. splitting
   d. scrolling

E 8. Using the Task Reference, determine the number of different ways that you can do the same tasks as those performed with these SmartIcons and write down at least one other method for each SmartIcon:

   a.

   b.

   c.

   d.

Tutorial Assignments

Launch 1-2-3 and open the worksheet T4GTR1.WK4 for Goodtread Tire & Rubber Company (GTR). This worksheet is used to analyze the components of GTR's cost of goods sold. The costs are entered in millions of dollars. Review the worksheet. Prepare a bar chart and a pie chart by performing the following:

1. Create a pie chart of 1997 cost of goods sold as sketched in Figure 4-51. Select appropriate colors and patterns to differentiate the slices before you print this chart.

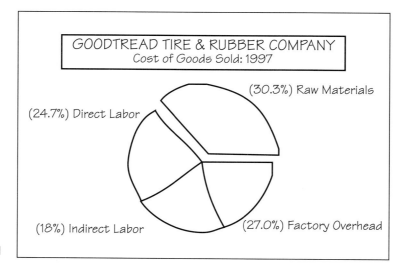

Figure 4-51

2. Save the worksheet as S4GTR2.WK4. Preview and print the pie chart.

E   3. Create the 3-D stacked bar chart specified by the rough sketch in Figure 4-52. Select appropriate colors and patterns to differentiate the bars when you print this chart.

4. Select point sizes, then use boldface and italics with the titles to improve the chart's appearance.

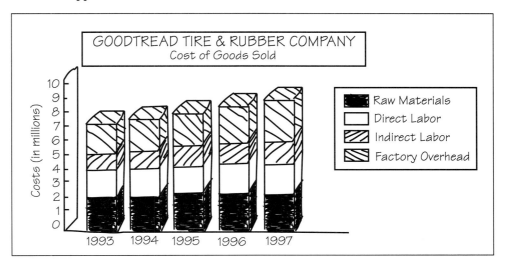

Figure 4-52

5. Save the worksheet as S4GTR3.WK4. Preview and print the worksheet and chart. Launch 1-2-3 and open worksheet T4FIC1.WK4 for the Fortune 500 Industry Comparisons. This worksheet is used by financial analysts to assess the performance of various industries in 1994. A financial analyst creates charts like these to compare an individual company's performance versus its respective industry's performance. Review this worksheet. Prepare bar, pie, and line charts for comparing the industry data by performing the following:

6. Create the bar chart following the rough sketch in Figure 4-53. Make sure you include all labels and titles as shown.

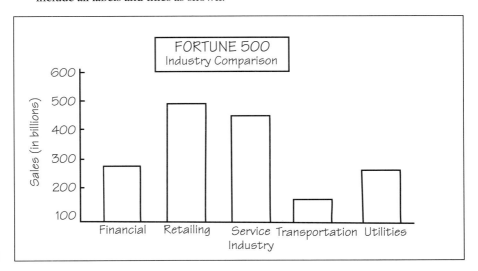

Figure 4-53

7. Save the worksheet as S4FIC2.WK4. Preview the chart and worksheet, then print them both.

E

8. Develop a 3-D pie chart following the rough sketch in Figure 4-54. Make sure you include all headings and titles as shown in the design sketch. Use fill patterns, boldface, and italics to improve the appearance of the chart.

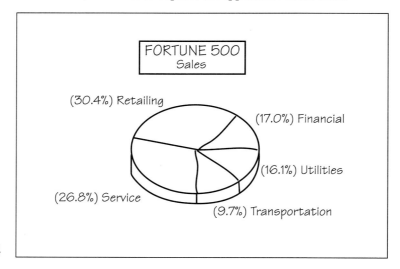

Figure 4-54

9. Save the worksheet as S4FIC3.WK4. Preview the chart, then print it.
10. Create the line chart comparing sales per employee among the industries as indicated by the rough sketch in Figure 4-55. Title the y-axis "Sales/Employee (in thousands)." Did you use the procedures for selecting a collection of columns in preparing this chart?

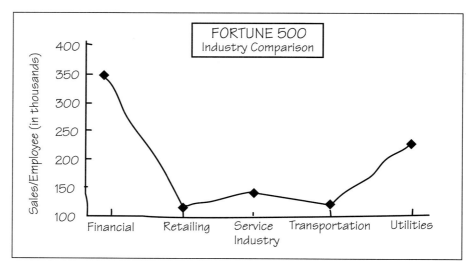

Figure 4-55

11. Add the text "Wow! Efficient!" to the line chart. Change the line style on the box surrounding the text to none and center the text.

E

12. Surround the text with a rounded rectangle.
13. Add an arrow pointing from the rounded rectangle to the marker for Financial on the line chart.
14. Save the worksheet as S4FIC4.WK4. Preview and print the chart with the comment.

Launch 1-2-3, open the C4YCC1.WK4 worksheet for Yamasuka Chemical Company, then save it as S4YCC5.WK4. Brian and Migiwa have reviewed the charts for the presentation. Migiwa would like to have several other charts and a copy of the worksheet data that emphasizes the Sales by Sector in 1999. Develop these additional materials for Migiwa's presentation by performing the following:

E
15. Prepare a 3-D comparison stacked bar chart of Operating Income from 1995 to 1999. Include a descriptive title, and label both the x-axis and y-axis, as appropriate. Use point size, typeface, boldface, and italics to improve the chart's appearance.

16. Select patterns and colors for the data ranges so they are easily identified in the chart. Add the text "More Emphasis Needed" with an arrow that points to the 1999 data for Consumers. Save the worksheet as S4YCC5.WK4. Preview and print this chart.

E
17. In the worksheet area that contains Brian's data, add a rounded rectangle that surrounds the Sales by Sector data for the three sectors for 1999. If necessary, change the fill pattern of the drawn object so both the data and rectangle appear on the report. Add the text "Approaching Goal" with an arrow that points to the rectangle surrounding the Sales for 1999. Preview and print the report area of the worksheet including the notation and rectangle.

E
18. Prepare a line chart that plots the Total Sales by Sector and the Total Operating Income by Sector for 1995 through 1999. Use the Ranges dialog box to specify the individual ranges. Place the Sales data in the A data series, the Operating Income data in the B data series, and the years in the X data series for the chart.

E
19. Label the y-axis "Yen in Billions." Change the legend to identify the data as "Sales" and "Operating Income." Position the legend at the bottom of the chart. Add the title "Sales and Operating Income" to the chart. Select colors, styles, and widths so the lines are easy to see on your printed chart. Save the worksheet as S4YCC6.WK4. Preview and print this chart.

E
20. Design a chart of your choice; it can be a chart you see in a magazine or newspaper or you can use one of the worksheets on your Student Disk to design the chart. Include at least one drawn object. Create and print the chart you design. Save the worksheet as S4***7.WK4. You can use your initials for the three-letter descriptive abbreviation to replace the asterisks. Write a paragraph explaining what message the chart communicates.

Case Problems

1. Work Sampling for Guardian Mutual Insurance

Guardian Mutual Insurance (GMI) is a large, nation-wide insurance company that sells insurance for both individuals and businesses. Guardian employs a staff of 127 computer programmers to build and maintain management information systems to serve their agents.

Steve Michaels was recently hired by Susan Gentry as a junior systems analyst for the Claims Management System (CMS) at GMI. Susan's staff is classified into three different levels, SA2, SA3, and SA4. The SA2 staff level, Steve's classification, is generally new hires; the SA3 staff level consists of analysts with two to five years of experience; and the SA4 staff level is made up of systems analysts with six or more years of experience. Susan wants to measure the productivity of her staff. She asks Steve to conduct a work sampling study to determine how the different staff levels spend their day. Work sampling is a procedure in which an individual's activities are recorded at random times throughout the day to determine the relative amount of time spent on each activity. Steve collects the data for this study and summarizes the information in a 1-2-3 worksheet. He meets with Susan to review the worksheet. She is pleased with Steve's results, but she thinks that charts would better communicate the information from the work sampling study. In preparation for creating these charts, Steve develops his planning analysis sheet (Figure 4-56).

Steve is now ready to create the charts for Susan's upcoming staff meeting.

Planning Analysis Sheet

My goal:
Prepare charts showing the time spent on various job activities performed by systems analysts at different job classification levels.

What results do I want to see?
A bar chart showing the results of the work sampling study.
A pie chart showing the average time spent on various activities throughout the day by all job classification levels.

What information do I need?
The results of the work sampling study.

Figure 4-56

1. Launch 1-2-3 and open the worksheet P4GMI1.WK4, which contains the summary of Steve's work sampling study. Save the worksheet immediately as S4GMI1.WK4 in case you want to start over.
2. Review Steve's worksheet. Notice that Steve formatted the cells as *percentages* and included a row containing the *average* for each job activity.
3. Create a bar chart of the three staff levels and their respective percentages for a typical work day. Include the titles "Typical Work Day" and "Work Sampling" on your chart. Select appropriate colors and patterns to differentiate the bars.
4. Add the y-axis title "Percent of Day" and x-axis title "Job Activity." Format the y-axis range as a percentage with zero decimal places.
5. Change the font size of the title to 14 and the subtitle to 12. Add boldface and/or italics to enhance these titles.
6. Save the worksheet as S4GMI2.WK4. Preview and print both the worksheet and the bar chart.
7. Using the same chart, change the chart orientation from vertical to horizontal.
8. Change the color of the SA2 bars to black, the SA3 bars to white with black striped cross-hatching, and the SA4 bars to white.
9. Print the chart only, then save the worksheet as S4GMI3.WK4.
10. Create a pie chart of the average portion of each day spent on the six activities in the Typical Work Day.
11. Place the title "Typical Work Day" on the chart. Select a different font for the chart title and change the point size to 18.
12. Label the slices of the pie chart using the six daily activities. Explode the slice that shows the average program coding percentage. Is this less than half of a systems analyst's typical work day activities?
13. Save the worksheet as S4GMI4.WK4. Print the worksheet and the pie chart. What's wrong with the chart—are you able to see the separate slices of the pie? Fix this problem and print again.

E

14. Compare the vertical and horizontal bar charts. Which chart do you feel is the easiest to understand? Why?

E 15. Create a comparison stacked bar chart with each bar as one job classification and each activity as one data range. That is, the job activity data series are arranged by column. When you create the chart by selecting the range containing this data, the 1-2-3 default is to create the chart by row because there are more columns than rows. Use the Assign ranges option of the Ranges dialog box to switch the default By row assignment to a By column assignment. Select the legend from the range B8..G8 using the All ranges Series option in the Legend dialog box. Add appropriate titles and cross-hatching to the chart. Change point sizes and typefaces together with using boldface and italics to improve the appearance of the chart. Save the worksheet as S4GMI5.WK4 and print the chart. Why is the total height of each stacked bar the same? What does this represent?

E 16. Susan visits a number of college campuses each year speaking to groups such as the student chapters of the Data Processing Management Association (DPMA). Many of these students believe that systems analysts spend most of their time coding programs. Does the data from Steve's work sampling study support this opinion? Explain your answer.

2. Managing Quality for Antel Computer Chips

Antel Computer Chips (ACC) manufactures computer memory chips for several IBM clone computer manufacturers. The reputation of ACC has been built upon their high-quality memory chips sold at a low cost. Antel emphasizes product quality through a Total Quality Management (TQM) system, which was implemented in the mid-1980s. As each batch of memory chips is manufactured, a sample of chips is tested to establish the portion of defectives. Kathy Bowden performs these tests and plots the data on a control chart to determine if any significant changes have taken place in the quality of the chips produced. If a change is detected, Kathy makes corrective actions in the manufacturing process. A control chart consists of three lines: the upper control limit (UCL), the lower control limit (LCL), and the fraction of defectives in each sample from a batch. The UCL and the LCL are calculated using a common statistical formula for control charts that provides a measure of the expected variation of the fraction of defectives among the batches. Control charts are used to spot trends in the number of defectives. Whenever the fraction of defectives falls outside either the upper or lower control limits, corrective action is usually required.

Kathy has generally performed these tests and drawn the control charts by hand; however, she believes that using 1-2-3 would produce more accurate control charts. Kathy has built the worksheet in which the control charts will be created. Create the necessary control charts for Kathy by performing the following:

1. Launch 1-2-3 and open the P4ACC1.WK4 worksheet, which Kathy built for developing the control charts.

E 2. Prepare a control chart as shown in the sketch in Figure 4-57. Change the colors and styles so the lines for the UCL and LCL are black and contain no symbols, while the line for the Defectives is different from the UCL and LCL lines and includes symbols. Use the Help menu if necessary to alter the symbols for the UCL and LCL lines. Save the worksheet as S4ACC2.WK4. Preview and print the control chart.

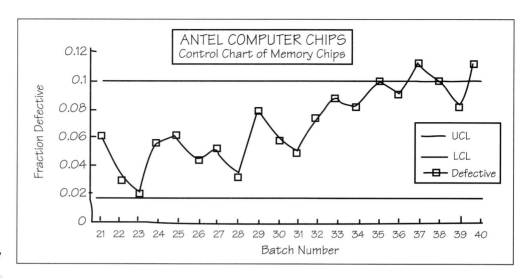

Figure 4-57

E   3. Review the control chart. Does there appear to be a problem with the memory chip manufacturing process? Explain your interpretation of this control chart.

E   4. To indicate that a problem with the memory chip manufacturing process might exist, add the text "Increasing Defectives" with arrows pointing to appropriate data points on the chart. Surround this text with a geometric shape of your choice. Save the worksheet as S4ACC3.WK4. Preview and print the revised control chart.

E   5. Review the control chart. Describe how the chart appears useful in determining problems in the memory chip manufacturing process. Write a short paragraph describing other features that could be used to further enhance the chart.

3. Stockholder Reporting for Nike, Inc.

Nike, Inc. is a world-wide manufacturer of athletic shoes, clothing, and accessories. The past five years have been extremely successful for Nike from a variety of standpoints. First, revenues and net income have grown rapidly, over 30% from last year. Also, Nike has continued to gain market share in both the footwear and the apparel divisions. Finally, the public image of Nike has continued to strengthen, largely because of high-image spokespeople such as Michael Jordan.

You are the administrative assistant in the CEO's office and need to prepare several charts to present to the company's shareholders. Nike is having their annual shareholders' meeting next week. You want the charts to clearly portray Nike's financial performance. Examine the selected financial data from Nike's 1990 Annual Report shown in Figure 4-58. A worksheet that contains the key data for the charts has already been created. Review the figures for accuracy. You are now ready to create the charts for the CEO to use at the upcoming shareholders' meeting.

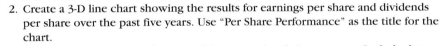

NIKE, INC.
Selected Financial Data

(Expressed in millions, except per share amounts)

	1990	1989	1988	1987	1986
Income Statement Data					
Revenue	2,235.0	1,710.0	1,203.0	877.0	1,069.0
Net Earnings	242.9	167.1	101.7	35.9	59.2
Earnings per Share	6.42	4.45	2.70	0.93	1.55
Cash Dividends per Share	0.75	0.55	0.40	0.40	0.40
Balance Sheet Data					
Current Assets	837.7	638.4	521.9	638.4	578.3
Current Liabilities	273.2	215.9	223.1	313.2	299.5
Working Capital	564.5	422.5	298.8	325.2	278.8
Total Assets	1,094.5	825.4	709.1	511.8	476.8
Long-term Debt	25.9	34.1	30.3	35.2	15.3
Shareholders' Equity	784.2	561.8	411.8	338.0	316.8

Figure 4-58

1. Launch 1-2-3 and open the worksheet P4NIK1.WK4, which contains the information obtained from Nike's 1990 Annual Report. Review the worksheet.
2. **E** Create a 3-D line chart showing the results for earnings per share and dividends per share over the past five years. Use "Per Share Performance" as the title for the chart.
3. **E** Specify "$ per Share" as the y-axis title, no x-axis title is necessary. Include data labels for both ranges. Place the legend for the chart in the upper-left corner of the outline frame, which contains the line chart.
4. Change the color scheme and make sure it is easy to see the lines.
5. Save the worksheet as S4NIK2.WK4. Preview and print both the worksheet and the 3-D line chart as a single report.
6. Using the same worksheet, create a 3-D bar chart showing the increase in Net Earnings over the past five years. Use "Earnings Comparison" as the title for the chart.
7. Title the y-axis as "Dollars in millions" then delete the x-axis title.
8. Change the colors and patterns of the bars to enhance the appearance of this chart.
9. Add "Great Growth!" to the chart as text. Place a geometric shape of your choice around this text.
10. Add an arrow that points from the text "Great Growth!" to the net earnings in 1990. Select an appropriate line width and style for this arrow.
11. Save the worksheet as S4NIK3.WK4. Preview and print the chart only.
12. **E** Create a mixed chart with current assets as the bar and current liabilities as the line. Use "Current Balance Sheet Items" as the title for this chart.
13. Add the title "Dollars in millions" to the y-axis then delete the x-axis title. Change the color scheme so the chart background is white, the bar color is white, and the line color is black.
14. Save the worksheet as S4NIK4.WK4. Preview and print the chart.
15. **E** Do these charts convey a message of strong growth for Nike? Why? What other data could you chart for the CEO to help with the upcoming presentation at the shareholders' meeting? Explain why these charts would be useful.

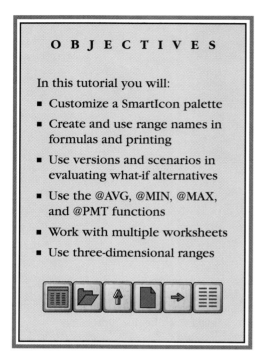

OBJECTIVES

In this tutorial you will:

- Customize a SmartIcon palette
- Create and use range names in formulas and printing
- Use versions and scenarios in evaluating what-if alternatives
- Use the @AVG, @MIN, @MAX, and @PMT functions
- Work with multiple worksheets
- Use three-dimensional ranges

Preparing and Examining What-If Alternatives

Developing an Operating Plan

CASE

Walnut Creek Products Shannon Mariner is a staff accountant at Walnut Creek Products (WCP). She joined WCP soon after graduating from college because she was familiar with WCP's quality products and impressed by the benefits and career potential WCP had to offer.

The principal product manufactured by WCP is the multi-media storage rack (model #WR3). This product can hold compact disks, audio cassettes, videotapes, and video game cartridges. Shannon bought this storage rack even before she began working at WCP and uses it to keep her CDs, videotapes, and cassettes organized. The storage rack is popular because it allows you to organize the various media in a single unit, it has quality hardwood construction and a stylish walnut finish, and it is affordable.

Shannon has been working with John Hirschi, the operations manager, to help him plan next year's production. In a meeting to discuss the goals for next year, John asks Shannon to prepare a **projected income statement**, a tool commonly used by accountants, which will list WCP's expected revenues and expenses for next year.

This projected income statement will help John determine how many racks to produce, how much to charge for each rack, how much money WCP needs to spend to produce the racks (the cost of goods), and how much money WCP needs to spend on marketing, general office administration, and so on (the operating costs) in order to maintain maximum profitability. He will use the projected income statement as WCP's operating plan for next year.

John gives Shannon a list of the line items and data values he wants entered into the worksheet. These include the number of racks sold, the price per rack, the cost of goods, the operating expenses, and the earnings before taxes. John is most interested in the **return on sales**, also known as profitability. He explains to Shannon that the return on sales is calculated by subtracting expenses from revenues and dividing by net sales. John uses the return on sales as a critical success factor that measures how much of every dollar of sales results in the "bottom line" earnings for WCP. At last month's production meeting, his management team set a target of 12% for this critical success factor. With Shannon's help John needs to create a plan for next year that has at least a 12% return on sales.

Shannon has all the information she needs so she gets right to work on the draft of the projected income statement (Figure 5-1), which includes a pie chart showing John where each dollar of sales goes.

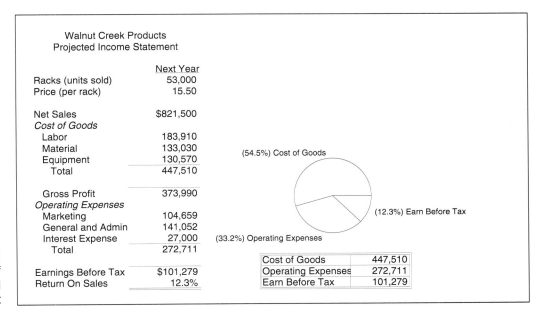

Figure 5-1
Shannon's draft of
WCP's projected
income statement

Later that afternoon Shannon reviews her worksheet with John, who notes how helpful it will be. Then he explains that this set of numbers is the first situation, or **base case**. In other words, this set of numbers will be a standard against which other alternatives will be measured. Shannon and John discuss several other sets of numbers that John wants to evaluate. For example, what would happen if WCP produced 61,000 racks and charged more for them—would WCP still have over a 12% return on sales?

John asks Shannon to create a worksheet that contains the projected income statement for analyzing three what-if alternatives. This will help John to determine which set of what-if values offers the most profitability for WCP. Shannon already has the base case, so by inserting the new numbers that John gives her she can determine the best case and the worst case. A common business practice is to evaluate the **best case**, or most optimistic situation when everything seems to go right, and the **worst case**, or most pessimistic situation when everything seems to go wrong. By examining these cases John will gain an understanding of the variations that might take place in WCP's revenues and costs.

John gives Shannon the other two alternative sets of numbers. In addition to modifying the number of racks produced and the price per rack, he has also modified the equipment costs. The formula for calculating the equipment cost is Price (per rack) * Racks (units sold) + the cost of owning the machine for one year. The price per rack is a **variable cost** because it changes in direct proportion to the number of racks produced. For example, the more racks produced, the higher the electricity bill (it takes a certain amount of electricity to run a machine to produce each rack). The cost of owning the machine for one year is a **fixed cost** because it remains the same regardless of the number of racks produced. John is considering using equipment with two different production capacities and, as part of his evaluation, needs to determine which equipment is most appropriate for next year's expected production. For the smaller capacity production equipment, he estimates the price per rack to be $1.69 and the cost of owning the machine to be $41,000 for the year. For the higher capacity equipment, he estimates the price per rack to be $1.49 and the cost of owning the machine to be $63,000 for the year.

Shannon returns to her desk and creates a planning analysis sheet in preparation for evaluating John's alternative sets of numbers (Figure 5-2). She doesn't need to sketch the worksheets for these alternatives because they have the same design as the base case.

Figure 5-2
Shannon's planning
analysis sheet

Planning Analysis Sheet

<u>My goal:</u>
Prepare alternative plans for units produced, price per unit, and equipment costs for next year

<u>What results do I want to see?</u>
Projected income statement for each alternative

<u>What information do I need?</u>
Base Case: Racks = 53000
              Price = 15.50
              Equipment = 1.69 * racks + 41000
Best Case: Racks = 61000
              Price = 16.25
              Equipment = 1.69 * racks + 41000
Worst Case: Racks = 53000
              Price = 15.50
              Equipment = 1.49 * racks + 63000

In this tutorial you will produce Shannon's worksheet and learn how to use 1-2-3 to interpret different sets of data. You will learn how to create and organize several worksheet solutions in order to make better business decisions.

Customizing the SmartIcon Palette

Before Shannon begins her worksheet, she wants to modify an existing SmartIcon palette to include the SmartIcons she will need for this assignment. She wants to add the Versions SmartIcon to help her track the different what-if alternatives. Because she plans to set up a summarized analysis with several alternatives, she wants to add SmartIcons that will help her work with multiple worksheets—Display Contiguous, Next Worksheet, and Previous Worksheet. You will learn how to create versions and scenarios and how to use multiple worksheets later in this tutorial. Also, Shannon decides to include the Range Name SmartIcon to help her name the ranges that will contain the what-if values.

So far in this book, each tutorial used a predefined SmartIcon palette that contained the icons specifically for that tutorial. When you create your own worksheets, you might want to customize your own palette to include the SmartIcons you use most frequently. To do this, you can modify any existing palette.

REFERENCE WINDOW

Customizing a SmartIcon Palette

- Click Tools, then click SmartIcons... to display this dialog box.

- Click the drop-down list arrow to display the list of available palettes you can customize, then click the palette you want to change to display the set of SmartIcons for that palette. (Note that this step is optional—the palette might already be displayed.)

- Click the Save Set... button to display the Save Set of SmartIcons dialog box.

- In the Name of set text box, type the name you want for the new palette, press [Tab], type the filename for the new palette in the File name text box, then click the OK button.

- To add a SmartIcon to the palette, drag the icon from the Available icons list to the palette list, positioning the icon where you want it in the list.

- To remove a SmartIcon from the palette, drag the icon anywhere outside the palette list.

- To change the location of the SmartIcon palette in the worksheet window, click the Position drop-down list arrow, then click the position you want.

- Click the OK button when you complete customizing the palette.

Let's modify the Tutorial 4 SmartIcon palette to create a customized set of SmartIcons for you to use as you carry out Shannon's what-if analyses. Note that if you do not have write access to the hard drive, you cannot customize your own SmartIcon palette. Instead, you can use the SmartIcon palette selector in the status bar to select the Tutorial 5 SmartIcon palette, and skip to the section entitled "Retrieving the Worksheet."

To modify a set of SmartIcons for this tutorial:

❶ Launch 1-2-3, and if you have write access to the hard drive, select the Tutorial 4 SmartIcon palette by using the SmartIcon palette selector ▦ in the status bar. This is the set you will modify. It is not necessary to open a worksheet file before you begin to customize your set of SmartIcons.

TROUBLE? If you do not have write access to the hard drive, select the Tutorial 5 SmartIcon palette, then skip to the section entitled "Retrieving the Worksheet."

❷ Click **Tools**, then click **SmartIcons...** to display this dialog box. See Figure 5-3. Notice the arrangement of the icons in the Available icons list box and the current set of icons for Tutorial 4.

available icons →

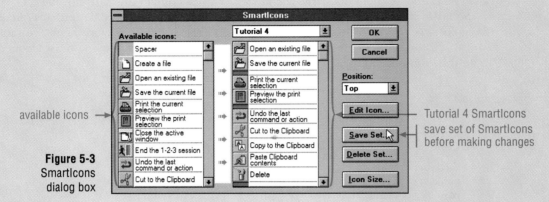

Figure 5-3
SmartIcons
dialog box

❸ Click the **Save Set... button** to display the Save Set of SmartIcons dialog box. You need to save this set of SmartIcons and give it a new name *before* you make any changes or the Tutorial 4 SmartIcon palette will be permanently changed.

❹ Type **My Icons** in the Name of set text box, press **[Tab]** to move to the File name text box, type **myicons** as the filename, then click the **OK button**. Lotus 1-2-3 automatically adds the .SMI file extension. See Figure 5-4. Remember filenames do not contain spaces. Note that the directory where the SmartIcons are stored might be different on your computer.

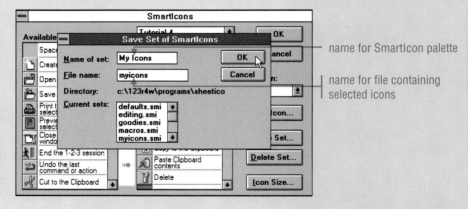

Figure 5-4
Save Set of
SmartIcons
dialog box

TROUBLE? If a warning dialog box appears saying that the MYICONS file already exists, and asks if you want to overwrite the existing file, click the OK button. Someone else used your computer and already saved a SmartIcon set with that filename.

Now, remove the SmartIcons that you don't want from the palette:

❺ Scroll the list of icons until you see Bold data. See Figure 5-5.

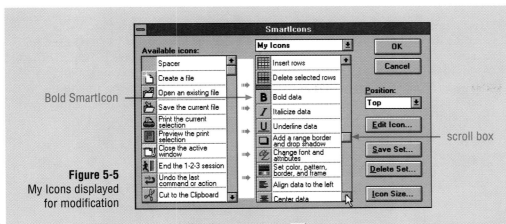

Bold SmartIcon

Figure 5-5
My Icons displayed
for modification

scroll box

❻ Drag the **Bold SmartIcon** ⓑ to the left until it is anywhere outside the My Icons list box, then release the mouse button to remove this SmartIcon from the set.

❼ Remove the following icons from the My Icons list box: Italicize data; Underline data; Add a range border and drop shadow; Change font and attributes; Set color, pattern, border, and frame; Align data to the left; Center data; Align data to the right.

With the unwanted SmartIcons removed, you are ready to add the icons to the palette that you will need for this tutorial. They are described as: Create and delete range names (Range Name SmartIcon); Work with versions and scenarios (Version SmartIcon); Select a range, drawn object, or query table (Go To SmartIcon); Display contiguous worksheets (Display Contiguous SmartIcon); Go to the next worksheet (Next Worksheet SmartIcon); Go to the previous worksheet (Previous Worksheet SmartIcon); and Go to the top left cell (Home SmartIcon). Let's begin by adding the Range Name SmartIcon to the palette.

To add the SmartIcons you will use in this tutorial to the My Icons palette:

❶ Scroll the Available icons list box until Create and delete range names (the Range Name SmartIcon) appears.

❷ Drag the **Range Name SmartIcon** ▦ from the Available icons list box and place it on top of the Insert Rows SmartIcon in the My Icons list box, then release the mouse button. The icon is added to the My Icons list box above the Insert Rows SmartIcon. See Figure 5-6.

icon added from
Available icons
list box

drag icon from here

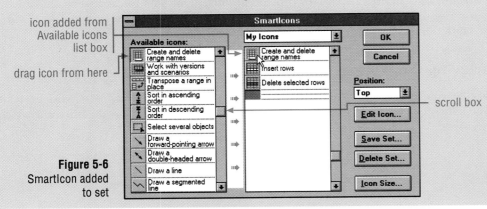

scroll box

Figure 5-6
SmartIcon added
to set

❸ Refer to Figure 5-7, and continue to add icons to the My Icons list. The Spacer, which you obtain from the very top of the Available icons list box, can be used to separate some of the icons. Notice that the position for this palette is "Top." Lotus 1-2-3's default palette location is at the top of the worksheet. You can also have a palette appear along the left or right side of the screen, along the bottom of the worksheet, or floating anywhere on the worksheet. Because the top position for the SmartIcon palette usually causes the least amount of interference, this is the location used throughout this book.

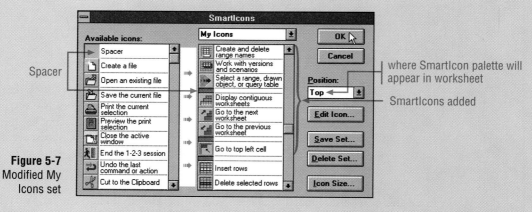

Figure 5-7
Modified My
Icons set

TROUBLE? If a SmartIcon in the My Icons list box is in the wrong location, drag the icon to the correct position.

❹ Click the **OK button** to complete the customization of your set of SmartIcons and return to Ready mode. The new set of SmartIcons appears. See Figure 5-8.

Figure 5-8
My Icons palette
ready for use

Customized SmartIcon palettes provide a convenient way for accessing those icons that you use frequently. When you modify an existing palette, make sure you save it first with a different name before adding or subtracting any SmartIcons.

Retrieving the Worksheet

Now that you've customized or selected a palette to work with Tutorial 5, you are ready to open Shannon's projected income statement worksheet and set up the different what-if alternatives.

To open Shannon's worksheet:

❶ Open C5WCP1.WK4, located on your Student Disk. Then, immediately save it as
S5WCP1.WK4 in the event that you need to restart this tutorial. Review Shannon's
worksheet and observe that the Return On Sales for the Base Case is 12.3%. See
Figure 5-9.

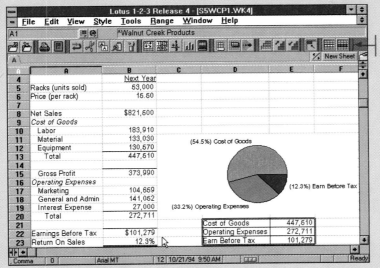

Figure 5-9
Shannon's projected
income statement
worksheet

❷ Verify that the My Icons/Tutorial 5 SmartIcon palette is displayed along the top of
the worksheet.

TROUBLE? If the palette is not displayed, use the SmartIcon palette selector in the
status bar to select either the My Icons palette or the Tutorial 5 palette.

Introduction to Range Names

Shannon plans to name the ranges that will contain the what-if values. Naming ranges will
make it easier for Shannon and John to evaluate the alternative what-if values. A **range
name** is a word or phrase that you use to substitute for a cell address like A5 or a cell
range like A5..A10. Anywhere that you would use a cell address or cell range you can use
the range name instead. Range names describe the data contained in the cells and are easier to remember. For example, if you want to add the cost of goods, you could specify
B9..B13 as the range to use in the @SUM formula, or you could name the range "COST OF
GOODS" and then select that range name from the list of ranges for summation.

You name ranges either by typing the name or by using a label in an adjacent cell.
Range names can be up to 15 characters long and can include letters, numbers, spaces,
and underscores (_) but not any other special characters. You should *not* begin a range
name with a number or try to create names that look like cell addresses, such as Q4 for
Quarter 4 or FY95 for Fiscal Year 1995. This can be confusing in formulas.

Once a range is named, you can use that name in formulas, reports, and charts. Using
range names instead of cell addresses is quicker for building formulas, selecting data, and
printing specific areas of a worksheet. Range names reduce the need to modify worksheet
formulas and help to avoid errors when specifying a range of cells. Range names are saved

automatically with the worksheet when you save it, but they do not alter the appearance of cell contents.

Using Range Names in Formulas

Range names allow you to use descriptive words instead of cell addresses in formulas. Descriptive words are more meaningful in a formula because they remind you of the purpose of the calculation. For example, the formula @SUM(COST OF GOODS) is easier to understand than @SUM(B10..B12). Shannon wants to include range names in her worksheet to make the formulas easier for John to review.

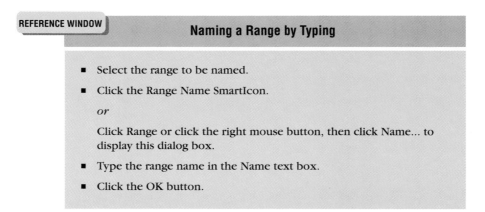

REFERENCE WINDOW

Naming a Range by Typing

- Select the range to be named.
- Click the Range Name SmartIcon.

  or

  Click Range or click the right mouse button, then click Name... to display this dialog box.
- Type the range name in the Name text box.
- Click the OK button.

Let's assign the range name TOTAL COSTS to cell B13.

To assign a range name to cell B13 by typing:

❶ Click **B13**. This is the single cell range that you want to name.

❷ Click the **Range Name SmartIcon** 🔲 to display the Name dialog box.

❸ Type **total costs** in the Name text box. See Figure 5-10. Note that you can type the range name in uppercase or lowercase letters. Regardless of how you enter a range name, 1-2-3 always converts the letters to uppercase after you click the OK button.

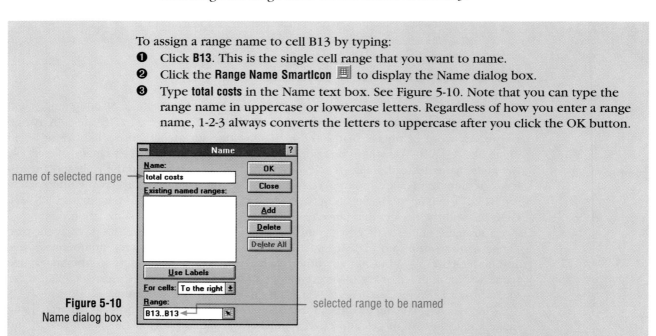

name of selected range

Figure 5-10
Name dialog box

selected range to be named

❹ Verify that the range B13..B13 is displayed in the Range text box.

❺   Click the **OK button** to complete the range name.

❻   Click **B15** and notice that in the cell contents box the range name TOTAL COSTS appears in the cell formula that calculates gross profit.

TROUBLE? If you misspelled the range name, click 🔳, click the misspelled range name in the Existing named ranges list box, click the Delete button to remove the unwanted name, then repeat Steps 3, 4, and 5.

Now let's assign the name COST OF GOODS to the range B10..B12, which contains the data values for the cost of goods line items, so these data values can be easily referenced.

To assign a range name to range B10..B12 by typing:

❶   Select the range B10..B12.

❷   Click the **Range Name SmartIcon** 🔳 to display the Name dialog box. See Figure 5-11. Notice that TOTAL COSTS appears in the Existing named ranges list box because you named this range in the previous set of steps.

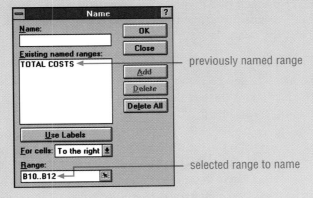

Figure 5-11
Name dialog box with previous entry

previously named range

selected range to name

❸   Type **COST OF GOODS** in the Name text box.

❹   Verify that the correct range appears in the Range text box.

❺   Click the **OK button** to complete naming this range.

❻   Click **B13**. Note that in the cell contents box, the cell formula is now @SUM(COST OF GOODS). Lotus 1-2-3 substituted the range name for the cell addresses in the formula @SUM(B10..B12). This will make it easier for John to understand the formulas in Shannon's worksheet.

You can name the range B8 using a label in an adjacent cell instead of typing the range name. You can use this method only if there is a label for each adjacent single cell range—for example, the label in cell A8 to name range B8 or the labels in cells A8, A9, and A10 to name ranges B8, B9, and B10.

REFERENCE WINDOW

Naming a Range Using a Label in an Adjacent Cell

- Select the range containing the label that will be used as the range name for the adjacent cell. (The range can contain more than one label.)
- Click the Range Name SmartIcon.

  or

  Click Range or click the right mouse button, then click Name....
- Select the appropriate For cells option.
- Click the Use Labels button to assign the cell label as the range name.
- Click the OK button.

Let's use the label in cell A8, "Net Sales," to name the range B8. When you use this method, you select the cell that contains the label you want to use as a range name and 1-2-3 automatically assigns this range name to the cell adjacent to it. In other words, you don't have to select the range itself.

To assign a range name to cell B8 using a label in an adjacent cell:

❶ Click **A8**, which contains the label that Shannon wants to use to name range B8.

❷ Click the **Range Name SmartIcon** ▦ to display the Name dialog box.

❸ Verify that the Range list box displays the correct A8..A8 range and that the For cells list box displays "To the right." This means that 1-2-3 will automatically name the range to the right of the selected range. You don't have to select it.

❹ Click the **Use Labels button** to assign the label in A8 as the range name of cell B8.

❺ Click **NET SALES** in the Existing named ranges list to verify that range B8 is assigned the range name NET SALES. See Figure 5-12. Then click the **OK button** to complete the specification and return to READY mode.

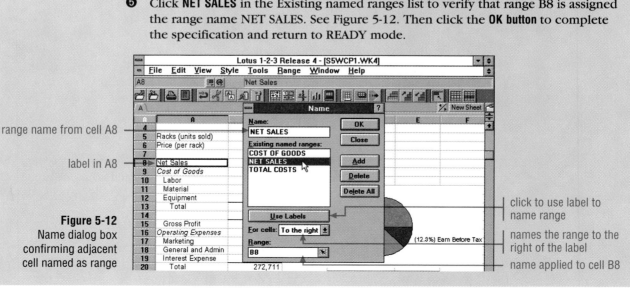

range name from cell A8

label in A8

Figure 5-12
Name dialog box
confirming adjacent
cell named as range

click to use label to name range

names the range to the right of the label

name applied to cell B8

⊙ Click **B15**. Note that in the cell contents box, the formula for Gross Profit is now +NET SALES-TOTAL COSTS. Again, 1-2-3 updated the formula to include the range names. Now the formulas will be easier for Shannon to review with John.

Now name two other ranges Shannon needs for use in evaluating her what-if alternatives.

❼ Name the SALES range (B5..B6) and the EQUIPMENT range (B12) using the typing method.

As these examples indicate, when you name a range, 1-2-3 automatically updates any formulas to include the new range name. Once you've named a range, you can also include the range name when you first enter a formula.

Using Range Names in Reports

Range names are useful in reports as well as formulas. One common use for including range names in reports is to reduce the time it takes to print the worksheet. Shannon wants to include a range name in her report so that each time she enters a new set of what-if values, she can quickly print the report to see the results. She might also want to print only the chart, so she plans to name that range, too.

Let's name the ranges Shannon plans to print frequently and then print the ranges to make sure the range names work.

To name the ranges to use in reports:
❶ Select the range A1..B24, which contains the projected income statement.
❷ Click the **Range Name SmartIcon** ⊞ .
❸ Type **INCOME REPORT** to name this range. Remember a range name can have a maximum of 15 characters, and you can use spaces in the name.
❹ Click the **OK button** to complete naming the range.
❺ Press **[Esc]** to unselect the currently highlighted range. This range no longer needs to be selected to continue with any other worksheet activities—you can use the range name instead.

Next, let's assign a range name for printing Shannon's pie chart.

❻ Select the range C9..F25, which contains both the pie chart and summary table, then assign it the range name PIE CHART using an appropriate method for naming this range.

Now let's print Shannon's report using the newly named range.

To print the reports using the range names:
❶ Click the **Print SmartIcon** ⊟ to display the Print dialog box.
❷ Click the **Selected range option button**, then click the **Selected range text box**.
❸ Press **[F3]** (Name) to display the Range Names dialog box. See Figure 5-13.

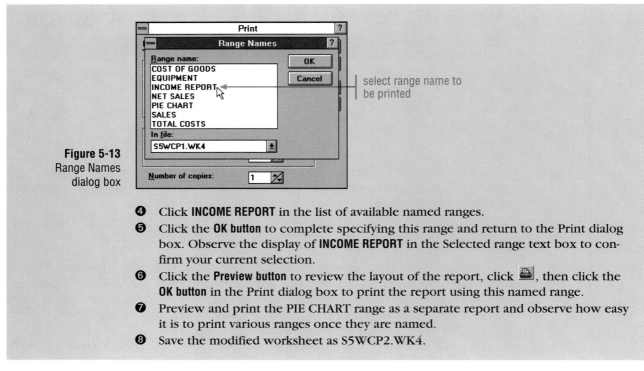

Figure 5-13
Range Names
dialog box

select range name to
be printed

❹ Click **INCOME REPORT** in the list of available named ranges.

❺ Click the **OK button** to complete specifying this range and return to the Print dialog box. Observe the display of **INCOME REPORT** in the Selected range text box to confirm your current selection.

❻ Click the **Preview button** to review the layout of the report, click 🖨, then click the **OK button** in the Print dialog box to print the report using this named range.

❼ Preview and print the PIE CHART range as a separate report and observe how easy it is to print various ranges once they are named.

❽ Save the modified worksheet as S5WCP2.WK4.

If you want to take a break and resume the tutorial at a later time, you can exit 1-2-3 by double-clicking the Control menu box in the upper-left corner of your screen. When you resume the tutorial, launch 1-2-3, and place your Student Disk in the disk drive. Open the S5WCP2.WK4 worksheet file, select the My Icons or Tutorial 5 SmartIcon palette, then continue with this tutorial.

■   ■   ■

Introduction to Versions and Scenarios

Shannon needs to perform various what-if analyses with her worksheet in order to develop the operating plan for next year. You know that a what-if analysis is conducted whenever one or more data values are revised and the effect of this change is observed on other calculated cells. Shannon plans to use a feature of 1-2-3 called **Version Manager** to organize and track the different what-if alternatives. In order for Version Manager to work, the data that will change with each new what-if analysis has to be in a named range. Then, in order to determine which ranges of data offer the most profitability for WCP, Shannon will save different versions. **Versions** are different sets of data used for the same named range. Finally, she will choose the best case scenario based on the different what-if versions. A **scenario** is a named group of versions.

Creating Versions

With all of the ranges named, Shannon is ready to use Version Manager to organize her what-if analyses. You use Version Manager to create a version of the worksheet that consists of one set of data in a named range and to give the version a name. Using Version Manager is like storing the data values in a named range on a piece of tape, as illustrated in Figure 5-14. Once you create a version, you can select it, and the data values in that version will be pasted over the ones currently in the range of the worksheet. In this way, Version Manager allows you to store and view a number of different what-if alternatives.

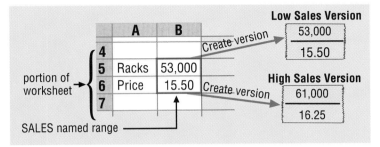

Figure 5-14
Version Manager stores alternative what-if data values for use in the worksheet

According to Shannon's planning analysis sheet in Figure 5-2, she needs to create two versions—one for the High Sales alternative and one for the Low Sales alternative. The Low Sales version is the set of numbers already in the worksheet in the SALES range. All Shannon has to do is name that version. Then, she will create the High Sales version by entering the what-if values in the SALES range and then naming that version.

REFERENCE WINDOW

Creating Versions

- Name the range of cells that contains the data values for the version, if the range hasn't been named previously.

- Enter the what-if data values for the version in this range.

- Click the Range SmartIcon, then double-click the range name for the version.

  or

  Click the range name selector, then click the range name for the version.

- Click the Version SmartIcon to display the Version Manager dialog box.

  or

  Click Range, then click Version... to display the Version Manager dialog box.

- Click the Create... button to display the Create Version dialog box.

- Type the name of the version.

- Type any comment that you want to describe the version.

- Click the OK button.

- Click the Close button in the Version Manager dialog box.

Let's create these two SALES versions for Shannon's what-if analysis.

To create the Low Sales version using the existing data values in the named range:

❶ Click the **Go To SmartIcon** to go to the SALES range. The Go To dialog box appears. See Figure 5-15.

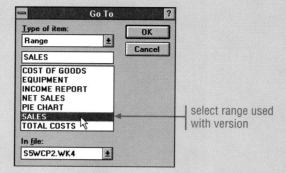

Figure 5-15
Go To dialog box

❷ Click **SALES** in the list of named ranges, then click the **OK button** to select this range of data for analysis. Since you don't want to alter these values for the Low Sales version, you are now ready to use this version.

❸ Click the **Version SmartIcon** to display the Version Manager dialog box. Notice that the dialog box is covering part of the pie chart.

   TROUBLE? If the Version Manager Index dialog box appears instead of the Version Manager dialog box, click the To Manager button to display the Version Manager dialog box.

❹ Move the **Version Manager** dialog box to the right so both the report and pie chart areas are visible on your screen. See Figure 5-16.

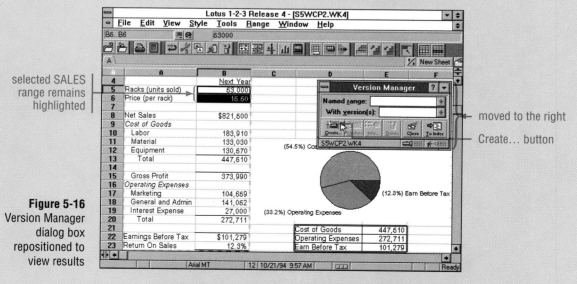

Figure 5-16
Version Manager
dialog box
repositioned to
view results

❺ Click the **Create... button** in the Version Manager dialog box to create and name this version. The Create Version dialog box appears with a default version name. See Figure 5-17.

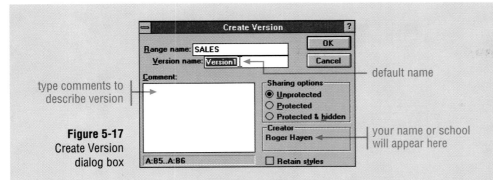

type comments to
describe version

Figure 5-17
Create Version
dialog box

default name

your name or school
will appear here

TROUBLE? If the default range name of RANGE1 or another range name appears in the Range name text box, you did not select the SALES range before accessing the Version Manager. Click the Cancel button, then repeat Steps 1, 2, and 5. The Version Manager dialog box remains displayed.

➏ Type **Low Sales** in the Version name text box to name this version.

➐ Press **[Tab]** to move the cursor to the Comment text box, then type **Worst sales projection for next year**. This will help you and anyone else looking at your worksheet to know what this version is for.

➑ Click the **OK button** to complete creating and naming this version and return to the Version Manager dialog box.

➒ Click the **Close button** in the Version Manager dialog box to close this dialog box and return to the worksheet window.

Now Shannon needs to create her High Sales version. First, she will enter the what-if values and then she will create and name a version that includes those what-if values. Let's enter the what-if values using the Best Case values from Shannon's planning analysis sheet (Figure 5-2) and name this version "High Sales."

To perform a what-if analysis and name this version "High Sales":

➊ Click **B5** then enter **61000**. Notice that as you change the data value the report is automatically recalculated and the pie chart is updated.

➋ Click **B6** then enter **16.25**. Again, the report is updated.

Now you are ready to create and name this version.

➌ Click the **Version SmartIcon** to display the Version Manager dialog box. See Figure 5-18. The Low Sales version name appears in the With version(s) list box because it also uses the SALES range. However, the version name appears in italics with a line through the checkmark to indicate that it does not contain the values currently entered in the worksheet area.

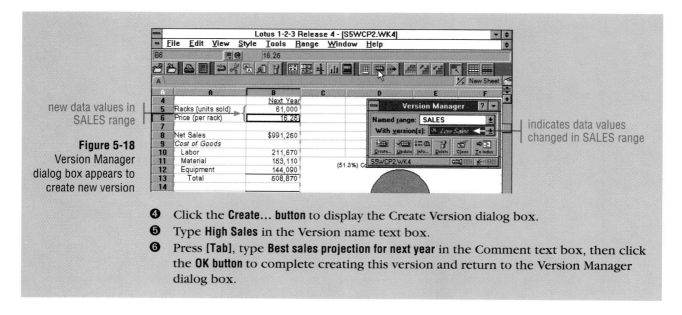

new data values in SALES range

Figure 5-18
Version Manager dialog box appears to create new version

indicates data values changed in SALES range

❹ Click the **Create... button** to display the Create Version dialog box.

❺ Type **High Sales** in the Version name text box.

❻ Press **[Tab]**, type **Best sales projection for next year** in the Comment text box, then click the **OK button** to complete creating this version and return to the Version Manager dialog box.

Once versions are set up, it is easy to view the various what-if solutions. Let's change from the currently selected High Sales version to the Low Sales version.

To change versions using the Version Manager:

❶ Click the **With version(s) drop-down list arrow** to display the list of available versions for the SALES named range. See Figure 5-19.

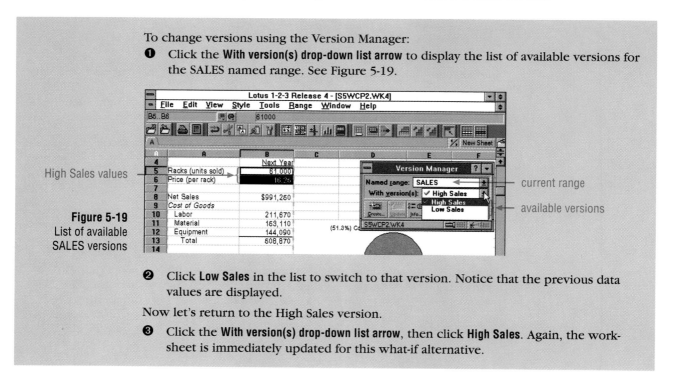

High Sales values

Figure 5-19
List of available SALES versions

current range

available versions

❷ Click **Low Sales** in the list to switch to that version. Notice that the previous data values are displayed.

Now let's return to the High Sales version.

❸ Click the **With version(s) drop-down list arrow**, then click **High Sales**. Again, the worksheet is immediately updated for this what-if alternative.

Besides the two SALES alternatives, Shannon's planning analysis sheet (Figure 5-2) includes two different equipment costs—a low and a high alternative. These alternatives, which are calculated using a formula, can be added to the list of versions. Since the equipment cost is in a separate range that was previously named EQUIPMENT, Shannon is ready to create these two versions. Let's add the EQUIPMENT versions to Shannon's worksheet. Again, the Low Costs version uses the values already in the worksheet, whereas the High Costs version uses what-if values.

To create the Low Costs version:

❶ Click the **range name selector** 🔲, also known as the navigator, to display the list of range names. See Figure 5-20.

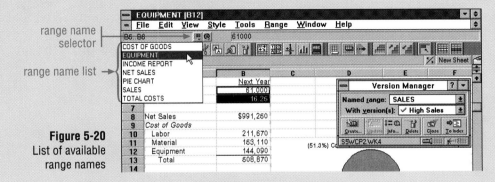

Figure 5-20
List of available range names

❷ Click **EQUIPMENT** to select this named range.

❸ Click the **Create... button** in the Version Manager dialog box to display the Create Version dialog box with EQUIPMENT appearing as the range name. See Figure 5-21. The cell pointer positions itself at the named range.

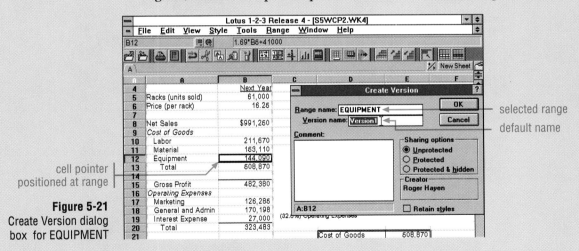

Figure 5-21
Create Version dialog box for EQUIPMENT

❹ Type **Low Costs** in the Version name text box.

❺ Press **[Tab]**, type **Best cost projection for next year** in the Comment text box, then click the **OK button** to complete creating this version.

Next, let's enter the what-if values to revise the formula that calculates Equipment for the High Costs version and then create this version.

To enter the what-if values and name the version "High Costs":

❶ Click **B12** to select this cell while the Version Manager dialog box is displayed.

❷ Edit this cell so it contains the formula 1.49*B5+63000 as specified by Shannon's planning analysis sheet (Figure 5-2).

Now you can create the version.

❸ Click the **Create... button** in the Version Manager dialog box.

❹ Type **High Costs** in the Version name text box.

❺ Press **[Tab]**, then type **Worst cost projection for next year** in the Comment text box. See Figure 5-22.

❻ Click the **OK button** to complete this specification for the High Costs alternative for Equipment, and return to the Version Manager dialog box.

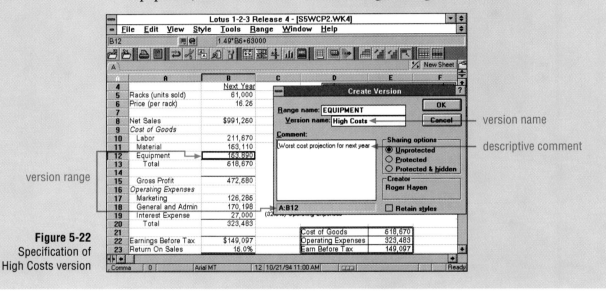

Figure 5-22
Specification of
High Costs version

Using Version Manager, you can easily view the best case alternative, which would be High Sales and Low Costs. Let's view the best case alternative.

To change the currently displayed version to the best case alternative:

❶ Verify that EQUIPMENT is displayed in the Named range list box of the Version Manager dialog box, then click the **With version(s) drop-down list arrow** to display the list of available versions for EQUIPMENT.

❷ Click **Low Costs**.

❸ Click the **Named range drop-down list arrow** to display the list of available named ranges, then click **SALES**. See Figure 5-23.

Figure 5-23
List of available
ranges with versions

❹ Click the **With version(s) drop-down list arrow** to display the list of available versions for the selected named range, then click **High Sales** to obtain the results for the best case alternative with a Return On Sales of 16.0%.

Now save this version with the worksheet.

❺ Save the worksheet as S5WCP3.WK4. Print both the projected income statement and the pie chart for the best case alternative.

Once you create a version, 1-2-3 allows you to edit it or delete it at any time using one of the buttons in the Version Manager dialog box.

Creating Scenarios

A **scenario** is a named group of versions. For example, the best case alternative with the High Sales version for the SALES range and the Low Costs version for the EQUIPMENT range can be grouped to form the Best Case scenario, as illustrated in Figure 5-24. Similarly, the Worst Case scenario can be created, as shown in Figure 5-25. When a scenario is selected, *all the ranges* in the scenario display the data values for the versions that make up that scenario. As Shannon sketched out in her planning analysis sheet, she wants to prepare three scenarios—Base Case, Best Case, and Worst Case. Creating a scenario is similar to creating a version—once you get to the right dialog box, all you have to do is name the scenario, add any comments you might have, then select the versions that make up the scenario.

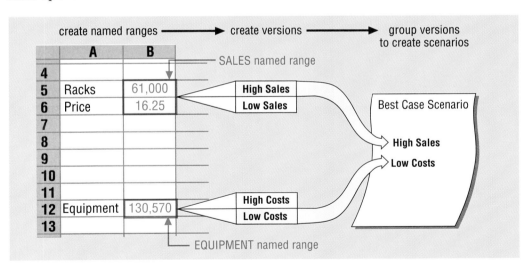

Figure 5-24
Best case senario
created from
versions

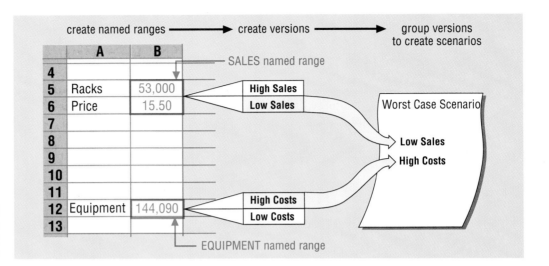

Figure 5-25
Worst case senario
created from
versions

Creating Scenarios

- Click the Version SmartIcon to display this dialog box.

- Click the To index... button to display the Version Manager Index dialog box.

- Click the Scenario... button to display the Create Scenario dialog box.

- Enter the name of the scenario.

- Enter any comments that you want to describe the scenario.

- Scroll through the Available versions list box to find the versions you want to make up the scenario, then select those versions by double-clicking them.

- Click the OK button to return to the Version Manager Index dialog box and display a list of the versions included with the newly created scenario.

- Click the Show button to select the scenario for viewing. This is optional.

- Click the Close button if you want to close the Version Manager Index dialog box.

Let's create Shannon's three scenarios. Then any one of them can be selected from the Version Manager Index in order to view the results appearing in the projected income statement. The **Version Manager Index** is a listing of the scenarios with the version included in each scenario.

To create the Base Case scenario:

❶ Verify that the Version Manager dialog box appears on your screen. If it is not displayed, then click the **Version SmartIcon** 🔲.

❷ Click the **To index button** in the Version Manager dialog box to display the Version Manager Index dialog box. Reposition the dialog box, if necessary, so that the entire dialog box is displayed. See Figure 5-26. This index is currently blank because no scenarios have been created.

Scenario name
Sort button

Scenario... button

Figure 5-26
Version Manager
Index dialog box

no scenarios

TROUBLE? If the index is not blank, the Version name Sort button will appear in place of the Scenario name Sort button. If this happens, click the Version name Sort button and select Scenario name Sort from the list.

❸ Click the **Scenario... button** to display the Create Scenario dialog box. See Figure 5-27. Notice that the default scenario name Scenario1 appears in the Scenario name text box.

type comments to
describe scenario

specify versions in
this scenario

Figure 5-27
Create Scenario
dialog box

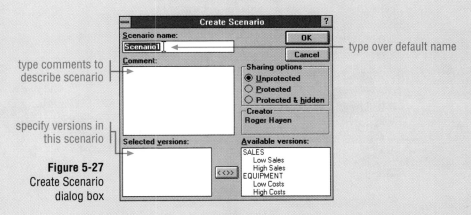

type over default name

❹ Type **Base Case** in the Scenario name text box.

TROUBLE? If the name Base Case does not replace Scenario1, double-click Scenario1, then enter the name again.

❺ Press **[Tab]** then type **Base case projection for next year** in the Comment text box.

Now you can select the versions to include with this scenario.

❻ Click **Low Sales** in the Available versions list box, then click the **<< button** to copy this version to the Selected versions list box. Remember that Low Sales was the Base Case. You could also double-click Low Sales to copy it to the Selected versions list box.

TROUBLE? If you select the wrong version, double-click that version in the Selected versions list box to remove it from the list, then repeat Step 6.

❼ Double-click **Low Costs** in the Available versions list box to copy it to the Selected versions list box. See Figure 5-28. Notice that the Selected versions list box lists both the range names and the version names.

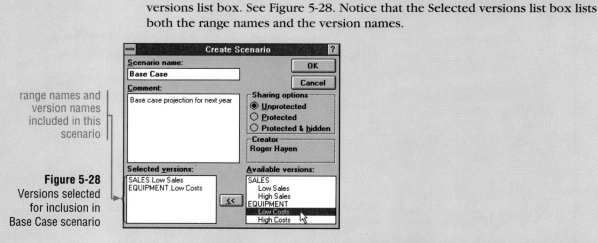

range names and
version names
included in this
scenario

Figure 5-28
Versions selected
for inclusion in
Base Case scenario

❽ Click the **OK button** to return to the Version Manager Index dialog box, which displays a summary of the versions that make up this Base Case scenario, then click the **Show button** to calculate the selected scenario and verify that the Base Case Return On Sales of 12.3% appears in the worksheet. See Figure 5-29.

TROUBLE? If you specify the wrong scenario, click the Delete button in the Version Manager Index dialog box, then click the OK button to confirm deletion of the scenario. Now, click the Scenario... button and repeat Steps 4 through 8.

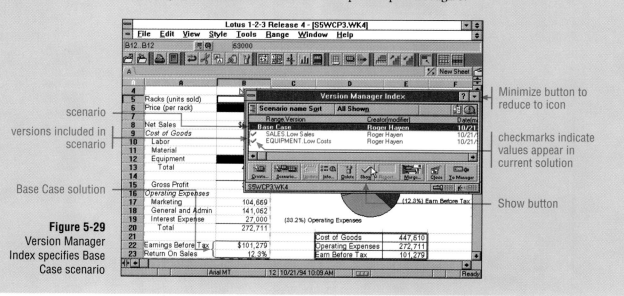

scenario

versions included in
scenario

Base Case solution

Figure 5-29
Version Manager
Index specifies Base
Case scenario

Minimize button to
reduce to icon

checkmarks indicate
values appear in
current solution

Show button

Because the Version Manager Index dialog box takes up a large area of your screen, you can minimize the dialog box to icon size in order to review your worksheet results. Let's minimize this dialog box and move the minimized Version Manager Index icon out of the way so it is not on top of the worksheet results.

To minimize the Version Manager Index dialog box and reposition its icon:

❶ Click the **Minimize button** for the Version Manager Index dialog box to reduce it to an icon.

❷ Drag the **Version Manager Index icon** from the lower-left corner of your display to cell **D4** in the worksheet. See Figure 5-30.

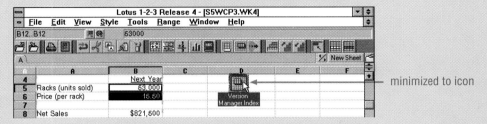

Figure 5-30
Version Manager
Index icon
repositioned to view
solution

minimized to icon

❸ Examine the entire worksheet result for the Base Case scenario, then print this report using the INCOME REPORT named range to produce a copy for John's review.

Next, let's create the Best Case and Worst Case scenarios using the same procedure.

To create the Best Case scenario:

❶ Double-click the **Version Manager Index icon** to display this dialog box.

❷ Click the **Scenario... button** to display the Create Scenario dialog box.

❸ Type **Best Case** in the Scenario name text box.

❹ Press **[Tab]** then type **Best case projection for next year** in the Comment text box.

❺ Double-click **High Sales** in the Available versions list box, then double-click **Low Costs** in the same list to copy the versions to the Selected versions list box.

❻ Click the **OK button** to return to the Version Manager Index dialog box, where you can now display the Base Case and Best Case scenarios by scrolling the index window. See Figure 5-31.

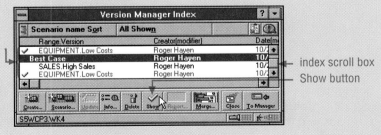

index window

Figure 5-31
Version Manager
Index displays Best
Case scenario

index scroll box
Show button

❼ Click the **Show button** to calculate the selected scenario, then verify that the Best Case Return On Sales of 16.0% appears in the worksheet by clicking any cell in the worksheet area and scrolling the window to display row 23, which contains the Return On Sales. This is almost a 4% increase in Return On Sales.

❽ Print this report using the INCOME REPORT named range to produce a copy of the scenario for John's review.

Finally, let's create the Worst Case scenario.

To create the Worst Case scenario:

❶ Double-click the **Version Manager Index icon** to display this dialog box.

❷ Create the scenario and name it "Worst Case." Enter **Worst case projection for next year** in the Comment text box, then include the **Low Sales** and **High Costs** versions in the Selected versions list box.

❸ Click the **OK button** to return to the Version Manager Index dialog box, where you can now display information about the three scenarios by scrolling the index window. See Figure 5-32.

Figure 5-32
Version Manager
Index displays Worst
Case scenario

index window →

index scroll box
Show button

❹ Click the **Show button** to calculate the selected scenario, then verify that the Worst Case value for Return On Sales is 10.9% by clicking any cell in the worksheet area and scrolling the window to display the Return On Sales.

❺ Print this report using the INCOME REPORT named range to produce a copy of the scenario for review.

As with versions, once you have set up your scenarios, it is easy to switch between different scenarios.

To change the scenario calculated in the worksheet:

❶ Double-click the **Version Manager Index icon** to display this dialog box.

❷ Double-click **Best Case** in the index window to calculate this solution and notice that the Return On Sales is now 16.0%.

❸ Double-click **Base Case** in the index window, then watch as the Return On Sales changes to 12.3%.

Shannon has successfully named ranges, created versions, and created the three scenarios to help John develop next year's operating plan. She brings her three printouts to John's office, and they both review the what-if scenarios. John tells Shannon that she did a great job preparing this worksheet and explains how helpful it will be.

Let's close the Version Manager Index dialog box so only the worksheet is displayed.

To close the Version Manager Index dialog box:

❶ Click the **Close button** in the Version Manager Index dialog box.

❷ Save the worksheet as S5WCP4.WK4. As with the range names, your scenarios are saved with your worksheet.

If you want to take a break and resume the tutorial at a later time, you can exit 1-2-3 by double-clicking the Control menu box in the upper-left corner of your screen. When you resume the tutorial, launch 1-2-3 and place your Student Disk in the disk drive. Select the My Icons or Tutorial 5 SmartIcon palette, open the S5WCP4.WK4 worksheet, then continue with this tutorial.

▪   ▪   ▪

Applying Functions

John would like Shannon to add a cost of goods summary section to WCP's projected income statement that includes the largest cost, the smallest cost, and the average cost. Shannon can obtain these values by using the statistical functions @MAX, @MIN, and @AVG. These functions are described in Figure 5-33 along with some of the more common 1-2-3 functions such as @SUM, @DATE, and @ROUND. Lotus 1-2-3 contains more that 100 different functions and they are classified into ten types of functions, some of which you have already used: Calendar (for example, @DATE), Database, Engineering, Financial, Information, Logical, Lookup, Mathematical (for example, @SUM and @ROUND), Statistical, and Text. By using the @function selector and the List All selection, you can display a list of all the 1-2-3 functions and obtain a description of each function.

Function	Description
@ABS(formula)	Calculates absolute value of the formula result
@AVG(range)	Calculates average of values
@COS(formula)	Calculates cosine of expression
@COUNT(range)	Counts nonblank cells in a range
@DAY(date)	Displays the day number of date
@INT(formula)	Displays the formula result as an integer
@LN(formula)	Finds the natural logarithm of the formula result
@MAX(range-list)	Finds maximum value in list
@MIN(range-list)	Finds miminum value in list
@MONTH(date)	Displays the month number of date
@NPV(interest-rate,range)	Calculates net present value of cash flows
@PMT(principal,rate,term)	Calculates loan payment
@ROUND(formula,decimals)	Rounds to specified decimal places
@SIN(formula)	Calculates sine of expression
@SLN(cost,salvage,life)	Calculates straight-line depreciation
@SQRT(formula)	Performs square root of the formula result
@STD(range-list)	Calculates standard deviation of values
@SUM(range-list)	Adds the values in the range
@TODAY	Displays today's date from the computer's clock
@YEAR(date)	Displays the year number of date

Figure 5-33
Selected 1-2-3 functions

Using the @MAX, @MIN, and @AVG Functions

Let's add the summary section to Shannon's worksheet. First, you need to enter the labels for the summary section in the worksheet, then you can enter the functions you will need for the summary.

To create the summary section in Shannon's worksheet:

❶ Scroll the worksheet so cell A10 is in the upper-left corner of worksheet area.

❷ Enter the labels in A26..A29, as shown in Figure 5-34. Make sure you include spaces in front of the labels in cells A27, A28, and A29 so that they will be indented, as shown in Figure 5-34.

labels for summary

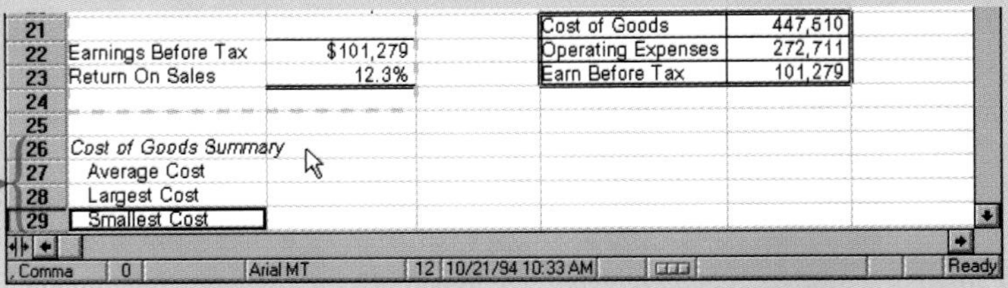

Figure 5-34
Cost of Goods
Summary section
of report

				Cost of Goods	447,510
21					
22	Earnings Before Tax	$101,279		Operating Expenses	272,711
23	Return On Sales	12.3%		Earn Before Tax	101,279
24					
25					
26	Cost of Goods Summary				
27	Average Cost				
28	Largest Cost				
29	Smallest Cost				

Comma   0   Arial MT   12 10/21/94 10:33 AM   Ready

REFERENCE WINDOW

Using Range Names in Functions

- Click the cell where you want the formula with the function to appear.

- Click the @function selector to display the list of available functions, then select the desired function.

  or

  Type @ and press [F3] (Name), then select the function you want.

  or

  Type the function name including the open parenthesis.

- Click the range name selector, then select the named range.

  or

  Use pointing to select the correct range.

- Click the Confirm button or press [Enter] to complete the specification.

Let's enter the functions for Shannon's cost summary using a few different methods.

To calculate the average cost using the @AVG function:

❶ Click **B27**.

❷ Click the **@function selector** 🔘 then click **AVG**.

❸ Select the range B10..B12, which contains the costs to be averaged.

❹ Click the **Confirm button** or press **[Enter]** to complete entering the function and display the result. What is displayed as the cell's content? Because B10..B12 is a named range, its name appears in this function.

Next, let's add the function for calculating the largest cost of goods.

To use the @MAX function to find the largest value:
❶ Click **B28**.
❷ Type **@MAX(** to begin the formula.
❸ Select the range B10..B12, which contains the costs from which the largest value will be calculated.
❹ Click the **Confirm button** or press **[Enter]** to complete the cell entry. It is not necessary to type the closing parenthesis, since no other arithmetic is included with this function. What is the amount of the largest cost?

Now let's add the function for calculating the smallest cost of goods.

To use the @MIN function to find the smallest value:
❶ Click **B29**.
❷ Type **@MIN(** to begin the formula.
❸ Click the **range name selector** ▦ to display the range names.
❹ Click **COST OF GOODS**, the range that contains the costs from which the smallest value will be derived.
❺ Click the **Confirm button** or press **[Enter]** to complete the cell entry. The final results for the Cost of Goods Summary are displayed. See Figure 5-35.

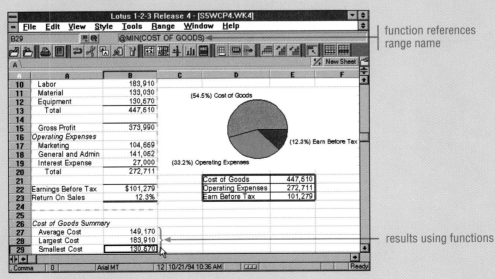

Figure 5-35
Cost of Goods
Summary with
values calculated
using functions

Now that you have completed the report, save the worksheet.

❻   Save the worksheet as S5WCP5.WK4, then preview and print the results. Make sure your printed result includes the newly added Cost of Goods Summary.

Calculating a Loan Payment with @PMT

John has a new project for Shannon. He has been looking for a new finishing machine that would produce a higher quality walnut finish for the multi-media storage rack at a lower cost. He found one but it costs $1,500,000. John is considering financing this machine with a bank loan, and he wants Shannon to determine what his monthly payments would be. He estimates that they can finance the entire cost of the equipment with a loan at a yearly interest rate of 9% and a repayment period of eight years.

Shannon knows that 1-2-3 has a financial function that is perfect for this type of calculation—@PMT. The syntax of the @PMT function is:

@PMT(principal,interest,term)

The **principal argument** is the total amount of the loan. The **interest argument** must be specified as a period interest rate that matches the **term argument**, or duration of the loan. For example, if the term is in months, then the interest rate must be a monthly rate. It is your responsibility to carefully match the period interest rate to the term of the loan in months or years.

Shannon planned, sketched, and partially completed the worksheet for the loan analysis. Let's open Shannon's partially completed worksheet for the new finishing machine.

To open the loan analysis worksheet:
❶   Close any other worksheet files that might be open.
❷   Open Shannon's partially completed worksheet, C5WCP2.WK4, then immediately save it as S5WCP6.WK4.
❸   Review the contents of the worksheet. How is the interest rate entered?

In Shannon's worksheet the interest rate period matches the term of the loan; however, they are both set up as yearly amounts. Shannon will have to convert them to monthly amounts in order to calculate the monthly payment using the @PMT function.

REFERENCE WINDOW

Using @PMT to Calculate a Monthly Payment

- Click the cell where you want to display the monthly payment amount.

- Click the @function selector, then click List All....

- Click the Category drop-down list arrow, click Financial, click PMT, and click the OK button.

- Click the cell containing the loan amount, or principal.

- Highlight the interest temporary argument, click the cell containing the interest rate entered as a decimal, then type /12.

- Highlight the term temporary argument, click the cell containing the term in years, then type *12.

- Click the Confirm button or press [Enter].

Instead of selecting the function from a list, you can type @PMT(and use pointing to specify the cell addresses for the loan amount, interest rate, and/or term.

Now let's add the loan payment calculation to Shannon's worksheet.

To calculate the monthly loan payment using the @PMT function:

❶ Click **B7**. This is where you want the monthly loan payment to be calculated.

❷ Click the **@function selector** 🔘 to display the list of frequently used @functions, then click **List All…** because the PMT function is not on the list.

❸ Click the **Category drop-down list arrow**, then click **Financial**, since PMT is a financial function.

❹ Scroll through the list of financial @functions, then double-click **PMT**. The @PMT function appears in the worksheet with the temporary arguments of principal, interest, and term. See Figure 5-36. The principal temporary argument is automatically selected.

@function selector ——

principal selected ——

Figure 5-36
@PMT function
selected from list
with temporary
arguments displayed

temporary
arguments displayed

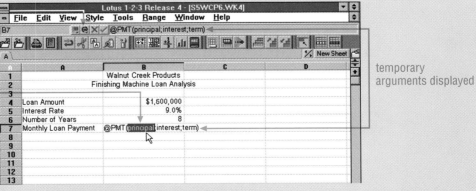

❺ Click **B4** to specify the loan amount, or principal.

❻ Highlight the **interest** temporary argument using the I, click **B5** to specify the annual interest rate, then type **/12** to convert the annual interest rate to a monthly interest rate.

TROUBLE? If ERR appears in the cell when you click the cell containing the interest rate, you highlighted a semi-colon (;) when you selected the interest temporary argument. Double-click the cell containing the @PMT function to edit it, reselect only the interest temporary argument, then either type the cell address or point to the cell containing the interest rate.

❼ Highlight the **term** temporary argument using I, click **B6** to specify the term in years, then type ***12** to convert the number of years to the number of months.

TROUBLE? If you highlight the wrong temporary argument or enter an incorrect cell address, just edit the contents of cell B7 and make your corrections.

❽ Press **[Enter]** or click the **Confirm button** to complete the function and display the loan payment. See Figure 5-37.

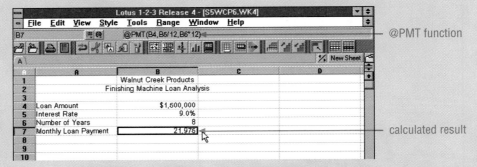

Figure 5-37
The loan payment
for the new
finishing machine

❾ Save the worksheet as S5WCP7.WK4, then preview and print the loan payment analysis.

If John wanted to make a yearly payment and *not* a monthly payment, Shannon would not have had to convert the annual interest rate to a monthly interest rate or the number of years to the number of months. The data for the @PMT function was already set up to calculate a yearly payment. When using the @PMT and other financial functions, you must match the time period of the interest rate with the time period of the term of the loan.

Introduction to Multiple Worksheets

Recently, a number of WCP's multi-media storage racks were returned because they were damaged in shipment. After investigating this problem, John believes a new machine would improve packaging and reduce damaged shipments. He is considering financing this machine with a different loan from that used for the finishing machine. He wants Shannon to prepare a report for this loan as she did for the finishing machine. He also wants her to include a summary of the total amount of the loans and the monthly payments for both pieces of equipment. Because John wants a summary, Shannon can't treat this second loan as a what-if evaluation and merely enter different data for the new loan. She needs to create a worksheet that contains the data for both loans together with the summary.

The basic 1-2-3 worksheet displays data in two dimensions. However, 1-2-3 offers you a new dimension for displaying data and creating reports. You can create multiple worksheets, also referred to as just **sheets**. The sheets are stored in a *single* 1-2-3 worksheet file. A summary of several detail plans, like Shannon's two loans, is a common application of the multiple worksheet feature. Shannon can create a separate sheet for each of the two loans and then use a third sheet for the summary, all in the *same* worksheet file.

Creating a Second Worksheet

When creating a worksheet for a second analysis like the packaging machine loan, it is a good idea to create the worksheet for the first analysis, verify its contents, and then copy the worksheet to another sheet for the other analysis. This helps to ensure that the same formulas are used in both worksheets. Remember, both sheets will be created in one worksheet file, S5WCP7.WK4.

Shannon is ready to expand her current worksheet for the finishing machine loan into a multiple worksheet file that includes the loan analysis for both pieces of equipment. Because the monthly loan payments are calculated using the *same* formulas, Shannon can duplicate the worksheet for the packaging machine from that for the finishing machine. Duplicating is *not* a 1-2-3 command but is the process of copying all the labels and formulas from one sheet to another one, so that you can perform the same analysis but with different data. When multiple sheets are used in a single worksheet file, each sheet is identified by its worksheet letter A, B, C, and so on. A worksheet tab appears for each sheet that is included in your worksheet file.

REFERENCE WINDOW   **Adding a New Sheet to the Current Worksheet File**

- Click the tab of the worksheet *after* which the new sheet is to be added.
- Click the New Sheet button.

First, let's create the second worksheet for the packaging machine loan.

To create the second worksheet in the same worksheet file:
❶ Verify that S5WCP7.WK4 with the loan analysis for the finishing machine is your current worksheet.
❷ Click the **New Sheet button** to create the new worksheet identified as sheet B. See Figure 5-38 on the following page.

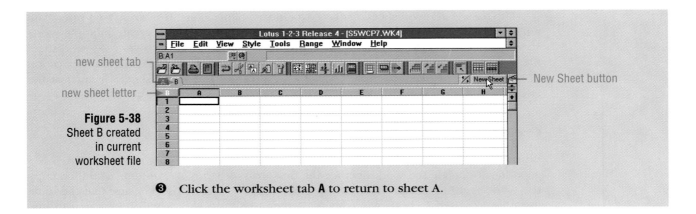

new sheet tab

new sheet letter

Figure 5-38
Sheet B created
in current
worksheet file

New Sheet button

❸ Click the worksheet tab **A** to return to sheet A.

Now that you have a new sheet (B), you can duplicate sheet A by copying the contents of sheet A to sheet B. After you duplicate the sheet, you will delete the existing data, then enter the data values for the new loan.

To duplicate sheet A:

❶ Select the range A:A1..A:B7 on sheet A. Notice that the worksheet letter appears with the cell address in the selection indicator because there is now more than one sheet in the file.

❷ Click the **Copy to Clipboard SmartIcon** 🔲 to copy the cell contents of this sheet.

❸ Click worksheet tab **B** or the **Next Worksheet SmartIcon** 🔲 to go to sheet B.

❹ Click **A1** to match the upper-left corner of the range that you copied from sheet A. This positions the contents of sheet B so it is an *exact image* of sheet A.

❺ Click the **Paste from Clipboard SmartIcon** 🔲 to copy the cell contents to sheet B. See Figure 5-39. What's wrong with this copy?

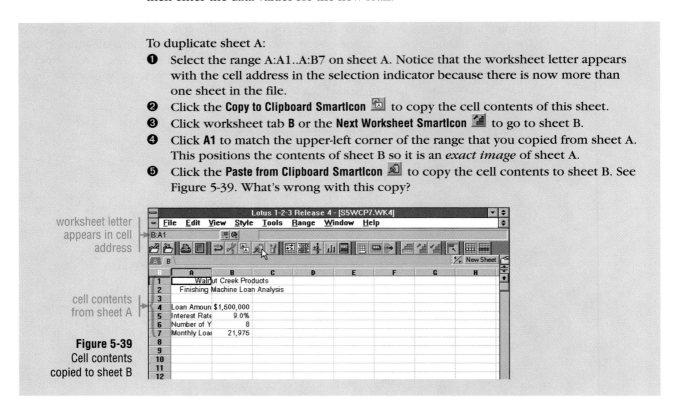

worksheet letter
appears in cell
address

cell contents
from sheet A

Figure 5-39
Cell contents
copied to sheet B

Formatting with Group Mode

Although copying places the correct cell contents from sheet A in the cells of sheet B, the default column widths and formats were *not* copied and need to be set. Let's make these changes to sheet B by using the Group mode option in the Worksheet Defaults dialog box. The Group mode applies the default formats and column widths from the *current* worksheet to *all* other sheets in a multiple-worksheet file. Therefore the formats you apply to sheet B will also be applied to sheet A.

To format the new sheet with the column widths and formats of the current worksheet using Group mode:

❶ Click worksheet tab **A** to make this the current worksheet. You want to apply the defaults from this worksheet to sheet B.

❷ Click **Style** then click **Worksheet Defaults...** to display this dialog box. See Figure 5-40. Note the other default settings you can specify using this dialog box.

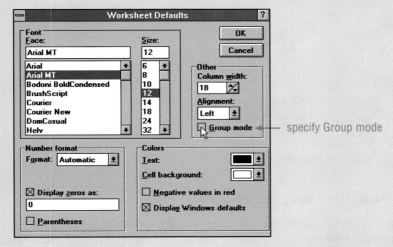

Figure 5-40
Worksheet Defaults
dialog box for
selecting Group
mode

❸ Click the **Group mode check box** to select this option, then click the **OK button** to complete this specification causing the current worksheet's defaults to be used with *all* the other worksheets in the file.

   TROUBLE? If you click the Group mode check box when sheet B is displayed, you will change the column widths and formats of sheet A to those of sheet B, which you don't want. *Immediately* click the Undo SmartIcon ⏎ then repeat Steps 1 through 3.

❹ Click worksheet tab **B** to display sheet B and observe that this sheet now uses the same column widths and formats as sheet **A**.

You have completed duplicating sheet A. Next, let's make changes to sheet B for the packaging machine loan.

To make the data changes to sheet B for the packaging machine loan:

❶ Verify that you are on sheet B (if necessary click worksheet tab **B**).

❷ Edit cell B2 to change the label to "Packaging Machine Loan Analysis."

❸ Enter the following data values for the packaging machine loan:

Loan Amount	2300000
Interest Rate	.078
Number of Years	10

Also notice that "Group" appears in the status bar, indicating that Group mode is in effect. See Figure 5-41 on the following page.

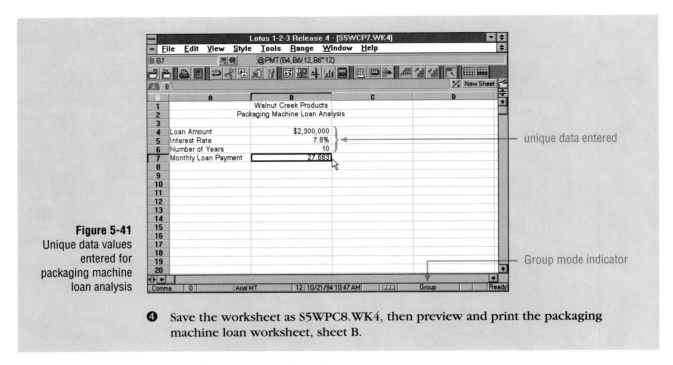

Figure 5-41
Unique data values
entered for
packaging machine
loan analysis

❹ Save the worksheet as S5WPC8.WK4, then preview and print the packaging machine loan worksheet, sheet B.

Using the Perspective View

Worksheet tabs allow you to view one worksheet at a time. Lotus 1-2-3 includes a **Perspective view** that allows you to display up to three adjacent sheets at one time in your worksheet window. Let's look at the two sheets (A and B) in the Perspective view.

To display multiple sheets in one worksheet window using the Perspective view:

❶ Click the **Display Contiguous SmartIcon** ▦ to display the two sheets (A and B) in the Perspective view. See Figure 5-42.

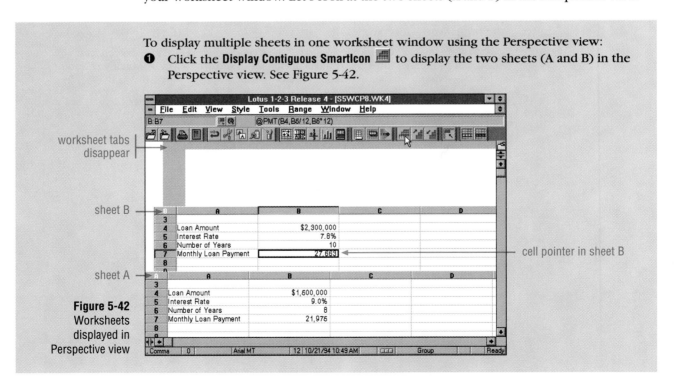

Figure 5-42
Worksheets
displayed in
Perspective view

❷ Scroll sheet B so that rows 4 through 7, which contain the loan analysis data, are displayed. Watch how sheet A scrolls at the same time. This occurs because scrolling is synchronized. However, you can change this option in the Split dialog box by selecting Split... from the View menu, then selecting the Perspective option.

❸ Click any cell in sheet B to select this worksheet and display the cell pointer if the cell pointer no longer appears on your screen because of scrolling.

❹ Click ▦ to return to the single worksheet view. This SmartIcon acts as a toggle between the two views.

❺ Click the **Previous worksheet SmartIcon** ▦ to display sheet A for the finishing machine loan, then save the worksheet as S5WCP8.WK4.

Shannon has the results she wants for both loans in the same worksheet file. She can easily toggle between these two sheets as she reviews the results and prepares printed reports for these loans to help John with his analysis.

Creating the Summary Sheet

Shannon's third sheet for the loan analysis contains formulas that do the summary calculations using the @SUM function. The summary is developed by (1) creating the third sheet, (2) duplicating the labels from either sheet A or B, (3) entering formulas with the @SUM function to calculate the summary results, and (4) entering labels for those planning items that don't make sense when they are added together, such as the interest rate.

Let's add sheet C for the summary, duplicate the worksheet contents from sheet A, and remove the unwanted formulas in preparation for the summary.

To set up the summary sheet:

❶ Click worksheet tab **B** to select sheet B because the new sheet is to be inserted as sheet C *after* sheet B.

❷ Click the **New Sheet button** to cause sheet C to be inserted.

❸ Click worksheet tab **A** to access this sheet as the source for duplicating the cell contents to sheet C.

❹ Select the range A:A1..A:B7, then click the **Copy to Clipboard SmartIcon** ▦ to copy the cell contents of this range to the clipboard.

❺ Click worksheet tab **C** to go to that sheet, click **A1**, then click the **Paste from Clipboard SmartIcon** ▦ .

Now turn Group mode off to revise sheet C. This will prevent you from removing the formatting from all of the sheets.

❻ Click **Style**, click **Worksheet Defaults...**, then click the **Group mode check box** to turn off Group mode.

❼ Click the **OK button**.

❽ Revise sheet C by changing the report title and deleting the cell contents, as shown in Figure 5-43.

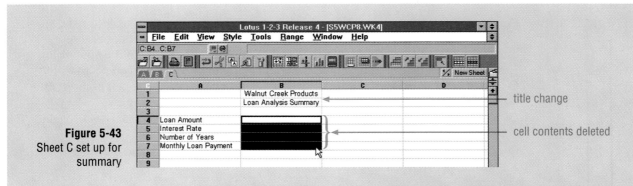

Figure 5-43
Sheet C set up for
summary

Now you can turn Group mode back on to apply the formats in sheet A to the other sheets.

❾ Click worksheet tab **A**, click **Style**, then click **Worksheet Defaults....**

❿ Click the **Group mode check box**, then click the **OK button**.

Using Three-Dimensional Ranges

Now Shannon can add the formulas for the summary to sheet C. The formulas can sum across sheets using a three-dimensional range. A **three-dimensional range** spans two or more consecutive sheets in the same worksheet file.

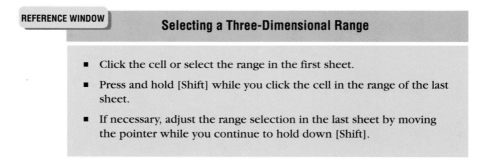

REFERENCE WINDOW

Selecting a Three-Dimensional Range

- Click the cell or select the range in the first sheet.
- Press and hold [Shift] while you click the cell in the range of the last sheet.
- If necessary, adjust the range selection in the last sheet by moving the pointer while you continue to hold down [Shift].

First, let's add the formula that sums the loan amount to sheet C.

To enter a formula with a three-dimensional range that sums across the sheets:

❶ Click the **Display Contiguous SmartIcon** 🔲 for the Perspective view, then scroll the worksheet to display the loan data in each sheet. This allows you to view all three sheets at the same time.

❷ Click **C:B4** to position the cell pointer at this location for the first summary formula.

❸ Type **@SUM(** to begin this formula.

❹ Click **A:B4** to specify a beginning cell for the three-dimensional range.

❺ Press and hold **[Shift]** while you click **B:B4** to specify the ending cell of the three-dimensional range. You could also type the three-dimensional range in your cell formula rather than use pointing.

TROUBLE? If you specify the wrong three-dimensional range for the @SUM formula, repeat Steps 4 and 5.

⑥ Click the **Confirm button** or press **[Enter]** to complete the @SUM formula and display the result of the three-dimensional range summation. See Figure 5-44.

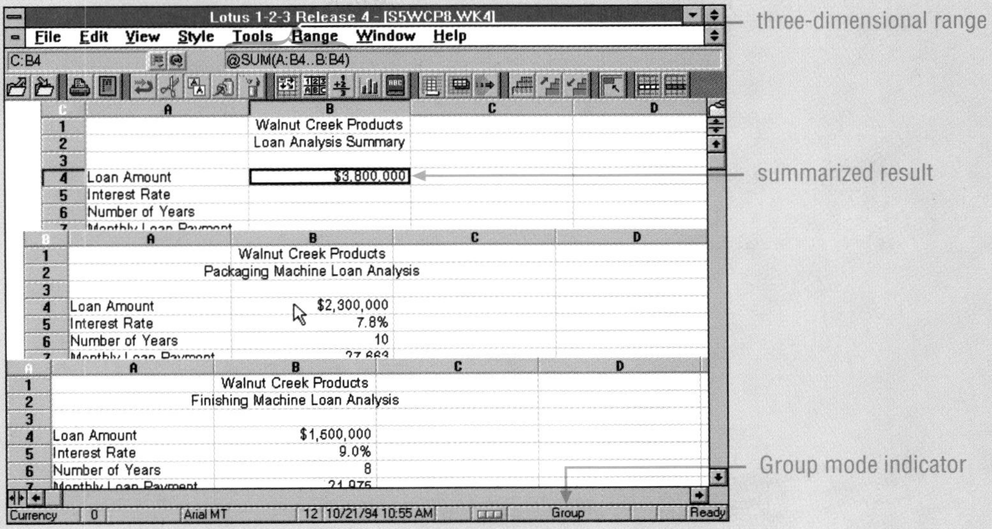

three-dimensional range

summarized result

Group mode indicator

Figure 5-44
Result of
three-dimensional
range summation

Now let's complete Shannon's loan analysis summary sheet by entering the formula to sum the monthly loan payments and by including comments for the interest rate and number of years, which don't make any business sense when they are added together.

To complete the summary sheet:

❶ Enter the formula in cell C:B7 that sums the Monthly Loan Payment for both loans using the same procedure you used for the Loan Amount.

❷ Enter the right-aligned label "See individual loan" by typing it in both cells C:B5 and C:B6. *Do not copy* the label you enter in C:B5 to C:B6, or you will change the cell format of B6 in sheets A and B because Group mode is still in effect.

TROUBLE? If you copied the label from C:B5 to C:B6, then click the Undo SmartIcon 🔄 and repeat Step 2.

❸ Save the worksheet as S5WCP8.WK4, then preview and print the sheet containing the Loan Analysis Summary.

The summary is complete. Shannon has created the analysis for both loans with the summary that John wants.

Naming Multiple Sheets

The worksheet tabs A, B, and C do not give Shannon and John a very good description of the contents of each of these sheets. You can change a sheet name by double-clicking the worksheet tab and typing a new name. A sheet name can contain up to 15 characters.

Let's change the worksheet tabs to display more descriptive names, which will make this multiple worksheet file easier for Shannon and John to use.

To change the worksheet tabs to more descriptive names:

❶ If the worksheet is displayed in the Perspective view, click the **Display Contiguous SmartIcon** 🏢 to return to the single sheet view and display the worksheet tabs.

❷ Double-click worksheet tab **A** to select this tab, type **Finishing**, then press **[Enter]** to change the name.

❸ Double-click worksheet tab **B**, type **Packaging** to change the sheet name, then press **[Enter]**.

❹ Double-click worksheet tab **C**, type **Summary** for the sheet name, then press **[Enter]**. The names that you enter also replace the sheet names in the formulas. See Figure 5-45.

TROUBLE? If you entered the wrong name for a worksheet tab, double-click the tab, then edit the name to correct it.

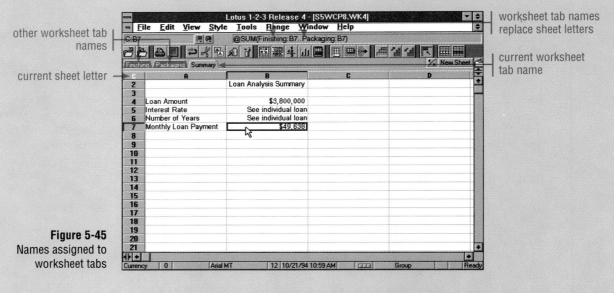

Figure 5-45
Names assigned to worksheet tabs

Now let's save this revised worksheet with the named tabs.

❺ Save the revised worksheet as S5WCP9.WK4.

Doing a What-If Analysis with Multiple Sheets

John wants Shannon to prepare a what-if alternative by revising the number of years for the packaging machine loan to 15 years to see what happens to the total monthly loan payment. Let's make this change and observe the results.

To perform a what-if analysis with multiple worksheets:

❶ Click the **Display Contiguous SmartIcon** 🏢, if necessary, to display the sheets in the Perspective view.

❷ Click **B:B6** to enter the new what-if data value in this cell.

❸ Enter **15** and observe the results. Is the summary automatically updated for this what-if analysis?

❹ Preview and print this alternative. Now what is the total monthly loan payment?

▪   ▪   ▪

Shannon has completed preparing her loan analysis for the proposed new equipment. She reviews her reports and decides that they provide the information John requested to support their decision making. John thinks the total monthly loan payment is acceptable and plans to go ahead with the new equipment purchase.

Questions

1. Suppose cell B8 is assigned the range name SALES and cell B10 the range name COSTS. Cell B12 contains the formula for profit, which is the difference between sales and costs. When you enter this formula, what is displayed as the cell contents for B12?
   a. +B8-B10
   b. @SUM(B8..B10)
   c. +SALES-COSTS
   d. @AVG(SALES..COSTS)
2. Which of the following is *not* a reason for using range names?
   a. easier to remember than cell addresses
   b. change the appearance of cell contents
   c. help avoid specifying incorrect cell ranges
   d. quicker means of printing specific worksheet areas
3. Which of the following allows you to create multiple sets of data values that can be stored and selected individually for use with the same named range in a single worksheet?
   a. what-if
   b. multiple ranges
   c. versions
   d. alternatives
4. A 1-2-3 scenario is a:
   a. named group of versions
   b. multiple range definition
   c. collection of alternative sheets
   d. combined chart and worksheet
5. The @COUNT function is used to find the:
   a. absolute value of a formula
   b. natural logarithm of a formula
   c. number of nonblank cells in a range
   d. square root of a formula
6. When you use the @PMT function to calculate a monthly loan payment, which pair of arguments must have a match between their time periods?
   a. principal amount and interest rate
   b. principal amount and term
   c. interest rate and term
   d. none; only the interest rate needs to be specified as monthly

7. When you use a multiple worksheet file, this feature allows you to apply the worksheet defaults from one sheet to all other sheets in the file:
   a. Group mode
   b. View preferences
   c. Number format
   d. Range version

E
8. Using the Task Reference, write down at least one other method of performing the tasks specified by the following SmartIcons:

   a.

   b.

   c.

   d.

Tutorial Assignments

Launch 1-2-3 and open the T5AFC1.WK4 worksheet file for Altman Fabricating Company (AFC). AFC is entering labor negotiations with its local labor union. To prepare for the negotiations, Mary Stone, manager of Human Resources, uses a 1-2-3 worksheet. Mary created the worksheet but does not have time to complete all of the alternatives. She wants you to finish the worksheet for her upcoming negotiations meeting by performing the following:

1. Review Mary's worksheet. What is the total contract cost in cell B69? Review the range names that Mary already created. What is the range name for cells B34..C34? Notice how Mary has used the label in one cell in the range to identify the contract option while the other cell contains the data value for that option.

2. Mary started to create her versions and scenarios. She created the Basic Contract scenario with the Low Cost versions for medical insurance and dental insurance combined with the High Cost version for the wage increase. You will create the High Cost versions for medical insurance, which equals $2,600 (cell C34), and dental insurance, which equals $440 (cell C37), and the Low Cost version for wage increase, which equals 4% (cell C12). Identify these versions on your worksheet by placing the label "High" in cells B34 and B37, and the label "Low" in cell B12 as the options that are included in the named ranges for each of the three versions.

3. Create a Prime Contract scenario that consists of the High Cost versions for the medical insurance and dental insurance and the Low Cost version for the wage increase. (*Hint*: Total Contract Cost = $1,155,270.)

4. Save the worksheet as S5AFC2.WK4. Preview and print both scenarios (Basic Contract and Prime Contract).

5. What if the labor union will only accept a 5% wage increase with the High Cost versions of medical and dental insurance? Use 1-2-3's Version Manager to perform this what-if analysis by first showing the Prime Contract scenario and then using the Version Manager to select the High Cost version for wage increase. (*Hint*: Total Contract Cost = $1,312,317.)

6. Save the worksheet as S5AFC3.WK4. Preview and print the results.

Launch 1-2-3 and open the T5TCL1.WK4 worksheet file for Traverse City Leasing (TCL). TCL is buying three new automobiles for its leasing fleet. Hiromi Surdu, TCL's purchasing manager, would like you to calculate the monthly payment for each automobile along with a total monthly payment for all three vehicles, the least expensive payment, the most expensive payment, and an average payment. Complete the following:

E
7. Using the @PMT function, calculate the payment of each auto using the information supplied by Hiromi. (*Hint*: Payment for Audi = $820.11.)

8. Create the range name of "PAYMENT" for the monthly payment amount of all three automobiles.

9. Save the worksheet as S5TCL2.WK4. Preview and print the worksheet, but do not print the items below row 11.

10. Use the @SUM function and the range name created in Assignment 8 to calculate the total payments. Then use the appropriate function to calculate the lowest payment, highest payment, and average payment. Place these formulas in the cells immediately to the right of their respective labels. What formula is displayed as the contents of cell B12? (*Hint*: Total Payments = $2,643.20.)

11. Save the worksheet as S5TCL3.WK4. Preview and print the entire worksheet.

Launch 1-2-3 and open the S5WCP9.WK4 worksheet file, which is the loan analysis for WCP created in this tutorial. Immediately save this file as S5WCP10.WK4. If you did not create this worksheet, then do so before you continue. John wants Shannon to revise WCP's loan analysis to include the purchase of one more piece of equipment. John is considering buying a woodworking machine for $920,000, which he would finance with a seven-year loan at an interest rate of 6.9%. John wants to know the monthly payment for this additional loan together with the total monthly payment for all three loans. Revise Shannon's loan analysis worksheet by doing the following:

E 12. Insert a new sheet *after* the Finishing sheet (sheet A). Duplicate the formulas for this new sheet from sheet A. Enter the data unique to the woodworking machine loan. Revise the report title so the second line is "Woodworking Machine Loan Analysis." Change the worksheet tab name to "woodworking." Save the worksheet as S5WCP10.WK4. Then preview and print the report for the woodworking machine.

E 13. Display the sheets in the Perspective view and use the Previous Worksheet and Next Worksheet SmartIcons to navigate through the four sheets.

E 14. Review the Summary sheet (now sheet D). What changes need to be made to this sheet so the new equipment loan is included in the summary? Make those changes. Then preview and print the Summary report with the results for all three loans. What features of 1-2-3 made it easy to add this third loan? If you had added the sheet for the woodworking machine *after* that for the packaging machine, what changes would you need to make in the Summary sheet?

Launch 1-2-3 and open the T5CCS1.WK4 worksheet file for Cellular Communication Specialists (CCS), which markets cellular telephones for both businesses and individuals in the Seattle and Portland metropolitan areas. The cellular industry is very competitive, thus, CCS likes to keep close track of weekly operations. Prepare a summary of CCS's weekly operations by doing the following:

15. Review the worksheet and its formulas. How are weekly total sales calculated?

E 16. Create range names for the following ranges:

Planning item name	Range name for data value	Cell range
Administrative Salaries	ADMIN	A:B16..B:B16
Units Sold	UNITS	A:B6..B:B6
Total Labor Cost	LABOR COST	A:B14..B:B14
Total Sales	SALES	A:B8..B:B8

E 17. Display the worksheet in the Perspective view, then add formulas to sheet C that summarize the Seattle and Portland operations. Use the @SUM function to calculate the totals for the planning items in Assignment 16. Use the formula for Total Sales divided by the Units Sold to calculate an average for all the sales, because it doesn't make business sense to add the average sales for the Seattle and Portland operations. Use the @AVG function to calculate the average of the billing rate for the three labor cost items. Copy the formula for Operating Income from either worksheet A or B for this calculation in worksheet C. (*Hint*: Operating Income = $9,870.)

18. Save the worksheet as S5CCS2.WK4. Preview and print the three worksheets.

19. Perform the following what-if analyses, then print the three worksheets after each analysis:
    a. What happens to CCS's total operating income if the base hourly rate for both Seattle and Portland is $5.25? (*Hint:* Operating Income = $9,798.)
    b. Using the new base hourly rate from Assignment 19-a, what if the phone installation rate increases to $35 at both locations? (*Hint:* Operating Income = $8,959.)
    c. What happens to CCS's total operating income if time per unit is increased to 2.75 hours at both locations? (*Hint:* Operating Income = $7,990.)
20. Save the worksheet as S5CCS3.WK4.

E

21. Using the already defined three-dimensional ranges for base hourly rate (HOURLY RATE), phone installation rate (INSTALL RATE), and time per unit (TIME PER UNIT), create the following Low and High versions:

		Low	High
Base Hourly Rate	Seattle =	4.25	5.25
	Portland =	4.25	4.75
Phone Installation Rate	Seattle =	30	40
	Portland =	28	35
Time per Unit	Seattle =	1.75	2.75
	Portland =	2.25	3.25

22. Create the High scenario that consists of each of the High versions. (*Hint:* Operating Income = $7,221.)
23. Save the worksheet as S5CCS4.WK4. Preview and print the worksheet file.

Case Problems

1. Financial Performance Reporting for Hot Wheels Manufacturing

Hot Wheels Manufacturing (HWM) supplies steel and aluminum wheels to world-wide auto makers such as Alfa Romeo, BMW, Ferrari, Honda, Chrysler, and Ford. HWM owns manufacturing plants worldwide, and is regarded as an industry leader in both quality and styling. HWM has experienced explosive growth resulting in a stock price that more than tripled in the last three years. However, a weakened global economy caused this year's sales to be sluggish, and HWM management is concerned about stock-holder's reactions.

Dan Sanchez is a financial analyst for HWM. His boss, Michelle Bierer, asked him to take last year's financial performance report worksheet and add a contract that has just been signed to make sales appear higher to the shareholders, so HWM's stock price does not decrease. The stockholders like to see at least a 10% increase in the return on sales amount each year. While earning his undergraduate degree from UCLA, Dan took several classes on business ethics, and he is considering whether what he has been asked to do is ethical. Ethics involves the use of good moral conduct in business operations.

HWM's customary policy for recording sales is that the sale is recorded when delivery is made. This policy is in accordance with generally accepted accounting prin-ciples (GAAP), the guidelines that accountants follow in stating a company's financial position. HWM's books closed on December 31, and the delivery date of the new con-tract is not until January 27.

Dan doesn't know what to do. He is anxious to prove himself in this new job, but doesn't want to do anything unethical. He decides to edit Michelle's worksheet to include the revised numbers since 1-2-3 makes such revisions very easy. But, he plans to prepare two reports. One with the actual performance numbers *and* one with the revised numbers. He'll create two scenarios in order to *document both sets of numbers* in his worksheet. That way, it will be clear that the revised numbers don't merely replace the actual numbers. Dan also plans to talk to Michelle, but he's not sure of what to say yet. Dan's first step is to develop a planning analysis sheet (Figure 5-46).

Planning Analysis Sheet

My goal:
Develop alternatives to improve the stock price based on this year's financial performance.

What results do I want to see?
Return On Sales should meet the shareholders' expectation for last year, which is 10%.

What information do I need?
Last year's worksheet file. This file needs to have range names, versions, scenarios, and @ROUND functions.

How will the new contract affect key financial numbers?
- The wheel prices would increase from 65 Steel and 95 Aluminum, to 70 Steel and 105 Aluminum as a result of the substantially higher prices of the new contract.
- The new contract would cause Total Wheels Sold to increase from a minimum of 680,000 units to a maximum of 725,000 units.

Figure 5-46

Make the necessary adjustments to Dan's worksheet to reflect the new contract with the automaker to determine if it meets the shareholder's objective of a 10% return on sales for Michelle.

1. Launch 1-2-3 and open the worksheet P5HWM1.WK4, which contains last year's financial performance *without* the new contract. Save the worksheet as S5HWM1.WK4.
2. Review the worksheet. Notice the worksheet has a key assumptions area, and all dollar amounts are stated in thousands, except the prices per unit.
3. Create the named range PRINT REPORT for the range A1..C44, which is the report of the financial results. Then create these named ranges for the planning item names:

Planning item name	Range name for data value	Cells
Return On Sales	RETURN ON SALES	B43
Total Wheels Sold	WHEELS SOLD	B15
Steel and Aluminum Wheel Prices	WHEEL PRICES	B8..B9

4. Use the @ROUND function, which you learned in Tutorial 2, to eliminate any potential rounding errors that might exist in the worksheet. (*Hint*: Total Expenses = 43,559.)
5. Save the worksheet as S5HWM2.WK4. Preview and print your worksheet using the named range for the financial results.
6. Perform the following what-if alternatives. Preview and print the worksheet after each alternative.
   a. What would the return on sales be if the total wheels sold is 680, which reflects the new contract Michelle informed Dan about? (*Hint:* Return On Sales = 9.5%.)

   b. What if the total wheels sold was 725? (*Hint*: Net Income = 5,960 using rounding.)

   c. Save the worksheet as S5HWM3.WK4.

7. Create the following versions:

   a. Versions for the range WHEELS SOLD with version names of "Actual" (Total Wheels Sold = 632) and "Revised" (Total Wheels Sold = 725)

   b. Versions for the range WHEEL PRICES with version names of "Actual" (Steel = 65, Aluminum = 95) and "Revised" (Steel = 70, Aluminum = 105)

8. Now create the scenarios for Actual, using the data prior to the new contract, and for Revised, using the data introduced by the new contract. (*Hint*: Return On Sales = 8.4% for the Actual scenario and 11.5% for the Revised scenario.)

9. Save the worksheet as S5HWM4.WK4. Preview and print each scenario.

E 10. Add one more named range to the worksheet with the name of TITLE for cell A2. Create an Actual version with the title "Income Statement—Actual" and a Revised version with the title "Income Statement—Revised." Include these versions in their respective scenarios. Save the worksheet as S5HWM5.WK4. Preview and print each scenario. If these are the reports that Dan gives to Michelle, will they help with his dilemma? Are these reports better than just having the scenarios in the worksheet file? Why?

E 11. Numbers are easily changed in a 1-2-3 worksheet. Versions and scenarios allow both an original and revised set of numbers to be saved in the same worksheet. But, is ease of change sufficient reason to make the change? Is the addition of the new contract to the income statement ethical? Should Dan say something to Michelle or just make the changes she requested? Why? What would you do if you were in Dan's position? Other than restating financial results, what could Michelle do in her report to the shareholders?

2. Equipment Leasing for Rainier Metals Company

Rainier Metals Company (RMC) is a world-wide manufacturer of aluminum and aluminum products. The aluminum industry has become overloaded with competitors. Rainier has been able to maintain their sales level, but the increased competition has caused prices to drop the last several years, reducing net income. The Board of Directors of RMC concluded that an investment in more efficient machinery would help increase net income.

Ray Jones is a purchasing assistant in the Production Engineering Department for RMC. His boss, William Burke, purchasing manager, asks him to research the available production equipment to find a casting machine that best meets the needs of RMC. He tells Ray that RMC plans to lease this equipment so they won't have to pay the full purchase price. They will pay a monthly fee for use of the equipment, which is similar to making a loan payment, and at the end of the term of the lease, give the machine back. Therefore, Ray needs to evaluate the lease payment, lease length or life, and the savings from reduced production costs. From his research Ray narrows the search down to two machines that are fairly equal in overall value and would reduce raw material costs through more efficient production methods. Ray presents his preliminary results to William, who is pleased with the research but wants a more detailed explanation of how each machine could potentially increase net income over the next five years.

Ray decides to create a 1-2-3 worksheet to show the effects of leasing either of the two machines. He will need a copy of the next five-year projected income statement to analyze the effect of leasing the machine on net income. First, he develops a planning analysis sheet (Figure 5-47) and then he is ready to build the worksheet.

Planning Analysis Sheet

My goal:
Develop a worksheet to show the effects of purchasing either machine.

What results do I want to see?
The effect of the machine purchase on net income.

What information do I need?
The projected income statement, purchase price of each machine, interest rate, period of loan repayment, and the change in cost of product sold percent.

What are the leasing factors for each machine?

	Machine 1	Machine 2
Lease Amount (in millions)	$120.1	147.5
Interest Rate	8.4%	8.9%
Number of Years	10	8
Raw Material Percent	39%	37%
Purchase Price	$160.1	$196.6

Note: The Lease Amount is determined by taking 75% of the Purchase Price to account for the value of the machine at the end of the lease period. This factor is similar to that used with other equipment that RMC has leased.

Figure 5-47

Revise the worksheet for Ray to present to William by performing the following:

1. Launch 1-2-3 and open the worksheet P5RMC1.WK4, which contains RMC's five-year projected income statement. Immediately save the worksheet as S5RMC1.WK4.
2. Review the worksheet. Notice that the worksheet contains a key assumption area used in calculating two accounts: raw materials cost and equipment cost. How are the values used in the formulas in the worksheet?
3. In the Machine Lease table Ray already included in the worksheet, enter the appropriate data and formulas to calculate the annual lease payment for Machine 1. Enter the data in column B immediately to the right of the labels.
4. Modify the formula for the equipment cost in each of the five years to add the annual lease payment to the current cost. Change the raw material percentage to the value that represents the production gains by installing Machine 1. (*Hint*: Net Income [1999] = $115.6 million.)
5. Save the worksheet as S5RMC1.WK4. Preview and print the worksheet.
6. Create the following named ranges:

Planning item name	Range name for data value	Cells
Raw Material Percent	RAW MATERIAL	B27
Machine Lease Lease Amount Interest Rate Number of Years	LEASE	B30..B33

E

7. Ray wants to be able to present each alternative clearly and easily to William, so you need to create the following versions:

   a. Versions for the range RAW MATERIAL with the version names of "Original," "Machine 1," and "Machine 2." These versions should contain the appropriate data values for each alternative. The initial raw material percentage is 43%.

   b. Versions for the range LEASE with the version names "Original," "Machine 1," and "Machine 2." Place the name of the version in cell B30 as a means of identifying the data used when a report is printed. For the Original version, use a lease amount of zero rather than modifying other formulas in the worksheet.

8. Create a scenario of Original, Machine 1, and Machine 2. Each scenario combines the versions with the same name. (*Hint*: Net Income [1999] : Original = $68.3, Machine 1 = $115.6, and Machine 2 = $139.7.)

9. Save the worksheet as S5RMC2.WK4. Preview and print each of the three scenarios.

E

10. Using your printouts, compare the three scenarios. Which scenario is the best alternative for Ray to recommend to William? Why? Explain your answer.

3. Summarizing Operations for Environmental Biotech

(Adapted from: Garbage, *March 1993, pages 16-19.)*

In 1986 an entrepreneur acquired the technology to use bacteria to dissolve grease, known as bioremediation. **Bioremediation** is a system that uses 13 species of vegetative bacteria to dissolve the grease left over from deep-fried foods, such as french fries. The bacteria actually consume the grease and convert it into the more environmentally friendly components of carbon dioxide gas and water. Prior to bioremediation, restaurants stored the grease in either 55 gallon drums or underground pits. The grease was then hauled away by contractors. Bill Hadley is an entrepreneur who helped develop the bacteria technology. After acquiring this new technology, Bill created Environmental Biotech Company (EBC), a company that contracts with restaurants to use the bacteria to solve the grease problem rather than storing it and later hauling it away.

EBC has grown quickly and has just added another division. Bill asked Deb Fitzgerald, EBC's accounting assistant, to create a 1-2-3 worksheet that summarizes the individual results for the two divisions into an overall company report. Deb decided the best way to develop a solution was to use the multiple worksheet feature of 1-2-3, so that the results for the individual division and the company summary would be available in one worksheet. She began by developing her planning analysis sheet (Figure 5-48).

Planning Analysis Sheet

My goal:
Develop a multiple sheet file that summarizes the results for Environmental Biotech's two divisions

What results do I want to see?
A summary income statement for Environmental Biotech

What information do I need?
Income statement numbers for each division

Figure 5-48

Your task is to create the multiple worksheet for EBC. To build this worksheet, perform the following:

1. Launch 1-2-3 and open the worksheet P5EBC1.WK4, containing the income statements for both divisions. Immediately save the worksheet as S5EBC1.WK4.

2. Review this worksheet. Notice that the two divisions are on worksheets A and B respectively.

E 3. Create the following range names to be used for the consolidated worksheet:

Planning item name	Range name for data value
Number of accounts	ACCOUNTS
Bacteria	BACTERIA
Delivery	DELIVERY
General and Admin	GENERAL
Sales	SALES

These range names should be three-dimensional across the sheets. In other words, the range name ACCOUNTS should include the planning items for both worksheet A and B.

4. Save the worksheet as S5EBC2.WK4.

5. Add a new worksheet (C) to the worksheet file. This worksheet is used to summarize the information from worksheets A and B.

6. Add formulas for the summary to sheet C. Use the @SUM function for all line items except Fee per Account and Net Income. Calculate the fee per account from the summarized results. Use the formula: sales divided by the number of accounts. Copy the formula for net income from sheet A. Include "Summary" in the report heading in place of the division name. (*Hint*: Net income = $169,158.)

E 7. Review the @SUM formulas for sales and each of the expense items in the summary worksheet (sheet C). What is the effect of using the three-dimensional range names?

8. Save the worksheet as S5EBC3.WK4. Preview and print all three worksheets.

E 9. Does this worksheet provide the information Deb can present to Bill? Why? Would it be easy to add other divisions to this worksheet file that are included in the summary? Why? How could this be done?

OBJECTIVES

In this tutorial you will:

- Plan a print macro and a what-if data entry macro
- Record a macro in the Transcript window
- Play back a recorded macro
- Place a macro in the worksheet
- Name a macro
- Document a macro
- Run a macro from a list
- Create a macro button and run a macro using a button
- Edit a recorded macro
- Debug a macro

Creating and Using Macros

Preparing a Staffing Plan

CASE

Godfather's Pizza* Linda Walden is the owner of a chain of Godfather's Pizza Restaurants. She operates a dozen restaurants in the suburban Omaha area. Recently, she promoted Charles "Chuck" Surdu to manager of the restaurant located in the Old Market Mall. Chuck developed a staffing plan worksheet in 1-2-3 that he uses to explore what-if alternatives to establish a target staffing level that assists him in hiring. He developed this plan because at certain times of the year sales are high and he needs more staff, and at other times of the year, sales are low and he doesn't need as many employees. With proper planning, he can avoid laying off good employees during those times of the year when sales are low.

Linda thinks that Chuck's worksheet for the Old Market Mall restaurant can be set up so the managers of the other eleven restaurants can use it. That is, Linda would like Chuck to provide the other managers with a 1-2-3 worksheet template for evaluating staffing plan alternatives. A **template** is a worksheet that already contains the labels and formulas needed for analysis and can be readily used with other sets of data. Because the other managers are not as experienced with 1-2-3 as Chuck, he needs to make this template easy for them to use.

*Adapted from: *Personal Computing*, "Financial Modeling," pp 69-77, April, 1987.

Chuck decides to create two macros that will convert his worksheet into a template the managers can use for their staff planning. Remember from the Guided Tour that a macro is a recorded set of 1-2-3 commands used to automate frequently performed tasks. The first macro Chuck plans to create is a print macro to enable the other managers to print the staffing plan quickly and easily. Then, because the other managers will need to evaluate their own staffing levels with this worksheet, Chuck wants to create a what-if data entry macro to make entering the staffing data equally efficient.

He prepares his planning analysis sheet and modifies his current worksheet to include his plans for the template (Figures 6-1 and 6-2). Note that the values for Weekly Sales are entered manually for each restaurant in preparation for analyzing alternative plans using Chuck's macro. He placed these values in the template as an example. The Weekly Hours and Number of Associates are calculated using formulas Chuck included in the template. The other restaurant managers will need to experiment with the values for Sales per Employee Hour, Manager Hours per Week, and Associate Hours per Week to determine the best values for their restaurants. Chuck reviews his plans with Linda. She gives her approval and asks Chuck to complete this project for her upcoming meeting with the managers.

Figure 6-1
Chuck's planning
analysis sheet

Planning Analysis Sheet

My goal:
Create a template worksheet that can be easily used by any of the restaurant managers

What results do I want to see?
Staffing plan by quarter for next year

What information do I need?
Staffing plan worksheet for one restaurant
Macros for managers to easily run the template

What macros do I want?
Print completed staffing plan and chart
Guided data entry for key input factors

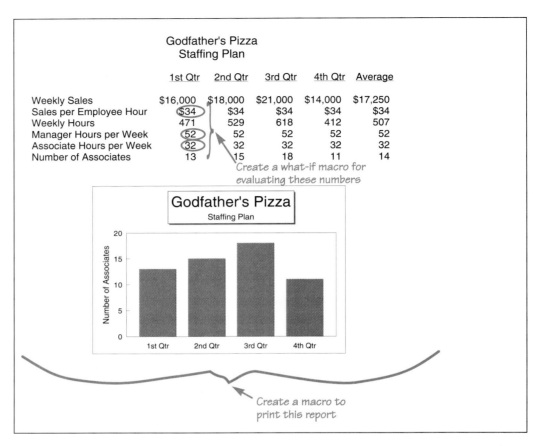

Figure 6-2
Chuck's plan to
convert his
worksheet into
a template

In this tutorial you will modify Chuck's worksheet to include macros that will make it easy for the other restaurant managers to use the template in preparing their own plans. You will learn how to create and run macros to automate repetitive what-if solutions that support making better business decisions.

Introduction to Macros

A **macro** is a series of commands that are stored as cell entries so they can be "played back," or executed, on demand in order to automate a 1-2-3 task. There are a number of situations where macros are useful in automating worksheet activities. If you type the same label, such as a company or report name, in the same worksheet several times, a macro can be used to enter this label. If you repeat a sequence of commands several times when developing a worksheet, macros can simplify entering these commands. If your worksheet contains several reports and each report has a different print specification, macros can store these specifications. Another reason for creating a macro is if someone with little experience with 1-2-3 needs to print or enter data into the worksheet. If so, macros can make working with 1-2-3 easy for a new user. The two macros Chuck plans to develop meet the criteria for creating a macro because the tasks will be performed a number of times by less experienced 1-2-3 users.

With macros, instead of repeating a task, you do it once and record it as a series of macro commands. Then, you store the recorded macro commands in your worksheet. Whenever you want to repeat the series of stored commands, you merely run the macro.

Once you decide a macro would be useful for your worksheet, you should follow these steps in creating the macro:

- plan the macro
- record the macro
- play back and test the macro
- place the macro
- name the macro
- document the macro
- run and test the macro
- debug, or correct, any problems with the macro
- save the worksheet including the macro

Now that you are more familiar with macros, you are ready to create the print macro and the what-if data entry macro. First, you need to open Chuck's staffing plan worksheet and select the SmartIcon palette created for use with this tutorial. Let's do that now.

To open the worksheet and select the Tutorial 6 SmartIcon palette:

❶ Launch 1-2-3.

❷ Select the Tutorial 6 SmartIcon palette by using the SmartIcon palette selector ▦ in the status bar.

❸ Open Chuck's staffing plan worksheet, C6GFP1.WK4, located on your Student Disk, and immediately save it as S6GFP1.WK4. Review the worksheet.

Planning the Macro

To create an effective and easy-to-use macro, you need to plan it. First, decide what you want the macro to do. Once you know the purpose of the macro, walk through the steps needed to complete the task of the macro. Going through each step is known as a **dry run**. This might seem like extra work, but it reduces the number of errors in the macro. Finally, write down the steps the macro will perform—each menu selection, mouse click, and keyboard press—to create your macro planning sheet. In this case, Chuck wants a macro that prints the staffing plan and chart. He has already completed a dry run and his macro planning sheet, as shown in Figure 6-3.

Figure 6-3
Chuck's macro planning sheet for printing the staffing plan

Print Macro Planning Sheet	
Action	Result
Click the Home SmartIcon	Positions the cell pointer at A1
Select the range A1..F30	Selects the range for printing
Click the Print SmartIcon	Displays the Print dialog box
Click the OK button	Prints the selected range
Click the Home SmartIcon	Positions the cell pointer at A1 and unselects the cell range

After you plan the macro, you enter, or record, the macro commands.

Recording the Macro

There are two ways to enter macro commands. You can perform the task and have 1-2-3 record your actions as macro commands, or you can type the macro commands yourself as a series of labels. The preferred method is to have 1-2-3 record your keyboard and mouse actions as macro commands. This method reduces the number of errors in the macro and eliminates the need to memorize which macro command corresponds to which action—1-2-3 does it for you. However, understanding the general syntax of a macro command is helpful because you will be better prepared to find any errors in your macro if something goes wrong. The general syntax of a macro command is shown in Figure 6-4, together with an example of the print macro.

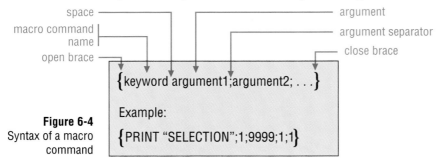

Figure 6-4
Syntax of a macro
command

The entire macro command is enclosed in braces ({ }). Some macro commands require the use of arguments. An **argument** is data such as a number, cell name, cell range, or menu option that you provide for 1-2-3 to use with certain macro commands. You will look more closely at macro commands after you record the print macro and when you edit a macro command later in this tutorial.

When you record a macro, the macro commands are recorded in a special window called the **Transcript window.** You need to open the Transcript window before you can record any commands. Once you open the Transcript window, you can switch back and forth from the Transcript window to the worksheet window as needed. This allows you to click or select the appropriate cells in the worksheet and check what macro commands are recorded in the Transcript window.

Let's open the Transcript window in preparation for recording Chuck's macro that prints the staffing plan and chart.

To open the Transcript window:
❶ Click the **Transcript Window SmartIcon** 🔳 to open the Transcript window. See Figure 6-5. The size of the worksheet window is adjusted automatically by 1-2-3. It is no longer maximized so you can switch between the two windows easily.

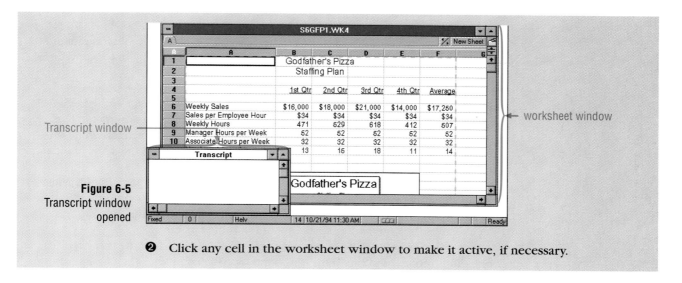

Transcript window ←

worksheet window →

Figure 6-5
Transcript window
opened

❷ Click any cell in the worksheet window to make it active, if necessary.

Once the Transcript window is open, you can then start and stop recording macro commands. When you start a 1-2-3 session, macro recording is turned off by default. So, you need to turn it on before 1-2-3 can record any commands.

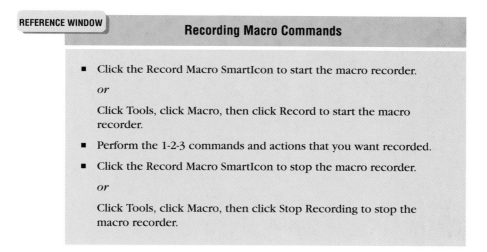

REFERENCE WINDOW

Recording Macro Commands

- Click the Record Macro SmartIcon to start the macro recorder.

  or

  Click Tools, click Macro, then click Record to start the macro recorder.

- Perform the 1-2-3 commands and actions that you want recorded.

- Click the Record Macro SmartIcon to stop the macro recorder.

  or

  Click Tools, click Macro, then click Stop Recording to stop the macro recorder.

Let's record the macro for printing the staffing plan, including its chart. Make sure your printer is on and has paper because 1-2-3 will execute the commands as you record them.

To record the macro for printing Chuck's report with the chart:
❶ Click the **Record Macro SmartIcon** 🔲 to start the macro recorder. Notice that "Rec" appears in the status bar. Lotus 1-2-3 executes the commands as you perform each step and records the commands at the same time. Each command appears on a single line in the Transcript window.

Now perform the actions listed in Chuck's macro planning sheet and, as you do, watch the Transcript window as well.

❷   Click the **Home SmartIcon** 🔲 to position the cell pointer at A1. The first command {HOME} is recorded in the Transcript window. It is surrounded by braces and does not contain any arguments.

❸   Select the range A1..F30, which is the range you want to print. The command {SELECT A1..F30;A1} is recorded in the Transcript window. SELECT is the keyword followed by a space, which separates the keyword from the first argument. The first argument is A1..F30, which identifies the range selected. A semicolon (;) separates the first argument from the second argument, A1, which is the starting location of the cell pointer when the range is selected.

❹   Click the **Print SmartIcon** 🖨 to display the Print dialog box, then click the **OK button** to print the worksheet and the bar chart. The PRINT command is recorded in the Transcript window with its printer specifications as the arguments. Remember, 1-2-3 executes the commands, so a copy of the report prints.

❺   Click 🔲 to position the cell pointer at A1 and unselect the print range. The {HOME} command is recorded in the Transcript window. This completes the commands to be recorded. See Figure 6-6.

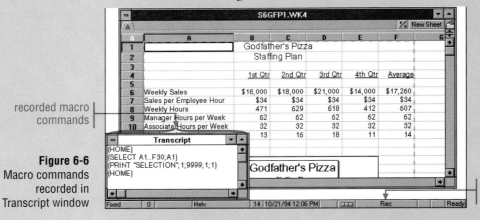

recorded macro commands

Figure 6-6
Macro commands
recorded in
Transcript window

indicates macro
recorder is turned on

❻   Click 🔳 to stop the macro recorder. "Rec" disappears from the status bar. Review the recorded macro commands in the Transcript window.

TROUBLE? If you make a mistake entering any of the commands, click the Transcript window, click Edit, then click Clear All to erase the contents of this window. Then repeat Steps 1 through 6.

Once you record the commands you need for the macro, you must copy the commands from the Transcript window to the worksheet. Then, when you save the worksheet, the macro commands are saved with the worksheet. If you quit 1-2-3 before copying the commands into the worksheet, you will lose the commands because the Transcript window is cleared and the commands are erased. Before you copy the commands, let's check to see if the macro is correct by testing it.

Playing Back a Recorded Macro

Lotus 1-2-3 allows you to "play" a macro after you record it but before you copy it into your worksheet. This gives you an opportunity to test the macro and make sure it runs correctly.

REFERENCE WINDOW

Playing Back a Recorded Macro

- Select the macro commands in the Transcript window.
- Click the Playback Transcript SmartIcon.

  or

  Click Transcript, then click Playback.

Let's play back the print macro to see if it is correct. Once Chuck knows it works, he can place it in his staffing plan worksheet.

To play back the recorded macro commands as a test:

❶ Click the **Transcript window** to make it active.

❷ Select all the commands in the Transcript window. See Figure 6-7. Make sure your selection includes the open brace ({) that starts the first {HOME} command.

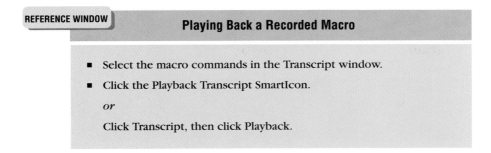

Figure 6-7
Selecting macro commands recorded in Transcript window

❸ Click the **Playback Transcript SmartIcon** to test how the macro executes. Wait for another copy of the report to print.

TROUBLE? If another copy of the report is not printed, the macro did not execute correctly. Click Edit, click Clear All to delete all the macro commands in the Transcript window, record the macro again, then repeat Steps 1,2, and 3.

The print macro works, so Chuck is ready to place the macro in his worksheet.

Placing the Macro

A macro can be placed in any single column range of cells in your worksheet. However, some locations are better than others. You don't want the macro to write over other data in the worksheet and you don't want the macro to be affected when you are inserting or deleting rows and columns or moving data. Therefore, you want to position the macro area away from the data area, and use range names in your macros instead of specific cell references. Figure 6-8 indicates a good arrangement for placing macros below and to the right of the data area. You can name a cell at the beginning of the macro area with a range name, such as MACROS. This makes it easy to move quickly between the macros area and the data area when they are in the same worksheet. If your file contains multiple sheets, it is a good idea to put macros in a separate sheet, and name the worksheet tab MACROS. This makes it easy to access the sheet containing the macros.

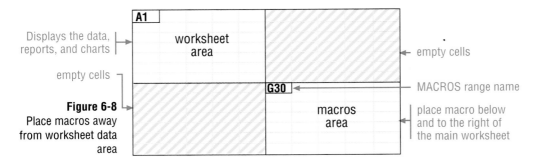

Figure 6-8
Place macros away
from worksheet data
area

Displays the data,
reports, and charts

empty cells

empty cells

MACROS range name

place macro below
and to the right of
the main worksheet

Now that Chuck's macro has been recorded and tested, Chuck is ready to copy and paste it into the worksheet as part of the worksheet file. Chuck has already assigned the range name MACROS to cell G30, the upper-left corner of the area where the macros will be placed. This will allow him to move from the worksheet area to the macro quickly.

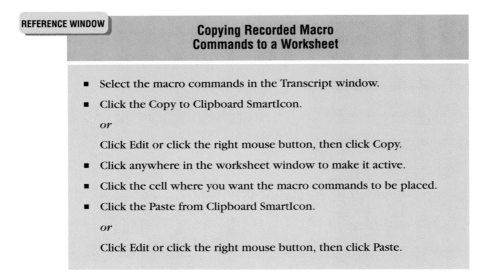

REFERENCE WINDOW

**Copying Recorded Macro
Commands to a Worksheet**

- Select the macro commands in the Transcript window.
- Click the Copy to Clipboard SmartIcon.

or

Click Edit or click the right mouse button, then click Copy.

- Click anywhere in the worksheet window to make it active.
- Click the cell where you want the macro commands to be placed.
- Click the Paste from Clipboard SmartIcon.

or

Click Edit or click the right mouse button, then click Paste.

Let's copy Chuck's recorded macro commands to the worksheet so they are stored with the worksheet for future use.

To copy the macro commands from the Transcript window to the worksheet:

❶ Click the **Transcript window** to make it active.
❷ Select all the commands recorded in the Transcript window.
❸ Click the **Copy to Clipboard SmartIcon** 🖼 to copy the commands to the clipboard.
❹ Click any cell in the worksheet window to make it the active window.
❺ Click the **range name selector** 🔲 to display the list of range names, then click **MACROS** to position the worksheet area at cell G30.
❻ Click **H37,** which is the location for this macro.
❼ Click the **Paste from Clipboard SmartIcon** 🗐 to place the macro commands in this location. See Figure 6-9.

TROUBLE? If you place the macro commands in the wrong cells, select all the cells containing the commands, then move them using 🖐 to the correct location in the worksheet.

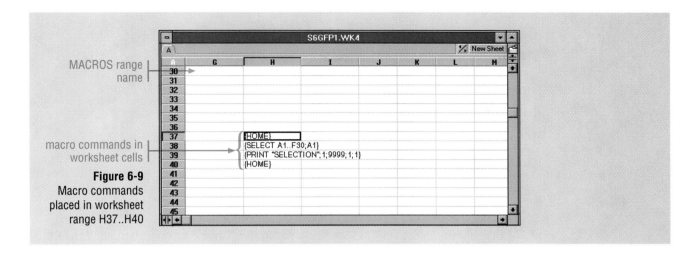

MACROS range name

macro commands in worksheet cells

Figure 6-9
Macro commands placed in worksheet range H37..H40

Naming the Macro

Now that you have copied the macro commands to the worksheet, you need to name the macro. You can't execute a macro located in a worksheet without giving it a name first. Because the commands are located in a range of cells, you assign the macro a range name. The macro range name can consist of up to 15 characters, such as PRINT REPORT, or it can consist of a backslash (\ ) and a single letter, such as \P for a print macro. The use of the backslash with a letter allows you to run the macro by pressing [Ctrl] and the letter. However, giving the macro a descriptive name makes it easier to remember what the macro does. Because the other managers are unfamiliar with the worksheet and with 1-2-3, Chuck prefers to use a descriptive name to make it easier for them to run the macro.

With either naming method, you assign the range name to only the *first cell* of the macro. This is because 1-2-3 reads *down* the column of stored macro commands and executes each command until it reaches an empty cell.

You name a macro range in exactly the same manner as you name any other range in your worksheet. Let's assign the range name PRINT REPORT to Chuck's macro, which prints the staffing plan for an individual restaurant.

To assign a range name to the first cell of the macro:
❶ Click **H37**, the first cell in the macro range.
❷ Click the **Range Name SmartIcon** ▦ to display the Name dialog box.
❸ Type **PRINT REPORT** in the Name text box. Remember, 1-2-3 converts the name to uppercase after you press [Enter] or click the OK button. See Figure 6-10.

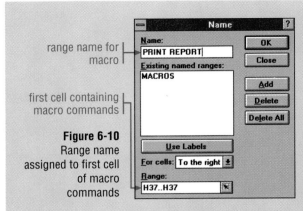

range name for macro

first cell containing macro commands

Figure 6-10
Range name assigned to first cell of macro commands

❹ Verify that the range H37..H37 is displayed in the Range text box, then click the **OK button** to complete naming the range.

Documenting the Macro

The next step in creating a macro is to document the macro. **Documenting** the macro means to place the name of the macro and the action it performs next to the column containing the macro. This allows you and other users to quickly find out the name of the macro and what it does. Chuck used the macro name PRINT REPORT because it describes the action carried out by this macro. He thinks this is enough documentation and plans to place this descriptive macro name immediately to the left of the first cell of his macro commands. Let's add this documentation to the worksheet.

To document the macro:
❶ Click **G37**, the cell immediately to the *left* of the first cell in the series of macro commands.
❷ Enter the label **PRINT REPORT** to document the name and action of this macro. See Figure 6-11.

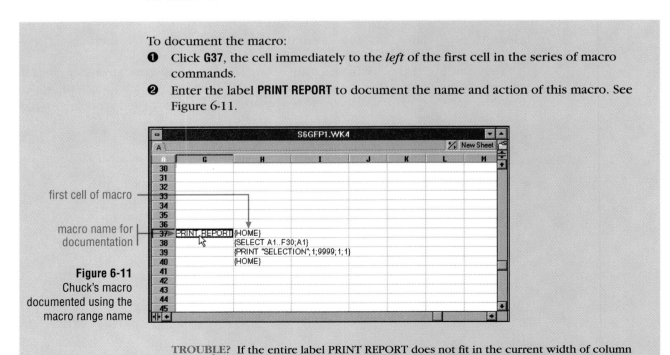

first cell of macro

macro name for documentation

Figure 6-11
Chuck's macro documented using the macro range name

TROUBLE? If the entire label PRINT REPORT does not fit in the current width of column G, use ✛ to increase the width of the column.

Chuck is convinced this macro will make it easier for the other restaurant managers to print their alternative staffing plans.

Executing a Macro

Now Chuck is ready to run the PRINT REPORT macro. There are three ways to execute a macro. First, if you named the macro with a backslash (\ ) and a letter, you can press and hold [Ctrl] while pressing the letter to run the macro. Or, if you used a descriptive range name, you can run the macro by selecting the range name from the Macro Run dialog box. The third method is to create a macro button. A **macro button** is a button you draw and name; then you click the macro button to run the macro.

Because Chuck used a descriptive name, he decides to run the PRINT REPORT macro by selecting the range name from a list in the Macro Run dialog box.

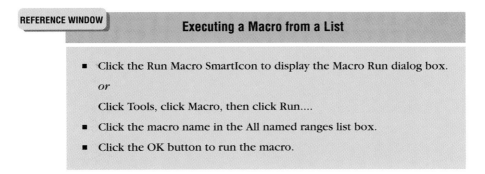

REFERENCE WINDOW

Executing a Macro from a List

- Click the Run Macro SmartIcon to display the Macro Run dialog box.
  or
  Click Tools, click Macro, then click Run....
- Click the macro name in the All named ranges list box.
- Click the OK button to run the macro.

Let's run Chuck's print macro by selecting its range name from a list.

To run the PRINT REPORT macro by selecting its range name:
❶ Click the **Run Macro SmartIcon** 🔳 to display the Macro Run dialog box. See Figure 6-12.

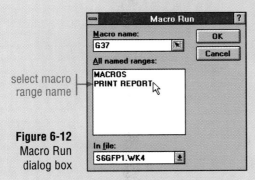

select macro range name

Figure 6-12
Macro Run
dialog box

❷ Click **PRINT REPORT** in the All named ranges list box to select it, then click the **OK button** to run the macro. "Cmd" (for command) displays in the status bar while the macro runs.

TROUBLE? If the report does not print when you run the macro, you either did not copy all the macro commands from the Transcript window, or you did not assign the range name to the first cell containing the macro commands. Review the macro commands displayed in the worksheet and compare them to the commands in the Transcript window. If they are not the same, repeat copying and pasting the macro commands. Otherwise, repeat the steps for assigning the range name PRINT REPORT to the macro.

The report with the chart is printed and ready for Chuck and Linda to use in analyzing the staffing requirements. However, Chuck thinks that creating a macro button to execute the print macro would make it even easier for the other store managers to print their staffing plans. Let's create a macro button next.

Creating a Macro Button

A **macro button** is a 1-2-3 drawn object that enables you to run a macro simply by clicking the button. You can place a macro button anywhere in a worksheet. However, as with the placement of the macro commands, it is a good idea to place the button away from the worksheet data. You use the Macro Button SmartIcon to draw the button and specify its location and size. You also need to specify the text that you want to appear on the button; this text identifies what the button does.

REFERENCE WINDOW

Creating a Macro Button

- Click the Macro Button SmartIcon.

  or

  Click Tools, click Draw, then click Button.
- Position the pointer at one corner of the location for the button.
- Drag the pointer to the opposite corner to specify the size and location of the button, then release the mouse button.
- Click the Assign macro from drop-down list arrow, then click Range.
- Select the range from the list of available range names.
- Enter the text that describes the button in the Button text box.
- Click the OK button to complete creating the button.
- Click any cell other than the macro button to unselect the button and return to Ready mode.

Let's create a macro button for Chuck's PRINT REPORT macro and assign the macro to the button.

To create a macro button and assign it to the PRINT REPORT macro:

❶ Click the **range name selector** 🔢, then click **MACROS** to position the worksheet area for locating the macro button.

❷ Click the **Macro Button SmartIcon** to begin creating the button. The pointer changes to ⁻¦⁻ for specifying the location and size of the macro button.

TROUBLE? If you move the ⁻¦⁻ too close to the row numbers, it will change to ✚ and you will not be able to draw the button. Move the pointer back into the worksheet area.

❸ Click **G32** and hold down the mouse button. This is the upper-left corner of the macro button.

❹ Drag the pointer to **G34** and release the mouse button. This is the lower-right corner of the macro button. The Assign to Button dialog box appears. See Figure 6-13.

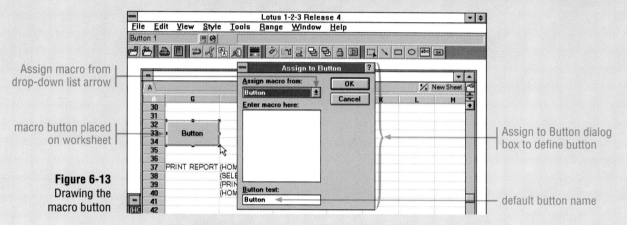

Assign macro from drop-down list arrow

macro button placed on worksheet

Assign to Button dialog box to define button

default button name

Figure 6-13
Drawing the macro button

❺ Click the **Assign macro from drop-down list arrow**, then click **Range** to indicate that the macro resides in a named range.

❻ Click **PRINT REPORT** to select the macro range name.

❼ Highlight **Button** in the Button text box ("Button" is the default button name), then type **PRINT REPORT**, the text you want to appear on the button. See Figure 6-14.

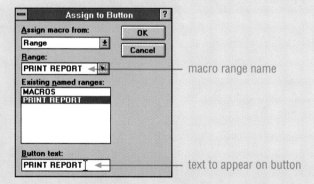

macro range name

text to appear on button

Figure 6-14
Assign to Button dialog box with Chuck's specifications

❽ Click the **OK button** to complete creating the macro button, then click any cell in the worksheet other than the macro button to unselect the button.

TROUBLE? If you enter the wrong text for the button name, position 🖑 on the button, then click the *right* mouse button to select the macro button and display the Quick menu. Select Assign Macro to redisplay the Assign to Button dialog box, then repeat Steps 7 and 8.

With the macro assigned to the PRINT REPORT button, Chuck is ready to try executing the macro using this button.

Executing a Macro Using a Macro Button

If a macro is assigned to a button, you run the macro by clicking the button.

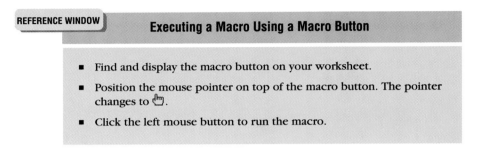

REFERENCE WINDOW

Executing a Macro Using a Macro Button

- Find and display the macro button on your worksheet.
- Position the mouse pointer on top of the macro button. The pointer changes to 🖐.
- Click the left mouse button to run the macro.

Let's run the macro that prints Chuck's staffing plan and chart.

To run the macro assigned to the PRINT REPORT macro button:

❶ Click the **range name selector** 🔢, then click **MACROS** to position the worksheet area and display the macro button.

❷ Move the pointer on top of the **PRINT REPORT macro button**. The pointer changes to 🖐, indicating the button can be selected. See Figure 6-15.

❸ Click the **PRINT REPORT macro button** to run the macro.

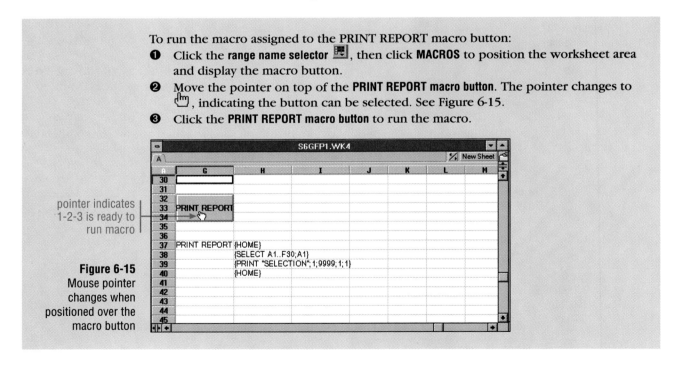

pointer indicates 1-2-3 is ready to run macro

Figure 6-15
Mouse pointer changes when positioned over the macro button

Saving the Macro

Macro commands that have been placed in your worksheet are saved when you save the worksheet file. As mentioned earlier, any macro commands you have not copied from the Transcript window to your worksheet are lost when you exit 1-2-3. Let's save Chuck's macro commands with his worksheet, then print the worksheet to check that the printout of the macro matches the macro planning sheet.

To save the macro commands with the worksheet then print the macro commands:
❶ Click the **Home SmartIcon** 🖾 to position the cell pointer at the worksheet before saving the file.
❷ Save the worksheet as S6GFP2.WK4, then print the range G35..K41, which contains the macro.

If you want to take a break and resume the tutorial at a later time, you can exit 1-2-3 by double-clicking the Control menu box in the upper-left corner of your screen. When you resume the tutorial, launch 1-2-3 and place your Student Disk in the disk drive. Open the S6GFP2.WK4 worksheet file, select the Tutorial 6 SmartIcon palette, then continue with this tutorial.

▨   ▨   ▨

Creating a Macro for What-If Data Entry

Next, Chuck needs to create the second macro that he planned according to his planning analysis sheet in Figure 6-2. This will be a guided data entry macro that the other store managers can use to enter their staffing numbers into the template as they conduct their own what-if analyses. The macro positions the cell pointer at the appropriate location and then pauses, allowing you to enter a new data value. A macro that pauses during execution is called an **interactive macro**. The cell pointer then moves to the next location for another data value, and the process continues until all the data values are entered.

Chuck walks through the actions he wants the macro to perform and prepares the macro planning sheet (Figure 6-16). He knows that in order to have a macro pause, he has to include the Pause command {?} in the macro commands. However, he wants to record the macro by performing the steps and having 1-2-3 record them, rather than typing each macro command. Therefore, he won't be able to include the Pause commands he wants. To solve this problem, he decides to enter test values as placeholders for the Pause command as he records his macro. **Test values** are example data values that might be entered by another store manager. Then, after he follows the various steps to record and place the macro, Chuck will edit the macro to include the Pause commands that he needs.

	What-If Macro Planning Sheet	
Action	Comment
Click the Home SmartIcon	Positions the cell pointer at A1
Click B7	Selects the cell for sales per employee hour
Enter 38 (test value)	Enters amount for sales per employee hour
Press [↓] [↓]	Positions the cell pointer for next entry
Enter 48 (test value)	Enters amount for manager hours per week
Press [↓]	Positions the cell pointer for next entry
Enter 34 (test value)	Enters amount for associate hours per week
Click the Home SmartIcon	Positions the cell pointer at A1

Figure 6-16
Chuck's what-if macro planning sheet

Clearing the Transcript Window

In preparation for creating the data entry macro, Chuck needs to clear the Transcript window to remove the previously recorded macro commands. Although this step is not required by 1-2-3, clearing all the old recorded commands helps to separate the commands that are used for a particular macro.

<table>
<tr><td>REFERENCE WINDOW</td><td>**Clearing the Transcript Window**</td></tr>
</table>

- Click the Transcript window to make it the active window. If the Transcript window isn't open, click the Transcript Window SmartIcon to open it.
- Click Edit, then click Clear All to erase the window's contents.

Let's clear the Transcript window and remove the macro commands for printing the worksheet in preparation for recording the commands for Chuck's second macro.

To clear the Transcript window:

❶ Click the **Transcript window** to make it the active window.

   TROUBLE? If your Transcript window isn't open, click the Transcript Window SmartIcon ▥ to open it.

❷ Click **Edit**, then click **Clear All** to erase the current contents of the Transcript window. If you took a break and exited from 1-2-3, the Transcript window was automatically cleared and no commands appear in it.

Recording the What-If Data Entry Macro

Now that the Transcript window is empty, Chuck is ready to record the guided data entry macro for doing the what-if analysis. You will record this macro in the same manner as you recorded Chuck's PRINT REPORT macro. Let's record this macro following the procedure written in Chuck's macro planning sheet (Figure 6-16).

To record the macro for guided data entry:

❶ Click any cell in the worksheet window to make it the active window.

❷ Click the **Record Macro SmartIcon** ▥ to start the macro recorder. "Rec" is displayed in the status bar.

Now carry out the steps according to Chuck's macro planning sheet.

❸ Click the **Home SmartIcon** ▥ to position the cell pointer at A1.

❹ Click **B7** to position the cell pointer at the location for entering the first test value. See Figure 6-17.

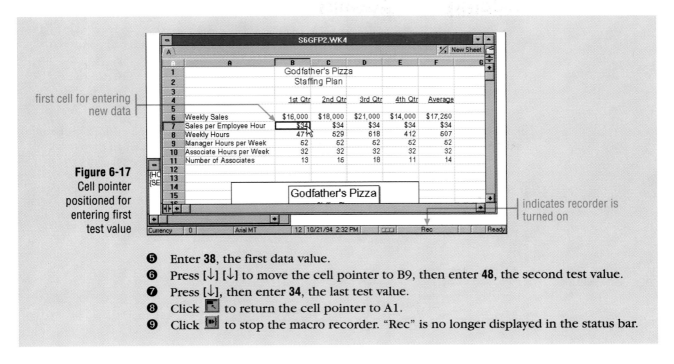

Figure 6-17
Cell pointer
positioned for
entering first
test value

first cell for entering new data

indicates recorder is turned on

❺ Enter **38**, the first data value.
❻ Press [↓] [↓] to move the cell pointer to B9, then enter **48**, the second test value.
❼ Press [↓], then enter **34**, the last test value.
❽ Click ▣ to return the cell pointer to A1.
❾ Click ▣ to stop the macro recorder. "Rec" is no longer displayed in the status bar.

Now the macro is ready to play back to make sure it was entered without any mistakes. However, since the macro includes the test values, the same values will be used automatically during the play back. You will not enter another set of test values. Let's test Chuck's macro by playing it back from the Transcript window.

To test the execution of the what-if data entry macro:
❶ Click the **Transcript window** to make it the active window.
❷ Scroll to the top of the window, then select all the commands in the Transcript window.
❸ Click the **Playback Transcript SmartIcon** ▣ to test the macro command execution and obtain the same results as when you initially recorded the macro.

TROUBLE? If the macro did not execute correctly, click the Undo SmartIcon ▣ to return the worksheet to its original condition. Make sure the Transcript window is active, click Edit, then click Clear All to delete all the macro commands. Record the macro again.

Next you can copy the recorded and tested macro to the worksheet, name it, then execute it.

To copy the macro from the Transcript window to the worksheet window:
❶ Click the **Transcript window** to activate it.
❷ Scroll to the top of the window, then select all the commands recorded in the Transcript window. Make sure you include the open brace. Click the **Copy to Clipboard SmartIcon** ▣ to copy these macro commands to the clipboard.
❸ Click any cell in the worksheet window to make it the active window.

④ Click the **range name selector** 🔲, then click **MACROS** to position the cell pointer at the location of the macros.

⑤ Click **H43**, then click the **Paste from Clipboard SmartIcon** 📋 to place the macro instructions at this location. Remember the macro must be placed in a column.

Now you can document the macro.

⑥ Click **G43**, then enter **WHAT IF** to document the macro's name and action. This completes placing the macro in the worksheet. Scroll the worksheet so all the commands for the WHAT IF macro are displayed and review them. See Figure 6-18.

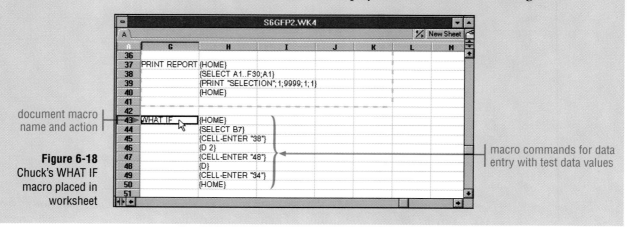

document macro name and action

macro commands for data entry with test data values

Figure 6-18
Chuck's WHAT IF macro placed in worksheet

Next, let's name the macro range WHAT IF. Again, Chuck wants to use a descriptive name so that the other managers will know what the macro is used for.

To assign a range name to this data entry macro, which begins in cell H43:

❶ Click **H43**, the first cell in the macro range that you assign the name to.

❷ Click the **Range Name SmartIcon** 🔲 to display the Name dialog box, type **WHAT IF** in the Name text box, verify that the range H43..H43 is displayed in the Range text box, then click the **OK button** to complete entering the range name.

The guided data entry macro is ready to run. Let's execute Chuck's macro for entering another set of factors for a different staffing plan.

To run the WHAT IF macro by selecting it from a list:

❶ Click the **Run Macro SmartIcon** 🔲 to display the Macro Run dialog box.

❷ Click **WHAT IF** in the All named ranges list box to select it, then click the **OK button** to run the macro. The macro runs but, like the play back test, still doesn't pause for entering new data values. This is because the Pause command is not included in the set of macro commands.

Let's fix the macro by replacing the commands that enter the test values with Pause commands, so that new data values can be entered each time the macro is executed.

Editing Macro Commands

Macro commands are recorded and stored as labels in cells in your worksheet. They can be modified by editing them in the same way that you edit any other 1-2-3 label. To edit them, you might want to replace the command with another command, as in Chuck's case, or you might want to change an argument or cell address. A list of all the macro commands can be viewed by clicking the Macro Command SmartIcon. This list helps you understand the syntax of each command and makes it easier for you to edit a command.

REFERENCE WINDOW

Using Help to Learn About Macro Commands

- Click the Macro command SmartIcon to display the Macro Keywords dialog box.

- Scroll the Macro name list, then click the macro keyword.

- Click the ? button in the upper-right corner of the dialog box to display the Help window that describes the macro's syntax including a description of the arguments.

Chuck needs to include the Pause command in his set of macro commands. He will do this by entering {?} in the places where the test values are located currently. When 1-2-3 reads {?}, it temporarily stops, or pauses, the macro so you can manually enter a data value or range name, move the cell or menu pointer, or complete a command for the macro to process. When you use the pause command in a macro, you must complete the cell entry with a tilde (~), which represents the Enter key. The macro continues processing only when you press [Enter]. Let's edit the data entry macro by deleting the macro commands that insert test values and replacing them with the Pause command.

To modify the WHAT IF macro to make it interactive:

❶ Click the **range name selector** 🔣, click **MACROS** to position the cell pointer where the macros are located, then scroll the window to display all the WHAT IF macro commands.

❷ Click **H45**, the cell containing the first macro command you need to revise.

❸ Click the **Macro Command SmartIcon** 🔲 to display the Macro Keywords dialog box, which contains a list of the available 1-2-3 macro commands. See Figure 6-19.
Notice that "Edit" appears in the status bar to indicate you are editing a command.

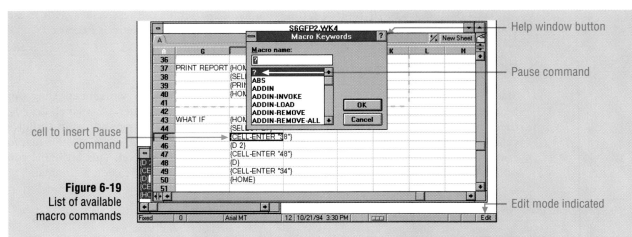

cell to insert Pause
command

Figure 6-19
List of available
macro commands

Help window button

Pause command

Edit mode indicated

❹   Click **?** (question mark) in the list of commands to select the Pause command.

   TROUBLE? If you click the ? button in the upper-right corner of the dialog box, the 1-2-3
   Help window appears. If this occurs, close the Help window, then repeat Step 4.

❺   Click the **OK button** to select this macro command. The dialog box disappears and {?
      appears in cell H45.

❻   Type } ~ (close brace and tilde) to complete the command, then press **[Enter]** to fin-
      ish specifying this macro command.

❼   Copy the Pause command from cell H45 into cells H47 and H49 to complete edit-
      ing the macro. See Figure 6-20.

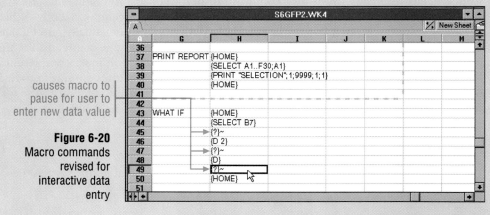

causes macro to
pause for user to
enter new data value

Figure 6-20
Macro commands
revised for
interactive data
entry

❽   Run the WHAT IF macro using the Run Macro SmartIcon [icon], and enter these new
      test data values:

      Sales per Employee Hour: **32**
      Manager Hours per Week: **44**
      Associate Hours per Week: **30**

❾   Run the PRINT REPORT macro to print a report with this data.

❿   Save the worksheet as S6GFP3.WK4—the macros are automatically saved with the
      worksheet. Print the range G35..K52, which contains the macros.

      Chuck has completed his data entry macro, which Linda and the other managers can
use to explore alternative staffing plans. But what if the macro does not execute correctly?

Stopping Macros

Suppose you run a macro, then discover it is the wrong macro. You can stop the execution of the macro and return to Ready mode by pressing [Ctrl][Break]. Stopping a macro's execution and returning to Ready mode is different from using the Pause command, which *temporarily* suspends the execution of the macro while you enter data or complete an action. Remember with the Pause command, once you press [Enter], the macro continues. Whenever you press [Ctrl][Break], execution of the macro stops completely and you are returned to Ready mode. You must run the macro again.

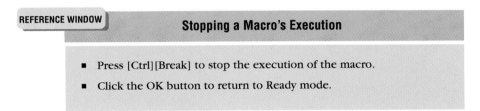

REFERENCE WINDOW

Stopping a Macro's Execution

- Press [Ctrl][Break] to stop the execution of the macro.
- Click the OK button to return to Ready mode.

Let's run Chuck's interactive macro, then stop its execution.

To stop the execution of a macro:

❶ Click the **Run Macro SmartIcon** 📄, click **WHAT IF**, then click the **OK button** to execute this macro.

❷ Press **[Ctrl][Break]** to stop the macro and display the message for the break. See Figure 6-21. Notice that you can press [F1] or click the ? button to get Help.

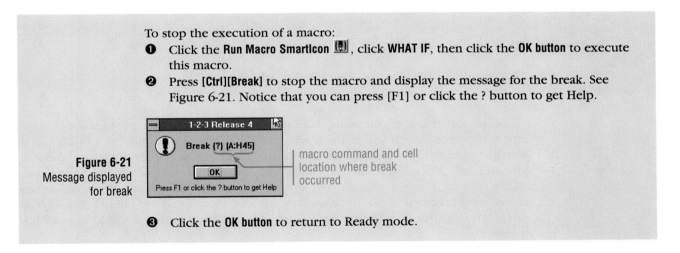

Figure 6-21
Message displayed
for break

macro command and cell
location where break
occurred

❸ Click the **OK button** to return to Ready mode.

The execution of the macro is stopped and you are ready for your next activity.

Debugging Macros

Sometimes when you first try to run a macro, it might not do what you expect, or 1-2-3 might display an error message. This occurs when the macro contains a syntax error, a typing mistake, or a spelling error. When a macro doesn't run correctly, you need to debug it. **Debugging** is the process of removing errors from your macros. By recording macros instead of entering macro commands manually, you avoid making many errors. However, when you edit a macro you recorded, you can cause an error. Let's make an intentional error in the data entry macro and see what happens when you try to execute it.

To place an intentional error in the WHAT IF macro:
1 Click the **range name selector** , click **MACROS**, then scroll the worksheet window to display all the WHAT IF macro commands.
2 Click **H47**, the cell that contains one of the Pause commands.
3 Edit this cell so it contains only {? by removing the close brace (}) and tilde (~).

Now let's run the macro to see what happens.

To run the macro with the intentional error and observe the result:
1 Click the **Run Macro SmartIcon** , click **WHAT IF**, then click the **OK button**.
2 Enter **35** in cell B7.
3 Observe the error message as the cell pointer moves to cell B9. See Figure 6-22.

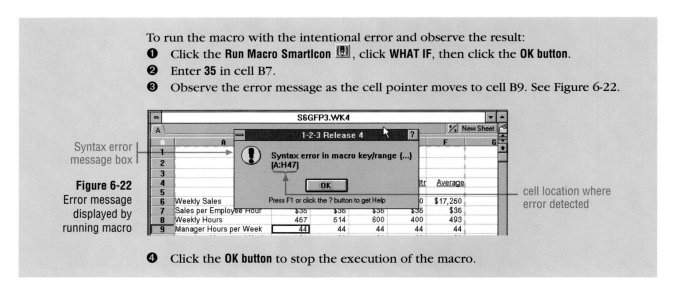

Syntax error message box

Figure 6-22
Error message displayed by running macro

cell location where error detected

4 Click the **OK button** to stop the execution of the macro.

When an error is encountered, 1-2-3 displays an error message and indicates the cell where the error occurred. Because macro commands execute so quickly, it is difficult to watch the execution of each macro command individually as you try to locate the errors. The Step and Trace modes in 1-2-3 allow you to observe the macro's execution. **Step mode** runs the macro one command at a time, whereas **Trace mode** displays the command being executed in the Trace window. Although you could use the two modes separately, you can see the command as you control its execution when you use them together.

Using Step and Trace Modes to Debug a Macro

- Click the Step Mode SmartIcon to activate Step mode.

  or

  Click Tools, click Macro, then click Single Step.
- Click the Trace Mode SmartIcon to activate Trace mode.

  or

  Click Tools, click Macro, then click Trace.
- Run the macro by pressing [Spacebar] to step through the macro commands one at a time.
- Locate the command where the error occurs, with the Syntax error message displayed in a dialog box, then click the OK button to stop execution of the macro.
- Click the Step Mode SmartIcon to deactivate Step mode.

  or

  Click Tools, click Macro, then click Single Step.
- Click the Trace Mode SmartIcon to deactivate Trace mode.

  or

  Click Tools, click Macro, then click Trace.

Let's use Step and Trace modes to find the intentional error in the revised data entry macro.

To use Step and Trace modes to debug the macro:
1. Click the **Step Mode SmartIcon** to activate this feature and display "Step" in the status bar.
2. Click the **Trace Mode SmartIcon** to activate this feature and open the Macro Trace window.
3. Click the **Run Macro SmartIcon**, select **WHAT IF**, then click the **OK button** to run the macro. Note that the {HOME} command is displayed prior to execution in the Macro Trace window. See Figure 6-23.

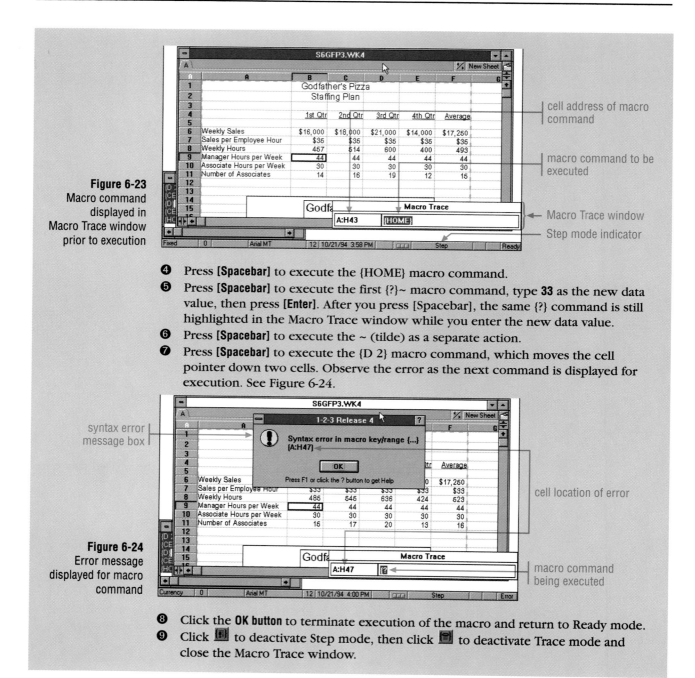

Figure 6-23
Macro command
displayed in
Macro Trace window
prior to execution

Figure 6-24
Error message
displayed for macro
command

❹ Press **[Spacebar]** to execute the {HOME} macro command.

❺ Press **[Spacebar]** to execute the first {?}~ macro command, type **33** as the new data value, then press **[Enter]**. After you press [Spacebar], the same {?} command is still highlighted in the Macro Trace window while you enter the new data value.

❻ Press **[Spacebar]** to execute the ~ (tilde) as a separate action.

❼ Press **[Spacebar]** to execute the {D 2} macro command, which moves the cell pointer down two cells. Observe the error as the next command is displayed for execution. See Figure 6-24.

❽ Click the **OK button** to terminate execution of the macro and return to Ready mode.

❾ Click ▦ to deactivate Step mode, then click ▦ to deactivate Trace mode and close the Macro Trace window.

Now, let's correct the error in the guided data entry macro by editing the cell that contains the intentional error.

To correct the intentional error:

❶ Click the **range name selector** ▦, click **MACROS**, then scroll the window to display all the WHAT IF macro commands.

❷ Click **H47**.

❸ Edit this cell so it contains the {?}~ macro command.

❹ Run the WHAT IF macro and refer to the data in Figure 6-16 to verify that you corrected the error.

TROUBLE? If the error still occurs, repeat Steps 2 through 4.

The intentional error has been found and corrected. Be careful not to alter a command's syntax when you make changes to recorded macros. However, if you do, now you know how to find the error and fix it.

Chuck has completed the staffing plan worksheet template and has reviewed the macros. Both macros work and meet the requirements specified by his design. The template worksheet with its macros will make it easy for the managers to print the staffing plan report and to enter what-if alternatives. The macro buttons will allow the managers with little 1-2-3 experience to do their own what-if evaluations. Linda is confident this worksheet will assist the managers in preparing better staffing plans for next year.

Questions

1. Performing each of the menu, keyboard, and mouse actions before you record a macro helps avoid errors in the macro. This activity is known as a:
   a. play back rehearsal
   b. dry run
   c. macro execution
   d. syntax plan
2. Which of the following is *not* a reason for using macros?
   a. several different reports are printed from a single worksheet
   b. the worksheet is used by someone with little 1-2-3 experience
   c. a series of 1-2-3 commands is used only once
   d. different sets of data are entered in the same cells for several what-if alternatives
3. Macro commands are recorded in which of these windows:
   a. active worksheet
   b. designated worksheet
   c. Transcript
   d. play back
4. When a macro is placed in the same worksheet as your data and reports, inserting rows can create problems with the macro unless the macro is placed in this preferred location:
   a. below and to the right of the data and reports
   b. to the left of the data and reports
   c. beginning in cell HA100
   d. anywhere in column A
5. Before a macro in your worksheet can be executed it must be named. The first cell in the macro is named:
   a. using the Macro Name dialog box

b. always beginning with the letter M

c. using special reserved macro names

d. the same as any other worksheet range

6. Which macro command causes the execution of a macro to pause so you can enter a data value?

a. {PAUSE}

b. {?}

c. {HALT}

d. {WAIT}

7. When are macro commands that have been placed in your worksheet saved?

a. upon exiting from 1-2-3

b. whenever the macro is run

c. when the worksheet file is saved

d. when you click File, then click Macro Save

8. How do you edit macro commands that have been recorded and stored in the worksheet?

a. using the Macro Editor

b. the same as any other 1-2-3 label

c. the same as any other 1-2-3 drawn object

d. using the Macro Trace window

E

9. Using the Task Reference, determine the number of different ways that you can do the same tasks as those performed with the following SmartIcons. Write down at least one other method for each SmartIcon:

a.

b.

c.

d.

Tutorial Assignments

Launch 1-2-3 and open the worksheet T6MMM1.WK4 for Montana Mining and Manufacturing (MMM). Talia Pinard built a quarterly Projected Income Statement for MMM. Your task is to create a template worksheet for Talia with a print macro and a what-if macro by performing the following:

1. Review Talia's worksheet. You can locate the macro area using the MACROS range name, which she has already specified. Which cell does the range name MACROS bring you to?

2. Perform a dry run and write out a macro planning sheet for a print income macro that prints the Projected Income Statement and its summary chart. Create this macro and place it in the worksheet, beginning at cell H55, then document the macro in cell G55 by entering the label PRINT INCOME. Run this macro.

3. Create a macro button in cells G51..G53, and assign it to the PRINT INCOME macro. Run this macro using the macro button.

4. Save the worksheet as S6MMM2.WK4.

5. Develop a what-if macro that guides entering new data values for evaluating alternatives with different amounts for net sales and for general and administration in each of the four quarters. Perform a dry run and write out a macro planning sheet. Create the macro and place it in cell H63. Then document the macro by entering its name, "WHAT IF" in cell G63. (*Hint*: Remember to use the tilde ~ .)

6. Create a button for the WHAT IF macro in cell I51..I53, and assign the macro to this button.

7. Run the WHAT IF macro using this test data:

Planning item	Qtr 1	Qtr 2	Qtr 3	Qtr 4
Net Sales	3,371	3,216	3,279	3,198
General and Admin	901	867	701	763

8. Save the worksheet as S6MMM3.WK4. Preview and print the report using your PRINT INCOME macro. Then, preview and print the macro area of the worksheet.

E 9. Relocate the macro commands for the PRINT INCOME and WHAT IF macros to a new sheet in the S6MMM3.WK4 file by clicking the New Sheet button, cutting the macro commands to the clipboard and pasting them in sheet B at cell A1. Rename the worksheet tab B "Macros." Now, run the WHAT IF macro and use your own test values. Then run the PRINT INCOME macro to produce a hard copy of the report. Where are the macro buttons located? Do they still run the macros?

10. Save the worksheet as S6MMM4.WK4. Preview and print the Macros sheet.

Chuck and the other managers of the Godfather's Pizza restaurants have been using the staffing plan worksheet template to evaluate different alternatives for the number of hours worked each week. However, they would also like to examine the impact of changes in the weekly sales for each of the four quarters. Chuck decides to make several additional improvements to his template worksheet. To make these enhancements, perform the following:

11. Launch 1-2-3 and open the S6GFP3.WK4 worksheet template created in this tutorial. If you did not create the worksheet, then do so before you continue.

12. Develop a second what-if macro that lets you interactively change the weekly sales. Name the macro "WEEKLY SALES." This macro should position the cell pointer for entering a new data value for weekly sales for each of the four quarters. To create this macro, perform a dry run, prepare a macro planning sheet, record the macro, edit the data entry commands, assign a range name to the macro, document the macro, create a macro button to display the range name, and run the macro using your own test values. Then, run the PRINT REPORT macro and print the macro commands for this new macro. Save this worksheet as S6GFP4.WK4.

E 13. Linda would like each of the managers to include the location of their restaurant on the staff planning report. Insert a row above row 3, then in cell A3, enter the label "Old Market Mall" and center it across columns A through F. Run the PRINT REPORT macro. Then examine the SELECT macro command in cell H39 that specifies the print range. Was the print range in this macro changed when you inserted the new row? What problem might this cause?

E 14. Name the range A1..F31, which contains the report including the chart, as STAFF PLAN. Edit the SELECT macro command in cell H39 and replace A1..F30 with "STAFF PLAN"; be sure to include the quotes surrounding STAFF PLAN in this change. Insert another row above row 3 to provide better spacing of the report title. Run the PRINT REPORT macro. Save this worksheet as S6GFP5.WK4. Check the cell range designated by the STAFF PLAN macro. What is the cell range assigned to this range name? Was this range revised when you inserted the row? If so, how is this helpful in creating macros?

E 15. Review Chuck's template worksheet for the staffing plan. What other macros would you suggest to include in this template? Explain why you think they would be useful.

Case Problems

1. Calculating Monthly Payments for Mortgage Brokers Association

Mortgage Brokers Association (MBA) is an originator of home mortgages. In addition to making first-time loans on homes, MBA also is very active in writing second mortgages or remortgaging homes as interest rates change. Despite the relatively small staff at MBA, they still manage to process hundreds of mortgages a week. Juan Santiago is a loan officer for MBA. Juan wants to create a template based on MBA's current worksheet, which calculates mortgage payments, to simplify its use. Besides calculating the mortgage payment, Juan and the other loan officers want to produce a loan payment schedule for the first two years of the loan. Juan thinks this template would help speed up the process of closing a mortgage. To create the template, perform the following:

1. Launch 1-2-3 and open the P6MBA1.WK4 worksheet file. Review Juan's worksheet and its formulas. Look at the LOAN PAYMENT macro Juan created in the MACROS named range and then run this macro.
2. What is wrong with the LOAN PAYMENT macro? Edit the macro so the macro will run correctly.
3. Create a LOAN PAYMENT macro button. Assign this button to the range name LOAN PAYMENT. Run the macro using test data with a $150,000 loan amount, 8.25% yearly interest rate, and 30 year length of loan.
4. Save the worksheet as S6MBA2.WK4. Preview and print the loan calculation and payment schedule area of the worksheet.
5. Perform a dry run and write out a macro planning sheet for a LOAN SCHEDULE macro that prints Juan's loan calculation and payment schedule. Create this macro and assign the range name "LOAN SCHEDULE" to it. Document this macro.
6. Create a macro button for the LOAN SCHEDULE macro. Assign the LOAN SCHEDULE macro to this button.
7. Save the worksheet as S6MBA3.WK4. Run the LOAN SCHEDULE macro using the macro button.

E

8. To prevent the LOAN PAYMENT and LOAN SCHEDULE macros from being accidentally deleted or altered, Juan wants to move them to a separate sheet. Name the worksheet tab "Macros." The macro buttons should still appear in sheet A. Rename the worksheet tab A "Loan." Test the relocated macros by running them, then save the worksheet as S6MBA4.WK4. Preview and print the macro commands.

E

9. What do you think are the advantages and/or disadvantages of placing the macros on a separate sheet within the same worksheet file?

2. Preparing Receipts for the International Red Cross

In 1863, Henry Dunant established the International Red Cross, which is now a federation of over 145 national societies around the world dedicated to helping victims of natural disasters and political turmoil. These Red Cross societies are non-profit organizations, which rely on the donations of time and money from individuals and corporations alike. Thousands of monetary donations come in daily, each requiring a receipt to be sent to the donor.

Sarah Barton volunteers 10 hours a week to help her local chapter prepare these receipts. She knew that using a 1-2-3 worksheet for preparing receipts would help decrease the time used to process donations. Sarah developed a template that can be completed with all the necessary information. Now she wants to add macro commands to the template so it can be used easily by the other volunteers. She would like one macro command to print the receipt and the other to guide the volunteers in entering the data for the receipt. Create these macros for Sarah by performing the following:

1. Launch 1-2-3 and open the P6IRC1.WK4 worksheet. Then review Sarah's donation receipt template. Notice how the template requires input of both text and numeric data. Save the worksheet as S6IRC1.WK4.

2. Determine a good location on your worksheet for placing the macros and create a MACROS range name as a means to quickly display this worksheet area.

3. Develop a PRINT RECEIPT macro that prints the donation receipt, and create a macro button to run it. Make sure you document your macro.

4. Save the worksheet as S6IRC2.WK4, then execute the macro using the button and print the macro area.

5. Develop a DONOR ENTRY macro that guides the user through entering donor information in the template receipt. The data items that are entered are:
   - Received From
   - Address
   - City, State Zip
   - Amount
   - Payment Method
   - Check Number

   The data item "City, State Zip" is entered as one label. An "x" is placed in the appropriate payment method and a space is used for the other two methods. Create a macro button for running this macro. Complete the macro by documenting it. (*Hint*: Do not forget the tilde ~ .)

6. Run the DONOR ENTRY macro using this test data:

Data Item	Donor Data
Received from	Beth Walters
Address	632 Halsted Road
City, State Zip	Farmington Hills, MI 48331
Amount	$250
Payment Method	Check
Check Number	1173

7. Save the worksheet as S6IRC3.WK4. Preview and print the macro commands for both macros.

E 8. What other macros could make the receipt preparation process more efficient? Describe how they would be useful.

E 9. Create a third macro, DO RECEIPT, that does both the guided data entry and the receipt printing. Copy the macro commands from your other two macros into the appropriate cells for this new macro. Create a macro button to run it and include documentation. Run this macro using your own test data. Save the worksheet as S6IRC4.WK4, then print the macro area.

3. Setting Rates for Commonwealth Electric Company

Commonwealth Electric Company (CEC) provides electricity to customers in New England for home and industrial use. The production and sales of electricity are measured in megawatt hours (MWH), which is the equivalent of one million kilowatt hours. Customer bills are based on their status of either residential or commercial and their MWH usage. CEC charges commercial accounts a higher rate, which then reduces the cost of electricity to residential customers. As a public utility, CEC's rates are regulated by state government. CEC is reviewing its rates and needs to evaluate new sets of proposed rates with the expected demand for electricity. Any change in rates must be approved by the Public Utility Commission (PUC), which bases its decision on CEC's return on investment.

Jane Taft works with three other tariff and rate analysts in the Tariffs and Regulations Department. They are responsible for developing forecasts to ensure that CEC is able to meet the demand for electricity and to conform with PUC regulations. In developing forecasts, Jane and her coworkers constantly make changes to the proposed customer electric rates (residential rate and commercial rate), the ratio of residential demand to commercial demand (residential percent), the production cost percent, and the total electricity sold for the year (the amount in the Total column). Jane created a 1-2-3 worksheet that allows her to develop alternative forecasts. She wants to add macros so the worksheet is easier for the other analysts to use as they prepare a forecasted income statement for an upcoming rate hearing with the PUC. Your assignment is to perform the following to create the macros for Jane's worksheet:

1. Launch 1-2-3 and open the P6CEC1.WK4 worksheet. Review the formulas Jane created for the forecasted income statement and examine how the formulas reference the key factors.

2. Create a MACROS named range to identify the location of macros in the worksheet.

3. Plan and record the FORECAST macro for preparing what-if alternatives with the guided data entry of selected key factors in Jane's worksheet. Have the macro ask for new residential rates, commercial rates, production cost percent, and total electricity sold for the year in the Total column.

4. Create a macro button for this macro. Run the macro with the following updated information:

Planning Item	New Amount
Residential Rate	77
Commercial Rate	94
Production Cost Percent	71%
Total Electricity Sold [Total]	2,411

5. Save the worksheet as S6CEC2.WK4. Preview and print the forecasted income statement.

6. Create a PRINT FORECAST macro that uses a range name as the selected range. Assign FORECAST REPORT to the range that contains the report you want to print. When creating your macro, the report's range name should be selected *before* you execute the command that prints the report.

7. Create a macro button for PRINT FORECAST and execute the macro.

8. Save the worksheet as S6CEC3.WK4.

9. Create a PRINT STATEMENT macro by recording the steps to print the FORECAST REPORT range together with a header. The header contains the user's name in the upper-left corner as "Prepared by: your name" and the current date in the upper-right corner. The date can be inserted automatically by 1-2-3 in the header by clicking the Insert Date button in the Page Setup dialog box. What symbol appears in the Header box to indicate the date will be displayed? Execute the macro to print the report with your name in the header.

10. Save the worksheet as S6CEC4.WK4. Preview and print the macro commands for all three macros in the worksheet.

11. Jane and her associates believe the maximum return on investment (ROI) they can expect from the PUC for next year is 8%. Does the solution for the what-if alternative obtained by running the macro fall within this maximum expectation?

12. Could any other macros be created that would be useful? Explain why.

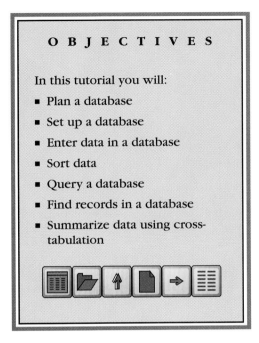

OBJECTIVES

In this tutorial you will:
- Plan a database
- Set up a database
- Enter data in a database
- Sort data
- Query a database
- Find records in a database
- Summarize data using cross-tabulation

Creating and Using a Worksheet Database

Managing Inventory

CASE **Fast Forward Video** Fast Forward Video specializes in selling and renting home video tapes of popular movies. Since Jodi Lopez and Bruce Kanno opened the doors of Fast Forward in 1984, their business has continued to expand as the popularity of home videos has grown. Jodi directs the overall activities, while Bruce manages the day-to-day operations. Jodi would like Bruce to improve their inventory management by developing a database to keep track of the movies and to produce several reports. A **database** is a collection of information organized into related groups. This information provided by the database helps you run your business more efficiently.

Bruce conducted an analysis of Fast Forward's requirements for movie management and determined that the information described by the data definition in Figure 7-1 needs to be maintained for each movie. A **data definition** describes the information that you want to include in your database. From this data definition, Bruce knows he can produce several reports, which include a movie list, an order list, and a category analysis. His movie list contains all of the movies grouped together by category. He could prepare an order list for reordering movies when the quantity in stock falls below a certain level. Finally, he could produce a category analysis to show the number of movies by category from each film maker.

Field Name	Description
Movie	Name of movie
Maker	Film maker
Year	Year produced
Category	Category of movie: Comedy, Drama, Suspense, Horror (category is coded by the first three letters COM, DRA, SUS, HOR)
Rate	Rating: G, PG, R, X, NR (not rated)
Price	Selling price
Qty	Inventory quantity
Loc	Storage location code
TV	Yes (Y) or no (N), indicating whether movie has been shown on television

Figure 7-1
Data definition for a
Movies database

To develop a worksheet containing a Movies database, Bruce prepares his planning analysis sheet and reviews it with Jodi (Figure 7-2).

Planning Analysis Sheet

My goal:
Review the movie videos database to determine which videos need to be reordered and the category of movies produced by different film makers

What results do I want to see?
List records in database by movie name, category, and within category by movie name
List movies that need to be reordered
Report of the number of movies by film maker and category

What information do I need?
Database of movies stocked in inventory

What calculations will I perform?
Count movies by film maker and category

Figure 7-2
Bruce's planning
analysis sheet

In this tutorial, you will develop a Movies database for Fast Forward Video. You will learn how to create and manipulate the data in a database to produce reports that support making better business decisions.

Introduction to 1-2-3 Databases

A database is a collection of related data, such as the movies at Fast Forward Video. Businesses use databases to do the recordkeeping to **track**, or maintain, the status of inventories, customers, members, sales, personnel, purchase orders, accounts receivable, accounts payable, payroll, and other standard business functions. Frequently, lists are prepared from these databases, which report the current status of these business activities, such as the movie list and order list Bruce wants to prepare for Fast Forward.

Recordkeeping is performed by managing the data in a database. **Data management** refers to the tasks required to maintain and manipulate a database. Data management tasks typically include: entering new data, updating current data, sorting data, searching for information, and creating reports.

A 1-2-3 **database table**, or simply a **database**, is used to manage data in a worksheet. The database table is a worksheet range containing data arranged as fields and records (Figure 7-3). A **field** is a column containing a single data item that describes some attribute or characteristic of an object, person, or place, such as a movie's name. A **record** is a row containing related data items for each field, such as the movie name, film maker, year produced, and price. A collection of related records makes up the database. The first cell in each column of the database table must contain the **field name**, a label that identifies the data item in the column.

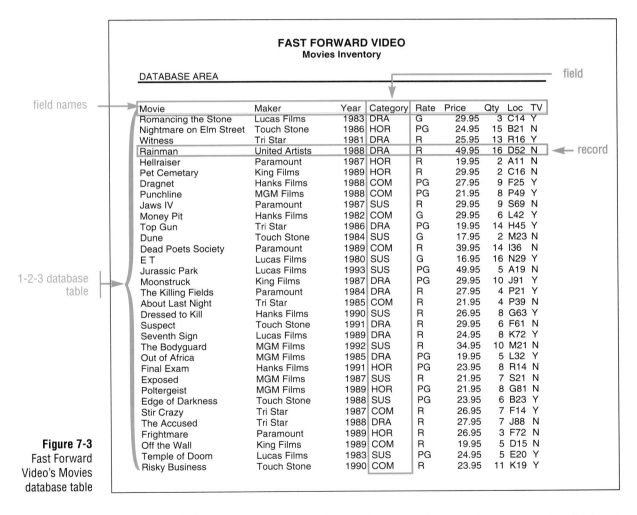

Figure 7-3
Fast Forward
Video's Movies
database table

The worksheet range containing the database must be organized so that the fields are in columns, while the records are entered in rows—1-2-3 does not permit you to reverse this arrangement of columns and rows.

Your first step in creating the Movies database is to retrieve the worksheet Bruce started, which contains a report title and designates an area for the database. Let's open Bruce's worksheet and select the Tutorial 7 SmartIcon palette.

To open the worksheet and select the Tutorial 7 SmartIcon palette:

❶ Launch 1-2-3 and select the Tutorial 7 SmartIcon palette by using the SmartIcon palette selector 🖿 in the status bar.

❷ Open Bruce's C7FFV1.WK4 worksheet file located on your Student Disk, then immediately save it as S7FFV1.WK4. Review this worksheet.

Creating a 1-2-3 Database

Similar to the process of creating other worksheets, several activities are necessary in creating a database, and the effort results in better information to support business operations. To create a database you must perform these activities:

- planning the database
- setting up the database
- entering data in the database

Planning the Database

When you plan a database, you need to determine what information you want the database to include. Bruce wants a database that provides information about Fast Forward's movie inventory. As you think about the data, list each field by name and describe its contents in a data definition, like the one Bruce outlined in Figure 7-1. Next, you need to decide whether the data in the field will be a label or a numeric value. Try *not* to mix labels and values in the same field. Then, decide how wide each field should be and the number of decimal places for those fields that will hold numeric values. Although you can make changes to the database after you enter the data, it is best to determine the database structure first. Finally, record your descriptions and decisions in a database planning sheet as you prepare to create the database, as Bruce has done in Figure 7-4.

		Database Planning Sheet	
Field Name	Data Type	Column Width for Largest Value	Decimal Places
Movie	Label	20	
Maker	Label	15	
Year	Value	5	0
Category	Label	8	
Rate	Label	5	
Price	Value	7	2
Qty	Value	4	0
Loc	Label	4	
TV	Label	3	

Figure 7-4
Database planning
sheet for the
Movies database

From this planning sheet, you can easily determine the format settings for the fields containing the numeric values. You'll need to set the format for the Year and Qty columns to Fixed with no decimal places to the right, and set the Price column to Fixed with two decimal places.

Setting Up the Database

You can place a database anywhere you want in a 1-2-3 worksheet. However, some database commands require two blank rows and two blank columns surrounding the database, so 1-2-3 can recognize this worksheet area as a database table. When your worksheet contains only a database table, column A is a convenient location for your first database field; however, you should still include two blank rows above the field names and two blank columns to the right of the database table in the event that you add other data, not included in the database table, to the worksheet. If there are other data areas in the worksheet besides the database table, include two blank rows and two blank columns on the sides of the database table that border the other areas.

When you create a 1-2-3 database table, remember these rules:
- The first row of the database must contain the field names. Subsequent rows immediately below the field names must contain the records. Do *not* insert any blank rows or divider lines between the field names (first row) and the records.
- Do *not* leave any blank rows between records in the database.
- The entries in a field must be either *all* labels or *all* values. Do *not* enter values in some records and labels in other records in the same field.
- Field names in a database must be unique. Do *not* use field names that look like cell addresses, such as P12 or Q4.
- Include at least two blank rows and two blank columns on the sides of the database table to separate other worksheet areas.

When working with a 1-2-3 database, you often need to select the area of your worksheet that contains the database. For this reason, you should assign a range name to your database table so you can select it quickly and easily. As you complete the steps of this tutorial, you will see the benefits of using a range name for your database table.

Let's create the database in 1-2-3 using Bruce's database planning sheet, as shown in Figure 7-4. After you create the database, you can enter the movie data.

To enter the field names, set column widths, establish number formats, and assign a range name to the database table:
1. Click **A7**, then enter **Movie** as the first field name. Enter the other field names as labels in row 7 (see the database planning sheet in Figure 7-4).
2. Adjust the column widths as specified by the database planning sheet using ✛.
3. Adjust the column widths of columns J and K to 1 character each; these are the blank columns needed to separate the database table from other worksheet areas.
4. Set the number formats as follows:

Column C	Fixed 0
Column F	Fixed 2
Column G	Fixed 0

5. Select the range A7..I54, click the **Range Name SmartIcon** ▦, then assign the range name **DATABASE**.
6. Click anywhere in the worksheet to unselect the range. See Figure 7-5. Notice that this range includes more rows than records, in case you need to add records to the database later on, such as when Fast Forward adds new movies to their inventory.

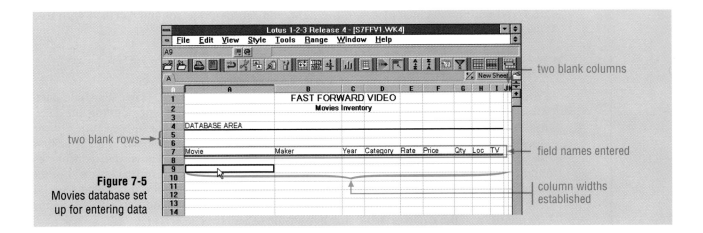

two blank columns

field names entered

column widths
established

two blank rows

Figure 7-5
Movies database set
up for entering data

Once you create the database, you are ready to begin entering data.

Entering Data in the Database

Entering data in a database is the same as entering any other labels and values into a 1-2-3 worksheet. Let's enter the data for the first four records of the Movies database.

To enter records in a database table:

❶ Click **A8**, the location for the first record immediately below the field name. Remember that you should *not* include a blank row between the field name and the first record.

❷ Enter the record for the movie *Romancing the Stone* using the data shown in Figure 7-3.

❸ Continue entering the records for the next three movies only using the data from Figure 7-3. Remember that [End]+[←] is a quick way to return the cell pointer to column A using the keyboard, once you enter the data for a record.

❹ Save the partially completed worksheet database as S7FFV2.WK4, then print the range A1..I20, which contains the report title and database, so that you have a printout of your work.

❺ Close the worksheet.

Now you know how to plan a database, create a database, and enter data in a database. You don't have to enter the remaining data in the database; one of Bruce's associates completed the data entry and saved the worksheet file as C7FFV3.WK4.

Sorting Data

When you initially enter records in a database, they are listed in the order in which you entered them. For example, when Fast Forward receives new movies, Bruce adds these records to the database at the end of the table. However, the reports that Bruce wants require the records to be arranged in alphabetical order by movie name.

To rearrange the records in a database, you must **sort** them. When you sort records, you designate a field as the **sort key**, or **key field**. To sort the records in alphabetical order by movie name, Bruce has to designate the Movie field as the sort key. Because there is only one field being used as a key field, the Movie field is the **primary key**, or **primary sort key**. By sorting the records, 1-2-3 will determine the new order for the database records, in this case listing the movies by name in alphabetical order.

Bruce also wants to sort the database by category, and within each category by movie name. To do this sort, Bruce will need to designate the Category field as the primary key. He also will need to designate *another* key field, called the **secondary key**, or **secondary sort key**. Bruce needs a secondary key to determine the sort order because the same category occurs for more than one movie, which will result in a tie. The secondary key can then act as a tie breaker for the primary key, determining the sequence of the records. Lotus 1-2-3 allows you to use several additional key fields, depending on the number of fields that you expect might result in ties.

Lotus 1-2-3 sorts data in either ascending or descending order. **Ascending order** arranges labels alphabetically from A to Z and values numerically from the smallest to largest number. Also, numbers precede letters and blanks are first in the sort sequence. **Descending order** arranges labels alphabetically backwards from Z to A and values numerically from the largest to smallest number, with blanks appearing last in the sort sequence.

If you are sorting using one key field, you can use the Sort Ascending and Sort Descending SmartIcons, and you can include the field names in the sort selection. But, if you are sorting using more than one key field, you cannot use the SmartIcons; instead, you must use the Range Sort menu selections. When you use the Range Sort menu selections, *do not* include the field names in the sort range. You can use the Range Sort menu selections on any range in a worksheet, since these options are not limited to a database area.

Sorting on a Single Key Field

Bruce wants to produce a movie list with the movie names arranged alphabetically. This list will make it easier for the associates at Fast Forward to look up a movie for a customer. He will use the Movie field as the sort key to sort the database. Because this is the only field he plans to sort by, it is a single key field. You can use the SmartIcons to perform this sort.

REFERENCE WINDOW

Sorting on a Single Key Field

- Click any cell in the column that contains the field you want to use for the sort.
- Click the Sort Ascending or Sort Descending SmartIcon to perform the sort.

Let's produce Bruce's movie list by sorting the Movies database alphabetically by movie name. First, you need to open the worksheet that Bruce's associate completed for him, then sort the database.

To open the worksheet and sort the database records using a single key field:

❶ Open the worksheet C7FFV3.WK4 located on your Student Disk, then immediately save it as S7FFV3.WK4.

❷ Click **A8**, or any other cell in column A of the database table, to sort by the Movie field.

❸ Click the **Sort Ascending SmartIcon**. Wait for the database records to be arranged in alphabetical order. See Figure 7-6.

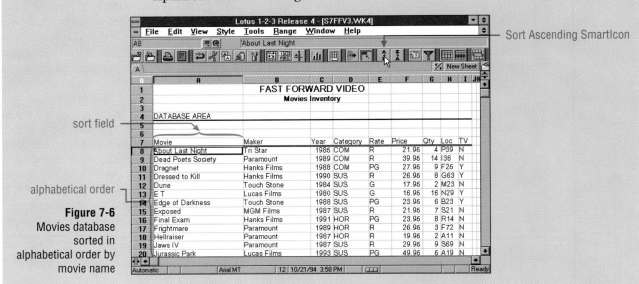

Figure 7-6
Movies database
sorted in
alphabetical order by
movie name

Sort Ascending SmartIcon

sort field

alphabetical order

TROUBLE? If your database is not in the same order as in Figure 7-6, you might have sorted the records in descending sequence or by the wrong field. Repeat Steps 2 and 3.

❹ Preview and print this arrangement of the Movies database including the report heading in rows 1 through 6. If the print area remains selected, click any cell to unselect the print range.

Sorting on More than One Key Field

Bruce wants a movie list that has movies arranged alphabetically by category first, then alphabetically by movie name within the category. In this way, when a customer wants a movie from a particular category, the associates can use this list to look for the movie. This arrangement requires a sort on two fields, with the Category field being the primary key and the Movie field being the secondary key. A sort SmartIcon is not available for sorting more than one field. These sorts must be done using the Range Sort menu selections. Once a sort is performed, 1-2-3 remembers the range containing the data that was sorted, so the range can be used with subsequent sorts. When using the Range Sort menu selections, make sure the field names are *not* included in the sort range.

Sorting on More Than One Key Field

- Select the range containing the database table for the sort. Do not include the database field names in the sort range.

- Click Range, click Sort, then click the Reset button to remove any previous sort specifications, if necessary.

- Use the range selector to specify the Sort by field, then select the sort sequence option.

- Click the Add Key button for the next sort field, then specify the next Sort by field and its sort sequence, continuing until all sort fields are selected.

- Verify and, if necessary, change the sort range so it does *not* include the database field names.

- Click the OK button to initiate the sort.

Let's prepare Bruce's movie list with the movies arranged first by category and then by movie name within category. Because the database was just sorted, 1-2-3 remembers the range containing the database from the other sort.

To sort the database on more than one key field:
❶ Click **Range**, then click **Sort...** to display the Sort dialog box. See Figure 7-7.

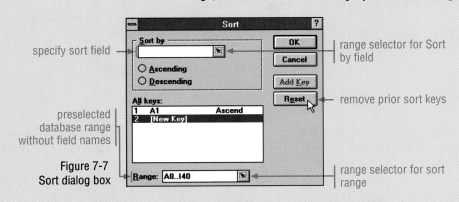

specify sort field

range selector for Sort by field

remove prior sort keys

preselected database range without field names

Figure 7-7
Sort dialog box

range selector for sort range

❷ Click the **Reset button** to remove any previous sort specifications, because this is a new sort.
❸ Click the **range selector** for the Sort by text box to specify the field, then click any cell in the Category field (column D). This field is the primary key. The Ascending option is selected automatically. You can change this by clicking the Descending option button.
❹ Click the **Add Key button** to specify the secondary key.
❺ Click the **range selector** for the Sort by text box to specify the next field, then click any cell in the Movie field (column A). This field is the secondary key.

⑥ Verify that the sort range is A8..I40, which 1-2-3 remembers from the previous sort. If the range is different, enter the correct range by typing it or by using the range selector. Do not include any blank rows in the selected sort range.

⑦ Click the **OK button** to sort the database.

⑧ Click **A8** to unselect the sort range, then scroll the screen to display the field names. See Figure 7-8.

secondary sort key ——— primary sort key ———

Figure 7-8
Movie list report
arranged by category
and movie name

	Movie	Maker	Year	Category	Rate	Price	Qty	Loc	TV
7	Movie	Maker	Year	Category	Rate	Price	Qty	Loc	TV
8	About Last Night	Tri Star	1986	COM	R	21.95	4	P39	N
9	Dead Poets Society	Paramount	1989	COM	R	39.95	14	I36	N
10	Dragnet	Hanks Films	1988	COM	PG	27.95	9	F25	Y
11	Money Pit	Hanks Films	1982	COM	G	29.95	6	L42	Y
12	Off the Wall	King Films	1989	COM	R	19.95	5	D16	N
13	Punchline	MGM Films	1988	COM	PG	21.95	8	P49	Y
14	Risky Business	Touch Stone	1990	COM	R	23.95	11	K19	Y
15	Stir Crazy	Tri Star	1987	COM	R	26.95	7	F14	Y
16	Moonstruck	King Films	1987	DRA	PG	29.95	10	J91	Y
17	Out of Africa	MGM Films	1985	DRA	PG	19.95	5	L32	Y
18	Rainman	United Artists	1988	DRA	R	49.95	16	D62	Y
19	Romancing the Stone	Lucas Films	1983	DRA	G	29.95	3	C14	Y
20	Seventh Sign	Lucas Films	1989	DRA	R	24.95	8	K72	Y
21	Suspect	Touch Stone	1991	DRA	R	29.95	6	F61	N
22	The Accused	Tri Star	1988	DRA	R	27.95	7	J88	N
23	The Killing Fields	Paramount	1984	DRA	R	27.95	4	P21	N
24	Top Gun	Tri Star	1986	DRA	PG	19.95	14	H45	Y
25	Witness	Tri Star	1981	DRA	R	26.95	13	R18	Y
26	Final Exam	Hanks Films	1991	HOR	PG	23.95	8	R14	N

TROUBLE? If the field names were sorted with the database records, click the Undo SmartIcon 🔁 to return the database to its prior sequence. Repeat Steps 1 and 6 to select the correct sort range without the field names or any blank rows, then repeat Step 7.

⑨ Save the sorted 1-2-3 database as S7FFV3.WK4, then print the movie list including the title in rows 1 through 6. If the print range remains selected, click any cell to unselect it.

Now, Bruce has a current movie list, which the associates at Fast Forward Video can use to look up a movie for a customer. He has completed two of the four reports he needs according to his planning analysis sheet in Figure 7-2.

If you want to take a break and resume the tutorial at a later time, you can exit 1-2-3 by double-clicking the Control menu box in the upper-left corner of your screen. When you resume the tutorial, launch 1-2-3 and place your Student Disk in the disk drive. Open the S7FFV3.WK4 worksheet file, select the Tutorial 7 SmartIcon palette, then continue with this tutorial.

Querying a Database

Bruce has sorted the Movies database and produced two movie lists, but he still needs two more reports. For these reports, Bruce does not need to work with all the records in the database—he wants to know which movies should be reordered. To find this out, he will query the database. To **query** a database means to ask questions of the database using criteria that you specify. The **criteria** are the conditions that you use to determine which records you want to work with. By specifying the criteria, you work with only those records that match the conditions. Bruce needs to query the database to determine the records that meet the criteria for reordering, which is when the quantity in stock is less than seven units.

When you query a 1-2-3 database, the criteria act as a filter, as illustrated in Figure 7-9. Only the records satisfying the criteria are copied to a query table located elsewhere on your worksheet. A **query table** contains the selected data that is filtered from your database table. The query table is similar to a chart or a drawn object that you place on a worksheet. Bruce can use a query table to produce an **exception report**—a report that contains only the records selected by the query. The query table will let Bruce see which movies he needs to reorder without having to look at all the records in the database.

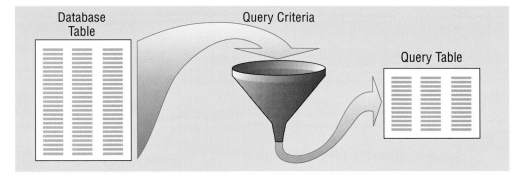

Figure 7-9
Query criteria filters
records from
database

Relational operators are used when you specify the criteria for a query (Figure 7-10). They indicate the comparison that is to be made, such as those Movies with Qty < 7 (that is, the quantity in stock is less than seven).

Operator	Symbol
Equal to	=
Not equal to	<>
Less than or equal to	<=
Less than	<
Greater than or equal to	>=
Greater than	>

Figure 7-10
Relational operators

Creating a Query

Creating a query involves several steps. First, you select the fields that you want to include in the query table. Bruce wants all the fields in his database included in the query, although he could specify any subset of the fields. Next, you select the criteria that you want to use as a filter by specifying the fields, operators, and values. For example, Bruce needs to tell 1-2-3 that he wants a list of movies with a quantity less than seven (Qty < 7). Then, you need to select the area of the worksheet where you want to place the query table. Remember that if any data exists at that location, it will be overwritten by the query table. Bruce wants his query table to appear immediately to the right of the database table. This will allow him to move quickly between the two areas using [Tab] and [Shift][Tab]. Finally, Bruce will tell 1-2-3 to perform the query. Bruce is creating a new query; however, once a query has been created, you can change or modify it with different data.

REFERENCE WINDOW

Querying a Database

- Click the range name selector to display the list of range names, then click the range name of your database table. If you didn't name the database range, name it now.
- Click the Create Query SmartIcon to display the New Query dialog box.
- Click the Choose Fields button to display this dialog box, select the fields to be included in the query table, then click the OK button.
- Click the Set Criteria... button to display this dialog box.
- Using the Field list box, select the field you want.
- Using the Operator list box, select the relational operator you want.
- Using the Value list box, select the value you want, then click the OK button.
- Using the select location range selector, specify where you want the upper-left corner of the query table to appear in the worksheet.
- Click the OK button to produce the query table as a 1-2-3 object.

Let's query the Movies database and produce Bruce's exception report—the order list for those movies with less than seven units in stock.

To query the database and extract selected records as a query table in order to produce an exception report:

❶ Click the **range name selector** 🖾 then click **DATABASE** to select the database table for performing the query.

❷ Click the **Create Query SmartIcon** 🖾 to display the New Query dialog box. See Figure 7-11.

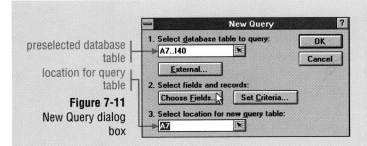

preselected database
table

location for query
table

Figure 7-11
New Query dialog
box

> **TROUBLE?** If range A7..I40 does not appear, the database range might not be selected. Click the Select database table to query text box, press [F3] to display the Database Names dialog box, then click DATABASE.

Now, select the fields to be displayed in the query table.

❸ Click the **Choose Fields... button** to display the Choose Fields dialog box. See Figure 7-12.

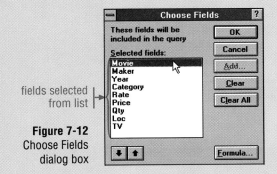

fields selected
from list

Figure 7-12
Choose Fields
dialog box

Select all the fields in the Selected fields list box, then click the **OK button** to return to the New Query dialog box.

Next, specify the criteria for selecting records.

❹ Click the **Set Criteria... button** to display the Set Criteria dialog box. See Figure 7-13. The criteria list box displays the default values, which are the first selections in the Field, Operator, and Value list boxes.

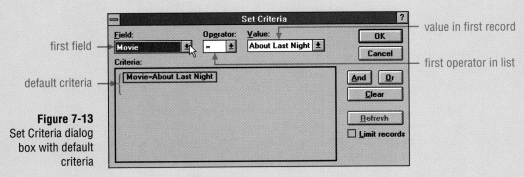

first field

default criteria

Figure 7-13
Set Criteria dialog
box with default
criteria

value in first record

first operator in list

❺ Click the **Field drop-down list arrow**, then click **Qty** to select it.
❻ Click the **Operator drop down list arrow**, then click **<** (less than) to select it.

❼ Click the **Value drop-down list arrow**, then click **7** to select it as the last specification for the criteria.

TROUBLE? If you selected the wrong field, operator, or value, click the appropriate drop-down list arrow, then make the correct selection.

❽ Click the **OK button** to complete specifying the criteria and return to the New Query dialog box.

Once the criteria are specified, you are ready to indicate the location of the query table on your worksheet.

❾ Click the **range selector** for the Select location for the new query table list box, scroll to L7, then click **L7** to specify this cell as the upper-left corner of the query table. You need to specify only the upper-left corner—1-2-3 will take as much space as it needs for the query table.

This completes specifying the query. You are now ready to have 1-2-3 extract the records from the database that meet the criteria and place them in the query table.

❿ Click the **OK button** to perform the query. Scroll the screen to display the query table. See Figure 7-14. Lotus 1-2-3 surrounds the query table with a line to identify it as a query. Note that the SmartIcon palette now displays the SmartIcons used most often with a query, that "Query 1" appears in the selection indicator as the default query name, and that the query table is highlighted, indicating it is selected.

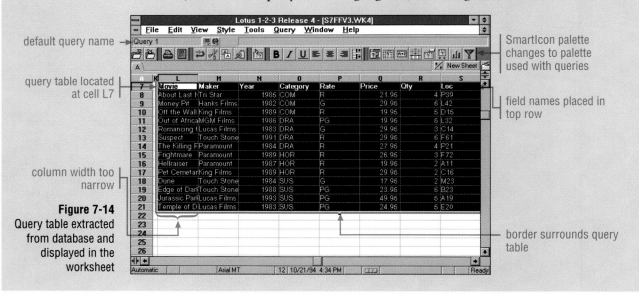

default query name →

SmartIcon palette changes to palette used with queries

query table located at cell L7

field names placed in top row

column width too narrow

Figure 7-14
Query table extracted from database and displayed in the worksheet

border surrounds query table

What's wrong with the query? The column widths used for the database table are *not* repeated in the query table. You need to set these column widths separately. You can set them as you did for the database by using ✛, or you can set them to the width of the longest label or the largest value in each column. Let's set the column widths to accommodate the widest cell entry in each column.

To set the column size to accommodate the widest cell entry:

❶ Verify that the query table is selected. If necessary, click the border of the query table to select it.

❷ Click the **Size Column SmartIcon** 📇 to change the column width for the widest cell entry. See Figure 7-15.

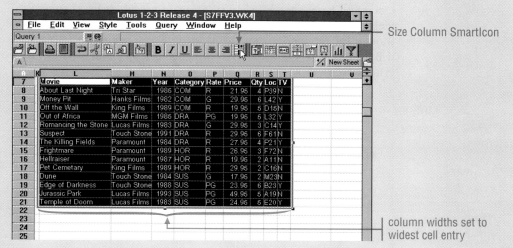

Size Column SmartIcon

column widths set to widest cell entry

Figure 7-15
Query table with column widths set

Bruce wants to add a title to his exception report, so when he prints it and shows it to Jodi, she will also know what the report is for. Let's enter a report title for the exception report. Before you can enter the title you need to unselect the query table.

To unselect the query table and enter a report title:

❶ Click any cell in the extracted records to select the cell and unselect the query table.

❷ Enter the report title and subtitle in column L, as shown in Figure 7-16. Center the titles across columns L through T, boldface them, then increase the size of the main title to 14 points.

report title and subtitle

query table

Figure 7-16
Completed exception report ready for printing

❸ Save the worksheet as S7FFV4.WK4, then print the exception report located in the range L1..T30. If the print range remains selected, click any cell to unselect it.

Changing an Existing Query

Once you have created a query, you can modify it by changing the query criteria. Bruce feels that only those movies with less than five units in stock should be reordered. Even though the demand for movies is great, Bruce knows that Fast Forward Video's movie distributor responds quickly; therefore, the delivery time is short. Bruce wants to change the criteria for the query he created.

REFERENCE WINDOW

Changing an Existing Query

- Select the existing query table by clicking any cell located in the query table.
- Click the Set Query Criteria SmartIcon to display the Set Criteria dialog box.
- Use the appropriate list box—Field, Operator, or Value—to select the field, operator, or value you want to modify.
- Change the criteria as necessary.
- Click the OK button to produce the new results in the query table.

Let's modify the query criteria for Bruce's order list so it contains only those movies with less than *five* units in stock.

To change the data displayed in the query table:

❶ Select the query table by clicking any cell located in it.
❷ Click the **Set Query Criteria SmartIcon** 🗟 to display the Set Criteria dialog box.
❸ Click the **Value drop-down list arrow**, then select **5**. See Figure 7-17.

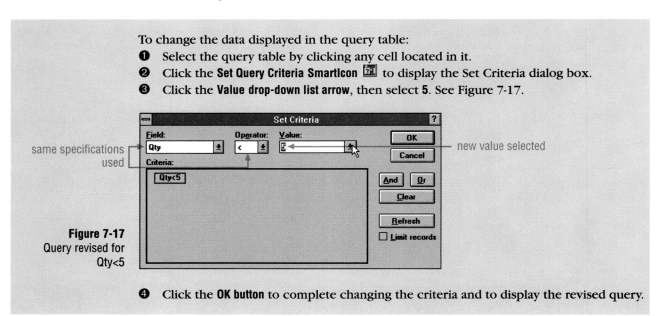

same specifications used

new value selected

Figure 7-17
Query revised for
Qty<5

❹ Click the **OK button** to complete changing the criteria and to display the revised query.

⑤ Print the revised order list, including the report title. If the print range remains selected, click any cell to unselect it.

Bruce has the order list he wants and is ready to phone the distributor to obtain more of these movies.

Finding Records in a Database

You can find records in a database by having 1-2-3 locate the records for you based on the criteria you specify. This saves you from scrolling through an entire database to find a single record or a specific number of records. A common use of this 1-2-3 find operation is when you want to make changes to certain records in your database. You do *not* need to copy the selected records to a separate area of the worksheet because 1-2-3 highlights the records as it finds them in the database table.

REFERENCE WINDOW

Finding Records in a Database

- Click the range name selector to display the list of range names, then click the range name of your database table.
- Click Tools, click Database, then click Find Records....
- Select the field name, operator, and/or value from the appropriate drop-down lists.
- Click the OK button to highlight the selected records in the table.
- If necessary, move through the selected records using [Ctrl][Enter].

Finding a Single Record

When a field contains a data value that uniquely identifies a record, you can perform a find to locate that one record in the database. For example, since each movie has a unique name, a find performed on a movie name locates the record that matches the find criteria you specify.

Top Gun is a popular movie, which people frequently rent and also buy. Bruce decides to check on its price and location so he will be able to answer customer questions quickly. Let's look up the price and location of the movie *Top Gun*.

To find the *Top Gun* record in the Movies database:

❶ Click the **range name selector** 🔲, then click **DATABASE** to select the database table for performing the find.

❷ Click **Tools**, click **Database**, then click **Find Records...** to display the Find Records dialog box. See Figure 7-18. The Movie field name appears in the Field list box and the Operator list box displays = (equal sign).

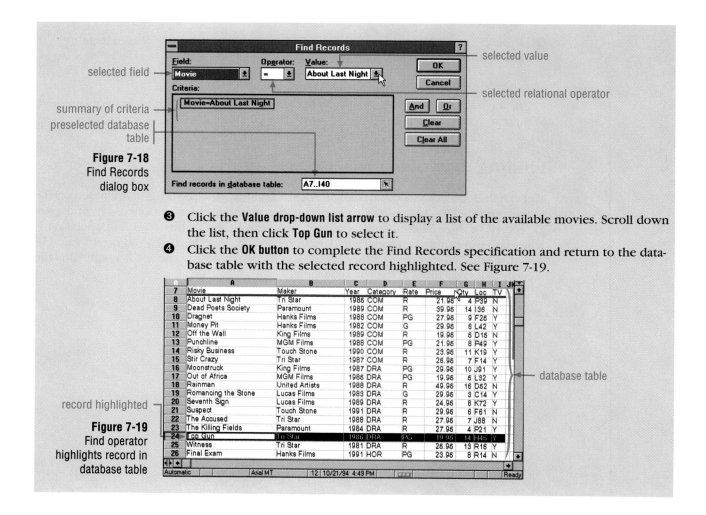

Figure 7-18
Find Records
dialog box

selected field
selected value
summary of criteria
preselected database table
selected relational operator

❸ Click the **Value drop-down list arrow** to display a list of the available movies. Scroll down the list, then click **Top Gun** to select it.

❹ Click the **OK button** to complete the Find Records specification and return to the database table with the selected record highlighted. See Figure 7-19.

record highlighted

Figure 7-19
Find operator
highlights record in
database table

database table

Bruce can see that *Top Gun* has a price of $19.95 and is stored in location H45. Knowing this information will allow him to help his customers more quickly.

Finding Several Records

When several records match the find criteria, 1-2-3 highlights each of them. You can navigate through the series of selected records by using the keys illustrated in Figure 7-20.

To Do This	Press
Go to next record	[Ctrl][Enter]
Go to previous record	[Ctrl][Shift][Enter]
Go to next cell in a record	[Enter]
Go to previous cell in a record	[Shift][Enter]
Edit data in a record	[F2] (EDIT), make your change, and press [Enter]
Unselect highlighted records	[Esc] or click any cell

Figure 7-20
Navigating through
records selected
with find

Because some customers prefer movies produced by certain film makers, Bruce wants to look up the film makers whenever he is asked. Let's look up which films were made by Lucas Films for customers who like this film maker's special effects.

To find all movies in Fast Forward Video's inventory made by Lucas Films:
❶ Click the **range name selector** 🔳, then click **DATABASE**.
❷ Click **Tools**, click **Database**, then click **Find Records...** to display this dialog box.
❸ Click the **Field drop-down list arrow** to display a list of the available fields. Click **Maker** to select it. Observe that the Operator list box displays an equal sign (=), so no additional selection is necessary.
❹ Click the **Value drop-down list arrow** to display a list of the available film makers.
❺ Click **Lucas Films** to select it, completing the find specification. See Figure 7-21.

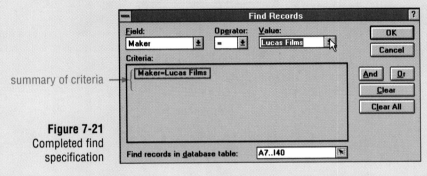

summary of criteria →

Figure 7-21
Completed find
specification

❻ Click the **OK button** to perform the find operation. The selected records are highlighted in the database table. See Figure 7-22.

records highlighted →
Figure 7-22
Records meeting
find criteria
highlighted in
database table

15	Stir Crazy	Tri Star	1987 COM	R	26.95	7 F14	Y
16	Moonstruck	King Films	1987 DRA	PG	29.95	10 J91	Y
17	Out of Africa	MGM Films	1985 DRA	PG	19.95	5 L32	Y
18	Rainman	United Artists	1988 DRA	R	49.95	16 D52	N
19	Romancing the Stone	Lucas Films	1983 DRA	G	29.95	3 C14	Y
20	Seventh Sign	Lucas Films	1989 DRA	R	24.95	8 K72	Y
21	Suspect	Touch Stone	1991 DRA	R	29.95	6 F61	N
22	The Accused	Tri Star	1988 DRA	R	27.95	7 J88	N
23	The Killing Fields	Paramount	1984 DRA	PG	27.95	4 P21	Y
24	Top Gun	Tri Star	1986 DRA	PG	19.95	14 H45	Y
25	Witness	Tri Star	1981 DRA	R	25.95	13 R16	Y
26	Final Exam	Hanks Films	1991 HOR	PG	23.95	8 R14	N

Automatic   Arial MT   12 10/21/94 4:57 PM   Ready

❼ Press **[Ctrl][Enter]** to move to the next record that matches the find criteria. Continue pressing [Ctrl][Enter] until you have looked at all five records for Lucas Films. You can navigate through the selected records using the keys described in Figure 7-20. Then, press **[Esc]** to terminate the find operation.

Using Crosstab to Summarize a Database

Bruce and Jodi would like to know the number of movies they stock in each category produced by each film maker. That is, do they have more comedy (COM) movies from some film makers than they have suspense (SUS) movies from another film maker? Generating a list of the mix of movies they carry in stock will help them decide whether or not they need to purchase additional movies to improve the variety of movies in stock.

In 1-2-3, the crosstab feature produces a cross-tabulation of the data in a database. A **cross-tabulation** is a table that summarizes the data for one field for each combination of data values for any other two fields. This summary is not a copy of the data values from the database but contains calculations performed using the data values. For example, Bruce wants to summarize the movie data for each combination of category and film maker data values by counting the number of records that exist for each combination (Figure 7-23). Lotus 1-2-3 automatically places the crosstab table in a new sheet within the worksheet file.

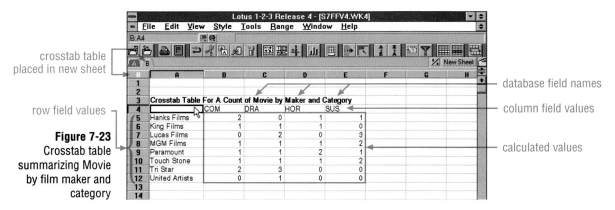

Figure 7-23
Crosstab table summarizing Movie by film maker and category

crosstab table placed in new sheet

row field values

database field names

column field values

calculated values

REFERENCE WINDOW

Summarizing Data with Crosstab

- Click the range name selector to display the list of range names, then click the range name of your database table.

- Click the Cross-tabulate SmartIcon to display the Crosstab Heading Options dialog box.

- Select the correct field in the Row headings and Column headings list boxes.

- Click the Continue button to display the Crosstab Data Options dialog box.

- Select the correct field in the Summarize field list box.

- Click the appropriate Calculate option button.

- Click the Continue button to carry out the cross-tabulation.

Let's use the crosstab feature to produce Bruce's report of a count of movies by film maker and category.

To cross-tabulate a count of the movies by film maker and category:

❶ Click the **range name selector** ⊞, then click **DATABASE** to select the database table.

❷ Click the **Cross-tabulate SmartIcon** ▼ to display the Crosstab Heading Options dialog box. See Figure 7-24.

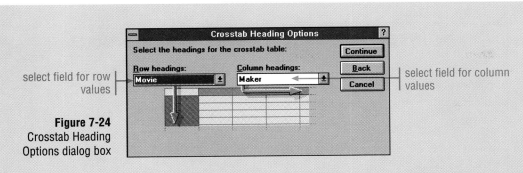

Figure 7-24
Crosstab Heading
Options dialog box

❸ Click the **Row headings drop-down list arrow**, then click **Maker**.
❹ Click the **Column headings drop-down list arrow**, then click **Category**.
❺ Click the **Continue button** to display the Crosstab Data Options dialog box and observe that Movie is already selected as the field to summarize. See Figure 7-25. If the correct field was not selected, you would need to select it now.

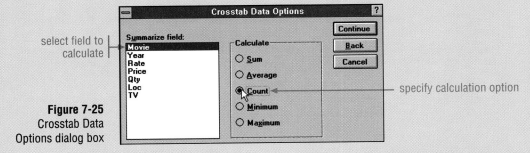

Figure 7-25
Crosstab Data
Options dialog box

❻ Click the **Count option button**, which is the correct calculation method. Because the Movie field contains labels, it doesn't make sense to sum or average them. However, it would make sense to sum the Qty field. Notice the other options you have for calculating the summary.
❼ Click the **Continue button** and wait for the summary to be processed. See Figure 7-26. Notice that the crosstab table is placed on a separate sheet, which *immediately follows* the sheet containing your database.

TROUBLE? If you selected the wrong fields or summary option, click Edit, click Delete, click Sheet, and click the OK button to remove the sheet with the crosstab table. Then, repeat Steps 1 through 7.

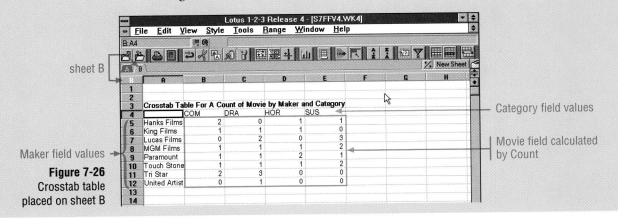

Figure 7-26
Crosstab table
placed on sheet B

❽ Using the column letter, adjust the width of column A to 12 characters to display the entire name of each film maker and complete the report (see Figure 7-23).

Now you are ready to print Bruce's summary. Let's print the crosstab table and return to sheet A where the database table is located.

To print the crosstab table and return to the database sheet:
❶ Select the range A1..E20 in sheet B, then print the range.
❷ Click worksheet tab **A** to return to the database.
❸ Save the worksheet file with the two sheets as S7FFV5.WK4.

Bruce has completed the development of the Movies database and produced the movie list and order list. He created a summary of movies by film maker and category to consider changes in these selections. Jodi and Bruce are confident that this worksheet database will help them manage their inventory better for increased profitability.

Questions

1. This is a description of the data that you want to include in your database table:
   a. field name
   b. data definition
   c. data record layout
   d. file design layout
2. When setting up a 1-2-3 database, which is a rule you should *not* follow:
   a. The first row of the database table must contain the field names.
   b. Do not leave any blank rows between records in the database.
   c. The field names should look like cell addresses.
   d. The entries in a field must be either all labels or all values.
3. To sort customer names in Z-to-A order, which sorting option would you use?
   a. ascending
   b. descending
   c. backward
   d. reverse
4. You need to include two blank rows and two blank columns on the sides of your database table that border other worksheet areas when using this SmartIcon:
   a. 🔲   c. 🖨️
   b. 🔲   d. 🔲
5. When sorting a database using two key fields, which field is the tie breaker:
   a. breaker key
   b. primary key
   c. secondary key
   d. value field
6. When working with a selected set of records from a 1-2-3 database, the conditions you use to specify which records you want are known as the:

a. display values
b. criteria
c. match points
d. filter values

7. Which one of these database commands produces a copy of specified records at another location in the same worksheet?
   a. Find Records
   b. New Query
   c. Sort
   d. Crosstab

8. Which one of these database commands lets you look at selected records in the database without making a copy of them?
   a. Find Records
   b. New Query
   c. Sort
   d. Crosstab

E 9. Using the Task Reference, determine the number of different ways that you can do the same task as those performed with the following SmartIcons. Write down at least one other method for each SmartIcon:

   a. ▢   c. ▢

   b. ▢   d. ▢

Tutorial Assignments

Launch 1-2-3 and open the worksheet T7CPE1.WK4 for Circuits Plus Electronics (CPE). CPE is a mail-order catalog electronics dealer. CPE is clearing out obsolete merchandise from its warehouse. This merchandise will be placed on sale in the upcoming catalog. Mary Matalin has created a 1-2-3 database that includes the inventory for the sale. When creating her database, Mary used the data definition shown in Figure 7-27.

Field Name	Description
Part	Part number of close-out item
Brand	Maker of close-out item
Description	Description of close-out item
Retail	Retail price
Sale	Sale price
Savings	Difference between Retail and Sale price
Quantity	Quantity of item in stock for sale

Figure 7-27

Mary has entered all the data for the close-out items, but she has not arranged them in any specific order. Complete the following tasks to organize Mary's database:

1. Sort the database alphabetically by brand name. Print the sorted database, then save the worksheet as S7CPE2.WK4.

2. Produce a report of all items on sale for less than $300 by performing a query. Place the query table in cell K8. Adjust the columns by using the Size Column SmartIcon.

E 3. Sort the query table in ascending order on the Sale field by using the SmartIcon that sorts records in a query table. Place a title above the query table, indicating that the table lists sale items costing less than $300. Print the query table, then save the worksheet as S7CPE3.WK4.

4. Redo the query for items costing more than $300. Sort the query table in descending order using the Sale field. Then add an appropriate title identifying the table. Print the query table, then save the worksheet as S7CPE4.WK4.

Launch 1-2-3 and open the worksheet S7FFV5.WK4. If you did not create this worksheet in the tutorial, then do so before you continue. Bruce and Jodi have been using the Movies database to manage their inventory. After gaining experience with this application, they would like to refine their queries and add another management report. Help them to manage their inventory better by performing the following:

5. List the movies produced by Lucas Films and place the list in cell W7 in the worksheet. Adjust the column widths as necessary. Sort this list by the Movie field. Add an appropriate title for this movie list report, then print it.

E

6. Revise the first query so that in addition to retrieving all movies with a quantity of less than five, it also retrieves only those movies that have been shown on television. Use the And option in the Set Criteria dialog box to formulate this query by adding the new criterion. Print this revised order list report, including the report title in columns 1 through 6. Then modify the query table and produce a list of movies that have a quantity of less than 10 and that have *not* been shown on television. Print this revised order list.

E

7. Modify the criteria from Assignment 6 using the Or option in the Set Criteria dialog box to produce a list of movies that *either* have a quantity of less than five *or* that have been shown on television. Print this order list report, then compare it to the one from Assignment 6. Is there a difference? If so, what is it?

E

8. Create a cross-tabulation of the sum of the quantity of films by film maker and category. Total each row and column of the cross-tabulation. Print this crosstab report. Save the worksheet as S7FFV6.WK4. What number is displayed in the lower-right corner of this table with the row and column totals?

Case Problems

1. Payroll Processing for Partners in Grime Maintenance

Partners in Grime Maintenance (PGM) provides janitorial services to clients in the Houston Metroplex. Otis Anderson and his wife Christa founded PGM in 1976 when they saw a need for professional janitorial services in the area. Otis felt they could provide better services at a lower price than other companies. Over the years as PGM's business has grown, its number of employees has increased to meet this growth. Christa is responsible for preparing PGM's weekly payroll. With a current staff of about 20 employees, preparing the payroll has become a time-consuming task. A simple error in any one calculation is often difficult to track down. Christa developed a payroll database in 1-2-3 to improve processing the weekly payroll. She uses the database to calculate the gross pay, various deductions, and net pay for each employee. Because PGM has a relatively high employee turnover, using a 1-2-3 database allows Christa to manipulate and change records easily.

The Payroll Register database that Christa set up contains fields described in her data definition, as shown in Figure 7-28.

Field Name	Description
Name	Employee name (last, first)
SSN	Employee social security number
Rate	Hourly pay rate
Reg	Hours worked at regular pay rate
OT	Hours worked that qualify for overtime pay of 1.5 times regular pay rate
Gross	Total pay for weekly pay period
Federal	Federal income tax withholding amount
FICA	Social security contribution amount
State	State income tax withholding amount
Med	Medical insurance employee contribution
Net	Pay for pay period afer all deductions

Figure 7-28

The employees of PGM are asked to choose either a family or individual medical insurance plan. The family plan costs $30 per week, whereas the individual plan costs $18 per week. Since PGM employs several part-time janitors, these employees are allowed to choose only the individual medical insurance plan. Also, the Payroll Register database is set up to include total information required for the completion of the federal and state 941s. (A 941 is a form that is filed summarizing the payroll deduction tax deposits.)

Because the Payroll Register database contains several fields whose values are calculated, Christa set up the database fields in two groups, as shown in Figure 7-29.

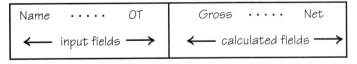

Figure 7-29

All the calculated fields contain formulas, except for the Med field (medical insurance). Christa included the Med field in this group because this is where she wants it to appear in her payroll report. Christa used the following methods to determine the calculated fields in the payroll register:

- Gross—multiply the pay rate by the regular hours worked plus 1.5 times the overtime hours worked
- Federal—multiply 15.8% of the weekly gross pay for each employee
- FICA—multiply 7.8% of the weekly gross pay for each employee
- State—multiply 6.5% of the weekly gross pay for each employee

Christa is preparing to write the payroll checks for this week's payroll. Update the Payroll Register database and summarize the payroll data by performing the following:

1. Launch 1-2-3 and retrieve Christa's P7PGM1.WK4 worksheet file. Immediately save the worksheet as S7PGM1.WK4.
2. Review the database and its field structure. Examine the formulas used for the various calculations. Prepare a database planning sheet from the fields defined in the worksheet.
3. Add the following records to the Payroll Database:

Name	SSN	Wage	Reg	OT	Med
Foster, Gregg	413-98-8902	6.90	40	0	18
Butler, Miriam	312-90-2647	6.55	20	0	18
Diorio, Doris	364-65-7381	7.15	40	5	30
Wackerle, Tiffany	377-97-9076	7.15	40	7	18

Make sure you copy the formulas for the fields that are calculated. Sort the database table alphabetically by name, including the calculated fields. Save the worksheet as S7PGM2.WK4. Preview and print the worksheet. What did you do to make the social security numbers appear correctly?

4. Otis wants to know which employees worked 40 regular hours last week. Produce a report of only these employees. Include an appropriate report title, then print the report. Save the worksheet as S7PGM3.WK4.

E 5. After reviewing the report of those employees who worked 40 regular hours, Otis would like a second report that lists the employees who worked 40 hours and have a wage rate higher than $7.00 per hour. Create a query table using the And option to produce this report. Adjust the column widths, include an appropriate report title, then print the report. Save the worksheet as S7PGM4.WK4.

6. Christa wants a summary report that displays the total gross pay by the regular (Reg) hours worked and the pay rate per hour. Create and print this report. Save the worksheet as S7PGM5.WK4.

E 7. Christa needs to transfer money to the checking account on which the payroll checks are drawn. How much money does she need to transfer this week? She needs to issue checks to the Internal Revenue Service, the State Treasurer, and Blue Care Health for the federal withholding tax, FICA, state withholding tax, and medical insurance. What are the amounts of these checks? What is an advantage of placing the totals above the database table?

2. Applicant Tracking for Seeing Eyes University

The Seeing Eyes University (SEU), started by Dorothy Harrison Eustis in 1929, was the first guide-dog school for the visually impaired in the United States and is accredited by the National Federation of the Blind. SEU trains a guide dog for three months, then trains the guide dog and its owner as a team for one month. SEU uses a variety of dogs; no one breed is better than another. Currently, 7,000 guide dogs are in use throughout the United States. With an estimated 500,000 blind Americans, guide-dog schools have been unable to train enough dogs to meet the demand of the visually impaired.

Jay Kirchner is in charge of allocating guide dogs to qualified applicants for SEU. Jay allocates guide dogs based on the age of the applicant, the activity level of the applicant, and the length of time the applicant has been impaired. Lukas Franck, the school's dean and Jay agree that a 1-2-3 database would help with the recordkeeping activities Jay needs to perform for guide-dog placement. Jay prepared the following data definition, which describes the necessary fields for this database (Figure 7-30).

Field Name	Description
Applicant	Name of applicant
Age	Age of applicant
Activity	Activity level of applicant in everyday life
Duration	Number of years applicant has been visually impaired
Breed	Breed of dog best suited for applicant
Date	Date delivery of guide dog is expected

Figure 7-30

1. Prepare a database planning sheet, then create the guide-dog database using the following records:

Applicant	Age	Activity	Duration	Breed	Date
Gerald Carter	42	Low	12	Retriever	09/02/95
Holly Spencer	19	High	1	Shepherd	12/15/95
Eve Bundridge	56	Medium	11	Retriever	01/09/96

Mark Gorski	28	High	4	Shepherd	12/29/95
Anita Braxton	33	High	5	Shepherd	12/01/95
Bob Jackson	59	Low	14	Labrador	01/31/96

Add an appropriate title and assign a range name to the database table.

E 2. Prepare a report that displays a count of applicants by activity and breed. Add totals for the activity levels and breeds to this summary data in the crosstab table. Save the worksheet as S7SEU1.WK4. Preview and print the database table and the summary report. Close the worksheet.

3. Retrieve the worksheet P7SEU2.WK4, which Jay completed, containing all the current data. How does Jay's database differ from the one you created? Write out the database planning sheet for this database. Add the field name "Sex" in column B to indicate the sex of the applicant, and in column F add the field name "Dog" for the guide dog's name.

E 4. Jay needs to know which guide dogs are to be delivered before 12/31/95. Create this exception report. Adjust the column widths if necessary. Include an appropriate report title. Sort this report in ascending order by date. Save the worksheet as S7SEU3.WK4. Preview and print the report.

E 5. Create three separate reports for each breed of dog trained by SEU. Place an appropriate title on each of these reports. Save the worksheet as S7SEU4.WK4. Preview and print each of the reports.

E 6. What other reports could Jay produce from this database to help him manage the placement of guide dogs? How would each report support his management activities?

3. Membership List Maintenance for Bay Area Personal Watercraft Association

The Bay Area Personal Watercraft Association was formed in the summer of 1992 to bring together people who enjoy personal watercrafts. The association organizes weekend outings to fit the interests of all members. Some members are interested in touring the shorelines of the Pacific Ocean or Mission Bay. Other members prefer to develop freestyle performances. The remaining members like to compete with other members in slalom course racing. Rick Thomas started the association and is in charge of maintaining a membership list, which includes each member's main riding style interest. He uses a 1-2-3 database for this recordkeeping activity. The fields for the database are described in the data definition shown in Figure 7-31.

Field Name	Description
Lname	Member's last name
Fname	Member's first name
Street	Street address
City	City name
ST	State
Zip	Postal zip code
Phone	Telephone number
PWC	Watercraft model owned
Int	Interest in riding style that member prefers (Tour = touring, Free = freestyle, or Slal = slalom)
Mem	Membership type (Ind = individual or Fam = family)
Dues	Membership fee

Figure 7-31

Rick is planning a weekend retreat for the members of the Bay Area Personal Watercraft Association. He needs to mail an information packet to each member as they phone in their reservations for the outing. Help Rick prepare a membership list and the necessary mailing labels by performing the following:

1. Launch 1-2-3 and open the P7BAP1.WK4 worksheet. Review Rick's Membership database.
2. Rick just received several new memberships in the mail; add these to his database. Make sure the named range DATABASE contains these additions.

Philips, Dan	Jones, Wendy	Toshi, Li
234 Euclid Ct	4492 Opal Ave	1143 Royce
San Francisco, CA	Oakland, CA	Sacramento, CA
94118	94609	92804
(415)437-0084	(510)585-8480	(916)672-9370
X2	VXR	WR3
Free	Slal	Free
Ind	Ind	Fam
25	25	35

3. Prepare a membership list arranged by last name. Print the updated membership list and save it as S7BAP2.WK4.
4. As Rick works on planning different events, he wants a summary of the number of members according to their riding interests and type of membership. How many individual members prefer slalom racing in group outings? Include a title for this report. Print a report containing the table with this breakdown. Save the worksheet as S7BAP3.WK4.

E   5. Create an exception report based on criteria that you determine, sort this data as you determine appropriate, and print this report. How is the report useful? Save the worksheet as S7BAP4.WK4.

E   6. Create a crosstab table using fields and a calculation option that you determine and print the summary table. How is this summary useful? Save the worksheet as S7BAP4.WK4.

E   7. Create a macro that produces a single mailing label for any one of the records in Rick's Membership database. Create range names for the MACROS area, for the MAILING macro, and for the LABEL area. The macro should allow Rick to select a record by using the cursor movement keys to point to the last name of the member. The macro should then copy the contiguous fields Lname, Fname, Street, City, ST, and Zip as a row from the database table to a separate work area. A work area is a range of cells in the worksheet that you use to temporarily store cell contents that you want to use elsewhere in the worksheet. By using a work area, you can copy a database record to this range and then always refer to the range when you do other processing. Therefore, you use the same work area regardless of the record selected. Then, the macro should copy the individual fields from the single row work area to a three-line mailing label area, then print the mailing label. (*Hint*: After recording your macro, replace the recorded selection command {SELECT A:A8..A:D8;A:A8} with the generalized command {?}~{ANCHOR}{R 5}~, where the range A8..F8 is the range for whatever row you would have selected when recording your macro.)

E   8. Execute the MAILING macro using the record for Innis, Chaz. Use the cursor movement keys to move to this record during the macro execution, and press [Enter] to select and print the mailing label for Chaz. Print the macro commands separately. Save the worksheet as S7BAP5.WK4.

E   9. What other macros might be useful in manipulating Rick's Membership database? Describe the macro(s) and explain your answer.

Exploring Advanced What-If Alternatives

Determining a Product Mix

CASE

Micro Overflow Corporation* Don Dalton started Micro Overflow Corporation (MOC), a full-service personal computer outlet for the disabled, in his garage four years ago. MOC sells **turnkey systems**, complete computer systems that include all the necessary hardware, software, and training so their owners can immediately begin to use them.

Don's goal in starting MOC was to remove obstacles for the physically challenged in the workplace. Don is paralyzed from the neck down and confined to a wheelchair—he experienced firsthand the need for this type of product. MOC's computer systems are unique because they are configured with special hardware and software for the specific needs of each user. Some MOC systems are sold with optical readers that scan documents and then "read" the words aloud, thus enabling the visually impaired to receive printed information. Other MOC systems include accessors that allow users to control the computer with voice commands, eye movements, or special purpose keypads, rather than the standard keyboard.

*Adapted from: "A PC Revolution: Aided by Computers, Many of the Disabled Form Own Businesses," *Wall Street Journal*, October 8, 1993, page 1.

Don's goal is for MOC to reach $4 million in sales in the next four years. He needs to determine if and how this will be possible by developing a business plan. His business plan will show how many turnkey systems MOC needs to sell in order to cover the cost of Don's ten-room office suite and the payroll, which has expanded to nine people, *and* to make a profit. Although each system is configured to the special needs of each user, Don classifies the systems into two general categories—readers and accessors. In preparing his business plan, Don needs to explore his product mix; that is, the number of each of these two categories of systems he expects to sell.

Another factor Don needs to include in his business plan is the cost percent. The **cost percent** is the cost of goods compared to the total sales in dollars (not units). As MOC sells more systems, it can buy the specialized equipment it uses in greater volumes, which will reduce costs. In other words, as sales go up, the cost of goods goes down.

Don asks his assistant, Kris Retzke, to help him prepare a projected income statement to allow him to explore alternative revenues and expenses for the next four years. Don and Kris discuss the line items and data values they need in the worksheet. These include the expected number and selling price of each type of system together with the cost of goods, the operating expenses, and the earnings before taxes. The cost of goods consists primarily of the hardware and software used in each system. Kris gathers all the information she needs and prepares a draft of the projected income statement with an initial product mix of reader and accessor computer systems (Figure 8-1).

Micro Overflow
Projected Income Statement

	1995	1996	1997	1998
Systems sold				
Readers	120	146	179	218
Accessors	90	119	157	207
Prices per unit				
Readers	8,500	8,600	8,700	8,800
Accessors	10,500	10,650	10,800	10,950
Sales revenue				
Readers	1,020,000	1,259,040	1,553,890	1,917,535
Accessors	945,000	1,265,220	1,693,613	2,266,618
Net sales	$1,965,000	$2,524,260	$3,247,502	$4,184,154
Cost of goods	1,218,300	1,565,041	2,013,451	2,594,175
Gross Profit	746,700	959,219	1,234,051	1,589,979
Operating expenses				
Salaries	372,000	409,200	450,120	495,132
Benefits	104,160	114,576	126,034	138,637
Marketing	157,200	201,941	259,800	334,732
General and admin	49,125	63,107	81,188	104,604
Interest expense	11,000	11,000	11,000	11,000
Total	693,485	799,823	928,141	1,084,105
Earnings before tax	$53,215	$159,395	$305,910	$505,873
Return on sales	2.7%	6.3%	9.4%	12.1%

Figure 8-1
Kris's draft of MOC's projected income statement

Kris reviews her worksheet with Don. He thinks it looks good and explains that next they need to do several what-if analyses to calculate the cost of goods based on cost percents that change with the number of systems they sell. They discuss the range of sales for each type of system that might occur next year. What would happen to operating costs and profit as more readers and accessors are sold? Which product mixes are most profitable? Kris considers these questions and develops a planning analysis sheet in preparation for evaluating Don's alternative product mixes (Figure 8-2).

Planning Analysis Sheet

My goal:
Prepare alternative analyses to determine the best product mix of computer systems sold and to evaluate reduced costs from increasing systems sold

What results do I want to see?
Projected income statement for each of the following alternatives:
—Reduced costs from volume purchasing
—Product mix for break-even
—Varied product mix options

What information do I need?
Decision tables for volume purchasing that specify cost percents for different amounts of net sales

Range of product mix alternatives for 1995
—Readers   80 to 160 systems
—Accessors   70 to 110 systems

What other calculations will I perform?
Cost of sales = net sales * cost percent
Cost percent = select percent based on net sales amount

Figure 8-2
Kris's planning
analysis sheet

In this tutorial you will use Kris's worksheet and learn how to use 1-2-3 to explore various what-if alternatives.

Retrieving the Worksheet

First you need to retrieve and examine Kris's worksheet in preparation for exploring alternative what-if analyses.

To select the Tutorial 8 SmartIcon palette and open the worksheet:

❶ Launch 1-2-3 and select the Tutorial 8 SmartIcon palette using the SmartIcon palette selector ▥ in the status bar.

❷ Open Kris's worksheet file, C8MOC1.WK4, located on your Student Disk.

❸ Immediately save the worksheet as S8MOC1.WK4 in the event you want to restart the tutorial.

In calculating the number of systems sold and the price per system in the projected income statement for MOC, Kris used constants for the first year of the plan. For the remaining years, she used a growth rate for the number of systems sold and an annual dollar amount increase for the price per unit. These values were then used to calculate the sales revenue for each type of system, which were then summed to determine the net sales amount. The cost of goods was calculated by multiplying the cost percent by the net sales. Let's examine Kris's worksheet and the formulas she used to calculate these planning items.

To review Kris's worksheet and examine the formulas used in calculating net sales and cost of goods:

❶ Click **B6**. This cell contains a constant. Examine the contents of cells B7, B9, and B10.

❷ Click cells **C6**, **D6**, and **E6**. Note that the annual growth rate for the number of readers sold is the same each year.

❸ Click cells **C7**, **D7**, and **E7** to see that the annual growth rate for the number of accessors sold is the same each year.

❹ Click cells **C9**, **D9**, and **E9** to see that the expected annual increase in the price per reader is the same.

❺ Click cells **C10**, **D10**, and **E10** to see that the anticipated annual increase in the price per accessor is the same.

❻ Examine the formulas in cells B12 through E14, which calculate the sales revenue and net sales.

❼ Click **B16**, the cell containing the formula used to calculate the cost of goods using a constant for the cost percent. Click cells **C16**, **D16**, and **E16** to see that the same constant is used every year.

❽ Inspect other cells in the worksheet and review the formulas used in their calculations.

Kris reviews her worksheet before performing any analyses.

Auditing the Worksheet

As Kris looks over her worksheet, she notices the Circ indicator in the status bar (Figure 8-3).

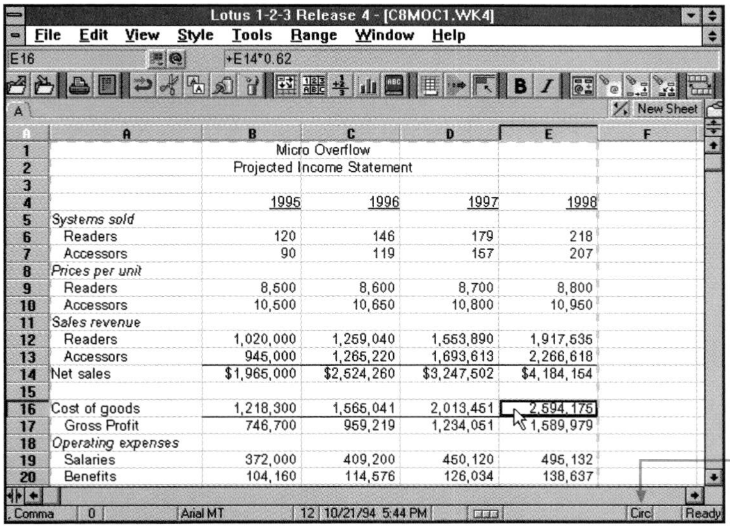

Figure 8-3
Kris's worksheet
with Circ indicator

Lotus 1-2-3 detected a circular reference in the worksheet. A **circular reference** is a cell address in a formula in which the calculated value of the formula in the cell depends on the value in that same cell. Because the cell does not initially contain a value, zero is used in the formula the first time the worksheet is calculated. Each time a value is entered in a cell, the worksheet is recalculated, including the cell with the circular reference. Depending on the formula, the calculated result might change each time the worksheet is recalculated—usually not a desirable situation. Although there are some advanced applications in which circular references are desirable, most circular references are the result of an incorrect cell address in a formula, and these need to be detected and corrected.

Lotus 1-2-3's audit feature helps you find the cell containing the error. The audit feature helps you inspect the overall logic of a worksheet. It helps you find and analyze formulas, circular references, and links to other worksheet files or applications. If you are using a worksheet that someone else created, the audit feature can quickly identify cells that contain formulas. When your own worksheets start to get large and complex, the audit feature can help you review its organization. The audit feature can also make what-if analyses easier by identifying cells that will change when a new what-if value is entered. It can also let you know if a specific cell or range of cells is referenced by any formulas elsewhere in the worksheet.

Let's find the cell containing the circular reference and fix it now.

To find and correct the circular reference:

❶ Click the **Circ indicator** in the status bar. The cell pointer moves to cell E24. Note that the formula is @SUM(E19..E24). The cell is referencing itself. As necessary, scroll the worksheet window so cell A18 is also visible.

❷ Press **[F9]** (CALC) to recalculate the worksheet, and observe the result in cell E24. This value will continue to increase each time the worksheet is recalculated because of the circular reference.

❸ Edit the formula in cell E24 so it is @SUM(E19..E23). The Circ indicator in the status bar disappears.

❹ Click the **Save SmartIcon** to save the changes made to this worksheet.

Figure 8-4 lists additional audit situations that 1-2-3's audit feature can help you with. *Note:* These audit activities, other than circular references, are available only in the commercial version of the software.

Audit Activity	Description
All formulas	Identifies all cells in the worksheet that contain formulas to distinguish input data values from calculated values
Formula precedents	Examines cells whose results are used in calculating a selected cell
Cell dependents	Identifies cells that are calculated using the result from the selected cell
Circular references	Inspects cells involved in a circular reference in which the calculated value for a cell depends on the value in that same cell
File links	Identifies formulas that refer to data in other 1-2-3 worksheet files
DDE links	Checks formulas that refer to a file created with another Windows application

Figure 8-4
Audit analyses

Building in Decisions

The current cost percent (62%) will decrease if total sales increase. Based on her discussion with Don, Kris sketched a decision table (Figure 8-5). A **decision table** details various conditions that can occur and the appropriate action to take for each condition.

If conditions	Then actions
Net Sales	Cost Percent
Less than $2,000,000	62%
$2,000,000 or more	58%

Figure 8-5
Decision table for
cost percents

Lotus 1-2-3 provides two methods for building the logic of a decision table into formulas: the @IF and @VLOOKUP functions.

Using the @IF Function

In 1-2-3 the @IF function allows you to make comparisons, like those in Kris's decision table, that test a condition to determine which action 1-2-3 should take. The @IF function has this general form:

@IF(*expression-1 relational operator expression-2, true-expression, false-expression*)

An **expression** is a formula or value. Values can include text strings such as "yes" or "no." The **relational operators** are the same as those used with queries (refer to the section "Querying a Database" in Tutorial 7). An @IF function is evaluated by 1-2-3 in this manner:

- Calculate the values for expression-1 and expression-2.
- Compare the results of expression-1 and expression-2 using the relational operator and obtain either a "true" or "false" outcome.
- If the outcome is "true," calculate and display the result of the true expression.
- If the outcome is "false," calculate and display the result of the false expression.

Examples of several @IF functions and their components are illustrated in Figure 8-6.

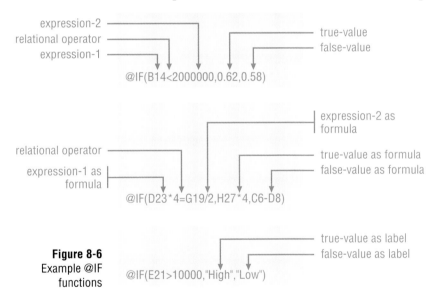

Figure 8-6
Example @IF
functions

Kris decides to set up a key assumption area to display the cost percent values, then to reference these values in the @IF function. Although the values could be entered directly into the @IF function, this arrangement makes it easier for Kris and Don to review and change the cost percent values. Let's set up the key assumption area for the cost percents, as shown in Figure 8-7.

Figure 8-7
Key assumption
area set up with
cost percents

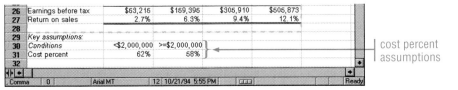

To set up the key assumption area for the cost percents used in the decision table:

❶ Move the cell pointer to cell A29. Then enter the labels, "Key assumptions:," "Conditions," and "Cost percent" as shown in Figure 8-7. Italicize the Key assumptions: and Conditions labels.

❷ In cells B30 and C30, add the labels identifying the conditions under which each cost percent should be used, as shown in Figure 8-7.

   TROUBLE? If the 1-2-3 Classic menu appeared when you typed <, press [Esc], then in cell B30, enter '<$2,000,000. The apostrophe will identify the entry as a label.

❸ Select the range B31..C31. Change the cell format to Percent with zero decimals.

❹ Click **B31**, then enter **.62**, the first cost percent from the decision table.

❺ Click **C31**, then enter **.58**, the second cost percent from the decision table.

Now that Kris has set up her decision table values as key assumptions, she is ready to enter the @IF formula to calculate the cost of goods.

REFERENCE WINDOW

Building in Decisions Using the @IF Function

- Click the cell where you want to display the result of the decision.

- Use the @function selector to choose IF, then specify the condition, replace the true temporary argument (x) with the true expression, and replace the false temporary argument (y) with the false expression.

  or

  Type the @IF formula.

- Type any additional arithmetic to be performed with the result of the @IF function.

- Click the Confirm button or press [Enter].

Let's enter the @IF formula that implements Kris's decision table.

To include the decision table using the @IF formula:

❶ Click **B16**, then enter the formula **@IF(B14<2000000,B31,C31)*B14**.
   (Remember that you can use the @function selector to enter the @IF function, pointing to specify the cell addresses, and the F4 (ABS) key to add absolute referencing.) This formula checks the value of net sales in cell B14. If the value is less than $2,000,000, the formula multiplies that value by the true-condition value, the cost percent in B31 (62%). If the value is equal to or greater than $2,000,000, the formula multiplies the value in cell B14 by the false-condition value, the cost percent in cell C31 (58%).

❷ Select the range B16..E16, then click the **Copy Current Cell SmartIcon** to copy the @IF formula into cells C16, D16, and E16.

❸ Click **E16** to make sure the @IF formula appears. See Figure 8-8. Note that the first and last variables in the formula are relative references and changed accordingly, but the references to the cells containing the cost percents did not change because they are absolute references.

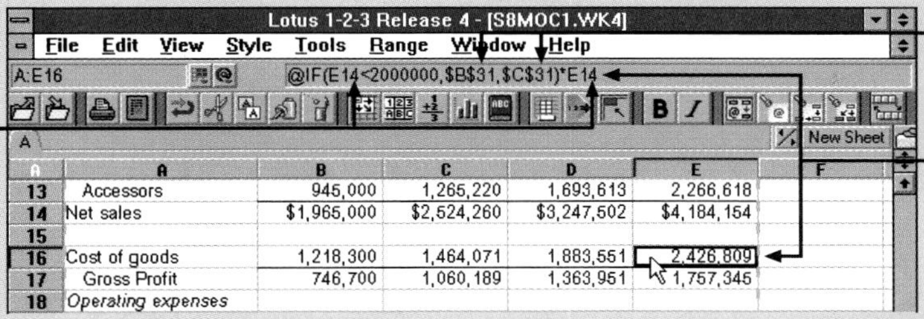

relative references

absolute references

formula with
@IF function

Figure 8-8
@IF formula
implements
decision table

TROUBLE? If cells C16, D16, and E16 contain zeros, you did not include the absolute references for the cost percents. Edit the formula in cell B16 so that it matches the formula in Step 1, then repeat Steps 2 and 3.

❹ Save this modified worksheet as S8MOC2.WK4. It is not necessary to print this worksheet at this time.

After reviewing Kris's worksheet, Don and Kris decide that sales, which have been increasing steadily, could surpass $3 million. They formulate a revised decision table to include a reduction in costs when purchases exceed $3 million (Figure 8-9).

If conditions	Then actions
Net Sales	Cost Percent
Less than $2,000,000	62%
$2,000,000 or more and less than $3,000,000	58%
$3,000,000 or more	55%

Figure 8-9
Decision table for
cost percent
with additional
volume discount

Because this decision table contains three conditions, two @IF functions are necessary for its implementation. The false-condition value is actually another @IF function nested inside the first one. First, a new cost percent value is added to the key assumption area, then the cost of goods formula is modified so it considers all three conditions. Let's make these changes to Kris's worksheet now.

To modify the decision table to include three conditions:

❶ Click **C30**, then enter '**<$3,000,000** as the new condition label for the cost percent of 58%.

❷ Click **D30**, then enter '**>=$3,000,000** as the third condition label.

❸ Click **D31**, then enter **.55** as the cost percent and format this cell as Percent with zero decimals.

❹ Click **B16**. Replace the false-condition in the formula (C31) with @IF(B14<3000000,C31,D31). The complete formula should now read @IF(B14<2000000,B31,@IF(B14<3000000,C31,D31))*B14. The second @IF function is evaluated only if the first @IF function is evaluated as false. This means the net sales amount in cell B14 must be greater than $2,000,000 in order for the second @IF function to be evaluated.

TROUBLE? If the cost of goods is calculated as 1, you did not type two closing parentheses before the multiplication operator, and 1-2-3 automatically inserted a close parenthesis after the B14 cell address at the end of the formula. Edit the formula by placing the two closing parentheses before the multiplication operator and removing the closing parenthesis at the end of the formula after the B14 cell address.

Now copy the @IF formula to the other three years of the plan.

❺ Select the range B16..E16, then click the **Copy Current Cell SmartIcon** to copy the formula into cells C16, D16, and E16.

❻ Click **E16** to confirm that the formula with the nested @IF function appears in this cell. See Figure 8-10.

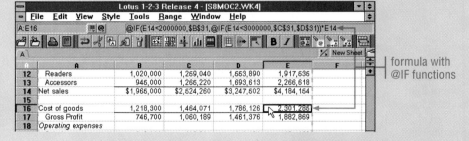

formula with @IF functions

Figure 8-10
Expanded decision
table implemented

❼ Save this modified worksheet as S8MOC3.WK4, then close the worksheet file.

Using a Table Lookup

Kris and Don meet with their purchasing manager, Sara Binder, to further review and refine the costs associated with buying the hardware and software for the readers and accessors. Sara suggests they expand the decision table to include the additional conditions shown in Figure 8-11.

If conditions	Then actions
Net Sales	Cost Percent
Less than $2,000,000	62%
$2,000,000 or more and less than $3,000,000	58%
$3,000,000 or more and less than $4,000,000	55%
$4,000,000 or more and less than $5,000,000	53%
$5,000,000 or more	51%

Figure 8-11
Expanded decision
table for cost percent

This decision table could be implemented using a total of four nested @IF functions with each subsequent @IF function acting as the false-value for the previous @IF function. This would be a rather complex formula to set up. Lotus 1-2-3 provides another method for implementing complex decision tables like this. First, you enter a table of values, known as a **lookup table**, in a convenient cell range. Lotus 1-2-3 then uses an input value to look up another value in the table; this is called a **table lookup**.

Lotus 1-2-3 performs table lookups with the @VLOOKUP and @HLOOKUP functions. @VLOOKUP searches down a column until it finds the input value, then it looks across to the right for the lookup value. @HLOOKUP searches across a row until it finds the input value, then it looks down for the lookup value. Only the @VLOOKUP function is discussed here.

The syntax of the @VLOOKUP function is:

@VLOOKUP(*expression, lookup table range, column-offset*)

The **expression** is the input value. Lotus 1-2-3 searches down the left-most column in the table, column 0 (zero), until it finds a value that is equal to or *less than* the input value. The **lookup table range** is the range in the worksheet containing the lookup table. The **column-offset** is the column number of the lookup table that 1-2-3 should look in after it finds the input value. The first column is always numbered zero. A lookup table can have as many columns as you choose, but the first column must always contain the input values.

Building in Decisions Using the @VLOOKUP Function

- Click the cell where you want to display the result of the table lookup.

- Use the @function selector to choose VLOOKUP, then use pointing to specify the expression (x) and lookup table (range), and type the column-offset number.

  or

  Type the @VLOOKUP formula.

- Specify any additional arithmetic performed with the result of the @VLOOKUP formula.

- Click the Confirm button or press [Enter].

Kris decides it would be easier to add this lookup table to the worksheet if she used her original worksheet before the @IF formulas were added to it, so that she doesn't need to remove the information she entered for the @IF formulas.

To prepare for implementing the lookup table:

❶ Open the S8MOC1.WK4 worksheet and immediately save it as S8MOC4.WK4.

❷ Click the **Go To SmartIcon** [icon] then enter **A29** to position the cell pointer.

❸ Enter **Lookup table for Cost percent:** as the table's title. Enter **Net sales** in cell A30 and **Cost percent** in cell B30 as column headings. Use italics, underlining, and alignment as appropriate. See Figure 8-12.

table title

lookup table

Figure 8-12
Lookup table for
cost percents

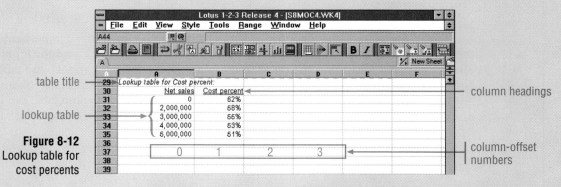

column headings

column-offset
numbers

❹ Format cells B31..B35 (the cost percent values) as Percent with zero decimals. Enter the data values shown in Figure 8-12 for Net sales and Cost percent. Remember to enter the cost percent values as decimal numbers. Your screen should look like Figure 8-12.

With the table in place, Kris is ready to add the @VLOOKUP functions to the formula for calculating the cost of goods.

To include a decision table for the cost percent using the @VLOOKUP function:

❶ Click the **Go To SmartIcon** ▣ then enter **A11** to position the worksheet area for modifying the cost of goods formula that is calculated using the cost percent from the lookup table.

❷ Click **B16**. Enter the formula **@VLOOKUP(B14,A31..B35,1)*B14**. (Remember to use pointing and the F4 (ABS) key as appropriate.)

This selects the desired cost percent from the lookup table and multiplies it by the net sales to calculate the cost of goods.

Now, you need to copy the formula with the @VLOOKUP function to the cells that calculate the cost of goods for the other three years of the plan.

❸ Copy the formula from cell B16 to cells C16..E16.

❹ Click **E16** to confirm that the @VLOOKUP formula appears in this cell. See Figure 8-13.

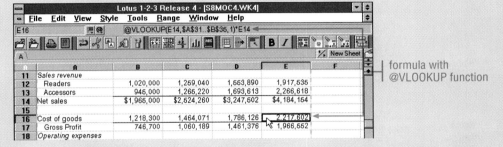

Figure 8-13
@VLOOKUP formula
used to calculate
cost of goods

❺ Click the **Save SmartIcon** 🖫 to save this modified worksheet as S8MOC4.WK4. Then close the worksheet file.

If you want to take a break and resume this tutorial at a later time, you can exit 1-2-3 by double-clicking the Control menu box in the upper-left corner of your screen. When you resume the tutorial, launch 1-2-3, place your Student Disk in the disk drive, and select the Tutorial 8 SmartIcon palette, then continue with this tutorial.

■   ■   ■

After looking over this version of the worksheet, Don decides that it is more realistic to project sales only up to $3,000,000, so he will do further what-if analyses with the S8MOC3.WK4 worksheet, which contains the nested @IF functions.

Protecting the Worksheet

Kris realizes that when she and Don start exploring what-if alternatives using their worksheet, they are going to be changing values in various cells, and she doesn't want any of her formulas to be deleted inadvertently. She decides to protect the worksheet so that the cells containing formulas cannot be changed.

When you **protect**, or **seal**, a worksheet, data in the file cannot be changed except in the cell ranges you specifically *un*protect before the file is sealed. Once a worksheet is sealed, you cannot insert or delete rows or columns, and you can't change cell contents or attributes, column widths, row heights, drawn objects, or query tables.

Using protection is a two-step process. First you need to identify the cells that are *not* to be protected, and then you turn on protection by sealing the file.

REFERENCE WINDOW

Turning on Protection

- Select the collection of cells to remain unprotected.
- Click Style then click Protection... to display this dialog box.
- Click the Keep data unprotected after file is sealed check box, then click the OK button or press [Enter].
- Click File then click Protect... to display this dialog box.
- Click the Seal file check box, then click the OK button or press [Enter].
- In the Set Password dialog box, type your password, press [Tab], then type your password a second time to verify it.
- Click the OK button or press [Enter].

Kris knows that Don wants to explore what-if alternatives with the number of systems sold and the prices per unit in 1995, so she unprotects those cells so that they can be modified after the worksheet is sealed.

To specify the unprotected cell ranges:
1. Open the S8MOC3.WK4 worksheet and immediately save it as **S8MOC5.WK4**.
2. Click the **Home SmartIcon** to display the desired worksheet area.
3. Select the range collection B6..B7 and B9..B10, which contains the input data values for 1995. (Remember that after you select the first range, press and hold down [Ctrl] while you select the other range that makes up the collection.)
4. Click **Style** then click **Protection...** to display this dialog box.
5. Click the **Keep data unprotected after file is sealed check box**. See Figure 8-14. Verify that the Range text box displays the correct collection.

Figure 8-14
Unprotecting
selected cells

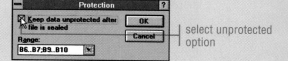

select unprotected option

➏ Click the **OK button** or press **[Enter]** to complete specifying the cells that are to remain unprotected, then press **[Esc]** to unselect the collection.

➐ Click **B6**. Notice that the text in the unprotected cells changes color, and that the status bar displays a "U" to indicate the current cell is unprotected.

Now let's seal the worksheet so only the unprotected cells can be modified.

To seal the worksheet and protect cells from changes:
➊ Click **File** then click **Protect...** to display this dialog box.
➋ Click the **Seal file check box**, then click the **OK button** or press **[Enter]** to display the Set Password dialog box.
➌ Type **DON** in the Password text box (asterisks appear rather than the text you type). Press **[Tab]** to move to the Verify text box, then type **DON** again. See Figure 8-15. Be sure to remember your password, so you will be able to unseal the file later on. Also note that 1-2-3 is case sensitive (the password is in uppercase letters).

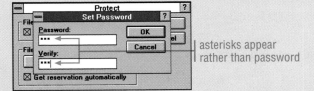

Figure 8-15
Entering password
to seal a file

asterisks appear
rather than password

TROUBLE? If a dialog box appears telling you the passwords do not match, you might have pressed [Enter] instead of [Tab] or you typed the password incorrectly in either the Password text box or the Verify text box. Click the OK button, then repeat Step 3.

➍ Click the **OK button** or press **[Enter]** to complete the password and seal the file.
Now let's try to enter a new value in a protected cell.

➎ Click **C6**. Notice that "Pr" appears in the status bar to indicate the cell is protected.

➏ Type **150**. Because the cell is protected, you cannot enter the new data value and a message for the protected cell displays. See Figure 8-16.

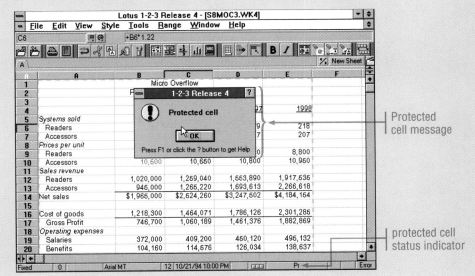

Figure 8-16
Message displays
for protected cell

Protected
cell message

protected cell
status indicator

❼ Click the **OK button** or press **[Enter]** to close the Protected cell dialog box and return to Ready mode.

Note that to unprotect cells, you choose Protection... from the Style menu, and to seal the worksheet, you choose Protect... from the File menu.

Once a file has been sealed, you need to unseal it before any changes can be made to the protected cells. In order to unseal a worksheet file, you need to know the password used to seal it.

REFERENCE WINDOW

Turning off Protection

- Click File then click Protect... to display this dialog box.

- Click the Seal file check box, then click the OK button or press [Enter].

- In the Get Password dialog box type your password, then click the OK button or press [Enter].

Let's unseal the worksheet.

To unseal the worksheet:
❶ Click **File** then click **Protect...** to display this dialog box.

❷ Click the **Seal file check box** to unselect it, then click the **OK button** or press **[Enter]** to display the Get Password dialog box.

❸ Type **DON** then click the **OK button** or press **[Enter]** to complete the password entry and turn off protection.

TROUBLE? If a dialog box appears telling you that your password is incorrect, you mistyped the password. Click the OK button then repeat Steps 1 through 3. Remember to use uppercase letters because 1-2-3 is case-sensitive. If you continue to get the incorrect password, close the worksheet file without saving it, and then reopen it.

❹ Click cell **C6**. Notice that "Pr" no longer appears in the status bar. Type **150** then press **[Enter]**. The new data value is entered in the cell because it is no longer protected.

❺ Click the **Undo SmartIcon** 🔙 to replace the constant data value that you just entered with the original formula.

Let's leave the worksheet unprotected for now.

Hiding Data

Kris and Don go over the worksheet together. Don wants to perform what-if analyses that address these questions:
- How many reader systems need to be sold in 1995 to reach a target return on sales of 20% in 1998 when all other key assumptions in the four-year plan remain the same?
- What is the product mix of readers and accessors that need to be sold in 1995 for MOC to break even?

Because Don is focusing his attention on 1995 and 1998, he wants to hide the columns for the other two years. That way, he can focus on next year's plan and the expected results for the fourth year.

Hiding data is a means of making an entire column or worksheet disappear from the worksheet display. When data is hidden, the attention of worksheet users is focused on only what you want them to see and not on distracting or confidential data. Formulas that refer to data in hidden columns or worksheets continue to work correctly. A hidden column or worksheet can be redisplayed at any time, unless the worksheet is sealed after the columns are hidden. Then the worksheet needs to be unsealed before the hidden data can be redisplayed.

Let's hide the columns for 1996 and 1997 in Kris's worksheet to focus on Don's planning activities.

To hide columns C and D, which contain the data for 1996 and 1997:

❶ Move the pointer to the line that separates column D from column E in the worksheet frame. The pointer changes to ↔.

❷ Drag the pointer left to the line between columns B and C until columns C and D disappear. See Figure 8-17.

columns C and D
are hidden

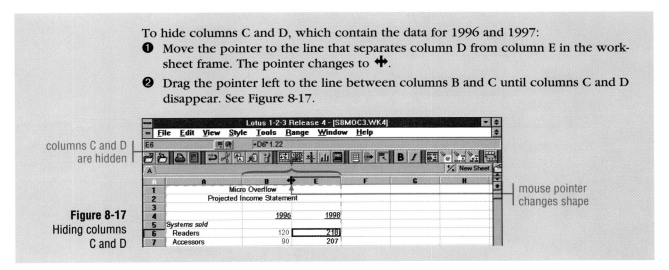

mouse pointer
changes shape

Figure 8-17
Hiding columns
C and D

This gives Don a report that focuses on the desired years of his plan. Now he's ready to explore his what-if questions.

Examining Alternatives with Goal Seeking

Don and Kris decide to use goal seeking, also known as backward solving, to evaluate their questions. **Goal seeking** is the process of changing a constant used in calculating a formula until the formula yields the result you want. The constant is in the **adjust cell**, and the formula that is calculated using that constant is in the **target cell**.

Don wants to see how many more readers need to be sold to make the return on sales in 1998 equal to 20%. The number of readers sold in 1998 is dependent on the number of readers sold in 1995. Don does not want to change any formulas, only constants, so he will adjust the number of readers sold in 1995 until the return on sales in 1998 is 20%.

There are two methods you can use to obtain a goal seeking solution. With the **trial-and-error** method of goal seeking, you manually change the value of the constant in the adjust cell and look for the goal value in the target cell. With 1-2-3's **Backsolver**, an add-in program, a built-in mathematical procedure automatically carries out a series of trial-and-error solutions.

Using the Trial-and-Error Method to Perform Goal Seeking

The trial-and-error method of goal seeking is exactly what it sounds like. Values are entered in the adjust cell until the goal value is attained in the target cell. Don and Kris will adjust the number of readers in 1995 until the return on sales in 1998 equals 20%.

REFERENCE WINDOW

Performing Trial-and-Error Goal Seeking

- If necessary, split the worksheet window so the target and adjust cells are both visible.

- Click the adjust cell to select it.

- Enter a new trial value and observe the result in the target cell.

- Repeat entering new trial values in the adjust cell until the desired goal result appears in the target cell.

Let's use Kris's worksheet to evaluate Don's goal seeking alternative for a 20% return on sales in 1998.

To use the trial-and-error method of goal seeking:

❶ Split the worksheet window horizontally and scroll the worksheet as necessary so that rows 4 through 15 appear in the top window, and rows 23 through 27 appear in the bottom window. Note that cell E27 contains the return on sales for 1998. See Figure 8-18.

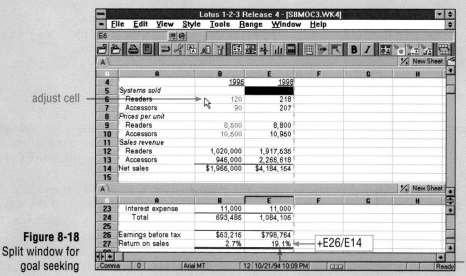

Figure 8-18
Split window for goal seeking

❷ Click **B6**, the adjust cell.

❸ Enter **130**. The return on sales in 1998 changes to 19.7%.

The sales in 1995 need to be higher. Let's try 140.

❹ Enter **140**. The return on sales in 1998 is 20.2%.

This is more than the desired goal value, so the sales in 1995 need to be between 130 and 140.

❺ Enter **135**. The return on sales in 1998 is 19.9%, which is just slightly less than the desired goal value.

❻ Enter **136**. The return on sales is now 20%, which is the desired goal.

❼ Click the **Save SmartIcon** 🖺 to save the worksheet. Preview and print the worksheet.

Although trial-and-error is not the most elegant way to do goal seeking, it does produce the desired result without rewriting any formulas. With some practice, goal seeking by trial-and-error provides a reasonable method for exploring what-if alternatives where a goal value is known for a formula. Lotus 1-2-3 does provide a means for obtaining a more organized series of solutions by using a what-if table, as described later in this tutorial.

Using Backsolver to Perform Goal Seeking

Lotus 1-2-3 Release 4 for Windows provides the Backsolver feature, which automatically calculates a goal seeking solution. With Backsolver, all you need to do is specify the target cell, its desired goal, and the adjust cell or cells. Lotus 1-2-3 quickly carries out a series of trial-and-error solutions to arrive at the specified goal value.

You can have Backsolver adjust more than one cell in a single solution to attain the desired goal value. In this situation, Backsolver changes the values in all the adjust cells *by the same percentage*.

REFERENCE WINDOW

Using Backsolver for Goal Seeking

- If necessary, split the worksheet window so the target and adjust cells are both visible in the worksheet window.

- Click Range, click Analyze, then click Backsolver... to display this dialog box.

- Enter the target cell address in the Make cell text box.

- Enter the goal value for the target cell in the Equal to value text box.

- Enter the adjust cell address(es) in the By changing cell(s) text box.

- Click the OK button or press [Enter].

Don wants to explore his second what-if alternative. He wants to find the product mix that provides him with a break-even point during the first year of his plan. **Break even** occurs when revenues are equal to expenses; that is, the earnings before tax and return on sales are zero. Under these conditions, Don expects that the relationship between the number of reader and accessor systems sold would be the same as the initial ratio of 120 to 90, that is, 4 readers to each 3 accessors.

To find a break-even solution for the first year:

❶ Scroll the top window so that rows 6 through 17 appear.

❷ Click **B6** then enter Don's initial value of **120**. This is necessary to preserve the ratio of 120 readers to 90 accessors in his initial plan.

❸ Click **Range**, click **Analyze**, then click **Backsolver...** to display this dialog box.

Next you need to choose the target cell, called the "Make cell" in Backsolver.

❹ Enter **B27** in the Make cell text box.

Now enter the goal value.

❺ Enter **0** in the Equal to value text box, which is the break-even target value.

Now enter the adjust cells.

❻ Enter **B6..B7** in the By changing cell(s) text box.

❼ Click the **OK button** or press **[Enter]** to obtain the goal seeking solution. See Figure 8-19.

break-even product mix

break-even profit goal

Figure 8-19
Product mix for break even in 1995

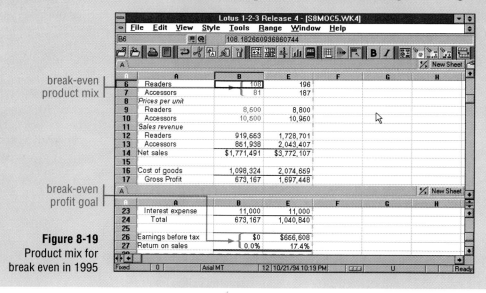

Now let's redisplay the hidden columns.

find break-even point during first year

On the assignment Subway Sandwich Rick wants to know the annual weekly sales for break even.

To redisplay hidden columns:

❶ Move the pointer to the line that separates column B from column E in the worksheet frame. Again, the pointer changes to ✛.

❷ Drag the pointer to the right until you reach the right edge of column E. When you release the mouse button, column D appears and is set to a width of 11 characters. See Figure 8-20. When redisplaying hidden columns in this manner, you need to display them one at a time.

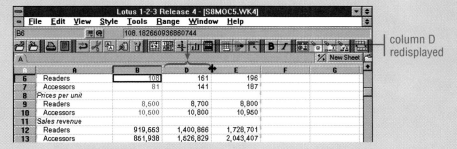

column D redisplayed

Figure 8-20
Redisplay of
previously hidden
column D

TROUBLE? If you try to redisplay both columns at one time, column D will be set to a width of 22 characters. Use the pointer to reduce the width to 11 characters, then continue with the next step.

Next column C can be redisplayed.

❸ Move the pointer to the line between columns B and D, then drag the pointer to the right until you reach the right edge of column D. Again, when you release the mouse button, column C appears and is set to a width of 11 characters.

❹ Click the **Save SmartIcon** 🖫 to save the modified worksheet. Preview and print the worksheet, then close this file.

If you want to take a break and resume this tutorial at a later time, you can exit 1-2-3 by double-clicking the Control menu box in the upper-left corner of your screen. When you resume the tutorial, launch 1-2-3 and place your Student Disk in the disk drive. Select the Tutorial 8 SmartIcon palette, then continue with this tutorial.

Exploring Alternatives with What-If Tables

Don and Kris consider the different alternatives that have been explored. In each situation, a single solution was produced and the results printed. Although this gives Don a good idea of how different product mixes affect the potential profitability of MOC, he needs to look at several different worksheets to compare the alternatives. Don would like to be able to compare these alternatives in one report.

Don decides to use a what-if table, also known as a data table, to display the different alternatives in one worksheet. A **what-if table** lets you calculate and display results for a series of what-if alternatives all at one time. The table shows the results of a formula using a series of input data values for a selected cell. You place the table in a conveniently located cell range in your worksheet so you can easily review and compare the results of the different what-if alternatives. A one-variable what-if table, sometimes called a one-way data table, allows you to change one input data value and capture calculated values for one or more different formulas. A two-variable what-if table, or a two-way data table, lets you change two input data values and display the calculated results for a single formula.

Don and Kris decide to prepare a what-if analysis to evaluate alternative numbers of systems sold during their four-year plan. The questions they want to address are:

- What are the earnings before tax for each year when the number of reader systems sold in 1995 ranges from 80 to 160 in increments of 10, while all other key assumptions remain unchanged?
- What are the earnings before tax in 1995 when the number of reader systems sold ranges from 80 to 160 in increments of 10 *and* the number of accessor systems sold varies from 70 to 100 in increments of 10, while all other key assumptions remain unchanged?
- Which product mixes of reader and accessor systems sold are profitable in the first year of the plan, that is, which combinations exceed break even?

One-Variable What-If Table

First, Don and Kris want to determine the earnings before tax for each of the four years when the number of reader systems sold in 1995 varies from 80 to 160. Because they will change the value in only one cell, they can use a what-if table with one variable.

In general, a one-variable what-if table is arranged as illustrated in Figure 8-21. The table resides in a cell range with a series of input values in the first column of the table. The top row of the table contains one or more formulas that are evaluated using each input data value. The results for each formula are displayed in the same column as the formula in the rows immediately below it. The upper-left corner of a one-variable what-if table can either be blank or contain a label for documentation. The input cell is the cell whose value is replaced by the series of input values. When the what-if table is calculated, the input cell is temporarily given each of the data values from the series of input data values in the leftmost column of the what-if table. The entire worksheet is recalculated and the results of each formula are then stored in the appropriate row of the what-if table.

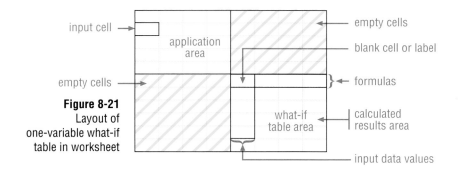

Figure 8-21
Layout of
one-variable what-if
table in worksheet

input cell → application area → empty cells → blank cell or label → empty cells → formulas → what-if table area → calculated results area → input data values

Using a One-Variable What-if Table

- Set up the table in a convenient cell range with the input data values in the left-most column and the formulas to be calculated in the top row.

- Click Range, click Analyze, then click What-if Table... to display this dialog box.

- Click the Number of variables drop-down list arrow, then select 1.

- Click the range selector for the Table range text box, then select the range that includes the left-most column of input values and the top row of formulas.

- Click the range selector for the Input cell 1 textbox, then select the input cell for the input data values.

- Click the OK button or press [Enter].

The first thing you need to do is to select an area of your worksheet for the what-if table. Don and Kris decide to use the area immediately below the projected income statement.

Let's begin constructing a one-variable what-if table to address Don's question—What are the earnings before tax each year when the number of reader systems sold in 1995 varies from 80 to 160 in increments of 10? Kris again decides the worksheet with the nested @IF functions is most appropriate for this analysis.

To enter a title for the table and label the table's left-most column for documentation:
➊ Open the **S8MOC3.WK4** file and immediately save it as **S8MOC6.WK4**.
➋ Click the **Home SmartIcon** [⬚], then split the worksheet window horizontally and scroll it so the systems sold are shown in the top window and the range that will contain the what-if table (rows 33 to 43) is in the bottom window.
➌ Enter the labels in cells A33 and A34, as shown in Figure 8-22.

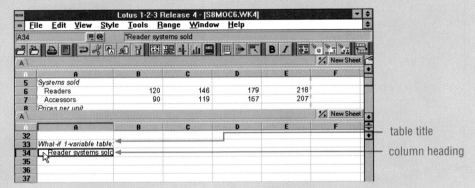

Figure 8-22
Documentation
for one-variable
what-if table

Next let's enter the input data values in the left-most column of the table using Fill by Example to create the series of values.

To enter the what-if table input data values using Fill by Example:
➊ Enter **80** and **90** in cells A35 and A36, respectively.
You input two values to give 1-2-3 the increment value.
➋ Select the range A35..A43, then click the **Complete Sequence SmartIcon** [⬚] to fill this range with values incremented by 10.

Now let's set up the formulas whose values will be stored in the what-if table when it is calculated—in this table, the earnings before tax for each of the four years. The cell formulas +B26, +C26, +D26, and +E26 provide a convenient method for collecting these values from the application area of the worksheet. Rather than displaying the data values for these formulas in the top row of the what-if table, let's display the formulas as text to serve as a reminder of how the results are obtained.

To enter formulas for calculating the results for the what-if table:
➊ Enter the formula **+B26** in cell B34.
➋ Select the range B34..E34, then click the **Copy Current Cell SmartIcon** [⬚] to place, in these cells, formulas that reference the formulas calculating the earnings before tax for each year.

find out earning before tax for each year.

❸ Format these four cells as Text so the formulas appear rather than the results of the formulas. See Figure 8-23.

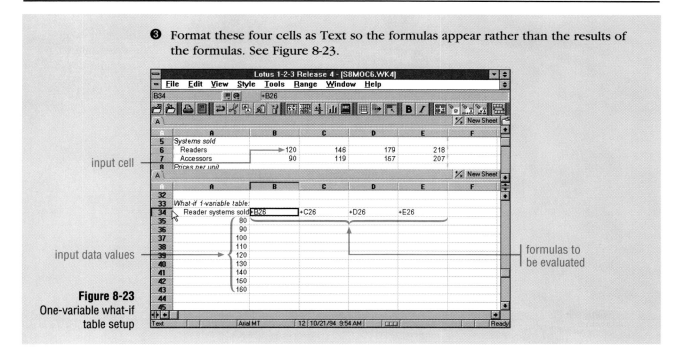

input cell

input data values

formulas to be evaluated

Figure 8-23
One-variable what-if table setup

Once the what-if table is set up, it is ready to receive the calculated results. Let's recalculate the worksheet using the input data values from the what-if table.

To calculate and place the results in the what-if table:

❶ Click **Range**, click **Analyze**, then click **What-if Table...** to display this dialog box.

❷ Click the **Number of variables drop-down list arrow**, then select 1 because this table has only one input cell.

❸ Click the **range selector** for the Table range text box, then select the range A34..E43.

Next, you need to select the input cell. This is the cell whose value is replaced by the input data values in the table's first column before the worksheet is recalculated.

❹ Click the **range selector** for the Input cell 1 text box, then click **B6**, the input cell, to complete specifying the what-if table. See Figure 8-24.

indicates what-if table with one variable

includes input data value column and formula row

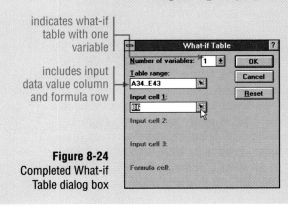

Figure 8-24
Completed What-if Table dialog box

❺ Click the **OK button** or press **[Enter]** to calculate the what-if table. This might take a while because the entire worksheet is recalculated for each of the input data values. Scroll the bottom worksheet window as needed to display the what-if table. See Figure 8-25.

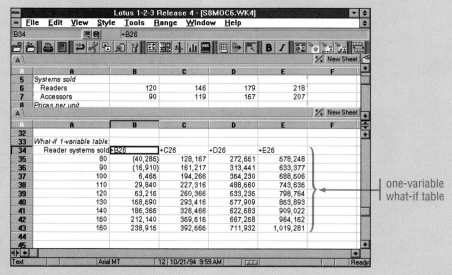

Figure 8-25
Completed
one-variable
what-if table

❻ Click the **Save SmartIcon** to save this as file S8MOC6.WK4. Then preview and print the one-variable what-if table.

In reviewing the what-if table, Don sees that all combinations of reader systems sold are profitable except those for 80 and 90 systems in 1995. He decides to take a closer look at the profitable product mixes in 1995.

Two-Variable What-if Table

Don and Kris want to evaluate the profitability of various product mixes of reader and accessor systems to be sold in 1995. This what-if evaluation involves two input data values.

In general, a two-variable what-if table is arranged as illustrated in Figure 8-26. The table contains one series of input data values in the left-most column of the table and the second set of input data values in the table's top row. The upper-left corner of the two-variable what-if table holds the single formula, whose results are recorded in the what-if table for each pair of input values from the left column and the top row. Note that you can evaluate only one formula in a two-variable what-if table. When the what-if table is calculated, 1-2-3 places each pair of input data values into the designated input cells in the application area, then recalculates the entire worksheet. The results of the formula are then placed in the calculated results area of the what-if table. When you create a two-variable what-if table, you are prompted for the what-if table range and the two input cells in the application area. The values in the left-most column go into *input cell 1*, while those in the top row are placed into *input cell 2*. As with a one-variable what-if table, the input data values and output formula need to be laid out in the what-if table range *before* the two-variable what-if table is calculated.

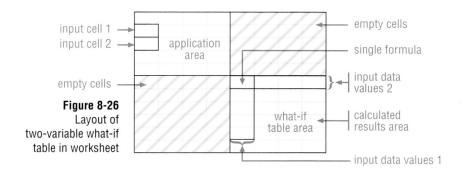

Figure 8-26
Layout of
two-variable what-if
table in worksheet

Don and Kris can use the same worksheet area they used for the one-variable what-if table, because the same number of reader systems sold will be one of the input data values. However, the what-if table setup needs to be modified for the second input.

REFERENCE WINDOW

Using a Two-Variable What-if Table

- Set up the table in a convenient cell range with the first series of input data values in the left-most column, the second series of input data values in the top row, and the formula to be calculated in the upper-left corner of the table range.

- Click Range, click Analyze, then click What-if Table... to display this dialog box.

- Click the Number of variables drop-down list arrow, then select 2.

- Click the range selector for the Table range text box, then select the range that includes the left-most column and the top row of input data values, and the formula in the upper-left corner.

- Click the range selector for the Input cell 1 text box, then select the input cell for the first series of input data values.

- Click the range selector for the Input cell 2 text box, then click the input cell for the second series of input data values.

- Click the OK button or press [Enter].

Let's set up the what-if table area with the second series of input data values using Fill by Example.

To set up the second input data series using Fill by Example:

❶ Select the range B34..E43, then press **[Del]** to remove the formulas in the top row and the previous what-if calculated results.

❷ Click **A33**, then edit the label to read "What-if 2-variable table."

❸ Enter **70** and **80** in cells B34 and C34, respectively.

❹ Select the range B34..F34, then click the **Complete Sequence SmartIcon** 🔲 to fill this range with the data values for the number of accessor systems sold.

Next let's enter the formula for displaying the calculated results in the upper-left corner of the what-if table range.

To enter the formula for displaying the calculated results that appear in the what-if table:

❶ Click **A34**, then enter the cell formula **+B26**, which references the cell where earnings before tax in 1995 is calculated.

❷ Format cell A34 as Text so the formula appears rather than the result of the formula.

Now, let's name the range containing the formula that calculates the earnings before tax in 1995.

❸ Scroll the bottom window, as necessary, then click **B26**. Then click the **Range Name SmartIcon** 🔲 to display the Name dialog box and enter **EBT [1995]** as the range name identifying this cell. Note that the range name for cell B26 is now displayed in cell A34. Naming the range helps document the data values that will be displayed in the what-if table.

This completes the setup of the two-variable what-if table. See Figure 8-27.

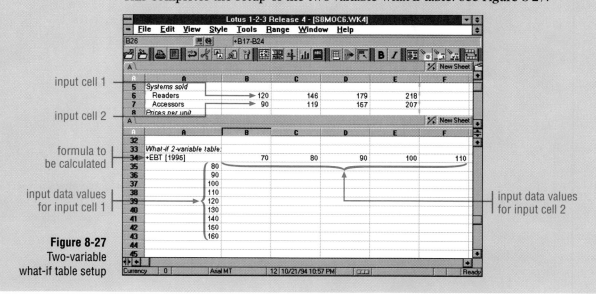

Figure 8-27
Two-variable what-if table setup

The table is ready for calculating the results.

To calculate and store the results in the two-variable what-if table:

❶ Click **Range**, click **Analyze**, then click **What-if Table...** to display this dialog box.

❷ Click the **Reset button** to remove the previous what-if table settings.

❸ Click the **Number of variables drop-down list arrow**, then select **2**. This tells 1-2-3 that the table has two input cells.

❹ Click the **range selector** for the Table range text box, then select the range **A34..F43** for the table area.

❺ Click the **range selector** for the Input cell 1 text box, then click **B6**, the input cell for the input data values in the left-most column of the table.

❻ Click the **range selector** for the Input cell 2 text box, then click **B7**, the input cell for the input data values in the top row of the table.

❼ Click the **OK button** or press **[Enter]** to calculate the what-if table. Scroll the bottom worksheet window to display the what-if table. Your screen should look like Figure 8-28.

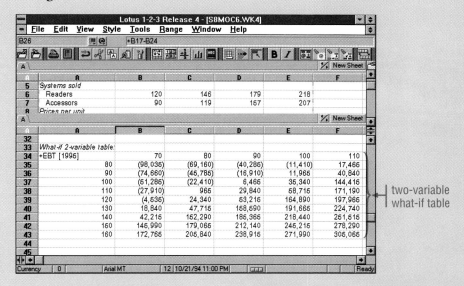

Figure 8-28
Completed
two-variable
what-if table

❽ Unsplit the worksheet window and save the worksheet as file S8MOC7.WK4. Then preview and print the two-variable what-if table.

Don reviews the results in the what-if table and learns the product combinations of reader and accessor systems that must be sold in order for MOC to be profitable next year. These are product mixes with an earnings before tax that are positive numbers in the what-if table.

Kris and Don review the what-if analyses prepared with goal seeking and what-if tables. The alternative product mixes they explored have identified potential areas of concern in their business plan, but overall, Don feels that the outlook for the future of MOC is bright, and he is confident they can cover the cost of their office suite and payroll, and make a profit.

Questions

1. A table that lists conditions that occur and actions to take for each condition is a:
   a. lookup chart
   b. decision table
   c. decision paradigm
   d. spreadsheet matrix

2. A function that performs a comparison and then chooses one of two possible values is:
   a. @PMT
   b. @CHECK
   c. @IF
   d. @IRR

3. The use of an @IF function as either the true-expression or false-expression of another @IF function is known as _____ @IF functions.
   a. looped
   b. nested
   c. interior
   d. recurring

4. In the formula @VLOOKUP(B14,A31..D35,2), the column-offset of 2 specifies that the desired value will be found in which column of the worksheet?
   a. A
   b. B
   c. C
   d. D

5. A formula in 1-2-3 that includes a cell reference directly or indirectly to itself is known as a:
   a. circular reference
   b. group calculation
   c. simultaneous equation
   d. spherical reference

6. When a worksheet is _____ , you can prevent accidentally entering data values where formulas should be located.
   a. bound
   b. padlocked
   c. secured
   d. sealed

7. _____ is the situation where you know the desired value for a cell that is calculated by a formula and you want to find the value of an input cell that results in the desired value for the formula.
   a. Aiming
   b. Goal seeking
   c. Reverse solving
   d. Inverse solving

E   8. Using the Task Reference, write down at least one other method of performing the tasks specified by the following SmartIcons:
   a.
   b.
   c.
   d.

Tutorial Assignments

Launch 1-2-3 and open the T8FAP1.WK4 worksheet, which contains the annual year-end bonuses for the sales and marketing staff in each of Fitness Arts Products (FAP) four marketing regions. Marti Lonestar, FAP's assistant marketing manager, laid out the basic worksheet with a key assumption area that contains the cost percent and bonus percent. Note that the cost of sales is equal to the sales multiplied by the cost percent. Finish Marti's analysis by performing the following tasks:

1. Modify Marti's worksheet to include the decision table shown in Figure 8-29 for determining the bonus rate that is applied to the sales in each region. The bonus is then calculated by multiplying the gross profit by the bonus rate for each region. (*Hint:* Total Bonus = $7.1 million.)

If conditions	Then actions
Sales (in millions)	Bonus Percent
Less than $100	1.0%
$100 or more and less than $200	3.0%
$200 or more	6.0%

Figure 8-29

2. Save this worksheet as S8FAP2.WK4. Preview and print the worksheet.

E 3. Marti believes that the maximum bonus pool for FAP is only $6 million this year. She wants to know what bonus percent should be used with the sales in each region to achieve this goal. Use Backsolver to find the new bonus percents. The bonus percents must retain the same *relative relationship* (1:3:6) as those in the decision table. Save this worksheet as S8FAP3.WK4. Preview and print the worksheet. Then close the worksheet.

4. The cost percent, which is used to calculate the cost of sales and gross profit, has not been finalized. The current estimate is between 75% and 85%. Marti is concerned about how the final numbers could affect her bonus plan. Open her S8FAP2.WK4 worksheet. Create a one-variable what-if table that contains the bonus amounts for each region and their total for 1% increments of the estimated cost percent. Place the what-if table below the key assumption area of the worksheet. Apply the Text format to the top row of the what-if table containing the formulas.

5. Save the worksheet as S8FAP4.WK4. Preview and print the worksheet including the what-if table.

Launch 1-2-3 and open the T8HEP1.WK4 file. This worksheet calculates the payroll for employees of Home Energy Products (HEP), a company that markets and installs insulation, thermal windows, and storm doors. Renee Salinas is responsible for preparing the weekly payroll report. Revise her worksheet by completing the following:

6. Change the pay rate for Mike Phillips to $11.25. What happens when you attempt to make this change? Why can't you change the pay rate?

7. Change the regular hours worked for Brigid Rodriquez to 38. What happens when you attempt to make this change?

E   8. Turn off protection by unsealing the worksheet. The password is HEP. Repeat the change in Tutorial Assignment 6.

9. Enter the withholding tax table in Figure 8-30 to Renee's worksheet. Name the range that contains the table "TAX TABLE."

Withholding Tax Table

Gross Pay	Federal Tax Rate	State Tax Rate
Less than $200	5%	0%
$200 or more and less than $400	9%	2%
$400 or more and less than $700	11%	5%
$700 or more and less than $1,000	15%	6%
$1,000 or more	18%	8%

Figure 8-30

E   10. The federal and state tax withheld is calculated by multiplying the selected tax rate from the table by the gross pay for each employee. Modify the worksheet to include the formulas that calculate taxes withheld. (*Hint:* Total Net Pay = $2,869.14.) Save the worksheet as S8HEP2.WK4.

E   11. Preview and print the worksheet including the decision table for the withholding tax. If your printer allows, print the report in landscape orientation.

Launch 1-2-3 and open T8MOC1.WK4, a worksheet Don created for MOC. Before moving into the new office suite, Don needs to have several leasehold improvements made, such as building a reception area and modifying work areas so they are accessible for the physically challenged. Don plans to finance these improvements, and he created a worksheet to help evaluate combinations of interest rates and loan durations. Complete the following:

12. Review Don's worksheet. What is the expected cost of the leasehold improvements and the current estimated monthly loan payment for them? Is the correct formula used for calculating the monthly loan payment?

13. Create a two-variable what-if table that displays the monthly loan payment when the annual interest rate varies from 7% to 12% in increments of 1% and the loan life varies from 10 years to 20 years in increments of 5 years. Position this table so its upper-left corner is in cell A10. Format cell A10 as text.

14. Save the worksheet as S8MOC8.WK4. Preview and print the entire worksheet including the what-if table.

E   15. Do a what-if analysis by increasing the cost of the leasehold improvements to $200,000, then recalculate the what-if table. Why did you need to recalculate the what-if table?

16. Save the worksheet as S8MOC9.WK4. Preview and print the entire worksheet including the table. Close the worksheet file.

17. What combination of interest rates and loan durations results in a monthly payment that is less than $2,000? Circle them on your printed report.

Case Problems

1. Evaluating Training Benefits for Upland Electric

Upland Electric Industries (UEI) is a diversified electric utility holding company that provides essential services in energy, financial services, freight transportation, and real estate development to the people of the Midwest. Heidi Yun manages the Information Center within the Information Systems Department at the corporate headquarters of UEI. She is considering expanding the services provided by the Information Center to include additional training in the use and application of personal computer (PC) software tools such as presentation graphics and desktop publishing. Heidi's proposed training facility would accommodate up to 12 participants in one class with a PC available for each participant.

An important aspect of personnel and human resource management for any training program like Heidi's is an evaluation of training effectiveness. Heidi wants to evaluate her program using a cost/benefit analysis that compares the costs of providing training with the expected increases in employee productivity. Training costs include instructors, equipment, materials, facilities, and participant's time. Potential training benefits include the dollar value of productivity increases, turnover rate reductions, and absenteeism rate reductions. In order to obtain approval for her training program, the benefits must be greater than the costs; that is, the cost/benefit ratio must be less than one. Heidi has developed a worksheet containing the cost/benefit analysis for next year's operation of the training program. Although she carefully estimated the costs and benefits, these might vary due to changes in business conditions. Heidi wants to obtain a better understanding of these variations by using what-if tables to answer the following questions:

a) What are the total costs, total benefits, net benefits and cost/benefit ratio when the number of trainees varies from 30 to 42 in increments of 2 trainees?

b) What are the total costs, total benefits, net benefits and cost/benefit ratio when the training days per trainee varies from 6 to 10 in increments of one day?

c) What are the net benefits when the number of trainees described in question a) is combined with the training days per trainee in question b)?

d) What is the cost/benefit ratio when the number of trainees described in question a) is combined with the training days per trainee in question b)?

Heidi also wants to know the number of trainees required to break even when the costs are equal to the benefits; that is, when net benefits are zero. Complete the following to answer these questions:

1. Launch 1-2-3 and open the worksheet P8UEI1.WK4, which contains Heidi's cost/benefit analysis. Immediately save the worksheet as S8UEI1.WK4.
2. Review Heidi's worksheet and examine the formulas used to calculate the expected costs and benefits. What is the current cost/benefit ratio? Is this ratio acceptable? That is, is it less than one?
3. Use goal seeking to determine the number of trainees needed to break even; that is, when the net benefits are zero and the cost/benefit ratio is one. Preview and print the worksheet for this solution. Then return the number of trainees to its original value (36).
4. Enter a what-if table to calculate the answer to question a). Save this as S8UEI2.WK4, then preview and print the worksheet including the what-if table. Circle the minimum number of trainees required for total benefits to just exceed total costs on your printed report.
5. Create a what-if table to calculate the answer to question b). Save this as S8UEI3.WK4, then preview and print the worksheet including the what-if table. On your printed report, circle the minimum training days per trainee necessary for total benefits to just exceed total costs.

6. Enter a what-if table to calculate the answer to answer c). Save this as S8UEI4.WK4, then preview and print the worksheet including the what-if table.

E 7. Create a chart that compares the net benefits for the training days per trainee with the number of trainees using the results from the what-if table for question c). Plot the number of trainees on the x-axis. Title the chart and both the x-axis and y-axis. Label the legend appropriately. Save this in the same S8UEI4.WK4 file and print the chart.

E 8. Develop the what-if table for question d). Create a chart like the chart in Problem 7, except plot the cost/benefit ratio on the y-axis. Save this as S8EUI5.WK4, then preview and print the worksheet including the what-if table and the chart. Close the worksheet file.

E 9. Compare the results for Problems 3 and 4 above. How does the break-even value you found in Problem 3 compare with the result you circled in Problem 4? What is the difference between the two results?

E 10. Formulate a goal seeking question. Why is this goal seeking? Open the P8UEI1.WK4 file and save it as S8UEI6.WK4. Then perform the goal seeking analysis and print a report of the solution. Write a summary that explains the goal seeking results.

E 11. Formulate another two-variable what-if table by selecting the input cells and the range of values to be explored for each. Describe why you selected these inputs to explore using a what-if table. Open the P8UEI1.WK4 file and save it as S8UEI7.WK4. Then create this what-if table. Produce a chart from the what-if table data and include appropriate titles and legends. Print the final report including the what-if table and the chart.

2. Profit Planning for Subway Sandwich Shops

(*Adapted from:* Sandwich-Shop Chain Surges, but to Run One Can Take Heroic Effort, Wall Street Journal, *September 16, 1992, page 1.*)
Subway Sandwich Shops has more than 7,000 franchises worldwide. Frederick DeLuca, co-founder of Subway Sandwich Shops, helps many would-be entrepreneurs fulfill their dream of owning their own business by setting them up with a Subway franchise. A typical Subway shop is a 1,000 square-foot space with yellow decor and fake plants, doing mostly takeout business. Each Subway shop is evaluated by measuring the weekly sales. This is known as the critical success factor (CSF). Although weekly sales vary throughout the year, the average weekly sales is the principal CSF used to gauge store performance.

Ricardo Kanno is considering buying a Subway franchise, which he will locate in the Campus Mall. A typical franchise costs about $60,000 depending on the leasehold improvements, which include interior renovations, seating, and equipment. Rick obtained data on operating a typical Subway shop and built a projected income statement worksheet to analyze its expected annual profitability. Before Rick signs the franchise agreement, he wants to evaluate several alternatives to determine their effect on his expected profitability. Complete the following analyses to produce the information that Rick wants so he can gain a better understanding of this business opportunity:

1. Launch 1-2-3 and open the worksheet P8SSS1.WK4, which contains the projected income statement that Rick created. Save the worksheet as S8SSS1.WK4.

2. Review Rick's worksheet. Notice that his plan is prepared by quarter with an annual total for the year. Most of his calculations are based on the CSF of average weekly sales. Other than those cells containing labels, all but five of the numeric data values are calculated using formulas.

3. Add the decision table in Figure 8-31 to Rick's worksheet. As his weekly sales vary from quarter to quarter, the cost of the ingredients used in the submarine sandwich change, as indicated by the cost percents in his decision table. The cost percent is multiplied by the sandwich revenues to calculate the sandwich cost of sales in each quarter. Use these cost percents to revise the cost of sales calculation for sandwiches. Save this worksheet as S8SSS2.WK4, then preview and print the worksheet. (*Hint:* Return on sales [Annual] = 3.23%.)

If conditions	Then actions
Weekly Sales	Cost Percent
Less than $4,500	51%
$4,500 or more and less than $5,500	49%
$5,500 or more	46%

Figure 8-31

E 4. Use the audit feature to determine which cells contain the input numeric values. If you do not have the auditor available, then examine each data value in the Annual column to find these five cells. Unprotect the five cells that contain the input numeric data values for Rick's plan.

5. Seal the worksheet using the password "SUBWAY." Are changes to the calculations limited to the five cells that contain the input numeric data once the file is sealed? Test this and describe your test. Do a what-if analysis to determine the annual return on sales by changing the annual weekly sales to $6,000. Preview and print the worksheet.

6. Rick wants to know the annual weekly sales for break even. Use the trial-and-error method or Backsolver to do this analysis. Save the worksheet as S8SSS3.WK4, then preview and print the worksheet. What is the owner/manager salary that Rick has planned for himself with this break-even plan? Circle the break-even annual weekly sales.

E 7. Rick talked to his finance professor at Babson College about his possible investment in a Subway shop. His professor advised him that, by working long hours and taking no vacation, he could expect to earn $49,000 for the year. Complete a what-if analysis that changes the owner/manager salary to this amount. Then, use goal seeking to find the new annual weekly sales needed for break even. Preview and print a report of this analysis. Rick obtained sales information from other franchises, with similar locations, indicating he should expect the CSF for the year to be between $5,000 and $6,000. If Rick wants to receive the salary of $49,000, does this appear to be a good business venture for him? Why or why not?

8. Because of the importance of the weekly sales in evaluating this potential business opportunity, Rick wants to further explore the expected annual earnings before tax and annual return on sales as the annual weekly sales vary from a low of $4,000 to a high of $8,000 in increments of $500. Unseal the worksheet, then create a what-if table for this analysis. Format the data appropriately in your what-if table. Save this worksheet as S8SSS4.WK4. Preview and print the worksheet including the what-if table. Review the what-if table. Does this information change your evaluation of this venture from Problem 7? If so, how and why? If not, why not?

E   9. Rick believes he should look at the annual earnings before tax with different combinations of annual weekly sales and annual owner/manager salary. Create a what-if table for this analysis. Vary the annual weekly sales as specified in Problem 7. Select an appropriate range and increment for the Annual Owner/manager salary. Save the worksheet a S8SSS5.WK4. Preview and print the results including the what-if table.

E   10. Produce a chart from the what-if table you created in Problem 9. Include appropriate titles and legends on the chart. Save the worksheet and print the chart. Review your results. Now, does this look like a good business opportunity for Rick? Why or why not? Based on your analysis, if you had $60,000 to invest, would you open the Subway Sandwich Shop at the Campus Mall? Why?

3. Product Pricing for Rollerblade, Inc.

(*Adapted from:* Fast Track, World Traveler, *November, 1993, pages 21-26.*)

Rollerblade, Inc. (RBI) introduced the first in-line skates just over a decade ago. In-line skates are now one of the fastest-growing segments of the sporting goods industry. In-line skates look something like a ski boot with three or four wheels lined up in a row, rather than two in front and two in back like traditional roller skates. RBI is preparing to introduce the all-new Bravoblade line of skates, which incorporates an innovative braking mechanism called Active Brake Technology (ABT). ABT allows a skater to brake by simply moving the braking foot forward with all wheels on the ground.

Noel Shadko, a product analyst in RBI's Marketing Department, is responsible for analyzing the expected operating results for the new Bravoblade line of skates. She prepared a projected statement of operations to analyze next year's expected profitability of this product line. However, the number of skates sold, the price per pair of skates, and the manufacturing costs could vary. Noel wants to examine these conditions to better understand the risks associated with this new product rollout. Complete the following to produce the information Noel wants:

1. Launch 1-2-3 and open the P8RBI1.WK4 worksheet, which contains the projected statement of operations that Noel developed. Save the worksheet as S8RBI1.WK4 and review its content.

2. Find the number of pairs of Bravoblades that need to be sold to just break even. Save the modified worksheet as S8RBI2.WK4, then preview and print the worksheet.

3. Reset the number of skates sold to the initial value of 75,000 pairs, then find the price per pair that RBI needs for break even. What is this price?

E   4. Reset the price per pair to the initial value of $76. The cost of goods sold table in Figure 8-32 reflects the lower costs experienced as the production volume increases. Add this lookup table to the worksheet on sheet B so it is separated from the current report. Name the range that contains the table as "COST OF GOODS" for reference in the formulas you use to implement this decision table. Include the appropriate formulas that calculate the raw materials and the direct labor costs for next year by selecting the correct cost percent from the lookup table for use in place of the constants currently used in these formulas. Save the worksheet as S8RBI3.WK4. Then preview and print the worksheet including the decision table for the cost of goods sold.

Cost of Goods Table

Sales	Raw Materials (% of Sales)	Direct Labor (% of Sales)
Less than $3,000,000	49%	24%
$3,000,000 or more and less than $4,000,000	46%	21%
$4,000,000 or more and less than $5,000,000	44%	19%
$5,000,000 or more and less than $6,000,000	42%	17%
$6,000,000 or more	39%	16%

Figure 8-32

5. Examine the relationship between skates sold and price per pair by creating a what-if table that displays the earnings before tax as the number of skates sold varies from 40,000 pairs to 90,000 pairs in increments of 10,000 pairs and the price per pair varies from $72 to $80 in increments of $2. Save this worksheet as S8RBI4.WK4. Preview and print the what-if table.

E   6. Create a chart from the what-if table in Problem 5. Include appropriate titles and legends on the chart. Save the worksheet and print the chart. Review your results. The market research for the new Bravoblades indicates that RBI should expect to sell at least 50,000 pairs of these skates. What combinations of price per pair and volume (number of skates sold) provide a positive earnings before tax? Circle these on the report from Problem 5 and indicate these combinations by marking them on your chart.

E   7. Revise the what-if table to contain results for the earnings before tax as a percent of sales. Modify the chart to display the new results. Save this worksheet as S8RBI5.WK4. Preview and print the projected statement of operations and the revised chart. Close the worksheet file.

8. Noel examined her market research information and created a second worksheet with the Bravoblade skates presented as two models—the Coolblade and the Powerblade. Open P8RBI2.WK4 and immediately save it as S8RBI6.WK4. Using goal seeking, determine the product mix of Coolblades and Powerblades for break even. This solution should maintain the current ratio of 3 pairs of Coolblades to 2 pairs of Powerblades. Save the worksheet, then preview and print the report with this break-even solution.

E   9. Formulate a goal seeking question using the worksheet from Problem 8. Why is this goal seeking? Perform the goal seeking analysis and print a report of the solution. Save this worksheet as S8RBI7.WK4. Write a summary interpreting your goal seeking results.

E   10. Develop and sketch a decision table for use with the Projected Statement of Operations. Your sketch of the decision table should be similar to those illustrated in this tutorial. Describe the business situation represented by your decision table. Implement this decision table. Save this worksheet as S8RBI8.WK4. Preview and print the results.

E   11. Formulate a two-variable what-if table by selecting the input cells and the range of values to be examined for each. Describe why you selected these inputs to explore using the what-if table. Create this what-if table. Save this worksheet as S8RBI9.WK4. Preview and print the worksheet including the what-if table.

E   12. Produce a chart from the what-if table data in Problem 11. Include appropriate titles and legends. Save the worksheet, then print the chart. Review the results from the what-if table and chart. Write a summary that explains these results.

Combining and Integrating Worksheet Applications

OBJECTIVES

In this tutorial you will:

- Combine multiple worksheet files
- Link worksheet files
- Do drill down
- Paste, link, and embed objects between Windows applications
- Use 1-2-3 in client and server applications
- Use Write as a client application
- Use Paintbrush as a server application

Providing Executive Information

CASE

Omega Mutual Life   Omega Mutual Life (OML) is a full-service life insurance company that provides for the financial security and economic protection of millions of policy holders. Its life insurance products are organized into three categories: individual, credit, and group policies. Individual policies are purchased by individuals for themselves. Credit policies are purchased by financial institutions for credit-related consumer purchases such as automobile loans. These policies provide coverage that will pay off the unpaid balance of the loan. Group policies are purchased by employers for their employees.

Dawn Fernandez is an information specialist at OML. She is developing an executive information system for the senior management of OML. An **executive information system**, or EIS, provides senior management with the current status of key factors critical to running a business, such as revenues, expenses, and profits.

Dawn is working with Eileen Gabriel, OML's chief financial officer, to determine what information is needed in the EIS. The two meet to discuss the requirements. Eileen explains that, in addition to the EIS containing the correct information, she also wants a chart showing the total premium income by quarter.

Eileen explains to Dawn that OML is divided into two regions, East and West. Each region sells and services its own policies. The EIS should **consolidate**, or add, the results from each region to determine the performance of the company as a whole. The worksheet needs to include the premium income, which is the total revenues collected on the insurance policies, and the insurance in force, which is the total amount of all the current insurance policies issued by OML. For example, if you paid a quarterly premium of $200 for a $50,000 life insurance policy, the $200 is premium income and the $50,000 is the amount of insurance in force. The worksheet also includes a row that sums the number of policies in each quarter, and a row that calculates the average policy amount. Eileen also wants the total number of policies and the average policy by quarter.

Dawn considers these requirements and develops a planning analysis sheet in preparation for completing the EIS (Figure 9-1). She brings her plan to Eileen for her approval. Eileen thinks all the critical information is present and approves Dawn's plan.

Planning Analysis Sheet

My goal:
Develop an EIS that displays critical information for review by senior management

What results do I want to see?
Current reported results for premium income, insurance in force, number of policies, and average policy by quarter, summarized at the corporate level

What information do I need?
Current results from each region in a separate worksheet file that uses an arrangement of data which is suitable for combining results to produce the corporate summary

What calculations will I perform?
Add the results of each region to yield the corporate summary

---

Figure 9-1
Dawn's planning
analysis sheet

Based on her planning analysis sheet, Dawn designs a worksheet that presents the critical information thoroughly and clearly. Figure 9-2 shows Dawn's corporate worksheet sketch for the EIS. You'll examine the formulas used later.

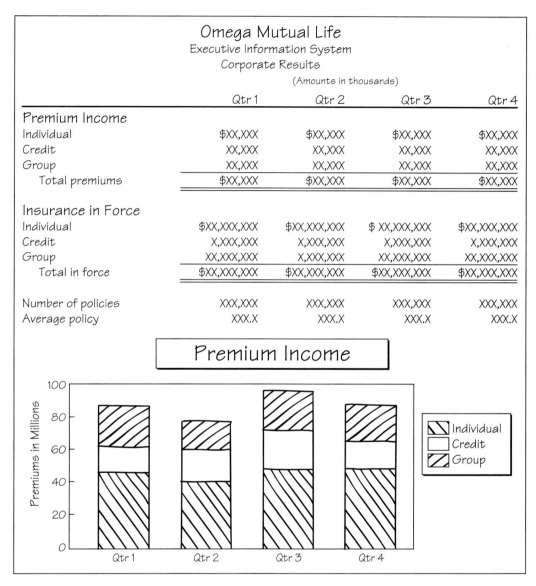

Figure 9-2
Dawn's corporate
worksheet sketch

Knowing that she needs the same information from each region, Dawn decides to create a template. As defined in Tutorial 6, a template is a worksheet that already contains the labels and formulas needed for analysis and can be readily used with other sets of data. After Dawn creates and saves the corporate template worksheet, she changes the title and saves it under a new filename for each region. It is easier to consolidate worksheets if the worksheets to be consolidated and the final worksheet are *exact images* of each other, as provided by Dawn's templates. She sends region worksheet files to the regional offices where the data for the region will be entered.

In this tutorial you will use Dawn's template worksheet and the worksheets from the East and West regions to learn how to use 1-2-3 to combine worksheet results.

Retrieving the Worksheets

In this tutorial you need to select the SmartIcon palette for Tutorial 9, then retrieve and examine the worksheet Dawn prepared for summarizing the results from the files furnished by the regions.

To select the Tutorial 9 SmartIcon palette and retrieve the worksheet:
1. Launch 1-2-3.
2. Select the Tutorial 9 SmartIcon palette using the SmartIcon palette selector ▦ in the status bar.
3. Open Dawn's worksheet C9OML1C.WK4 on your Student Disk.
4. Immediately save this corporate template worksheet as S9OML1C.WK4 in case you want to restart the tutorial. See Figure 9-3.

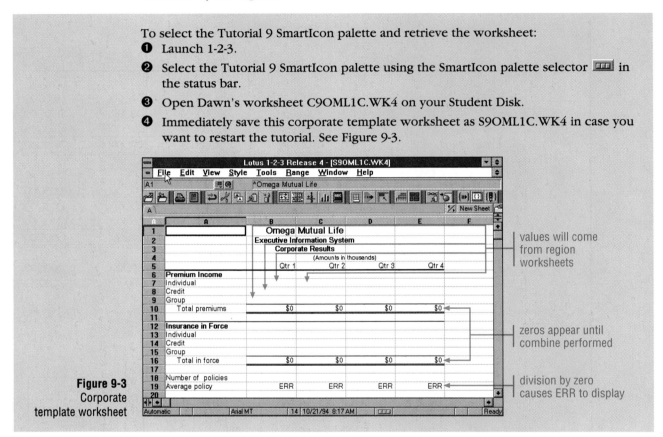

Figure 9-3
Corporate
template worksheet

Dawn's corporate template worksheet does not contain any data because it will receive data from the region worksheet files. Let's review Dawn's template worksheet and the worksheets from the East and West regions.

To review the formulas used to calculate total premiums, total in force, and average policy, and the design of the chart:

❶ Click **B10**. The @SUM formula in this cell sums the income from the three types of policies.

❷ Click **B16**. The @SUM formula in this cell sums the total insurance in force. These values are zero now because there is no data to sum.

❸ Click **B19**. The average policy is calculated by dividing the total in force by the number of policies.

❹ Press **[PgDn]** to display the Premium Income chart. The chart appears empty because the worksheet contains zeros.

Now let's examine the worksheet that Dawn has received from the West region.

To examine the West region worksheet:

❶ Open the C9OML1W.WK4 worksheet file located on your Student Disk, and immediately save it as S9OML1W.WK4 in case you want to restart the tutorial. See Figure 9-4. Note that all the data values are constants except the values in the cells that calculate the totals and the cells containing the average policy values.

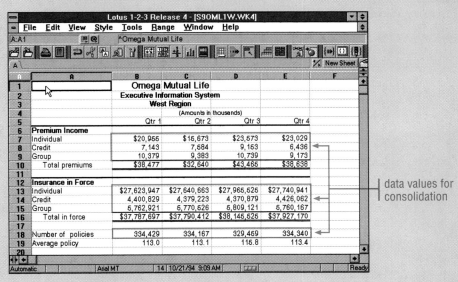

Figure 9-4
Performance results
for the West region

❷ Click the **range name selector** [⊞] to display the range names, then select **REGION**. This range contains the data that will be consolidated with the East region's data to obtain the corporate results.

Next, let's review the worksheet for the East region.

To examine the East region worksheet:

❶ Open the C9OML1E.WK4 worksheet file located on your Student Disk. Immediately save this file as S9OML1E.WK4 in case you want to restart the tutorial. See Figure 9-5. Inspect the cell contents to verify the use of constant values and formulas.

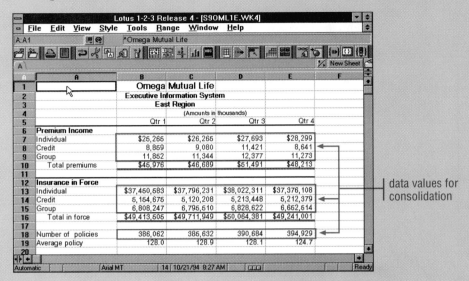

data values for consolidation

Figure 9-5
Performance results
for the East region

❷ Click the **range name selector** [icon], then select **REGION**. Note that this range is the same as the range in the West region worksheet.

Now that Dawn has the completed worksheets from both regions she's ready to consolidate them into one worksheet.

Combining Multiple Worksheet Files

When you combine worksheets in 1-2-3, the values that are combined can *replace*, *be added to*, or *be subtracted from* a value in the current worksheet file (Figure 9-6).

Effect in Current File	Action
Replace values	Formulas, data values, and labels from the source file are copied to the current worksheet and replace existing cell contents
Add to values	Numeric values from the source file are added to the constants or blank cells in the current worksheet file
Subtract from values	Numeric values from the source file are subtracted from constants or blank cells in the current worksheet file

Figure 9-6
File combine effects

When you execute the File Combine command, you specify the range in the source file that will be combined with the destination file. The **source file** is the file that supplies the data. The **destination file** is the current worksheet, the file that receives the data. The location in the current worksheet of the incoming data from the source file is determined by the position of the cell pointer in the current worksheet. The cell pointer designates the upper-left corner of the range where the incoming data will be located.

Using File Combine Add with a Data Range

- Click the cell that is the upper-left corner of the range where you want data from the source file located.

- Click the Open File SmartIcon to display the Open File dialog box.

- Click the Combine button to display the Combine 1-2-3 File dialog box.

- Click the Range button, then type the range name or the cell address in the source worksheet that contains the incoming data.

- Click the Add to values button.

- Click the OK button to add to the numeric values in the current worksheet.

Dawn wants the results from the source files for each region to be added to the worksheet to produce consolidated corporate results. Let's consolidate the data from the East and West regions into the corporate worksheet.

To consolidate data for the East region:

❶ Click **Window** to display the Window menu, then click **S9OML1C.WK4** to make the corporate template worksheet the current worksheet. The other open worksheet filenames are displayed in the menu. The files for the East and West regions do not need to be closed before carrying out the file combine.

TROUBLE? If you closed the S9OML1C.WK4 file, its name does not appear in the menu. Open this file now.

❷ Click the **Home SmartIcon** 🔲.

❸ Click **B5** to position the cell pointer at the upper-left corner of the range where the data from the source file will be located. Remember that the regional worksheets and the corporate template worksheet are exact images of each other, and the range REGION in both the East and West regional worksheets encompasses the range B5..E19.

❹ Click the **Open File SmartIcon** 📂 to display the Open File dialog box.

❺ Scroll the File name list box, then click **C9OML1E.WK4** to select this file. Note that this is the original file you renamed in the preceding steps—it is not the open East region file.

TROUBLE? If you double-clicked the filename, 1-2-3 opened the file. Close the C9OML1E.WK4 file, then repeat Steps 4 and 5.

❻ Click the **Combine button** to display the Combine 1-2-3 File dialog box. See Figure 9-7.

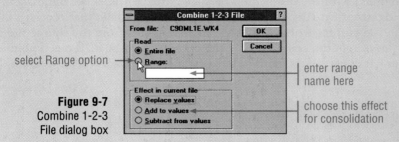

select Range option ──→

enter range
name here

choose this effect
for consolidation

Figure 9-7
Combine 1-2-3
File dialog box

Dawn wants to combine a range from the source file, not the entire file.

❼ Click the **Range button**, then type **REGION**. This is the name of the range in the C9OML1E.WK4 file to be combined. You also could have typed the cell addresses of the range, in this case B5..E19.

❽ Click the **Add to values button** to select this effect in the current file.

❾ Click the **OK button** to add the numeric values in the source file to the current worksheet file. Dawn's corporate worksheet now displays the performance results for the East region, as shown previously in Figure 9-5.

TROUBLE? If "East Region" appears as the report heading in your S9OML1C.WK4 file, then you selected the wrong option in the Combine 1-2-3 File dialog box. Click the Undo SmartIcon ⤴, then repeat Steps 2 through 9.

The results of the East region have been successfully consolidated into the blank template worksheet for the corporate results. Now let's consolidate the results for the West region.

To consolidate data for the West region:
❶ Verify that the cell pointer is still located at cell B5, the upper-left corner of the range where the data from the West region file will be located.

❷ Click the **Open File SmartIcon** 📁 to display this dialog box.

❸ Scroll the File name list box, then click **C9OML1W.WK4** to select this file.

❹ Click the **Combine button** to display the Combine 1-2-3 File dialog box.

❺ Click the **Range button**, then type **REGION** as the name of the range in the C9OML1W.WK4 file to be combined.

❻ Click the **Add to values button**.

❼ Click the **OK button** to add the numeric values in the source file to those in the current worksheet file. The corporate worksheet now displays the totals of the two regions. See Figure 9-8.

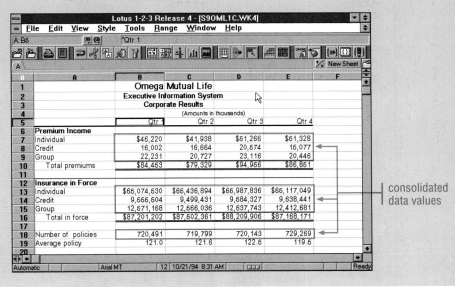

Figure 9-8
Consolidated
corporate results

consolidated
data values

Now that the region worksheets have been combined, let's look at the Premium Income chart and print the consolidated report.

To review the consolidated results:

❶ Scroll down the worksheet window to display the Premium Income chart, which Dawn set up initially.

❷ Click the **Home SmartIcon** when you are finished examining the chart.

❸ Save the worksheet with the consolidated results as S9OML1C.WK4, then preview and print both the worksheet and the chart. Your report should look like Figure 9-9 on the following page.

❹ Close all the worksheet files without saving them again.

Omega Mutual Life
Executive Information System
Corporate Results
(Amounts in thousands)

	Qtr 1	Qtr 2	Qtr 3	Qtr 4
Premium Income				
Individual	$46,220	$41,938	$51,266	$51,328
Credit	16,002	16,664	20,574	15,077
Group	22,231	20,727	23,116	20,446
Total premiums	$84,453	$79,329	$94,956	$86,851
Insurance in Force				
Individual	$65,074,530	$65,436,894	$65,987,836	$65,117,049
Credit	9,555,504	9,499,431	9,584,327	9,638,441
Group	12,571,168	12,566,036	12,637,743	12,412,681
Total in force	$87,201,202	$87,502,361	$88,209,906	$87,168,171
Number of policies	720,491	719,799	720,143	729,269
Average policy	121.0	121.6	122.5	119.5

Figure 9-9
Printout of
completed EIS

Dawn has the EIS with the consolidated results that Eileen wants, and they are ready to review it.

Linking Worksheet Files

Dawn sits down with Eileen at Eileen's computer and demonstrates the consolidation using the File Combine command. Eileen is pleased with the worksheet and her ability to review the results directly or to print the report with the chart. She asks Dawn if there is some way to set up the worksheet so that when she receives updated files from the regions, the results would automatically appear in the corporate worksheet file. Then, whenever Eileen is using the EIS, she knows it will contain the most current information.

To make the updated region worksheet files immediately and automatically available to Eileen, Dawn decides to *link* the region worksheet files to the corporate worksheet file. To link these worksheets, Dawn needs to build a linking formula. A **linking formula** is one that references cells in another file. The formula includes a file reference. The **file reference** is the filename and range. The file can be an open file or a file on disk. A formula with a file reference automatically obtains the value from the linked worksheet when you open the file.

To facilitate the link, Dawn creates a multiple sheet file with three sheets: Corporate, East, and West. She will then link the region files to the East and West sheets in the multiple sheet file. This will allow Eileen to have all the results in one file so she can more easily examine and compare the corporate results with those for the regions.

When creating a formula with a file reference that links two worksheets, you should open both worksheet files and tile the windows so they are arranged side-by-side. This ensures that the correct file reference is used.

Dawn creates her new multiple sheet file based on the design of the original template. Let's open Dawn's new worksheet file and the East region file, then arrange them side by side in preparation for linking them.

To tile worksheet windows for easy reference:

❶ Open the C9OML2C.WK4 worksheet file and immediately save it as S9OML2C.WK4 in the event you want to restart the tutorial. This is Dawn's file containing the three sheets.

❷ Review this multiple sheet file. Notice that Dawn has already set up the region sheets with the desired labels and that the consolidation in the Corporate sheet uses the @SUM function.

❸ Open the S9OML1E.WK4 file, which contains the data for the East region.

❹ Click **Window**, then click **S9OML2C.WK4** to display this open worksheet in the active window.

❺ Click the **Arrange Side by Side SmartIcon** ⊞ to display the multiple sheet worksheet and the East region worksheet in adjacent windows. See Figure 9-10. Notice that the active window appears on the left.

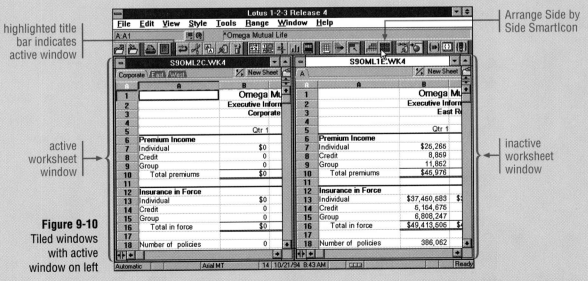

highlighted title bar indicates active window

Arrange Side by Side SmartIcon

active worksheet window

inactive worksheet window

Figure 9-10
Tiled windows with active window on left

Let's display the East sheet because it is the sheet to which you'll be linking the data.

❻ Click the **East worksheet tab** to display that sheet of the S9OML2C.WK4 file.

Dawn needs to link the East and West region worksheets to their respective sheets in the multiple sheet file. To do this, you need to place a linking formula in the multiple sheet file. The linking formula identifies the worksheet and the range from which the data will be retrieved. The format of a linking formula is:

$$+<<filename.WK?>>range$$

The **filename.WK?** is the name and extension of the file. It might include its disk drive identifier and path. The **range** is the cell address or range name of the data you want to retrieve from the specified file.

Using Formulas to Link 1-2-3 Worksheet Files

- Tile the worksheets for the linked formula reference.
- Select the range in the worksheet that is to be linked.
- Click the Copy to Clipboard SmartIcon.
- Click the upper-left corner of the range in the worksheet where you want the linked formulas to be copied.
- Click the Paste Link SmartIcon.

Let's create the linking formulas in the East sheet of the multiple sheet file that reference data in the East region's worksheet file (S9OML1E.WK4).

To create linking formulas in the East sheet:
1. Select the range B7..E9 in the S9OML1E.WK4 worksheet to choose this range for the file linking formulas.
2. Click the **Copy to Clipboard SmartIcon** 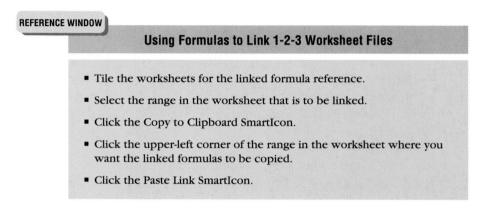.
3. Click **B:B7** in the S9OML2C.WK4 worksheet. This cell will contain the first linking formula.
4. Click the **Paste Link SmartIcon** to complete copying the formulas. See Figure 9-11. Notice that the complete formula in the cell contents box contains the filename S9OML1E.WK4 before the cell address.

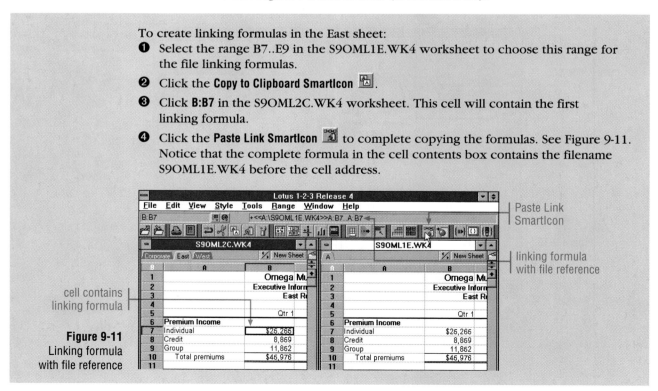

Figure 9-11
Linking formula
with file reference

Instead of using the SmartIcons to create the linking formula with the file reference, you can use pointing or type the entire formula. When typing the formula, be careful to include the correct path.

Let's finish linking the data from the East region worksheet to the S9OML2C.WK4 worksheet.

To complete the link between the East sheet and the East region worksheet file:

❶ Select the range B13..E15 in the S9OML1E.WK4 file. Click the **Copy to Clipboard SmartIcon** 🔳 to copy the values for insurance in force.

❷ Click **B:B13** in the East sheet of the S9OML2C.WK4 file. Click the **Paste Link SmartIcon** 🔳 to complete the link.

❸ Select the range B18..E18 in the S9OML1E.WK4 file, then click 🔳 to copy the number of policies.

❹ Click **B:B18** in the East sheet of the S9OML2C.WK4 file, then click 🔳. This completes creating the linking formulas with the file references to the East region worksheet.

❺ Save the worksheet on the left with the default filename S9OML2C.WK4.

❻ Close the S9OML1E.WK4 worksheet without saving it again.

Now, let's create the linked file references for the West region.

To create the linked file references for the West region:

❶ Open the S9OML1W.WK4 worksheet. This window appears on top of the S9OML2C.WK4 worksheet window and is the active window. See Figure 9-12.

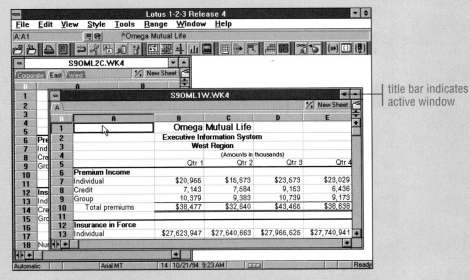

Figure 9-12
West region worksheet in the active window

❷ Click the S9OML2C.WK4 worksheet title bar or anywhere else in the exposed area of the window to make it the active window.

❸ Click the **Arrange Side by Side SmartIcon** 🔳 to place the windows side by side with the S9OML2C.WK4 window on the left.

❹ Click the **West worksheet tab** to display sheet C for the West region.

❺ Build the linking formulas in the West sheet of the S9OML2C.WK4 file. These formulas are created in the same manner as those for the East sheet.

❻ Save the updated S9OML2C.WK4 worksheet file. Then preview and print the corporate worksheet.

Dawn shows Eileen the new multiple sheet file. She explains that linking formulas with file references preserve the data integrity among the linked files so the files all display exactly the same data values. Dawn demonstrates this by making a change in one of the source worksheets.

To demonstrate the data integrity of calculations between linked files:

❶ Click **B14** in the S9OML1W.WK4 worksheet for the West region.

❷ Type **4,601,000** then press **[Enter]**. Observe that the values in cells B14 and B16 in the S9OML2C.WK4 worksheet are immediately updated. See Figure 9-13. If both worksheet files were not open at the same time, the values in the S9OML2C.WK4 file would be updated when you open the file or when you use the Edit Links command.

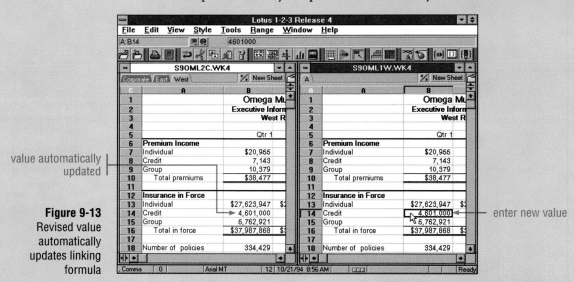

Figure 9-13
Revised value automatically updates linking formula

❸ Click the **Undo SmartIcon** to return the original value in cell B14. Again, the formula with the file reference is updated in the corporate sheet.

❹ Close the S9OML1W.WK4 worksheet file without saving the changes. Then click the **Maximize button** of the S9OML2C.WK4 worksheet to fill the worksheet window with the worksheet.

Dawn knows that setting up the linking formulas takes more work than just combining data. However, the file with the linking formulas will provide Eileen with the automatic updates she wants, which are not available with the File Combine command.

Dawn can use the criteria shown in Figure 9-14 to help her decide whether to use the File Combine command or the linking formula method.

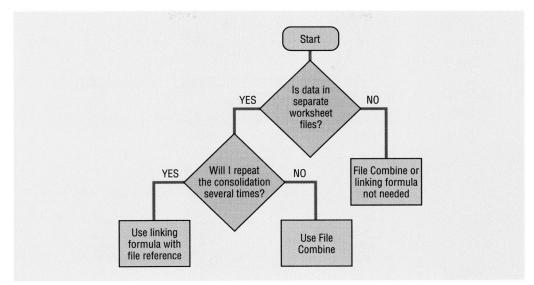

Figure 9-14
Strategy for combining
or linking worksheets

Doing Drill Down

Drill down is the ability to quickly display related information in an EIS at lower levels of detail. Drill down is not a 1-2-3 command or menu choice; however, it enables you to see how consolidated data arranged in a multiple sheet file is used to understand a business condition. As Eileen examines the corporate results for premium income of individual policies in the second quarter, she notices they are somewhat lower than the other three quarters. She wants to know whether this dip in premium income is for one or both of the regions. Let's see how drill down can be used to examine these results.

To use drill down in examining results in a multiple sheet file:
❶ Click the **Corporate worksheet tab**, then click **A:C7** with the single sheet view of sheet A displayed. This is the amount that Eileen wants to explore using drill down.
❷ Click the **Display Contiguous SmartIcon** 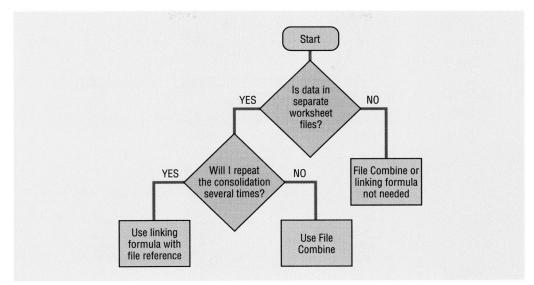 to switch to the perspective view.

❸ Click the **Go To SmartIcon** to display the Go To dialog box, then click the **OK button** because the desired cell address appears in the dialog box. This scrolls the sheets so the corporate and regional premium incomes of individual policies are all displayed. See Figure 9-15.

Eileen notices that the dip in premium income was caused by a low value in the West region.

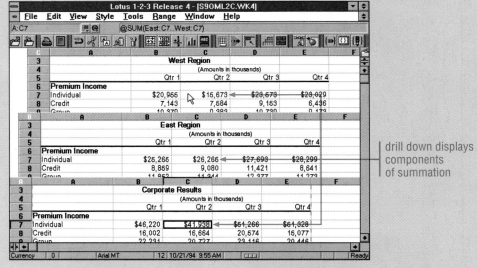

drill down displays components of summation

Figure 9-15
Consolidated and region premium income displayed for comparison

❹ Click to return to the single sheet view.

If you want to take a break and resume this tutorial at a later time, you can exit 1-2-3 by double-clicking the Control menu box in the upper-left corner of your screen. When you resume the tutorial, launch 1-2-3, place your Student Disk in the disk drive, select the Tutorial 9 SmartIcon palette, and open the files S9OML2C.WK4 and S9OML1W.WK4, then continue with this tutorial.

Eileen examines the premium income. She wonders what occurred in the second quarter to cause the drop in the West region's income.

Integrating Windows Applications

Eileen decides to send a memo to Paul Yang, the West region's manager. She wants Paul to review the West region's data and provide her with an explanation of the dip in the region's premium income. Eileen wants to include the premium income data in her memo so Paul can verify that the correct information for the West region was sent to her.

She prepares the memo using Microsoft Write, the word processing application included with Microsoft Windows. A **word processing** application, or **word processor**, allows you to create, edit, format, and print documents. A **document** is any written item, such as a letter, memo, or report. Some examples of word processing software are Lotus AmiPro, Microsoft Word for Windows, and WordPerfect for Windows. Because she also needs to verify the data from the West region, Eileen wants to include in her memo data from her 1-2-3 worksheet. To do this, Eileen needs to integrate the two applications.

Integrating applications is the transferring and sharing of data among different software tools, both Windows and non-Windows applications. An **object** is a package of information, such as a 1-2-3 range, that can be used in another application. The object is copied from the **source**, or **server**, application, and a copy of the object is pasted into the **destination**, or **client**, application. For Eileen's integration, 1-2-3 is the server application, and Write is the client application.

Not every Windows application has client and server capabilities. Lotus 1-2-3 is both a server and a client, but Microsoft Write can only be a client and Microsoft Paintbrush can only be a server.

There are three methods for transferring and sharing information among Windows applications: pasting, linking, and embedding. When you **paste** an object from a source application into a destination application, a copy of the selected object is placed in the destination document. When you **link** an object from a source application to a destination application, a communication path is established between the object from the server application and the copy of the object in the client application. When you **embed** an object from a server application into a client application, a copy of the *entire* file that contains the object is attached to the file in the client application.

In general, the process of integrating Windows applications is a two-step procedure. First, you have to copy the data from the source application to the Windows clipboard, then you have to paste, embed, or link the data into the destination application, as illustrated in Figure 9-16.

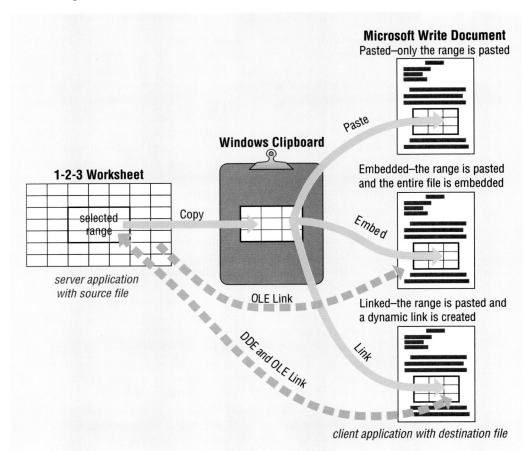

Figure 9-16
Using the clipboard to integrate data

When you *paste* a copy of an object from a source application into a destination application, you have no connection to the document file from which you transferred the object. Once the paste is completed, any direct relationship to the source document is lost. If you want to change the object, you need to locate the original source document file, make the desired changes using the appropriate application, then replace the old copy of the object in the destination application with the revised copy of the object.

When you *link* an object to the client application, you create a reference, or a link, between the client file and the *original* document file. A **link** is a dynamic connection between a file in a server application and another file in the client application. If you edit the original object in the server application, your changes also appear in the copy of the object in the client file. This is similar to the link that is established between worksheets in 1-2-3 when you use linking formulas.

When you *embed* an object, the data for the object is copied to the destination application together with a copy of the *entire* source file that is attached to the destination file. You can click on the embedded object, open the source application, then edit the embedded object. Unlike editing a linked object, editing an embedded object will not change the original data file. Because the copy of the entire source file resides in the destination file, you can move the destination application file with the embedded data to another computer as a *single* file. As long as the computer to which you move the file has a copy of the source application you used to create the embedded data, you can use that application's facilities to edit the embedded data. On the other hand, if the source file is very large, considerable disk storage space can be used up saving the copy of the entire file with the embedded object.

In the Windows environment, linked and embedded objects share information between applications based on Dynamic Data Exchange (DDE) and Object Linking and Embedding (OLE, pronounced ohLAY). DDE and OLE establish different connections to the source document from which the copy of an object in the destination document is obtained. **DDE** is the connection between documents that supplies data to the client application when a change occurs in the server application. **OLE** is a feature that allows the client application to "remember" the server application where the linked or embedded object originated.

OLE was introduced in Microsoft Windows version 3.1; consequently applications developed before that version do not have OLE capabilities. To determine if a Windows application you are using has OLE capabilities, you can check the application's documentation or on-line Help facility.

Whenever you use an application with OLE client capabilities, you can use the Insert Object command to display a list of available server applications on your computer system. The Insert Object command is usually listed on the Edit menu.

REFERENCE WINDOW

Listing Server Applications

- Click Edit in the menu bar.

- Click Insert Object... to display this dialog box.

- Use the scroll bar to review the list of available server applications.

- Click the Cancel button to complete examining the list.

Let's use the Insert Object command to list the servers available to 1-2-3.

To list the servers available to 1-2-3:

❶ Click **Edit** then click **Insert Object...** to display the Insert Object dialog box, which lists the server applications for 1-2-3. See Figure 9-17. You might not have the same servers shown in the figure. Your list of servers depends on the applications that are installed on your system. Notice that Microsoft Write is not an available server for 1-2-3.

Figure 9-17
List of available servers for current client application

your list might
be different

❷ If a scroll bar is visible, use it to scroll through the list of server applications.

❸ Click the **Cancel button** after you have finished viewing the available server applications.

Linking an Object from a 1-2-3 Worksheet

Eileen decides to link the worksheet to the memo rather than pasting or embedding it. When you copy an object using object linking, the linked object appears in the destination document, but the data for the object resides in the file where it was originally created. The advantage of linking is that if you edit the *original* object, the changes you make will be reflected in all client applications to which the object is linked. This is especially handy when you are working on a number of documents that all contain the same object. By linking the 1-2-3 data to the Write document, Eileen can be sure the data in her memo will automatically be updated if changes to the worksheet are made. If the data was embedded in the Write document, she would have to update the data in both documents each time there is a change.

There are several ways to create links. The easiest method is to copy and paste the link from the server application.

You have already used the Windows clipboard in 1-2-3 to copy and paste data within a worksheet; now you will use it to copy and paste data between two applications, in this case 1-2-3 and Microsoft Write.

Let's link Eileen's 1-2-3 worksheet data to her Write memo by first copying the cell range to the clipboard then using the Paste Link command in Write.

To copy a 1-2-3 object to the clipboard:

❶ If necessary, click **Window** then click **S9OML1W.WK4** to make this the active file.

TROUBLE? If you closed the S9OML1W.WK4 file, its name does not appear in the menu. Open this file now.

❷ Select the range A5..E10, which contains the premium income data to be linked to the memo.

❸ Click the **Copy to Clipboard SmartIcon** ⬛ to copy the worksheet range object to the Windows clipboard.

Eileen now needs to launch Microsoft Write so she can integrate the data into her memo.

Opening Multiple Applications

You can launch another application in Windows without exiting the application you are currently working in. Windows places the new application on top of the current application window when you open the second application. To move among the open applications, you press [Alt][Esc] or [Alt][Tab]. Each time you press [Alt][Esc] you switch to the next application window. When you hold down [Alt], each time you press [Tab] you display the title of an open Windows application you can switch to. Release [Alt] when the name of the application you want to switch to appears.

Let's launch the Write application.

To launch the Write application:

❶ Press **[Alt][Esc]** to switch to the Program Manager window.

TROUBLE? If the Program Manager window does not appear, continue pressing [Alt][Esc] until it does.

❷ Look for the Accessories group icon or the Accessories group window. If you see the Accessories group icon, double-click it to open the Accessories group window. See Figure 9-18.

Write icon ────→

Figure 9-18
Accessories
group window for
launching Write

❸ Look for the Write icon in the Accessories group window. If necessary, scroll the Accessories group window to bring the Write icon into view.

❹ Double-click the **Write icon** to open the Write window, then click the **Maximize button**, if necessary, to enlarge the Write window. See Figure 9-19.

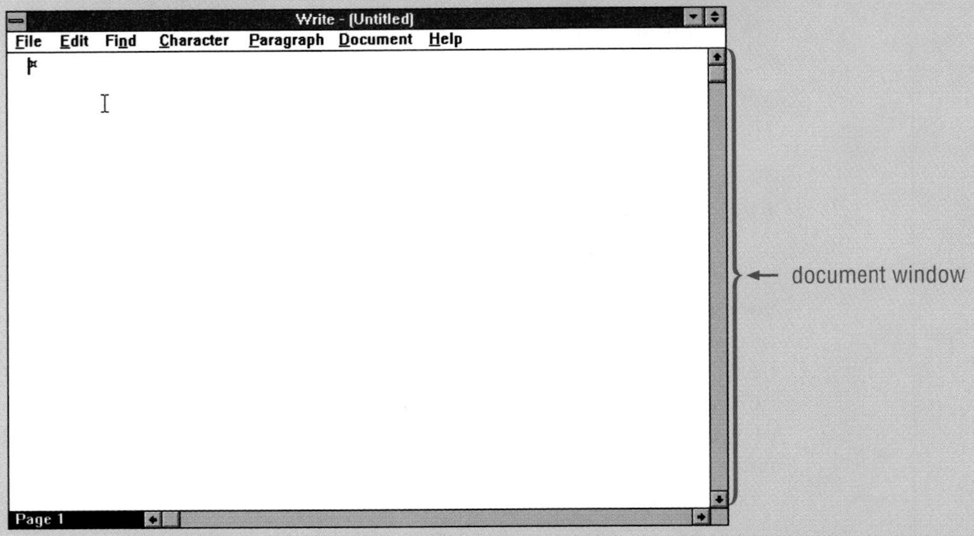

Figure 9-19
Write Untitled
document window

Now Eileen is ready to open her memo.

Opening a Write Document

Opening a Write document file is similar to opening a 1-2-3 worksheet. Note that Write uses the file extension "WRI" to identify its files. Let's open the file C9OML3.WRI, which contains Eileen's memo.

To open Eileen's memo:
❶ Click **File** then click **Open...** to display the Open dialog box.
❷ Click the **Drives drop-down list arrow** to select the drive where your Student Disk is located.
❸ Click **C9OML3.WRI** in the File Name list box to select this file, then click the **OK button** to open the file. See Figure 9-20.

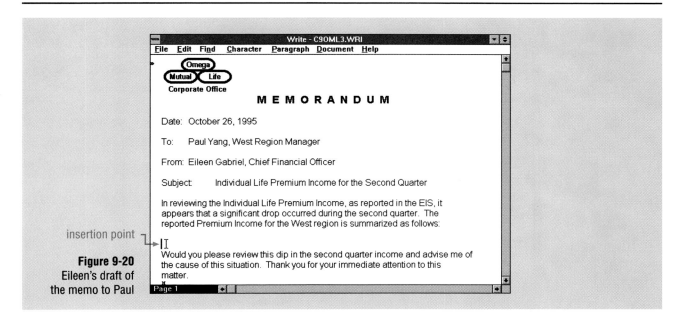

Figure 9-20
Eileen's draft of
the memo to Paul

Linking a 1-2-3 Object to a Write Document

In Write, by using the Paste Link command, you establish a DDE link between the Write document file and the 1-2-3 worksheet file. Now, any changes you make to the original worksheet data will also appear in the Write document. When you link the data from 1-2-3 to Write, 1-2-3 is the server and Write is the client.

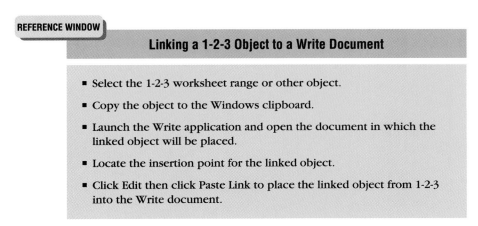

REFERENCE WINDOW

Linking a 1-2-3 Object to a Write Document

- Select the 1-2-3 worksheet range or other object.
- Copy the object to the Windows clipboard.
- Launch the Write application and open the document in which the linked object will be placed.
- Locate the insertion point for the linked object.
- Click Edit then click Paste Link to place the linked object from 1-2-3 into the Write document.

Eileen can now link her object, the table of worksheet data, into her memo to Paul. Remember, this object is still held temporarily in the Windows clipboard. Let's link the West region's worksheet to Eileen's memo.

To link a 1-2-3 object into the Write document:

❶ Move the insertion point to the blank line directly above the last paragraph in Eileen's memo, then click. See Figure 9-20.

> **TROUBLE?** If you click the wrong location for the insertion point, move I to the desired location and click, or press [↑] or [↓] to reposition the insertion point.

❷ Click **Edit** then click **Paste Link** to copy the contents of the clipboard at the insertion point using linking. See Figure 9-21.

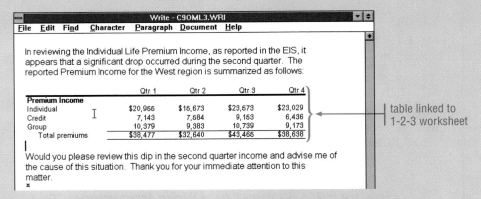

Figure 9-21
Eileen's memo
with linked table

Eileen wants the table centered between the right and left margins.

❸ Click I anywhere on the inserted table to select it.

❹ Click **Paragraph** then click **Centered** to center Eileen's table.

Eileen has successfully integrated the data from her 1-2-3 worksheet into her Write document.

Printing a Write Document

After reviewing her memo, Eileen is ready to print her memo to Paul. Let's do that next.

To print the Write document:

❶ Check that your printer is ready.

❷ Click **File** then click **Save As...** to save this document as S9OML3.WRI.

❸ Click **File** then click **Print...** to display the Print dialog box. The default print settings are acceptable.

❹ Click the **OK button** to print the document.

Satisfied with the memo, Eileen faxes it to Paul.

Editing a Linked Object

Paul calls Eileen as soon as he receives her fax. He tells her that one of the data values is incorrect. The individual premium income in the second quarter should actually be $25,673. Because Eileen is still in Write, she decides to edit the data from there. When you use object linking to copy a table from 1-2-3 to Write, the data remains in 1-2-3, but the table also appears as an object in Write. Linked objects are edited in the server application. You can edit a linked object by starting from either the server application or the client application. In either case, the *original source document file* is edited in the server application. Because a DDE link is set up between the two applications, any changes to the data in 1-2-3 will change the table in Write.

Frequently, when working in the client application, you might want to change some aspect of the linked object. In this case, it is easier to initiate the edit from the client application, rather than take the extra steps to launch the server application and open the source file.

REFERENCE WINDOW

Editing a 1-2-3 Object Linked to a Client Application

- Double-click the linked object to launch 1-2-3 and open the worksheet file that contains the selected object.

  or

  Launch 1-2-3, then open the worksheet file that contains the object.

- Make the desired edit changes to the object in 1-2-3.

- Save the revised worksheet.

- Click File then click Exit to switch back to the client application.

  or

  Double-click the 1-2-3 Control menu box to return to the client application.

Eileen needs to correct the error in the corporate results worksheet. Let's edit the data in the 1-2-3 source file by accessing it from Write, the client application.

To edit the object from within the linked source document:

❶ Double-click the **data table object** to access the object in the server application (1-2-3). If 1-2-3 had not been launched, it would be launched and the source document file opened. Any changes made at this point would be saved both in the source document file and in the destination file.

❷ Click **C7** then change the value in the cell to 25673.

❸ Save this with the default name of S9OML1W.WK4, so the DDE link is updated, then close this file.

Now let's check to see if the change was made in the client application.

To view the update in the client application after changing the server application:

❶ Press **[Alt][Esc]** as many times as necessary to switch back to Write.

❷ Click anywhere outside the table to unselect it and observe the change in the table in the Write document where the individual premium income now reads $25,673. See Figure 9-22.

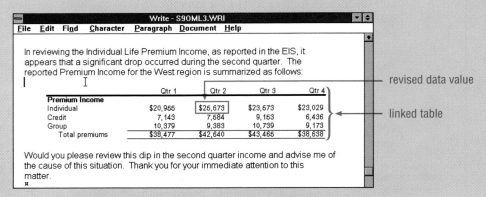

Figure 9-22
Linked data in
Write memo

When objects are linked, you can determine the sources of the links from within the client application. Let's examine the link between Eileen's Write document and her 1-2-3 worksheet.

To observe the link to Write as the client from 1-2-3 as the server:

❶ Click **Edit** then click **Links...** to display the Links dialog box for Write. See Figure 9-23.

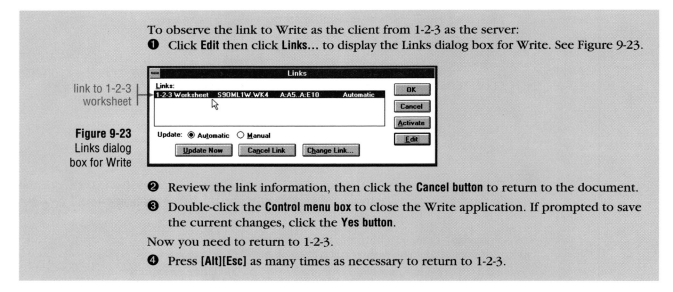

Figure 9-23
Links dialog
box for Write

❷ Review the link information, then click the **Cancel button** to return to the document.

❸ Double-click the **Control menu box** to close the Write application. If prompted to save the current changes, click the **Yes button**.

Now you need to return to 1-2-3.

❹ Press **[Alt][Esc]** as many times as necessary to return to 1-2-3.

Embedding an Object into 1-2-3

When Dawn created the corporate results worksheet, she also created a logo for OML using Microsoft Paintbrush, the drawing application that is included with Windows. Eileen wants to include the logo in the worksheet for her EIS.

Launching Microsoft Paintbrush

First Eileen needs to launch Paintbrush so she can copy the logo to the clipboard.

To launch the Paintbrush application:
❶ Press **[Alt][Esc]** to switch to the Program Manager window.

❷ Look for the Accessories group icon or the Accessories group window. If you see the Accessories group icon, double-click it to open the Accessories group window.

❸ If necessary, scroll the Accessories group window to find the Paintbrush icon. Double-click the **Paintbrush icon** in the Accessories group window to open the Paintbrush window. Click the **Maximize button**, if necessary, to enlarge the Paintbrush window. See Figure 9-24.

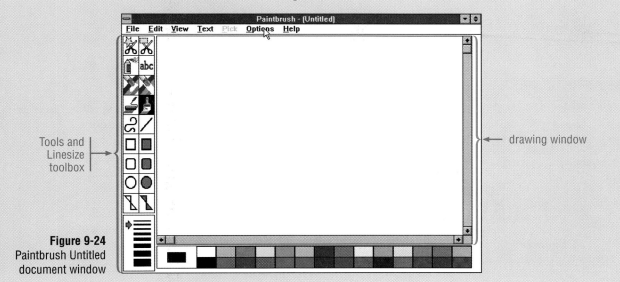

Tools and Linesize toolbox

drawing window

Figure 9-24
Paintbrush Untitled document window

Opening a Paintbrush Document

Now Eileen is ready to open Dawn's logo.

To open the Paintbrush document containing the logo:
❶ Click **Options** then click **Image Attributes...** to display the Image Attributes dialog box. Type **1.4** in the Width text box and **0.70** in the Height text box, then click the **OK button**. This revises the size of the drawing area so the picture in Paintbrush is limited to the approximate size of the space available for it in the worksheet.

❷ Click **File** then click **Open...** to display the Open dialog box. This is similar to the 1-2-3 Open File dialog box.

❸ Click the **Drives drop-down list arrow** to select the drive where your Student Disk is located.

❹ Click **C9OMLOGO.BMP** in the File Name text box to select this file, then click the **OK button** to open the file. See Figure 9-25.

Pick tool —

Figure 9-25
OML logo in
Paintbrush

— logo

Now let's copy the logo to the Windows clipboard before transferring it to Eileen's 1-2-3 worksheet.

To copy the selected Paintbrush object to the Windows clipboard:

❶ Look for the Tools and Linesize toolbox. If this does not appear, click **View** then click **Tools and Linesize**.

Now you need to select the object you want to copy.

❷ Click the **Pick tool** [icon].

❸ Move the mouse pointer to the upper-left corner of the drawing until the pointer changes to $+$. Then click and drag the pointer to the lower-right corner. A dashed box surrounds the logo to indicate the object is selected. See Figure 9-26.

TROUBLE? If the dashed box does not surround the entire logo, repeat Steps 2 and 3.

Figure 9-26
Selected logo object

| dashed box
| indicates selection

❹ Click **Edit** then click **Copy** to copy the selected object to the Windows clipboard. The selected object can now be pasted, embedded, or linked to the 1-2-3 worksheet.

❺ Press **[Alt][Esc]** to return to the 1-2-3 application. You might have to press [Alt][Esc] more than once to return to 1-2-3.

Embedding an Object in a 1-2-3 Worksheet

Once the object, OML's logo, is copied to the Windows clipboard from the server application, you can embed it in the 1-2-3 worksheet, the client application.

Embedding an Object into 1-2-3

- Launch the server application, select or create the desired object, then copy it to the Windows clipboard.

- Use [Alt][Esc] or [Alt][Tab] to switch back to 1-2-3.

- Click the cell that is the upper-left corner of the worksheet area where you want the embedded object to appear.

- Click Edit then click Paste Special... to display this dialog box.

- Click the appropriate embedded object clipboard format to select it.

- Click the Paste button.

Now let's embed Dawn's logo as an object in Eileen's 1-2-3 worksheet.

To embed the object in the worksheet:

❶ Click the **Home SmartIcon** 🔲 to position the cell pointer at the desired location.

❷ Click **Edit** then click **Paste Special...** to display the Paste Special dialog box. See Figure 9-27. Notice that Windows automatically provides three clipboard formats for your selection. The format you select controls whether the object is pasted, embedded, or linked.

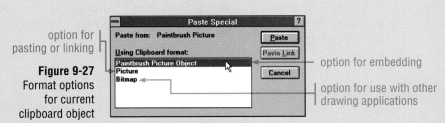

option for pasting or linking

Figure 9-27
Format options
for current
clipboard object

option for embedding

option for use with other drawing applications

TROUBLE? If BITMAP is the only available file format, your installation of Paintbrush does not produce the necessary formats for embedding the logo. This could result if you have Version 3.0 of Paintbrush, rather than Version 3.1. See your instructor or technical support person for assistance.

❸ Click **Paintbrush Picture Object** to select this as an embedded object, then click the **Paste button**. The object is embedded in the worksheet as indicated by the Embedded 1 selection indicator. See Figure 9-28. Notice that 1-2-3 placed a frame with a drop shadow around the object to indicate it is an embedded object.

indicates embedded object

logo object embedded in worksheet

Figure 9-28
Logo object from Paintbrush embedded in 1-2-3 worksheet

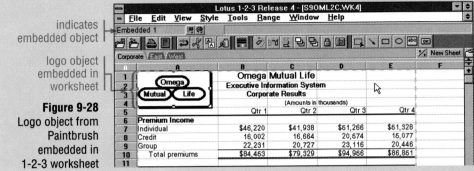

Editing an Embedded Object

Windows makes switching between DDE and OLE applications easy. To make changes to an embedded object, you simply choose that object in the destination file by double-clicking the object. The application in which the object was created opens, and you can make any necessary changes. Remember, the entire source file as well as information identifying the server application, not just the copied data, are embedded in the destination file. For example, to return to Paintbrush from 1-2-3 after embedding the logo, you double-click the logo. If Paintbrush is not already launched, it will be launched and the attached file containing the logo will be opened for editing. You no longer need to use [Alt][Esc] or [Alt][Tab] to switch between applications to view or change different kinds of information—you can perform all these operations by starting from within the one document for the client application.

REFERENCE WINDOW

Editing an Embedded Object

- Double-click the embedded object to open the server application.

- Make the desired changes to the object in the server application.

- Click File then click Update in the server application to place the changes in the source file.

- Click File then click Exit & Return to... to switch back to the destination file.

or

Double-click the Control menu box of the server application to return to the destination file.

Once an object like the logo is embedded in a worksheet document, the object can be revised in the server application. Let's try it.

To switch to the server application to edit an embedded object:

❶ Double-click the **logo object** to open the Paintbrush application with the file that contains the logo. See Figure 9-29. Any desired editing changes could now be made to the logo.

client application

server application

Figure 9-29
Paintbrush opened
with logo file

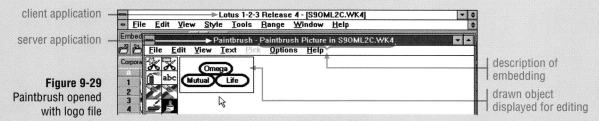

description of
embedding

drawn object
displayed for editing

TROUBLE? If you double-click the logo and the Lines & Colors dialog box appears, the object is pasted and not embedded in the worksheet. Click the Cancel button and press [Del] to remove the pasted object. Then repeat Step 1 through Step 3 in the section "Embedding an Object in a 1-2-3 Worksheet." Now repeat Step 1 above.

At this point, you could edit the object. After making your changes, you need to update the object in the client application.

❷ Click **File** to display this menu, which now contains commands to Update the object in the client application or to Exit and Return to the client file. See Figure 9-30.

Figure 9-30
File menu with
commands for
embedded objects

new menu
selections

❸ Click **Update** to place any changes in the 1-2-3 worksheet.

❹ Click **File** then click **Exit & Return to S9OML2C.WK4** to switch back to 1-2-3 and close the Paintbrush application.

❺ Preview and print the corporate results worksheet, which now includes the logo object. Save the worksheet with the default filename, S9OML2C.WK4, then close the worksheet and exit from 1-2-3.

■   ■   ■

Eileen is pleased with the final version of the EIS. She commends Dawn for her hard work. Eileen can select and integrate EIS data to support her communication activities within OML. Dawn is confident that the EIS, with its direct data transfer, will help Eileen monitor OML's operations for increased profitability.

Questions

1. The process of adding together the results from multiple business units such as regions, divisions, or departments, is called:
   a. concentration
   b. affiliation
   c. consolidation
   d. amalgamation

2. When separate 1-2-3 worksheet files are combined, it is best to design the ranges that are combined as _____ images.
   a. mirror
   b. exact
   c. glass
   d. critical

3. When files are combined, the cell pointer designates the _____ of the range where the incoming data is placed in the worksheet.
   a. name
   b. upper-right corner
   c. size
   d. upper-left corner

4. Sharing results among different applications, both Windows and non-Windows, is known as _____ applications.
   a. synthesizing
   b. blending
   c. integrating
   d. harmonizing

5. When you _____ a copy of a 1-2-3 worksheet range to another client application, a DDE is established between the original worksheet of the server application and the copy in the client application.
   a. embed
   b. link
   c. paste
   d. implant

6. A package of information, such as a 1-2-3 worksheet range or graphic, that can be used in another application is a(n):
   a. victim
   b. article
   c. target
   d. object

7. When you _____ a copy of a 1-2-3 worksheet range in another application, a copy of the entire worksheet file is attached to the document file of the other application.
   a. embed
   b. link
   c. paste
   d. implant

E 8. Using the Task Reference, write down at least one other method of performing the tasks specified by the following SmartIcons:
   a.
   b.

Tutorial Assignments

Launch 1-2-3 and open the T9APT1CO.WK4 worksheet file for Aqua Pure Technologies (APT). Cesar Gonzalez, APT's assistant operations manager, uses 1-2-3 to plan and coordinate production of the Aqua Clarifier purification system. He receives a worksheet file that contains the aggregate production plan from the planners at each of APT's manufacturing operations in North America (NA), South America (SA) and the Pacific Rim (PR). Cesar needs to consolidate the plans from each of these manufacturing operations to produce the corporate aggregate production plan. He received the worksheet files with the individual plans and has laid out a summary worksheet for consolidating the production plans, which you will complete by performing the following:

1. Review Cesar's worksheet for the corporate summary. In preparation for doing the consolidation, notice that the range for the quarterly data is blank and that formulas are used in the total column to calculate these values after the consolidation is performed. Examine the range named PLAN. Does this range include the cells for all the quarterly data?

2. Open the worksheet files from the planners at each manufacturing operation. These files, identified by the last two characters of the filename, are T9APT1NA, T9APT1SA, and T9APT1PR. Examine each worksheet including the range named PLAN, which contains the data for consolidation. If you want, you can preview and print each of these worksheets. Are the PLAN ranges in the three individual operation worksheets and the corporate summary exact images? Close each worksheet when your review is finished.

3. Use the File Combine command to consolidate the production plans for the three manufacturing operations in the corporate summary worksheet. Save the worksheet as S9APT1CO.WK4. Preview and print the corporate aggregate production plan. Circle the total production requirement and the total number of production hours required for APT's worldwide manufacturing operations on the worksheet.

E 4. Cesar created the T9APT2CO.WK4 template as a multiple sheet file. Open this template, then choose the Entire file and Replace values options in the Combine 1-2-3 File dialog box to place the production plan for each manufacturing operation in its respective sheet. Save this worksheet as S9APT2CO.WK4, then preview and print the corporate aggregate production plan sheet.

E 5. Use drill down to examine the demand forecast in the third quarter. Click this cell in the North American sheet before changing the view. What is the demand forecast during this quarter for the three manufacturing operations?

E 6. Copy the range A:A9..A:F13, which contains the corporate aggregate production plan, to the clipboard. Launch Write and open the T9APT1.WRI document. Place the contents of the clipboard at the designated location in this document using the Paste Link command on the Edit menu. Save the document as S9APT1.WRI, then print the memo that includes the worksheet table. Close the Write application and return to 1-2-3.

Launch 1-2-3 and open the T9GCE1CO.WK4 worksheet file for Gulf Coast Energy (GCE), whose business activities include petroleum exploration, production, refining, and marketing. GCE is organized into two business units, the Oil & Gas Production Group (OG) and the Refining & Marketing Group (RM). Paula Chen is responsible for obtaining the operating income statements from each of these groups and then preparing the consolidated statement of operating income. Each group submits a separate worksheet file to Paula for her use in preparing the corporate summary. She just received the year-end statements from each group's accountant, and she is ready to prepare the consolidated statement, which you will do by completing the following:

7. Review Paula's worksheet for the consolidated statement. This is a variance report with the budget and actual data consolidated and then the variance and percent variance calculated from the consolidated amounts. Examine the formulas for calculating the gross profit, operating profit, other deductions and earnings before tax, variance and percent variance in her template worksheet. The incoming data from the groups for the budget and actual amounts is placed in the range named INCOME. Which cells are included in this range?

8. Open the two worksheets for the business groups. These files, identified by the last two characters of the filename as OG and RM, are T9GCE1OG and T9GCE1RM. Examine each worksheet including the range named INCOME. If you want, preview and print both worksheets. Is the INCOME range an exact image in all three worksheets? Close both of the group worksheets when your review is completed.

9. Use the File Combine command to consolidate the budget and actual operating income data for both groups in the consolidated statement worksheet. Save this worksheet as S9GCE1CO.WK4. Preview and print the consolidated statement of operations. Examine the content of the budget and actual cells for gross profit, operating profit, and other deductions. Do they contain formulas or numeric constants? Why? What is the consolidated actual earnings before tax?

E 10. Because the Oil & Gas Production Group includes some sales to the Refining & Marketing Group, they are counted twice in the consolidated statement of operating income. Paula created a third worksheet, T9GCE1EL.WK4, which contains the intracompany sales for correcting these overstated results. The adjustment for sales between business units, known as the intracompany eliminations, needs to be subtracted from the consolidated results for both groups. Open the T9GCE1EL.WK4 worksheet and review its contents. Using the INCOME named range, subtract the elimination data from the previously consolidated results in the S9GCE1CO.WK4 worksheet. Save this consolidated statement with the eliminations as S9GCE2CO.WK4. Preview and print the revised consolidated statement. Then close both worksheets.

E 11. Paula created the T9GCE2CO.WK4 template as a multiple sheet file. Open this template, then review the contents of each sheet and examine the formulas for the consolidated statement. Which formula calculates the consolidation? Use the Entire file and Replace values options in the Combine 1-2-3 File dialog box to place the data for the Refining & Marketing Group and for the intracompany eliminations in their respective sheets in the file. Use linking formulas to display the data values for the Oil & Gas Production Group in its sheet. Save this worksheet as S9GCE3CO.WK4. Preview and print the sheet that contains the consolidated statement.

12. Launch Paintbrush and open the T9GCELOG.BMP file, which contains GCE's logo. Embed this logo in the upper-left corner of the consolidated statement sheet in the S9GCE3CO.WK4 file. Save the worksheet file, then preview and print the consolidated statement including the embedded logo. Close the Paintbrush application.

13. Paula needs to send a memo to Stanton Dent, GCE's chief financial officer. The memo will include the consolidated net sales, cost of sales, and gross profit. She prepared a draft of the memo and saved it in the Write document file T9GCE1.WRI. Copy the range A:A7..A:E10 in the S9GCE3CO.WK4 worksheet to the Windows clipboard. Launch Write and open Paula's memo. Place the contents of the clipboard at the specified location in this document using linking. Save the document as S9GCE1.WRI, then print the memo, which includes the consolidated income data. Double-click the linked object to return to 1-2-3.

Launch 1-2-3 and open the S9OML2C.WK4 worksheet file for Omega Mutual Life (OML). If you did not create this worksheet in the tutorial, then do so before you continue. Eileen is pleased with her EIS but needs to expand its operation by including some enhancements. Complete the following:

E 14. When Dawn initially created the EIS, she did not include the South region, which was in the process of being organized. Eileen now wants to include this new region in the EIS. Open the T9OML1S.WK4 file, which contains the plan for the South region, and review the contents of this worksheet. Then make S9OML2C.WK4 the active worksheet. Activate Group mode and insert a new sheet between the East and West sheets, then deactivate Group mode. Name the worksheet tab "South."

15. Use the File Combine command to place the results from the T9OML1S.WK4 file into the South sheet. Are the results for the South included in the corporate summary? Why or why not? If they are not, make the necessary revisions so that the results for the South region are included in the corporate summary. Save this worksheet as S9OML3C.WK4. Preview and print the Corporate sheet and the South sheet.

E 16. Eileen wants to include a copy of the chart that summarizes OML's premium income in her memo to Paul. Copy the Premium Income chart to the Windows clipboard. Launch Write and open the S9OML3.WRI file. Immediately below the current 1-2-3 worksheet table object, add this paragraph:

> Compare the premium income for the West region to the overall OML premium income for the year as summarized in this chart:

Place the chart immediately below this paragraph using the Paste Link command on the Edit menu. Center the chart. Save this document as S9OML4.WRI, then print it. Which files are currently linked to this Write document? Why? Why is it best in Eileen's situation to use linking rather than embedding? Close the Write application.

E 17. Eileen asked Dawn to set up a macro to automate combining the regional worksheet files into the corporate results worksheet. Dawn's macro is in the T9OML4CM.WK4 worksheet. Open the worksheet file and review its contents. If your Student Disk is in a drive other than A, locate the FILE-COMBINE macro commands and change the disk drive letter. Use the range name selector to go to the OPTIONS range, which contains the macro buttons. Execute the Consolidate macro and watch the file processing, then execute the Print Report macro. Use the range name selector to locate the macros and print them. Close the worksheet without saving it. What is an advantage of using a macro to do the consolidation with the File Combine Add command?

Case Problems

1. Tracking Bonuses for John Connolly & Sons

John Connolly & Sons has been a publisher of textbooks since 1945. John Connolly was the original founder of the publishing company and was later joined by his sons, Mark and Brian, when they graduated from college. Over the past fifty years, John Connolly & Sons has established itself as a leading publisher of mathematics and statistics textbooks, which are distributed through the company's University and Junior College divisions.

John has since retired and turned the control of the family-owned and operated company to Mark, the oldest son. Mark concentrates on the financial area of the company. Brian maintains responsibility for the sales and marketing functions of the company. He is particularly focused on the management of key personnel. Brian recognizes that in order to achieve sales growth in the publishing industry, outstanding sales associates are needed.

Brian meets regularly with his University and Junior College division managers, Mary Monzo and Brad Anderson. Mary and Brad each manage the sales associates for their respective divisions. Mary's sales associates are responsible for sales to four-year universities. Brad's staff serves the same group of clients except at junior colleges and technical schools. At the start of each year, Mary and Brad meet with each of their sales associates and set a quota. A five percent bonus is paid to each associate based on the excess sales for the four quarters and the quota for that sales associate. The payment of a bonus as an incentive has improved the productivity of the sales associates.

At the last meeting between Brian, Mary, and Brad, Brad discussed a system that would track bonuses for each division and sales associate. Your task is to create this system for Brian and his division managers by completing the following:

1. Launch 1-2-3 and open the P9JCS1JC.WK4 and P9JCS1UN.WK4 worksheet files, then save them as S9JCS1JC.WK4 and S9JCS1UN.WK4. Review the worksheets. Preview and print each worksheet for your reference.

E   2. Open the P9JCS1CO.WK4 worksheet, which summarizes the bonuses paid to each division. Use formulas with file references to link the totals from the TOTAL row in each of the division worksheets to the summary worksheet. Save this worksheet as S9JCS1CO.WK4, then preview and print the summary. Why is linking formulas with file references a good method for including the data in this summary worksheet?

3. Copy the bonus totals from the summary worksheet to the clipboard. Launch Write and open the P9JCS1.WRI document. Use linking to place the contents of the clipboard at the specified location between the first and second paragraphs. Save the document as S9JCS1.WRI, then print the memo with the division bonus totals.

4. Mary needs to revise her quarterly sales numbers for several associates. She received the P9JCS2UN.WK4 file, which contains these changes from Accounting. Although the Accounting staff members followed a similar arrangement for the new data, their worksheet does not contain the bonus amount or the totals. The quota and quarterly sales data need to be replaced for each associate in Mary's S9JCS1UN.WK4 worksheet. Return to 1-2-3, open the P9JSC2UN.WK4 file, then review it, including the named range. Use the File Combine command to replace the quota and sales data in the S9JCS1UN.WK4 worksheet with that from the P9JCS2UN.WK4 worksheet.

5. Return to Write and review the table from the summary data. Was it updated? Print the S9JCS1.WRI document.

2.   Analyzing Work Centers for Merritt Laboratories, Inc.

In 1956, Dr. Joseph P. Merritt founded Merritt Laboratories, Inc (MLI). Dr. Merritt worked as a research chemist for a leading pharmaceutical company prior to founding MLI. He is recognized as one of the premier researchers in the areas of cardiovascular, neural, and respiratory systems. Since its founding, MLI has grown to become one of the worldwide leaders in the manufacturing of prescription drugs. MLI patents most of its pharmaceutical products, which provides product differentiation in the competitive pharmaceutical industry. Currently, MLI sells over 100 different prescription and non-prescription pharmaceutical products.

The pharmaceutical industry is regulated by the U.S. Food and Drug Administration (FDA). The FDA approves new products only after extensive testing. The FDA also maintains a close watch on the production and effectiveness of existing drugs. MLI produces all of its products at its production facility in Providence, Rhode Island. A work center approach is taken in the production of all of MLI's pharmaceuticals. A work center is made up of a set of machines and machine operators. Each work center works on one batch of a product at a time until that batch is complete. MLI production is separated into two groups, the Caplet and Tablet groups. Each group maintains the same work centers in different parts of the factory.

Gabriela Dietz is MLI's production manager. At the end of each month, Gabriela prepares a work center analysis that calculates the amount of machine time available and the efficiency of labor. Machine time available is the amount of time that a machine is not used. Gabriela has set a goal of 7% to 15% machine time available and 90% efficiency of labor. Gabriela generally presents the results of this analysis at the monthly production review meeting. This month Gabriela is going to be out of town and is preparing a memo to present at the meeting. Gabriela would like you to complete this memo by performing the following:

1. Launch 1-2-3 and open the P9MLI1CA.WK4 and P9MLI1TA.WK4 worksheet files for the MLI work centers. Review the worksheets. How are machine time available and efficiency of labor calculated?

E 2. Construct a third worksheet that can be used as the consolidated worksheet. This worksheet should be similar in structure to the worksheets for the Caplet and Tablet groups. Can you create this worksheet from a copy of a worksheet for either the Caplet or Tablet group? How is this useful? Do you need formulas to calculate the machine time available and efficiency of labor? Why? Save this worksheet as S9MLI1WC.WK4.

3. Consolidate the Caplet and Tablet groups into the summary worksheet. Did you combine the entire file or a cell range? Explain. What could be done to make this more efficient? Save this worksheet as S9MLI2WC.WK4. Preview and print the consolidated report for the work centers. What is the total machine capacity? Circle the total efficiency of labor.

E 4. Using the consolidated data, create a bar chart of efficiency of labor. Add the appropriate titles and headings. Save this worksheet as S9MLI3WC.WK4. Preview and print the bar chart. Based on the efficiency of labor, which work center should Gabriela investigate more closely? Why?

5. Launch Write and open the P9MLI1.WRI document. Review the document. From the consolidated worksheet, place a table of the work centers, machine hour capacity, machine hours used, and machine time available above the Figure 1 caption. Place the bar chart from the consolidated worksheet above the Figure 2 caption. Did you use embedding or linking? Explain. Save this document as S9MLI3.WRI. Preview and print the document.

E 6. Return to 1-2-3 and the consolidated worksheet. To automate the consolidation process, create a macro and macro button that will consolidate the Caplet and Tablet work groups. Save this worksheet as S9MLI4WC.WK4. Execute the macro, then print the macro commands as documentation.

3. Reporting Operating Profits for SeaWest Industries

SeaWest Industries (SWI) manufactures, constructs, and manages wind farms. A wind farm consists of several hundred wind turbine generators that churn silently in a breeze producing electricity. SWI recently completed construction of a wind farm in Tehachapi, California which, at the time of completion, was the largest single wind project of its kind. SWI manufacturing operations are organized in two divisions—Micon Wind Turbines in Copenhagen, Denmark and Mitusbishi Wind Turbines in Yokohama, Japan—which make up the Wind Turbine Manufacturing business unit.

Niels Rydder, vice president and chief financial officer of SWI, asked Lisbeth Hether, a financial analyst, to develop a worksheet for preparing the quarterly statement of consolidated operating profit for Wind Turbine Manufacturing. The statement of operating profit is a variance report that includes the budget, actual, variance, and percent variance for each line item. Each quarter the two manufacturing divisions use electronic mail to transmit a worksheet file containing their operating profit data to the corporate office in San Diego. These files contain data obtained directly from each division's general ledger system and are in local currency—Danish Krone (DKK) or Japanese Yen—with the appropriate currency exchange rate included in the worksheet. The worksheet that Lisbeth created includes the operating profit data for each division in local currency and in U.S. dollars (USD). The consolidated statement of operating profit uses USD, because the different local currencies do not produce meaningful results when consolidated. Lisbeth has set up the consolidation worksheet and has just received the two worksheets from the manufacturing divisions. Niels needs the consolidated statement of operating profit for a meeting tomorrow. Perform the following tasks to produce the information Niels wants:

1. Launch 1-2-3 and open the worksheet P9SWI1.WK4, which is a multiple sheet file that contains the quarterly statement of operating profit that Lisbeth created. Save the worksheet as S9SWI1.WK4.

2. Review Lisbeth's worksheet by examining each of the three sheets. Notice that the local currency operating statements are immediately to the right of the USD statements so you can use [Tab] and [Shift][Tab] to move quickly between the two statements. What formula is used in the Wind Turbines sheet to do the consolidation for the budget and actual amounts? In general, what is the formula for performing the currency conversion to USD for each division? Why is "ERR" displayed in the cells that calculate the percent variance? Notice that the budget and actual columns in the local currency statements are blank in preparation for receiving the data from the division files. Try using the range name selector to access the local currency statements.

E 3. Open the P9SWI1DK.WK4 and P9SWI1JP.WK4 worksheets for the manufacturing operations in Copenhagen and Yokohama, respectively, and examine their contents. If you want, print these two files. Compare these worksheets to the line items in the local currency statements. Do the rows and columns of data in the division files match the corresponding data in the operating profit statements?

4. Use the File Combine command to place the local currency data in its respective statement. Where does the cell pointer need to be located while the File Combine is being done? Save the worksheet as S9SWI2.WK4, then preview and print all three USD reports and the two local currency reports. (*Hint:* Wind Turbine Operating Profit Variance = $2,151.)

5. Lisbeth wants to send Niels a memo that contains the Wind Turbines operating profit. Copy the range A:A7..A:E24 to the clipboard for use in her memo. Launch Write and open the P9SWI1.WRI document. Use object linking to place the operating profit data at the specified location in the memo. Save this document as S9SWI1.WRI, then print the memo.

E 6. Create a macro that lets Lisbeth do the file combine of the division worksheets and print all five of the operating profit statements. Have the macro print all the USD reports first and then the local currency reports. Place the macro on a separate sheet and name that sheet "Macros." Include a macro button on the Macros sheet for executing the macro. Save this worksheet as S9SWI3.WK4. Execute the macro. Print the macro commands. Is there an advantage to using a macro to do file combines? Why or why not?

E 7. SWI is considering establishing a third manufacturing division, which would be located in Southern California. What changes would need to be made to Lisbeth's worksheet to include the reporting for this third division? If the sheet for this new division is a duplicate of those for the other two divisions, what is an easy way to handle the currency exchange rate?

E 8. Create a separate 1-2-3 worksheet for the proposed Southern California division. This should include the same line items as those used with the other two divisions. Make up the budget and actual data for this division. Save this worksheet as S9SWI4SC.WK4, then print the file. Open the S9SWI2.WK4 worksheet and save it as S9SWI4.WK4. Revise the S9SWI4.WK4 worksheet to include the changes you described in Problem 7 for adding the Southern California division. Use the File Combine command to include the California data in the revised worksheet. Save this worksheet, then preview and print the Wind Turbine and Southern California operating profit reports.

OBJECTIVES

In this tutorial you will:

- Use macro commands that prompt for data entry
- Use macro commands that check data values
- Use macro commands that build loops
- Use subroutines to group macros as a unit
- Create user-defined macro menus

Developing Advanced Macro Applications

Tracking Revenues and Expenses

CASE

Berkshire Teddy Bears   Two years ago, Tiffany Barrett gave birth to a son and decided to resign her executive position at Fairfield Financial in favor of something that would demand less of her time. She founded Berkshire Teddy Bears (BTB) with her sister Erika. They got the idea when Erika went shopping for a teddy bear for her new nephew and was unable to find the kind of high-quality bear she cherished as a youngster. Unable to find such a bear, she handcrafted one herself to give to her nephew. Soon, Erika and Tiffany were using the sewing hobby they'd enjoyed since their teens to make bears and sell them at boutiques, church bazaars, and craft shows. BTB quickly grew profitable.

Tiffany and Erika gambled that loving parents and grandparents would pay a bit more for a hand-crafted bear. Each of BTB's 14-inch bears are signed and numbered to verify their origin. Tiffany and Erika catered to their customers by opening a "hospital" for wounded bears, so that if the family pet plays a little rough with "Teddy," parents can return it to BTB for repairs. They perform the surgery, then mail the bear—now wearing a hospital gown and carrying a certificate of health from the house doctor—home to recuperate.

As budding entrepreneurs, Tiffany and Erika have quickly learned that to run a successful business, they need to manage cash flow. Cash is the lifeblood of most small businesses because cash is required to meet their current obligations. Successfully managing cash flow relies on the use of technology as a survival strategy.

Tiffany and Erika discussed their requirements for tracking revenues and expenditures. They decided to use a checkbook ledger to keep them informed of their cash flow. A **checkbook ledger** is a database that contains a listing of all cash transactions conducted by a business. Using 1-2-3, Erika set up a checkbook ledger worksheet (Figure 10-1). The data definition for BTB's ledger is shown in Figure 10-2.

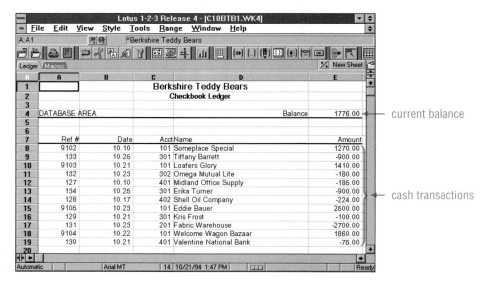

Figure 10-1
Checkbook ledger
worksheet

Field Name	Description
Ref #	Check or deposit number; 9000 numbers are deposits
Date	Date of transaction entered in mm.dd format
Acct	Account number identifies type of transaction
Name	Name to whom check was made out or from whom money was received
Amount	Amount of transaction—deposits (revenues) are positive and checks (expenses) are negative

Figure 10-2
Data definition of
checkbook ledger
database

In their database, Tiffany and Erika track cash flow by using a chart of accounts. A **chart of accounts** is simply a list of the accounts, identified by account numbers, used by a business. Tiffany used her accounting background from Fairfield Financial to set up the chart of accounts for BTB (Figure 10-3). Account numbers, like 301 and 302, are easier to use to classify and track transactions than account names, like Salaries and Health insurance.

```
Account
Number      Description
  101       Sales
  201       Cost of sales
  301       Salaries
  302       Health insurance
  401       Office expense
  402       Automobile expense
```

Figure 10-3
Chart of accounts

Now that the ledger is set up, Erika and Tiffany decide to make the ledger easier to use. They want to include macros that will prompt whoever is entering a transaction and that will sort and print the database. Erika develops her planning analysis sheet based on these requirements (Figure 10-4).

Planning Analysis Sheet

My goal:
Develop macros for entering transactions in the ledger database, and for sorting and printing the database

What results do I want to see?
List of revenues and expenses recorded in ledger database and available for printing reports

What information do I need?
Ledger database worksheet for recording transactions

What tasks will the macros perform?
1. Go to the ledger database
2. Insert a row in the database range for the transaction
3. Prompt user for a data value for each field of the transaction and enter the value into the database
4. Sort the database
5. Print the database

Figure 10-4
Erika's planning
analysis sheet

With this completed, Erika develops the macros.

Introduction to Advanced Macro Commands

In Tutorial 6 you learned how to create and use macros by recording macro commands and playing them back. Lotus 1-2-3 has many advanced macro commands that help to develop sophisticated, automated spreadsheet applications. These advanced macro commands are not worksheet actions that you can record and playback. You must manually enter the keyword and arguments of each macro command, which make up the command's syntax, as labels in cells (refer to Figure 6-4, if necessary). You can group the advanced macro commands into five categories:

- *Data manipulation.* These commands select, enter, edit, copy, erase, and recalculate data.
- *Interactive.* These commands suspend the running of a macro for user input, control the timing of a macro, and prevent the user from stopping the macro.
- *Flow of control.* These commands direct the sequence of executing macro commands using branching, subroutine calls, looping, and conditional processing.
- *Screen control.* These commands control various parts of the screen display, including changing the mode indicator or screen size, making the computer beep, and manipulating the control panel.
- *File manipulation.* These commands open, close, and combine worksheet files.

Now that you are more familiar with the advanced macro commands, you are ready to examine the worksheet Erika prepared for the checkbook ledger that tracks revenues and expenses.

Retrieving the Worksheet

First, you need to select the SmartIcon palette for this tutorial, which is the same SmartIcon palette you used in Tutorial 6, and then open Erika's worksheet.

To select the Tutorial 6 SmartIcon palette and open the worksheet:

❶ Launch 1-2-3, and select the Tutorial 6 SmartIcon palette using the SmartIcon palette selector ⊞ in the status bar.

❷ Open Erika's C10BTB1.WK4 worksheet located on your Student Disk. Immediately save this file as S10BTB1.WK4 in case you want to restart the tutorial.

❸ Review the worksheet. Notice that the Ledger sheet contains only the database, and the Macros sheet contains all the macros. Use the range name selector to examine each of the named ranges in both sheets. See Figure 10-5.

Range Name	Description
BALANCE	Identifies the cells that are summed in the Amount field
DATABASE	Identifies the rows that contain records for each transaction, but excludes field names
REPORT AREA	Specifies the report heading and database area for printing
INPUT	Specifies the range name for the data input macro
REPORT	Specifies the range name for the print report macro and prints the Ledger sheet (performs the same tasks as the PRINT REPORT macro in Tutorial 6)
SORTER	Specifies the range name for the sort macro
MACROS	Designates cell A1 on the macro sheet for directly locating the macros

Figure 10-5
Range names in
Erika's worksheet

❹ Click the **Macros worksheet tab** then click the **Home SmartIcon**. The macro buttons for executing the macros Erika developed and the macro commands for the Input macro are displayed in the window. See Figure 10-6.

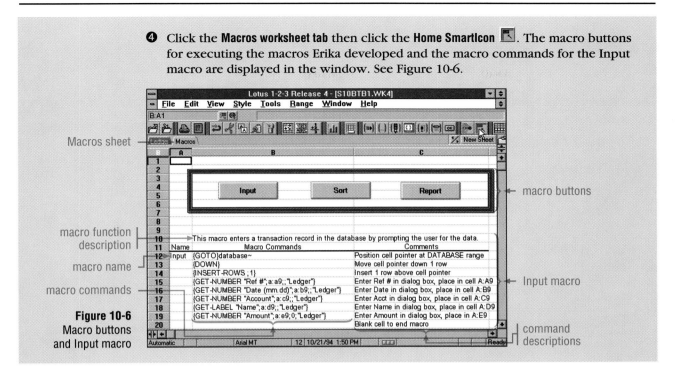

Figure 10-6
Macro buttons
and Input macro

You'll learn the details of the macro commands after you execute the macros and observe their operation.

Documenting Advanced Macros

Erika documented her Input macro, as shown in Figure 10-6. Although 1-2-3 does not require documentation for the macro's execution, the documentation is helpful when someone tries to understand what the macro does long after it was created. Erika described the function of the macro, identified the macro's range name, and added comments that describe the action of each macro command.

Prompting Data Entry: the {GET-NUMBER} and {GET-LABEL} Commands

Erika and Tiffany wanted to make their data entry simple. The Input macro Erika wrote prompts the user for input for each data value in a transaction. Let's execute Erika's Input macro to observe its operation.

To execute the data entry macro:
❶ Click the **Input macro button** to execute the macro. The cell pointer moves to cell A9, the second row of the database, and the Ledger dialog box prompting data entry for the Ref # field displays. See Figure 10-7.

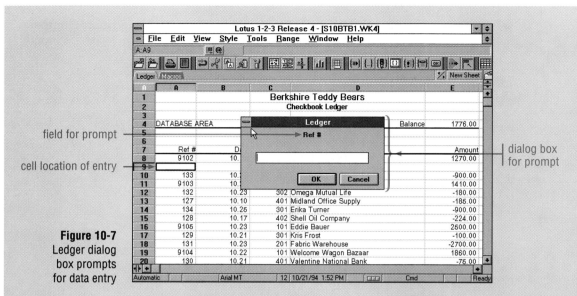

field for prompt

cell location of entry

Figure 10-7
Ledger dialog
box prompts
for data entry

When you add a record to a database that is identified by a named range, the range must be expanded to include the new record (row). If you insert the record immediately above or below the named range, the new record is *not* included in the range. However, by inserting the new record as the *second* row of the database, you expand the named range to include the newly inserted record.

❷ Enter **135**, the data value for the Ref # field.

❸ Enter the data values for the other four fields in their respective dialog boxes as follows:

Date	**10.26**
Account	**201**
Name	**Burlington Mills**
Amount	**-870**

Notice how you must enter the date as a decimal number (mm.dd). If you enter the date as mm/dd, 1-2-3 will divide the number and place the result in the cell, even if the cell has a date format. Your screen should now look like Figure 10-8.

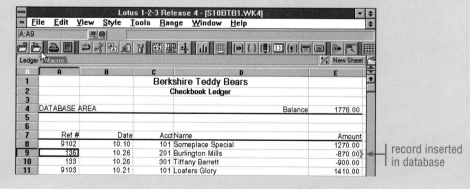

Figure 10-8
New transaction
added to Ledger
database

record inserted
in database

Now let's review the macro commands to see how Erika instructed 1-2-3 to perform these steps.

To review the Input macro commands:

❶ Click the **Macros worksheet tab,** or click the **range name selector** 🔲 then click **Macros** to display the macro sheet.

❷ Scroll the window, as necessary, to view the Input macro commands, as shown previously in Figure 10-6.

Erika's Input macro uses these advanced macro commands: {GOTO}, {INSERT-ROWS}, {GET-NUMBER}, and {GET-LABEL}. Figure 10-9 describes these commands. Lotus 1-2-3 also provides the {FORM} and {APPENDBELOW} macro commands as an alternative method for prompted data entry. You can find descriptions of these commands in the Macro Reference and 1-2-3's on-line Help.

Macro Command	Description
{GOTO}*location*~	Moves cell pointer to specified location
	location is a range name or cell address
{INSERT-ROWS [*location*]; [*number*]}	Inserts the desired number of rows at the current or specified location
	location is a range name or cell address, if omitted the current location of the cell pointer is used
	number is the rows to be inserted, if omitted the number of rows specified by the location is used
{GET-LABEL [*prompt*];*location*; [*default*];*title*}	Displays a dialog box and waits for the user to enter a data value in the cell as a label
	prompt is the text or a cell address containing the text that appears at top of the dialog box, with a text argument enclosed in quotation marks
	location is the range name or cell address where you want the data stored
	default is an initial value that appears in the text box, without a default value the text box is blank
	title is the text or a cell address containing the text that appears in the title bar of the dialog box, with a text argument enclosed in quotation marks
{GET-NUMBER [*prompt*];*location*; [*default*];*title*}	Displays a dialog box and waits for user to enter a data value in the cell as a number

Figure 10-9
Syntax of macro commands used for prompting data entry

The arguments enclosed in brackets are optional; however, if you skip an argument, the semicolon is still needed. You do *not* type the brackets when entering the optional arguments.

The {GET-NUMBER} command performs data editing on the input data values. **Data editing** is a check of an input data value to determine if it meets specified conditions. The {GET-NUMBER} command edits the data value entered in the dialog box to determine whether it is a numeric value. If it's not a number, ERR appears at the specified cell location to indicate a number was not entered. The {GET-LABEL} command places the input data value in the cell as a label without data editing.

Using Special Keys in Macros

When you write a macro, you have to use special entries to represent many keystrokes. In Erika's macro, {GOTO} specifies the F5 key, the tilde (~) represents the Enter key, and {DOWN} indicates the [↓] key. Figure 10-10 lists special keys you can use in creating advanced macros.

Key Indicator in Macro	Substitute for Key or Keystroke Action
{LEFT} or {LEFT n} {L} or {L n}	Moves cell pointer one or *n* cells to the left
{RIGHT} or {RIGHT n} {R} or {R n}	Moves cell pointer one or *n* cells to the right
{UP} or {UP n} {U} or {U n}	Moves cell pointer one or *n* cells up
{DOWN} or {DOWN n} {D} or {D n}	Moves cell pointer one or *n* cells down
{BIGLEFT}	Moves cell pointer one screen to the left
{BIGRIGHT}	Moves cell pointer one screen to the right
{HOME}	Moves cell pointer to cell A1
{END}	With {LEFT}, {RIGHT}, {UP}, or {DOWN} moves cell pointer to next blank or nonblank cell
{PGUP}	Moves cell pointer up one page
{PGDN}	Moves cell pointer down one page
{EDIT}	Edits current cell
{NAME}	Lists range names
{ABS}	Creates an absolute cell reference
{GOTO}	Cell pointer moves to specified cell
{WINDOW}	Switches between split windows in a worksheet
{QUERY}	Repeats last database query
{CALC}	Recalculates the worksheet
{ALT}, {MENUBAR} or {MB}	Accesses menu bar
~	Executes the Enter key
{ALT}	Executes the Alt key
{BACKSPACE} or {BS}	Executes the Backspace key
{DEL}	Executes the Delete key
{ESC}	Executes the Esc key

Figure 10-10
Special keys
in macros

Entering Advanced Macro Commands

You enter advanced macro commands as labels in the desired location in the worksheet, such as in Erika's separate Macros sheet. You enter these commands by using the Macro Command SmartIcon, or the F3 (Name) key, or by typing the entire command.

REFERENCE WINDOW

Entering Advanced Macro Commands

- Click the cell where you want the macro command to appear.

- Click the Macro Command SmartIcon to display the Macro Keywords dialog box.

  or

  Type { then press [F3] (NAME) to display the Macro Keywords dialog box.

- Type the beginning letters of the macro command to scroll the list.

- Click the desired macro keyword.

- Click the OK button to place the keyword in the cell.

- Type the remainder of the macro command, then click the Confirm button or press [Enter] to complete entering the macro command.

  or

- Type the entire macro command in the desired cell, then press [Enter].

Erika decides she wants to see the balance after entering a new transaction. Let's enter the {GOTO} macro command to the end of Erika's Input macro to move the cell pointer to cell E4, the cell containing the balance.

To enter a macro command using the Macro Command SmartIcon:

❶ Click **B:B20** to select the cell where you want the macro command.

❷ Click the **Macro Command SmartIcon** to display the Macro Keywords dialog box, then type **GO** to scroll the list to the macro commands beginning with "GO." See Figure 10-11.

type "GO" here to scroll list

Figure 10-11
Macro name list
scrolled to GOTO

❸ Click **GOTO** in the list to select it, then click the **OK button** to place an open brace and the GOTO keyword into cell B:B20.

❹ Type **)a:e4~** to finish the macro command, then press **[Enter]** to complete entering the macro command.

You could have typed the macro command in the cell, but by using the Macro Command SmartIcon, you avoid misspelling the macro keyword.

❺ Move the comment in cell B:C20 to cell B:C21, then enter a comment in cell B:C20 to describe the macro command. See Figure 10-12.

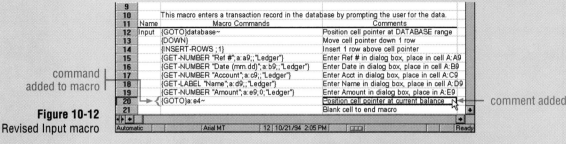

command added to macro

Figure 10-12
Revised Input macro

comment added

❻ Test the revised Input macro using the following test data values:

Ref #	**9106**
Date	**10.27**
Account	**101**
Name	**Country Mouse**
Amount	**940**

❼ Save this revised worksheet as S10BTB1.WK4.

Sorting the Database: the {SORT} Command

After new records are inserted in the database, Erika thinks it would be helpful to sort the database by account number and then by date. This way, she and Tiffany can see at a glance how much money comes in and how much is spent on specific items.

Erika named the range for the sort macro "Sorter" "rather than "Sort." Lotus 1-2-3 range names need to be different from macro keywords or other 1-2-3 reserved words because 1-2-3 commands take precedence over range names. This means that if you use a 1-2-3 keyword or reserved word as a range name in a macro, 1-2-3 executes the command rather than the macro.

Let's execute the Sorter macro, which sorts the database with Acct as the primary sort key and Date as the secondary sort key.

To execute the sort macro and arrange the database by account and date:
❶ Click the **Macros worksheet tab** to return to the Macros sheet.
❷ Click the **Sort macro button** to execute the sort. Review the results of the sort. See Figure 10-13.

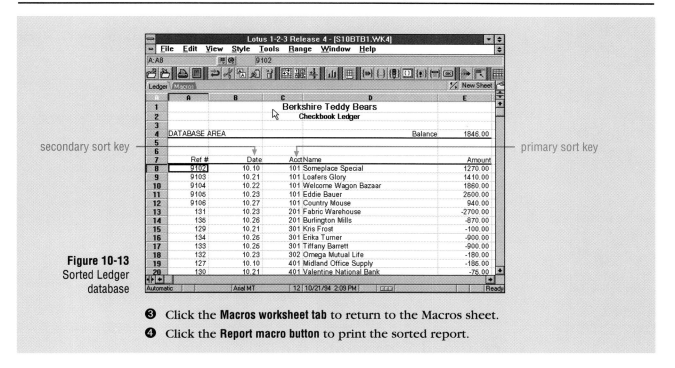

Figure 10-13
Sorted Ledger
database

secondary sort key

primary sort key

❸ Click the **Macros worksheet tab** to return to the Macros sheet.

❹ Click the **Report macro button** to print the sorted report.

Now let's review the Sorter and Report macros to see how Erika instructed 1-2-3 to perform these actions.

To review the Sorter macro:

❶ Click the **Macros worksheet tab** to return to the Macros sheet.

❷ Scroll down the worksheet to display the Sorter and Report macros. See Figure 10-14. Review each macro command.

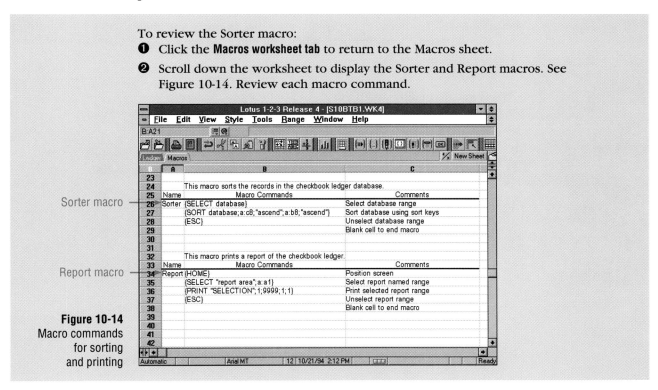

Sorter macro

Report macro

Figure 10-14
Macro commands
for sorting
and printing

The Sorter macro uses two advanced macro commands: {SELECT} and {SORT}. These commands are described in Figure 10-15.

Macro Command	Description
{SELECT *range*;[*location*]}	Selects the specified range and the initial location of the cell pointer
	range is specified range name or cell address
	location is where the cell pointer is positioned when range is unselected
{SORT *range*;[*key1*];["*order1*"]; [*key2*]["*order2*"];[*key3*];["*order3*"]}	Sorts the specified range using the sort keys and specified sort order
	range is the range to be sorted
	key is the field used for the sort
	order is specified as "ascend" or "descend" for the desired arrangement and is required for each sort key

Figure 10-15
Syntax of macro commands used for sorting

Conditional Statements: the {IF} Command

As Erika looks over her Input macro, she realizes that if someone runs the Input macro and enters a label instead of a number when the {GET-NUMBER} command requests data values for the Ref#, Date, Acct, and Amount fields, 1-2-3 will place the ERR value in the cells, but won't otherwise notify the user that there is a problem. Let's run the Input macro and observe what happens when you enter the wrong type of data in response to the prompts.

To observe data editing with the {GET-NUMBER} command:
1. Scroll the Macros sheet to display the macro buttons.
2. Click the **Input macro button** to display the Ledger dialog box.
3. Enter **abc** as the data value for the Ref # field. Note that ERR appears in cell A:A9.
4. Enter the data values for the next four fields in their dialog boxes as follows:

Date	**Oct 26**
Account	**29B**
Name	**1234**
Amount	**ten**

See Figure 10-16. Look at the results with ERR entered in row 9.

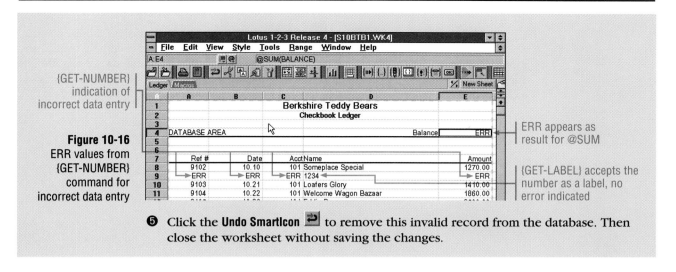

Figure 10-16
ERR values from
{GET-NUMBER}
command for
incorrect data entry

❺ Click the **Undo SmartIcon** to remove this invalid record from the database. Then close the worksheet without saving the changes.

Erika wants the macro to detect a data input error as soon as it occurs so the user can correct the error before entering the data value for the next field in the record. This means that if a data entry error occurs, Erika wants the dialog box redisplayed immediately so the user can enter the number correctly the second time. This requires the use of *conditional logic* to test for the occurrence of the ERR value. Erika revises the Input macro to include the {IF}, {BRANCH}, and {BEEP} commands, which are described in Figure 10-17.

Macro Command	Description
{BEEP [*tone-number*]}	Sounds one of four tones through the computer's speaker
	tone-number is a value of 1 through 4 that specifies the tone
{BRANCH *location*}	Causes a macro's execution to continue at the specified location rather than with the command in the next cell down the column
	location is a range name or cell address of the next macro command that is executed
{IF *condition*}*true-macro-commands*	Tests the condition and executes the *true-macro-commands* when the condition is true, otherwise these commands are not executed and the commands in the cell immediately below the {IF} command are executed
	condition is a comparison using a relational operator, like those used with the @IF function, or a logical function
	true-macro-commands are those macro commands executed when the condition evaluates to true

Figure 10-17
Syntax of macro
commands used for
conditional checking
of input data

When Lotus 1-2-3 evaluates a condition in an {IF} statement, it directs the flow of the next macro command executed based on the results of the condition (Figure 10-18). If the condition is true, the macro command in the same cell as the {IF} command is executed. If the condition is false, 1-2-3 skips the macro command in the cell with the {IF} command and executes the macro command in the cell immediately below the {IF} command.

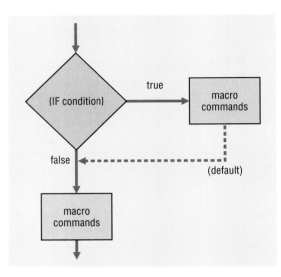

Figure 10-18
Alternative paths of
an {IF} command

Erika made the revisions to her macro in the C10BTB2.WK4 worksheet. Let's open the worksheet and examine the macro.

To review the revised Input macro:

❶ Open Erika's C10BTB2.WK4 worksheet located on your Student Disk.

❷ Click the **Macros worksheet tab**, if necessary, then click the **Home SmartIcon** and scroll the worksheet window to display the entire revised Input macro. See Figure 10-19.

Input macro ———
conditional logic ———

Figure 10-19
Revised Input
macro with {IF},
{BRANCH}, and
{BEEP} commands

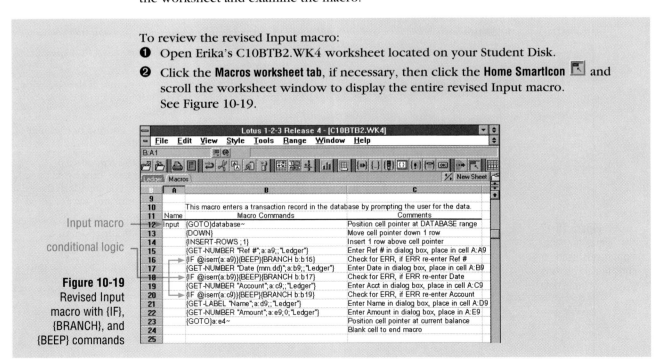

Erika used the {IF} and {BRANCH} commands in rows 16, 18, and 20 with the @ISERR function. The @ISERR function is true when a cell contains the ERR value, otherwise it's false. If the cell referenced by the @ISERR function contains the ERR value, 1-2-3 executes the {BEEP} command to sound an audible alarm, then executes the {BRANCH} command, which in this case, causes the previous {GET-NUMBER} command to be re-executed. If the {BRANCH} command was not used, the {BEEP} command would produce the tone, but the error could not be corrected because 1-2-3 would execute the command following the {IF} command.

Figure 10-20 lists several functions that test cell contents and return true or false.

Function	Description
@ISERR(cell-reference)	Tests for ERR and returns true (1) or false (0)
@ISNA(cell-reference)	Tests for NA and returns true (1) or false (0)
@ISNUMBER(cell-reference)	Tests for a number (value) and returns true (1) or false (0)
@ISRANGE(cell-reference)	Tests for valid range name and returns true (1) or false (0)
@ISSTRING(cell-reference)	Tests for a string (label) and returns true (1) or false (0)

Figure 10-20
Selected 1-2-3
functions for testing
cell contents

Let's execute the revised Input macro with the conditional test to observe its operation.

To execute the revised macro with the conditional statements for error checking:

❶ Click the **Home SmartIcon** 🔲, or scroll the worksheet window to display Erika's macro buttons.

❷ Click the **Input macro button** to execute the macro.

❸ Enter **abc** as the data value for the Ref # field. ERR appears in cell A:A9, the computer beeps, and the Ledger dialog box for Ref # displays. See Figure 10-21.

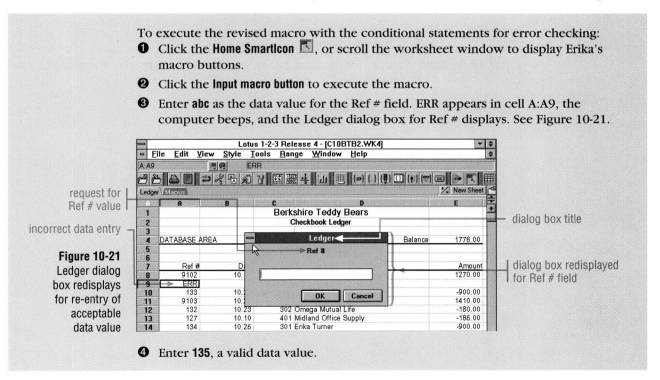

request for
Ref # value

incorrect data entry

Figure 10-21
Ledger dialog
box redisplays
for re-entry of
acceptable
data value

dialog box title

dialog box redisplayed
for Ref # field

❹ Enter **135**, a valid data value.

❺ Use your own unacceptable test data values for the Date and Acct fields. Then enter the valid data values as follows:

Date   **10.26**

Acct   **201**

Name   **Burlington Mills**

Amount   **-870**

TROUBLE? If you make a mistake entering the correct data values, click the Undo SmartIcon 🔄, repeat Step 2, then enter the valid data values from Steps 4 and 5.

❻ Close the worksheet without saving the changes.

Erika has processed her transaction for BTB with data editing to ensure numeric data was entered in the appropriate fields.

If you want to take a break and resume this tutorial at a later time, you can exit 1-2-3 by double-clicking the Control menu box in the upper-left corner of your screen. When you resume the tutorial, launch 1-2-3, place your Student Disk in the disk drive, and select the Tutorial 6 SmartIcon palette, then continue with this tutorial.

◼   ◼   ◼

Creating a Loop: the {BRANCH} Command

Erika and Tiffany usually enter several transactions at a time. The Input macro stops after one transaction is entered. Erika wants to be able to enter one transaction after another until she is done. She decides to use a loop. A **loop** allows macro commands to be repeated, like those for entering several transactions (Figure 10-22).

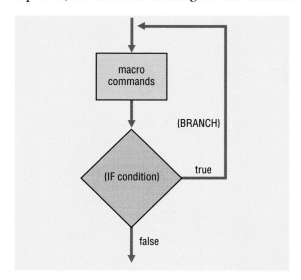

Figure 10-22
Loop repeats a
series of macro
commands

When you use a loop, you need a way to stop the loop, that is, to signal the macro that the task is finished. An easy way for Erika to signal she has entered all her transactions is to enter a specific data value. For ending her data entry, Erika picks a Ref # of 9999 for her "done" indicator value. She chooses this value because it's a number that will be accepted for that field and because she does not expect to have a transaction with that number.

Erika made these changes to her macro in the C10BTB3.WK4 worksheet. Let's open that worksheet and review her revised macro.

To review the revised Input macro, which contains a loop:

❶ Open Erika's C10BTB3.WK4 worksheet located on your Student Disk.

❷ Click the **Macros worksheet tab**, if necessary, then click the **Home SmartIcon** 🔳 and scroll down the worksheet window to display the revised Input macro. See Figure 10-23.

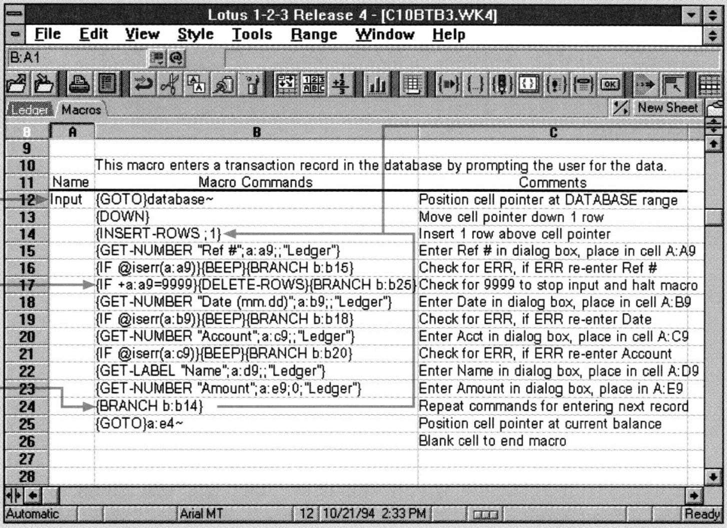

Figure 10-23
Revised Input macro with loop

Labels on figure:
- Input macro → (row 12)
- {IF} command to exit loop (rows 16–17)
- {BRANCH} command to repeat commands to enter one record (rows 23–24)
- loop returns control to row 14

Worksheet contents:

	A	B	C
10		This macro enters a transaction record in the database by prompting the user for the data.	
11	Name	Macro Commands	Comments
12	Input	{GOTO}database~	Position cell pointer at DATABASE range
13		{DOWN}	Move cell pointer down 1 row
14		{INSERT-ROWS ;1}	Insert 1 row above cell pointer
15		{GET-NUMBER "Ref #";a:a9;;"Ledger"}	Enter Ref # in dialog box, place in cell A:A9
16		{IF @iserr(a:a9)}{BEEP}{BRANCH b:b15}	Check for ERR, if ERR re-enter Ref #
17		{IF +a:a9=9999}{DELETE-ROWS}{BRANCH b:b25}	Check for 9999 to stop input and halt macro
18		{GET-NUMBER "Date (mm.dd)";a:b9;;"Ledger"}	Enter Date in dialog box, place in cell A:B9
19		{IF @iserr(a:b9)}{BEEP}{BRANCH b:b18}	Check for ERR, if ERR re-enter Date
20		{GET-NUMBER "Account";a:c9;;"Ledger"}	Enter Acct in dialog box, place in cell A:C9
21		{IF @iserr(a:c9)}{BEEP}{BRANCH b:b20}	Check for ERR, if ERR re-enter Account
22		{GET-LABEL "Name";a:d9;;"Ledger"}	Enter Name in dialog box, place in cell A:D9
23		{GET-NUMBER "Amount";a:e9;0;"Ledger"}	Enter Amount in dialog box, place in A:E9
24		{BRANCH b:b14}	Repeat commands for entering next record
25		{GOTO}a:e4~	Position cell pointer at current balance
26			Blank cell to end macro

Erika used the {BRANCH} and {IF} commands to create her loop. The new {IF} command in row 17 checks to see if the Ref # is 9999. If it isn't, the macro continues with row 18. If the Ref # is 9999, the macro deletes the current row ({DELETE-ROWS}), then branches to the {GOTO} command at the end of the macro (row 25). The {BRANCH} command in row 24 returns control to the {INSERT-ROW} command for entering the next transaction—this creates the loop. Let's execute Erika's macro and use the loop to enter several records.

To execute the Input macro with a loop for entering several transaction records:

❶ Click the **Home SmartIcon** 🔳 or scroll the worksheet window to display Erika's macro buttons.

❷ Click the **Input macro button** to execute the macro and display the prompted data entry dialog box.

❸ Use your own test data values and enter appropriate values for at least two records.

❹ Enter **9999** as the data value for the Ref # field to terminate the macro's execution.

❺ Close the worksheet without saving the changes.

In addition to the {IF} and {BRANCH} commands, 1-2-3 provides the {FOR} and {FORBREAK} macro commands as an alternative method for implementing a loop. You can find descriptions of these commands in the Macro Reference and 1-2-3's on-line Help.

Using Subroutines: the {subroutine} Command

Erika's worksheet contains three macros that are each executed individually. Because Erika and Tiffany frequently do all three tasks of entering, sorting, and reporting the ledger, they would like a macro that does all three processing activities in sequence. Erika can implement this type of macro using macro subroutines. A **subroutine** is a series of macro instructions grouped as a unit to perform a specific task. Subroutines can include recorded macro commands, key names, and advanced macro commands. A subroutine is executed using a subroutine macro command to **call**, or reference, the macro commands that make up the subroutine.

The syntax for the {subroutine} command is described in Figure 10-24.

Macro Command	Description
{*subroutine*}	Calls a macro for execution
	subroutine is the range name that identifies the macro to be executed

Figure 10-24
Syntax of subroutine macro

Erika created an All macro with subroutine calls to the Input, Sorter, and Report macros. These three macros are each a series of macro instructions grouped as a unit to perform a particular task—input records, sort the database, and print the report. Erika added the All macro to her C10BTB4.WK4 worksheet. Let's open that file and review her new macro.

To review the All macro for updating the ledger database using subroutines:

❶ Open Erika's worksheet C10BTB4.WK4 located on your Student Disk.

❷ Click the **Macros worksheet tab**, if necessary, then click the **Home SmartIcon** 🔲 to display the revised set of macro buttons. See Figure 10-25.

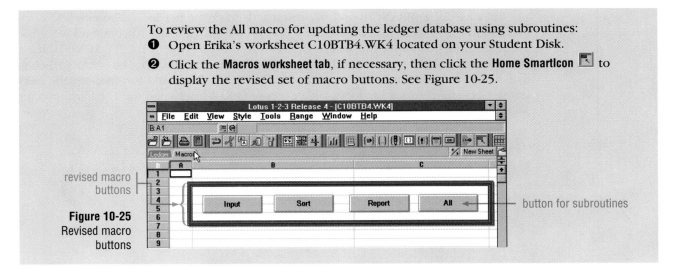

Figure 10-25
Revised macro buttons

❸ Scroll the worksheet window to view the All macro, which contains the three subroutine calls. See Figure 10-26.

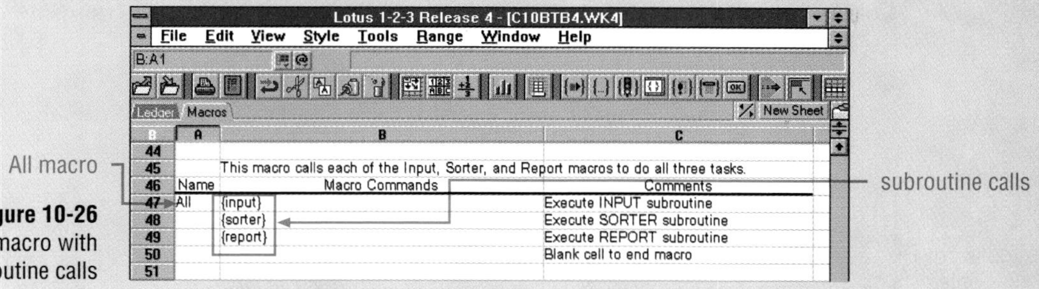

All macro

Figure 10-26
All macro with
subroutine calls

subroutine calls

Each subroutine call in Erika's All macro will execute each of the other macros in sequence. Let's do that.

To execute the All macro for entering, sorting, and printing the ledger:
❶ Click the **Home SmartIcon** 📄 or scroll the worksheet window to display the macro buttons.
❷ Click the **All macro button** to execute it.
❸ Use your own test data values and enter appropriate values for at least two records.
❹ Enter **9999** as the data value for the Ref # field to end the Input macro's execution.
❺ Wait for the database to sort and the report to print, then close the worksheet without saving any changes.

Tiffany is pleased with the All macro button for executing all three macros, but Erika thinks that their part-time bookkeeper might not want to sort and print the database each time she makes a new entry. Erika decides to create a menu with the three macros as menu choices, which the bookkeeper can choose to execute individually.

Applying User-Defined Menus: the {MENUBRANCH} Command

Lotus 1-2-3 has macro commands that allow you to create several different macro menus. One type of macro menu gives you a dialog box for making menu selections. This customized menu is referred to as a **user-defined menu**. When you execute a menu macro, the menu choices and descriptions of their actions appear in a dialog box. You select the menu choice for execution in the same manner as you make any dialog box selection.

Erika created the menu macro in her C10BTB5.WK4 worksheet. Let's open that worksheet and execute the macro menu to observe its operation.

To execute the user-defined menu:

❶ Open Erika's C10BTB5.WK4 worksheet located on your Student Disk.

❷ Click the **Macros worksheet tab** to display the macro button that executes the menu macro.

❸ Click the **Ledger menu macro button** to display the dialog box with the user-defined menu. The menu choices appear in the list while a description of the highlighted menu choice appears above the list. See Figure 10-27.

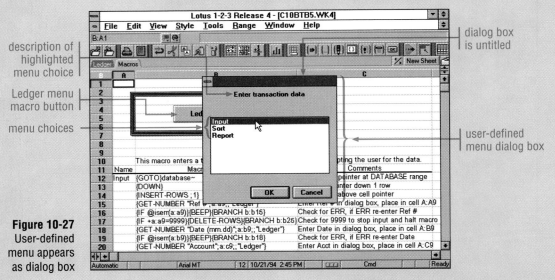

description of highlighted menu choice

dialog box is untitled

Ledger menu macro button

menu choices

user-defined menu dialog box

Figure 10-27
User-defined menu appears as dialog box

❹ Click the **Sort menu choice** to display its description, then click the **Report menu choice** for its description.

❺ Click the **Input menu choice**, then click the **OK button** to initiate execution of the Input macro. Use your own test data values and enter appropriate values for at least two records, then enter **9999** for the Ref # value to terminate input and return to the user-defined menu dialog box.

❻ Double-click the **Sort menu choice** to execute that macro, then double-click the **Report menu choice** to print the ledger.

❼ Click the **Cancel button** to close the user-defined menu dialog box and return to Ready mode.

Let's look at how Erika set up the macros for the user-defined menu.

To review the user-defined menu macro commands:

❶ Click the **Macros worksheet tab**, if necessary, then click the **Home SmartIcon** [icon] to redisplay the macro button.

❷ Press [Tab] and scroll the worksheet to display the menu macros. See Figure 10-28. These macro commands are below and to the right of the other commands because columns of a different width are needed for displaying the macro commands on the worksheet.

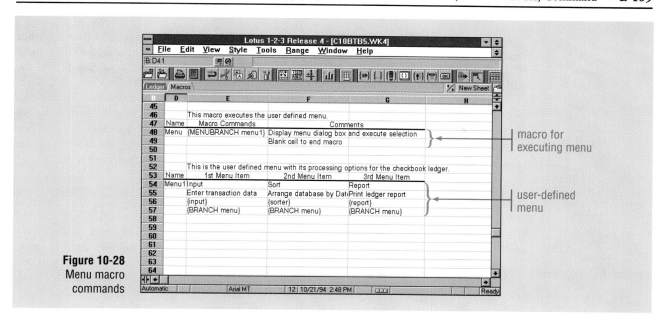

Figure 10-28
Menu macro
commands

Erika's user-defined menu requires two named ranges. The first range, MENU, is a macro containing the {MENUBRANCH} command, which causes the menu to be displayed. The syntax of this command is shown in Figure 10-29.

Macro Command	Description
{MENUBRANCH *location*}	Displays a dialog box containing a list of user-defined menu choices, waits for a selection, and then executes the macro commands for the selected menu choice
	location is the range name or cell address that specifies the user-defined menu choices and their macro commands

Figure 10-29
Syntax of macro
commands for
user-defined menu

The second named range, MENU1, contains both the entries for the user-defined menu and the macro commands that are executed when that menu choice is selected. Lotus 1-2-3 requires that these are located in adjacent columns. The blank column, column H on the right, is necessary to indicate the end of the menu items. The general structure of the macro menu is as follows:

Row 1	*Menu choice 1*	*Menu choice 2*	*Menu choice 3 ...*
Row 2	*Description 1*	*Description 2*	*Description 3 ...*
Row 3	*Macro command*	*Macro command*	*Macro command ...*

A user-defined menu must have the menu choice in the first line, the menu choice description, which appears at the top of the dialog box, in the second line, and the beginning of the macro command to be executed in the third line. Notice how Erika used the {BRANCH} command to redisplay the user-defined menu for the next selection.

Although Erika set up her menu with subroutine calls for the macro commands that are executed when a menu choice is selected, she could have included the commands with the menu. However, by placing the commands in a separate macro, she can test each macro individually and document those macros with comment statements in the adjacent columns. For these reasons, she prefers her design with the subroutine calls.

■　　　　　■　　　　　■

The advanced macro commands make it easier for Tiffany and Erika to use their checkbook ledger to keep track of revenues and expenses. The macros also make it easier for less experienced 1-2-3 users to operate their systems by guiding them through the processing tasks. Erika and Tiffany are confident that this worksheet provides them with the information they need to monitor their cash flow and make better business decisions.

Questions

1. With prompted data entry, this macro command causes a dialog box to be displayed and checks the input value to ensure it is numeric:
   a. {GET-LABEL}
   b. {FORM-CHECK}
   c. {DIALOG-VALUE}
   d. {GET-NUMBER}
2. When *inserting* rows in a worksheet that are immediately above or below a named range, the new rows are:
   a. included in the named range
   b. included below the named range
   c. not included in the named range
   d. not inserted in the worksheet and an error message displays
3. Which of the following is *not* a special key entry used in macro commands:
   a. {DOWN}
   b. {BIGRIGHT}
   c. {END-RUN}
   d. {DEL}
4. Checking an input data value to determine if it is numeric is known
   as _____.
   a. limit setting
   b. data editing
   c. macro testing
   d. internal validation
5. The {BRANCH} and {IF} commands can be used to create a loop that causes macro commands to be:
   a. repeated
   b. copied
   c. renewed
   d. duplicated

6. A series of macro instructions grouped as a unit to perform a specific task is a(n):
   a. loop
   b. program
   c. subroutine
   d. object
7. When creating a user-defined menu, this command causes the menu to be displayed in a dialog box:
   a. {MENUBAR}
   b. {MENU-DIALOG}
   c. {USER-MENU}
   d. {MENUBRANCH}

E   8. Using the Task Reference, write down at least one other method of performing the tasks specified by the following SmartIcons:
   a.
   b.
   c.

Tutorial Assignments

Launch 1-2-3 and open the T10ASM1.WK4 worksheet file for Apollo Strategic Mapping (ASM),which develops and markets a geographic information system (GIS)— a computer setup that makes it possible to view and analyze data on digitized maps. Mapping is a down-to-earth way to interpret data that was previously available only as computer printouts. Scott Fox, ASM's assistant office manager, uses 1-2-3 to maintain the equipment inventory. When creating his database, Scott used the data definition shown in Figure 10-30.

Field Name	Description
Tag #	Equipment identification tag number, unique number assigned by ASM
Date	Date of purchase entered in yymmdd format
Serial #	Manufacturer's serial number
Description	Description of equipment
Cost	Purchase cost of equipment

Figure 10-30

Scott has set up the database and entered data for several pieces of equipment. Complete the following tasks to enhance the operation of Scott's worksheet by using macros:

1. Review Scott's worksheet. Locate the macro area using the MACROS range name or the Macros worksheet tab. Which macro is ready for you to use in Scott's worksheet? Which cell was assigned a range name for executing this macro?
2. Complete the development of the Input macro in Scott's worksheet by entering the missing macro commands. The actions of these commands are specified in the macro's comments. Make up appropriate test data values and execute the macro using this data.
3. Finish the Sorter macro for the worksheet by entering the macro commands specified by its comment statements already in the worksheet. This data should be sorted in ascending order by the Tag # field. Run this macro to arrange the equipment inventory list.

    4. Run the Report macro to print a copy of the completed result.

    5. Save the worksheet as S10ASM1.WK4, then print the sheet that contains the macro commands.

    6. Revise the Input macro so that the user is requested to re-enter any Tag #, Date, or Cost data value that is not a numeric value. Insert rows in the macro for these additional commands. Include comments for all your macro commands. Run this macro and use data with unacceptable values to test it. Print a copy of the results using the Report macro. Then delete the row with the unacceptable data from the database.

    7. Save the worksheet as S10ASM2.WK4, then print the sheet that contains the macro commands.

    8. Use the {IF} and {BRANCH} commands to modify the Input macro so it includes a loop allowing several records to be entered until a "done" indicator value is entered, which you picked and built into the macro. Insert rows in the macro for these commands, as necessary. Test this macro using appropriate data values that you make up. Sort the database and print a copy of the results using the Sorter and Report macros.

    9. Save the worksheet as S10ASM3.WK4, then print the sheet that contains the macro commands.

E 10. Plan and create a macro that saves the worksheet under the current filename. Use a dry run, described in Tutorial 6, to help you develop this macro. Add a macro button to the Macros sheet for executing this macro. Document the macro, test it, and print a copy of it.

  11. Locate the partially completed user-defined menu macro in columns D through H of the Macros sheet. Finish this user-defined menu by including options to input records, sort the database, print the report, or save the worksheet. Save this worksheet as S10ASM4.WK4. Test the macro and then print a copy of the macro commands for the user-defined menu.

As an assistant loan officer at the State Employees Credit Union (SECU), Nancy O'Neil is responsible for preparing loan payment schedules for credit union members. She uses a 1-2-3 worksheet to prepare these schedules. Your task is to enhance the operation of her loan payment worksheet by performing the following:

  12. Launch and open Nancy's T10SEC1.WK4 worksheet for SECU. Review her worksheet. Locate the macro area using the MACROS range name or the Macros worksheet tab. Which range name identifies the loan payment schedule? Use other range names as appropriate in creating your macros.

  13. Locate the partially completed macro that prints the loan payment schedule. Add the commands described by the comments to finish the macro. Create a macro button for executing the report macro and place it in column F of the loan payment schedule on the Schedule sheet. This makes it easy for Nancy to run the macro from the sheet with the loan payment schedule. Test your macro.

  14. Create the Input macro that prompts the data entry for the loan amount, the interest rate, and the length of the loan using a dialog box by entering the macro commands as specified by the comments for this macro. Include data edit checks in the macro so that Nancy can enter only numeric data. If an inappropriate data value is entered, the dialog box should be redisplayed so an appropriate value can be entered. Create a macro button for executing the macro and place it in column F of the loan payment schedule near the button for printing the report. Test the macro using your own data values. Print the loan payment schedule with your test data.

  15. Save this worksheet as S10SEC2.WK4. Print a copy of the macro commands.

E 16. Run the macro, then print a report with one set of test data values for a loan with a life of less than three years. What do you notice about the schedule displayed after the length of the loan is reached? How is this implemented in Nancy's schedule? Why is this a desirable feature of her worksheet?

Erika and Tiffany reviewed the options for their checkbook ledger at Berkshire Teddy Bears. Before settling on the final design, they would like to evaluate several additional enhancements to their macro processing. To make these desired changes, do the following:

17. Open the C10BTB5.WK4 file. Create a second sort macro and name it SORTER2. Design this macro so that the database is arranged by date in ascending order and then within date by account in ascending order. Run this macro using one of the methods you learned in Tutorial 6. Print the database report, then print the revised macro.

18. Revise the user-defined menu so that it contains menu choices for both sort options. Use appropriate menu choices and descriptions to identify each sort option. Execute the macro to test its operation and then print the revised macro. Save this worksheet as S10BTB5.WK4.

E 19. Create a macro to delete a transaction record from the ledger database. This macro should pause to allow the user to move the cursor to the record to be deleted and then press [Enter]. Use the command you learned in Tutorial 6 for pausing the macro's execution. Test this macro. Add this delete macro to the macro menu and test the revised user-defined menu. Print the macros for deleting the selected record and the revised user-defined menu. Save and then close the worksheet.

E 20. Review the macros in Erika's S10BTB5.WK4 worksheet. What other macros would you suggest for the checkbook ledger? Explain why you think they would be useful.

Case Problems

1. Tracking Employee Skills for Automated Business Systems

Automated Business Systems (ABS), founded in 1979, offers services to the computer and communications industries. Like many of its competitors, ABS assumes the duties of processing the accounts receivable, accounts payable, inventory, and payroll of its clients. Because these services provide a low-cost alternative for information services, ABS has attracted many industry leading companies as their customers.

In providing information services, ABS uses a "team" concept. Velshona Wilcox, manager of the Client Services Division (CSD), initiated the use of teams seven years ago to bring about a more creative approach to solving customer problems. Within CSD, systems consultants are assigned to a team to design a computer system to solve a client's information problem. Each design team is made up of systems consultants with different expertise. After the design is complete, the Client Applications Division assumes the day-to-day operation of the new system. The diverse expertise of the consultants makes CSD's team concept so valuable.

Since the implementation of the team concept seven years ago, the number of systems consultants has greatly increased. This rapid growth makes it more difficult for Velshona to keep track of the areas of expertise of the systems consultants and to maintain diversified teams. Velshona decides that the best method for tracking employee skills is to use a 1-2-3 database (Figure 10-31).

```
Field
Name          Description
Consultant    Name of systems consultant
Certified     Indicates system consultant's certification
EXP_1         Indicates consultant's primary area of expertise
EXP_2         Indicates consultant's second area of expertise
EXP_3         Indicates consultant's third area of expertise
Years         Number of years of experience consultant has in systems design
Team          Identification of consultant's current team assignment
```

Figure 10-31

The database allows Velshona to track the skills of each consultant and team to maintain diversified, problem-solving teams. Velshona wants to make the database easier to use. Your task is to improve her worksheet by completing the following:

1. Launch 1-2-3 and open the P10ABS1.WK4 worksheet, which contains the employee skill tracking database. Review Velshona's worksheet. What range names have been created? Why is it useful to have range names for these items?

2. Velshona plans on hiring several new consultants. Complete the development of Velshona's prompted data entry macro, which allows her to enter new consultants without having to make changes to the named ranges. The action of these commands are specified in the macro's comments. Assign INPUT as the range name and create a macro button for this macro. Execute the macro using the following test data values:

Consultant:	Loring, Chad
Certified:	CSP
Exp_1:	Cobol
Exp_2:	System W
Exp_3:	Lotus 1-2-3
Years:	6
Team:	C

Save this worksheet as S10ABS2.WK4.

E 3. Complete the Sorter macro, which sorts the database using the Team field as the primary sort key and the Consultant field as the secondary sort key. The action for each macro command is indicated by its comment. Use the named ranges in place of cell addresses when specifying the sort keys. Assign the specified range name to this macro and create a macro button for executing it. Execute the macro.

E 4. Finish the Report macro, which prints the database. The macro should sort the database prior to printing. Use the Sorter macro from Problem 3 as a subroutine for this sort. Assign the specified range name to this macro and create a macro button for its execution. Save this worksheet as S10ABS3.WK4, then execute the macro.

E 5. Do these macros make the operation of the Employee Skill Tracking worksheet easier? What other advanced macro commands could be used to improve the operation of this worksheet? Explain how you would use them.

2.   Scheduling Production for Yasuka Communication Products

Yasuka Communication Products (YCP) is a manufacturer of specialized electronics equipment used by a variety of businesses. YCP custom builds each order. Although many components are similar, the exact specifications and configurations change from one order to the next. As a result, the complexity and scope of an order cause the amount of processing time to vary. Each order is produced using a job shop production configuration. In this arrangement, an order, or job, is assigned to a work center for completion. When one job is finished, the next job is started.

The growth in customer orders has strained the production capacity at YCP and created a number of problems. The number of customers complaining about late orders has increased 40%. One major customer, Sky Pagers, had to delay opening service in a major metropolitan area because YCP could not deliver equipment on time. Sky Pagers' president is threatening to stop ordering equipment from YCP.

Tom Peters, YCP's superintendent of manufacturing, meets with Shannon Taylor, his assistant in charge of production scheduling, to discuss this problem. They talk about how YCP should use the earliest due date (EDD) to establish the priority for selecting which job is started first in their job shop manufacturing. The EDD method concentrates on customer satisfaction by meeting as many due dates as possible during a schedule period. With EDD, orders are processed starting with the next job that has the earliest due date.

Shannon returns to her office and begins developing a 1-2-3 database that contains a list of jobs awaiting processing (Figure 10-32). This will allow YCP to organize its job sequencing to increase the number of jobs completed on schedule. Shannon includes a calculation for the current backlog of orders so the sales staff can advise customers of the increased time it might take to complete their orders.

Figure 10-32

Field Name	Description
Job #	Unique number assigned to each job scheduled for production
Cust #	Unique number assigned to each customer, where a customer could have more than one scheduled job
Description	Description of the product being manufactured for the order
Order	Date of the order, entered in the form mm.dd as a number
Due	Due date of the order, entered in the form mm.dd as a number
Days	Number of days required for completion of the job

Shannon meets with Tom again to review their production scheduling database. He is pleased with the information for better control of the job shop schedule. However, he would like a worksheet that is easier to use and agrees that Shannon should improve its operation by creating several macros. Your task is to enhance the production scheduling worksheet for Shannon and Tom by completing the following:

1. Launch 1-2-3 and open the P10YCP1.WK4 worksheet, then immediately save it as S10YCP1.WK4. Review the worksheet.
2. Set up named ranges for the report area containing the company name heading and the database, and for each of the three macros specified on the Macros sheet.
3. Create a macro for printing the report area. Place this macro in the specified area of the Macros sheet. Include documentation of the macro commands. Test this macro.

4. Create a macro that sorts the database area, without the field names, in ascending order of (1) due date, (2) production days within order date, and (3) order date within production days. Place this macro in the area indicated on the Macros sheet. Document these macro commands and test the macro. Print the product scheduling report after sorting the database.

E 5. Modify the Input macro, which prompts the user for the data for a new order and inserts that data in the database. Change the macro to use the field names from the database area as cell addresses for the prompts, rather than entering the field names as text in the macro commands. Test the macro using your own data values.

6. Modify the Input macro by adding appropriate data editing checks on all the fields that contain numeric data. If an inappropriate data value is entered, redisplay the dialog box so the user can enter an appropriate data value. Insert rows in the macro for these additional commands. Document the commands you added to the macro. Test the macro using your own data values. Print the production scheduling report after entering and sorting the test data. Save this worksheet as S10YCP2.WK4, then print the sheet that contains the macro.

7. Modify the Input macro using {IF} and {BRANCH} commands to include a loop for entering orders in sequence. Design this loop so that the user can exit from the loop when a "done" indicator value is entered. Insert rows in the macro for the additional commands. Document the commands you added to this macro. Test the macro using your own data values. Sort the data and print the report. Save the worksheet as S10YCP3.WK4.

E 8. Create a macro to delete an order from the database. While the macro is being executed, it should pause so the user can move the cursor to the record to be deleted and then press [Enter]. Document this macro. Test the macro by deleting one of the records containing the data values you entered. Print the report after testing the macro.

9. Locate the partially completed user-defined menu macro in columns D through H of the Macros sheet. Finish this macro menu so it contains choices for entering a record, deleting a record, sorting the database, and printing the production schedule. Assign appropriate range names for this macro. Create a macro button that initiates the execution of the user-defined menu. This button should be placed in a convenient location on the Macros sheet. Include appropriate documentation for the user-defined menu macro commands. Test the user-defined menu to verify that it works correctly.

10. Save the worksheet as S10YCP4.WK4. Print each of the macros you created in Problems 7 through 9.

E 11. Write user instructions that Shannon can give to Tom explaining how to operate their production scheduling worksheet. Assume Tom knows how to access 1-2-3 and open a worksheet, but does *not* know how to create or run macros.

E 12. What other macros might be used with YCP's production schedule? Explain why.

3.   Contract Bid Proposal for Northwest Pipeline

Northwest Pipeline (NWP) is a diversified natural gas company that began operations in 1926. NWP's original business was as a small "wildcatting" firm. Wildcatting involved the exploration and production of oil and gas deposits. NWP concentrated its efforts in the northwest region of the United States, primarily Oregon and Idaho. From its original wildcatting operations, NWP has evolved into a multifaceted company that currently operates businesses in oil and gas exploration, natural gas transmission and distribution, and construction. The construction business segment builds natural gas pipelines for both its own use and for the use of other natural gas transmission companies.

Natural gas was a key addition to NWP's corporate identity because of the new focus on alternative energies. Natural gas is one of the favored fuels for the future because it provides energy without the harmful pollutants that crude oil and other energies produce. Natural gas is by no means a new energy source, rather one whose good physical properties are being discovered. NWP currently operates 5,700 miles of its own natural gas pipelines in Oregon and Idaho. NWP constructed these pipelines because other construction companies were reluctant to build through the Rocky Mountain landscape. By building its own pipeline, NWP discovered several methods that eased the construction of the pipeline. These new methods made NWP's pipeline construction business a success.

Steve Blackmar, a chief financial analyst for the pipeline construction division, manages a group of analysts that perform cost studies of bid proposals to build new natural gas pipelines. NWP is currently putting together several bid proposals for natural gas pipelines in the Grant Canyon and Bacon Flat, Nevada regions for several large natural gas companies. The preparation of this bid proposal is very similar to other proposals. Karen St. Jean, a junior financial analyst in Steve's group, suggests building a 1-2-3 worksheet for use in developing bid proposals. Steve agrees to Karen's idea and instructs her to begin immediately. Complete the bid proposal worksheet by completing the following:

1. Launch 1-2-3 and open the P10NWP1.WK4 worksheet file for the bid proposal worksheet. Review Karen's worksheet. Why do zeros appear in column B?

2. Create a separate sheet for the macros and name this worksheet tab "Macros."

3. Create a macro that prompts the user for the necessary information to compute the total contract cost. This macro should use the @ISERR command to verify that the user enters numeric values in the appropriate cells. This and all other macros should be placed on a separate Macros sheet. Execute the macro with the following data values:

Contract bid for:	Grant Canyon
Length of pipeline:	79,300
Terrain rating:	4
Number of workers:	75
Equipment costs:	763,500
Inspection costs:	39,200
Permits costs:	77,250

   Save the worksheet as S10NWP2.WK4.

4. Create a print macro that prints the bid proposal. Document and test this macro.

5. Create a third macro that executes both the prompted data entry macro and the print macro. Document this macro and test it using the data values from Problem 3.

6. Karen feels the bid proposal worksheet would be easier for other analysts to operate if it contained a user-defined menu. Create a menu that gives the user the option of running either the data entry or print macro. Create a macro button that initiates the execution of the menu. Include appropriate documentation for the macro. Execute this macro with the following data values:

Contract bid for:	Bacon Flat
Length of pipeline:	119,550
Terrain rating:	2
Number of workers:	85
Equipment costs:	1,089,000
Inspection costs:	34,800
Permits costs:	93,750

Save the worksheet as S10NWP3.WK4. Then preview and print the bid proposal.

7. Print the macro sheet that contains all the macros you have created.

E 8. Create an auto-execute macro for the user-defined menu system. An auto-execute macro executes the assigned macro when a worksheet file is initially opened. An auto-execute macro is given the special range name of \0 (zero). The \0 range name should name the same range that executes the {MENUBRANCH} command. Unprotect only those cells where data is placed, and seal the worksheet. Save the worksheet as S10NWP4.WK4, then close it.

E 9. Open the S10NWP4.WK4 worksheet file. Did the user-defined menu macro automatically start? Why would this be useful to include in a worksheet? How is protection helpful if only selected data values are changed?

10. What other macros might be useful for the bid proposal worksheet? Explain how those macros would enhance use of the bid proposal worksheet.

Additional Case 1

Sales Invoicing for Island Dreamz Shoppe

CASE   **Island Dreamz Shoppe**   Like many entrepreneurs, Nicole Richardson discovered the old-fashioned way to make money: pick something you like to do, keep costs low and quality high, and make teamwork a priority. This prescription has led to her success with the Island Dreamz Shoppe, a gift gallery featuring the crafts from artists throughout the Caribbean. Their crafts capture the spirit of the islands in jewelry, paintings, and embroidered giftware.

Since it opened two years ago, business has been brisk. At the request of many of her customers, Nicole expanded her business to include mail orders. When customers visit the Shoppe, they get a catalog to take with them. Many customers find it more convenient to order items after they get home, rather than trying to cram extra gifts into an already overstuffed suitcase.

On a good day, Nicole receives about a dozen phone calls from customers wanting to place orders. With this number, she doesn't need a full-blown order-entry system, but she would like to automate her invoice preparation. She decides to use a 1-2-3 template worksheet for her sales invoices. Once the template is set up, all she needs to do is enter the data for each order and print the invoice.

Nicole's completed invoice for a recent customer order from Rachel Nottingham is shown in Figure 1. Using this paper invoice as a model, Nicole prepares her planning analysis sheet (Figure 2), so she can identify the labels, formulas, and attributes she wants to use in her template worksheet. The calculations needed in the template include the current date, the dollar amount for each item ordered, the total amount for all items, the sales tax, the shipping amount, and the total amount of the order.

Island Dreamz Shoppe
1001 Anchor Cove
Montego Bay, Jamaica, B.W.I.

		Date	21-Oct-95
		Invoice No	1097

Name: Rachel Nottingham
Address: 2741 Landsdowne Road
City: Victoria, BC   Postal Code: V8R 3P6
Country: Canada

Item #	Description	Quantity	Unit Price	Extended Price
21	Summer Beach Scene	3	$25.00	$75.00
27	Sea Scape Watch	2	36.00	72.00
47	Spanish Ducat Key Chain	1	12.00	12.00
63	Raindrop Crew Neck T-shirt	2	14.00	28.00
67	Stone-washed Twill Jacket	3	54.00	162.00
			Total Sale	$349.00
			Sales Tax	24.43
			Shipping	25.00
			TOTAL	**$398.43**

Payment Method	
	Check
	Visa
X	MasterCard
	Discover
	American Express

Credit Card #	4799123456789001	Expiration	03/97

Thank you for your order!

Figure 1
Island Dreamz Shoppe sales invoice

Using her planning analysis sheet and the original paper invoice, Nicole sketches the template she wants to create with 1-2-3 (Figure 3). For each item ordered, she plans to enter the item number, description, quantity, and unit price. She wants 1-2-3 to do the calculations described in her planning analysis sheet (Figure 2). The encircled numbers are guides to help you relate Nicole's sketch to the required calculations.

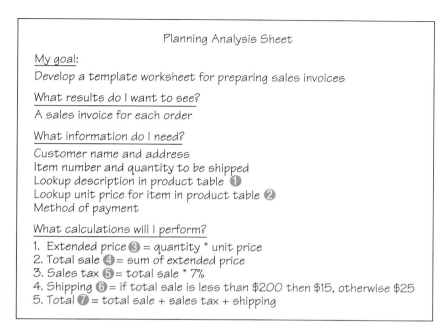

Figure 2
Nicole's planning
analysis sheet

Planning Analysis Sheet

My goal:

Develop a template worksheet for preparing sales invoices

What results do I want to see?

A sales invoice for each order

What information do I need?

Customer name and address
Item number and quantity to be shipped
Lookup description in product table ❶
Lookup unit price for item in product table ❷
Method of payment

What calculations will I perform?

1. Extended price ❸ = quantity * unit price
2. Total sale ❹ = sum of extended price
3. Sales tax ❺ = total sale * 7%
4. Shipping ❻ = if total sale is less than $200 then $15, otherwise $25
5. Total ❼ = total sale + sales tax + shipping

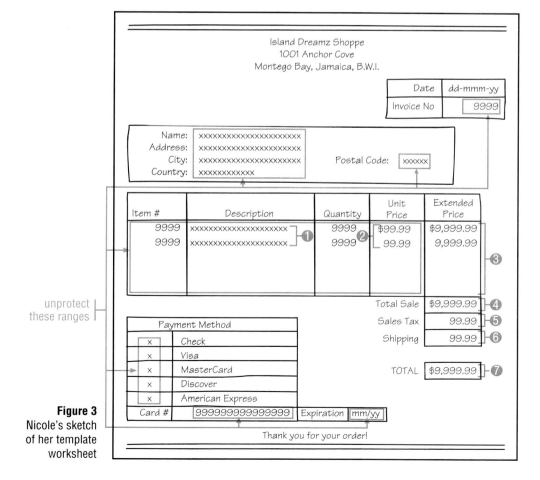

Figure 3
Nicole's sketch
of her template
worksheet

Nicole also sketches a table that lists the items Island Dreamz sells (Figure 4). The table includes the item number, product description, and unit price of each product. Nicole uses this information in preparing her invoices.

Item #	Description	Unit Price
21	Summer Beach Scene	25.00
27	Sea Scape Watch	36.00
31	Victorian Walking Stick	28.00
47	Spanish Ducat Key Chain	12.00
63	Raindrop Crew Neck T-shirt	14.00
67	Stone-washed Twill Jacket	54.00
78	Island Can Coolers	6.00

Figure 4
Island Dreamz
product table

Complete the following to create Nicole's sales invoice template worksheet:

1. Create the sales invoice for Island Dreamz by entering the labels for the invoice template worksheet. Adjust the column widths as necessary. The placement of the labels should correspond to Nicole's sketch, but do not need to be an exact match.

2. Enter the formulas specified by Figure 2 into the worksheet. Obtain the date from the computer's clock using the appropriate function.

3. Format the cells as shown in Figure 3. Remember to format the cell containing the expiration date as a label. Also, note that the first cell in the Unit Price and Extended Price columns is formatted differently from the rest of the cells in those columns.

4. Add lines and attributes as illustrated in Figure 1. Save the template worksheet as SC1IDS1.WK4.

5. Launch Paintbrush and open the XC1IDS1.BMP file, which contains the Island Dreamz logo. Paste the logo on the invoice as illustrated in Figure 1. Remove the line that surrounds the logo.

6. Create a macro for printing the invoice and place the macro on a separate sheet. Assign the macro to a button on the same sheet for executing this macro. Assign the name "Macros" to this sheet, and assign the name "Invoice" to the sheet with the invoice.

7. Apply protection as indicated in Figure 3 so that only those cells where data is entered can be changed. Seal the worksheet to turn on protection. Make sure you remember your password. Save the revised template worksheet without any data entered in it.

8. Test the operation of the worksheet by entering the data for the order shown in Figure 1. Note how the values in the Extended Price column are calculated automatically as you enter the data. Use the macro to print this invoice.

9. Enhance the appearance of Nicole's invoice by using additional fonts, attributes, and lines of your choice. Describe why you selected these characteristics. Delete the data for Rachel's order, then save the worksheet as SC1IDS2.WK4. Test the operation of the worksheet with data values that you make up. Print your enhanced worksheet, then close it without saving it again.

10. Open the SC1IDS1.WK4 worksheet and unseal it in preparation for modifying it. Insert a new sheet between the Invoice and Macros sheets. Assign the name "Product" to the new sheet. Create the product table that contains the product information shown in Figure 4. Give this table, excluding the column headings, the range name "PRODUCTS." Print a copy of this sheet.

E 11. Nicole wants 1-2-3 to automatically look up the description and unit price in the product table when an item number is entered in the worksheet. If fewer than eight items are entered in the worksheet, the Description, Unit Price, and Extended Price columns should be blank. This is accomplished by combining the @IF function and @VLOOKUP function. The @IF function tests for an empty cell for Item #. If this cell is empty, nothing is placed in the Description, Unit Price, and Extended Price cells. The test for an empty cell uses two successive quotation marks (""). A null, or empty, value is displayed in a cell using the same set of quotation marks. The @VLOOKUP function uses the item number to obtain the appropriate description and unit price from the product table. Place appropriate formulas in the Description, Unit Price, and Extended Price cells. Test the worksheet with at least two different orders with different numbers of items. Save the worksheet as SC1IDS3.WK4. Use the print macro to print these invoices.

E 12. Change the protection for the Description and Unit Price cells so that they are protected. Seal the worksheet to turn on protection. Test the worksheet with data that you make up. Describe how you tested the protection for the Description, Unit Price, and Extended Price cells. Save the worksheet as SC1IDS4.WK4.

13. Write user instructions for operating Nicole's sales invoice worksheet.

14. What other changes or enhancements could Nicole make to improve the use of her sales invoice worksheet?

E 15. Nicole wants to include an order form with her catalog. A customer writes an order on this form and sends it to Island Dreamz. Design this catalog order form. You might want to research order forms in catalogs that you have received for ideas to use with your design. Create the form using 1-2-3. Save this worksheet as SC1IDS5.WK4, then print a copy of the blank order form.

16. Arrange and clearly identify the printouts and answers for all the Problems in this case as your documentation for the case.

OBJECTIVES

In this case you will:
- Create a multiple sheet file
- Enhance worksheets with attributes
- Combine worksheet files
- Link worksheets
- Develop a macro for a file combine
- Create charts from summary data
- Develop a print macro
- Create a user-defined menu macro
- Use Write as a client application

Additional Case 2

Performance Reporting for Boston Scientific

CASE

Boston Scientific* Boston Scientific is on the cutting edge of medical cost reduction. The company develops and manufactures catheters and other products that are used as alternatives to traditional surgery. As described by CEO Peter Nicholas: "We were one of the first companies to articulate the concept of less invasive procedures." This is possible because medical imaging techniques now allow physicians to see inside the body and manipulate instruments through a natural opening or a tiny incision. Boston Scientific aggressively markets its products for these medical procedures. For example, a traditional coronary bypass surgery often costs from $50,000 to $70,000, including the hospital stay and weeks of recovery time. By contrast, clearing out a clogged artery with one of Boston Scientific's catheters, which is inserted under the skin of a patient's arm, takes just a few hours and costs roughly $12,000.

*Adapted from: *Fortune*, "Boston Scientific," p. 97, April 5, 1993.

Although many of Boston Scientific's products are expensive relative to the cost of a scalpel, they enable a patient to leave the hospital much sooner, saving huge hospital bills. For this reason, their products are popular and sales continue to increase rapidly. Another important element in Boston Scientific's growth is the company's ability to leverage technology across its four largely autonomous divisions: Medi-Tech (radiology), Mansfield (cardiology), Microvasive Endoscopy (gastroenterology), and Microvasive Urology.

Willow Shire joined Boston Scientific last year as a junior accountant. Her responsibilities include preparing the quarterly performance report that consolidates financial results of the four divisions. Willow created a template worksheet for reporting quarterly financial results. She sent a copy of the template to the controller at each division, where that division's data was entered in it. Willow just received the worksheet files from the four divisions. She now needs to prepare the consolidated statement of operation summarizing the division results. You'll prepare this statement by completing the following:

1. Read through all the problems for this case and develop a planning analysis sheet in preparation for building the consolidation worksheet for Boston Scientific. Use your planning analysis sheet to guide your activities in preparing your 1-2-3 solution.

2. Open and review each of the worksheets for the four divisions: XC2BOSMT.WK4 (Medi-Tech), XC2BOSMF.WK4 (Mansfield), XC2BOSME.WK4 (Microvasive Endoscopy), and XC2BOSMU.WK4 (Microvasive Urology).

3. Create a multiple sheet file that contains a consolidation sheet and a sheet for each of the divisions. Include the title, "Consolidated Statement of Operations," on the consolidated sheet. Use the File Combine command to place the results for each division in its sheet of the multiple sheet file. Assign each sheet an appropriate name using the worksheet tab. Include appropriate formulas in the consolidation sheet to add the division results as the corporate total. Enhance the title for each sheet by applying appropriate attributes. Save the worksheet as SC2BOS1.WK4. Print the Consolidated Statement of Operations sheet.

4. Create a macro that lets Willow do the file combines of the division worksheets and print all five of the statements of operation. Place the macro on a separate sheet named "Macros." Include a macro button on the Macros sheet for executing the macro. Save the worksheet as SC2BOS2.WK4. Execute the macro. Print the sheet that contains the macro commands.

E   5. Create a comparison stacked bar chart that includes the operating earnings for each division. Place this chart in a convenient location on the sheet containing the Consolidated Statement of Operations. Save the worksheet. Print the chart. Write a description of what this chart shows.

E   6. Create a pie chart that compares the operating earnings for the year (that is, those in the total column) for the four divisions. Place this chart on the sheet containing the Consolidated Statement of Operations. Save the worksheet, then print the chart.

7. Develop a macro that prints the two charts. Place the macro on the Macros sheet. Include a macro button on this sheet for executing the macro. Test the macro. Save the worksheet. Print the macro.

8. Create a user-defined menu macro that lets Willow replace the data for a selected division by doing a File Combine with that division's file, or that lets her redo the entire consolidation for all four divisions. On the Macros sheet, include a macro button for executing this macro. Test the macro. Save the worksheet as SC2BOS3.WK4. Print your user-defined menu macro.

9. Launch Write and create a memo to Mr. Nicholas that includes the chart from Problem 5. This memo should include your summary of the results displayed in the chart. Use object linking to include the chart in the memo. Save the document as SC2BOS2.WRI. Print the document with the chart.

10. Willow needs a summary report that contains only the product sales and operating earnings data. She wants the report to list the product sales by division with a corporate total and then list the operating earnings by division with a corporate total. Prepare a sketch of this report. Create the report as a separate worksheet file. Use appropriate fonts and attributes to enhance your title for this report. Use file linking to obtain the necessary data values from each of the individual division worksheet files. Save the worksheet as SC2BOS4.WK4. Print this summary report.

11. Revise your memo from Problem 9 by adding the summary report from Problem 10 as a table in the memo document. The memo should now include both the chart from Problem 5 and the summary table from Problem 10. Did you use linking or embedding to place the summary table in the memo? Explain your choice. Save the document as SC2BOS4.WRI, then print the document.

12. What else could Willow include in the consolidation worksheet to make it more useful? Explain your answer.

13. Write user instructions on how to operate the consolidation worksheet. Assume the user knows how to access and run 1-2-3, but not how to do a consolidation.

14. Arrange and clearly identify the printouts and answers for all the problems in this case as your documentation for the case.

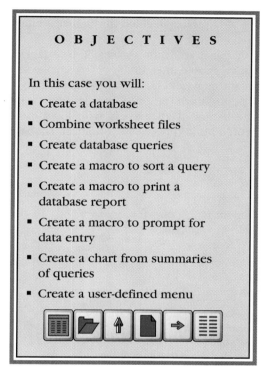

Additional Case 3

Negotiating Salaries for the National Basketball Association

OBJECTIVES

In this case you will:

- Create a database
- Combine worksheet files
- Create database queries
- Create a macro to sort a query
- Create a macro to print a database report
- Create a macro to prompt for data entry
- Create a chart from summaries of queries
- Create a user-defined menu

CASE

National Basketball Association   When Dr. James Naismith nailed a peach basket to a pole, he could not possibly have envisioned the popularity of the sport that he founded. Since those early days of peach baskets and volleyballs, basketball has become one of the most popular sports in the world—most certainly in America.

The National Basketball Association (NBA) has become home to some of the greatest athletes in the world. The popularity of the NBA has soared over the last decade thanks to players like Michael Jordan, Julius Erving, "Magic" Johnson, and Larry Bird. This popularity has resulted in larger attendance at games, larger television viewing audiences, and an increase in advertising sponsorships which, in turn, has led to increased player salaries.

While growing up, Troy Jackson wanted to be a professional basketball player. However, while in his senior year of college, Troy had reconstructive knee surgery, ending his chances to ever play competitive basketball again. Troy was still determined to make it into the NBA one way or another. Upon graduation, Troy was offered a job in the NBA head offices in New York, where he works on Commissioner David Stern's staff.

Commissioner Stern and his staff have become concerned with the large number of player salaries being decided through arbitration. Salary arbitration is the process of negotiating a contract when both sides cannot agree to a specific dollar amount. The arbitration process is conducted through an independent third party that listens to arguments from both sides and then makes a final determination as to the terms of the contract. Over the past several years the number of contracts decided through arbitration has more than tripled.

To help the NBA head office keep track of these arbitration cases, Troy suggests developing a 1-2-3 database that lists the information shown in Figure 5.

The commissioner agrees that a database like this would be useful in maintaining a watchful eye over the salaries being decided through arbitration. Commissioner Stern asks Troy to build the database and include a listing of all players who have gone through arbitration over the past three years. You'll build the salary arbitration database by completing the following:

Figure 5
Data definition for a salary arbitration database

Field Name	Description
Player	Name of player involved in arbitration
Position	Position player plays (guard, center, forward)
Team	Name of team that is involved in arbitration
Player Bid	Amount that player is asking for
Team Bid	Amount that team is willing to pay
Settle	Amount that arbitrator feels is "fair"

1. Read through all the problems for this case and develop a planning analysis sheet in preparation for creating, modifying, and manipulating the database. Use your planning analysis sheet to guide the development of your 1-2-3 solution.
2. Create the salary arbitration database using the data definition in Figure 5. List the field names in the same order as specified in the data definition. Include an appropriate title centered at the top of your worksheet. Select a typeface and point size for the title. Bold and underline the field names.
3. Add the records in Figure 6 to the salary arbitration database. Save the worksheet as SC3NBA1.WK4.

Figure 6
Records for the salary arbitration database

Player	Position	Team	Player Bid	Team Bid	Settle
Miller, Reggie	Guard	Indiana	4450000	3850000	4270000
Smith, Charles	Forward	New York	2350000	1580000	2200000
Perkins, Sam	Center	Seattle	2450000	2100000	2390000
Gamble, Kevin	Forward	Boston	2650000	1950000	1960000

4. Open the XC3NBA2.WK4 worksheet file and view its contents. This file contains the current listing of players and teams that entered into arbitration over the past three years. Make SC3NBA1.WK4 your active worksheet. Combine the contents of the XC3NBA2.WK4 worksheet file into the salary arbitration database. Save the worksheet as SC3NBA3.WK4. Preview and print the worksheet.
5. Assign a range name to the database and other appropriate ranges for use with this database. Which ranges did you name? Why?
6. Between the database field headings and the worksheet title, add a row that contains the averages for the three salary fields. Use functions and named ranges in calculating these averages. Save the worksheet as SC3NBA4.WK4. Preview and print the salary arbitration database.

7. Create three separate query reports, one each for the guards, forwards, and centers. Arrange each report in alphabetical order by player. Place an appropriate title above the query. Below each query add formulas that average the salary fields for that query. Save the worksheet as SC3NBA5.WK4. Preview and print each report separately.

E 8. Create a bar chart summarizing the averages for each position. This chart should compare the player bid, team bid, and settle contract prices for each position (guard, forward, and center). Include the appropriate headings, labels, and legends.

E 9. Create three separate print macros. One macro should print the entire database. A second should sort each of the three queries by team and player and then print these reports. The final macro should print the bar chart. Use range names as appropriate for printing these reports. Place these macro commands on a separate worksheet. Save the worksheet as SC3NBA6.WK4. Execute the macro that prints the bar chart. Print the sheet containing the macros.

10. Troy wants to be able to enter new player records in the database when the players are involved in an arbitration dispute. Create a prompted data entry macro that allows Troy to enter the new records. Place this macro on the same sheet with your other macros. Test the macro using the following data:

Player	Edwards, Blue
Position	Forward
Team	Milwaukee
Player Bid	2050000
Team Bid	1700000
Settle	1810000

Save the worksheet as SC3NBA7.WK4. Print the database using the print macro.

E 11. Compare the Forwards report on your screen to the report in Problem 7. Did the report include the new record just added? Modify the input macro in Problem 10 to include the macro command that refreshes the queries. This command can be retrieved from the list of macro commands. (*Hint:* Before the query refresh command is executed in the macro, you need to select the query table.) Execute the input macro again using the following data:

Player	Chapman, Rex
Position	Guard
Team	Washington
Player Bid	1550000
Team Bid	1200000
Settle	1310000

Save the worksheet as SC3NBA8.WK4. Execute the macro that prints the individual position queries. Were the queries updated?

12. To make the operation of the salary arbitration database smoother, create a user-defined menu for executing the macros that you have developed. Test the menu using test data values that you make up. Save the worksheet as SC3NBA9.WK4. Preview and print the macro commands for all macros.

E 13. Formulate a fourth query on the database. Describe why you selected this query. Create the query table for this query. Use an appropriate title for a report containing this query. Save the worksheet as SC3NBA10.WK4. Preview and print the report of the query.

14. What else could be included in the database to make it more useful? Explain your answer. Are there other macros or charts that would be beneficial for the database to include? Describe how they would benefit the users of the database.

15. Write user instructions on how to operate this worksheet. Assume the user knows how to access and run 1-2-3, but not how to use the salary arbitration database.

16. Arrange and clearly identify the printouts and answers for all the problems in this case as your documentation for the case.

OBJECTIVES

In this case you will:

- Create macros to sort a database and print reports
- Ask what-if questions about a completed worksheet
- Link worksheets
- Perform goal seeking
- Implement a decision table
- Create versions and scenarios
- Create a what-if table
- Include worksheet data in a Write document

Additional Case 4

Managing Tours for Executive Travel Services

CASE

Executive Travel Services   Executive Travel Services (ETS) of San Diego is a travel booking agency that specializes in selling packaged tours to business executives from Fortune 500 companies. ETS was started in 1982 by Tom Williams, a retired executive from a Fortune 500 company. As an executive, Tom often wished he could socialize with other top executives in an informal setting for several days. Using this idea, Tom founded ETS. ETS books tours that vary in duration from one to three weeks. The tours are designed to let the executives enjoy a variety of activities, as well as become acquainted with other executives.

In the last several months, the number of available tour requests by executives has nearly doubled. ETS accidentally overbooked several of their more popular tours, such as the Orient Express. Tom discussed the overbooking problem with Melissa Merron, a recently hired travel associate at ETS. They agreed that a 1-2-3 database could be used to develop a tour management system, which would provide them with information necessary to avoid future overbooking problems. Tom asked Melissa to analyze the requirements for the database. She worked with Tom and the other ETS associates to develop the data definition shown in Figure 7.

Field Name	Description
Tour	Tour name
Month	Month tour is scheduled to start
Type	Type of tour: Fish, Golf, Photo, or Relax
Sold	Number of seats sold for tour
Open	Number of seats still open for sale
Price	Price of tour

Figure 7
Data definition for
the Tours database

Melissa has already set up the database. Tom would like her to make several changes to improve the operation of their tour management system, by completing the following:

1. Read through all the problems for this case and develop a planning analysis sheet in preparation for creating, modifying, and operating the tour management system. Use your planning analysis sheet to guide the development of your 1-2-3 solution.

2. Open the XC4ETS1.WK4 worksheet file for ETS. Review the Tours database. Examine the named range. What is missing from the database?

3. Add the appropriate field names as described in the data definition. The field names should go in the same order as listed in the data definition. Center and bold each field name.

4. Enhance the appearance of the report title and subtitle:
   a. Bold both titles
   b. Italicize the subtitle
   c. Increase the point size of the title to 14
   Print the Tours database. Save the worksheet as SC4ETS2.WK4.

5. Sort the database with the Type field as the primary sort key and the Tour field as the secondary sort key. Save the worksheet as SC4ETS2.WK4. Preview and print the database.

6. Create a macro on a separate worksheet that will do the sort described in Problem 5. Assign the macro to a macro button and test its execution.

7. Create a macro that will print the Tours database using a named range. Assign the macro to a macro button. Execute the macro and save the worksheet as SC4ETS3.WK4.

E

8. Tom wants to know how much revenue the tours are producing. Add a Total Revenue field to the database and place it immediately to the right of the Price field. Total revenue is calculated as the number of seats sold for a tour multiplied by the price charged for the tour. Add a formula that uses a named range to sum the total revenue for all tours. Place the formula so that additional records can be added easily to the database. Save the worksheet as SC4ETS4.WK4. Print the Tours database. Circle the total revenue on the printout.

9. Produce a report of all golf tours with a price less than $1,000 by doing a query. Adjust the column widths as needed. Place a title describing the query table's contents above the query table. Sort the query table in ascending order by price. Print the query table, then save the worksheet as SC4ETS5.WK4.

10. Open the XC4ETS6.WK4 worksheet file. This is ETS's projected income statement. What is missing from the income statement? How can you solve this problem?

11. Using a linking formula, include the total revenue from the Tours database in ETS's projected income statement.

12. Add a rent expense in the amount of $12,000 in a new row, which you insert immediately below the administrative expense. What is the net income for ETS? Create a macro that will print the income statement. Save the worksheet as SC4ETS6.WK4. Execute the print macro to produce a copy of the income statement.

13. Based on the expected revenue from the Tours database, and taking into consideration the added rent expense, what commission rate could ETS pay and still realize a net income of $15,000?

E 14. Develop high cost and low cost scenarios for expenses. Create at lease two versions that are used for these scenarios. Select appropriate expense items and/or key assumptions for inclusion in the versions. Print a report with each scenario. On the printouts, circle the values that are used with the versions for each scenario. Save the worksheet as SC4ETS7.WK4. Write a summary comparing the versions.

E 15. Formulate a goal seeking question using the worksheet from Problem 14. Why is this goal seeking? Perform the goal seeking analysis and print a report of the solution. Save the worksheet as SC4ETS8.WK4. Write a summary interpreting your goal seeking results.

E 16. Develop and sketch a decision table for use with the projected income statement. Describe the business situation represented by the decision table. Implement this decision table. Save the worksheet as SC4ETS9.WK4. Preview and print the results.

E 17. Formulate a two-variable what-if table by selecting the input cells and the range of values to be examined for each. Describe why you selected these inputs to explore using the what-if table. Create the what-if table. Save the worksheet as SC4ETS10.WK4. Preview and print the what-if table.

E 18. Produce a chart from the what-if table data in Problem 17. Include appropriate titles and legends. Save the worksheet, then print the chart. Review the results from the what-if table and the chart. Write a summary that explains these results.

E 19. Launch Write and create a memo to Tom that includes tables you obtain from both the Tours database and the projected income statement. This memo should list only the tours that are still available and the net income of ETS. Use a query to produce the list of available tours. Save the document as SC4ETS11.WRI. Print the document.

20. What other information could Melissa produce from either the Tours database or the projected income statement? How would these reports support ETS management decision-making?

21. Arrange and clearly identify the printouts and answers for all the problems in this case as your documentation for the case.

References

1 1-2-3 Commands

2 @Functions

3 Macros

4 SmartIcons

1-2-3 Commands

This reference section describes commands in the main menu. To display Help about any 1-2-3 command, highlight the command and press [F1] (Help). To display Help about the Help window commands, choose Help Using Help.

File Commands

```
File
New
─────────────────────
Open...          Ctrl+O
Close
─────────────────────
Save             Ctrl+S
Save As...
Protect...
Send Mail...
─────────────────────
Print Preview...
Page Setup...
Print...          Ctrl+P
Printer Setup...
─────────────────────
Exit
```

New Creates and opens a new worksheet file.

Open Opens 1-2-3 files, files created in other programs such as Excel, and text files. Also incorporates data from a worksheet, text, or graphics file on disk into the current file.

Close If the worksheet window is active, closes the current file and lets you save changes to it. Updates data embedded in another Windows application file if the data had been modified. If the Transcript window is active, closes it.

Save Saves the current file. If you edited 1-2-3 data embedded in another Windows application file, Save changes to Update. If you're working with a shared file containing versions and scenarios, Save changes to Save Versions.

Save As Saves all or part of the current file using the name, directory, drive, and file type you want. Also lets you assign a password to 1-2-3 files. If the current window contains an embedded worksheet, Save As changes to Save Copy As.

Protect Protects all worksheets in the current file and seals it with a password. Also gets, releases, or changes the network reservation for the file.

Send Mail Sends 1-2-3 data using cc:Mail, Lotus Notes, a VIM mail application, or Microsoft Mail running under Windows for Workgroups Version 3.1.

Print Preview Shows the current selection as formatted for printing. Also lets you change the page layout and print the selection.

Page Setup Sets margins, print titles, headers and footers, and page orientation for printing. Also sizes data to fit the printed page, hides and shows worksheet elements in print, and saves page settings.

Print Prints or previews the selection. Lets you change the page layout and the number of copies you print.

Printer Setup Sets the printer and printer settings.

Exit   Ends the 1-2-3 session and lets you save modified files. If you edited 1-2-3 data embedded in another Windows application file, Exit changes to Exit & Return. Exit & Return saves changes to the embedded data and returns you to the other application.

(File Name)   Lists the last five named files you used and lets you open them quickly from the menu without choosing File Open.

Edit Commands

```
┌─────────────────────────┐
│ Edit                    │
├─────────────────────────┤
│ Undo              Ctrl+Z│
├─────────────────────────┤
│ Cut               Ctrl+X│
│ Copy              Ctrl+C│
│ Paste             Ctrl+V│
│ Clear...             Del│
│ Paste Special...        │
│ Paste Link              │
├─────────────────────────┤
│ Arrange               ▶ │
├─────────────────────────┤
│ Copy Down               │
│ Copy Right              │
├─────────────────────────┤
│ Insert...         Ctrl + │
│ Delete...         Ctrl - │
├─────────────────────────┤
│ Find & Replace...       │
│ Go To...             F5 │
├─────────────────────────┤
│ Insert Object...        │
│ Links...                │
└─────────────────────────┘
```

Undo   Reverses your most recent action or command.

Cut   Deletes cell contents and styles, drawn objects, query tables, or recorded instructions, and puts them on the clipboard.

Copy   Copies the current selection to the clipboard.

Paste   Copies the clipboard contents to the current location in the worksheet or Transcript window.

Clear   Deletes cell contents, styles, or both without using the clipboard. Also deletes drawn objects, query tables, and recorded instructions.

Clear All   Appears on the Edit menu when the Transcript window is active. Deletes all items from the Transcript window without using the clipboard.

Paste Special   Pastes either cell contents or styles, or converts formulas to values. Pastes a query table as either a new query table or worksheet data. Also creates a DDE or OLE link in the current file, or embeds data from another Windows application.

Paste Link   Links cells in a file or across files. Also links cells and drawn objects between 1-2-3 and other Windows applications.

Arrange   Opens a submenu that lets you place drawn objects in front of or behind one another, flip them horizontally or vertically, rotate and group them, lock them to prevent accidental change, and fasten them to underlying cells.

Copy Down   Copies the contents of the top row of a range to the remaining rows in the range.

Copy Right   Copies a range's left-most column to the rest of the range.

Copy Left   Appears when you press [Shift] and then choose Edit. Copies the contents of the right-most column of a range to the rest of the range.

Copy Up   Appears when you press [Shift] and then choose Edit. Copies a range's bottom row to the rest of the range.

Copy Back   Appears when you press [Ctrl] and then choose Edit. Copies data from the front worksheet of a three-dimensional range backward through the rest of the range.

Copy Forward   Appears when you press [Ctrl] and then choose Edit. Copies data from the last worksheet of a three-dimensional range forward through the rest of the range.

Insert   Inserts a range, rows, columns, or worksheets in the current file.

Delete   Deletes a range, rows, columns, or worksheets in the current file.

Find & Replace   Finds and replaces characters in a range, query table, or file.

Go To   Finds and selects a range, chart, drawn object, or query table in an active file.

Insert Object   Lets you start another Windows application from 1-2-3, create data, and then embed it in the current 1-2-3 file.

Links   Creates and manages DDE and OLE links between the current 1-2-3 file and other Windows application files. Also updates 1-2-3 file links.

View Commands

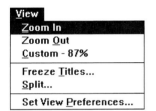

Zoom In   Increases the display size of worksheet cells by 10%.

Zoom Out   Decreases the display size of worksheet cells by 10%.

Custom - XX%   Resets the display size of worksheet cells to the default.

Freeze Titles   Freezes rows and columns so they remain in view as you scroll the worksheet. If you freeze rows or columns, Freeze Titles changes to Clear Titles.

Split   Divides a worksheet window horizontally or vertically into two panes, or displays three contiguous worksheets in Perspective view. If you split the window, Split changes to Clear Split.

Set View Preferences   Hides or shows the worksheet frame, tabs, gridlines, scroll bars, page breaks, charts, drawn objects, and pictures. Also hides or shows SmartIcons, the edit line, and the status bar. Sets the frame type, gridline color, and displayed cell size.

Style Commands

Number Format   Changes the display of values in cells, chart axes, and query tables.

Font & Attributes   Changes the typeface, point size, attributes, and color of text. Lets you specify the style of text in cells, chart elements, text blocks, macro buttons, and query tables.

Lines & Color   Lets you enhance ranges, charts, drawn objects, and query tables. Depending on the current selection, sets the line or edge style, changes the color and pattern, adds borders and designer frames, and changes the symbols in a line chart.

Alignment   Aligns values and labels in cells and query tables, and text in text blocks. Also wraps data in a cell, and changes the orientation and angle of cell contents.

Gallery   Formats a range or collection using a 1-2-3 style template.

Named Style   Saves a cell's styling as a named style, and lets you apply named styles to other ranges.

Column Width Sizes worksheet columns or query table fields. You can select the number of characters you want or have each column or field automatically accommodate its widest entry. Also resets columns or fields to the default width.

Row Height Sizes rows in the worksheet or in a query table. You can select the number of points you want or have each row automatically accommodate the largest font it contains.

Protection Turns cell protection off for a range before you seal a file with File Protect. Reprotects the range after you unseal the file.

Hide Hides and shows selected columns or worksheets.

Page Break Inserts and deletes page breaks.

Worksheet Defaults Sets default styles for the current worksheet including font, alignment, number format, and column width. Also sets text and background color in cells, lets you display negative values in red, turns Group mode on and off.

Tools Commands

Chart Creates a chart using a selected range or collection.

Draw Opens a submenu that lets you create lines, polylines, arrows, rectangles, arcs, ellipses, polygons, text blocks, and buttons that run macros. You can also draw freehand.

Database Opens a submenu that lets you query database tables, find, delete, and append records, and cross-tabulate data. You can also connect to and create external database tables, and send commands to an external database.

Spell Check Finds and corrects misspelled or duplicated words.

Audit Finds formulas, formula precedents, cell dependents, and circular references. Also finds file and DDE links.

SmartIcons Lets you choose which icons to display, and reposition them. You can also customize icons and size them.

User Setup Lets you turn on drag-and-drop, automatic formatting and file saving, Undo, autoexecute macros, and error beeps. Also lets you change the user name, default directory, number of filenames displayed on the File menu, international settings, and recalculation.

Macro Opens a submenu that runs a macro, turns on Step mode, and opens the Macro Trace window. Also lets you control macro recording, show or hide the Transcript window, and assign a macro to a button on the worksheet.

Add-in Loads and removes add-ins.

Range Commands

Note: The Range commands appear when you're working with data on the worksheet.

Version   Lets you enter, view, and manage different versions of data in a named range, and group them to create scenarios. You can also share files and consolidate data from other users.

Fill   Enters a sequence of values, dates, or times in a range.

Fill by Example   Enters a sequence of data in a range based on a data pattern in the range. Also lets you create custom sequences.

Sort   Sorts data in a range.

Parse   Separates a column of labels into columns of labels, values, dates, or times.

Transpose   Transposes rows and columns, columns and worksheets, or rows and worksheets.

Name   Creates and deletes range names.

Analyze   Opens a submenu that lets you perform what-if and regression analyses, solve problems with Solver and Backsolver, create frequency distributions, and work with data matrices.

Chart Commands

Note: The Chart commands appear when you're working with a chart.

Type   Changes the chart type. Also lists values plotted in the chart, changes its orientation, and repositions the plot frame.

Ranges   Assigns and plots data ranges by column, row, or individual range. Also lets you plot data against a second y-axis, and plot a range as a line, area, or bar.

Headings   Adds, changes, or repositions the title, subtitle, and note.

Legend   Adds, changes, or repositions the legend entries.

Data Labels   Creates and positions labels to identify data points. Also lets you explode slices in a pie chart.

Grids   Shows or hides x-, y-, and second y-axis gridlines.

Axis   Opens a submenu that lets you customize the x-, y-, and second y-axes including the titles, axis type, scale, and units. You can also position tick marks and labels.

Name   Renames a chart.

Set Preferred   Changes the default chart style using the type and settings of the selected chart.

Use Preferred   Changes the selected chart to the default style.

Numeric Color   Sets the color and pattern for data series using values you enter in the worksheet.

Query Commands

Note: The Query commands appear when you're working with a query table.

Set Criteria   Lets you define query criteria, limit the number of records in a query table, and refresh the records in a query table.

Choose Fields   Lets you select and arrange fields in a query table. Also lets you use a formula to create a computed column.

Sort   Sorts the data in a query table.

Aggregate   Aggregates a group of values in a query table. Also names the field containing the aggregate value.

Show Field As   Lets you rename a field in a query table.

Name   Lets you rename a query table.

Set Options   Lets you replace original records, exclude duplicate records in a query table, show sample values in the Set Criteria dialog box, and refresh the query table automatically.

Show SQL   Displays the equivalent Structured Query Language (SQL) command for selecting the records in the current query table.

Set Database Table   Lets you query a different database table.

Join   Joins additional database tables with the currently selected database table, or removes a joined database table.

Update Database Table   Replaces original records in a database table with edited records from a query table.

Refresh Now   Updates the data in a query table.

Transcript Commands

Note: The Transcript commands appear when the Transcript window is active.

Playback   Runs selected items in the Transcript window as a macro.

Record Relative   Records range selections as relative references.

Minimize on Run   Reduces the Transcript window to an icon when you run recorded items as a macro.

Window Commands

Tile   Sizes and places open windows side by side.

Cascade   Sizes and stacks open windows diagonally.

(Window Name)   Lists up to nine open windows, with a check mark next to the active window. Makes a different window active.

More Windows   If more than nine windows are open in the 1-2-3 window, lists their names in a dialog box and lets you change the active window.

Help Commands

Contents   Displays Help topic categories.

Search   Lists Help topics that match a keyword you type.

Using Help   Describes how to use 1-2-3 Help.

Keyboard   Gives information about 1-2-3 keyboard shortcuts. Also describes function, navigation, editing, and other keys.

How Do I?   Lists common 1-2-3 tasks and explains how to perform them.

For Upgraders   Describes new features, new user interface, 1-2-3 Classic, and parts of the 1-2-3 window.

Tutorial   Starts the 1-2-3 Tutorial.

About 1-2-3   Gives information about 1-2-3, including the release number and copyright.

@Functions

@Function Categories

Lotus 1-2-3 @functions can be grouped into ten categories.

Calendar @functions Calculate values that represent dates and times. Date @functions use **date-numbers**, consecutive numbers that correspond to dates from January 1, 1900 (date-number 1) to December 31, 2099 (date-number 73050). Time @functions use **time-numbers**, consecutive decimal values that correspond to times from midnight (time-number 0.000000) through 11:59:59 PM (time-number 0.999988). Choose an appropriate format so 1-2-3 displays them as actual dates and times.

The date @functions include @DATE, @DATE-VALUE, @DAY, @MONTH, and @YEAR. The time @functions include @HOUR, @MINUTE, @NOW, @SECOND, @TIME, and @TIMEVALUE.

Database @functions Perform statistical calculations and queries in 1-2-3 databases. All database @functions have three arguments: input, field, and criteria. *Input* is the range that contains the database. *Field* is the name from the database table enclosed in quotation marks. *Criteria* is a range you create to specify selection requirements. Each criteria range must include database field names from the input range and the criteria you want 1-2-3 to use.

The database @functions include @DAVG, @DCOUNT, @DMAX, @DMIN, @DSTD, @DSUM, and @DVAR.

Engineering @functions Perform engineering calculations and advanced mathematical operations. Engineering @functions include @BETA, @DECIMAL, @GAMMA, and @HEX.

Financial @functions Calculate loans, annuities, and cash flows. When using financial @functions, follow these guidelines:
- Within an @function, express the term and the interest rate in the same unit of time.
- Lotus 1-2-3 accepts interest rates as either percentages or decimal values. The percent is automatically converted to a decimal.
- The financial @functions assume that annuities are ordinary annuities, in which the payments are made at the end of each time interval.

Financial @functions can be grouped into four categories: capital budgeting tools include @IRR and @NPV; depreciation includes @DDB, @SLN, and @SYD; ordinary annuities include @FV, @PMT, @PV, and @TERM; and single-sum compounding includes @CTERM and @RATE.

Information @functions Obtain information about cells, ranges, the operating system, and some 1-2-3 tools, or mark places where information is missing or incorrect. Information @ functions can be divided into two categories: cell and range information includes @CELL, @CELLPOINTER, @COLS, and @ROWS; and error checking includes @ERR and @NA.

Logical @functions Calculate the results of conditional (logical) formulas. Logical @functions include @FALSE, @IF, @ISERR, @ISNA, @ISNUMBER, @ISSTRING, and @TRUE.

Lookup @functions Find the contents of a cell, such as looking up a value in a table. Lookup @functions include @CHOOSE, @HLOOKUP, @INDEX, and @VLOOKUP.

Mathematical @functions   Perform a variety of calculations with values. Angles that you enter as arguments (for @COS, @SIN, and @TAN) must be expressed in radians. To convert degrees to radians, multiply the number of degrees by @PI/180. Some mathematical @functions—@ACOS, @ASIN, and @ATAN—produce angle values in radians. To convert radians to degrees, multiply the number of radians by 180/@PI.

Mathematical @functions include @ABS, @ACOS, @ASIN, @ATAN, @COS, @EXP, @INT, @LN, @LOG, @MOD, @PI, @RAND, @ROUND, @SIN, @SQRT, and @TAN.

Statistical @functions   Perform calculations on lists of values. Each statistical @function has an equivalent database @function. Statistical @functions include @AVG, @COUNT, @MAX, @MIN, @STD, @SUM, and @VAR.

Text @functions   Manipulate text strings—labels, string formulas, or literal strings (any sequence of letters, numbers, or symbols enclosed in quotation marks). Text @functions include @CHAR, @CLEAN, @CODE, @EXACT, @FIND, @LEFT, @LENGTH, @LOWER, @MID, @N, @PROPER, @REPEAT, @REPLACE, @RIGHT, @S, @STRING, @TRIM, @UPPER, and @VALUE.

@Function Descriptions

This section contains descriptions and examples of the 1-2-3 @functions listed alphabetically. @Function names appear in uppercase letters, but they can be entered in either uppercase or lowercase letters.

@@   @@(*location*) returns the contents of a single cell to which *location* refers. The location acts as a pointer to another cell, whose contents @ returns.

@ABS   @ABS(*x*) calculates the absolute (positive) value of *x*. *X* can be any value.

@ACCRUED   @ACCRUED(*settlement*;*issue*;*first-interest*;*coupon*;[*par*];[*frequency*];[*basis*]) calculates the accrued interest for securities with periodic interest payments. @ACCRUED supports short, standard, and long coupon periods.

@ACOS   @ACOS(*x*) calculates the arc cosine of a value. The arc (or inverse) cosine is the angle, measured in radians, whose cosine is *x*. The result of @ACOS is a value from 0 to π. *X* can be any value from –1 to 1.

@ASIN   @ASIN(*x*) calculates the arc sine of a value. The arc (or inverse) sine is the angle, measured in radians, whose sine is *x*. The result of @ASIN is a value from π/2 to –π/2. *X* can be any value from –1 to 1.

@ATAN   @ATAN(*x*) calculates the arc tangent of a value. The arc (or inverse) tangent is the angle, measured in radians, whose tangent is *x*. The result of @ATAN is a value from π/2 to –π/2. *X* can be any value.

@AVEDEV   @AVEDEV(*list*) calculates the average of the absolute deviations of a *list* of values.

@AVG   @AVG(*list*) averages the values in *list*. List can be any combination of values and ranges.

@BINOMIAL   @BINOMIAL(*trials*;*successes*;*probability*;[*type*]) calculates the binomial probability mass function or the cumulative binomial distribution.

@CELL   @CELL(*attribute*;*location*) returns information about the first cell in *location*.

@CELLPOINTER   @CELLPOINTER(*attribute*) returns information about an *attribute* for the current cell.

@CHAR   @CHAR(*x*) returns the character of the Lotus Multibyte Character Set (LMBCS) that corresponds to the number *x*.

@CHIDIST   @CHIDIST(*x*;*degrees-freedom*;[*type*]) calculates the chi-square distribution.

@CHITEST   @CHITEST(*observed-range*;[*expected-range*]) returns the chi-square probability for either Goodness of Fit or Independence.

@CHOOSE   @CHOOSE(*x*;*list*) finds the value or label, represented by *x*, from *list*.

@CLEAN   @CLEAN(*text*) removes nonprinting characters from *text*.

@CODE   @CODE(*text*) returns the Lotus Multibyte Character Set (LMBCS) code that corresponds to the first character in *text*.

@COLS   @COLS(*range*) counts the number of columns in *range*.

@CORREL   CORREL(*range1*;*range2*) calculates the population correlation coefficient.

@COS @COS(*x*) calculates the cosine of an angle (*x*) measured in radians. The result of @COS is a value from –1 to 1. *X* can be any value.

@COUNT @COUNT(*list*) counts the nonblank cells in a *list* of ranges.

@COV @COV(*range1*;*range2*;[*type*]) calculates either the sample or population covariance.

@CTERM @CTERM(*interest*;*future-value*;*present-value*) calculates the number of compounding periods it takes for an investment (*present-value*) to grow to a *future-value*, earning a fixed *interest* rate per compounding period.

@DATE @DATE(*year*;*month*;*day*) calculates the date-number for the specified *year*, *month*, and *day*.

@DATEDIF @DATEDIF(*start-date*;*end-date*;[*format*]) calculates the number of years, months, or days between two date-numbers.

@DATEVALUE @DATEVALUE(*text*) calculates the date-number for the date specified in *text*.

@DAVG @DAVG(*input*;*field*;[*criteria*]) calculates the average of the values in a *field* of the *input* range that meet criteria in the *criteria* range.

@DAY @DAY(*date-number*) extracts the day of the month (an integer from 1 to 31) from *date-number*.

@DAYS @DAYS(*start-date*;*end-date*;[*basis*]) calculates the number of days between two dates using a specified day-count basis.

@DAYS360 @DAYS360(*start-date*;*end-date*) calculates the number of days between two dates based on a 360-day year, according to the standards of the U.S. securities industry.

@DB @DB(*cost*;*salvage*;*life*;*period*) calculates depreciation allowance using the fixed declining balance method.

@DCOUNT @DCOUNT(*input*;*field*;[*criteria*]) counts the nonblank cells in a *field* of a database table that meet specified *criteria*.

@DDB @DDB(*cost*;*salvage*;*life*;*period*) calculates the depreciation allowance of an asset for a specified *period*, using the double-declining balance method.

@DMAX @DMAX(*input*;*field*;[*criteria*]) finds the largest value in a *field* of a database table that meets specified *criteria*.

@DMIN @DMIN(*input*;*field*;[*criteria*]) finds the smallest value in a *field* of a database table that meets specified *criteria*.

@DSTD @DSTD(*input*;*field*;[*criteria*]) calculates the population standard deviation of the values in a *field* of a database table that meet specified *criteria*.

@DSTDS @DSTDS(*input*;*field*;[*criteria*]) calculates the sample standard deviation of sample values in a *field* of a database table that meet specified *criteria*.

@DSUM @DSUM(*input*;*field*;[*criteria*]) calculates the sum of the values in a *field* of a database table that meet specified *criteria*.

@DVAR @DVAR(*input*;*field*;[*criteria*]) calculates the population variance of the values in a *field* of a database table that meet specified *criteria*.

@DVARS @DVARS(*input*;*field*;[*criteria*]) calculates the variance of sample values in a *field* of a database table that meet specified *criteria*.

@ERR @ERR returns the value ERR (error). @ERR is seldom used by itself, but is often used with @IF to indicate an ERR value under certain conditions.

@EVEN @EVEN(*x*) rounds a value away from 0 to the nearest even integer.

@EXACT @EXACT(*text1*;*text2*) compares two sets of characters. If the two sets match exactly, @EXACT returns 1 (true); if the two sets are not the same, @EXACT returns 0 (false).

@EXP @EXP(*x*) calculates the value of *e* (approximately 2.718282) raised to the power *x*.

@FALSE @FALSE returns the logical value 0 (false). Use @FALSE with macros or @functions such as @IF that require a logical value of 0 (false).

@FDIST @FDIST(*x*,*degrees-freedom1*;*degrees-freedom2*;[*type*]) calculates the *F*-distribution.

@FIND @FIND(*search-text*;*text*;*start-number*) calculates the position in *text* at which 1-2-3 finds the first occurrence of *search-text*, beginning at the position indicated by *start-number*.

@FTEST @FTEST(*range1*;*range2*) performs an *F*-test and returns the associated probability.

@FV @FV(*payments*;*interest*;*term*) calculates the future value of an investment, based on a series of equal *payments*, earning a periodic *interest* rate, over the number of payment periods in *term*.

@FVAL @FVAL(*payments*;*interest*;*term*;[*type*]; [*present-value*]) calculates the future values of a series of equal *payments* earning a periodic *interest*.

@GEOMEAN @GEOMEAN(*list*) calculates the geometric mean of a *list* of values.

@GRANDTOTAL @GRANDTOTAL(*list*) adds all cells in a *list* that contain @SUBTOTAL in their formulas.

@HLOOKUP @HLOOKUP(*x*;*range*;*row-offset*) finds the contents of a cell in the specified row of a horizontal lookup table, a range with either value information in ascending order or labels in the first row.

@HOUR @HOUR(*time-number*) extracts the hour, an integer from 0 (midnight) to 23 (11:00 PM), from *time-number*.

@IF @IF(*condition*;*x*;*y*) evaluates *condition* and takes one of two actions. If *condition* is true, @IF returns *x*; if *condition* is false, @IF returns *y*.

@INDEX @INDEX(*range*;*column*;*row*;[*worksheet*]) returns the contents of a cell located at the intersection of a *column*, *row*, and (optionally) *worksheet* of a *range*.

@INT @INT(*x*) returns the integer portion of *x*, without rounding the value. *X* can be any value.

@IPAYMT @IPAYMT(*principal*;*interest*;*term*;*start-period*;[*end-period*];[*type*];[*future-value*]) calculates the cumulative interest portion of a periodic payment.

@IRATE @IRATE(*term*;*payment*;*present-value*;[*type*];[*future-value*];[*guess*]) calculates the periodic interest rate necessary for an annuity (*present-value*) to grow to a *future-value* over the number of compounding periods in *term*.

@IRR @IRR(*guess*;*range*) calculates the internal rate of return (profit) for a series of cash-flow values generated by an investment. The internal rate of return is the percentage rate that equates the present value of an expected future series of cash flows to the initial investment.

@ISERR @ISERR(*x*) tests *x* for the value ERR. If *x* is the value ERR, @ISERR returns 1 (true); if *x* is not the value ERR, @ISERR returns 0 (false).

@ISNA @ISNA(*x*) tests *x* for the value NA. If *x* is the value NA, @ISNA returns 1 (true); if *x* is not the value NA, @ISNA returns 0 (false).

@ISNUMBER @ISNUMBER(*x*) tests *x* for a value. If *x* is a value, NA, ERR, or a blank cell, @ISNUMBER returns 1 (true); if *x* is text, @ISNUMBER returns 0 (false).

@ISSTRING @ISSTRING(*x*) tests *x* for text or a label. If *x* is text or a cell that contains a label or a formula that results in a label, @ISSTRING returns 1 (true); if *x* is a value or blank cell, @ISSTRING returns 0 (false).

@LARGE @LARGE(*range*;*n*) finds the *n*th largest value in *range*.

@LEFT @LEFT(*text*;*n*) returns the first *n* characters in *text*.

@LENGTH @LENGTH(*text*) counts the number of characters in *text*.

@LN @LN(*x*) calculates the natural logarithm of *x*. Natural logarithms use the number *e* (approximately 2.718281) as a base.

@LOG @LOG(*x*) calculates the common logarithm (base 10) of *x*.

@LOWER @LOWER(*text*) converts all uppercase letters in *text* to lowercase.

@MATCH @MATCH(*cell-contents*;*range*;[*type*]) finds the relative position of a cell with specified contents.

@MAX @MAX(*list*) finds the largest value in *list*.

@MEDIAN @MEDIAN(*list*) returns the median value in *list*.

@MID @MID(*text*;*start-number*;*n*) returns *n* characters from *text*, beginning with the character at *start-number*.

@MIN @MIN(*list*) finds the smallest value in *list*.

@MINUTE @MINUTE(*time-number*) extracts the minutes, an integer from 0 to 59, from *time-number*.

@MIRR @MIRR(*range*;*finance-rate*;*reinvest-rate*) calculates the modified internal rate of return (profit) for a series of cash-flow values generated by an investment.

@MOD @MOD(*x*;*y*) calculates the remainder (modulus) of *x*/*y*. *X* can be any value. If *x* is 0, @MOD returns 0.

@MONTH @MONTH(*date-number*) extracts the month from *date-number* as an integer from 1 (January) to 12 (December).

@N @N(*range*) returns the entry in the first cell in *range* as a value. If the cell contains a label, @N returns the value 0.

@NA @NA returns the value NA (not available). **Note:** *You cannot substitute the label NA for the value NA in formulas. For example, the formula +A2+34 = NA when A2 contains @NA, but equals 34 when A2 contains the label NA.*

@NORMAL @NORMAL(*x*;[*mean*];[*std*];[*type*]) calculates the normal distribution function for *x*.

@NOW @NOW calculates the value that corresponds to the current date and time on the computer's clock.

@NPER @NPER(*payments*;*interest*;*future-value*;[*type*];[*present-value*]) calculates the number of compounding payment periods in an annuity.

@NPV @NPV(*interest*;*range*) calculates the net present value of a series of future cash-flow values discounted at a fixed, periodic *interest* rate.

@ODD @ODD(*x*) rounds a value away from 0 to the nearest odd integer.

@PAYMT @PAYMT(*principal*;*interest*;*term*;[*type*]; [*future-value*]) calculates the periodic payment for an annuity.

@PERCENTILE @PERCENTILE(*x*,*range*) calculates the *x*th sample percentile among the values in *range*.

@PI @PI returns the value π (calculated at 3.1415926536); π is the ratio of the circumference of a circle to its diameter.

@PMT @PMT(*principal*;*interest*;*term*) calculates the payment on a loan (*principal*) at a given *interest* rate for a specified number of payment periods (*term*).

@PMTC @PMTC(*principal*;*interest*;*term*) is a special form of @PMT that supports Canadian mortgage conventions.

@POISSON @POISSON(*x*;*mean*;[*cumulative*]) calculates the Poisson distribution.

@PPAYMT @PPAYMT(*principal*;*interest*;*term*; *start-period*;[*end-period*];[*type*];[*future-value*]) calculates the principal portion of a periodic payment.

@PRANK @PRANK(*x*;*range*;[*places*]) finds the percentile of *x* among the values in a *range*.

@PRICE @PRICE(*settlement*;*maturity*;*coupon*; *yield*;[*redemption*];[*frequency*];[*basis*]) calculates the price per $100 face value for securities that pay periodic interest.

@PROPER @PROPER(*text*) capitalizes the first letter of each word in *text* and converts the remaining letters to lowercase.

@PUREAVG @PUREAVG(*list*) calculates the average of a *list* of values, ignoring all cells that contain labels.

@PURECOUNT @PURECOUNT(*list*) counts the cells in a *list* of ranges excluding cells that contain labels.

@PUREMAX @PUREMAX(*list*) finds the largest value in a *list*, ignoring all cells that contain labels.

@PUREMIN @PUREMIN(*list*) finds the smallest value in a *list*, ignoring all cells that contain labels.

@PURESTD @PURESTD(*list*) calculates the population standard deviation of a *list* of values, ignoring cells that contain labels.

@PURESTDS @PURESTDS(*list*) calculates the standard deviation of a *list* of values, ignoring all cells that contain labels.

@PUREVAR @PUREVAR(*list*) calculates the population variance of a *list* of values, ignoring cells that contain labels.

@PV @PV(*payments*;*interest*;*term*) calculates the present value of an investment, based on a series of equal *payments*, discounted at a periodic *interest* rate over the number of periods in *term*.

@PVAL @PVAL(*payments*;*interest*;*term*[*type*]; [*future-value*]) calculates the present value of an annuity.

@QUOTIENT @QUOTIENT(*x*;*y*) calculates the result of *x/y*, truncated to an integer.

@RAND @RAND generates a random value between 0 and 1. Each time 1-2-3 recalculates your work, @RAND generates a new random value.

@RANGENAME @RANGENAME(*cell*) returns the name of the range in which a *cell* is located.

@RANK @RANK(*item*;*range*;[*order*]) calculates the relative size or position of a value in a range relative to the other values in a range.

@RATE @RATE(*future-value*;*present-value*;*term*) calculates the periodic interest rate necessary for an investment (*present-value*) to grow to a *future-value* over the number of compounding periods in *term*.

@REGRESSION @REGRESSION(*x-range*;*y-range*;*attribute*;[*compute*]) performs multiple linear regression and returns the specified statistic.

@REPEAT @REPEAT(*text*;*n*) duplicates *text* the number of times specified by *n*.

@REPLACE @REPLACE(*original-text*;*start-number*;*n*;*new-text*) replaces *n* characters in *original-text*, beginning at *start-number*, with *new-text*.

@RIGHT @RIGHT(*text*;*n*) returns the last *n* characters in *text*.

@ROUND @ROUND(*x*;*n*) rounds the value *x* to the nearest multiple of the power of 10 specified by *n*.

@ROUNDDOWN @ROUNDDOWN(*x*;[*n*];[*direction*]) rounds the value *x* down to the nearest multiple of a specified power of 10.

@ROUNDM @ROUNDM(*x*;*multiple*;[*direction*]) rounds the value *x* to the nearest specified multiple.

@ROUNDUP @ROUNDUP(*x*;[*n*];[*direction*]) rounds the value *x* up to the nearest multiple of a specified power of 10.

@ROWS @ROWS(*range*) counts the number of rows in *range*.

@S @S(*range*) returns the entry in the first cell in *range* as a label.

@SCENARIOINFO @SCENARIOINFO(*option*; *scenario*;[*creator*]) returns information about the attributes of a scenario.

@SCENARIOLAST @SCENARIOLAST(*filename*) returns the name of the last displayed scenario.

@SEC @SEC(*x*) calculates the secant of an angle.

@SECOND @SECOND(*time-number*) extracts the seconds, an integer from 0 and 59, from *time-number*.

@SEMEAN @SEMEAN(*list*) calculates the standard error of the sample mean for a *list* of values.

@SHEETS @SHEETS(*range*) counts the worksheets in a *range*.

@SIGN @SIGN(*x*) returns 1 if *x* is a positive value, 0 if *x* is 0, and –1 if *x* is a negative value.

@SIN @SIN(*x*) calculates the sine of an angle (*x*) measured in radians. *X* can be any value.

@SLN @SLN(*cost*;*salvage*;*life*) calculates the straight line depreciation allowance of an asset with an initial value of *cost*, an expected useful *life*, and a final value of *salvage*, for one period.

@SMALL @SMALL(*range*;*n*) finds the *n*th smallest value in a *range*.

@SQRT @SQRT(*x*) calculates the positive square root of *x*. *X* can be any positive value or 0.

@STD @STD(*list*) calculates the population standard deviation of the values in *list*.

@STDS @STDS(*list*) calculates the sample standard deviation of a *list* of values.

@STRING @STRING(*x*;*n*) converts the value *x* to a label with *n* decimal places.

@SUBTOTAL @SUBTOTAL(*list*) adds the values in *list*. Use @SUBTOTAL to indicate which cells @GRANDTOTAL should sum.

@SUM @SUM (*list*) adds the values in *list*.

@SUMSQ @SUMSQ(*list*) calculates the sum of the squares of a *list* of values.

@SUMXMY2 @SUMXMY2(*range1*;*range2*) subtracts the values in a corresponding cell in two ranges, squares the differences, and then sums the results.

@SYD @SYD(*cost*;*salvage*;*life*;*period*) calculates the sum-of-the-years-digits depreciation allowance of an asset for a specified period.

@TAN @TAN(*x*) calculates the tangent of an angle (*x*) measured in radians. *X* can be any value.

@TDIST @TDIST(*x*;*degrees-freedom*;[*type*]; [*tails*]) calculates the student's *t*-distribution.

@TERM @TERM(*payments*;*interest*;*future-value*) calculates the number of periods required for a series of equal *payments* to accumulate a *future-value* at a periodic *interest* rate.

@TIME @TIME(*hour*;*minutes*;*seconds*) calculates the time-number for the specified *hour*, *minutes*, and *seconds*.

@TIMEVALUE @TIMEVALUE(*text*) calculates the time-number for the time specified in *text*.

@TODAY @TODAY calculates the date-number that corresponds to the current date on your computer.

@TRIM @TRIM(*text*) removes leading, trailing, and consecutive space characters from *text*.

@TRUE @TRUE returns the logical value 1 (true).

@TRUNC @TRUNC(*x*;[*n*]) truncates a value to a specified number of decimal places.

@TTEST @TTEST(*range1*;*range2*;[*type*];[*tails*]) performs a student's *t*-test and returns the associated probability.

@UPPER @UPPER(*text*) converts all letters in *text* to uppercase.

@VALUE @VALUE(*text*) converts a number entered as *text* to its corresponding value.

@VAR @VAR(*list*) calculates the population variance in a *list* of values.

@VARS @VARS(*list*) calculates the sample population variance in a *list* of values.

@VDB @VDB(*cost*;*salvage*;*life*;*start-period*;*end-period*;[*depreciation-factor*];[*switch*]) calculates the depreciation allowance of an asset with an initial value of *cost*, an expected useful *life*, and a final value of *salvage* for a period specified by *start-period* and *end-period*, using the variable-rate declining balance method.

@VERSIONCURRENT @VERSIONCURRENT (*range*) returns the name of the current version for a *range*.

@VERSIONDATA @VERSIONDATA(*option*; *cell*;*version-range*;*name*;[*creator*]) returns the contents of a cell in a version.

@VERSIONINFO @VERSIONINFO(*option*;*version-range*;*name*;[*creator*]) returns information about the attributes of a version.

@VLOOKUP @VLOOKUP(*x*;*range*;*column-offset*) finds the contents of the cell in a specified column of a vertical lookup table.

@WEEKDAY @WEEKDAY(*date-number*) extracts the day of the week from a *date-number*.

@WEIGHTAVG @WEIGHTAVG(*data-range*; *weights-range*;[*type*]) calculates the weighted average of values in *data-range*.

@YEAR @YEAR(*date-number*) extracts the year, an integer from 0 (1900) to 199 (2099), from *date-number*.

@YIELD @YIELD(*settlement*;*maturity*;*coupon*; *price*;[*redemption*];[*frequency*];[*basis*]) returns the yield for securities that pay periodic interest.

@ZTEST @ZTEST(*range1*;*mean1*;*std1*;[*tails*]; [*range2*];[*mean2*];[*std2*]) performs a *z*-test and returns the associated probability.

Macros

Special Keys for Macro Commands

Key Indicator in Macro	Substitute for This Key
Cursor Movement Keys	
{LEFT} or {LEFT *n*} {L} or {L *n*}	[←] cursor movement one or *n* cells
{RIGHT} or {RIGHT *n*} {R} or {R *n*}	[→] cursor movement one or *n* cells
{UP} or {UP *n*} {U} or {U *n*}	[↑] cursor movement one or *n* cells
{DOWN} or {DOWN *n*} {D} or {D *n*}	[↓] cursor movement one or *n* cells
{BIGLEFT}	[Ctrl][←]
{BIGRIGHT}	[Ctrl][→]
{HOME}	[Home]
{END}	[End]
{PGUP}	[PgUp]
{PGDN}	[PgDn]
{NEXTSHEET} or {NS}	[Ctrl][PgUp]
{PREVSHEET} or {PS}	[Ctrl][PgDn]
Function Keys	
{HELP}	[F1] select Help
{EDIT}	[F2] edit current cell

(continued in next column)

Key Indicator in Macro	Substitute for This Key
{NAME}	[F3] list range names
{ABS}	[F4] absolute cell reference
{GOTO}	[F5] move to cell
{WINDOW}	[F6] switch between split windows in a worksheet
{QUERY}	[F7] repeat last database query
{TABLE}	[F8] recalculate what-if table
{CALC}	[F9] recalculate the worksheet
{ALT}, {MENUBAR} or {MB}	[F10] access menu bar
Other Special Keys	
~	[Enter]
{ALT}	[Alt]
{BACKSPACE} or {BS}	[Backspace]
{DELETE} or {DEL}	[Delete]
{ESC}	[Esc]
{INSERT} or {INS}	[Insert]
{TAB}	[Tab]

Macro Command Descriptions

This section lists the macro commands alphabetically by keyword. You will be able to use the information in this section most effectively if you have some programming experience or at least some familiarity with programming concepts (such as conditional processing, subroutines, and for loops).

As you read through the macro command descriptions, keep in mind the following conventions:

- Macro command keywords appear in upper-case letters, but you can enter them in upper-case or lowercase.
- Brackets [ ] around an argument mean the argument is optional. For example, {PROTECT [range]} means the {PROTECT} command works even if you don't specify a range.
- When an argument is italicized, it means you must substitute something else when you write the command. For example, {BRANCH *location*} means you must include a location in the command.

{?} {?} suspends macro execution to let you move the cell pointer, complete part of a command, or enter data for the macro to process. When you press [Enter], the macro continues. To have 1-2-3 enter what you typed while macro execution was suspended, follow the {?} command with a ~ (tilde).

{ALERT} {ALERT *message*;[*buttons*];[*icon-type*];[*results-range*]} displays a message box and waits for you to choose OK or Cancel.

{APPENDBELOW} and **{APPENDRIGHT}** {APPENDBELOW *target-location*;*source-location*} copies the contents of *source-location* to the rows immediately below *target-location*. {APPENDRIGHT *target-location*;*source-location*} copies the contents of *source-location* to the rows immediately to the right of *target-location*.

{AUDIT} {AUDIT *audit*;[*files*];[*result*];[*report-range*];[*audit-range*]} highlights or produces a report of all formulas, or the relationships of values and formulas, in the current file or in all active files; also highlights or produces a report on circular references, file links, or DDE links.

{BACKSOLVE} {BACKSOLVE *formula-cell*;*target-value*;*adjustable-range*} finds values for one or more cells that make the result of a formula equal to a value you specify.

{BEEP} {BEEP} sounds the Windows beep.

{BLANK} {BLANK *location*} erases the contents of *location*, which can be a cell or a range. {BLANK} does not change the formatting of the cells in *location* and does not force recalculation.

{BRANCH} {BRANCH *location*} transfers macro control from the current macro cell to *location* for further macro instructions.

{BREAK} {BREAK} produces the effect of pressing [Ctrl][Break] in Menu mode, so you can return 1-2-3 to Ready mode. {BREAK} simulates pressing [Esc] one or more times; it will not interrupt a macro.

{BREAKOFF} and **{BREAKON}** {BREAKOFF} and {BREAKON} have no connection to the {BREAK} macro keyword. {BREAKOFF} disables [Ctrl][Break] while a macro is running. Normally, you can stop a macro at any time by pressing [Ctrl][Break]. While {BREAKOFF} is in effect, however, you cannot use [Ctrl][Break] to stop the macro. {BREAKON} restores the use of [Ctrl][Break], undoing a {BREAKOFF} command.

{CELL-ENTER} {CELL-ENTER *data*;[*target-location*]} enters *data* in *target-location*.

{CHOOSE-FILE} {CHOOSE-FILE *file-type*;*results-range*;*title*} displays a Windows common dialog box that contains a list of files and waits for you to select one.

{COLUMN-WIDTH} {COLUMN-WIDTH *width*;[*range*]} adjusts each column in *range* to the specified *width* in the default font and size.

{COLUMN-WIDTH-FIT-WIDEST} {COLUMN-WIDTH-FIT-WIDEST [*range*]} adjusts columns to the width of the widest entries included in *range*.

{COLUMN-WIDTH-RESET} {COLUMN-WIDTH-RESET [*range*]} returns each column in *range* to the default width defined with Style Worksheet Defaults Column Width.

{CROSSTAB} {CROSSTAB *database-table*;*row-headings*;*col-headings*;*summary-field*;*summary-method*} creates a cross-tabulation table.

{DATA-TABLE-1} {DATA-TABLE-1 [*output-range*];[*input-cell-1*]} substitutes values for one variable in one or more formulas and enters the results in *output-range*.

{DATA-TABLE-2} {DATA-TABLE-2 [*output-range*];[*input-cell-1*];[*input-cell-2*]} substitutes values for two variables in one formula and enters the results in *output-range*.

{DATA-TABLE-3} {DATA-TABLE-3 [*output-range*];[*input-cell-1*];[*input-cell-2*];[*input-cell-3*];[*formula*]} substitutes values for three variables in one formula and enters the results in *output-range*.

{DATA-TABLE-RESET} {DATA-TABLE-RESET} clears the ranges and input-cell settings for all what-if tables in the current file.

{DATABASE-APPEND} {DATABASE-APPEND *source-range*;*database-table*} adds new records to *database-table*.

{DATABASE-DELETE} {DATABASE-DELETE *database-table*;*criteria*} deletes the records from *database-table* that meet *criteria*.

{DATABASE-FIND} {DATABASE-FIND *database-table*;*criteria*} locates and selects records in *database-table* that meet *criteria*.

{DELETE-COLUMNS} {DELETE-COLUMNS [*range*];[*delete-selection*]} deletes all of each column that includes cells in *range*; or deletes only the part of the columns covered by *range*.

{DELETE-ROWS} {DELETE-ROWS [*range*]; [*delete-selection*]} deletes all of each row that includes cells in *range*; or deletes only the part of the rows covered by *range*.

{DELETE-SHEETS} {DELETE-SHEETS [*range*]} deletes all of each worksheet that includes cells in *range*.

{DIALOG?} {DIALOG? *name*} displays a 1-2-3 dialog box, and waits for you to choose OK or press [Enter].

{DISTRIBUTION} {DISTRIBUTION [*values-range*];[*bin-range*]} creates a frequency distribution that counts how many values in *values-range* fall within each numeric interval specified by *bin-range*.

{EDIT-CLEAR} {EDIT-CLEAR [*selection*];[*property*]} deletes data and related formatting from the worksheet without moving it to the clipboard.

{EDIT-COPY} {EDIT-COPY [*selection*];[*format*]} copies data and related formatting from the worksheet to the clipboard.

{EDIT-COPY-FILL} {EDIT-COPY-FILL *direction*;[*range*]} copies the contents of one row, column, or worksheet in *range* to all of *range*, based on a specified *direction*.

{EDIT-CUT} {EDIT-CUT [*selection*];[*format*]} cuts data and related formatting from the worksheet to the clipboard.

{EDIT-FIND} {EDIT-FIND [*search-for*];[*look-in*];[*search-through*]} finds the first instance of specified characters in labels, formulas, or both.

{EDIT-GOTO} {EDIT-GOTO *name*;[*part*];[*type*]} selects all or part of a range, query table, chart, or other drawn object, and then scrolls to it. Any items in the same file that were previously selected become unselected.

{EDIT-PASTE} {EDIT-PASTE [*selection*];[*format*]} copies data and related formatting from the clipboard into the active worksheet file.

{EDIT-PASTE-LINK} {EDIT-PASTE-LINK [*destination*];[*format*];[*reference*]} creates a link between a 1-2-3 for Windows worksheet file and the file referenced on the clipboard.

{EDIT-QUICK-COPY} {EDIT-QUICK-COPY *destination*;[*source*]} copies data and related formatting from the *source* range to the *destination* range, without using the clipboard.

{EDIT-QUICK-MOVE} {EDIT-QUICK-MOVE *destination*;[*source*]} moves data and related formatting from the *source* range to the *destination* range, without using the clipboard.

{FILE-CLOSE} {FILE-CLOSE [*discard*]} closes the current file.

{FILE-COMBINE} {FILE-COMBINE [*how*];*file-name*;[*password*];[*source*]} combines data and number formats from a 1-2-3 worksheet (.WK*) file on disk into the current file, starting in the current cell.

{FILE-EXIT} {FILE-EXIT [*discard*]} ends the 1-2-3 session.

{FILE-EXTRACT} {FILE-EXTRACT [*filename*];[*file-type*];[*password*];[*backup*];[*extract-range*];[*properties*]} saves a range to another file.

{FILE-NEW} {FILE-NEW [*filename*];[*where*]} creates a new file on disk and in memory, places the new file in a window, marks the window current, and displays a blank worksheet with the cell pointer in cell A1.

{FILE-OPEN} {FILE-OPEN *filename*;[*password*];[*read-only*];[*where*];[*how*]} reads a file into memory, makes it the current file, and moves the cell pointer to the cell it was in when you last saved the file. You can also use File Open to open a sheet file from Excel Versions 2.1, 3.0, and 4.0.

{FILE-OPEN?} {FILE-OPEN?} displays the File Open dialog box.

{FILE-SAVE} {FILE-SAVE [*filename*];[*filetype*];[*password*];[*backup*]} saves the current file.

{FILE-SAVE-AS?} {FILE-SAVE-AS?} displays the File Save As dialog box.

{FILE-SEAL} {FILE-SEAL [*password*]} controls the reservation for the current file and seals the file.

{FILE-UNSEAL} {FILE-UNSEAL [*password*]} unseals the current file and releases its network reservation setting.

{FILE-UPDATE-LINKS} {FILE-UPDATE-LINKS} recalculates formulas in the current file that contain links to other files.

{FILL} {FILL [*range*];[*start*];[*step*];[*stop*];[*units*]} enters a sequence of values in a specified *range*.

{FILL-BY-EXAMPLE} {FILL-BY-EXAMPLE [*range*]} fills *range* with a sequence of data. 1-2-3 creates a pattern for the sequence, based on data you include in the *range*.

{FOR} {FOR *counter;start;stop;step;subroutine*} creates a "for loop"—it repeatedly performs a subroutine call to *subroutine*.

{FORBREAK} {FORBREAK} cancels a "for loop" created by a {FOR} command. You must use {FORBREAK} only within a "for loop." Using {FORBREAK} anywhere else causes the macro to terminate with an error.

{FORM} {FORM *input-location*;[*call-table*]; [*include-list*];[*exclude-list*]} suspends a macro temporarily so you can enter and edit data in the unprotected cells in *input-location*.

{FORMBREAK} {FORMBREAK} ends a {FORM} command, canceling the current form. Use {FORMBREAK} only within a {FORM} command.

{FRAMEOFF} and **{FRAMEON}** {FRAMEOFF} and {FRAMEON} have no effect in 1-2-3 Release 4.

{GET} {GET *location*} suspends macro execution until you press a key, then records your keystroke as a left-aligned label in *location*. You can press any key except [Ctrl][Break].

{GET-FORMULA} {GET-FORMULA [*prompt*]; *result*;[*default*];[*title*]} lets you enter a formula.

{GET-LABEL} {GET-LABEL [*prompt*];*result*; [*default*];[*title*]} lets you enter anything that you want 1-2-3 to store in the worksheet as a left-aligned label.

{GET-NUMBER} {GET-NUMBER [*prompt*]; *result*;[*default*];[*title*]} lets you enter a number or a numeric formula. {GET-NUMBER} enters the number in the worksheet or evaluates the formula and enters the result as a number.

{GET-RANGE} {GET-RANGE [*prompt*];*result*; [*default*];[*title*]} lets you enter a range name or address. {GET-RANGE} enters the name or address in the worksheet as a left-aligned label.

{HIDE-COLUMNS} {HIDE-COLUMNS [*range*]} hides all columns in *range*.

{HIDE-SHEETS} {HIDE-SHEETS [*range*]} hides all worksheets in *range*.

{IF} {IF *condition*} evaluates *condition* as true or false. If *condition* is true, 1-2-3 continues to the macro instruction immediately following the {IF} command in the same cell. If *condition* is false, 1-2-3 goes immediately to the next cell in the column, skipping any further instructions in the same cell as the {IF} command.

{INDICATE} {INDICATE [*text*]} displays *text* in the title bar until 1-2-3 reaches another {INDICATE} command or until you end the 1-2-3 session.

{INSERT-COLUMNS} {INSERT-COLUMNS [*range*];[*number*];[*insert-selection*]} inserts one or more blank columns in the current file or inserts only the part of the columns covered by *range*.

{INSERT-ROWS} {INSERT-ROWS [*range*];[*number*];[*insert-selection*]} inserts one or more blank rows in the current file, or inserts only the part of the rows covered by *range*.

{INSERT-SHEETS} {INSERT-SHEETS [*where*]; [*number*];[*range*]} inserts one or more blank worksheets in the current file.

{LET} {LET *location,entry*} enters a number or left-aligned label in *location.*

{LINK-CREATE} {LINK-CREATE *link-name*; *app-name;topic-name;item-name;*[*format*];[*mode*]; [*branch-location*]} without using the clipboard, creates a link between the current worksheet file and another Windows application that supports DDE or OLE as a server.

{LINK-UPDATE} {LINK-UPDATE [*link-name*]} updates DDE and OLE link, or activates and updates links deactivated with {LINK-DEACTIVATE}.

{MENU-CREATE} {MENU-CREATE *menu-description-range*} replaces the current 1-2-3 menu bar with a customized menu bar.

{MENUBRANCH} and **{MENUCALL}** {MENUBRANCH *location*} displays a dialog box that contains a list of menu commands; waits for you to select one and then choose OK or Cancel; and then branches to the macro instructions associated with the command you select. {MENUCALL *location*} displays a dialog box that contains a list of menu commands; waits for you to select one and then choose OK or Cancel; and then performs a subroutine call to the macro instructions associated with the command you select.

{PANELOFF} and **{PANELON}** {PANELOFF} freezes the control panel until 1-2-3 encounters a {PANELON} command or the macro ends. {PANELON} unfreezes the control panel and status line.

{PRINT} {PRINT [*what*];[*from*];[*to*];[*start*];[*copies*]} prints the current file according to the current page settings.

{PRINT?} {PRINT?} displays the File Print dialog box.

{PROTECT} {PROTECT [*range*]} turns protection back on for a *range* that has been unprotected.

{QUERY-ADD-FIELD} {QUERY-ADD-FIELD *field*} adds a *field* to the currently selected query table. The field is displayed as the last field in the query table.

{QUERY-AGGREGATE} {QUERY-AGGREGATE *function;field-name*} performs calculations on groups of data from a query table. For example, you can calculate sales by salesperson, by month of sale, or by account.

{QUERY-CHOOSE-FIELDS} {QUERY-CHOOSE-FIELDS [*field1*];[*field2*];...;[*field15*]} specifies the fields that you want to appear in the currently selected query table.

{QUERY-CRITERIA} {QUERY-CRITERIA [*criteria*]} specifies *criteria* to determine which records appear in a new or currently selected query table.

{QUERY-NEW} {QUERY-NEW *database-table;output-range;*[*criteria*];[*query-name*];[*record-limit*];[*field1*];[*field2*];...;[*field10*]} creates a query table that contains the records you extract from a database table.

{QUERY-SORT} {QUERY-SORT [*key1*];[*order1*]; [*key2*];[*order2*];[*key3*];[*order3*]} arranges data in the currently selected query table in the order you specify.

{QUERY-SORT-KEY-DEFINE} {QUERY-SORT-KEY-DEFINE *key-number;key-field;key-order*} defines a sort key to be used by a subsequent {QUERY-SORT} command.

{QUERY-SORT-RESET} {QUERY-SORT-RESET} clears all sort keys for the currently selected query table.

{QUIT} {QUIT} ends a macro immediately, returning keyboard control to you. Any instructions that follow a {QUIT} command in a macro are never completed. Even if you use {QUIT} in a subroutine, the command ends the entire macro, not just the subroutine.

{RANGE-NAME-CREATE} {RANGE-NAME-CREATE *range-name*;[*range-location*]} assigns a name to a range address.

{RANGE-NAME-DELETE} {RANGE-NAME-DELETE *range-name*} deletes a range name in the current file.

{RANGE-NAME-DELETE-ALL} {RANGE-NAME-DELETE-ALL} deletes all range names in the current file.

{RANGE-NAME-LABEL-CREATE} {RANGE-NAME-LABEL-CREATE [*direction*];[*label-range*]} assigns an existing label as the range name for a single cell immediately above, below, to the right of, or to the left of the label.

{RANGE-VERSION?} {RANGE-VERSION? [*option*]} displays the Version Manager window.

{RECALC} {RECALC *location*;[*condition*];[*iterations*]} recalculates the values in *location*, proceeding row by row. Use {RECALC} to recalculate formulas located below and to the left of cells on which they depend.

{REGRESSION} {REGRESSION [*x-range*];[*y-range*];[*output-range*];[*intercept*]} performs multiple linear regression analysis and also calculates the slope of the line that best illustrates the data.

{RETURN} {RETURN} affects flow of control in subroutines. In a subroutine called by {*subroutine*} or {MENUCALL}, {RETURN} immediately returns macro control from the subroutine to the location from which the {*subroutine*} or {MENUCALL} command was issued. In a subroutine called by a {FOR} command, {RETURN} ends the current iteration of the subroutine and immediately starts the next iteration. {RETURN} is optional in a subroutine. If a macro encounters a blank cell at the end of a subroutine, it interprets this as a {RETURN}.

{ROW-HEIGHT} {ROW-HEIGHT *height*;[*range*]} adjusts each row in *range* to a specified *height* in points.

{ROW-HEIGHT-FIT-LARGEST} {ROW-HEIGHT-FIT-LARGEST [*range*]} adjusts each row in *range* to the height of the largest font in that row.

{ROW-HEIGHT-RESET} {ROW-HEIGHT-RESET} resets row height to the default setting.

{SCENARIO-ADD-VERSION} {SCENARIO-ADD-VERSION *scenario-name*;[*scenario-creator*];*version-range*;*version-name*;[*version-creator*]} adds a version to a scenario.

{SCENARIO-CREATE} {SCENARIO-CREATE *name*;[*share*];[*comment*]} creates a scenario.

{SCENARIO-DELETE} {SCENARIO-DELETE *name*;[*creator*]} deletes a scenario.

{SCENARIO-SHOW} {SCENARIO-SHOW *name*;[*creator*]} displays in the worksheet the selected scenario.

{SCROLL-COLUMNS} {SCROLL-COLUMNS [*amount*]} scrolls horizontally by column in the current worksheet.

{SCROLL-ROWS} {SCROLL-ROWS [*amount*]} scrolls vertically by row in the current worksheet.

{SELECT} {SELECT *name*;[*part*];[*type*]} selects all or part of a range, chart, query table, or other drawn object, without scrolling to it. Any items in the same file that were previously selected become unselected.

{SELECT-ALL} {SELECT-ALL [*type*]} selects one of the following: the active area of the current worksheet; all charts or drawn objects in the current worksheet; all worksheets in the current file.

{SELECT-APPEND} {SELECT APPEND *name*;*part*} selects all or part of a range, chart, or other drawn object without deselecting those currently selected.

{SELECT-REMOVE} {SELECT-REMOVE *name*} removes a range, chart, or other drawn object from the currently selected collection.

{SHEET-NAME} {SHEET-NAME *new-name*;[*old-name*]} names a 1-2-3 worksheet in the current file.

{SHEET-NAME-DELETE} {SHEET-NAME-DELETE [*worksheet-name*]} deletes the name of a 1-2-3 worksheet in the current file.

{SHOW-COLUMNS} {SHOW-COLUMNS [*range*]} redisplays all hidden columns in *range*.

{SHOW-SHEETS} {SHOW-SHEETS [*range*]} redisplays all hidden worksheets in *range*.

{SMARTICONS-USE} {SMARTICONS-USE *set-name*} selects a set of SmartIcons to use with 1-2-3.

{SORT} {SORT [*range*];[*key1*];[*order1*];[*key2*]; [*order2*];[*key3*];[*order3*]} arranges data in *range* in the order you specify.

{SORT-KEY-DEFINE} {SORT-KEY-DEFINE *key-number*;*key-range*;*key-order*} defines a sort key to be used by a subsequent {SORT} command.

{SORT-RESET} {SORT-RESET} clears all sort keys for sorting range data.

{SPELLCHECK?}   {SPELLCHECK?} displays the Tools Spell Check dialog box and waits for you to choose OK.

{STYLE-BORDER}   {STYLE-BORDER *border*;*display*;[*range*];[*color*];[*style*]} controls borders for *range*.

{STYLE-EDGE}   {STYLE-EDGE [*color*];[*style*]; [*width*];[*arrowhead*]} changes the color, style, and width of the edge of entire charts, chart elements (plot frames, solid data series, titles, legends, and footnotes), text blocks, enclosed drawn objects, arcs, freehand drawings, polylines, OLE objects, and pictures created in other Windows applications.

{STYLE-FONT}   {STYLE-FONT *typeface*;[*range*]; [*font-family*];[*character-set*]} assigns a font to a *range*.

{STYLE-FONT-ALL}   {STYLE-FONT-ALL [*typeface*];[*size*];[*bold*];[*italic*];[*underline*];[*range*];[*underline-style*];[*font-family*];[*character-set*]} assigns a font and adds bold, italic, and underlining to *range*.

{STYLE-FONT-ATTRIBUTES}   {STYLE-FONT-ATTRIBUTES *attribute*;*on-off*;[*range*];[*underline-style*]} adds bold, italic, or underlining to *range*.

{STYLE-FONT-RESET}   {STYLE-FONT-RESET [*range*]} restores a worksheet default font, font size, attributes, and color to *range*.

{STYLE-FONT-SIZE}   {STYLE-FONT-SIZE *size*;[*range*]} assigns a point size to the fonts in *range*.

{STYLE-FRAME}   {STYLE-FRAME *display*;[*color*]; [*style*];[*range*]} adds or removes a frame for *range*.

{STYLE-GALLERY}   {STYLE-GALLERY *template*;[*range*]} formats *range* with one of fourteen style templates available in 1-2-3.

{STYLE-INTERIOR}   {STYLE-INTERIOR [*background-color*];[*pattern*];[*pattern-color*];[*text-color*];[*negatives*];[*range*]} adds colors and patterns to *range*.

{STYLE-LINE}   {STYLE-LINE [*color*];[*style*]; [*width*];[*arrowhead*];[*symbol*]} changes the color, style, and width of the selected line for drawn lines and chart lines including line data series, gridlines, and axes.

{STYLE-NUMBER-FORMAT}   {STYLE-NUMBER-FORMAT [*format*];[*decimals*];[*parentheses*]; [*range*]} sets the display of values in *range*.

{STYLE-NUMBER-FORMAT-RESET}   {STYLE-NUMBER-FORMAT-RESET [*range*]} resets the format of *range* to the current default format specified in Style Worksheet Defaults.

{subroutine}   {*subroutine* [*arg1*];[*arg2*];...; [*argn*]} performs a subroutine call. A subroutine is a discrete unit of macro instructions. A subroutine call causes 1-2-3 to complete the instructions in the specified subroutine before continuing the current macro instructions.

{UNPROTECT}   {UNPROTECT [*range*]} turns protection off for a *range*.

{VERSION-CREATE}   {VERSION-CREATE *version-range*;*name*;[*share*];[*retain-styles*];[*comment*]} creates a new version.

{VERSION-DELETE}   {VERSION-DELETE *version-range*;*name*;[*creator*]} deletes the specified version.

{VERSION-SHOW}   {VERSION-SHOW *version-range*;*name*;[*creator*];[*goto*]} displays in the worksheet the selected version.

{VERSION-UPDATE}   {VERSION-UPDATE *version-range*;*name*;[*creator*]} updates an already existing version with new data you enter in its named range.

{WAIT}   {WAIT *time-number*} suspends macro execution and displays Wait as the mode indicator until the time specified by *time-number*. When the specified time arrives, 1-2-3 removes the Wait indicator and continues the macro.

{What-if tables}   See {DATA-TABLE} entries

{WINDOW-ACTIVATE}   {WINDOW-ACTIVATE [*window-name*];[*reserved*];[*pane*]} makes a window the active window.

{WINDOW-ARRANGE}   {WINDOW-ARRANGE *how*} sizes open windows (worksheet and Transcript) and either places them side by side or arranges them one on top of the other, with just the title bars showing.

{WINDOW-STATE}   {WINDOW-STATE *state*} minimizes, maximizes, or restores the active window.

{WORKSHEET-TITLES}   {WORKSHEET-TITLES *direction*} freezes (or unfreezes) columns along the top of the worksheet, rows along the left edge of the worksheet, or both.

SmartIcons

File SmartIcons

Create a file

Open an existing file

Close the active window

Save the current file

Send data by electronic mail

Preview the print selection

Set up header, footer, margins, and other page settings

Set page orientation to landscape mode

Set page orientation to portrait mode

Fit the print selection on one page

Fit all columns in the print selection on one page

Fit all rows in the print selection on one page

Set columns as print titles

Set rows as print titles

Select the data to print

Print the current selection

End the current 1-2-3 session

Edit SmartIcons

Undo the previous action or command

Cut the current selection to the clipboard

Copy the current selection to the clipboard

Paste the contents of the clipboard in the worksheet

Delete styles from the current selection and leave data intact

Paste data from the clipboard, but not the styles

Paste styles from the clipboard, but not the data

Paste the results of formulas from the clipboard, not the formulas themselves

Paste the contents of the clipboard as a formula, file link, DDE line, or OLE link

Place selected drawn objects in front of all other drawn objects

Place selected drawn objects behind all other drawn objects

Flip a chart or other drawn object horizontally

Flip a chart or other drawn object vertically

Rotate a chart or other drawn object

Group or ungroup selected drawn objects

Lock (protect) or unlock selected drawn objects

Select several drawn objects

Select all drawn objects in the worksheet

Copy the contents of the top row in the selection to fill the entire selection

Copy the contents of the left-most column in the selection to fill the entire selection

Copy the contents of the top left cell to fill the entire selection

Copy a range's style to another range

Insert one or more columns to the left of the selected columns

Insert one or more rows above the selected rows

Insert a range

Insert a new worksheet after the current worksheet

Delete all columns in the selected range

Delete all rows in the selected range

Delete the selected range

Delete all worksheets in the selected range

Find or replace specified characters in labels and formulas

Display Go To dialog box to move to a range, chart, drawn object, or query table

Create and embed data in the worksheet

View SmartIcons

Increase the size of the contents of the window

Decrease the size of the contents of the window

Display the contents of the window in the default size

Display three contiguous worksheets in Perspective view

Show or hide worksheet elements

Style SmartIcons

$ Format values with the default currency symbol, the default thousands separator, and two decimal places

¥   Format values with the default currency symbol, the default thousands separator, and two decimal places

£   Format values with the default currency symbol, the default thousands separator, and two decimal places

0,0   Format values with the default thousands separator and no decimal places

%   Format values as percent with two decimal places

16   Enter today's date in the current cell

     Change the font, color, and attributes of data

N   Remove bold, italics, and underlining from data

B   Add or remove boldface

I   Add or remove italics

U   Add or remove underlining

U   Add or remove double underlining

     Change the color, pattern, lines, and frames in the current selection

     Draw an outline around a cell or range and add a drop shadow

     Add a border

     Align data to the left

     Center data

     Align data to the right

     Evenly align data with both the left and right edges of a range

abc   Set text at an angle

     Apply a style template to a range

B _I_ **u**   Create or apply a named style

     Size columns to fit the widest entry

     Insert a horizontal page break

     Insert a vertical page break

Tools SmartIcons

Create a chart using the data in the selected range

Draw a line

Draw a segmented line

Draw a forward-pointing arrow

Draw a double-headed arrow

Draw a rectangle or square

Draw a rectangle or square with rounded corners

Draw an arc

Draw an ellipse or circle

Draw a polygon

Create a freehand drawing

Create a text block

Create a button for starting a macro

Create a query table

Cross-tabulate values from a database table

Check spelling

Audit cells

Find formulas

Find formula precedents

Find cell dependents

Find links to 1-2-3 files

Find DDE links

Select and rearrange available SmartIcons

Select next set of SmartIcons

Recalculate the worksheet

Select a macro command

Run a macro

Turn Step mode on or off

Turn Trace mode on or off

Record a macro or stop recording

Show or hide the Transcript window

Range SmartIcons

Use Version Manager to work with versions and scenarios

Fill the selected range with a sequence of values

Fill the selected range with a sequence of data in a pattern established by the first cell in the range

Sort a range or database table in ascending order (A-Z and smallest to largest values) using the selected column as the key

Sort a range or database table in descending order (Z-A and largest to smallest values) using the selected column as the key

Transpose data from columns to rows, or rows to columns

Create or delete a range name

Use Solver to find solutions that meet constraints

Sum values in the selected or adjacent range, if you include empty cells below or to the right of the range

Query SmartIcon

Specify fields to appear in a query table

Chart SmartIcons

Select a chart type

Line chart

Area chart

Vertical bar chart

Horizontal bar chart

Horizontal stacked bar chart

Vertical stacked bar chart

Pie chart

XY chart

HLCO chart

Radar chart

Mixed chart

3-D line chart

3-D area chart

3-D vertical bar chart

3-D pie chart

Window SmartIcons

Arrange windows side by side

Stagger windows so that for all windows except the first, only the title bars show

Navigation SmartIcons

Go to the next worksheet

Go to the previous worksheet

Go to cell A1 in the current worksheet

Go to the lower-right corner of the worksheet's active area

Go up to the next cell that contains data and is next to a blank cell

Go down to the next cell that contains data and is next to a blank cell

Go right to the next cell that contains data and is next to a blank cell

Go left to the next cell that contains data and is next to a blank cell

Go to the first cell in the next range of a collection

Go to the first cell in the previous range of a collection

Index

prompting data entry,
L 393-396
titles for what-if tables, L 336
values, L 52-53
x- and y-axis titles, L 176-177
equal to operator (=), L 295
ERR values, data editing, L 401
errors. *See also* editing
canceling, L 49
correcting, L 54
data input, L 400-401
debugging macros, L 275-279
mode indicator specifying, L 15
exception report, L 295, L 299
executing. *See* running macros
executive information system (EIS),
L 351-381
combining multiple worksheet
files, L 353, L 356-360
consolidating information,
L 352, L 353
drill down, L 365-367
integrating Windows
applications. *See* embedding
objects; integrating
applications; linking objects
opening multiple applications,
L 371-374
planning, L 352-353
exiting Lotus 1-2-3 for Windows,
L 38-39
expenditures, L 118-119
expense schedule, detailed, L 44
exploding pie chart slices,
L 192-193
expressions, functions, L 319,
L 323

F

field names, L 287, L 289
entering, L 289-290
fields, L 287. *See also* key fields

File Combine command, L 357
file extensions
WK4, L 60
WRI, L 372
file links, audit activities, L 318
file manipulation commands, L 392
File menu, commands for
embedded objects, L 381
file references, L 360, L 361, L 362
creating, L 363-364
filenames
file references, L 360, L 362
saving worksheets, L 58
Student Disk, L 60-61
worksheets, L 14, L 15, L 60-61
files. *See also* charts; databases;
documents; worksheets
destination, L 357
linking. *See* linking objects;
linking worksheets
protecting (sealing), L 326-328
saving, L 11
source, L 357
Student Disk, L 60
Fill by Example, L 87-89
entering input data values in
what-if tables, L 336, L 340
fill patterns
charts, L 177-178, L 179, L 184
transparent, L 184
worksheets, L 142-144
Find Records dialog box, L 302
fixed cost, L 208
Fixed format, L 102
flipping drawn objects, L 185-186
flow of control commands, L 392
fonts
changing, L 176
selecting, L 136-140
footers, printing worksheets,
L 144-146
{FOR} command, L 406
{FORBREAK} command, L 406
{FORM} command, L 395

formats, L 101-106
cells, L 27-28
charts, L 162
dates, L 135-136
formatting multiple worksheets
with Group mode, L 238-240
number of decimals, L 101,
L 102
formulas, L 24, L 29-30
audit activities, L 318
cell addresses, L 29
copying formulas containing
absolute and relative
references, L 128
copying using relative
references, L 92-97
copying with rounding, L 107
entering, L 53-57
entering by pointing, L 89-92
entering for calculating results
of what-if tables, L 336-337,
L 340
entering with @ROUND
function, L 106-107
file references, L 360, L 361
for growth rate, L 84
linking, L 360, L 362
predefined. *See* functions
range names, L 214-217
@function selector, L 99-100
functions, L 24, L 30-31
applying, L 231-236
arguments, L 98
at sign (@), L 30, L 98
@AVG, L 231, L 232-233
@COS, L 231
@COUNT, L 231
@DAY, L 231
expressions, L 319, L 323
@function selector, L 99-100
@HLOOKUP, L 323
@IF, L 319-322
@INT, L 231
@ISERR, L 403

finding multiple records in databases, L 302

scrolling, L 19–21

special, in macros, L 396

keys (sort), primary and secondary, L 291, L 292

L

label prefixes, L 25–27, L 134

labels

adding to worksheet rows, L 123

cells, L 24–27

centered, L 26

editing, L 61–62

entering, L 49–52, L 123, L 134–135

left-justified, L 25

long, entering, L 134–135

naming ranges using labels in adjacent cells, L 215–217

pie charts, L 190–191

prefixes, L 25–27, L 134

right-justified, L 25–26

wide, L 56

x- and y-axis, L 162, L 163

landscape orientation, L 146

launching

Lotus 1-2-3 for Windows, L 9–11

Microsoft Paintbrush, L 377

Microsoft Write, L 371–372

ledger, checkbook, L 390–391

left-justified labels, L 25

left-to-right rule, precedence of operations, L 57

legend, L 163

less than operator (<), L 295

less than or equal to operator (<=), L 295

line charts, L 161, L 168

3-D, L 161

Lines & Color dialog box, L 178

linking formulas, L 360, L 362

creating, L 362–364

file references, L 360, L 361, L 362, L 363–364

linking objects, L 368, L 369, L 370–371

editing documents, L 375–376

editing objects, L 370

viewing links, L 376

to Write documents, L 373–374

linking worksheets, L 360–365

data integrity of calculations, L 364

drill down, L 365–366

@LN function, L 231

loan payments, calculating with @PMT function, L 234–236

long labels, entering, L 134–135

lookup table, L 322–325

lookup table range, L 323

lookup tables

column-offset, L 323

preparing to implement, L 324

loops, macros, L 404–406

Lotus 1-2-3 for Windows

exiting, L 38–39

integrating applications. See embedding objects; integrating applications; linking objects

launching, L 9–11

overview, L 4–6

Lotus Applications group window, L 9–10

M

macro buttons, L 265, L 393, L 406–407

creating, L 266–268, L 269–274

running macros, L 268

Macro Command SmartIcon, L 397–398

macro instructions. See macros

macro planning sheet, L 257

Macro Run dialog box, L 265

macros, L 254–279

advanced. See advanced macro commands; advanced macros

arguments, L 258

copying from Transcript window to worksheet window, L 271

copying recorded commands to worksheet, L 262–263

data entry, L 393–396

debugging, L 275–279

displaying names, L 397

documenting, L 264

editing commands, L 273–274

entering commands, L 258

function description, L 393

Help feature, L 273

interactive, L 269–274

menus, L 407–410

naming, L 263–264, L 272

placing, L 261–263

planning, L 257

playing back, L 260–261

range names, L 263–264

recording, L 258–261, L 270–272

repeating commands, L 404–406

reviewing commands, L 399, L 402, L 408–409

running, L 36–37, L 263, L 265–266, L 268, L 272

saving, L 268–269

stopping, L 275

syntax of commands, L 258

main menu bar, L 10–11

selecting commands, L 11

margins, changing, L 144

@MAX function, L 231, L 233

{MENUBRANCH} command, L 407–410

TASK	MOUSE	MENU	KEYBOARD
Absolute references, *L 127*			`F4`
Audit, cell dependents (not included in Student Version), *L 318*	[icon]	Click Tools, click Audit..., click Cell dependents, click the OK button	`Alt` `T` , `A` , `D` , `Enter`
Audit, circular references (not included in Student Version), *L 318*	Click Circ indicator	Click Tools, click Audit..., click Circular references, click the OK button	`Alt` `T` , `A` , `C` , `Enter`
Audit, DDE links (not included in Student Version), *L 318*	[icon], click DDE links, click the OK button	Click Tools, click Audit..., click DDE links, click the OK button	`Alt` `T` , `A` , `E` , `Enter`
Audit, file links (not included in Student Version), *L 318*	[icon], click File links, click the OK button	Click Tools, click Audit..., click File links, click the OK button	`Alt` `T` , `A` , `F` , `Enter`
Audit, formula precedents (not included in Student Version), *L 318*	[icon]	Click Tools, click Audit..., click Formula precedents, click the OK button	`Alt` `T` , `A` , `P` , `Enter`
Audit, locate formulas (not included in Student Version), *L 318*	[icon]	Click Tools, click Audit..., click All formulas, click the OK button	`Alt` `T` , `A` , `A` , `Enter`
Backsolver, *L 331*	See Reference Window: Using Backsolver for Goal Seeking		
Boldface cell contents, *L 138*	`B`	Click Style or [mouse], click Fonts & Attributes..., click Bold, click the OK button	`Ctrl` `B`
Cancel action	`X`		`Esc`
Cascade worksheets		Click Window, click Cascade	`Alt` `W` , `C`
Center cell contents, *L 135*	Select range, [icon]	Select range, click Style or [mouse], click Alignment..., click Center, click the OK button	Select range, `Alt` `S` , `A` , `C` , `Enter`
Center text across columns		Select range, click Style or [mouse], click Alignment..., click Center, click Across columns, click the OK button	Select range, `Alt` `S` , `A` , `C` , `O` , `Enter`
Chart, adjust size, *L 182*	Drag handles using [icon]		
Chart, create, *L 72*	Select range, [icon], click where you want chart to appear	Select range, click Tools, click Chart, click where you want chart to appear	Select range, `Alt` `T` , `C` , click where you want chart to appear

TASK	MOUSE	MENU	KEYBOARD
Chart, delete	Click chart, ☐	Click chart, click Edit, click Clear	Click chart, Del or Alt E, E
Chart, modify type, *L 167*	Click chart, select type: ☐, ☐, ☐, ☐, or ☐ Double-click chart or click chart, ☐, select type, click the OK button	Click Chart, click Type..., select type, click the OK button	Alt C, T, type chart type, Enter
Chart, move	Click and drag chart using ☐		
Chart object, select, *L 172*	Click object		
Clear cell contents	☐	Click Edit, click Clear	Del or Alt E, E
Close the worksheet, *L 38*	☐ or double-click worksheet Control menu box ☐	Click File, click Close	Alt F, C
Collection, select, *L 187*	See Reference Window: Selecting a Collection		
Color, add		Select range, click Style or ☐, click Lines & Color..., select color, click the OK button	Select range, Alt S, L, select color, Enter
Column width, adjust, *L 65*	Drag the column heading dividing line	Click Style, click Column Width..., click Set width to	Alt S, C, S
Column width, fit widest, *L 65*	Click column letter, ☐	Click column letter, click Style, click Column Width..., click Fit widest entry	Click column letter, Alt S, C, F
Column width, reset		Click Style, click Column Width..., click Reset to worksheet default	Alt S, C, R
Copy cell contents, *L 93*	Select range, press Ctrl and drag ☐ to new location Select range, ☐, select range, ☐	Select range, click Edit or ☐, click Copy, select range, click Edit or ☐, click Paste	Select range, Ctrl C, select range, Ctrl V

TASK REFERENCE

LOTUS 1-2-3 RELEASE 4 FOR WINDOWS

Italicized page numbers indicate the first discussion of each task. 🖱 *means to click the right mouse button.*

TASK	MOUSE	MENU	KEYBOARD
Crosstab table, *L 304*	📊, select database range, 🔽, select crosstab options	📊, select database range, click Tools, click Database, click Crosstab..., select crosstab options	F5, select database range, Alt, T, B, T, select crosstab options
Database, change query, *L 300*	See Reference Window: Changing an Existing Query		
Database, find records, *L 301*		📊 select database range, click Tools, click Database, click Find Records..., click Set Criteria, click the OK button	F5, select database range, Alt, T, B, F, click Set Criteria, Enter
Database, new query, *L 296*	See Reference Window: Querying a Database		
Date, include, *L 135*	@, click TODAY, ✓		Type @TODAY, Enter
Delete a row or column, *L 133*	📊 or 📊	Click Edit, click Delete, click Row or Column, click the OK button	Ctrl [−] (on numeric keypad), R or C, Enter
Drop shadow box, add, *L 140*	Select range, ⬛	Select range, click Style or 🖱, click Lines & Color..., click Outline, click Designer frame, click the OK button	Select range, Alt, S, L, O, D, Enter
Edit 1-2-3 object linked to another application, *L 375*	See Reference Window: Editing a 1-2-3 Object Linked to a Client Application		
Edit cell contents, *L 61*	Double-click cell		Move to cell, F2
Edit embedded object, *L 380*	See Reference Window: Editing an Embedded Object		
Embed object into 1-2-3, *L 379*	See Reference Window: Embedding an Object into 1-2-3		
Exit 1-2-3, *L 39*	🚪 or double-click 1-2-3 Control menu box ⬛	Click File, click Exit	Alt F4 or Alt F, X
File combine add, *L 357*	See Reference Window: Using File Combine Add with a Data Range		
Fill by example, *L 87*	Select range, 📊	Select range, click Range, click Fill by Example	Select range, Alt R, E
Footer, *L 144*	📄, click Page Setup..., type footer in line position box	Click File, click Print..., click Page Setup..., type footer in line position box	Ctrl P or Alt P, then S, Tab to line position box, type footer

TASK	MOUSE	MENU	KEYBOARD
Format comma, *L 103*	Select range, [0,0] Select range, click number format selector, click Comma	Select range, click Style or 🖱, click Number Format..., click Comma, click the OK button	Select range, [Alt] [S], [N], select Comma, [Enter]
Format currency, *L 103*	Select range, [$] Select range, click number format selector, click Currency	Select range, click Style or 🖱, click Number Format..., click Currency, click the OK button	Select range, [Alt] [S], [N], select Currency, [Enter]
Format date, *L 103*	Select range, click number format selector, click date format	Select range, click Style or 🖱, click Number Format..., select date format, click the OK button	Select range, [Alt] [S], [N], select date format, [Enter]
Format numbers, *L 103*	See Reference Window: Formatting Numbers in Cells		
Format percentage, *L 103*	Select range, [%] Select range, click number format selector, click Percent	Select range, click Style or 🖱, click Number Format..., click Percent, click the OK button	Select range, [Alt] [S], [N], select Percent, [Enter]
Formula, enter, *L 53*	Click cell, type arithmetic operators, click cell names, type constants, ☑		Move cursor to cell, type formula, press [Enter]
Function, enter, *L 106*	Click cell, [@], select function, complete function arguments, ☑		Move cursor to cell, type function, [Enter]
Go To a cell or range name, *L 23*	[→], type cell name or select range, click the OK button	Click Edit, click Go To..., type cell name or select range, click the OK button	[F5] or [Alt] [E], [G], type cell name or select range, [Enter]
Goal seeking, *L 331*	See Reference Window: Using Backsolver for Goal Seeking		
Header, *L 144*	📄, click Page Setup..., type header in line position box	Click File, click Print..., click Page Setup..., type header in line position box	[Ctrl] [P] or [Alt] [P], then [S], [Tab] to line position box, type header
Help, access, *L 64*	[?], select Help option	Click Help, select Help option	[F1] or [Alt] [H]

TASK	MOUSE	MENU	KEYBOARD
Help, close, *L 65*	Double-click Help window Control menu box ▭	Click File, click Exit	`Esc` or `Alt` `F`, `X`
Hidden column, display, *L 333*	Drag the column heading dividing line to the right until the column is set to the desired width	Click Style, click Hide..., click Column, type cell address for column in Range text box, click the Show button	`Alt` `S`, `H`, `C`, `Tab`, type cell address in column Range text box, `Tab`, `W`
Hide column, *L 329*	Drag the column heading dividing line to the left until the column disappears	Select columns, click Style, click Hide..., click Column, click the OK button	Select columns, `Alt` `S`, `H`, `C`, `Enter`
Insert a row or column, *L 122*	▦ or ▥	Click Edit, click Insert, click Row or Column, click the OK button	`Ctrl` [+] (on numeric keypad), `R` or `C`, `Enter`
Italicize cell contents, *L 138*	*I*	Click Style or 🖱, click Fonts & Attributes..., click Italics, click the OK button	`Ctrl` `I`
Label, enter, *L 50*	Click cell, type label, ✓		Move cursor to cell, type label, `Enter`
Launch 1-2-3, *L 9*	Double-click 1-2-3 Release 4 icon	Click File, click Run, click Browse, select 1-2-3 Release 4 directory, PROGRAMS, 123W.EXE, click the OK button, click the OK button	`Alt` `F`, `R`, select 1-2-3 Release 4 directory, PROGRAMS, 123W.EXE, `Enter`
Left-align cell contents	Select range, ▤	Select range, click Style or 🖱, click Alignment..., click Left, click the OK button	Select range, `Alt` `S`, `A`, `L`, `Enter`
Line style, select, *L 184*		Select range or click object, click Style or 🖱, click Lines & Color..., select Line style, click the OK button	Select range or click object, `Alt` `S`, `L`, `Y`, select Line style, `Enter`
Link 1-2-3 object to another application, *L 373*	See Reference Window: Linking a 1-2-3 Object to a Write Document		
Link worksheet files, *L 362*	See Reference Window: Using Formulas to Link 1-2-3 Worksheet Files		
List server applications, *L 369*	🗂, click the Cancel button	Click Edit, click Insert Object..., click the Cancel button	`Alt` `E`, `O`, `Esc`
Macro, enter commands, *L 397*	See Reference Window: Entering Advanced Macro Commands		
Macro, record, *L 259*	⏮	Click Tools, click Macro, click Record	`Alt` `T`, `M`, `C`

TASK	MOUSE	MENU	KEYBOARD
Macro, run, *L 265*	🔲, double-click macro range name Click user defined macro button	Click Tools, click Macro, click Run, double-click macro range name	Alt F3 or Alt T, M, R, Tab, ↓ to macro range name, Enter
Macro, terminate, *L 275*			Ctrl Break, Esc
Macro button, create, *L 266*	🔲, draw button, click Assign from range, type button text, click the OK button		
Macro button, modify	Position pointer on button, click 🖱, click Assign Macro..., click Assign from range, type button text, click the OK button	Position pointer on button, click 🖱, click Tools, click Macro, click Assign to button, then click Assign from range, type button text, click the OK button	Position pointer on button, click 🖱, Alt T, M, A, click Assign from range, type button text, Enter
Make a cell the active cell, *L 19*	Click the cell		Use ←, →, ↑, or ↓ to move to cell
Move cell contents, *L 131*	Select range, move pointer to edge of range until it changes to ✋, click and drag range to new location Select range, ✂, move pointer to new location, 📋	Select range, click Edit or 🖱, click Cut, move pointer to new location, click Edit or 🖱, click Paste	Select range, Ctrl X, move pointer to new location, Ctrl V Select range, Alt E, T, move pointer to new location, Alt E, P
Move down one window, *L 20*	Click in vertical scroll bar below scroll box		PgDn
Move left one window, *L 20*	Click in horizontal scroll bar to left of scroll box		Ctrl ← or Shift Tab
Move right, left, up, down, *L 20*			→ ← ↑ ↓
Move right one window, *L 20*	Click in horizontal scroll bar to right of scroll box		Ctrl → or Tab
Move up one window, *L 20*	Click in vertical scroll bar above scroll box		PgUp

TASK	MOUSE	MENU	KEYBOARD
Named range, create, *L 214*	Select range, ▦, type name, click the OK button	Select range, click Range, click Name..., type name, click the OK button	Alt R, N, type name, Enter
Named range, select, *L 217*	▦, click desired name	Click Range, click Name..., click desired name	Alt R, N, click desired name
New sheet, create, *L 237*	New Sheet	Click Edit, click Insert, click Sheet, click the OK button	Alt E, I, S, Enter
New sheet, select, *L 238*	Click worksheet tab	Click Edit, click Go To..., type worksheet letter with colon, click the OK button	Alt E, G, type worksheet letter with colon, Enter
Object, add, *L 184*	○, □ or ◣, specify location and size of object using mouse	Click Tools, click Draw, click the object and specify location and size of object using mouse	Alt T, D, press letter for desired object, specify location and size of object using mouse
Object, arrange, *L 185*	▦, ▦ or ◪	Click Edit, click Arrange, then click desired arrangement	Alt E, A, press letter for desired arrangement
Open a worksheet, *L 11*	📂	Click File, click Open...	Ctrl O or Alt F, O
Outline, add, *L 142*		Select range, click Style or 🖱, click Lines & Color..., click Outline, click the OK button	Select range, Alt S, L, O, Enter
Paste	Move pointer to location, 📋	Move pointer to location, click Edit or 🖱, click Paste	Move pointer to location, Ctrl V, or Alt E, P
Paste link, *L 362*	Move pointer to location, 📋	Move pointer to location, click Edit, click Paste Link	Move pointer to location, Alt E, K
Pattern, add, *L 142*		Select range, click Style or 🖱, click Lines & Color..., click Pattern, select pattern, click the OK button	Select range, Alt S, L, P, select pattern, Enter
Pattern, chart, *L 178*		Click chart object, click Style or 🖱, click Lines & Color..., click Pattern, select pattern, click the OK button	Click chart object, Alt S, L, P, select pattern, Enter
Point size, select, *L 140*	Select range, click point size selector, select point size	Select range, click Style or 🖱, click Fonts & Attributes..., select point size, click the OK button	Select range, Alt S, F, select point size, Enter

TASK	MOUSE	MENU	KEYBOARD
Print, area, *L 69*	Select range, 🖨️, click the OK button	Select range, click File, click Print, click the OK button	Select range, `Ctrl` `P` or `Alt` `P`, `R`, `Enter`
Print, chart, *L 170*	Click chart, 🖨️, click the OK button	Click chart, click File, click Print, click the OK button	Click chart, `Ctrl` `P`
Print preview, *L 69*	Select range, 📰, click the OK button	Select range, click File, click Print Preview..., click the OK button	Select range, `Alt` `F`, `V`, `Enter`
Print, worksheet	🖨️, click Current worksheet, click the OK button	Click File, click Print..., click Current worksheet, click the OK button	`Ctrl` `P`
Protect cells, *L 326*		Select cells, click Style, click Protection..., click Keep data unprotected after file is sealed, click the OK button	Select cells, `Alt` `S`, `P`, `K`, `Enter`
Protection, turning off, *L 328*	See Reference Window: Turning off Protection		
Protection, turning on, *L 326*	See Reference Window: Turning on Protection		
Quick menu, activate, *L 103*	Click 🖱️		
Right-align cell contents	Select range, ▤	Select range, click Style or 🖱️, click Alignment..., click Right, click the OK button	Select range, `Alt` `S`, `A`, `R`, `Enter`
Save worksheet with current name, *L 67*	💾	Click File, click Save	`Ctrl` `S` or `Alt` `F`, `S`
Save worksheet with a new name, *L 59*		Click File, click Save As...	`Alt` `F`, `A`
Scenario, create, *L 226*	⌨️, click the To Index button, click the Scenario button, type scenario name and select versions, click the OK button	Click Range, click Version..., click the To Index button, click the Scenario button, type scenario name and select versions, click the OK button	`Alt` `R`, `V`, `Alt` `S`, type scenario name and select version, `Enter`
Scenario, select, *L 230*	⌨️, click the To Index button, double-click scenario name	Click Range, click Version..., click the To Index button, double-click scenario name	`Alt` `R`, `V`, `Alt` `T`, `↑` or `↓` to select scenario name, `Alt` `W`
Seal file, *L 326*		Click File, click Protect..., click Seal file, click the OK button, type password, press `Tab`, type same password, click the OK button	`Alt` `F`, `R`, `S`, `Enter`, type password, `Tab`, type same password, `Enter`

TASK	MOUSE	MENU	KEYBOARD
Select a range, *L 67*	Click upper-left corner of range and drag mouse to lower-right corner of range		Press and hold Shift, move pointer with ←, →, ↑, and ↓
SmartIcons, customize palette, *L 209*		Click Tools, click SmartIcons..., drag icon to add or delete from palette	Alt T, I, drag icon to add or delete from palette
SmartIcons, select palette, *L 17*	▦, click palette name	Click Tools, click SmartIcons..., select palette from drop-down list	Alt T, I, select palette from drop-down list
Sort data, ascending, *L 291*	Click key field column, ↕	Click key field column, click Range, click Sort..., click Ascending, select sort range, click the OK button	Alt R, S, type cell name for desired sort column, Tab, A, R, type sort range, Enter
Sort data, descending, *L 291*	Click key field column, ↕	Click key field column, click Range, click Sort..., click Descending, select sort range, click the OK button	Alt R, S, type cell name for desired sort column, Tab, D, R, type sort range, Enter
Spell check (not included in Student Version), *L 63*	ABC	Click Tools, click Spell Check..., click the OK button	Alt T, S, Enter
Split-window, move to, *L 194*	Click window		F6
Split worksheet area, *L 194*	Click and drag ↕ or ↔	Click cell for split, click View, click Split..., click Horizontal or Vertical, click the OK button	Position cell pointer for split, Alt V, S, H or V, Enter
Sum a range of cells, *L 98*	Select range, ↕ @, click SUM, select range, click ✓		Type @SUM formula, Enter
Text block, add, *L 181*	See Reference Window: Adding a Text Block		
Tile worksheets, *L 361*	▦	Click Window, click Tile	Alt W, T
Typeface, select, *L 139*	Select range, click typeface selector, select typeface	Select range, click Style or 🖱, click Fonts & Attributes..., select typeface, click the OK button	Select range, Alt S, F, select typeface, Enter
Underline cell contents, *L 141*	U	Click Style or 🖱, click Fonts & Attributes..., click Underline, click the OK button	Ctrl U
Undo, *L 18*	↩	Click Edit, click Undo	Ctrl Z or Alt E, U

TASK	MOUSE	MENU	KEYBOARD
Unseal file		Click File, click Protect..., click Seal file, click the OK button, type password, click the OK button	Alt F, R, S, Enter, type password, Enter
Value, enter, *L 52*	Click cell, type value, ☑		Move cursor to cell, type value, Enter
Version, create, *L 219*	See Reference Window: Creating Versions		
Version, select, *L 222*	🔲, click the Named range drop-down list button, select range name, click the With version(s) drop-down list button, select version	Click Range, click Versions..., click the Named range drop-down list button, select range name, click the With version(s) drop-down list button, select version	Alt R, V, Alt R, use ↑ or ↓ to select range name, Alt V, use ↑ or ↓ to select version
View, clear split	Click and drag ↕ or ↔	Click View, click Clear Split	Alt V, S
View, perspective, *L 240*	🔲	Click View, click Split..., click Perspective, click the OK button	Alt V, S, P, Enter
What-if table, one-variable, *L 335*	See Reference Window: Using a One-Variable What-if Table		
What-if table, two-variable, *L 339*	See Reference Window: Using a Two-Variable What-if Table		